T0244211

A Noble Ruin

A Noble Ruin

Mark Antony, Civil War, and the Collapse of the Roman Republic

W. JEFFREY TATUM

OXFORD

UNIVERSITY PRESS

Oxford University Press is a department of the University of Oxford. It furthers
the University's objective of excellence in research, scholarship, and education
by publishing worldwide. Oxford is a registered trade mark of Oxford University
Press in the UK and certain other countries.

Published in the United States of America by Oxford University Press
198 Madison Avenue, New York, NY 10016, United States of America.

Library of Congress Cataloging-in-Publication Data
Names: Tatum, W. Jeffrey, author.
Title: A noble ruin : Mark Antony, civil war, and the collapse of the Roman republic / W. Jeffrey Tatum.
Description: New York, NY : Oxford University Press, [2024] |
Includes bibliographical references and index.
Identifiers: LCCN 2023020435 (print) | LCCN 2023020436 (ebook) |
ISBN 9780197694909 (hardback) | ISBN 9780197694923 (epub) |
ISBN 9780197694930
Subjects: LCSH: Antonius, Marcus, 83 B.C.?–30 B.C. |
Statesmen—Rome—Biography. | Nobility—Rome—Biography. |
Rome—History—Civil War, 43–31 B.C.
Classification: LCC DG260 .A6 T38 2024 (print) | LCC DG260 .A6 (ebook) |
DDC 937/.05092 [B]—dc23/eng/20230516
LC record available at https://lccn.loc.gov/2023020435
LC ebook record available at https://lccn.loc.gov/2023020436

DOI: 10.1093/oso/9780197694909.001.0001

Printed by Sheridan Books, Inc., United States of America

for Chris Pelling

Contents

Acknowledgements

It was Stefan Vranka who first suggested to me that I should write a biography of Mark Antony. In the long interval since then, he has remained a model of patience. And in his role as editor—after I finally disgorged a manuscript—he has been nothing less than invaluable. Others, too, have helped me with this book. I am grateful to audiences in the Americas, Australasia, and Europe who allowed me to try out some of my ideas, and I owe special thanks to my hosts on these occasions: Patricia Baker, Catalina Balmaceda, Henriette van der Blom, James Chlup, Robert Cowan, Monica Cyrino, Mary Ann Eaverly, John Marincola, Daniel Osland, Francisco Pina Polo, Daniel Pullen, James Rives, Cristina Rosillo-López, Lea Stirling, Frances Titchener, and Kathryn Welch. I also benefited from the Working Group in Roman History organized amid the COVID crisis by Celia Schultz; its members—Jane Chaplin, Evan Jewell, Rose Maclean, Gwynaeth McIntyre, Carlos Noreña, Josiah Osgood, Andrew Riggsby, Amy Russell, and Kathryn Welch—very kindly and helpfully discussed a draft of my chapter on the Perusine War. Robert Morstein-Marx allowed me to read, in advance of its publication, his fascinating book *Julius Caesar and the Roman People*, which teems with ideas. Tim Smith graciously answered multiple questions about aediles and the aedileship. David Levenson, Frederik Vervaet, and Hendrikus van Wijlick shared with me evidence I might easily have overlooked. My colleagues at Victoria University of Wellington, always encouraging, allowed me to teach (more than once) an undergraduate course on Antony and Cleopatra: the students in these classes, by way of reactions and discussions, did much to aid me in shaping this account of Antony's life. My research also received practical support from the Joint Research Committee and the Joint Leave Committee of the Faculty of Humanities and Social Sciences at Victoria University. And I was fortunate enough both to begin this book and, later, complete it in the congenial setting of the Institute for Classical Studies at the University of London.

My greatest debts are owed to Diana Burton, Jon Hall, Chris Pelling, and Robin Seager: they each of them read the whole of a draft of this book, were generous with their erudition, offered numerous valuable suggestions, and saved me from multiple blunders. I cannot thank them enough. As for local support, my New Zealand in-laws, nephews, and niece kept things lively. Likewise Jo and Jason and all the denizens of 14 Ingestre Street. Most of all, I am grateful to Diana Burton: her learning and generosity improved this book considerably; more importantly, she made life outside it and beyond it so much fun.

Few scholars have done more to advance our understanding of the sources for Antony and therefore our grasp of the man and his times than Chris Pelling. And from the beginning he has sustained a lively interest in the development of this biography. That is partly why this book is dedicated to him. Mostly, however, it is because he is my friend.

Preface

In his lifetime, Mark Antony was a famous man—and he played a leading role in the transformation of the Roman world. The fall of the Roman republic and the imposition of the Augustan age articulate a truly crucial epoch in European and Mediterranean history and culture. Antony was a central figure in this transformation. Consequently, he remains famous, or infamous, and an object of recurring academic study. His life—variegated, passionate, sensual, bold, tragic (in a sense)—inspires vigorous reactions. Nearly everyone has a view on Antony, and the habit began early. For Cicero, Antony was distasteful, a talented man who was also a bad man—and Cicero said so in vitriolic speeches, the *Philippics*, which soon became central to the ancient world's curriculum in oratory. Antony's enemies, not least Octavian, put Cicero's vituperation to work in fashioning him a dangerous failure, a Roman noble corrupted by his appetites and his lust for Cleopatra. Later historians adopted and adapted these themes, delivering their readers an Antony who was irresistibly depraved, startlingly brave, sometimes cunning, but almost always constitutionally incapable of choosing the right side of history. The biographer Plutarch, relying on the same material, crafted a life whose protagonist was great-natured but too philosophically inept—too simple and naive—to resist temptation, be it food and drink, levity, luxury, or feminine beauty: Plutarch's Cleopatra enduringly embodies all these dangerous attractions. She, and the deceptions lurking in what the Greek biographer deplores as oriental ostentation, lead Antony fatally astray. Plutarch's influence is nothing less than formidable—his Antony is very much the chivalrous and unstudied Antony of Shakespeare's *Antony and Cleopatra* and Ronald Syme's *The Roman Revolution*—and in reacting to it by emphasizing Antony's acumen and sophistication there is always a danger of forgetting that, in the end, Octavian won and Antony lost.

Investigations of Antony or topics involving Antony are legion. Nor can any fairminded person complain there are too few biographies of the man. Which raises the question: is another one otiose? Obviously, I hope not. Justifying a new account of Antony's life by cataloguing deficiencies in one's predecessors, however, is an exercise which is both unattractive and unfair. Indeed, many are superb. No biographer of Antony will ever excel the clarity and charm of Chamoux. The cleverness of Rossi and the acumen of Halfmann inspire admiration. English readers have long relied on Huzar's *Mark Antony: A Biography*. This book will soon be half a century old, which means that, through no fault of its own, its account misses recent discoveries and is unaffected by the many changes in our ways of thinking about the late republic that have taken place since its appearance. A new biography presents a fresh opportunity for taking advantage of what are undeniable advances in our understanding of the fall of the republic and the triumviral period which followed—and in our appreciation of the dynamics of Rome's government of the eastern Mediterranean, where Antony, for the last decade of his life, was master.

This biography is written for more than one audience. It is accessible to any reader, or at least I hope it is. In the body of the text, all Latin and Greek is translated or explained, and throughout this volume there is more than one excursion aimed at clarifying technical matters essential for understanding Antony's career. These are by no means digressions, but classicists and ancient historians may prefer to skip them. As for the apparatus of scholarship, that is reserved for the notes (some notes, however, furnish explanations and clarifications designed for the aid of general readers). I mostly eschew polemics and doxographies, which means I do not regularly point it out when I depart from prior assumptions or approaches. For each section of the biography, however, I furnish references to works which I regard as fundamental or which are both recent and important. Routinely included in these citations is a selection of standard, frequently cited biographies of Antony, where different takes on Antony are often to be found. By way of these references, the curious or conscientious can pursue earlier, sometimes quite different discussions on any matter in Antony's career. I confess that I have not read everything there is to read which is pertinent to Mark Antony. Nor, of what I have read, have I cited everything here. The omission of any previous scholarly work should not be viewed as an implicit criticism of it. Ancient historians, I hope, will find things in this book which they judge to be both new and true, but I do not expect mine to be the final word on Antony or the times in which he lived. The study of the past is always a work in progress and very little in Roman history is settled business. Most of what I have to say about Antony is necessarily provisional.

No biography of an ancient figure can furnish a reader with the kind of psychological depth one expects in modern life writing. We know too little of Antony's private world to try to unpack his personality by way of detailed descriptions of specific episodes or by way of applying sophisticated methodologies as a means of filling in the gaps. His inner being and its urges, so important for contemporary biographers, elude us and there is little we can do about it. Perhaps this is not such a bad thing after all. In John Lanchester's splendid novel *Capital*, one of its more adept operatives, a man who shares the company of many notable people, is keenly aware of the gap between celebrities and their public: 'Mickey knew plenty of things that people were desperate to know—most of them variations on the theme of "what is X really like?"—as if there were a special category of knowledge called "really likeness"—as if it were somehow the ultimate question'.[1] As if, indeed. What Antony was *really* like we shall never know, which puts us in the same position as the bulk of his contemporaries. Still, in trying to make sense of his career, we can certainly get glimpses of the person who played the part.

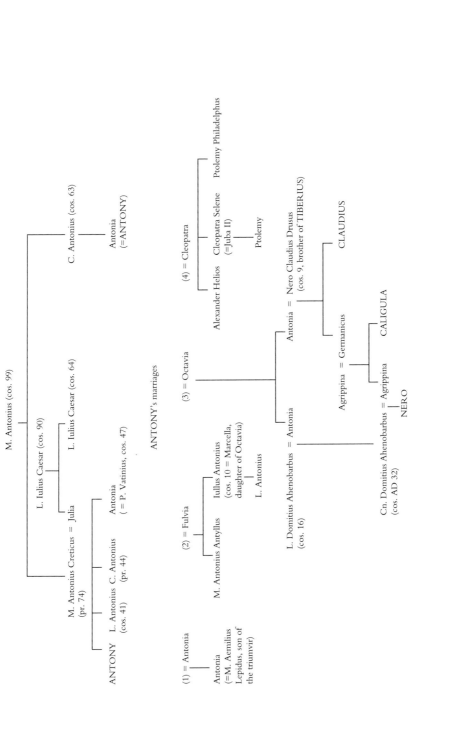

M. Antonius (cos. 99)

L. Iulius Caesar (cos. 90)

C. Antonius (cos. 63)

L. Iulius Caesar (cos. 64)

Antonia (=ANTONY)

M. Antonius Creticus = Julia
(pr. 74)

Antonia
(= P. Vatinius, cos. 47)

ANTONY   L. Antonius   C. Antonius
          (cos. 41)   (pr. 44)

ANTONY's marriages

(1) = Antonia

Antonia
(=M. Aemilius
Lepidus, son of
the triumvir)

(2) = Fulvia

M. Antonius Antyllus

Iullus Antonius
(cos. 10 = Marcella,
daughter of Octavia)

L. Antonius

(3) = Octavia

L. Domitius Ahenobarbus = Antonia
(cos. 16)

Antonia = Nero Claudius Drusus
(cos. 9, brother of TIBERIUS)

(4) = Cleopatra

Alexander Helios   Cleopatra Selene   Ptolemy Philadelphus
                   (=Juba II)

Ptolemy

CLAUDIUS

Agrippina = Germanicus

CALIGULA

Cn. Domitius Ahenobarbus = Agrippina
(cos. AD 32)

NERO

I
Beginning

Noble Antony

Mark Antony was a *nobilis*, a Roman noble. The Latin word means *noted* or *famous*, but *nobilitas* refers to fame of a distinctive brand. All Roman senators were distinguished men—by definition they were *optimi*, the best men of the city—but few were nobles.[1] Orators and jurists, and especially triumphant generals, garnered glory in abundance, celebrity which remained within the reach of any senator, if he was good enough. Nobility, however, was a property of birth. Although scholars still squabble over the exact definition of *nobilitas*, all agree that individuals descending from consuls or dictators were esteemed by the Roman public as *nobiles*.[2] Nobility, then, was an aristocracy of birth but one predicated on exceptional individual achievement in the service of the republic, an origin that imbued the nobility with a legitimacy grounded in what we might describe as a myth of meritocracy.[3]

Central to any Roman's claim to greatness was *virtus*, a word which fundamentally means *manliness*—and in patriarchal Rome that sense of the word was never lost—but *virtus* gathered to itself every facet of individual excellence in public life. Consequently, the concept was central to the ideology of the aristocracy. As one modern scholar has put it, for the Roman aristocrat *virtus* 'consisted in the winning of personal eminence and glory by the commission of great deeds in the service of the Roman state'.[4] It designated the right stuff, something possessed only by a few. And it ran in families: everyone in Rome tended towards the belief that *virtus* was hereditary. Hence the natural conclusion that the descendants of great men were possessed of a fibre superior to others even among the aristocracy. The fame of a *nobilis* was not mere glamour: it resided in the conviction of others that he was exactly the kind of man the republic needed.

The noble's excellence, a consequence of his birth, was manifest in his actions.[5] *Industria*, hard work, was also an aristocratic virtue in Rome, and all grandees were obliged to devote themselves to aiding their friends and dependents—by way of legal advice or advocacy, gifts to the needy, and sometimes by offering protection to anyone beleaguered by dangerous foes. A Roman aristocrat sought to become the refuge of many and exhibited his grandeur by holding court in his mansion: each day began with a morning levee called a *salutatio* at which all were welcome and no visitor's request too trivial to be heard.[6] Whereas the modern habit is to communicate one's importance to others by throwing up barriers and insisting on inaccessibility—and by exhibiting an inclination to say *no*—at Rome the great and the good acted otherwise, indeed so much so that ordinary people expected their betters to be available whenever they needed them and were angry on those occasions when their petitions were rejected.[7] Even as a young man, an aristocrat and a noble most of all was expected to be active in assisting others in the Forum, where trials and other legal business were transacted.[8] In exchange for this industry, an aristocrat expected esteem.

Roman aristocrats, and nobles especially, were rich men.[9] This wealth, which was principally landed wealth, set them apart for all the obvious reasons but also because it enabled its owner to devote himself to lavishing attention and benefactions on individuals at every level of society. Through what the historian Sallust called 'the might of their kindred and the multitude of their dependents', a noble, by being helpful in a way no one else could be, put himself in the centre of an extensive network of freedmen and clients, neighbours, friends, foreign connections, aristocratic clubs, even financiers and businessmen—each of whom owed him a favour, or more likely many favours.[10] A grandee's good works were by no means selfless: every benefaction shackled its recipient with an inevasible debt of gratitude, of *gratia*. Romans were obsessed with the practical and moral claims of gratitude—and ingratitude was abominated. It was very nearly impossible for anyone to deny a request from a man or woman to whom he owed a favour. *Gratia*, for this reason, was a key foundation of aristocratic clout.[11]

Glory and honour were earned not only by way of personal favours but also, indeed principally, through benefactions to the republic. The many civic labours undertaken by aristocrats—pleading or advising in the courts, serving in the legions as an officer—were acts of public service: these men did not take a salary, they strove for fame. Likewise when they held magistracies or sat in the senate: this, too, was a civic duty, not a job. A senator's recompense was power and admiration by a grateful public. Roman grandees relished their crowded levees, and boasted about them, and they invidiously observed any applause received by their peers. In everything they did, they strained themselves in seeking recognition for it. Prestige, *dignitas*, for most in the aristocracy, was their ultimate concern. This was truer for a noble than for anyone. A classic statement of the values and ambitions animating the Roman noble was the panegyric delivered by the noble Quintus Metellus at the funeral of his noble father, Lucius Metellus. Lucius, we learn, achieved 'the ten greatest distinctions in pursuit of which men with sound judgement devote their lives'. He made it his aim to be 'the best of warriors, the finest orator, the bravest general, the magistrate under whose auspices the greatest deeds are accomplished, holder of the republic's highest magistracy, to be supremely intelligent, to be recognised as the most distinguished senator, to obtain great wealth by honourable means, to leave behind many sons, and to be the most famous citizen in Rome'.[12] The noble, in this formulation, is not like anyone else and endeavours to be better even than his peers. His aim is to be recognized by all as the best man—the most valorous, the best educated, the most eloquent, the most statesmanlike—in the republic.

This noble pose is as idealized as it is ambitious. There were ugly sides to the nobility. Jealous rivals often depicted the nobility as an inert class, the abundant legacies of which permitted its members an easy ascent to greatness. Cicero can say of the noble Lucius Domitius Ahenobarbus that he had spent the whole of his life as a consul-designate.[13] Rivals of the nobility, especially politicians who lacked illustrious antecedents, grumbled over a noble's advantages: he was shielded by family fame, by credit for the deeds—the triumphs and the consulships—of his ancestors, by an abundance of wealth and personal connections, all of it inherited, none of it earned.[14] Some denounced the nobility for its pretensions. Sallust spoke for many when he complained how, for all their claims to *virtus*, too many nobles lacked real courage or even experience in warfare.[15] Instead, they devoted their energies towards decadent ends. Luxury and greed and debauchery were their true pursuits.[16] Worst of all, he complained, nobles were insufferably arrogant and even savage when protecting their paramountcy. In a letter to a provincial governor, Cicero urges him not to offend Antony's brother Lucius: slighting a young man who is formidable and a noble, he warns, will incite the enmity of many.[17] The orator was not alone in reckoning arrogance and condescension as hallmarks of noble conduct.[18] Indeed, aspersions of this kind reflected a widely shared view of the nobility. Rhetorical handbooks, for instance, put these negative premises to work when instructing an orator on the best means of stirring a jury's resentment against a Roman noble: a pleader is advised to draw attention to his 'overbearingness bordering on violence, clout, alliances, riches, his complete lack of inhibition in asserting superiority over others, his nobility, clients, contacts, networks, and kinsmen.'[19] Like the heroic figure emerging from Metellus' panegyric, this dark portrayal of the noble is also a stereotype. It will not do to split the difference, but doubtless many nobles in various ways combined qualities from both paradigms.

The Roman people were willing to take the bad with the good. Clearly, Roman voters accepted the claim that their nobles were superior men, the proof of which is that, during the last two centuries of the republic, the vast majority of consulships, Rome's highest magistracy, went only to men who were *nobiles*.[20] Only rarely did anyone from outside the nobility make it to the top. And it was even more uncommon for a man who was the first in his family to attain the rank of a senator, a *novus homo* or new man, to become a consul. In the view of the nobility, the anomaly of a new man's holding the consulship was nothing short of sacrilege: the office, they complained, was polluted by its association with any *novus homo*, however impressive his accomplishments.[21] Even after Cicero, a new man, reached this office—in the teeth of prevailing prejudices and outpolling his noble colleague, Gaius Antonius, Mark Antony's uncle—he was admired by the nobility but never really accepted by them.[22] And yet he ennobled his family. Great man though he was, Cicero remained a *novus homo* all his life. His son, by contrast, was nobly born—and he notoriously despised the glorious Marcus Vipsanius Agrippa, a new man.[23]

For all the success of the nobility, *nobilitas* was not and must never become a magic word. Most consuls were nobles, yes, but most nobles failed to make it to the consulship, so steep was the competition. Roman history is littered with noble failures, and it was actually remarkably rare for a noble family to preserve its political eminence over several generations.[24] Misadventure, misfortune, sloth, or sheer incompetence could blight even a noble's future. Which is why a noble, like everyone else in the aristocracy and notwithstanding his undeniable advantages, had to work very hard to hang on to his place at the top.[25] The demands of his heritage rendered it impossible for a noble to remain undisgraced by mediocrity: he must attain the consulship in the teeth of competition from his peers as well as ambitious and talented inferiors. For this reason, nobles were ferocious when defending their prestige. This was as true of Mark Antony as it was of any noble. In his fierce contest with Octavian, who was the son of a *novus homo*, Antony savagely ridiculed his enemy's obscure origins: his great-grandfather, he sneered, was a freedman from the countryside who made ropes, and his grandfather was a sordid money changer.[26] None of this was true: Octavian's family derived from the local aristocracy of Velitrae. But the point of Antony's acerbity was not accuracy but rather to underline with graphic brutality the enormous social gulf separating him from his upstart rival. In Rome, this gulf mattered very much.

Rome's Political Aristocracy

The civic life of Rome was animated by its two dynamic principles, the people's majesty and the senate's authority.[27] Only the people, in their various assemblies, were competent to pass legislation, and it was the people who elected the executive magistrates who went on to become senators. The people were, in a very real sense, sovereign. 'It is fitting', even Cicero concedes, 'that all powers, all commands, all commissions are granted by the Roman people'.[28] The people did not, however, draft or deliberate legislative proposals. Nor were the people responsible for supervising Rome's financial affairs, or its civic religion, or its foreign policy. These were matters that, by custom or law, had been handed over to the senate, the body of former magistrates who, by dint of their collective experience and wisdom, were deemed best equipped for addressing the realities of statecraft. Thus the senate's dominating influence resided principally in its prestige, its *auctoritas*: it tendered its advice to the people and the people's magistrates not by way of laws but by way of decrees. It was traditional, which is to say, it was very much a moral obligation, for both magistrates and the public to defer.

Neither the senate nor the people could act without the leadership of the magistrates. Only magistrates possessed the capacity for summoning and addressing the senate, for summoning and addressing the people, or for putting forward legislative proposals. In dealing with the people, a magistrate needed eloquence and social confidence. When he spoke before the public, and the administration of the republic often demanded these face-to-face encounters, he did so at an assembly known as a *contio*. Anyone could attend, and every speaker's audience enjoyed the liberty of cheering or jeering—or simply departing. Sometimes they threw things. In Rome, popular sovereignty was not an abstraction diluted by the realities of representative government. In the courts, which also operated outdoors and in public, in the provinces, and in warfare, magisterial leadership was indispensable and its responsibilities exacting. Their specific duties and powers varied. Aediles, for instance, maintained the fabric of the city and produced important religious festivals. Praetors presided over the courts and governed provinces. Consuls held sway in the city, sustained order, and presided over the senate. Tenure of these magistracies was limited to a single year, and a minimum age was prescribed for each. These offices could be held only in a prescribed sequence, nor could they be held in successive years—a rule designed to prevent any individual from holding unbroken power.

By Antony's day, a man animated by political aspirations stood for the quaestorship at around thirty or, in his early thirties, the office of tribune of the *plebs*. These were highly responsible positions. A tribune had the power to stymie any magisterial or governmental activity he deemed harmful to a citizen or detrimental to the good of the republic. Even popular legislation could be blocked if he forbade it through his veto. At the same time, tribunes could convoke the senate or propose and carry legislation. These offices offered a Roman entry into the senate. The most important of the magistrates, however, were the praetors and consuls: these men were invested with *imperium*, the capacity to command armies or administer justice.[29] The consulship was Rome's highest and most prestigious office, 'the supreme glory of a public career', as Cicero heralds it.[30] Only two men in each year were elected consuls, and only after they had advanced through the quaestorship and praetorship with enough distinction to surpass their rivals. Reaching the consulship was so momentous an achievement that ex-consuls, the *consulares*, enjoyed the first rank in the senate.[31] For a noble like Antony, this supreme glory was the object of his public career.

Not every Roman aristocrat aimed at a senatorial career. Those who did not remained members of the equestrian order.[32] They were the *equites*, or knights, the wealthy class who, the Romans believed, originally furnished the city with its cavalry. The differences between a senator and an equestrian were very real: a senator, employed in civic service, enjoyed greater prestige and superior honour. But despite these distinctions, senators and equestrians belonged to the same class. They inhabited the same social world, were products of the same brand of education, shared the same cultural pursuits. Both senators and equestrians could look back on younger days when both served as officers and held minor offices. Indeed, a senator *was* an equestrian at the start. It was only after he was elected quaestor or tribune and entered the senate that he surrendered his equestrian status. It was at that point in his career that his life diverged in important ways from his equestrian coevals. Still, they were hardly separate species. The relationship between senators and equites has been encapsulated neatly: 'there was more to unite the two orders than to divide them.'[33]

Eschewing a public career, an equestrian was free to spend his time as he liked. Some became fabulously wealthy financiers. Many, like Cicero's friend Atticus, invested widely, grew richer, and offered practical aid to busy senators, whose careers they helped to foster. Most remained devoted agriculturalists, even those who also engaged in manufacture or trade or finance. The individual contentiousness that characterized senatorial competition was unnecessary and often unhelpful for this branch of the aristocracy, which is not to say equestrians were unpolitical or irresponsible in civic affairs: every Roman jury, for instance, included a panel of knights, and collectively the equestrian order mattered a great deal in Roman elections. As individuals, moreover, because they were close, sometimes indispensable, to their senatorial friends and relations, they enjoyed considerable personal influence but were often, for this same reason, very much affected by senatorial politics. Equestrian actors are not always visible to us in our ancient sources: Atticus is the most conspicuous owing to Cicero's letters and Nepos' biography of the man. If his views and activities are any guide to the sentiments and preoccupations of his peers, then at least some equestrians remained close to the centres of power in Rome both by way of economic ties but also through bonds of high culture and shared political values.

What's in a Name?

The formal name of the man we know as Mark Antony was *M. Antonius M. f. M. n. Cor.*, Marcus Antonius, son of Marcus, grandson of Marcus, of the Cornelian tribe.

Every Roman belonged to one of the republic's thirty-five tribes. These were not affiliations founded on ethnicity or kinship but rather slices of society based on region and feelings of neighbourliness and which operated very much like modern voting districts.[34] As for embedding in one's name the identity of one's father and grandfather, this is a habit of nomenclature that exhibits Roman patriarchy in a way so obvious it requires no further comment. Every man had at least two names and most had three.[35] The first name, or *praenomen*, was a given name. The Romans had so very few of these that they could be abbreviated without causing confusion.[36] His second name, his *nomen*, indicated his *gens*, a word sometimes rendered *clan*. If a Roman had a third name, which Antony did not, that was his *cognomen*, originally a kind of nickname which was preserved to provide further definition for a family. Among the Claudians, for example, there were Claudii Pulchri, Claudii Nerones, and so forth. Romans recycled the same names over several generations and this can lead to confusion on our part. Women ordinarily had only a single name, the feminine form of their father's *nomen*. Antony's daughters were each of them *Antonia*.

Not everyone named Antonius was related to one another. Within each *gens* there were collateral branches so distant from one another that it makes no sense to talk about a relationship, and there were families the names of which became homonymous over time. Moreover, whenever a Roman freed a slave, that slave usually took as her or his name the *nomen* of his or her owner. When Marcus Tullius Cicero freed his learned slave Tiro, that man became Marcus Tullius Tiro. Newly enfranchised citizens also adopted a Roman *nomen*, often the name belonging to the agent of his enrolment. For this reason, not everyone named Antonius is a kinsman, even a distant kinsman, or even a loose connection of our Antony. Indeed, by the end of the first century, there were Antonii all over the Mediterranean world, most of whom never saw Rome. For these reasons, discerning the correct relationship between Antonians is not always easy. The early Antonii throw up this very problem.

Early Antonians

It is impossible to know who invented Anton, a son of Hercules and progenitor of the Antonii—or when, inasmuch as the predilection for tracing aristocratic ancestry back to the gods emerged early in the city's history. The appeal of any kinship with so mighty a hero is obvious. Elevated to divinity owing to his matchless valour and on account of his relentless devotion to the rescue of humanity, Hercules also attracted men's devotion because, for all he was courageous and adventurous, he remained susceptible to the enormities of mortal passion and appetite: he was a stout man, who became a god. A robust, even grandiose heritage, then, for the Antonii to claim as their own. Indeed, few of Rome's preeminent families, keen though they were to fabricate kinship with gods and heroes, made so bold as to arrogate to themselves this affinity with Hercules: only the Fabii made the same boast, perhaps later than did the Antonii.[37]

Unlike the patrician Fabii, who began to accumulate consulships in the early years of the republic, the plebeian Antonii supply visible senators only in the second century.[38] By then we can spy a very few Antonii active in Roman warfare and diplomacy, often working in conjunction with the resplendent noble family, the patrician Aemilii. But they leave little trace. One of them, however, a tribune of the *plebs* in 167, comes into clearer focus. During that year there was a fierce debate over Roman policy regarding the island of Rhodes, a long-standing ally whose loyalty had lately become suspect in some quarters of the senate. This Marcus Antonius interposed his veto to block a declaration of war, a bold act. In the same year, he put the powers of his office to work on behalf of the great Lucius Aemilius Paullus, the conqueror of Macedon whose recent victory in the east had rendered Rome the leading power in the eastern Mediterranean.[39] Glorious though he was, Aemilius Paullus had enemies and Antonius was clearly keen to take his side in the politics of the day. This energetic tribune, it is almost a certainty, was Mark Antony's great-great-grandfather.

It is sometimes suggested that Antony's family somehow derived from a distinguished, very ancient clan. The patrician Antonii Merendae enjoyed eminence early, during the first century of the republic. In 450, Titus Antonius Merenda was elected one of the *decemviri consulari imperio legibus scribundis*, the second installation of 'the ten men empowered with consular imperium in order to write the laws', a body charged with governing Rome and drawing up a legal code. And Quintus Antonius Merenda, very likely a son of the decemvir, was elected military tribune with consular power for 422. Now it is sometimes urged that this family must have been plebeian (and consequently potential ancestors of the later Antonii) on the assumption that *Antonius*, because it was a plebeian name in later Roman history, was always a plebeian name.[40] But this reasoning is far from conclusive. According to Dionysius of Halicarnassus, three members of the college of 450 were plebeian: not, however, Antonius, who is explicitly designated patrician. As for the military tribune with consular power, the date of his election is significant inasmuch as, according to Livy, the first plebeian to hold that office was elected only in 400.[41]

Admittedly, the events and the personalities of fifth-century Rome, including the relationship between patricians and elite plebeians, remain murky. Still, even if we cannot always be certain of the underlying reasons for the phenomenon, it is evident that homonymous *gentes*—one patrician, another plebeian—existed in Rome.[42] Nothing, then, stands in the way of our viewing the Merendae as a patrician clan which, by the second century if not before, had succumbed to extinction.[43] The plebeian Antonii, whatever their exact connection with these ancient patricians, were a different family, and it is notable that, notwithstanding assertions of ancient and heroic antecedents in the persons of Anton and Hercules, they never reprised the cognomen Merenda and never asseverated a nobility originating in the early republic.[44]

The Family of Mark Antony

The Antonii arrived among the nobility of Rome only in the first century and by way of the illustrious career of Marcus Antonius, a talented commander and spectacular orator.[45] Born in 143, he commenced his political career in 113, when he became quaestor, an office he held while serving in Asia, where he established lasting personal connections. There Antonius was delegated responsibilities weighty enough for him to bear the title quaestor *pro praetore*, an early distinction. In 102 he was sent out as praetor *pro consule*, in command of a large fleet, to suppress Cilician piracy, a duty which allowed him to expand his contacts in the east. After collecting additional troops and ships from Rome's eastern subjects and allies, Antonius campaigned by sea and land until 100,[46] when he returned to Rome to celebrate a triumph. This was glory sufficient to garner a consulship of 99, a success he later capped by reaching a censorship in 97. Further distinctions accrued, including an augurate, which installed Antonius as a member of Rome's most distinguished religious college.[47] His native honour now clad in magisterial and pontifical majesty, Antonius was a prince of the senate—and ennobled his line.

Antonius was one of the leading pleaders of his day, much admired by the young Cicero, who remained devoted to his memory.[48] Antonius eschewed publishing his speeches, preferring instead to write a treatise on rhetoric, which remained incomplete at the time of his death. In describing Antonius' oratorical skill, Cicero wittily resorts to the image of a conquering general—an *imperator*—strategically deploying, not battalions, but the elements of his eloquence.[49] Antonius was, Cicero insists, one of the speakers at Rome owing to whom Latin oratory finally arrived at a standing equal to Greek.[50] As for the man himself, Cicero tells us that, although he was learned and sophisticated, he endeavoured to give the impression of being unstudied.[51] A man of many parts, then, martial, political, smooth-tongued, and possessed of a well-stocked mind.

Not long after Antonius reached the pinnacle of his public career, the fortunes of Rome collapsed into tumultuous strife eventuating in bloody civil war. In the year 90, Rome's allies in Italy, their *socii*, long loyal and long-suffering, after being rebuffed in their solicitations for Roman citizenship, seceded in order to concoct a new nation, Italia. This was a development an imperious Rome could only regard as intolerable. The Social War intervened, a conflict so bitter and threatening that it tested the cohesiveness of Rome's aristocracy—and its competence. In the end, and only after carnage and destruction on a frightening scale, Rome vanquished Italia by yielding to the Italians' demand for citizenship. But this profound transformation of the Romans' citizenry introduced fresh incentives for political antagonism.[52]

We need not be detained by the particulars of the perturbations afflicting Rome as its old citizens quarrelled over what should be done with the new ones. It is enough to observe that this divisive issue provoked such intense public discord that it generated a baleful political environment marked by extreme distrust and sharp practice—even murderous violence. And it threw up an extraordinary bid by Gaius Marius to recover his past pre-eminence in Roman affairs. Marius, victor in the Jugurthine War, saviour of Italy in Rome's wars against the fearsome Cimbri and Teutones, and six times a Roman consul, had no equal in military glory or political accomplishment. But now, a man of nearly seventy and showing evidence of failing health, he resented any dimming of his lustre—especially when he observed the rise of Publius Cornelius Sulla, his former lieutenant but now his personal enemy.[53]

After distinguishing himself in the Social War, Sulla became consul in 88 and was assigned Rome's war against the formidable Mithridates VI of Pontus, who was violating the republic's eastern provinces and massacring Roman citizens and allies. Marius envied Sulla his command and, through the agency of a tribunician ally, persuaded the popular assembly that Sulla should be superseded by himself. This, however, the consul could not accept, and Marius' action provoked the obscene horror of a Roman army marching against the city itself. Sulla seized the capital, executing his enemies and reinstating himself as commander in the Mithridatic War. Marius fled to the safe shores of Africa, whence he returned after Sulla's departure in 87. Rome was again captured by Roman forces, and Marius went to work vengefully slaughtering any aristocrat perceived to be hostile or even uncooperative, a bloodbath that only ended in 86 when Marius, now consul for the seventh time, collapsed.[54]

Civil war was then suspended until 83, when Sulla, having settled eastern affairs to his own satisfaction, invaded Italy, took Rome for a second time, and published his abominable lists of proscribed citizens—rich Romans deemed enemies of the republic who could be killed with impunity while their property was seized and sold by the new regime. Domestic terrorism, however, was not Sulla's only ambition. He revised the Roman constitution, retired from public life, and handed the management of public affairs back to the senate, the leaders of which were mostly his past supporters and comrades. The political landscape of the republic would never again be entirely tranquil, but Sulla's administration, it was widely hoped, brought civil conflict to a lasting if grim conclusion. The scalding cruelties of the Sullan proscriptions, however, were never forgotten.[55]

It was in the aftermath of Marius' return in 87 that Antonius met his end, executed on the orders of the old general.[56] It remains unclear just what incited Marius' animosity. It is worth observing that, at the time of his death, one of Antonius' sons was serving as a junior officer under Sulla's command.[57] It has been suggested that Antonius had once been a beneficiary of Marian support but later changed loyalties, backing Sulla instead of his former ally. This cannot be excluded, but it is far from certain.[58] That Marius had grown to hate Antonius, however, is undeniable: he is said to have relished the report of Antonius' death, which he heard while gazing with glee at the man's severed head.

Antonius certainly had important connections with Arpinum, the Volscian town that was the birthplace both of Marius and Cicero. Lucius Tullius Cicero, the orator's uncle, served under Antonius when he campaigned against the pirates. So, too, did Marcus Gratidius, Antonius' close friend who was Marius' brother-in-law and also a relation of Cicero.[59] All these men—Antonius, Marius, Cicero, and the Gratidii—were joined by their tribal affiliation: each was a member of the Cornelian tribe. Perhaps, too, they were somehow connected by ties of neighbourliness that often led to personal affinity.[60] This is not to claim that the Antonii hailed from Arpinum—they certainly did not—but they probably owned property there and were clearly intimate with the local aristocracy.[61] It is in the context of these associations that Cicero came to know and admire Antonius. The friendship between the family of Cicero and the family of Mark Antony originated in the rise of the consul of 99. It survived the civil war between Sulla and his enemies. It also survived the civil war between Caesar and Pompey. It could not, however, withstand the pressures of Antony's consulship in 44, as we shall see.

Antonius left two sons, Marcus and Gaius, the father and the uncle of Mark Antony. The identity of their mother is lost. Nor can we say with certainty when they were born, though the elder cannot have born later than (or much before) 114 or the younger much later than 106. At the time of their father's death, Gaius was probably abroad, serving under Sulla, whereas Marcus, approaching thirty, was probably in Rome preparing to stand for a quaestorship.[62] How he reacted to his father's execution goes unmentioned in our sources: indeed, we hear very little of Marcus before his praetorship in 74. And yet it appears that, instead of taking flight, he remained in the city.[63] His eldest son, Mark Antony, was born in 83, but nowhere, not even in our most hostile sources, is it thrown in Antony's face that he was born a fugitive, nor is his father, also an object of abuse by ancient writers, ever denounced as a coward.

We know rather more about Antony's uncle than his father, and none of it is attractive.[64] Admittedly, this colouring reflects the hostile tone of our sources, which are mostly specimens of invective or works by historians with little choice but to rely on the invective of others. Nevertheless, Gaius' disreputable character and sheer incompetence remain unmistakable. Abusing his Sullan commission, Gaius intimidated and cheated numerous Greek dignitaries in Achaea, after which profiteering he rushed home to Rome in time to seize his opportunity for sordid enrichment during the proscriptions. In 76, to his public discomfiture, Gaius was confronted in court by the Greeks he had swindled in Achaea, the interests of whom were represented before the praetor by the young Julius Caesar. When the proceedings of the case went against him, Gaius made appeal to an accommodating tribune of the *plebs*, whose intervention rescued him from what was certain to be an adverse judgement.[65]

This dishonest evasion from justice was not forgotten, and in the census of 70 Gaius was expelled from the senate, a humiliation attributed to his mistreatment of Rome's allies and to his vast accumulation of debts. Undeterred by this disgrace, Gaius regained the senate by winning election as tribune, probably in 68, and went on to become urban praetor in 66, with Cicero's visible support. During his praetorship, he produced lavish and immensely popular games.[66] He was Cicero's colleague in the consulship in 63, proof of his popularity with voters, senatorial disapproval notwithstanding, and it was he who led the Romans' military campaign against Catiline.[67] When the rebellion was finally put down, Gaius was even hailed *imperator*, conquering general, although he had left the actual fighting to his legate, Marcus Petreius. As proconsul in Macedonia from 62 to 60, Gaius suffered multiple defeats at the hands of neighbouring enemies. Returned to Rome, he was prosecuted first for treason, then for extortion and, despite a vigorous defence by Cicero against the latter charge, condemned in 59.

The circumstances of Gaius' exile were anything but modest. He settled on Cephallenia, where he possessed properties so extensive that, we are told, he could treat the whole of the island as if it were his personal estate. Indeed, he kept himself busy by founding a new Cephallenian city. The ample wealth displayed by this lifestyle may have been acquired by way of the depredations he inflicted on Macedonia during his proconsulship. It is more likely, however, that Gaius became rich under Sulla and the allegations of financial embarrassment hurled against him by his enemies were simply unfounded. Exile was not the end for Gaius: he was pardoned by Caesar in 44 and in 42 became censor, largely owing to the influence of his nephew.

His brother was, in many respects, a more sympathetic figure, or at least a less objectionable one, although modern historians, unduly influenced by his military setbacks, have preferred censure.[68] Plutarch describes him as kindly, upright, and generous to a fault. Now this is not entirely Plutarch's invention: a similar characterization finds a less charitable formulation in Sallust, for whom Marcus was simply a congenital wastrel, heedless of any but his most pressing concerns.[69] Plutarch's Marcus, by contrast is all amiability, a trait that persists even when he is intimidated by his strong-willed wife. None of this need be untrue, but it is worth observing how, in his depiction of Marcus, Plutarch prepares his readers for what to his mind are the salient features of Antony's personality. Inherited similarities play their part in the structuring of Plutarchan biographies, in which ancillary characters tend to make their entrances largely in order to give definition to the central subject of the work.[70] Perhaps we should distrust Plutarch in this instance and settle for Sallust's spendthrift, whatever his degree of likeability. The type was, after all, far from exceptional amid late republican aristocrats. And, as we shall see, the real Marcus, far from being a simple soul, was very capable of exhibiting political sharp elbows. Nor, when he was in authority, was generosity his most conspicuous quality.

It was probably after his father's death that Marcus married Antony's mother, Julia, herself a survivor of Marian savagery. Better born than her husband—she descended from an ancient patrician family—she was the sister of Lucius Iulius Caesar, consul in 64. Her great-grandfather was the consul of 157 and her father was Lucius Julius Caesar, consul in 90 and censor in 89. Yet he, along with his brother, the brilliant Gaius Julius Caesar Strabo, was put to death during the Marian terror. Now Cicero, in one of his blistering attacks on Mark Antony's heritage, alleges that Marcus' first wife was Numitoria, the daughter of Quintus Numitorius Pulla. But this assertion is incredible. Pulla was a figure infamous for his betrayal of his native city, Fregellae, when it rebelled against Rome in 125 and was subsequently destroyed. Admittedly the man was, for this reason, something of a benefactor to Rome, but his deed remained repugnant—and consequently no daughter of his could have been either an attractive or likely match for the noble son of an ex-consul and ex-censor. The slur is Ciceronian invention and can safely be discarded. Julia, by contrast, was a brilliant and therefore suitable match for Marcus. Later events would prove her courage and boldness.[71] She bore her husband a daughter and three sons.

Marcus rose to prominence during his praetorship in 74, a remarkable year for Roman foreign policy.[72] In the west, Pompey the Great and Metellus Pius were still struggling to take back Spain from the Marian holdout Quintus Sertorius.[73] In the east, Mithridates of Pontus was again menacing Rome's eastern provinces. Another Mithridatic War was inevitable, the command of which ultimately fell to the consul Lucius Licinius Lucullus, but only after complicated and covert negotiations with senatorial powerbrokers.[74] Mithridates remained a formidable and cunning enemy, and one of his most damaging means of impeding the Romans lay in his sponsorship of Mediterranean piracy. Nor was piracy a danger limited to the east: in the west, too, pirates harassed Roman possessions, even (with Sertorius' cooperation) preventing desperately needed supplies from reaching Pompey and Metellus.[75] Consequently, it was decided to establish an extraordinary command against piracy anywhere in the Mediterranean. Marcus got the job.[76]

This command, extensive and unprecedented, will have been sought by many, which is why Marcus, like Lucullus, had to resort to senatorial intrigue in order to advance his interests. But Marcus also enjoyed the open endorsement of Marcus Aurelius Cotta, the other consul of the year.[77] Marcus' appointment signals the high esteem in which he was held by his senatorial peers.[78] Now because Marcus had to operate in the east and west simultaneously, he took on a large staff of officers. One of them, it appears, was Julius Caesar, who only a few years previously had hauled Gaius Antonius before the praetor on behalf of angry Greeks. His view of Marcus, it seems, diverged from his attitude towards Gaius, nor did he suffer any doubts about the usefulness of cultivating a relationship with him by way of military service.[79] All of which underscores the reality that, in gaining the command against the pirates, Marcus had achieved a stunning political success.[80]

From an administrative perspective, Marcus was responsible for a very complex operation, and an expensive one. He required not merely funds to cover his campaign's expenses but also ships, since much of Rome's navy had already been diverted to the fight against Mithridates.[81] Which perhaps explains the severity of his exactions from provinces and allies.[82] There were also complaints about personal corruption on the part of Marcus' officers as they enforced Rome's requisitions in Sicily and in the east, accusations that later extended to Marcus himself.[83] It is certainly clear to us that Marcus, wherever he operated, involved himself in local affairs. In Crete he established a significant network of alliances which he left behind to his sons.[84]

Marcus began in the west, campaigning along the coasts of Spain and Liguria, where his operations were successful in suppressing, although not eliminating, piratical interference in the Sertorian War.[85] The senate, by prolonging his command, registered its satisfaction with his results. By 72 Marcus arrived in the east, where he concentrated on Crete, whose support of Mithridates and piracy alike expressed itself in the island's contumacious refusal to cooperate with the Romans. When diplomacy failed, Marcus launched an attack on the island in 71 but was defeated. The Cretans, however, did not fail to perceive that this was a defeat Rome would never accept. Loath to wage a hopeless war against a superpower, the Cretans came to terms with Marcus in a face-saving agreement he chose to represent as a victory. He even went so far as to style himself Creticus in commemoration of his achievement.[86] It was while he was still on Crete that Marcus fell ill and perished. A Cretan embassy rushed to Rome to explain itself and assure that senate of its peaceable intentions. As for the campaign against piracy, no replacement for Marcus was named. His mission was apparently deemed accomplished. Antony's father, the point must be underlined, although hardly a sensational success, was by no means a failure. Indeed, for all practical purposes, he achieved Rome's immediate goals by suppressing piracy in the west and bringing Crete over to the republic. Antony's father, felled by illness in his early forties, met a dignified if premature end.[87]

Antony's Birthday

After Mark Antony's decisive defeat by Octavian at the battle of Actium, the senate declared the day of his birth a *dies vitiosus* (a depraved and inauspicious day)—in fact, the only *dies vitiosus* in the Roman calendar. The Romans marked many dark and ill-omened days, but none was worse than Antony's birthday. Any public act or private ritual performed on this day was tainted. Therefore the senate could not meet, assemblies could not gather, private couples should not be married, and so forth. So great an abomination was Antony, so the senate decreed—on orders from the victorious Octavian—that no other day could be worse than his birthday. Every year, if only to remind itself of its salvation by Octavian, the republic was commanded to shudder.[88]

It is owing to Octavian's vindictiveness that we know Antony was born on 14 January. But in which year? Our sources are unsure. Plutarch cannot decide between 86 and 83, and Appian accepts a tradition which dates his birth to 81.[89] The known facts of Antony's life conform best with the year 83 and this date is confirmed by Antony's coinage, if we are right in recognizing marks on some issues as indications of his age.[90] He was the eldest of three sons, all close in age and all destined for fame or notoriety. He also had a sister, who married Publius Vatinius, a staunch ally of Caesar.[91]

Making Sense of Our Sources: Bias, Misinformation, Disinformation

It becomes clear at the very start how difficult it is to put our evidence to work in recovering Antony's biography. Indeed, the fundamental obstacle lies in the nature of our sources. They are relatively few and usually very uneven in their coverage. All of them throw up problems. Documentary evidence, like coins, inscriptions, or papyri, are precious, invariably suggestive, but never unambiguous. Ancient correspondence, when we have it, is extremely valuable but by no means straightforward. Everyone who writes a letter does so for a reason, and posterity is rarely his principal audience. Our chief resources for getting at Antony's life are literary. Central among these are the speeches of Cicero, including the blistering *Philippics* which aimed at ruining Antony, the narrative histories of Appian and Cassius Dio, and Plutarch's biography. It is obvious that an oration, even when it is not a specimen of invective, is anything but objective. How best to unpack a speech for our purposes, however, is not always clear. No less affected by parti pris premises and every bit as determined to convey political or moralizing judgments to their readers are Appian and Dio. So, too, Plutarch, who composed his *Demetrius and Antony* as a medium for the moral improvement for his readers, who are advised to draw the right lessons from the careers of two formidable men who turned bad and succumbed to failure.

Plutarch, Appian, and Dio are writers from the imperial age. Each of them, however, consulted sources reaching back to contemporary accounts: they read Cicero's speeches, perhaps his letters; they knew Augustus' *Autobiography*; Quintus Dellius, one of Antony's principal lieutenants (until he went over to Octavian), composed a well-known history which included the campaign against Parthia and, possibly, events leading up to the battle of Actium; and Gaius Asinius Pollio, a close ally of Antony (until he shifted his loyalty to Octavian), was the author of a very influential history which covered Roman affairs from the formation of the First Triumvirate in 60 to the battle of Philippi, when Antony defeated Marcus Brutus, and perhaps carried on to some point in the late thirties. That Antony was a bad man was axiomatic in the Augustan Age and thereafter, and so it is unsurprising that imperial writers are unfriendly to Antony. But they are not always hostile. Dio, to be sure, regards Antony as decadent and dangerous. But nor does he exhibit much fondness for Cicero, and he

Fig. 1.1   Bust of Marcus Tullius Cicero, 1st cent. BCE bust in the Palazzo Nuovo of the
Capitoline Museums.
Source: Shutterstock.

deems Octavian a man determined from the start to make himself a despot in Rome.
Plutarch and Appian, by contrast, sometimes have good things to say about Antony.
Nevertheless, for the biographer and the historian alike, he is a figure of dubious morality, and the trajectory of his career is elaborated mostly by way of his personal dis-
sipation. In part, that was what they read in their sources: both Dellius and Pollio, it
is worth bearing in mind, defected to Octavian before they completed their histories. But the bias of their sources is not the whole story of the story which Plutarch or
Appian wrote. Each has more than one message to convey and a dramatic framework
to construct: Antony is a colourful figure they find useful, even indispensable, for its
literary elaboration. The sheer literariness of both authors, as we shall see, introduces
complexities and therefore difficulties for their interpretation.[92]

Antony's Boyhood in Cicero's Invective

Of Antony's childhood and younger days we know very little. Our principal source is a
brief, hostile passage in Cicero's *Second Philippic*.[93] It was a standard invective move in
Roman oratory to vituperate an enemy's life comprehensively, beginning in his boy-
hood and carrying on to the present moment. Cicero's account of the early Antony
is a typical specimen. There we learn that Antony was born into his father's poverty,
strained himself in lubriciousness and perversity, and, by way of irresponsible living,

accumulated massive debts—each of these a familiar trope in Greek and Roman calumniation but expressed by Cicero with passion, wit, and humour.[94] His Antony
blames his father for his financial embarrassment, pretends to be rich enough to sit in
seats reserved for the equestrian order, and earns what he can by prostituting himself.
Soon, however, he finds real romance as the passive sexual partner of Gaius Scribonius
Curio, son of the wealthy consul of 76. The father, however, like a figure from comedy
or erotic poetry, puts guards on the door to keep Antony out of his house. But he is
foiled when the clever fellow sneaks in at night by lowering himself through the com-
pluvium, the opening in the roof of a Roman house's atrium. Antony is a spendthrift,
but Curio guarantees his credit. Alas, the bill soon balloons to six million sesterces—
an astounding sum. On Cicero's advice, Curio *pater* pays it but banishes Antony from
his son's life. Plutarch read this passage with care—he was very aware of the preponderance of fiction in rhetorical denigration—and relied on it in his biography. He did
not believe everything he read. He ignored Antony's poverty—instead, Antony's father
is simply 'not very rich'—and his Antony is a figure whose early promise is blighted by
the baleful influence of Curio, a reversal of the dynamic in Cicero but one dictated by
the biographer's tendency to represent his subject as brilliant but reactive and easily
led astray.[95] In Plutarch, Antony is not Curio's lover. Instead, the pair of them descend
into carousing, multiple love affairs, and profligacy, a conventional constellation in in
every ancient writer's complaint about wayward young men.[96]

Invective was a central feature of Roman public life and for that reason influenced
the historical narratives which recorded it. Romans were good at saying bad things
about one another—'in the allegation of disgusting immorality, degrading pursuits
and ignoble origin the Roman politician knew no compunction or limit'—and doing
so was a skill so vital they learned it in school.[97] Romans resorted to calumniation in
order to shame their opponents and put themselves forward as champions of traditional morality. Style mattered as much as content. Vituperation, to be taken seriously,
had to be elegant and well-fashioned. Deprecation did not merely humiliate others: it demonstrated the intelligence and education of the denigrator. Doing invective
poorly—throwing out crude insults—was proof of man's stupidity or bad breeding.
In Rome, calumnies and slurs need not be, indeed rarely were, tethered to reality, but
they could not carry conviction or exhibit acuity if they were patently false. Romans
made fun of ugly people but insulting a handsome man as ugly was ludicrous; instead,
one was advised to insinuate that his beauty was a sign of his lustfulness.[98] This trivial
restriction did little to inhibit anyone's invention or imagination. And why should it?
Vituperation exhibited eloquence righteously and cleverly deployed in the articula-
tion of sound values made personal by way of pointing out an individual's failure to
enact them. It outraged and shamed an opponent. Truth barely entered into it, which
is why Plutarch distrusted Cicero's abuse of Antony. Even he, however, could not ignore it. It was, after all, nearly his only source for Antony's early years.

We should dismiss Cicero's passage as the malicious fantasy it is. In the matter
of Antony's early poverty, however, historians have been loath to do so. In Rome,
bankruptcy was a legal hazard and a moral failure, which is why the charge was so
commonly rolled out against an opponent and so easily dismissed.[99] Antony's case,
however, gives rise to credibility because it is widely believed that his father died a
failure. This, as we have seen, was not the case. But even if it were, it would be no reason

to conclude the man died in arrears. Nor can inferences regarding Antony's situation be drawn from the alleged financial difficulties of his uncle, who in 70 was ejected from the senate in part on the basis of his debts, and in 64, when competing with Cicero for the consulship, was pilloried by the orator for his poverty. Gaius Antonius was an unsavoury man, but a rich one, notwithstanding the talking points of Cicero's campaign rhetoric.[100] Plutarch, we observed, rejected the idea of Antony's poverty. So, too, did Dio, in a fictitious speech he furnishes for Antony's friend Quintus Fufius Calenus.[101] This is not to say Antony came into the world wealthy by senatorial standards. Furthermore, he was obliged to share his father's estate with two brothers and a sister. But apart from Ciceronian vituperation, there is no good reason to regard the financial circumstances of Antony's youth as in any way remarkable. At worst his patrimony, like Caesar's and others, was a modest one, but ample enough to launch a career.[102]

Putting aside Cicero's invective and its adaptation by Plutarch, we know next to nothing about Antony's childhood and early adulthood. But this is hardly unusual. Greek and Roman historians did not often discuss children, and ancient biographers, unlike their modern counterparts, tended to be uninterested in recording an individual's childhood.[103] This is not because Greeks and Romans doubted the importance of this period in anyone's life or were indifferent to the rearing of children. Rather, the prevailing view held that any healthy child equipped with the right heritage and furnished with a suitable education would, in the fullness of time, grow up to become a perfectly satisfactory adult. For them, unlike us, the categories of *right heritage* and *suitable education* and *satisfactory adult* were more or less uncontroversial. Even in the case of a moralizing author like Plutarch, whose *Demetrius and Antony* was composed in order to illustrate how two figures ostensibly enjoying the right heritage and a suitable education did *not* turn out to be entirely suitable adults, their childhoods are not examined. For Plutarch, Antony, like his father, was too easy-going and too easily influenced by strong women—and so his heritage, although splendid, was perhaps not *quite* right.[104] As for his education, it was not deficient but was spoiled by a curriculum which included the wrong brand of oratory, one which was popular and stimulated superficial ornamentation and bravado.[105] Explanations like these were sufficient for Plutarch's purposes, and in any case he, like us, had only Cicero to go on.

Antony's Education

For modern biographers of ancient figures, the usual reaction to this silence on the part of our sources is to furnish the reader with a rehearsal of what we know about the typical upbringing experienced by members of the elite classes in Rome. It was intense in its concentration on literary culture. Children became fluent in Greek as well as Latin and by the time they were teenagers were deeply familiar with the poetry of both languages. An education in prose works followed. All of this was preparation for training in rhetoric. Eloquence, again in both languages, was an essential tool in public life but also a quality which marked out a cultivated man. More than a few aristocrats also began to study philosophy during these years. High culture, which the Romans denominated as *humanitas*, was indispensable for an aristocrat, and elite Romans worked very hard in acquiring it. The intellectual demands of this slice of society are evident to us in the sophistication of its surviving correspondence. Roman letters, always crucial in sustaining aristocratic relationships, teem with literary allusions and recherché references to law, philosophy, and history—displays of erudition that exhibit the right kind of upbringing and education.[106] When Cicero fretted over his son's lack of seriousness when studying in Athens, he was profoundly reassured when at last he received a letter which he judged deeply classical in its diction: 'other things can be feigned', the orator writes to Atticus, 'but style is proof of one's learning'.[107] Romans of the senatorial and equestrian orders, even if they did not deliver speeches in public, were expected to become proficient in the composition of literature, an activity so important that not even the din of war constituted a legitimate distraction. While campaigning in Gaul, Caesar thought it important that he compose, in addition to his transparently political *Commentaries*, a treatise on linguistic theory. At the same time, Cicero's brother, one of Caesar's officers, strained himself in poetic composition. Neither was unique. On the eve of the battle of Philippi, even the reality of the next day's existential combat could not keep Marcus Brutus from literary industry: he was composing a Latin epitome of Polybius' history.[108]

At the same time, boys were obliged to take part in military exercises which prepared them for service in the legions. Nor were the banal practicalities of civilian life ignored. A rudimentary knowledge of Roman law, at the very least, was essential, and young men spent time in the Forum attending distinguished jurists, pleaders, and politicians, activities which forged valuable personal connections but also exposed them to real-life applications of the abstractions cultivated in the classroom.[109] The ambitious aimed at making an early start and, by the time a man was twenty, he was expected to be a familiar figure in the Forum. And some aristocrats were prodigies. At the age of seventeen, Lucius Sempronius Atratinus led the prosecution of Marcus Caelius Rufus: his opponents were Caelius himself, Marcus Licinius Crassus, and Cicero—three of Rome's most capable orators.[110]

But it was not all work and no play. The sons of the aristocracy—but not their daughters—enjoyed a high degree of license in accommodating their appetites for food, drink, excitement, and sex. These inclinations could run to excess, a recurring topic of Roman comedy and public moralizing, but complaints about objectionable adolescent antics were so commonplace that orators learned how to counter them with a boys-will-be-boys strategy known as the indulgence trope, the *locus de indulgentia*. And this argument, it appears, was usually effective because it reflected widely held views on the part of the kind of aristocratic men who sat on Roman juries. It was far from unusual, Cicero reminds the court at the trial of Caelius Rufus, for a man, after enjoying wanton good times during his youth, to put aside childish things and become a respectable, indeed an illustrious, leader of the republic. 'Nature herself', he observes, 'lavishes on the young a profusion of passions, and even if these passions should burst into the open, so long they do not ruin anyone's life or wreck anyone's home, we regard them as minor matters which are easy to put up with'.[111]

That Antony's youth involved this brand of intensive education and martial training, peppered along the way with parties, no one can doubt. His possession of high culture and his military career are proof of that. And his reputation for sensuality is legendary. Intriguingly, however, it is in the category of callow wantonness that Antony appears to have diverged from many of his high-spirited contemporaries. When he was very young, Antony appeared in court in support of a freedman, Quintus Fadius, who was locked in a dispute with an equestrian named Sicca (we do not know his full name), a friend of Cicero, who was present on Sicca's behalf. In a speech delivered much later, when he was consul, Antony threw this incident in Cicero's face as evidence of the orator's unfriendly behaviour. Cicero responded in his *Second Philippic*, but did so, we learn from a letter to Atticus, with hesitation: he was loath to embarrass Sicca by bringing the matter up, which suggests Sicca's case was either a dubious one or failed so abysmally that it did him no credit, background which also explains why Antony was keen to deploy the incident against the orator. Cicero, however, despite his concern for Sicca, simply could not resist returning to this episode because it gave him an opportunity to point out that Antony had fathered children with Fadius' daughter. Indeed, in the *Second Philippic* and elsewhere, Cicero insists that Antony was married to Fadia and therefore had a freedman for a father-in-law.[112]

Antony and Fadia

Antony's alleged marriage to Fadia has had a long run and continues to recur in discussions of Antony's youth. So gross a mésalliance, however, is unthinkable, and it is in any case clear from Cicero's letter to Atticus that it is the reality of the children, not the disgrace of an unsuitable match, that seizes his interest.[113] That the allegation of Antony's marriage to Fadia is a vituperative fiction is obvious to us.[114] It was also obvious to Plutarch, who omits it.[115] However, it is also clear that Cicero did not make up Antony's children by Fadia. They were real. Indeed, they are his entire incentive for concocting his version of the case of Fadius v. Sicca: it was not a virtuous exercise of noble duty by the young Antony, but the act of reprobate youth carried away by passion. Antony's children, disgracefully from a senatorial perspective, are the grandchildren of a freedman—for once an insult that is genuine. In a letter to Atticus, responding to his friend's concern on Sicca's account, Cicero cannot disguise his glee.

If the children are real, then a sexual relationship between Antony and Fadia is also real. If marriage is excluded—and it is—how is this to be explained? The solution, too often overlooked, was put forward long ago: here we have an example of concubinage.[116] Roman men took concubines for more than one reason. Elite men of mature years sometimes preferred concubines when seeking a stable sexual relationship unencumbered by the obligations of marriage. The emperor Vespasian, for instance, took Caenis as his concubine in order not to disrupt his relationship with his adult sons.[117] A younger man might take a concubine before marrying in order to evade the seamy and expensive society of a *meretrix*, a courtesan, or the hazards of adultery and fornication. Most concubines were freedwomen, but not all and there was nothing exceptional about a freeborn woman's becoming a concubine so long as she came from the lower orders of society. Concubinage was an institution the arrangements of which vaguely resembled marriage and in some instances was confounded with it by the poorly informed. But a concubine was not a wife. She was owed no serious social or legal obligations—even if she became pregnant. Any children were illegitimate and were not in any way the responsibility of their father.

The most famous instance of concubinage from antiquity comes for the *Confessions* of Augustine.[118] When he was a teenager, he took a concubine. She became pregnant and at the age of seventeen Augustine became a father of a son, Adeodatus. Although Augustine has much to say about this concubine and the son she bore him, he never mentions her name. At first, the son was an unwelcome nuisance, but in the end, when it became time for Augustine to marry, he dismissed his concubine but elected to keep Adeodatus, who died not long afterwards. The young Augustine was no saint, but his decision to keep a concubine was based on prudence. A similar and perhaps unexpected motive must underlie Antony's relationship with Fadia. She, like Augustine's concubine, bore Antony children, and Cicero claims Antony admitted they were his own. He may well have done so. He may even have provided something for their upkeep: after all, he was willing to aid Fadius in a court case. Unlike Augustine, however, Antony did not take these children into his household. We know nothing of their ultimate fate or the fate of their mother. Almost certainly, they were all of them deceased by the time of Cicero's *Second Philippic* if not long before that. Once Antony ended his relationship with Fadia, there was, in the world of republican Rome, no legal or moral obligation for him to look back on it. Still, in Rome this form of exploitation, although unattractive to modern sensibilities, was deemed a form of restraint. Antony's choice of a concubine instead of a series of affairs with courtesans, however, diverges from the stereotype of the young Roman roué and is not what one might predict of the young Antony. Perhaps his mother, whose strong personality is well documented, was something of a disciplinarian in these matters.[119]

Such a Face and Such a Mien

No writer mentions Antony's appearance as a boy. He does not come into view until he is a man. Descriptions of individuals furnished by Greek and Roman writers rarely aim at anything like realistic, photographic accuracy. Instead, they tend to list looks in order to portray character, good or bad, through the application of physiognomic assumptions or by way of subordinating details to an explicit interpretation of the effects of an individual's image.[120] Only Plutarch gives us a glance at Antony's face— his forehead was broad, his nose aquiline—but these details are mentioned only to prepare the reader for the biographer's extended comparison of Antony with his ancestor, Hercules. Like the god, Antony is virile and fond of food, carousing, and the company of warriors. Cicero has unflattering things to say about the implications of Antony's physique. He does not deny its athleticism—'that maw of yours, that torso, that hard build of yours, as strong as a gladiator's'—but the orator puts Antony's shape to work in degrading him (*gladiator* was always a term of abuse among the aristocracy) and denouncing him for gluttony, drunkenness, and public vomiting. It is obvious how Cicero's Antony is a dark version of Plutarch's. But neither is very interested in recording Antony's actual appearance. For their differing purposes, Antony must be robust and athletic.[121] We have no reason to doubt that he was.

Depictions in the plastic arts throw up similar difficulties for anyone wanting to see what Antony looked like. These media, too, aim at creating an effect. Image-making of this kind varies over time and from place to place. In the east, Roman grandees, like

Fig. 1.2 The Vatican Antony, a Flavian-era depiction often identified as Mark Antony, in the Vatican Museums.
Source: Wikimedia Commons.

the Hellenistic kings who preceded them, are routinely young, beautiful, and often take on divine qualities which signal their majesty. In Rome, great men shape themselves by assimilating features both from this Greek canon and traditional republican markers of authority. There, too, paintings, coinage, and sculpture were intended to provide viewers with an interpretation of a grandee's qualities, not a record of his real appearance. Many of the busts and statues which survive from antiquity are clearly portraits of an important Roman but cannot be identified further. This is why, even in the past, statues and coins, both in the west and the east, so often required labels. At the same time, individuation—a distinct hairstyle or combination of facial features—was sometimes employed to render certain men and women easy to recognize. Alexander the Great and Augustus are usually unmistakable. Individual Ptolemies or Seleucids, by contrast, often blur into one another.[122]

In the case of Antony, our only certain depictions appear on his coins. Because they are so small, portraits on coins are distorting and emphasize only a few features. Still, Antony's coins, notwithstanding a bit of variation, usually represent him with a thick neck, a jutting chin, a longish nose, a broad forehead, and thick hair. This image obtains in both the west and the east.[123] It is similar to Plutarch's portrayal and may reflect the biographer's familiarity with coins or even surviving statues of Antony. In any case, Plutarch is correct to see in Antony's official portraits an evocation of his

Herculean heritage. This portrait, because it *is* Herculean, also evokes stereotypical representations of athletes, especially boxers and wrestlers. Coins have the advantage of being labelled. Other small crafts, by contrast, tend not to name names. In addition to coins, numerous miniature pieces—gems, cameos, even paintings—have been viewed as depictions of Antony, mostly on the grounds that their subjects share this basic design, from thick neck through thick hair.[124] In each case, the identification remains possible but uncertain.

Nor can we be entirely certain that we possess even a single sculpture that depicts Antony. What is perhaps the most familiar portrait identified as Antony, a Flavian bust housed in the Vatican, is now generally and rightly regarded as a misidentification. Statues and busts which are linked to Antony nearly all share conspicuous similarities with Antony's coins and the concise descriptions in Cicero and Plutarch. The most famous of these are a muscular, full-length nude statue, now in the Cairo Egyptian Museum, and busts, some of them damaged, in Budapest, Narbonne, Thasos, and, in the Centrale Montemartini in Rome, a portrait currently tagged as either Antony or the Elder Cato. Different from these is a bust, also often identified as Antony, which now belongs to the Kingston Lacy Estate. This portrait was discovered in Egypt and its Antony is softer and less rugged, especially in its slender neck, than what we see in the coins or these other busts. In Alexandria, however, Antony may well have emphasized, in some images, his role as the New Dionysus and his associations with Osiris instead of his Herculean heritage.[125] Although there is a strong consensus in favour of accepting the Cairo nude and most of these busts as genuine depictions of Antony, each of these pieces, like Antony's coins but on a grander scale, operated principally as a projection of his personal authority.[126] For Antony, that authority was normally expressed by way of an image that was big and strong.

Antony and the Catilinarian Conspiracy

Antony was very young when, in 71, he lost his father. Owing to the demographics of ancient Rome, his situation was far from uncommon.[127] Its frequency, however, will hardly have rendered it painless. He and his siblings remained with their mother, and Julia, in accordance with traditional practices, took charge of her children's education. Soon after the death of Antony's father, she remarried.[128] Her new husband was Publius Cornelius Lentulus Sura, a noble patrician who in 71 held the consulship.[129] Their marriage probably took place in 70. During that same year, Lentulus was expelled from the senate in a notoriously harsh—and partisan—census. Antony's uncle, Gaius, as we have seen, was also excluded by these censors. Lentulus' expulsion was unfortunate. But despite this setback he remained an ex-consul and a highly influential member of the aristocracy. In 63 he was elected praetor for the second time, which was, because he had been praetor for the first time in 74, the earliest year in which he could legally hold that magistracy. Nor could he legally hold a second consulship before 60. It may have been his ambition to claim that office earlier, or perhaps his aspirations were grander, or more sinister, than that. For the events of 63 revealed that Lentulus was a leading figure in a conspiracy which aimed at seizing power in Rome.

Fig. 1.3 The Centrale Montemartini Antony, 1st cent. BCE bust identified as either Mark Antony or the Elder Cato in the Centrale Montemartini.
Source: Carole Raddato from FRANKFURT, Germany, CC BY-SA 2.0, via Wikimedia Commons.

The elections for 64 were dominated by the contest over the consulship. The principal candidates were Antony's uncle, Gaius Antonius, Lucius Sergius Catilina, whom we usually call Catiline, and Cicero. Gaius and Catiline were both nobles. Cicero, by contrast, was a new man. But he was by far the most gifted of the three and, so far anyway, the most successful. Gaius' foibles we have observed. Catiline was a far more capable man.[130] His family, although ancient and honourable, was in decline. But he restored its fortune during Sulla's proscriptions. Elected praetor for 68, he governed Africa for two years, where his corruption incited consternation in the senate and led to more than one trial upon his return. Nevertheless, Catiline survived it all. Still, his legal troubles left something of a tarnish. In the elections for 63, he lost to Cicero, who was elected at the top of the poll, and to Gaius, who only just edged him out. Catiline stood again for 62 and, once again, fell short.[131]

There was more than one reason for prosperous voters to prefer Cicero to his noble rivals. Chief among these was his reputation for probity and soundness. He was a talented orator who everyone knew would exert himself in defending the rights of capital and the propertied order. These qualities were especially to the fore at this time because Italy was plagued by debt and a serious shortage of credit; the urban poor were disturbingly restless; peasant farmers in Etruria, including veterans of Sulla's armies, were facing ruin; and many in Transalpine Gaul were rendered desperate owing to crushing indebtedness.[132] It was in this environment that Catiline and his allies, a collection of distinguished men who included Lentulus, began organizing a coup which came to be known as the Catilinarian Conspiracy.[133] Their ultimate goals remain unclear. It is unlikely that they aimed at autocracy, although that charge was naturally levelled against them, but it is reasonably certain that they aimed at abolishing debts and putting themselves into positions of redoubtable if temporary authority. A violent strike was planned in Rome, a shock which was to be followed by a march on the city by Sullan veterans in Etruria. The Catilinarians also endeavoured to persuade the Allobroges in Transalpine Gaul to rise up in rebellion.

Cicero uncovered this plot and by dint of bold and brilliant oratory rallied the senate, which resorted to its final decree, the *senatus consultum ultimum*, an appeal to the city's magistrates to rescue the republic. Gaius then took the field against Catiline and his army of veterans. In the city, Cicero, by obtaining incriminating documents furnished by a cooperative embassy from the Allobroges, managed to arrest five senators implicated in Catiline's conspiracy, one of whom was Lentulus. At Cicero's urging, the senate elected to put these men to death without a trial. This was a stunning violation of their rights as citizens, but in the panic of the moment—everyone was convinced there were other conspirators in the ranks of the senate and believed intimidating them was imperative—this decision was deemed a just one. Cicero was hailed as a saviour and declared *parens patriae*, father of his country.[134] In the following year, Gaius's army defeated Catiline's, for which victory he was acclaimed *imperator*.[135]

When later Antony and Cicero became enemies, he protested that Cicero refused to surrender Lentulus' body for burial, an act of cruelty against his mother, Julia. But that was not true.[136] And although Cicero showed Lentulus no mercy, he went to great pains to isolate the Antonii from any association with Lentulus' crimes. Throughout his consulship, Cicero advertised his friendship with Gaius, to whom he rendered every assistance, including making it possible for him to receive Macedonia as his province. In subsequent years, their friendship continued without interruption. Moreover, when delivering his *Fourth Catilinarian*, a speech he later published and was widely read, Cicero made it clear that Julia's brother, Lucius Caesar, voted to execute Lentulus *although* the man was his brother-in-law. In making this point, Cicero described Julia in highly complimentary terms: she is a *femina lectissima*, a very estimable woman, and clearly no part of her husband's nefarious enterprise.[137] Nor did this episode do anything to diminish Julia's subsequent reputation. Her children, too, were left untarnished by it.

Antony Fights for Rome

It is not impossible that Antony served under his uncle in the campaign against Catiline. It is almost certain that he joined him when, after he defeated Catiline, he entered Macedonia as its provincial governor. By then Antony had reached an age when he was ripe for active military service and provincial administration. For much of Rome's history young aristocrats were expected to undertake voluntary service in the cavalry, and any aspirant for high office was obliged to complete no fewer than ten annual campaigns. This legal requirement, the so-called *decem stipendia*, had lapsed by the late republic.[138] The ideology underlying it, however, subsisted: military experience—the exhibition of valour, the authority of command, and the honest profit of warfare—remained essential to aristocratic sensibilities and the public's high estimation of their governing class. As Cicero puts it in his magisterial *De Officiis*, 'a young man's first claim to fame should be won in warfare, if that is possible'.[139] As a young man Cicero had practiced what he preached when he was old: against the grain of his unbellicose temperament, he took his turn as a junior officer.[140] Even in the year of his consulship, at the height of his own glory, the orator openly conceded that 'the greatest prestige belongs to men who are celebrated as warriors'.[141]

The young men of Rome often distinguished themselves while on campaign. The future consul of 187, Marcus Aemilius Lepidus, at the tender age of fifteen slew an enemy soldier in battle and saved the life of a fellow citizen.[142] Cicero's teenaged son, doughtier than his father, was not much older than Lepidus when, serving as a cavalry officer during the civil war, he impressed Pompey with his bravery and horsemanship.[143] Julius Caesar, at about the age of twenty, was decorated for his valour at the storming of Mytilene.[144] And so it goes. Naturally not everyone garnered glory at the very onset of his military career: as Cicero recognized, such an achievement was not always possible. Nevertheless, we routinely spy Romans in responsible positions, including naval commands, at remarkably early ages. Military service was a duty all aristocrats recognized as fundamental to the social superiority they enjoyed by dint of their native *virtus*: for men aspiring to civic leadership and high office, it was indispensable.

Which is not to overlook the complexities of the Romans' attitudes towards warfare. The Roman people celebrated their greatest warriors, but they did not always honour them with consulships.[145] Nor, by Antony's day, did the city's populace, for all its martial fervour, personally serve the republic as soldiers: infantrymen were drafted in the countryside, and we have no evidence of any enthusiasm on the part of the urban *plebs* for joining their ranks.[146] Exemption from military service—*militiae vacatio*—was prized by Romans of every social order, or so we must infer from the fact that it is among the rewards proffered by Roman laws as an encouragement to their enforcement.[147] None of this subverts the reality that military greatness was central to Roman ideology or crucial to aristocratic identity. Still, it is clear enough that not every Roman possessed an appetite for combat, and perhaps more than a few young men preferred to fulfil their obligation to the republic in the relative security of garrisons in pacified provinces. Indeed, an aversion to military commands on the part of ex-magistrates, it has been suggested, gradually became a feature of the late republican aristocracy.[148]

Glory was not the only asset which attracted a young aristocrat to military service. There was much to be gained by way of acquiring expertise in the operations of Roman power abroad and there were valuable opportunities for improving and expanding the network of one's personal connections. This was true of any campaign and especially, by Antony's day, of military service carried out as part of the administration of a Roman province. Some young men received formal appointments on a governor's staff. Others came along as one of a governor's tent-mates, *contubernales*, in which group they mixed with senior, sometimes prominent, figures. Here they met not only senators but also the personnel who played important roles in supporting a Roman army and managing provincial finances—the *publicani*, for instance, rich financiers whose corporations supplied vital services to Rome's military and collected taxes in Rome's provinces.[149] Cultivating friendships with these men was of inestimable value to any noble's future career.

Immediate profiteering, too, was the aim of some young men. That there was baksheesh to be got by subalterns active in provincial service is rarely documented but nonetheless very clear to us. Gaius Antonius, as we have seen, while serving in the cavalry under Sulla, abused his position in order to defraud local businessmen in Achaea.[150] Gaius Publicius Malleolus, when he was quaestor in Cilicia, invested heavily in the province by making loans and perhaps engaging in commerce.[151] Cicero, in his prosecution of Verres for his corrupt administration of Sicily, emphasizes the potency of any governor's retinue and adduces multiple instances of dishonesty on the part of Verres' accomplices.[152] Not everyone, Cicero makes it clear, was a Verres: on more than a few occasions, he reminds his audience, governors felt compelled by a sense of decency to dismiss legates, prefects, tribunes, even quaestors, whose improbity went too far, a remark that reveals much about the realities of provincial administration.[153]

So pervasive was the expectation that provincial service should be profitable that, whenever it was disappointed, resentment over the matter could be nothing short of fierce. We see this in the poetry of Catullus, a rough contemporary of Antony. He complains bitterly of his subaltern tour of duty in Bithynia when the province was governed by Gaius Memmius, an unprofitable experience Catullus laments more than once and unfailingly by way of forceful Latin obscenities. He very nearly spits out the words *pete nobiles amicos*—'seek noble friends'—commonplace advice he despises as misleading and, in his case, detrimental.[154] Appointments like the one that so frustrated Catullus had normally to be sought out: one must indeed seek noble friends. In 54, for instance, Cicero wrote to Caesar on behalf of his equestrian friend, Gaius Trebatius Testa, a rising star among Rome's jurists. Cicero asked Caesar to add Trebatius to his staff in Gaul—in a letter which makes it clear how the orator expects Trebatius to emerge from his service with Caesar a richer man.[155] A young noble like Antony, however, unlike the equestrians Catullus or Trebatius, was himself an ornament in any proconsul's retinue. For that reason, he was likely to be sought out. In Antony's case, seeking noble friends was by no means a chore.

Antony was old enough to take up military service by 65 and he may have done so at any time after that. His complaints about Cicero's treatment of Julia in 63 need not imply that he was present in Rome at the time. In truth, we can only speculate about his first campaign or provincial appointment and perhaps we should simply admit our ignorance. However, one very obvious opportunity for Antony to go abroad as a young officer came when his uncle became governor of Macedonia.[156] If so, he may also have served in his uncle's campaign against Catiline. Gaius was governor of Macedonia until 60. There, after successfully invading Thrace, he met with more than one serious reversal, failures the disgrace of which was worsened by the man's singular corruption—for which crime he was, on his return to Rome, condemned, notwithstanding a stalwart defence by Cicero.[157] This trial perhaps helps to explain why, if Antony did in fact accompany his uncle, Cicero could not easily fold in tales of misconduct in Macedonia when he was confecting a disgraceful Antonian youth for insertion into his *Second Philippic*: the orator's very public friendship with Antonius, along with his full-throated rejection of any provincial irregularities on Antonius' part, rendered that phase of Antony's career untouchable. Naturally this can be no more than guesswork. Still, it remains likely enough that Gaius' governorship of Macedonia was the setting for Antony's first foray into provincial administration and fighting for Rome.

The First Triumvirate

While Antony was away from Rome, political developments of extraordinary and un-expected consequence took place.[158] Julius Caesar returned early from his Spanish province. He then made two requests of the senate: he sought the award of a triumph and the right to stand for the consulship without being obliged to enter the city to do so. It was a formal requirement for anyone seeking office to declare his candidature in the Forum, a procedure known as *professio*. Doing so, however, entailed crossing the city's sacred boundary, the *pomerium*. If, however, Caesar crossed the pomerium, he would thereby surrender his proconsular *imperium* and that would render him ineligible for a triumph. Hence the two, related requests to the senate. To his surprise and consternation, the exemption from *professio* was refused owing to forceful resistance by a faction of powerful senators centred round Marcus Porcius Cato. At that time, Cato was no more than an ex-tribune, but he was already a noble of formidable stature whose kin and connections possessed considerable wealth and influence. Their circle disliked and distrusted Caesar, and they denied his request for an exemption in order to blunt his glory or block his rise to the consulship. This tactic, which one modern scholar aptly describes as *Cato's Dilemma*, put Caesar in an awkward position: he must either abandon his hopes for a triumph or postpone his consular candidature.[159]

Caesar was not the only figure impeded by Cato and his circle. Pompey the Great returned to Rome at the end of 62 after achieving victory in the Third Mithridatic War, a conflict in which Pompey advanced Roman arms throughout the eastern Mediterranean, redrew the region's geopolitical map, and vastly enriched Rome's treasury.[160] He was now a man unparalleled in prestige, glory, and wealth. But instead of being greeted like the hero he was, he instead met with frustration after frustration as the senate, under the leadership of Cato and his allies, stymied his demands for lands to be assigned to his legions and only slowly and almost grudgingly took up the confirmation of his arrangements in the east. In late September of 60, Pompey celebrated his third triumph, the most sensational and luxurious display in Roman history. Even then, however, the senate continued to drag its feet on his eastern acts and his legions' rewards. Another grandee facing obstruction on Cato's part was Marcus Licinius Crassus. Although very influential in the senate, he remained unable to get past Cato's circle in a controversial matter: the wealthy equestrians who collected Rome's taxes, the *publicani*, were desperately seeking to renegotiate their contract for Asia, where they were in danger of taking a serious loss. Crassus was one of the champions of the *publicani*—Cicero was another—and the wealthy Crassus was also, it appears, personally invested in their Asian enterprise. Both his dignity and his money were put in peril by Cato and his obstructionist tactics.

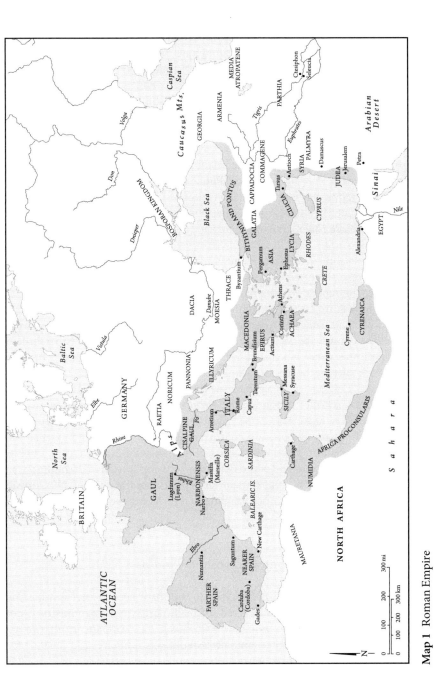

Map 1 Roman Empire

Crassus and Pompey abominated one another. But Caesar, who had ties to each, perceived how powerful the three of them could be if they united their political resources against the circle of Cato. Pompey and Crassus were persuaded to put pragmatism ahead of past animosities and the three men forged a friendship, an alliance known by modern scholars as the First Triumvirate, or, more often nowadays, the so-called First Triumvirate.[161] A fresh marriage tie also marked this association: Pompey married Julia, Caesar's daughter. Caesar's popularity, in combination with the clout of his new partners, propelled him into one of the consulships of 59. His colleague, however, was Marcus Calpurnius Bibulus, Cato's son-in-law and a long-standing enemy of Caesar. His election, proof of the influence of Cato's circle, made it inevitable that 59 would be marked by fierce clashes. Caesar's consulship, consequently, was a turbulent one, but he managed to carry legislation meeting the requirements of both Pompey and Crassus. A friendly tribune, Publius Vatinius, possibly already married to Antony's sister, introduced a law, the *lex Vatinia*, establishing Caesar in an extraordinary five-year command in Cisalpine Gaul (the northern region of modern Italy) and Illyricum (the coastal region of the Adriatic Sea reaching roughly from Slovenia to Albania).[162]

Caesar's consulship was effective but heavy-handed and often violent. By the middle of the year, the three dynasts, as they are routinely often called by modern historians, were unpopular with Romans of all classes. Worried that the following year would bring in magistrates willing to undo their programme, they threw all their resources behind candidates on whose support they could count. And they were very successful. The consuls for 58 were Lucius Calpurnius Piso, Caesar's father-in-law, and Aulus Gabinius, a man who had long been a close adherent of Pompey.[163] In addition to friendly consuls, the dynasts acquired a reliable ally in the college of tribunes. Publius Clodius Pulcher was a patrician who sought to become a plebeian so that he could hold the office of tribune of the *plebs*, a position which would allow him to introduce an ambitious programme of legislation. Transferring from patrician to plebeian status was a fraught process, controversial and unwelcome to the senatorial order. Sensing an opportunity for attaching to themselves a dynamic young noble, Caesar and Pompey facilitated Clodius' transfer to plebeian status. In gratitude, so they assumed, he would deploy his veto power in protecting their interests.[164] Early in 58, Caesar left Rome for his province. He did not return until the outbreak of the civil war in 49.

Antony, Cicero, and Clodius

During the year of Caesar's consulship, Antony will have been involved in lending support to his uncle, who was prosecuted for malfeasance in his administration of Macedonia.[165] The charge was brought by Caelius Rufus, with Cicero defending. Caelius was a talented prosecutor, and Gaius' guilt was doubtless too obvious for any jury to overlook. As a consequence, he was condemned and withdrew into exile. This trial became notable, however, because, in his speech, Cicero included harsh words about Caesar's consulship which alarmed the dynasts and prompted them to help Clodius in his effort to become a plebeian.[166] Nevertheless, Gaius' trial was not principally a contest between political factions. Furthermore, nothing suggests that the Antonii, collectively or individually, were preoccupied by or implicated in the struggle between the First Triumvirate and Cato's circle. Cicero's defence of Gaius was a reflex of his friendship with the man and his family. His criticism of Caesar, however, was not perceived at the time to be an expression of Gaius' political sentiments.

Gaius' trial, as we have seen, prodded the dynasts to lend their support to Clodius. When he became tribune for 58, he immediately promulgated an ambitious legislative programme consisting of four laws.[167] Two of these transformed Roman politics. One, the *lex Clodia de collegiis*, restored and even enhanced the right of poor and modest Roman citizens to form neighbourhood associations called *collegia*, a precious feature of social life among the lower orders which had been restricted in the sixties owing to urban unrest. The other, the *lex Clodia frumentaria*, provided for the monthly distribution of free grain to heads of households. This law's attraction to the poor is obvious. These two measures, one appealing to their dignity, the other to their welfare, were welcomed by the urban *plebs* with enthusiasm and abundant gratitude. Their passage rendered Clodius the most popular man in the city, and he soon developed techniques for putting his popularity to work: Clodius deployed the city's *collegia* as instruments for staging demonstrations on his behalf or, in some instance, riots against his political opponents. This was an unprecedented mobilization of popular agitation and violence in Rome and it elevated the tribune to an extraordinarily influential position.[168]

Antony, we know, was an early supporter of Clodius and his politics. So, too, were other young aristocrats, and it is not hard to see why: they hoped to acquire popularity with the people by way of an association with the tribune. Moreover, Clodius, at first anyway, directed his newfound clout in directions which suited the interests of the First Triumvirate. Early in 58, for instance, Vatinius was put on trial for alleged irregularities committed when he supported the dynasts during the previous year. He appealed to Clodius for aid—a tribune had the right and duty to offer his assistance, his *auxilium*, to any citizen whose rights were in threat of violation—and Clodius responded by staging a demonstration that so violently disrupted Vatinius' trial that its continuation was impossible. Antony, if Vatinius was already his brother-in-law, had personal reasons for wanting to see the man rescued.[169] At the same time, he was perhaps not disinclined to be involved with a tribune whose activities could only draw him closer to Pompey, Caesar, and Crassus.

Soon, however, Antony separated himself from Clodius.[170] Plutarch suggests that Antony soured on Clodius' policies and was concerned about the opposition they incited. This has the ring of truth, since it is highly likely that Antony broke with Clodius because he was unwilling to join in the tribune's attacks on Cicero.[171] The tribune and the orator were enemies of long standing. At the beginning of 58, however, Clodius gave assurances that he had no designs against Cicero. But, after he became formidable, he changed his mind. He began his campaign against the orator by first promulgating laws which furnished the consuls, Calpurnius Piso and Gabinius, with highly attractive provincial commands, a quid pro quo which guaranteed their complaisance. Next, he introduced a measure which made it a criminal act to put a citizen to death without a trial, a law the application of which was explicitly retrospective. Its obvious target was Cicero, whom Clodius (and others) held responsible for the execution of the Catilinarians in 63. Clodius made his intentions clear by marshalling demonstrations which threatened the orator. Soon Cicero was struggling for his safety and was persuaded to withdraw from the city. Thereafter he was condemned to exile by another Clodian law, a measure which also called for the confiscation of his property and the demolition of his house: on its site, Clodius erected a shrine to the goddess *Libertas*, Freedom. Cicero was, as we have seen, a loyal friend of the Antonii, but neither they nor anyone else could rescue him from Clodius. The orator remained in exile until 57, when Pompey assembled a coalition which carried legislation restoring his citizenship and his property.[172] Nonetheless, Antony, if he could not stop Clodius, also could not be a party to Cicero's persecution. Hence his break with the tribune. The young noble did what he could: he furnished the orator with generous loans.[173]

Study Abroad

By Antony's day it had become customary for young men to study abroad, in a centre of Greek culture, in order to put the finishing touches on their education.[174] There they attended lectures on rhetoric, practiced oratory under expert speakers, and studied philosophy—all in Greek. Athens was a popular centre, but so, too, was Rhodes. It was possible to spend time studying in both places, as the young Cicero did. We do not know where Antony took up residence. Even if he preferred to continue his education in Rhodes, doubtless he visited Athens en route. Later in his career, Antony attended philosophical lectures. Presumably he did so now. But it was rhetoric that was central to his curriculum. In Rome, style mattered.[175]

That Antony was a talented speaker is obvious and easy to document. Cicero describes him and his brothers as *non indiserti*, which is to say, *very eloquent*. His civic career was punctuated by important orations and eloquence was an attribute of a good general, so it is little surprise that he was remembered as a skilful speaker.[176] Plutarch, in his account of Antony's education in Greece, describes his style as Asianic, a critical term for a florid style marked by long and complicated phrasing, and typical of his times. It is not obvious, however, that Plutarch knew the text of any Antonian speech, nor does he appear to locate Antony's views on oratory within the first century controversy in Rome over Attic versus Asianic approaches to speechifying.[177] Instead, Plutarch takes up Antony's preference for a style he describes as boastful, arrogant, and superficial as a means of diagnosing the Roman's inner character.[178] As for the qualities of Antonian speechifying, he tells us little.

For members of the aristocracy, eloquence and fine writing were marks of character. Consequently, they were topics which invited praise and abuse. Plutarch did not know Antony's speeches, but he was aware of his enemies' criticisms of his prose style, and this is a likely source for the biographer's depiction of Antonian oratory as vapid, florid, and trendy. Suetonius tells us that in his later propaganda Octavian criticized Antony as a madman because he wrote to be admired rather than understood.[179] Octavian went on to complain about Antony's eclecticism not only in his prose but also in his oratory. But it is on his writing that Octavian concentrated his disapproval in a quotation furnished by the biographer:

Are you unsure whether you ought to copy Annius Cimber or Veranius Flaccus, so
that you can use words which Sallustius Crispus has excerpted from Cato's *Origines*?
Or would you prefer to translate into our language the verbose fatuity of Asiatic
orators?[180]

Suetonius probably excerpted this passage from a public letter composed by Octavian
during his propaganda war with Antony in the months leading up to the battle of
Actium. Here Octavian reprises a line of attack on Antony's style launched by Cicero.
In his *Philippics* he ridicules the formulation of one of Antony's edicts and concludes: 'who talks like that?'[181] Octavian, however, makes a closer reading of Antony's
style. He claims that Antony introduces anachronisms, like the historian Sallust, who
in the thirties was changing Roman historiography by writing in a spare, difficult
Latin which exhibited its connection with traditional values by recycling diction from
the elder Cato. At the same time, however, Antony, according to Octavian, inclines
towards the orotundity of what was then a contemporary style of Greek writing.

Now Octavian does not say there is anything wrong with Sallust's cutting-edge
Latin, or even with a florid style in Greek. What Octavian objects to is their incompat-
ibility: it is simply impossible to write in both styles at the same time. Antony, because
he fails to recognize this, makes his literary prose into something of a dog's dinner.
Furthermore, and this is Octavian's clear implication, because one's literary style, so
the Romans believed, revealed one's character, Antony's soul is marred by insensi-
bility and inconstancy.[182] The moral message is the important one. In another context,
Octavian attacked Antony's letters as vulgar and arrogant.[183]

Octavian probably adduced a few examples which he believed confirmed his animadversions. What survives of Antony's prose, which is only a very few letters, exhibits nothing like a Sallustian manner of expression or periods and florid expressions
suggesting the influence of an Asian style. The oddest moment in extant Antonian
prose comes in a public letter composed in 43 in which Antony describes Aemilius
Lepidus as 'the devotedest of men'—*piissimus* is the unexpected superlative Antony
uses here—a phrase Cicero makes fun of: 'not merely *devoted* but *devotedest*—you
introduce an entirely new word into the Latin language just so you can show off your
god-sent sense of devotion.'[184] Now there is no reason for us to accept that Antony
coined the word *piissimus*, but it does appear to be a word that was only just coming to
life in the late republic. Still, Cicero, too, used it in his letters, and by the time we reach
imperial Latin, it is reasonably frequent.[185]

Attacking an opponent's literary style was a common means of discrediting his education and character, yet another standard feature of Roman vituperation, and it is
clearly invective which animates Cicero's and Octavian's criticism of Antony's style.
There is no good reason to take their detraction seriously. Antony's success as an orator is clear enough from his political and military career. As for his letters, these constituted a central aspect of his public image during the triumviral period. After he
was installed in the east, it was by way of correspondence that Antony communicated
with Roman society. And during his propaganda contest with Octavian, it was by way
of public letters that he calumniated enemies and fashioned himself as Rome's better
hope for the future. As we shall see, Antony's letters at this time were so effective as
propaganda that Octavian and his allies were obliged to exert themselves in refuting

them. And so fascinating were Antony's letters that, even after his death, they continued to circulate.[186]

Whether he travelled to Athens or Rhodes, Antony left Rome sometime in the first half of 58. We do not know the names of his teachers or his fellow pupils. The events of his later life make it clear that Antony was a devoted admirer of Greek culture, a true philhellene, so we need not doubt the pleasure he took in living abroad and cultivating his Greek style. This intellectual divagation, however, did not last long because, in the next year, it was interrupted when Aulus Gabinius, preparing to take charge of the province of Syria, invited Antony to join his staff. Antony did not say yes immediately. But very soon he abandoned his studies for service as a cavalry prefect. It was the end of the beginning.

II

Fighting for empire

Aulus Gabinius

Aulus Gabinius, who derived from a praetorian family, established himself in Roman politics during his energetic tribunate in 67, the most consequential achievement of which was his law, carried against forceful opposition, creating an extraordinary command to combat piracy. This law, everyone knew, was meant for Pompey the Great, and it granted him far-reaching powers for carrying it out. Pompey's brilliant, rapid success against the pirates led directly to his appointment as commander in the Third Mithridatic War, the pinnacle of his military career. Gabinius' inventive and intrepid support earned him the great man's lasting friendship, and it was largely owing to Pompey's exertions that Gabinius was elected consul in 58.[1]

Gabinius owed his provincial command, as we have seen, not to Pompey but to Clodius Pulcher. During his tribunate in 58, as part of a strategy designed to isolate Cicero, Clodius promulgated legislation furnishing Gabinius and Calpurnius Piso with attractive and extended provincial assignments in exchange for their acquiescence in his designs against the orator. Under the terms of Clodius' law Gabinius became governor of Syria for at least three years, perhaps longer: our evidence on this point is inconclusive and in any case Gabinius' tenure was interrupted in 54, when another tribunician measure, advanced in 55 by Gaius Trebonius, assigned Syria to Crassus. Syria was a highly desirable province: it was very rich and, because it was also politically unstable, furnished ample opportunity for reform or exploitation. The province was strategically located on Rome's eastern frontier, and Clodius' law allowed Gabinius to levy fresh troops in addition to the two legions already assigned to the province.[2] Gabinius, it was obvious to everyone, was an ambitious man. And he had plans for Syria.

Gabinius invited Antony to join his staff. Every governor took with him a retinue of aristocrats. In order to administer his province, he assembled a staff comprising his quaestor and a number of *legati*, legates or deputies, as well as officers denominated by various titles, some of whom were elected, others appointed. The governor was also accompanied by men without formal assignments—his *comites*, or companions—who joined him as consultants or assistants. All these men, elected officers, legates, or companions, were of equestrian or senatorial status and served the governor without a salary (although their expenses were paid). They must not be confused with a governor's functionaries, like his lictors, scribes, heralds, and so forth, who were salaried employees of the republic. By modern standards, it will be obvious, Roman provincial administration was remarkably amateurish in character—there was no diplomatic corps nor a class of professional officers commanding the troops—and its ranks were modestly staffed.[3]

Gabinius was not, then, offering Antony a job. He was instead cultivating the kind of friendly relationship typical between members of Rome's aristocracy. Gabinius had good reason to do so: his father had served under Antony's grandfather as his quaestor in his campaign against the pirates. Gabinius' offer to Antony, then, was a reflection of their families' continued goodwill and constituted an entirely natural expression of comity on the part of the senior man.[4] Nor, despite Gabinius' hostile relationship with Cicero, need one detect in Antony's decision to join him any hint of an alignment against the orator.[5] Relationships among aristocrats were hardly so reductive as that: Cicero, for example, although he was Gabinius' bitter enemy, was also, like Gabinius, Pompey's friend. Far from being hostile to Cicero, Antony was, as we have seen, a supporter who furnished the orator with loans during his exile.[6] Antony joined Gabinius because his offer was a welcome one. And a highly traditional one.

Antony, Prefect of the Cavalry

According to Plutarch, Antony did not immediately agree. He insisted on an appointment as an officer and was satisfied when Gabinius offered him the rank of cavalry prefect.[7] By the first century, Rome no longer fielded a cavalry of its own citizens but instead relied on subject forces, *auxilia*, for horsemen. These units, however, were routinely commanded by Roman prefects, responsible officers who, in a province like Syria, were certain to see combat.[8] Antony's decision was a notable one because, in this period, prefectures, although appealing to members of the equestrian order, were no longer posts highly sought after by members of the nobility—if our scrappy evidence is a reliable guide in this matter.[9] Still, some young nobles shone as cavalry prefects. Crassus' son was invaluable in the role in Gaul, and during the civil war Cicero's son was an impressive prefect fighting under Pompey.[10] Antony, too, was attracted by the post: he was eager to shine in battle.

Valour, *virtus*, never ceased to matter in Rome. But in the case of nobles its presence was generally assumed. Which is why, in Antony's day, so many members of the nobility, confident in the splendour of their family's reputation, allowed themselves to develop priorities other than martial ones and so became less devoted than their ancestors to warfare.[11] New men, by contrast, keen to prove their merit, continued to view military service as a highly practical means of attaining a respectable place in senatorial society.[12] There was never a shortage of aristocrats prepared to take their turn as officers, but not everyone sought multiple deployments in combat zones or aimed at commanding armies in foreign wars. This change in aristocratic conduct, although real, should not be exaggerated. At the same time, it must not go overlooked, and it is germane to any estimation of Mark Antony's early career. By extending himself, surely for the second time, in provincial service, and in provincial service likely to be marked by combat, Antony revealed himself a Roman noble who preserved what had by his day become an old-fashioned sensibility.

We cannot, however, leave it at that. Romans viewed the office of cavalry prefect as an ideal appointment for provincial profiteering. That was a use to which Antony's uncle had put the post when he served under Sulla, as we have seen.[13] Cicero, in reporting a witticism by Quintus Mucius Scaevola, takes it for granted (it is the predicate of the joke) that a request for a prefecture is naturally based on a desire to exploit provincials.[14] And the rich equestrian Atticus was praised by his biographer because, although he accepted prefectures, he never actually went out to a province in order to exercise the office: 'he was satisfied with the honour; he disdained any increase in his personal fortune'.[15] Now the totality of Antony's career is sufficient evidence for the man's lack of scrupulosity in financial matters, including exploiting official positions for the sake of personal gain. And if it is true that Antony served under his uncle in Macedonia, then that time abroad was a lengthy tutorial in multiple forms of administrative corruption. Not that we must conclude that Antony was ever so rapacious a figure as his kinsman. Still, his prefecture, awarded by a proconsul of a highly friendly disposition, put Antony in a position to acquire more than military glory—even if our sources, which are entirely favourable for this episode in his life, concentrate solely on his military and diplomatic successes.[16]

Roman Provinces and Roman Empire

Antony made his way into Roman public life principally as an officer in the provinces. And he was destined to spend most of his career as a triumvir in administering the provinces of the eastern Mediterranean. Even as a triumvir, the exercise of his power in the east was shaped by the traditional duties and the prevailing circumstances of any Roman governor. A triumvir operated on a scale that was grander than a provincial governor's but his responsibilities and worries obtained under more or less the same conditions. Understanding something about the nature of Rome's empire and the operations of its administration, then, because it is essential for grasping the situation of Antony the junior officer and, later, Antony the triumvir, requires a brief digression here.[17] We shall begin with provinces and their place in the Romans' conception of their empire. Then we shall turn to the practicalities of administration.

In the Roman view of things, dominion over the wider world was a reality limited only by the extent of the city's sheer potency, might which by Antony's day was nothing short of prodigious.[18] Polybius insists that by 167 the Romans had, by extinguishing the kingdom of Macedon, subjected the whole of the Mediterranean to their authority. More than once he returns to what he deems the universal recognition that everyone, and not only peoples actually conquered by the Romans, must obediently submit to the authority of this new superpower.[19] That view was by no means held by everyone in the Mediterranean in 167, but Polybius' judgement without question reflects the prevailing Roman attitude. It was a disposition rooted in Roman sensibilities regarding the fundamental nature of conquest: in the aftermath of any victory, the vanquished were obliged to concede that their defeat constituted a permanent condition, the terms of which could be revisited only by the Romans.

When, for instance, in 153 the Celtiberian city of Segeda (in modern Spain) endeavoured to justify a complaint about Roman interference in its affairs by citing specific favourable conditions outlined in a treaty imposed by Rome more than two decades previously, the Romans quickly made it clear how this objection revealed the Segecans' misunderstanding of the true nature of their prior capitulation. As Appian, who reports the incident, reminds his reader, 'the senate, when it grants favours, always stipulates that they will be valid only so long as the senate and people wish it'.[20] This same principle is found in a well-known inscription which is our only extant text of a formal surrender by a defeated people: the otherwise unattested Seanoci (a people in Spain) are granted, by their otherwise unattested conqueror, Lucius Caesius, a complete restoration of their freedom and possessions—but, again, only so long as the senate and people wish it so.[21]

Because Roman conquest was understood by the Romans as a continuous state and not a momentary event that could fade into the past, they viewed their right to exercise authority over the conquered as unlimited, certainly in principle and very often in practice. Annexation, as a consequence, was beside the point. Rome did of course annex various territories throughout the Mediterranean—and these annexations they denominated provinces, *provinciae*—but when rehearsing the constituents of their empire, a not infrequent activity in Rome, orators and writers routinely listed, alongside their provinces, the city's free allies and neighbouring kings.[22]

Provincial Administration

Originally *provincia* referred to an official responsibility assigned to a magistrate or promagistrate, oversight of the treasury, for instance, in the case of a quaestor, or, for a peregrine praetor, jurisdiction over legal cases involving foreigners. A consul or praetor was often directed to carry out, as his *provincia*, a specific military task, a duty that entailed the deployment of *imperium* by way of commanding troops in waging war against Rome's enemies. This sense of the word—the *provincia* as an assignment, and especially as a military assignment—persisted even after the Romans began annexing territories which they subsequently articulated into provinces defined in terms of geography.[23] Within his province, a Roman governor, like any Roman general, held absolute, incontestable authority.

Gabinius' province, Syria, was a relatively new one. In 64 Pompey was aghast at the perturbation afflicting the region and fretful, perhaps, that its instability rendered it vulnerable to Rome's formidable eastern neighbour, the kingdom of Parthia, which extended from modern Iran into Armenia and so far east as Afghanistan. He consequently decided, as part of his reorganization of the near east in the aftermath of the Third Mithridatic War, to impose annexation.[24] The resulting Roman province included several significant cities—Antioch became its capital—and entailed supervision over numerous free cities as well as client kingdoms like Ituraea, Judea, Edessa, and various minor principalities. The province bordered the Nabateans and sundry Arab dynasts: they, too, were a responsibility of the Syrian governor, whose authority was bolstered by the presence of two Roman legions. He needed them: even after Pompey's pacification of the area, Syria remained deeply riven by local animosities and the province was harassed by constant banditry, all potentially serious military challenges.

The first duty of any governor was maintaining peace and security in his province. For this reason, all provincial assignments were military commands and all governors possessed *imperium*, which they exercised over Roman forces and any allied forces they decided to muster. Still, the conditions of antiquity rendered impossible anything like a totalitarian martial regime. Instead, the Romans managed their domains largely by relying on existing infrastructures for government and administration. Admittedly there were times when the Romans felt obliged to impose a new constitution on their subjects. In these instances, too, they looked to the social order which already dominated. This was true from the beginning of Rome's eastern interventions. When Titus Quinctius Flamininus, after the Third Macedonian War, organized the cities of Thessaly, 'he chose the council and magistrates mainly on the basis of their wealth and gave a preponderance in each city only to that class in whose interest it was that everything remain secure and quiet'.[25]

Local dignitaries received esteem, protection, and economic advantages from Rome in exchange for their cooperation in overseeing the cities and districts of the province. These figures, owing to their regional influence and authority, were essential in sustaining the good order which they, like the Romans, recognized as necessary for prosperity. Even if the fundamental basis of Roman rule lay in its overwhelming military force, the incessant application of this force in maintaining Roman control was costly and unwelcome. Intimidation was important, of course, but collaboration was always preferable to the violent deployment of legions. Hence the Romans' routine resort to native instruments of regulation, a technique that entailed a notable degree of local autonomy even in provincial cities. This limited autonomy, however, furnished the political space in which local elites could operate on behalf of Rome and in their own interests.[26]

The rule of Rome came at a cost. As Cicero reminded his brother, when Quintus was governor of Asia: 'inasmuch as it is absolutely impossible to maintain our empire without taxation, a province should deem it only fair that its perpetual peace and tranquillity be purchased at the price of some part of its revenues'.[27] This extraction of taxes and tribute was a vital responsibility for every governor. Depending on the republic's requirements, payments were made in cash or in kind. Often their collection was the responsibility of local communities, which remitted their taxes directly to Roman authorities. At other times, however, companies of tax-farmers, the *publicani*, were employed. These were rich men of the equestrian order who formed companies, *societates publicanorum*, in order to provide many of Rome's public services (or *publica*, hence the denomination *publicani*), such as provisioning Roman armies or managing Rome's various and scattered public properties, especially Rome's mines. The task with which they are most closely associated remains the collection of taxes.

All these enterprises demanded enormous financial resources. Consequently, the companies formed by *publicani* were large and complex, involving numerous investors and a large and international staff. So effective were the *publicani* at tax collection that provincial communities and even neighbouring dynasties sometimes procured their services.[28] Their operations, unfortunately, are not always fully visible to us. Still, it is obvious from Cicero's recurring commentary on the dignity and clout of the *publicani*, and his animadversions on their cupidity, how vital a part they played in Roman administration, even if their part was not always an edifying one.[29] That the interests of the tax-farmers and the interests of Rome's subjects could diverge is obvious, and it was the duty of a governor to preserve an honest balance between all parties. Still, he should not offend Rome's financial class: even the thoroughly upright Cicero advises his brother that, whenever any local constituency is pushing back too hard against the *publicani*, he should have a quiet word with the provincials and nudge them towards compliance—even if compliance comes at something of a cost to them.[30]

And yet justice remained an important element in the administration of the empire: provincials, certainly elite provincials, had to be convinced that Rome furnished a reliable and accessible and at least fundamentally fair jurisdiction. For this reason, a conspicuous feature of every governor's administration was his court of assizes, which circulated through the province in order to exhibit its accessibility. In every case, the governor had the power to deliver the final and incontestable judgement on any matter arising within his province. The governor and his staff routinely settled controversies affecting cities, important provincials, and any Roman citizens— businessmen, financiers, or even Roman settlers—resident or active within his province. It is unsurprising that, in affairs of this nature, competing parties strained their every capacity in attempting to influence the governor's verdict, circumstances which opened the door to disreputable transactions. This is why a governor's tenure was customarily marked by so many tokens of honour—including, in the east, sacred honours—and by emoluments. Cultivation of this kind began even before a governor arrived in his province: when Gabinius departed Rome for Syria, for instance, the *publicani* whose investments he would soon regulate accompanied him on horseback as a kind of honour guard.[31] This was prudent, for the governor, within the confines of his province, possessed absolute and unchallengeable authority.[32] As Cicero put it to his brother: 'multitudes of Roman citizens and provincial subjects, many cities, many principalities—they all gaze intently at the nod of a single man from whom there is no appeal'.[33]

For all his inevasible authority, however, every Roman governor contended with multiple and competing claims on his duty or loyalty or friendship, and these factors inevitably affected any judgements he rendered. Provincial elites were hardly isolated figures: they cultivated close, sometimes profound, friendships with powerful Romans, with whom they remained in constant contact. Consequently, whenever local dignitaries collided with one another, they could each of them call on the influence of their respective Roman supporters. And in Syria as in other provinces there were Roman businessmen and financiers who, influential in their own right, could also conjure the clout of grandees in the city.[34] Finesse was required, a reality underscored in Cicero's long, public letter to his brother on the political hazards inherent in governing a province.[35]

Taxation and Profiteering

Tax collecting was a profitable business. And yet even greater gains could be made by financiers from lending money to cities or even kingdoms lacking the liquidity required to meet their immediate commitments to Rome, loans frequently made at usurious rates. These financiers were often *publicani* who operated simultaneously as tax-gatherers and lenders. Senators, too, by way of the complicated trading and selling of partnerships in the publicans' societies, or by way of equestrian shell-lenders masking their involvement, could be parties to this profiteering. Nor were all local elites excluded from these dividends: through their cooperation or complicity, the chief men of a province who succeeded in cultivating the right relationship with their Roman superiors also advanced in wealth and prestige at the expense of their own cities.[36]

Transactions of this kind, although they were pervasive, are rarely visible to us. Let us begin with a modest affair the conclusion of which, it appears, was satisfactory to everyone involved. An inscription erected in 71 by the Peloponnesian city of Gythium relates the difficulties faced by this city during the previous year when a heavy financial contribution was imposed on the town by Marcus Antonius, the father of Antony, who was then carrying out his command against piracy.[37] The city was in a serious plight but was rescued through the generosity of the brothers Cloatius, whose munificence is gratefully commemorated on this stone. These men were Roman knights who resided in Gythium. They had previously lent the city money and been congenial when renegotiating the loan. They had also, more than once, interceded on the town's behalf with Roman authorities—often covering the city's obligations to Rome at their own expense. When Gythium could not meet Antonius' demand, the town again turned to the Cloatii, who bailed out the city by way of a new loan. Its terms set the interest at 48% compounded annually, a rate later reduced to 24% simple interest, at which time the Cloatii also remitted a notable portion of what the city owed them. So thankful were the citizens of Gythium that they declared the brothers honoured benefactors and granted them civic privileges which were to be passed on to future generations. Here we see Roman money-lending at its best and most welcome. Even on these terms, however, it was a highly profitable business, and Gythium's gratitude to the Cloatii can only signal the harsher reality of much Roman investment in the provinces.

On a much grander scale were the investments of Pompey the Great, who, victorious in the Third Mithridatic War, put his position and profits to work by way of loans, constructed in collaboration with equestrian investors, to cities and kingdoms throughout the east. The sums involved in some of these transactions were massive. By the fifties, Ariobarzanes III, the king of Cappadocia, so we learn from Cicero, could do no more than pay the interest on his loan, itself an astonishing thirty-three talents per month. Not all could manage even that: again we learn from Cicero how Pompey's equestrian partner, Cluvius of Puteoli, was struggling to recover what was owed to Pompey and his associates by Mylasa, Alabanda, Heraclea, Bargylia, and Caunus, all communities falling under the administration of the governor of Bithynia. In a letter to this governor Cicero makes it clear that Pompey is exercised over these unpaid bills, information that can only have added to the man's disquiet over involving himself in this affair.[38]

Matters sometimes turned truly ugly when Romans turned ruthless in their determination to claw back debts. When Cicero was governor of Cilicia, he found himself confronted with the brutal methods employed by Marcus Brutus, the future Liberator, and his agents in their efforts to force the city of Salamis in Cyprus to disgorge money owed by the city for a loan it had contracted at 48% annually. In 53 or 52, in order to recover his investment, Brutus persuaded his father-in-law, Appius Claudius Pulcher, who at that time was governor of Cilicia and therefore overseer of Cyprus as well, to appoint Brutus' equestrian partner to a military prefecture and assign the man squadrons of cavalry he could put to work threatening the leading men of the town.[39] Lethal violence supervened, but the debt remained unresolved. For its part, the city claimed to be ruined by Brutus' exactions, and when Cicero succeeded Claudius as governor he was beset on one side by desperate Salaminians and on the other by avaricious businessmen representing Brutus—as well as by fierce letters from Brutus and urgent ones from his friend Atticus, all pressing him to deploy soldiers if need be in order to execute the terms of Brutus' loan. The orator was appalled.[40] Nor should it be thought that Cicero was some kind of naïf, for he, too, was perfectly prepared, under circumstances he deemed suitable, to exert himself on behalf of Roman creditors: Brutus was also owed money by Ariobarzanes, and in this case—on the grounds that it was a business matter in a client kingdom and not in a provincial city—Cicero was willing to award a prefecture or tribunate to another one of Brutus' equestrian agents. And in this case Brutus was able to make at least a partial recovery of his investment.[41]

Now Cicero had proved himself quite good in negotiations of the kind demanded by the standoff between Salamis and Brutus' coalition of equestrian investors. When he first arrived in his province he discovered that many cities were in arrears in their obligations to the *publicani*, for various reasons including local graft; through the combination of a strict crackdown on provincial peculation with a significant reduction in the rate of interest applied to the cities' loans, he succeeded in restoring a good relationship between the cities and the financiers. As a result of these compromises, the cities' overall indebtedness was much reduced, their fiscal integrity was restored, and regular repayments to the *publicani* were renewed—to the satisfaction of everyone involved. When Cicero endeavoured to arrange what he deemed decent, respectable terms for Salamis and its creditors, however, he was rebuffed by Brutus' agent. But although it was within his power to compel both parties to accept his terms, Cicero was unwilling to alienate his influential friends: he left the dispute hanging for his successor.

Gytheum and Salamis alike relied on Roman financiers in order to meet Roman demands for immediate payments in cash. Their experiences, plainly, were strikingly different, and in large measure this was owing to the personal ethics of the Romans who furnished them with loans and the governors who regulated their repayment. It was amid a web of relationships of this kind—between provincial cities and the government of Rome, between provincial cities and financiers, and between the agents of these parties and the governor on the spot—that Rome's administration of its provinces operated. And it is clear how, for governors less self-consciously rectitudinous than Cicero, provincial administration offered an abundance of opportunities for self-enrichment. Even Cicero, whose fundamental integrity in financial matters we need hardly question, returned from Cilicia a richer man. After returning to the treasury the balance of his grant for expenses, Cicero declared his legitimate personal profit to be more than two million sesterces. Some of this sum he doubtless made through the sale of captives from his campaigns against Cilician brigands, but surely not all of it or even the bulk of it.[42] But this was small stuff. In order to spare themselves the unwelcome burden of billeting Roman troops, the cities of Cyprus paid Cicero's predecessor a bribe of nearly five million sesterces. Although Romans lamented provincial corruption and passed laws to put a stop to it, the realities of Roman government entailed an unmistakable element of sleaze.[43]

Gabinius' Governorship of Syria

Gabinius' province was rife with insurrection and conflict. Pompey, as we have seen, established this province owing to the absence of any dominant local power capable of maintaining even a modicum of regional stability. At that time Syria was afflicted by constant conflict among regional dynasts, and Judea was divided by a civil war between the brothers Aristobulus and Hyrcanus, each struggling for sovereignty. This contest naturally attracted the involvement of outside chieftains and principalities, each of whom sought influence over the realm. An important figure in the Judean civil war was Antipater, a wealthy and influential Idumenean attached to the cause of Hyrcanus. Under his guidance, Hyrcanus won Pompey's favour, whereas Aristobulus resorted to violence which resulted in the fall of Jerusalem.[44] Aristobulus was taken prisoner and transported to Rome, while the government of Judea was placed under the authority of his rival, whom Pompey confirmed as High Priest. Notwithstanding Pompey's installation of peace in Syria, however, the province and the region continued to be troubled by disorder and strife—even in the teeth of Roman occupation.[45]

For Gabinius, Syria was very familiar territory. As Pompey's legate in 64 he had profited substantially from his unseemly insertions into the contest between Hyrcanus and Aristobulus.[46] During the following year he remained in the country when Pompey captured Jerusalem.[47] In an atmosphere so charged with precariousness, opportunities emerged for Gabinius to establish local connections, which he, like any other prominent Roman, will have endeavoured to sustain. When he returned to Syria as its proconsul, we can be confident, he was already personally invested in the politics, if not also the finances, of the region. As events would quickly show, he entered the province prepared for action on multiple fronts, domestic and international.

And indeed Gabinius' governorship was an eventful one. The proconsul campaigned in Judea, where he reorganized its government. He also introduced major reforms to the mechanics of taxation within his province, activities that alienated many among the *publicani*. He invaded Parthia, waged war against the Nabateans, and, most sensationally of all, marched into Egypt, where he restored Ptolemy Auletes to the throne in exchange for a bribe alleged to be ten thousand talents, or 240,000,000 sesterces.[48] During his tenure abroad Gabinius was denounced in Rome by his personal enemies, including Cicero, and his intrusion into Egyptian affairs, a project of signal importance to the interests of Pompey and Caesar, made him an obvious target for senators hostile to the First Triumvirate. Even before he returned to the city in 54 Gabinius was indicted for treason, *maiestas*. Acquitted by a thin majority, owing in large part to the influence of Pompey, Gabinius was further indicted for electoral corruption, *ambitus*, and provincial extortion, *repetundae*. The charge of *ambitus* was soon discarded, but in the matter of extortion he was condemned, even after Cicero, succumbing to pressure from Pompey, spoke for the defence.[49] In all these events, or certainly in most of them, young Antony played a notable role.

Gabinius and Judea

In Syria, action came fast. At the time of Gabinius' arrival, Judea was again shattered by an outbreak of civil war. The son of Aristobulus, Alexander, stirred fresh rebellion against Hyrcanus. He seized Jerusalem and began refortifying older military installations previously dismantled by Pompey. Gabinius reacted forcefully by besieging Jerusalem. Alexander was dislodged from the city, and, after further reversals, quickly locked up in Alexandreion, one of his refurbished strongholds. He soon surrendered. In the aftermath of this war, Gabinius instituted a far-reaching resettlement of Judea. The monarchy was abolished and in its place he established five autonomous regions, each managed by a council composed of local aristocrats. Hyrcanus, although patently incompetent as dynast, could not, inasmuch as he was Pompey's appointment, be dishonoured. Consequently, he remained High Priest. His authority, however, was restricted to religious duties.[50]

According to the historian Josephus, this reform was welcome in Judea.[51] But it did nothing to instil order or stability. In the next year, Aristobulus, along with another son, Antigonus, escaped Rome and reached Judea. There they easily raised a large army, clear evidence that, Josephus' opinion notwithstanding, monarchy remained a popular institution. Aristobulus even succeeded in winning over past partisans of Hyrcanus. Nevertheless, this revolt, too, was rapidly put down. Gabinius shipped Aristobulus back to Rome. His sons, however, were treated mercifully, owing to the intervention of their influential mother, who had assiduously cultivated the Roman community in Syria.[52] But that was hardly the end of it. When, in 55, Gabinius marched into Egypt in order to restore Ptolemy, an expedition to which we shall return, Alexander instigated yet another rebellion. This commotion was not a civil war but instead an insurrection against Roman hegemony, and many Romans resident in Judea were massacred. Alexander's forces this time excelled those he or his father had fielded previously. But they were no more successful. In a major battle fought near Mt. Tabor, the rebels were crushed. Again, the proconsul reorganized Judea.[53]

Little is known of the particulars of this final settlement, but its primary beneficiary is made absolutely clear in our sources: 'Gabinius then arranged affairs at Jerusalem in accordance with the designs of Antipater.'[54] In the interval between Pompey's settlement and Gabinius' arrival, the Idumaean Antipater had advanced his influence both in Judea and with surrounding principalities. In the conflicts of 57 and 56—and in the expedition to Egypt—he made himself indispensable to the Romans. It was only natural, then, that Gabinius should entrust the stability of Judea to the authority of a leader whose capacity matched his loyalty. Hyrcanus remained High Priest, and it is perhaps the case that his stature was in some way elevated by Gabinius' reform. But Antipater was now the leading figure in Judea, and his fortunes were destined to rise still higher: his later services to Caesar earned him Roman citizenship and in 47 he was officially recognized as procurator of Judea.[55] It was during Gabinius' proconsulship that Antipater cultivated a close and warmly reciprocated friendship with the young Antony, and this connection extended to Antipater's son, the future Herod the Great.[56] Herod remained a devoted friend of Antony, and it was through Antony's influence that Herod was later made first tetrarch of Galilee and ultimately king of Judea.[57]

Antony and Antipater and Herod

Antony's close relationship with Antipater and Herod is pertinent to any attempt at recovering the reality of his exploits in Syria. According to Josephus, our principal source for Gabinius' Judean campaigns, Antony's role was nothing short of heroic. In the initial clashes with Alexander, it is Antony who leads the vanguard, a performance he repeats in the war with Aristobulus.[58] In the assault on Alexandreion, Antony excels himself: 'his nobility, always splendid, was nowhere so much so as here'.[59] In Plutarch's account, although he conflates events, confounding the Roman's strikes against Alexander with his combat against Aristobulus, Antony's courage remains unobscured: he is the first man to scale the enemy's fortifications, and later, outnumbered in the field, routs the rebel army, slaying all save a handful.[60] Here is Antony the superlative Roman warrior, a natural predator, 'brute beauty and valour and act', to filch a phrase from Gerald Manley Hopkins.

This is exciting stuff. But this brand of unqualified, indeed hyperbolic, celebration of any man's exploits must incite scepticism at least equal to the suspicions aroused by accounts animated by invective and vitriol. It is an attitude required here, where it is clear enough that Josephus and, ultimately, Plutarch are each of them relying on the *Historiae*, or *Universal History*, of Nicolaus of Damascus.[61] This remarkable man—philosopher, orator, historian—was an influential figure in the court of Herod the Great and more than once Herod's successful advocate when he fell under Roman suspicions. He was also active in triumviral Alexandria, where he was tutor to the children of Antony and Cleopatra. At the end of his career, by which time he had become a friend of Augustus, Nicolaus settled in Rome, where he composed our earliest biography of the emperor, a work that is unfriendly to Antony.[62]

But that was later. Nicolaus was at the court of Herod when he penned his *Universal History*, one obvious purpose of which was to glorify his king. Hence Nicolaus' close attention to the career of Antipater—and to Antipater's friend and Herod's great benefactor, Antony, who was naturally exhibited in a favourable light.[63] Herod's friendship with Antony, it is worth observing, did not dissolve in the aftermath of Actium: on the contrary, when defending himself before Octavian, Herod adduced his loyalty to Antony both as the justification for his kingdom's past actions and as proof of his future fealty to the new regime. Octavian was persuaded.[64] So useful was this posture to Herod that he never relinquished it: a key garrison in Jerusalem, designed in part to protect the temple of the Jews, Herod named the Antonia in honour of his great patron, and the name endured until the temple's destruction.[65] It was in this environment, with all its Antonian enthusiasm, that Nicolaus, who was in any case closely acquainted with Antony, recorded the events in which Antony distinguished himself so brilliantly.

There is, however, no obvious reason to doubt the reality of Antony's valour in Syria, nor to question his usefulness in Gabinius' campaign. Antony, we have seen, sought a prefecture in the expectation that by fighting and through leadership he should show his noble virtue to advantage. But it is worth our observing that, even on the evidence of Josephus, at least in his *Antiquities*, Antony was only one, even if in retrospect the most famous, of several officers whom Gabinius trusted, each of whom doubtless endeavoured to impress. It is reasonable, then, to qualify our sources' laudatory register and conclude that Antony's doughtiness, undeniably real and very much on display in Syria, did him credit at the time and perhaps even enhanced his reputation in some quarters in Rome—without, however, causing anything like a sensation.

Gabinius and the *Publicani*

Josephus, and doubtless Nicolaus before him, was impressed by Gabinius' achievement in quelling the rebellions of Alexander and Aristobulus, and Gabinius' legions hailed him as *imperator*, conquering general.[66] It is perhaps a useful corrective, then, to observe that, for all his success in the Judean campaigns, Gabinius' request for a *supplicatio*, a thanksgiving for his victories, was rejected by the senate, an unusual and therefore noteworthy decision on the part of that body.[67] Cicero, who detested Gabinius, was delighted by this sensational rebuff, which he thereafter exploited by routinely complaining of the man's military reversals, not least his cavalry losses.[68] But this is vituperation which we may safely dismiss. From our perspective, Gabinius' successes merited the honour he was denied—even the hostile Cicero appears to have been surprised by the senate's refusal—which suggests that in this instance the proconsul was foiled by political interests opposed to him and not to any grave concern about his management of Syria. That this was the case is made clear by the uneven success of Cicero's *De provinciis consularibus*, *On the consular provinces*, delivered in June 56, only weeks after the senate's rejection of Gabinius' request for a *supplicatio* (that debate took place on 15 May). In this speech, Cicero argued vehemently that the senate should demand the recall of Calpurnius Piso from Macedonia and Gabinius from Syria. Cicero got his way over Piso, but Gabinius the senate declined to replace.[69]

Clearly, then, the body retained confidence in this man, even if it deemed it appropriate to slight him by denying him a *supplicatio*, which they did on behalf of the *publicani*. Cicero makes it clear to his brother that he was not present and did not participate in the senate's debate on Gabinius. He also informs him that the proconsul's disgrace was well-received outside the senate, which probably does not refer to demonstrations on the part of the general populace but is rather the orator's take on the reaction of many in the equestrian order.[70] When Cicero looked back on the senate's decision, in denouncing Gabinius yet again during a senatorial speech in 55, he connected his enemy's failure in the senate with his ill-treatment of Roman knights and *publicani* in his province.[71] This became a favoured topic of Gabinian abuse.

Again and again, Cicero inveighed against Gabinius' treatment of the *publicani*, unleashing bitter and distorting rhetoric lamenting how the proconsul degraded his countrymen by way of elevating Rome's subjects: 'the wretched *publicani* he handed over to Jews and Syrians—as slaves!'[72] In reality, Gabinius appears to have revised or cancelled existing loan agreements and, in some areas, including Judea, substituted either his own or locally managed operatives in place of the apparatus of the tax-farmers. But on what scale we cannot know. His encroachment cannot have been trivial. It is generally agreed that Gabinius' reforms constituted an extraordinary, perhaps unprecedented, intrusion into the routine system of taxation, tribute, and finance in his province and that his policy undermined the predominance of equestrian financiers—and presumably their senatorial partners—in the region.[73] They reacted by opposing his interests in Rome.

The Syrian interests of the Claudii, it is plausibly suggested, were degraded by Gabinius' actions. This is perhaps unsurprising. Although Clodius had furnished Gabinius with his province, the two men fell out later in the year when Clodius turned against Pompey.[74] Claudian resentment did not abate: when Gabinius returned to Rome, Appius Claudius Pulcher, who was then consul, savaged him in the senate and ardently supported his indictment for treason.[75] The Claudii will not have been the only senators whose financial interests in Syria were adversely affected by Gabinius' reforms, and even senators who were not invested in the province will many of them have been receptive to the complaints of the *publicani*. The senate's refusal to award Gabinius a *supplicatio* suffices to show that his reforms must have been extensive enough to prove costly to capitalists influential in Rome.

Controversy persists over whether Gabinius' intentions were honourable—did the proconsul act to protect provincials from the depredations of the *publicani*?—or whether his innovations were instead designed to elbow the *publicani* out of the way so that he could enrich himself. Two laws plausibly attributed to Gabinius are perhaps relevant, a *lex Gabinia* which forbade making loans to foreign representatives when they were resident in Rome and another designating February the month in which the senate must receive embassies.[76] Each of these measures, which limited Roman opportunities for exploiting the vulnerability of subject states, was drawn up with the interests of provincials in mind, which prompts the conclusion that Gabinius' proconsular reforms were animated by a similar sensibility. Care, however, must be taken: standing up to usury was always a commendable posture in Rome, and it must be acknowledged that Gabinius' law on lending, because it was susceptible to exceptions granted by the senate, was easily got round.[77] And more than one Roman politician's career exhibits a sharp disparity between a figure's tribunician legislation and his subsequent career.[78] Both Cicero and Dio, the former admittedly a hostile source, insist that Gabinius profited handsomely from his administration of Syria.[79]

We should perhaps avoid insisting on too sharp a distinction between Gabinius the reformer and Gabinius the opportunist. As we have seen, this man had been profitably involved in Syrian affairs during his service under Pompey, which means that any limitations he imposed on the *publicani* very likely benefitted his material interests in the province, and if his reforms worked to the advantage of the local aristocracy, whose indebtedness Gabinius reduced and to whom it appears he was handing over much of the remunerative work of tax collection, he could certainly expect practical and tangible expressions of gratitude from that quarter. And we must remind ourselves that, when we speak of Gabinius' fraught relationship with the *publicani*, we mean only those *publicani* whose income he infringed on.[80] As we shall see, Gabinius later enjoyed a perfectly amiable relationship with those *publicani* who were heavily invested in the restoration of Ptolemy Auletes.

What, we must ask, was Antony's role in all this? Perhaps he resisted Gabinius' policy on behalf of the *publicani* in the hope of winning favour at Rome. Or perhaps he resisted Gabinius' policy on behalf of some financiers and not others, thereby exhibiting the value of his friendship even at this early stage in his career. Almost certainly, just as he cultivated a close relationship with a figure like Antipater, Antony seized his chance, amid the proconsul's collaboration with the elites of Syria's cities, to forge connections, presumably lucrative connections, within the provincial aristocracy. What is unthinkable, however, is that, in this environment of potentially profitable disruption, Antony remained aloof. Provincial governors reached decisions only by way of consulting the peers who aided them as friends and advisors, a standard aristocratic practice even in Rome.[81] As an officer and therefore a member of Gabinius' staff, it was Antony's inescapable duty to play a role in the formation and administration of the proconsul's policy.

Antony and Archelaus

Gabinius' military designs reached beyond the frontiers of his province. In neighbouring Parthia, the murder of its king, Phraates, sparked a conflict between his sons, Orodes and Mithridates, which resulted in the expulsion of Mithridates from the kingdom. This prince then appealed to Gabinius for aid. The Roman took an interest, and in Mithridates' plight he believed he found a legitimate reason to invade Parthia: Phraates was formally an ally of Rome and so the restoration of his son represented, at least in principle, a covenanted responsibility on the part of Rome's proconsul. A notice in Strabo indicates that Gabinius took the trouble to consult with the senate, which did not demur.[82] So serious an undertaking as a Parthian war required careful planning, stealthy diplomacy, even intrigue. A valuable regional partner emerged in Archelaus, the High Priest and ruler of Comana. This man's father, also named Archelaus, had served as a general under Mithridates of Pontus, later defected to Rome, was declared a friend and ally of the Roman people by Sulla, and acted as an advisor to Licinius Lucullus in the Third Mithridatic War.[83] The son was valued by Pompey, who installed him at Comana.[84] In the course of his collaboration with Gabinius, Archelaus became an intimate of Antony.[85]

Archelaus, however, had detractors in the senate who frowned on his participation in Gabinius' expedition.[86] Elsewhere he was more welcome. In Egypt, Berenice, a daughter of Ptolemy XII, reigned as queen. In order to strengthen her position, for the Alexandrian elite were well aware that her exiled father was determined to regain his throne, it was decided that she should marry, and, on the pretence that Archelaus' true father was actually Mithridates, greatest of the kings of Pontus, Archelaus was invited to become her husband. At first, however, Gabinius detained him in Syria—the restoration of Ptolemy XII, whom the Alexandrians had driven from the Egyptian throne, was at the time the official if moribund foreign policy of the senate (see below)—but a generous bribe paid to Gabinius enabled his departure and Archelaus duly became king in Egypt. This took place in autumn of 56.[87] For Gabinius, the matter was inconsequential: he was busy settling affairs in Judea and planning his attack on Parthia. Early in 55, he commenced his invasion. His energies, however, were soon diverted elsewhere.

Fig. 2.1 Bust of Ptolemy XII, father of Cleopatra VII, 1st cent. BCE bust in the Louvre.
Source: Wikimedia Commons.

Ptolemy XII and the Problem of Egypt

Instead of Parthia, Gabinius invaded Egypt in order to topple Archelaus and Berenice and place Ptolemy XII on the throne. His change in plan requires an explanation. Ptolemy's relationship with the Roman senate, or, more precisely, with Pompey and Caesar, involved issues of Roman policy, fierce political infighting, and extensive financial corruption—and Gabinius, a Pompeian loyalist, was, while governor in Syria, caught up in its culmination. Ptolemy's reign began in 80, but his right to rule was almost immediately challenged by the Alexandrian elite, with whom he grew increasingly unpopular. An additional threat lurked in Rome, where Marcus Crassus, during his censorship in 65, urged the senate to annex Egypt.[88] In order to steady his position, Ptolemy looked to the senate. During Caesar's consulship in 59, he secured formal recognition as king in Egypt and was designated *socius et amicus populi Romani*, ally and friend of the Roman people, by the senate. This did not come cheap: the senate was won over only by heavy bribery, of which Caesar and Pompey were the chief beneficiaries. Roman financiers, whose capital made Ptolemy's emoluments practicable, also benefitted: their loans to the king brought them a hefty income by way of interest.[89]

In 59, then, Ptolemy's throne appeared secure. But in 57 the king was driven from Alexandria by Egyptians unhappy with Ptolemy's manner of government, not least his kowtowing to Rome. The king took refuge with his Roman friends, from whom he sought restoration. He had on his side a strong moral claim for Roman support—he was after all a friend of the Roman people—and his position was more than amply bolstered by the precarity of his financial circumstances: Ptolemy owed great debts in Rome and could repay them only if he were returned to power. Pompey took Ptolemy in hand, installed him in his Alban villa, and vigorously set to work in arranging the sovereign's affairs, a settlement that entrained fresh loans. Ptolemy's creditors included senators as well as equestrian capitalists. Chief among them was the rich investor Rabirius Postumus.[90]

Pompey exhibited his usual efficiency: in spring he addressed the senate, raising the issue of the king's restoration. The government in Alexandria, alarmed by Ptolemy's success in Rome, attempted to counter the exile's case by sending an embassy of one hundred delegates. The king and his Roman abettors—one of them was the young Marcus Caelius Rufus—arranged for these ambassadors to be assaulted when they arrived in Italy. Some were murdered, the residue intimidated or corrupted.[91] Consequently, Ptolemy's case prevailed in the senate. It was soon decreed that in the next year the governor of Cilicia should restore him. That man was a consul of 57, Publius Lentulus Spinther. In November Spinther departed for his province, which was intended to be the base for his expedition to Egypt.[92] But although he enjoyed the public support of Pompey and others, Spinther was not the first choice of the king or his equestrian backers, who preferred Pompey for the job.

The prospect of Pompey's winning the glory of leading Roman legions into Egypt, however, stirred resentment and hostility from many quarters.[93] Contentiousness over the command escalated sharply and rapidly, until early in January of 56 lightning struck a statue of Jupiter on the Alban Mount, an omen which led to an official consultation of the Sibylline Books. There an oracle was discovered warning against either embracing or rejecting the king of Egypt and forbidding the monarch's restoration 'with a crowd', an expression that was unsurprisingly taken to mean 'with an army'.[94] This sacred intervention naturally blighted the attraction of this assignment, yet it did nothing to settle Roman policy. Pompey's alleged ambitions were savagely attacked in popular demonstrations led by Clodius, and the issue drove a sharp wedge between Pompey and Crassus. Various proposals for Ptolemy's restoration by way of diplomatic actions were ventilated in the senate, but none prevailed, and very soon Pompey and Spinther alike abandoned the project.[95] Frustrated, the king removed himself from Rome to Ephesus.[96]

But there was too much money at stake for Pompey, Caesar, or their capitalist associates to abandon Ptolemy. And, after Archelaus was installed as king in Egypt, time was clearly of the essence. Political developments in Rome further concentrated the attention of Ptolemy's supporters. Near the end of 56, the triumvirs reaffirmed their friendship and expanded their network of senatorial allies at the conference at Luca. By means of violence and intimidation, Pompey and Crassus were elected consuls for 55. But central to Crassus' decision to remain in the alliance was his insistence that he be awarded the province of Syria. Desperate to keep up with Caesar and Pompey in the contest for military glory, he aimed at a Parthian conquest. This meant Gabinius had to go, but it was a demand Pompey felt powerless to resist. Nor could Pompey or Caesar hope to persuade their colleague to exert himself in restoring Ptolemy to his throne: during his censorship, Crassus had argued for the kingdom's annexation—a campaign in Egypt could only be an act of inconstancy—nor was he now to be distracted from Parthia.[97] For the consortium of Ptolemy's creditors, the situation was becoming a truly desperate one.

At the same time, Crassus' Parthian ambitions supplied Pompey and Caesar with fresh leverage for persuading Gabinius to take up the job. Indeed, he must have appeared their last hope, inasmuch as Lentulus Spinther, still in Cilicia, remained unwilling to aid the king. Consequently, Rabirius Postumus, on behalf of the consortium, travelled to Ephesus in order to negotiate with Ptolemy. The king's circumstances required urgent, unwelcome measures. He had little choice but to agree that, once restored to power, he would grant Rabirius the authority to extract Egyptian funds for a quick repayment of his Roman debts. There is no reason to believe Gabinius, or any of his officers, was previously involved in making loans to Ptolemy, but the king now added them to his long list of creditors because it would be necessary for him to bribe Gabinius to make an invasion. Rabirius then made his way to Syria, where he handed Gabinius letters from the king and from Pompey and doubtless others, all pleading with him to invade Egypt.[98] Caesar, who was deeply invested in Ptolemy's predicament, intensified the pressure. He also agreed to furnish auxiliaries to augment Gabinius' forces.[99] Pompey and Caesar will also have informed Gabinius that legislation transferring Syria to Crassus' command would soon be carried, which meant that, short of a highly improbable blitzkrieg-style victory in Parthia, he would soon be superseded before he could realize anything in the way of a spectacular accomplishment there. Egypt, in other words, was Gabinius' only real option, unless he was satisfied with his achievements in Judea. And inasmuch as the hostility of the *publicani* whom he had edged out of Syria awaited him in Rome, this was no time to refuse his friends.

The political risk to the proconsul was obvious and real—restoring Ptolemy could only attract hostility and prosecution in Rome—but he would have formidable supporters, not least Pompey. And riches. It was alleged that Ptolemy was now offering 10,000 talents, or 240 million sesterces, in exchange for his reinstallation in Alexandria.[100] This sum, even if its preciseness is less than trustworthy, must reflect the scale of the money involved in this operation. This amount was almost certainly intended for distribution among the consortium of Ptolemy's creditors. Still, there is no question but that Gabinius' share was a considerable one. Finally, there was the coercive power of aristocratic *amicitia*: Gabinius' friendship with Pompey was a long-standing one, and he owed his elevation to the consulship to the great man. His obligation to accommodate his friend, even in extreme circumstances, was quite simply inescapable. Which is why Gabinius abandoned his Parthian campaign—and his Parthian allies—in order to turn his forces towards Egypt.

Invading Egypt

At first, however, the proconsul hesitated and took advice from his staff. As well he should, because any march into Egypt constituted a clear violation of Roman law: the *lex Cornelia de maiestate* (the Cornelian law on treason) and the *lex Iulia de repetundis*

Fig. 2.2 Pompey the Great, 1st cent. CE head in the Ny Carlsberg Glyptotek.
Source: Wikimedia Commons.

(the Julian law on provincial extortion) each forbade any governor from taking troops outside his province without permission from the Roman people or Roman senate.[101] Gabinius would later insist that his Egyptian campaign was conducted *rei publicae causa*, for the sake of the republic, but that excuse was fragile at best.[102] Nor could the formal urging, even instruction, of a sitting consul be deemed a clearly adequate legal basis for invading Egypt. Any decision to march on Alexandria, then, could only be a risky one. Hence this consultation.[103]

Now Ptolemy's generosity extended even to Gabinius' legions and therefore certainly to his officers, but according to Plutarch few of these were in favour of the expedition.[104] And with good reason. Gabinius' invasion of Parthia was by Roman lights a glorious undertaking, and one likely to prove profitable for rankers and commanders alike. Furthermore, it was sanctioned by senatorial authority, whereas Gabinius' officers, and indeed the proconsul himself, could be certain that an expedition against Egypt would lead to an indictment in Rome. Admittedly, only the proconsul would be liable to prosecution, but in such a trial any member of his official retinue could be subjected to obloquy and disgrace.[105] Gabinius' officers, or certainly a significant slice of them, preferred waging war in Parthia.

Antony, however, was keen to take on Egypt, an enthusiasm his biographer attributes to his ambition for great deeds.[106] But for glory Parthia should have sufficed.

If Antony was indeed a proponent of restoring Ptolemy, other factors must have influenced him: lucre, perhaps, or the prospect of ingratiating himself with Pompey and Caesar and others who were behind Rabirius. It is in any case clear that, in this instance, constitutional proprieties counted for little with young Antony: Cicero was not entirely off the mark when, in denouncing Antony in his *Second Philippic*, he complained that, by taking part in Gabinius' expedition to Alexandria, Antony displayed contempt for the authority of the senate, the republic, and civic religion.[107] One suspects here a degree of sheer adventurism: this noble son of a noble senator, like others of his kind in the late republic, deemed himself invulnerable to political perils that might ruin lesser men. And, as events would show, he was right to do so.

Once again Gabinius acted in cooperation with Antipater and Hyrcanus: Judea furnished troops and supplies, and Antipater joined in the campaign.[108] Antony was once more a commander in the army's vanguard, but the Romans' passage along the coast towards Egypt met with no resistance and so combat was unnecessary. Plutarch is eloquent in his description of the difficulties thrown up by the terrain and of Antony's skill in overcoming them, but his purpose is a literary one: to highlight his subject's natural capacity as a leader even in his youth. Which means there is no reason to surmise anything but a routine march to Pelusium, modern Tell el-Farama, the easternmost city of Lower Egypt and a strategic site guarding Egypt against enemy advances from the northeast. Here, too, there was no resistance: the garrison at Pelusium was dominated by Jews, who were soon persuaded by the blandishments of Antipater to admit the Romans. Antony, again according to Plutarch, was the Roman officer on the scene for this diplomatic success, and it is very likely that he played an important part in assuring the city of its safety if it yielded without a struggle. Ptolemy, we are told, preferred bloodshed when he arrived at Pelusium, but, in Plutarch's narrative, was forestalled by Antony, a version of events which probably compresses an episode in which Gabinius obliged the king to respect the prior negotiations of Antipater and Antony.[109]

This is not to say that Archelaus did not put up a stout resistance in defence of his crown. His familiarity with Gabinius' resources made him aware of his military inferiority, and so he sent ships to harass Syria—Gabinius would later adduce these naval attacks as a justification for his invasion—and doubtless he played a part in stirring up a fresh rebellion in Judea, all in the hope that Gabinius would be compelled to abandon his march into Egypt in order to restore the security of his province. When this strategy did not succeed, he confronted the Romans in combat but, although his forces fought fiercely—indeed, Archelaus fell in battle—the Egyptians quickly succumbed. Antony, Plutarch tells us, once more distinguished himself in the fighting, valour we need not exclude although it is doubtless underlined a bit too boldly by the biographer.[110]

Ptolemy, restored to power, straightaway executed his daughter and purged the government of his enemies. Antony, by contrast, exercised his influence by insisting on a proper burial for Archelaus, who had been his friend in Syria.[111] The Alexandrians were by no means pleased to see the hated Ptolemy returned to the throne, and the bloodbath that followed can only have provoked deep consternation among all classes.

Matters were made worse when Gabinius stationed Roman troops in Alexandria who remained at Ptolemy's disposal.[112] And if at this point it was known that Rabirius, a Roman knight, was to be appointed *dioecetes*, or chief of the royal treasury, then the conviction that Alexandria had become something akin to an occupied city, the true master of which was Rome, may have begun to seize its population.[113] It is hardly surprising, then, that in the midst of these dispiriting, frightening events, Antony's ceremonial gesture of respect to Egypt's former king won him acclaim and popularity in Alexandria. His chivalry was never forgotten.

One item requires inclusion here. Appian mentions a report that Antony, when serving under Gabinius, fell in love at first sight with Cleopatra, 'although she was only a girl'.[114] That Antony met Cleopatra during this campaign is a certainty: she was in exile along with her father and she, like her father, was restored to Alexandria by Gabinius. Cleopatra was fourteen at the time, just flirting with the lower limits of Roman notions of nubility, so this story, by ancient standards, is not quite so creepy as it appears when translated into modern terms. It is not altogether impossible, then, that Antony was instantly enamoured by the future queen. But it is extremely unlikely, and Appian's qualification makes it clear that he, for one, finds this account unnatural. The anecdote is better regarded as one of many tales that accumulated round the legend of Cleopatra's fatal attraction for Antony. Even Plutarch, with his fondness for prolepsis, ignores it.

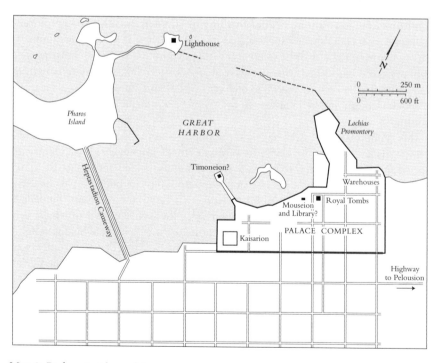

Map 2 Ptolemaic Alexandria

Coda

Gabinius, when he was still in Egypt, learned that Judea was again in revolt. Sending Antipater ahead, he soon followed and crushed the rebellion in a pitched battle. Gabinius' forces also clashed with marauding pirates, and he led a brief campaign against the Nabateans. Although Josephus is our source for these episodes, in none of them does he mention any role for Antony, which suggests, in view of this author's proclivities, that he had none.[115] Either Antony departed Gabinius' service in Egypt or did so soon after his return to Syria. This need not signal anything in the way of a falling out between the two men. It was simply obvious that Gabinius' tenure was reaching its end and, for Antony, new occupations beckoned.

As for Gabinius, his return to Rome was marked by an entirely predictable level of hostility and an array of prosecutions. Pompey did all he could. Crassus, virulently outspoken against Gabinius, was won over by a bribe. As for Cicero, Pompey, by employing the moral suasion of friendship, coupled with a degree of sharp compulsion, persuaded the orator to make his peace with Gabinius and become his advocate in the courts. The great man also strained himself in trying to win over senators and equestrians alike. But to no avail. Gabinius, although acquitted on a charge of treason, was condemned for provincial extortion—a charge that appears to have focused not on his actions in Syria but on his restoration of Ptolemy. Rabirius, too, was prosecuted for his role in receiving a share of Gabinius' ill-gotten gains. Amid this fervid litigation, one item is clearly pertinent to Antony. Among the men vying for the opportunity to prosecute Gabinius on the charge of extortion were Gaius and Lucius Antonius, Antony's younger brothers. Their application was unsuccessful. That was perhaps unsurprising: Cicero did not take them very seriously, and they may have been late in trying to become involved in the case. But their very presence in this affair requires comment.[116]

That Antony's brothers, young men in their twenties, should seek the limelight of a sensational prosecution is a perfectly natural phenomenon. Even the opportunity of delivering an oration in the *divinatio*, the contest over awarding the prosecution, was a welcome one. But the question is unavoidable: does their participation in this *divinatio* indicate that Antony had turned on Gabinius? In trials for provincial extortion, the subordinates of an indicted governor could sometimes be dragged into the case for abuse at the hands of prosecutors. This is one reason why it was not unknown for men, after completing their provincial service, to join in the prosecution of their former commanders. But such conduct was generally viewed as disreputable.[117]

As we have seen, the Antonii and Gabinii were families which had remained on good terms over a long period of time, and, in view of Antony's close collaboration with Gabinius in Syria and in Egypt, there was no obvious reason for his family to repudiate Gabinius now. Doing so could only offend Pompey and Caesar, and subsequent events demonstrate that Caesar, for one, was in no way alienated from Antony. It is better to conclude that the Antonii put themselves forward as covert accomplices of Gabinius' supporters: their intention was not to ruin the man but rather to stage a prosecution designed to fail, a cunning tactic so familiar in Rome that it had its own name, *praevaricatio*.[118] Although they never had an opportunity of putting their scheme into practice, the Antonii nevertheless made it clear to Gabinius, and to Pompey and Caesar, where their loyalties lay.

It was during his years in Syria, at least according to Plutarch, that Antony cultivated his distinctive style of leadership. Roman rankers expected their commanders to be brave and resolute, but different generals inspired their men in different ways. Some earned respect, if not affection, by way of severity. Others, like Caesar, applied a prudent combination of strictness and laxity in order to clarify their priorities and accommodate the personal needs of their soldiers. Antony, during his subaltern days in any case, despite the splendour of his birth, was fond of associating with his soldiers while they ate and drank, engaging in masculine ribaldry, and taking an interest in their personal lives, especially their romantic entanglements. He was also personally generous. All of this comes to us from Plutarch, for whom a generous Antony and Antony the elegiac lover are recurring motifs in his biography of the man.[119] But Antony's undeniable capacity as a military leader may well have had as one of its elements a willingness, at least on occasion, to treat his soldiers humanely instead of relying exclusively on the fundamental *de haut en bas* character of Roman social relationships.

Three aims motivated Antony's decision to join Gabinius. First, he hoped to enrich himself by way of the traditional opportunities associated with provincial service, and there is no reason to doubt that he did so. Second, he anticipated expanding his network of personal connections in the near east.[120] And again, he succeeded. Finally, Antony had insisted on a cavalry command in order to prove himself in combat and to shape his identity as a leader of men. That he did so is beyond question, even if we must temper the enthusiasm of our sources. The part played by Antony in Gabinius' invasion of Egypt was so well known in Rome that Cicero, more than a decade later, could make slighting references to it in his *Second Philippic*.[121] Antony's prefecture was a splendid success for the young noble. It is no surprise that he was soon serving at the side of Julius Caesar.

III

Quaestor, tribune, and guardian of Italy

After Egypt

After leaving Gabinius, Antony momentarily eludes our sources and we are poorly informed of his movements before 53, when he is again in Rome and a candidate for the quaestorship. By the end of 54, perhaps, or early in 53 he was with Caesar in Gaul. Cicero, in his *Philippics*, insists Antony could not be bothered to return to Rome, but this is a claim he introduces only to launch a riff on Antony's poverty: he had no home, the orator crows, to return to.[1] The interval between Gabinius and Caesar, however, may have been long enough for Antony to return to the capital or, just perhaps, travel to Cephallenia, where his uncle, Gaius, lived in luxurious exile as the island's virtual lord.[2] Antony was twenty-eight years old. His senatorial career lay before him. It was time to marry. A suitable wife, in Antony's circles, in addition to the charm, culture, and affection Romans prized in their partners, also possessed a distinguished pedigree or opulence, valuable for assisting her husband's lifestyle in public and private life. Ideally, she brought both qualities to a marriage.[3]

Antony married Antonia, one of his uncle's daughters and therefore his first cousin.[4] Marriage between first cousins was not common in the Roman aristocracy—men ordinarily preferred, by way of marriage, to expand their network of affinities—but nor was it illegal.[5] Gaius Antonius, it appears, was imaginative in the matter of marriage ties. His elder daughter he married to Lucius Caninius Gallus, a person of modest senatorial antecedents but impressive personal energy. Remarkably, he was one of the prosecutors who drove Antonius into exile in 59. Nevertheless, Antonius liked what he saw in the man. They were reconciled and joined by an unexpected marriage tie.[6] Caninius' career, however, was truncated. He, too, was charged with a crime, found guilty, and removed himself to Athens.[7] Still, Antonius' investment was a sound one for his family. Caninius' son, Antonius' grandchild, was destined for a consulship in 37, an appointment secured by Antony.[8] Nor was he the last Caninius Gallus to hold a consulship. In the case of Mark Antony, Antonius was able not only to attach his daughter to a rising noble but also, by marrying her to a cousin, keep a significant slice of his money and property in the possession of the Antonii. From Antony's perspective, affinity with his uncle brought him access to great wealth and an array of eastern contacts without binding him to any family implicated too deeply or dangerously in the political contentiousness of the fifties.

Antony very likely married Antonia in Rome.[9] Exactly when this marriage took place we do not know. However, we do know that Antony's daughter by Antonia was later betrothed to the son of Marcus Aemilius Lepidus: they married in late 38 or 37.[10] Aristocratic women were normally teenagers when they married for the first time. A birthdate in 53 for Antony's daughter, then, is reasonable and this fits neatly with a marriage between Antony and Antonia in 54. That is not the only possibility. Antony was certainly in Rome for nearly a year when he canvassed for the quaestorship, as we shall see, arriving by mid-53 and returning to Gaul by mid-52. If his daughter was born in 52 or 51, she was also, by Roman standards, of marriageable age in 38. A later birthdate, of course, need not imply a later marriage. The sad realities of ancient demographics entail a high infant mortality rate: young Antonia may not have been the first child born to this couple. We cannot exclude that Antony married on the very eve of his race for the quaestorship.[11] But a marriage in 54, when Antony was in his late twenties, more naturally suits the rhythms of aristocratic family life.

Service with Caesar

Very probably, then, it was as a married man that Antony joined Caesar in Gaul. How he gained his appointment we do not know. Caesar may have invited him. As a young man, he may have served under Antony's father, in which case he would naturally wish to reciprocate.[12] Or Antony may have proposed the idea—he had no reason to be shy—and he could summon the recommendations of influential friends keen to do a young noble a favour. Antony's uncle, the ex-consul Lucius Iulius Caesar, was on friendly terms with Caesar. He was an obvious choice for a recommendation. So, too, Cicero. His brother Quintus was one of Caesar's legates, and we know the orator sustained a steady correspondence with Caesar.[13] Nor should Gabinius be overlooked: he remained close to the dynasts and to the Antonii. Whatever the social lubrication that eased Antony's way into Caesar's command, there cannot have been any resistance. A young noble, even an inept one, was an ornament, and Antony's martial talents were not in doubt. In Gaul, Antony served alongside Lucius Munatius Plancus and Gaius Trebonius, each a future consul.[14] And the presence of Quintus Cicero allowed Antony to continue his cultivation of the great orator: the Tullii Cicerones, after all, were family friends.

After his splendid service in Syria, Antony was doubtless given a position of responsibility, but, again, we do not know what it was. Our first glimpse of him as an officer under Caesar does not come until 52, during the massive Gallic revolt against Rome led by Vercingetorix.[15] The scene is the brutal siege of Alesia, where the Gaul and his army were besieged by the Romans. The Romans, too, remained under fierce attack by Gauls struggling to relieve the siege. In reaction, Caesar constructed a strongly fortified system of doubled circumvallation, the double walls of which contained Vercingetorix in Alesia but also looked outwards, defending his legions from assaults by the Gallic relief force. It is amid this harsh conflict, during a bold night attack, that Antony comes into view. At this point, he was a legate: in cooperation with Trebonius, he was responsible for holding an important segment of Caesar's defensive line. But this moment came after Antony's election as quaestor, when he had returned to Gaul as quaestor-elect.[16]

Fig. 3.1 Bust of Julius Caesar, a 16th cent. CE bust by Andrea de Pietro di Marco Ferrucci in the Metropolitan Museum in New York.
Source: Wikimedia Commons.

Quaestor

By summer in 53, and almost certainly earlier than that, Antony was in Rome, where he intended to canvass for a quaestorship of 52.[17] He was now thirty, a natural and probably the minimum legal age for standing.[18] He possessed all the qualities of a plausible candidate: birth, military achievement, family connections; through his military service in the east he had acquired profits and friends abroad; his marriage to Antonia furnished him further funds and a personal profile suitable to a man of senatorial rank.[19] He was encouraged to stand by Caesar, who dutifully commended him to influential figures in Rome, one of whom was Cicero.

Although he later denied it, the orator was kindly disposed.[20] His family was attached to the Antonii, he was a confirmed friend of Antony's uncle and father-in-law (before they were competitors for the consulship, Cicero had supported Antonius' candidature for the praetorship, and once elected the two men were publicly reconciled; Cicero defended Antonius, unsuccessfully, in 59), and he was Antony's fellow tribesman, a traditional basis for electoral endorsement. During Cicero's exile, Antony had loyally furnished the orator and his brother Quintus with sorely needed loans.[21] Their friendship was long-standing and close: in a letter written in 49, Cicero

is perplexed that Antony, after arriving in the orator's neighbourhood, did not immediately call on him: that, Cicero observes to Atticus, was his regular habit.[22] By aiding Antony, Cicero could sustain, even enhance, their existing amity—and do Caesar
a favour. Indeed, there was no practical reason for the orator to be uncooperative.
Twenty quaestors were elected in each year, which meant that a noble like Antony was
a virtual shoo-in. By aiding Antony's canvass, Cicero—and doubtless other, unnamed
grandees—invested in their own future influence. Contentiousness animated races
for higher magistracies: in the case of the quaestorship, ordinarily only a new man,
or an abominable one, need fret over his chances. Cicero became a firm advocate of
Antony's election and expected to benefit from the association.[23]

Antony found himself in a disorderly, almost ungovernable city, where the circumstances of canvassing were anything but routine. In 54, canvassing for the magistracies
of the following year had been rife with sharp practice and corruption, a condition
worsened by the shocking revelation that the consuls, Appius Claudius Pulcher and
Lucius Domitius Ahenobarbus, had joined with two dishonest candidates for the consulship in a sleazy electoral conspiracy. This explosive scandal incited public outrage,
but the consuls, although tarnished, remained shameless. So, too, all the candidates,
who attacked one another with legal charges and countercharges. Elections were postponed more than once and finally abandoned until the next year. It was not until the
summer of 53 that magistrates for that year were, at last, elected.[24]

This was the fervid atmosphere in which Antony began his campaign for the quaestorship. After the elections for 53 were concluded, canvassing for 52 could commence
in earnest. But this soon turned very ugly. Clodius Pulcher was now a leading candidate for a praetorship of 52. His bitter enemy, Titus Annius Milo, was seeking a consulship. He was, it appears, the leading candidate and Clodius was determined to block
him. In opposing Milo, Clodius advanced not only his own interests but those of his
ally, Pompey the Great, who preferred other men.[25] He supported his former quaestor,
Publius Plautius Hypsaeus, and favoured a third candidate, Quintus Metellus Scipio,
a figure of unexcelled nobility soon to become Pompey's father-in-law.[26] Milo, however, enjoyed strong support among the senate's noble opposition against Caesar and
Pompey, nor, outside Clodius' urban following, was he unpopular with the public.

His cause was also championed by Cicero. Although closely aligned at this time with
Caesar and Pompey, Cicero was deeply in Milo's debt: as tribune the man had been instrumental in countering Clodius' urban violence and making possible Cicero's recall
from exile.[27] Cicero's probity and dignity demanded that he spare no effort on Milo's
behalf, a position Caesar and Pompey were obliged to respect and did respect. Soon,
Cicero was so closely identified with Milo's candidature that he became an object of
Clodian attacks. Searing invective, a routine facet of Roman canvassing, was usually
directed against one's rivals. But Clodius, when denouncing Milo in a speech delivered in the senate, seized the moment to devote much of his diatribe to vituperating
Cicero's career and character.[28]

Trash talk was topped by street fighting.[29] In one notorious episode, Clodius and
his gangs fell upon Milo on the Via Sacra. The man barely escaped with his life. Milo
fought back. Fearing his enemy would be returned as consul, Clodius continually disrupted every attempt at convening an assembly. That Clodius' enmity was concentrated on Milo he made clear by permitting elections for the tribunes of the *plebs* to

proceed, a concession which also exhibited his respect for the popular will. This gesture, however, was Clodius' only concession to public order: he appears even to have prevented the election of plebeian aediles, also chosen by the plebeian assembly (*concilium plebis*).[30] As for all other magistracies, because they could be elected only after consular elections had taken place, Clodius' obstruction blocked the creation of any executive government. So severe was the urban violence prevailing in Rome that, once again, magisterial elections were abandoned for the year.

Antony played a small but conspicuous part in the brutalities of 53—as a defender of Cicero. A friend of Caesar and therefore an ally of Pompey, Antony, if he felt an urge to become involved in the public hostilities racking Rome, might have been expected to show support for Clodius against Milo. But not everything in Rome was about Pompey and Caesar, as Cicero's devotion to Milo demonstrated. Antony was no friend of Clodius and, more importantly, was publicly allied with Cicero in his canvass for the quaestorship. He could not abandon him now. Perhaps, too, Antony was truly concerned for Cicero's safety. Clodius was a formidable and violent enemy and made it clear that Cicero was now a target. For these reasons, Antony took Cicero's side, a move which could hardly offend Pompey or Caesar. Antony's interest lay, not in deciding the outcome of the consular elections, but in making a show of protecting his friend.

More than once, Cicero recollects Antony's forceful exertions on his behalf. In his *Defence of Milo*, delivered when Antony opposed him as a prosecutor at Milo's trial for the murder of Clodius, an event we shall come to presently, Cicero adduced Antony's early and forceful hostility against Clodius:

> Recently, it was Mark Antony who inspired in all good citizens the highest hopes for our future salvation when he, a young man of the highest nobility, bravely took up the cause of the republic and snared that monster as he escaped the nets of a trial. O immortal gods, what a chance, what an opportunity that was![31]

Cicero goes on to allude obliquely to a moment when Antony fell upon Clodius, a scene he elaborates in the *Philippics* when he claims that Antony, brandishing a sword, chased the man through the Forum, his quarry managing an escape only by hiding under the stairs of a bookshop.[32] It is of course highly unlikely that Antony went round the Forum armed. Weapons were forbidden inside the pomerium, and even the most thuggish of Roman streetfighters relied on fists or clubs instead of knives and swords.[33] The two men's confrontation, in Cicero's over-the-top elaboration of it, is a fiction. But that does not mean Antony failed to confront Clodius in public, perhaps violently, or stopped short of threatening his life if he did not relent from attacking Cicero. Antony—on this point Cicero must be believed—made his forceful opposition to Clodius very public. That, after all, was the point.

Antony and Cicero's Election as Augur

Antony's service to Cicero was not limited to issuing threats. He took the orator's part when he was a candidate for co-option into the college of augurs. Roman civic life was inseparable from its civic religion, ceremonies and rituals regulated by the learning located in its priestly colleges. The most important of these priesthoods were the augurs, pontiffs, and quindecemvirs. Augurs were experts in taking the auspices, sacred techniques which allowed the Roman people to grasp the will of the gods and sustain the *pax deorum*, the republic's pact with its gods. The flights and activities of birds, occurrences of thunder and lightning, and other natural phenomena could, if interpreted rightly, act as omens. Because state actions like public assemblies or meetings of the senate required the correct and exact performance of ritual, augurs, as individuals and as a college, owing to their erudition in sacred matters, possessed important political as well as religious authority. If an augur recognized an ill-omen, to take the most prominent example of his public role, that judgement was beyond appeal: whenever he uttered the formula, *on another day*, any civic assembly must be dissolved immediately. Augurs, however, were not clergy. They were members of the aristocracy; indeed, they usually derived from Rome's finest families or were men who had made themselves into grandees. Nearly all were senators, although it was not uncommon for a scion of a noble house to be co-opted when very young. The college of augurs, in short, were a majestic and vital feature of the republic, its members key members of the governing class.[34]

On 9 June 53 Marcus Crassus' invading army was overwhelmingly defeated by the Parthians at the battle of Carrhae. Among the fallen was Crassus' gifted son, Publius Licinius Crassus. This man was an augur, and his death opened a vacancy in the college. By the late republic, augurs were chosen by the people in a *comitia sacerdotum*, a sacred assembly for electing pontiffs, augurs, or a member of the quindecemvirate. Candidates were nominated by the college: each member had the right to put forward an individual and no individual could receive more than two nominations. This procedure took place before the public in a *contio*. An election was then held in a special session of the tribal assembly at which only seventeen of the citizenry's thirty-five tribes participated: these were chosen by lot. Thereafter, the college of augurs formally co-opted its new member: this required an additional round of voting by the college, but only the candidate who was returned by the tribal assembly could be considered for the vacancy. Whenever it was necessary to create an augur in this way, the *comitia sacerdotum* was fitted into the schedule of assemblies between consular and praetorian elections.[35]

Cicero was co-opted in Crassus' place, an achievement of which he was justly proud.[36] Because elections in 53, held to furnish magistrates for 53, took place in July, it was probably too soon for Cicero's election to take place then. Elections for 52 should have taken place soon afterwards, but political perturbation, as we have seen, delayed them until the next year, when, under novel circumstances, they took place in March. That is a likelier time for Cicero's election. His formal nomination, however, could have taken place in the previous year, before it became obvious that elections were a lost cause.[37] If so, Cicero was also cultivating voters in 53 or certainly in 52, an operation he was able to carry out while acting as an advocate for other men seeking magistracies. He was nominated by Pompey and Quintus Hortensius Hortalus, the famous orator, and his only known rival was Gaius Lucilius Hirrus, a tribune of the *plebs* in 53 and later a failed candidate for an aedileship of 50. In view of Cicero's stature and

Pompey's endorsement, Cicero was almost certain to win selection, whatever the year of the election.

When they had become enemies, Antony boasted how he did Cicero a supreme kindness by not standing for this augurate himself.[38] In his *Philippics*, Cicero does not actually contradict Antony. Instead, he scoffs at the notion that Antony could have run any kind of capable race and he insists, falsely, that he was the college's only nomination. Antony's boast, then, was probably a true one—in a sense. When Crassus' death created a vacancy, it is highly likely that Antony's uncle, Lucius Iulius Caesar, who was an augur, at the very least offered to nominate his nephew. Antony, perhaps sensing the inevitability of a Ciceronian success—Cicero never lost an election in his life and was usually returned at the top of the polls—demurred. But he did not cover his lamp with a vessel: this was an action he could, and did, represent to others as a benefaction, a noble kindness, to Cicero during a time when Cicero's favour was important to him. At the time, it was an expression of wholesome Roman cooperation. Later, however, Antony deployed this episode in his depiction of Cicero as an ungrateful man.

Chaos in 52

On 18 January 52, Clodius was murdered on the Appian Way by Milo and his henchmen. On the next day, at his funeral, popular grief and rage, incited by populist tribunes and Clodius' widow, Fulvia, exploded into furious rioting.[39] The Curia was burned down, the neighbouring Basilica Hostilia badly damaged. The Forum remained occupied by an angry mob demanding justice for their hero. The senate hurriedly convened in an emergency session. There, in the absence of consuls, an *interrex* was appointed for the purpose of holding elections. The senate also carried a *senatus consultum ultimum*, its final decree appealing to the magistrates to rescue the republic from danger. But there were no magistrates. The body was consequently reduced to calling on the *interrex* and tribunes of the *plebs*, who could do little.[40] The senate also appealed to Pompey, who was proconsul, and directed him to assemble troops. But a proconsul could not legally enter the Forum. The city now desperately waited on the return of a normal government and the restoration of order, and only elections could make that possible.[41]

But it remained impossible to hold an undisrupted assembly. An *interrex* held office for five days. It was not the role of the first interrex to conduct elections: that duty belonged to his successor. But in 52 the second *interrex* was unable to do his job. Likewise his successors: holding elections remained impossible for *interrex* after *interrex*. During this time, Milo continued to press his candidature even in the teeth of hostility on the part of the masses. The destruction of the Curia and rioting in the Forum created a backlash when these enormities outraged members of the better-off classes whose votes determined the outcome of consular elections. These were men who possessed property in quantities sufficient to find its destruction abhorrent, and their revulsion at the Clodian riots unexpectedly resurrected Milo's aspirations. But the masses, refusing to let Clodius' killer escape punishment by way of the immunity conferred by holding office, now refused to allow the consular *comitia* to assemble so long as Milo was in with a chance. From some quarters it was urged that Pompey be created a dictator for conducting elections, but that presented further constitutional difficulties: only once before had an *interrex* nominated a dictator and that was in the case of Sulla, a baleful precedent.[42] It was not until the twelfth *interrex* was appointed—the learned jurist Ser. Sulpicius Rufus—that a solution was found, a novel strategy crafted by Sulpicius and Calpurnius Bibulus, who introduced it in the senate.

They proposed that the *interrex* name only a single candidate for the consulship, Pompey, who would also and irregularly be permitted to retain, as proconsul, his provinces; Pompey would also be exempted from the restriction disallowing the iteration of a magistracy until an interval of ten years elapsed; the new consul would immediately conduct elections but would not be permitted to nominate a colleague for two months following his election. In this way, it was hoped, partisans of the current candidates for the consulship would relent from further disruption. It will have been obvious to everyone that, at the appropriate juncture, Pompey would nominate Metellus Scipio, his future father-in-law, to be his colleague. Milo was thus excluded, and Plautius was dropped. No segment of society was likely to reject Pompey the Great when his nomination was advanced by a figure like Bibulus, a political opponent. The singularly competent Pompey, no one doubted it, would successfully restore order. Furthermore, Milo, now shut out of office, could be prosecuted for Clodius' murder, a result which would satisfy the urban masses. This motion was made in the senate by Bibulus and supported by its majority, including Cato.[43] Pompey's name was subsequently put before the people by Sulpicius and he was elected sole consul. He immediately, even harshly, imposed order on the city. He also endeavoured to display his close cooperation with senatorial adversaries. And he moved quickly to hold elections.[44]

Caesar, so far as we know, had no objections to the tactic. And in some quarters it was proposed that Caesar should be named Pompey's colleague.[45] But these thoughts evaporated quickly. Caesar suddenly faced serious difficulties in his province. The rioting and destruction that rocked Rome stimulated a violent revolt in Gaul, led by the redoubtable Vercingetorix. His conquests in jeopardy, Caesar concentrated all his energies on putting down the Gallic uprising. But he was not heedless of his future in Rome. While still in Ravenna, Caesar met with Cicero, who helped to broker the terms of a measure allowing Caesar, when his governorship ended, to stand for the consulship *in absentia*.[46] This is a matter to which we shall return. During Pompey's sole consulship, and in spite of the opposition of Cato, this measure was ultimately promulgated by all the tribunes (and consequently is designated the Law of the Ten Tribunes).[47] Amid the negotiations over this law, there is no suggestion that Caesar disapproved of Bibulus' proposal. And Caesar's later description of Pompey's actions in 52 is flattering.[48]

Caesar's Quaestor

Bibulus' motion attracted extraordinarily broad support and resolved a profound crisis. It also represented a notable and painful concession on the part of the circle of Cato and others hostile to the designs of Pompey and Caesar. For the sake of the republic, they elevated to a position of unparalleled glory a man they deemed their enemy. And, again for the sake of the republic, they jettisoned Milo, whose candidature

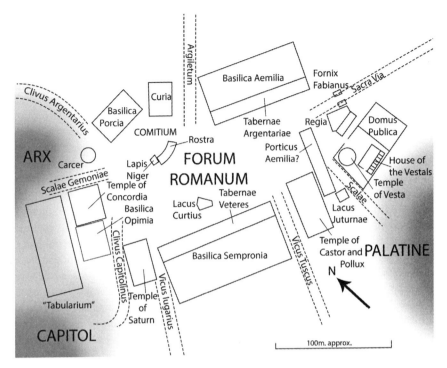

Map 3 The Roman Forum

they had so ardently supported. This radical, ad hoc transformation in Rome's political orientation threw up implications for Antony's electoral prospects. Owing to his confrontations with Clodius on Cicero's behalf, Antony feared that he might now be too closely associated with Milo in the public's mind—and he did not want to be tossed overboard along with him. Amid such volatile circumstances, Antony could hardly rely on drawing the fine distinction that he had been *Cicero's* friend and not *Milo's* ally.

The violent reaction of the urban *plebs* to Clodius' death was hardly nuanced, which could only be deemed a threat to Antony's electoral chances—especially because, in the tribal assembly that selected quaestors, the lower classes, Clodius' most devoted supporters, had so strong a voice. Nor, if he must be linked with Milo, could Antony expect any compensatory goodwill from senatorial grandees: they were leaving Milo to his fate and were keen to get all this trouble behind them. Pompey, too, was hostile to Milo. Cicero was not the only senator who remained steadfastly beside Milo, but there were not many others. Indeed, shortly after Pompey's election a majority in the senate joined in carrying a decree denouncing Clodius' death and the violence attending it as *contra rem publicam*, hostile to interests of the republic, a declaration associated with Pompey's *lex de vi*, his law on violence, crafted chiefly for Milo's prosecution.[49] Valuable though Cicero's recommendation clearly was, Antony no longer wanted to be tied to the orator's connection with Milo.

It was owing to these calculations that Antony decided not to compete for a quaestorship of 52. He *may* have got in, his was certainly a distinguished and respected name, but the disgrace of failure was simply too great to run any risk in an environment that remained so unsteady. Instead, he resolved to campaign for a quaestorship in 51.[50] His younger brother, Gaius, was also a candidate for this year and postponement allowed them to combine resources in a joint canvass.[51] Antony's deferral also gave him time to improve his image among the urban masses, which he did by joining Milo's prosecution.[52] This trial, the final day of which took place on 7 April, put Antony opposite Cicero, who, with Marcus Claudius Marcellus, made up Milo's defence. The situation was an awkward one—Cicero was still endorsing Antony's candidature—but it was not highly unusual for friends to take different sides in court.

Speaking for the prosecution allowed Antony, for the first time in his life so far as we know, an opportunity to deliver a speech before the Roman people. His *Against Milo* is Antony's only known forensic speech. It was never published, perhaps as a gesture of family *pietas*—the consul of 99 famously refused to publish his speeches—or perhaps because he did not wish to leave behind a memorial to his political volte-face. His speech must have been succinct: Milo's prosecutors were allotted only two hours for making their collective case. Nevertheless, because there were precious few occasions for a young aristocrat to deliver a public oration, any performance was a welcome opportunity—especially on the eve of an election. Antony's speech may have been brief but competing against Cicero in any trial was a sensational opportunity for raising one's domestic profile. It also furnished Antony a conspicuous setting for depicting himself both as a proponent of law and order and a champion of the popular causes Clodius stood for. The impression Antony made on the day can only have been enhanced by the coincidence that Cicero, the sole speaker for the defence, delivered a truly unsatisfactory performance. Milo was condemned and withdrew into exile. Owing to Cicero's lapse, Antony could bask in the glory of a forensic victory over Rome's greatest pleader.[53] It was enough to recover his supporters' confidence and repair any damage to his popularity. At the elections for 51, Antony was a winner.

The elections for 51 were held in late summer or early autumn. Caesar, before departing Ravenna, because he assumed Antony would be elected, arranged for him to be appointed his quaestor. Quaestorian assignments were a senatorial responsibility, but these could not officially take place before 5 December, when quaestors assumed office. Caesar, however, did not wish Antony to remain in Rome for that long. Gaul was in turmoil and he was needed there. Which is why, before his assignment was formalized, Antony left Rome while still quaestor-elect. Cicero later complained that in doing so Antony acted lawlessly, but this is misleading: Caesar, as we have seen, was not too shy to advertise Antony's presence at Alesia as a legate.[54] Cicero also alleges that Antony fled Rome in a move to elude debts, but that is no more than a conventional rhetorical slur.

Antony's long stay in Rome, and the complications he faced in attaining the quaestorship, were unexpected events. They reflect the political volatility of Rome in the fifties and especially the singular shattering of civic order caused by the murder of Clodius. For Antony, the way forward relied on a peculiar mixture of traditional loyalties and nimble adaptation to unexpected events in the Forum and senate. Antony was not, in 52, the only politician who had to think fast, but he certainly did not fall behind events. Amid a singularly difficult, perilous political landscape, Antony steered himself well. He could now return to fighting for Caesar.

Pompey in 52

A sequence of unpredictable misfortunes radically altered the relationship between the two dynasts.[55] In 54, Caesar's daughter Julia, to whom Pompey was deeply devoted, died in childbirth. Caesar proposed fresh affinities, but Pompey was unresponsive. Perhaps he was more affected by grief than was Caesar. Perhaps, less sentimentally, he believed there was more to be gained by the two friends through an expansion of their family ties.[56] In the next year, as we have noted, Crassus and the bulk of his legions perished at Carrhae, where his invasion of Parthia ended in disaster. His death further transformed the dynamics of Caesar's alliance with Pompey. Then, in 52, when the rioting and destruction incited by the murder of Clodius resulted in Pompey's extraordinary election as sole consul, Pompey became, not unfriendly to his ally, but certainly increasingly receptive to the blandishments of the leading senators centred round Cato, men like Calpurnius Bibulus, Domitius, the Claudii Marcelli, and others who, for personal or political reasons, abominated Caesar.[57] This shift did not mean Pompey wanted to break with his fellow dynast or rush into the arms of Caesar's enemies. In 52, he married Cornelia, daughter of Metellus Scipio, a man who was by no means close to Caesar but was certainly on very bad terms with Cato.[58]

Pompey's consulship, because its extraordinary purpose was the recovery of normality in civic affairs, obliged him and the senate to work closely together. In that body, Cato and his circle possessed a great deal of clout, for which reason alone Pompey's public posture involved conspicuous collaboration with his past rivals. He even went so far as to invite Cato to join his *consilium*, his body of consular advisors. Cato demurred.[59] Still, he and his allies, because they, too, sought a restoration of order, were willing, for now anyway, to concede the superiority of Pompey's position. Indeed, they were complicit in Pompey's elevation. As a mark of the republic's restored vitality and Pompey's personal eminence, it was in this year that the great man dedicated, to popular acclaim, his temple to Venus Victrix and shrines to Honos, Virtus, Felicitas, and Victoria, divinities which gave sacred shape to his magnificent theatre and defined the moral qualities of his public service.[60] In 52, powerful though he was, Pompey did not abuse or unduly exploit his singular position, and it became increasingly obvious to Caesar's enemies that he was a figure whose eminence they could endure easily enough or perhaps even turn to their advantage. They began to hope that, by cultivating Pompey and thereby opening a space between him and Caesar, they might weaken them both. Their designs did not go unperceived by Caesar.

Which is not to say Pompey did not look after his own interests. His command over the Spanish provinces was extended for five years, possibly by senatorial decree.[61] If so, this action can only have deepened Pompey's bond with the senate's leadership. For his part, Pompey displayed his respect for the senate by promulgating a law which reformed various aspects of Rome's regulation of its magistrates, including the assignment of provinces to former office holders.[62] Many stipulations of this law were traditional: for instance, it reaffirmed the requirement that men seeking office submit their application for candidature in person. This provision, however, because it appeared to some to endanger Caesar's rights under the Law of the Ten Tribunes, Pompey modified after its promulgation but before its passage by inserting a clause explicitly exempting Caesar. Perhaps Pompey's omission of Caesar's exemption was intentional: it allowed him, when complaints arose, to underline his loyalty to his friend—even amid close cooperation with the senate's leadership.

A key feature of this measure enacted into law a decree of the senate passed in the previous year. Pompey's law introduced a five-year interval between holding a magistracy and taking up a province. Hereafter provincial commands would be assigned to ex-praetors and ex-consuls who had not held such a post within the previous five years. This measure had more than one purpose. One was to curb electoral corruption: some candidates for office splashed out in donatives to voters in the expectation that they could recoup their costs by way of extortion and profiteering in the provinces. It hardly matters that this law was unlikely to deter provincial governors from continuing to exploit their position for gain: senators were always fretful about electoral corruption, and some may have believed this measure might improve the integrity of Rome's imperial administration—and so this law felt good. The senate was also concerned about the very different problem thrown up by the refusal of more and more magistrates to take up a province. This law was designed to establish over time a deep pool of potential governors who could not decently escape their duty. In the legislation superseded by Pompey's law, a *lex Sempronia* of 123, the assignment of provinces by the senate, because it was urgent business, was rendered immune to tribunician veto.[63] The new law, however, perhaps because it allowed the senate to conduct this business less hastily, omitted any exemptions along these lines. Hereafter provincial assignments were vulnerable to a veto. This technical detail carried profound, if inadvertent, political implications.

Although this *lex Pompeia* was not drafted with Caesar in mind, Caesar's position was not unaffected by it. A brief explanation is required. The *lex Pompeia Licinia* of 55, which extended Caesar's provincial command for five years, probably did so by forbidding his supersession before 50. In practical terms, that meant allocating Caesar's provinces to a magistrate (or magistrates) holding office in 50. This magistrate, presumably a consul, could not depart Rome until late in the year or early in 49. He had much to do: his provincial edict must be drafted, his staff assembled, his finances and forces organized, and so forth. Nor was the transfer of provincial authority from one governor to the next a simple or tidy procedure: the previous governor was entitled to remain in his province, after the arrival of his successor, for as long as thirty days in order to facilitate this complicated transition. As a consequence, when the *lex Pompeia Licinia* was carried, Caesar had no reason to expect that he would return to Rome before sometime in mid-49. Nor was this expectation altered by the Law of the Ten Tribunes.[64] Pompey's law, however, changed this timetable. Under its terms, when a successor to Caesar was named in 50, he could begin immediately to prepare for assuming control of his province. For this reason, Pompey's law, at least potentially, effectively shortened Caesar's command by months.[65]

Caesar's Enemies

Antony was Caesar's friend, a reality that soon threw him into conflict with Caesar's enemies. These men were keen to bring Caesar back from Gaul as soon as possible. In the elections for 51, in which Antony was elected quaestor, Cato put himself forward as a candidate for the consulship. He made it plain that, if elected, he would devote himself to recalling Caesar and putting him on trial. This ferocity attracted few votes. Instead, Sulpicius Rufus, the resourceful *interrex*, and Marcus Claudius Marcellus, Milo's advocate and like Cato an enemy of Caesar, were returned. The proconsul was not unaware of his enemies' strength. For this reason, Antony's was not the only candidature he favoured in 52. To protect his interests in the capital, he procured the loyalty of more than one tribune of the *plebs*. These men, Gaius Coelius, Publius Cornelius, Gaius Vibius Pansa, and Lucius Vincius, proved invaluable.[66]

At Alesia, Caesar won a victory so complete that the residue of the Gauls' resistance collapsed. In December, the senate, in recognition of this achievement, decreed a *supplicatio* (a thanksgiving to the gods) of twenty days. But Caesar's success became known in Rome well before that time, and this news prodded Marcellus to take hostile actions against the conqueror of Gaul. In spring, shortly after the fall of Alesia, he argued that Caesar's mission was accomplished, his army should be disbanded, and he should return to Rome. Marcellus went further: he demanded that the Law of the Ten Tribunes be discarded, both on the grounds that Caesar's recall (and subsequent triumph) meant he would be available for submitting his *professio* in 49 and because, Marcellus insisted, that law was in any case superseded by Pompey's provincial law. Marcellus' moves, clear violations of the *lex Pompeia Licinia* and the Law of the Ten Tribunes, met with learned criticism from Sulpicius, forceful opposition from Pompey, and vetoes and threats of vetoes from the tribunes. Nor could Marcellus win over a majority in the senate.[67] His failures, however, did nothing to reassure Caesar, who was well aware that the letter of the law was sometimes an inadequate shield from one's enemies. By the end of the year, and consonant with both the *lex Pompeia Licinia* and the Law of the Ten Tribunes, it was agreed that the matter of Caesar's successor and no other topic should occupy the senate on 1 March 50. This motion was made by Metellus Scipio and approved by Pompey.[68] The senate also carried a motion forbidding any further obstruction of this matter by tribunician veto. That proposal, predictably, was vetoed by Caesar's tribunes.

The consuls for 50 were Lucius Aemilius Lepidus Paullus, who was friendly to Caesar, and Gaius Claudius Marcellus, who was not. There were also censors in this year, Appius Claudius Pulcher, a kinsman of Pompey, and Lucius Calpurnius Piso, Caesar's father-in-law.[69] But all eyes were on Antony's friend, Scribonius Curio.[70] When a tribune-elect for 50 was condemned for electoral corruption, Curio stood for the vacancy and won. He was a vigorous and marvellously talented opponent of Pompey and Caesar, and his candidature gave cheer to their enemies. Even as tribune-elect, Curio was forward in denouncing the dynasts. We know too little about the tribunician college of this year to know whether any of its other members were partisans of Caesar. Almost certainly some were, but, in the end, it hardly mattered because, on the subject of Caesar's command, Curio soon changed his mind.

Curio was now married to Fulvia, Clodius' widow.[71] And, like Clodius, he intended to put his tribunate to work in advancing a wide-ranging and independent legislative programme. Unlike Clodius, however, Curio faced impediments, thrown up by Pompey and others in the senate, which proved too strong for him to overcome. In his frustration and humiliation—and perhaps, we may conjecture, under the influence of letters from Antony—he now took up Caesar's cause.[72] His detractors alleged, probably unfairly, that he had taken a bribe. By February he was an open advocate of Caesar. On 1 March, when Marcellus duly raised the question of Caesar's successor, Curio interposed his veto. And he made it clear that he would not relent until Caesar's rights were assured.

Caesar's Rights

Romans adored conquerors and Caesar's wars in Gaul made him a hero. By Roman standards, he had a right to expect his conquests to be celebrated by way of a triumph. He also had a right to expect to stand for a second consulship—unimpeded even by men who resented him—and no one could doubt his re-election. To refuse him these prizes at the end of his long war was, to any fair-minded Roman, indecent. Caesar, however, wanted more. He wanted to celebrate his triumph on the first day of his consulship—a glorious conjunction—and for this he sought a legal assurance and he got it in the Law of the Ten Tribunes. This measure meant he need not confront *Cato's Dilemma*: in 60, when Caesar returned from his proconsulship in Spain, because he hoped to celebrate a triumph, he sought the senate's permission to announce his candidature for the consulship without entering the city. This was necessary in order for him to preserve his *imperium*, the loss of which would render him ineligible for a triumph. The senate, with Cato taking the lead, refused, and Caesar was forced to choose between a triumph or standing for the consulship of 59.[73] Owing to the Law of the Ten Tribunes, however, when Caesar returned to the vicinity of Rome in 49, during which year, as we have seen, he expected his replacement as provincial governor to arrive and take command, he could remain outside the pomerium, win election to his second consulship, and celebrate his triumph in the brilliant manner of a Gaius Marius.[74]

Caesar's enemies could not prevent his celebrating a triumph or winning a second consulship. That reality, however, did not deter their efforts at spiking his glory. If Caesar could be compelled to return to Rome earlier than he expected, he would be obliged to sit outside the pomerium for months until his consulship in 48. There was nothing truly disgraceful in that—Pompey, by design, had done the same thing before celebrating his third triumph in 61—but Pompey had not intended to stand for office, nor did he face such implacable foes in the senate.[75] Caesar, very early on, came to the conclusion that, if he gave up his military command in order to return to the capital, he would be too vulnerable to his enemies' machinations.[76] He distrusted the likes of Cato and Marcellus: he had seen how willing they were to distort and discard the Law of the Ten Tribunes and he knew or suspected they harboured hopes of somehow hauling him into court, a humiliation for the returning hero even if in the end such an outrage failed to convict him.[77] At the same time, Pompey, according to Caelius, was truly afraid of the possibility of Caesar's election as consul while still in command of his army. Why this was the case is not entirely clear.[78] Caesar, in an attempt to defuse tensions, proposed standing for a consulship of 49.[79] A senatorial exemption could clear the way and, after his election, Caesar would begin to unwind his governorship and return to Rome. But this sensible solution provoked constitutionalist objections and was finally rejected by Pompey, who continued to insist Caesar separate himself from his armed forces.

Pompey, although by no means compliant, remained at least minimally loyal to Caesar's interests. Unlike Cato, he did not seek to see Caesar ruined. Quite the contrary. His influence and stature were more than sufficient to shield Caesar from his enemies, but Caesar was loath to rely for his protection on the goodwill of Pompey the Great. That was a posture that, in his view, diminished him and was unfair to a man of his achievements. Our sources, including Caesar himself, make it clear that he, like all Roman nobles, put a greater value on his *dignitas* than on his life.[80] At the moment of his greatest attainments, he was adamant in safeguarding his prestige. His enemies were determined to do all they could do to dent it. And Pompey sought to increase his own stature further by making himself at once the champion of the senate's authority and Caesar's necessary friend.

Curio was Caesar's advocate. At the same time, he was an independent, innovative politician. His sustained veto on the subject of Caesar's succession stymied the proconsul's enemies and paralysed the operations of the senate. He also offered a way forward by proposing that both Caesar and Pompey resign their extraordinary commands, actions that would free the republic from the dynasts' pressure and ensure Caesar's equality with his friend.[81] Curio's proposal, a brilliant stroke, drew sharp attention to the highly untraditional accumulation of powers and privileges enjoyed by Pompey. In so doing, he shifted the dynamics of Caesar's situation from a confrontation with his senatorial rivals to a contest between himself and Pompey. The idea of both dynasts stepping down was immediately popular with the bulk of the senate and many outside the senate who preferred peace and quiet to any confrontation between titans. Pompey naturally rejected Curio's proposition, as did Caesar's enemies. But again and again Curio brought it back. Despite its appeal to many, Curio's proposal, because it had no chance of success, made matters worse. Each ventilation exacerbated the distrust between Pompey and Caesar, which added to the toxic atmosphere generated by Caesar's enemies in the senate. More than ever, Caesar was convinced that he could not safely give up his army. And, more than ever, Pompey and the senate perceived a threat to the republic in Caesar's refusal to yield. By August, Marcus Caelius Rufus believed war was inevitable.[82] By the end of December, Pompey held the same view.[83]

Antony's Election as Tribune and Augur

In the summer of 50, amid this turmoil and anxiety, elections for 49 took place. The two men returned as consuls, Gaius Claudius Marcellus and Lucius Cornelius Lentulus Crus, were openly hostile to Caesar. His preferred candidate, Ser. Sulpicius Galba, failed. Election tampering was alleged. But although Caesar's enemies claimed these results exposed the public's repudiation of his demands, other factors, such as each individual's competence in canvassing, were also involved.[84] Their success, in other words, probably did not mark a reaction against Caesar among the propertied classes. Several of his allies, after all, including Marcus Aemilius Lepidus, the future triumvir, were elected praetor.[85] Still, in the new year Caesar would now be obliged to face formidable, unfriendly consuls who could at least claim a mandate. But Caesar was hardly helpless. By the time these consuls were returned, Caesar knew he had staunch allies in the tribunate: Quintus Cassius Longinus, a brother or cousin of Cassius the tyrannicide (no friend of Caesar, he, too, was elected tribune in this race)—and with him Mark Antony.[86]

As early as 51, Antony was openly planning to stand for a tribunate in 49.[87] Before the spring of 50, he left Caesar for Rome in order to begin canvassing.[88] He was all but certain to gain the office, but his campaign could not be treated as a mere formality. Elections were often unpredictable, and Curio's tribunate made it certain that Caesar's enemies would be keen to keep out Caesar's quaestor. Consequently, a diligent campaign was indispensable. Nor was Caesar unenergetic on Antony's behalf. He wrote to every colony and municipality in his province, urging them to travel to the capital in support of Antony's candidature. In summer, he began canvassing for Antony personally. Nor did Antony lack glamorous supporters in Rome: Curio worked the hustings on his behalf, splashing out with donatives paid for by Caesar. Caelius Rufus, a popular aedile in this year, also canvassed for Antony.[89]

In June, the distinguished orator, Quintus Hortensius Hortalus, died.[90] This created another opening in the augural college. There were two candidates: the ex-consul Lucius Domitius Ahenobarbus and Antony, who was almost certainly nominated by his uncle, Lucius Iulius Caesar. Lucius Caesar, now one of Caesar's legates in Gaul, will have travelled to Rome to participate in his nephew's campaign for the tribunate.[91] This meant that, at the time of Hortensius' death, he was on the scene and in a position to put Antony's name forward. This contest was a fierce one. An ex-consul and son of a pontifex maximus, Domitius, in normal times, would have been the strong favourite.[92] Which is not to say Antony did not also possess important recommendations: he was the grandson of an augur, and, unlike Domitius, had for weeks (if not longer) been working to win popular favour as a candidate for a tribunate. But this election was intensely suffused by the politics surrounding the issue of Caesar's return to Rome. In a letter to Cicero, composed in August, Caelius described this race as unattractively untraditional in the way personal ties were mostly overshadowed by factional affinities.[93] Domitius was Cato's brother-in-law and a leading figure among Caesar's enemies, Antony Caesar's quaestor. Caelius, at this time, was no partisan of Caesar, but for reasons of friendship supported Antony. So, too, did Curio. But Curio's high-profile participation must have rendered the political dimensions of this contest all the starker.

Tribunician elections came first and Antony was elected.[94] This success gave Antony welcome momentum. In the race for the consulship, as we have seen, only candidates backed by Cato and his circle were victorious. The contest between Domitius and Antony came next, and, as Caelius complained, it became a proxy struggle between Caesar and his enemies.[95] On the day of the election, the assembly was more than usually crowded. And there was violence. Antony won again. Domitius was visibly humiliated, as Caelius gleefully reports. The man's son, Gnaeus Domitius Ahenobarbus, immediately brought an accusation of political violence against one of Antony's partisans.[96] But that was small consolation for Domitius or Cato.

Helen of Troy

In the senate, Antony threw his support behind Curio. A dramatic moment came in early December, when Marcellus put two motions to a vote. The first was a resolution that Caesar resign his province. It carried but was vetoed by Curio. The second motion resolved that Pompey should resign. It failed. In reaction, Curio, with the strong backing of Antony and Caesar's father-in-law, Calpurnius Piso, then forced a third division on a motion resolving that both Caesar and Pompey give up their commands. This motion was passed overwhelmingly, by a vote of 370 to 22. This was a stunning and celebrated success for Curio, even if nothing came of the resolution. Presumably Marcellus imposed his consular veto.[97] Not for the first time, the consul wished something could be done to rid him of Curio's obstruction. But since spring, he and others had feared that any formal move aimed at suppressing the tribune would incite Caesar to come to his rescue at the head of an army.[98] It was owing to this anxiety that Marcellus, as consul, invested Pompey with the authority to take command of the two legions wintering in southern Italy and levy additional troops in the event Italy needed protection from an invasion.[99] So great a pitch of fear and distrust brought Rome closer than ever to open violence.

Antony entered his tribunate on 10 December. It appears that he immediately published an edict condemning Pompey's levy and military preparations as acts hostile to Caesar and therefore contrary to the welfare of the republic. Curio had issued similar complaints.[100] When Caesar sent a dispatch to the senate, in which he expressed his willingness to abide by the terms of Curio's proposal for disarmament, the consuls refused to allow its reading. In reaction, Antony held a *contio* on 21 December at which he first read Caesar's letter to the people, then delivered a blistering speech vituperating Pompey's life and career from the day he donned the toga of manhood. Antony recalled the sufferings of the Sullan civil war, the days when Pompey was feared as *adulescentulus carnifex*, Sulla's brutal boyish executioner, and, by reciting the horrors of that time, expressed his fear of Pompey's current, dangerous posture.[101] This speech was promptly published and circulated. On 25 December, Cicero and Pompey examined a copy. 'How do you imagine Caesar will act', Pompey put it to Cicero, 'should he gain control of the republic, if his quaestor, that pusillanimous pauper, dares to say such things?'[102]

Antony's oration, it is clear, went viral and did so to stunning effect. It did nothing, however, to move matters toward any kind of resolution. Pompey, after reading Antony's speech, no longer hoped for peace. On the day after his meeting with Pompey, Cicero wrote a letter to Atticus in which he rehearsed what he believed were probable scenarios for the coming year. The stalemate between Caesar and Pompey, he reckoned, was likely to continue in one of several possible configurations. War remained a possibility, but Caesar, Cicero observed, would require a reason. The rejection of his candidature, a violation of the Law of the Ten Tribunes, was a plausible justification. So, too, if a tribune obstructing the senate on his behalf or stirring up the populace should be expelled from Rome—or claim to have been expelled from Rome—and turn to him for refuge.[103] Doubtless Cicero had Antony in mind. Later, in his *Philippics*, Cicero put the blame for the civil war squarely on Antony, 'the first to furnish Caesar with a justification for waging war against his fatherland.'[104] Indeed, he went on to liken Antony to Helen of Troy: as she brought destruction there, the orator moaned, so Antony, in his turn, was the ruin of the republic.[105] It is a marvellous insult, but Plutarch viewed this conceit as over the top.[106] He recognized how, in this stage in his career, Antony, though forceful and bold, did not carry out his own designs. He acted as Caesar's agent. Even his methods were modelled on Curio's.

The senate met under new consuls on 1 January 49. Curio brought a letter from Caesar, but at first the consuls refused to read it. Antony and Cassius managed to change their minds. Nevertheless, there was no subsequent discussion of its contents.[107] In his letter, Caesar rehearsed his accomplishments and defended himself against his enemies; he once more proposed that he and Pompey resign their offices; otherwise, he made it clear, he would protect the interests of the republic—and himself. Its tone Cicero described as harsh and threatening.[108] Intense negotiations, in which Cicero was an ardent advocate of compromise, supervened. These were sometimes hopeful but, in the end, always frustrated. The senate convened on the second, fifth, and sixth of January, urgently ventilating a broad range of proposals. A motion by Metellus Scipio was carried: it required Caesar to dismiss his army by a fixed day or be declared an enemy of the republic. This resolution was immediately vetoed by Antony and Cassius. Acrimony ensued. Their veto was debated and attacked, but the tribunes remained resolute.[109] Finally, on 7 January, the senate carried its final decree. First, however, the consuls warned Antony and Cassius that, inviolable tribunes though they were, they must look after their safety and they must not impose a veto. In reaction to this threat, both men fled Rome, joined by Curio and Caelius Rufus. All dressed as slaves. This was done perhaps not so much to disguise themselves as to exhibit before the public their abject, illegal treatment by the senate. Nevertheless, after leaving the city they made a point of travelling by night.[110]

The Invasion of Italy

Antony and his companions paced themselves so as to ensure Caesar learned of events at Rome before their arrival. When reports of the tribunes' expulsion reached him, he marched into Italy (in violation of Roman law) at the head of his Thirteenth Legion. At Ariminum he greeted the tribunes, whose foul, disgraceful appearance he exhibited to his soldiers. This was a pageant, the first of many, the purpose of which was to justify the civil war. Caesar invaded Italy, so he insisted, not to inflict harm on anyone but to defend his dignity from the assaults of his enemies, to restore the dignity of the tribunes expelled from Rome, and to restore freedom, the *libertas* belonging to himself and to the Roman people, now oppressed by a narrow oligarchy of powerful men.[111] For the Romans, individual *dignitas* and political freedom were intimately related concepts, a reflex of their instinct for conflating individual personalities with ideological principles.[112]

The expression used by Caesar, in his *Civil War* and doubtless in his propaganda, *in libertatem vindicare*, to rescue and restore to freedom, he almost certainly borrowed from Sulla when that liberator invaded Italy.[113] The metaphor was an attractive one: this formula denoted the legal rescue of a free person wrongly relegated to slavery, and the *vindex*, the rescuer, in this operation was a private citizen acting selflessly and on his own initiative against someone perpetrating a horrible, uncivil action.[114] Caesar fought, then, as a liberator, and after his victory the dictator was indeed destined to be honoured as *Liberator*.[115] His enemies, however, also claimed to be the defenders of freedom.[116] *Libertas*, universal in its appeal, lay at the centre of their struggle. But freedom, then as now, was an inherently contestable value: what it meant and how it was realized were controversies igniting clashes, sometimes honest, sometimes contrived. Modern historians vary widely in the seriousness with which they take claims about *libertas* voiced by Roman statesmen, and they disagree over how deeply the Roman people were influenced by these claims.[117] That *libertas* was precious to Romans of all classes is undeniable. What, specifically, it meant to any individual must have depended on his circumstances and situation.

For the people of Italy, the outbreak of civil war was terrifying. The risk to life and property was real. Uncertainty, or perhaps even panic, also brought economic peril as moneys were hoarded and credit dried up. It was amid these practical realities that the propaganda of both sides was constrained to operate at every social level. The people of Italy shared the same values as their leaders. But their circumstances and immediate priorities were very different. In the municipalities, even the most distinguished remained wary of the political class in Rome: they looked to grandees not as embodiments of ideological principles but as friends who could shelter them from other senators' abuse or arrogance.[118] Cicero was certain the Italian aristocracy were more concerned about preserving their properties than defending any constitutional precept.[119] Nor did he expect anything different from financiers and capitalists in Rome. He put it to Atticus: 'do you believe they have any fears about living in a tyranny so long as they are left unmolested?'[120] As for the lower orders, for whom precarity was the natural condition of their daily lives, they, too, had much to fear from civil war. A contemporary historian later complained how ordinary Romans thought of *libertas* only when they were harangued by an orator, sold it cheap in exchange for a ration of grain, and deemed themselves free so long as they were not actually flogged.[121] This disdain was unfair, but it cannot be forgotten that the poverty and helplessness of the masses, which politicians like Clodius and others learned to exploit to their advantage, also instilled a powerful preference for stability and order.[122]

As for members of the senate, they, too, differed in their motives. Caelius Rufus, for instance, believed Pompey's side was the better cause but that Caesar's would win: hence his loyalty to the invader. Gaius Asinius Pollio, in a letter to Cicero, explains how it was only by joining Caesar that he could escape his political enemies.[123] His self-serving stance will not have been unique. Antony, a public spokesman for the legitimacy of Caesar's rights, emphasized the closeness of his friendship with Caesar. So, too, did others.[124] Later, when Caesar and others attempted to persuade Cicero to take their side, it was friendship, not policy, which they underlined.[125] And so it goes. Caesar's coalition was disparate, united solely by its members' adherence to one man, a true Party of Caesar (*Caesaris partes*), which, as we shall see, quickly dissolved after the Ides of March.[126] Matters were not radically different on the other side, denounced by Caesar as an oligarchic faction. The men lined up there were some of them behind Pompey, some behind Cato and his circle, and some simply against Caesar. Some believed in the authority of the senate, others feared Caesar's ambitions, still others placed their hopes in Pompey's good fortune. Marcus Brutus, who detested Pompey, believed Cato was a champion of the right values and so followed him.[127] Cicero, after lengthy deliberation, joined Pompey on the basis of principle. His brother, however, reached his decision in his own way, almost certainly more influenced by the orator than anything else.[128] Pompey was hardly the darling of all his allies. Rivalries, even fierce jealousies, persisted among Pompey's officers and constantly hampered his command. There were also men whose side in the war was determined entirely by accident: by chance they happened to be serving in an army or province that was taken over by Pompey.[129] On both sides, then, different senators were animated by different motivations, even if they shared a common vocabulary for articulating the principles at stake in the civil war. Many, to be sure, like Cicero acted, at least in part, because they were persuaded one side had stronger moral claims than its opposition.

Caesar in Italy

Pompey urged his supporters to join him in Brundisium.[130] It was his design to evacuate Italy for Greece. There he could gather his forces and exploit his extensive eastern connections. At the same time, by taking advantage of his naval superiority, he planned to impose an embargo on Italy. Blocking crucial shipments of grain, he was convinced, would exacerbate the Romans' misery under an occupying force and disrupt Caesar's administration of Italy.[131] This strategy eluded many: Cicero clearly did not grasp it and, when he did, despised it.[132] Indeed, Pompey had difficulty in gathering his flock. Because he lacked the authority to issue commands, he was sometimes reduced to pleading with his colleagues. Cicero was in no hurry to join him, and Domitius Ahenobarbus, in defiance of Pompey's requests, occupied Corfinium, a city he intended to hold and use as a base of operations against the invaders.[133] For his part, Caesar, perhaps still hoping for a reconciliation and in any case determined to keep Pompey onshore, hastened along Italy's eastern coast toward Brundisium.

The two tribunes, Antony and Cassius, as well as Curio and Caelius, were turned into officers in Caesar's invading army. As its main force marched toward Brundisium, Antony was dispatched, with five cohorts, to secure the loyalty of Arretium, a major city. There he expelled Pompey's legate, Lucius Scribonius Libo.[134] After rejoining Caesar, he was once more deployed to Sulmo. He was warmly greeted by the populace, while Pompey's officers on the scene fled or were captured. Antony completed this mission in a single day.[135] He was present with Caesar at the siege of Corfinium. This city, occupied by Domitius with a staff of distinguished senators and equestrians, stood in the way of Caesar's southern progress and could not safely be left in his rear. Domitius, however, lost his nerve and attempted to flee—only to be apprehended by men on his own side. The city now capitulated. Caesar made a great show of pardoning his foes and releasing them. He advertised this act of goodwill widely. It was, he insisted, a new policy, which he described as gentleness, *lenitas*, but which came to be known as Caesar's clemency, his *clementia*.[136] Curio and Caelius expressed their doubts about the genuineness of Caesar's merciful displays, and perhaps they were not alone, but this policy did much to calm fears in the municipalities and in Rome.[137] Caesar reached Brundisium just as Pompey was completing his preparations for departure. A tactical struggle ended with Caesar's failure to contain Pompey's fleet, which left Brundisium on 17 March. Frustrated, Caesar turned to Rome.

There, in April, Antony and Cassius, in the absence of the consuls, who had fled with Pompey, summoned the senate.[138] So that Caesar could be present, the body met outside the pomerium. It was not an impressive gathering. Many of Rome's most eminent senators were absent, some were with Pompey, others, like Cicero, remained aloof. Caesar spoke at length, justifying his actions before an indifferent audience. Several proposals were put before the fathers, including a motion allowing Caesar to extract funds from the treasury. A hostile tribune, Lucius Metellus, vetoed this measure and made a show of physically obstructing the entrance to the treasury. Caesar, Curio later admitted to Cicero, was so furious he nearly put the man to death.[139] Instead, however, he simply ignored him, mistreatment of a tribune of the *plebs* that did much to erode his popular support. Caesar was also frustrated in his attempt to be elected consul immediately. He very much wanted to be returned at an election conducted by Lepidus but doing so contravened augural law. Not even his supporters in the college, including Antony, could do anything to alter that, but Caesar was slow to drop the idea.[140] The attitude of the senate, too, was increasingly and openly unfavourable, and Caesar was soon out of humour.[141] In order to repair his standing in the city, he addressed the people, promising them grain and a bounty of three hundred sesterces for every citizen.[142] For many among the lower orders, this was an enormous sum, and its announcement, even if it was no more than a promise, was welcome. Despite this small success, however, Caesar's return to Rome was a disappointment.

He needed a victory and so quickly prepared a march to Spain, which remained under the control of Pompey's legates. The tribune Cassius accompanied him as an officer. Curio, by decree of the senate, received a grant of *imperium pro praetore*.[143] He was put in command of three legions and sent to take Sicily, important for provisioning the city, and thereafter to carry on to Africa, another province crucial to the grain supply. Antony's brother, Gaius, a legate, was directed to lead troops into Illyricum.[144] And, perhaps serving in concert with Gaius, Cicero's son-in-law, Publius Cornelius Dolabella, also a legate, now commanded a fleet in the Adriatic.[145] As for Antony, he became *tribunus plebis pro praetore*, tribune of the *plebs* with *imperium*, an extraordinary, even unnatural combination of powers which, perhaps like Curio's commission, was bestowed by a senatorial decree. Antony was charged with the administration and security of Italy during Caesar's absence. The city of Rome, however, was entrusted to the praetor Lepidus.[146]

Before his departure, Caesar attempted to win, if not the support of Cicero, then at least his neutrality. The orator received numerous letters urging him not to join Pompey, from Caesar personally, from Caesar's intimates Gaius Oppius, a Roman knight, and Lucius Cornelius Balbus, and from Caelius and Antony.[147] The letters from Caesar, Caelius, and Antony, which Cicero forwarded to Atticus, although suitably individuated, are so alike that it is clear they relied on an agreed set of talking points. Each letter politely stressed the importance of friendship, Cicero's dignity, his security, and the safety of his family. They also made it clear, taking pains not to give offence, that Caesar's patience with Cicero was wearing thin. Antony's letter registered its concern for Cicero by way of conceding a degree of awkwardness: he admits that, lately, he and Cicero had been less close than previously, a situation for which he blames himself, or, more specifically, his rivalry with Cicero.[148] His meaning is not immediately obvious to us and is variously interpreted. Its likeliest reference is to their recent clash at Milo's trial, where the young man naturally endeavoured to show up the great orator and where Cicero lost his case. In his letter, Antony extracts this episode from its fraught political context and renders it an instance of callow opportunism on his part, one element in his larger effort at persuading Cicero to ground his decision about staying or going on a personal, not a factional, basis.[149]

Encouraged by Antony's openness and warmth, Cicero, who was in Cumae, responded by feigning his agreement. He asked permission, however, to transfer himself to Malta, where, he claimed, he would wait out the war. This was a transparent fiction which made it clear to Antony that Cicero was now determined to join Pompey. Perhaps because he believed he was letting Caesar down by allowing Cicero to get away, Antony answered curtly, informing Cicero that, on Caesar's instructions, he was not permitted to allow him or any senator to leave Italy. He suggested Cicero write Caesar directly, but he did not, as good manners should have dictated, offer to intervene on his behalf. Antony's letter, a copy of which Cicero sent Atticus, is terse, ungracious, and for these reasons impolite. Cicero was naturally offended, not least because he recognized that, when Antony arrived in the Bay of Naples, as he was soon to do, he would be obliged to compromise his dignity in order to assure the tribune he would not betray his or Caesar's friendship. The orator was very unhappy about Antony's letter and made it clear to Atticus that it filled him with the social pain and outrage Romans denominated as *dolor*. Perhaps this is why, when he introduced this letter to Atticus, he angrily described it as tyrannical in its tone.[150]

It appears Antony regretted his letter. He arrived in Misenum on 3 May. Cicero expected him to call as a matter of courtesy: Cicero, a consular, was a grandee and decorum demanded Antony look in. In any case, it had always been Antony's habit, Cicero informs Atticus, to visit him whenever he could. But Antony did not come. Nor did he even send a note. Cicero found this odd and fretted over it. He concluded that Antony was avoiding him because he had unwelcome news to deliver or because he was avoiding an uncomfortable interview in which he would be unable to comply with Cicero's requests.[151] When Antony left Misenum for Capua, on 10 May, he at last sent a message apologizing for his failure to look in: it was indeed, he claimed, a sense of awkwardness that kept him away; he worried that Cicero was upset with him. Cicero seemed satisfied by this—doubtless he recognized Antony was unaccustomed to exercising authority over senior senators—and began making firm plans for leaving Italy.[152]

Tribunus Plebis pro Praetore

Caesar left for Spain in early April. Antony then commenced his administration of Italy. We know very little about it—our sources are focused on Caesar and

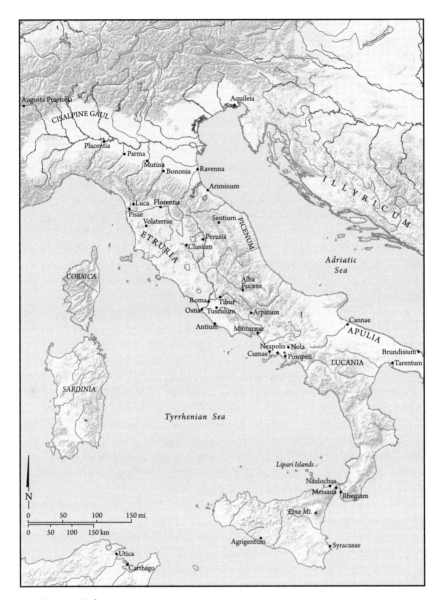

Map 4 Roman Italy

Pompey—but it must have entailed an enormous quantity of correspondence and frequent audiences. The municipalities will have sought instruction and reassurance, and normal business that might have been directed to magistrates in Rome was now, unusually, to be put before the tribune. His responsibilities were extensive and novel, and amid the anxieties incited by civil war his authority will have been viewed as nearly absolute. His chief task was to see to the security of Italy's port cities: senators must be confined, intruders halted. For these reasons, Antony began a tour of Italy, beginning with the cities of the coast. This progress, as we have seen, brought him to the Bay of Naples on 3 May, where Cicero's letters furnish a glimpse into his performance. In the orator's view, Antony did not impress: the powerful tribune was besotted by the love of pleasure and the love of sway.

Even before Antony arrived in Misenum, Cicero had heard rumours, which he passed on to Atticus, that he was travelling with the notorious courtesan, Volumnia Cytheris. She was carried with him in an open litter, 'a second wife'. And they were followed by other litters filled with girlfriends and other men whom Cicero describes, with clear distaste, as *friends*. We hear no more about the disreputable friends—perhaps they were actors and actresses and musicians, entertainment for Antony and his guests or even his hosts as he circulated through Italy—but we learn later that Cytheris was indeed Antony's companion.[153] Cicero disapproved, but it is not a scandal—not yet anyway. In his *Philippics*, by contrast, he paints a lurid portrait of Antony's decadent parade—Antony's mistress, he moans, was more highly honoured than his patrician mother Julia—dissolution elaborated even more starkly by Plutarch in his biography.[154] We may safely put aside these over-the-top purple passages. Doing so, however, does nothing to render Antony's conduct less remarkable. Cicero's letter makes it clear that Antony's retinue was inappropriate.

Volumnia Cytheris was the freedwoman of the wealthy freedman, Publius Volumnius Eutrapelus. This cultured, charming, and very witty man was a friend of both Cicero and Antony. After the Ides of March and until his victory at Philippi, Eutrapelus served under Antony as an officer.[155] Volumnia was a well-known mime-actress and therefore sexy, glamorous, and disgraceful. She was also one of Rome's most desired courtesans, high-class call-girls sought out as much for their sophistica-tion and elegant society as for their sensuality.[156] Before she was linked to Antony she was, so we are told, a lover of Gaius Cornelius Gallus, the equestrian marshal who was later Octavian's first procurator of Egypt. Gallus was also a founding figure in Rome's version of elegiac love poetry, and the beloved celebrated in his verse, Lycoris, was, ac-cording to later critics, modelled on Cytheris.[157] Marcus Brutus, the noblest Roman of them all, was also allegedly one of Cytheris' admirers.[158]

We get a guilty peek at her effect on Roman men in a letter Cicero wrote to his friend, Papirius Paetus, in 46.[159] Cicero is attending a dinner party hosted by Eutrapelus when unexpectedly Volumnia joins the company. The orator reaches immediately for his writing tablets, his version of a modern smartphone, and scribbles out to his friend a faux apology for finding himself in such an electric atmosphere. The letter is witty—Cicero pretends to blame Paetus for blaming him for keeping such company—but the senior consular is palpably pleased with himself, at once shocked and excited and feeling a bit edgy ('me, that sort of thing never appealed to me even when I was young, and certainly not now that I am old') but nonetheless entirely delighted.[160] After two thousand years, the frisson subsists.[161] It is not difficult to imagine the effect she made on the municipal aristocracy when she appeared alongside Mark Antony.

Now it was natural in Rome for young men to spend money on courtesans. It was a habit that could get out of hand, a recurring theme of Roman comedy and elegiac love poetry. But it was by no means exceptional. Nor was it unnatural or illicit even for a married man to enjoy the company of a courtesan.[162] It was, however, in the view of many, bad form for anyone of mature years, not least for a public official.[163] Cicero's astonishment at Antony's behaviour is not prudish. Instead, he is shocked that the man responsible for Caesar's government in Italy is so brazen and so unfocussed on his duty. If we are right in viewing the residue of Antony's bad company as actors and musicians and the like, his procession through Italy was certain to be sensational.[164] Perhaps he hoped, by exhibiting his earthy, un-martial side, to reassure anxious municipal aristocrats that his tour was not a threat to them. Even if this was true, however, there can be no doubting or overlooking Antony's undisguised hedonism.

Cicero was intrigued but unoffended by Cytheris. He was, however, disturbed by Antony's official treatment of his aristocratic peers.[165] Antony summoned senators who had ties with the Bay of Naples as well as magistrates from local municipalities. Courteous, they appeared at his residence early in order to attend his morning levee. But Antony did not rise until late. When informed that dignitaries from Naples and Cumae were present, two cities Caesar currently held in disfavour, he ordered everyone to leave and return the next day. He preferred, Cicero reports, to have a bath. This episode is curious, and Cicero's account of it is clearly intended to suggest that Antony, suffering from a hangover after a night of dissolution, seized upon any justification for ridding himself of his day's responsibilities. And that may be right. If so, it was disgraceful: Roman aristocrats, unlike modern powerbrokers, exhibited their grandeur by making themselves accessible, not by cancelling appointments. Perhaps, however, this highly unusual behaviour was designed to single out Cumae and Naples for criticism by way this relatively gentle expression of disapproval. If so, it had to strike many as arrogant. Whatever the reality of Antony's intentions, Cicero found his conduct frivolous.

We have no other independent accounts of Antony's administration of Italy.[166] That Cytheris remained his companion is certain. Whether he was always quite so cavalier in his treatment of municipal aristocrats we cannot know. Cicero, despite Antony's instructions, managed to make his way to Pompey, but of any serious disruptions in Italy there is no indication. The worst Cicero can say in his *Philippics* is that Antony inflicted Cytheris on every township in the country.[167] In reality, Antony must have been a busy man. Nor was the news from abroad always welcome. His brother, Gaius, was defeated and taken prisoner.[168] This reversal led to Dolabella's ejection from the Adriatic.[169] And in Africa, Curio perished in battle.[170] These were grave personal disappointments for Antony. At the same time, because reverses of this kind can only have dampened Caesar's support and even encouraged disaffected men still in Italy, these unwelcome reports demanded even more from him as he endeavoured to sustain order.

Caesar Returns to Rome

With remarkable efficiency, Caesar subjugated the city of Massilia and defeated Pompey's legates in Spain.[171] Before he returned to Rome, late in the year, he was named dictator by way of legislation carried by Lepidus. Caesar assumed this office, however, only when he entered the city. He then passed a series of laws, the most important of which were designed to alleviate Rome's debt crisis and stimulate renewed, desperately needed, sources of credit.[172] He solemnly celebrated the Feriae Latinae, the annual Latin Festival, an ancient and highly popular event.[173] Then, in his role as dictator, he conducted elections. Unsurprisingly, he was elected consul for 48 with Publius Servilius Isauricus at his colleague. The semblance of a normal Roman government was now restored. After only eleven days, Caesar abdicated his dictatorship and began preparations for his campaign against Pompey.[174]

In carrying his legislative programme, Caesar put Antony to work as a tribune.[175] He passed a law restoring the rights of the children of men proscribed during Sulla's dictatorship. Their unfortunate condition had long been recognized as an injustice.[176] This remedy, then, was welcome to many in the aristocracy and was intended to send a clear signal of Caesar's sincerity in the application of clemency. Antony also enacted a measure recalling men who had been exiled under Pompey's law on illegal electioneering, a crime designated by Romans as *ambitus*, which he carried during his sole consulship. Measures against *ambitus* were always deemed righteous in Rome, but Pompey's law was retroactive to 70, an unattractive feature that encouraged political score settling in the courts.[177] Men condemned under its terms could be represented as Pompey's victims, which meant that recalling them appeared another kindly act. Still, Antony's law did not supersede Pompey's; it simply corrected its misapplication. This remedy had been discussed by Caesar and his circle since spring, and, when he was in the Bay of Naples, Antony arranged to travel to Ischia, where he met with several exiles in order to assure them they would soon be recalled.[178] These Antonian laws naturally brought him credit from those who benefitted from them. But no one doubted that these measures reflected Caesar's programme, not independent political thinking on Antony's part.

Voluptuary though Antony may have been during his administration of the municipalities, it is nonetheless clear that, under his supervision, Italy remained stable and secure enough to meet Caesar's expectations. Antony's assignment, Caesar understood, can have been no easy task: Italy was politically unstable and its economy, racked by anxiety, was further weakened by debt crises and a credit crunch. When he returned late in the year and notwithstanding reports of Antony's undignified behaviour, Caesar continued to rely on him. Clearly, he was satisfied with Antony and untroubled by his carousing. Perhaps he even found it attractive. Although the circle of Caesar's friends was wide and diverse, there is no denying he had a soft spot for gifted but louche young men.[179] Caelius Rufus, Cornelius Dolabella, and Mark Antony, they all appealed to him.

Antony's open affair with Cytheris did not count against him, nor did his other appetites. Quite the contrary. When in 48 Caesar went east to confront Pompey, Antony was the legate on whom he reposed the most vital responsibilities. When Shakespeare's Brutus is planning his conspiracy, Cassius urges him to strike down Antony, 'so beloved of Caesar'. Brutus demurs, dismissing Antony as 'but a limb of Caesar'.[180] This poetic assessment aptly characterizes the historical events of 49. But by way of his robust and capable service to a man he clearly admired and loved—'no one is dearer to me than are you', Antony writes to Cicero, 'except my Caesar'—Antony became, while still a tribune, an imposing figure in Roman affairs.[181]

IV

Caesar's master of the horse

Victory at Pharsalus

Before the end of 49, Caesar abdicated his brief dictatorship and set out for Brundisium. Antony followed, no longer tribune of the *plebs*—that office lapsed on 10 December—but now serving as the proconsul's legate.[1] In the east, Pompey had exploited his enemy's divagation into Spain by assembling a large fleet; amassing a mighty host, including numerous auxiliary forces; and extruding funds from allies and subjects throughout Asia Minor. His army was far bigger than Caesar's and enjoyed an enormous advantage in resources. Furthermore, Pompey dominated the Adriatic Sea.[2] Earlier in the year, Scribonius Libo and Marcus Octavius defeated Caesar's forces in Illyricum and captured their leader, Antony's brother Gaius. This success allowed them to drive out the fleet commanded by Dolabella.[3] It was now early winter, the storms of which impeded sea crossings, and the Adriatic was patrolled by squadrons of warships under the admiralty of Bibulus.[4] Nevertheless, Caesar took his chance. In early January 48 he managed to cross to Epirus with seven depleted legions, a few hundred cavalrymen, and next to nothing in the way of provisions. He soon drew near Pompey's army in the vicinity of Dyrrhachium. Without reinforcements and provisions, however, his position was untenable, which is why his officers in Brundisium, including Antony, were directed to follow as soon as possible.[5]

This proved very difficult. After his arrival in Epirus, Caesar sent his transport ships back to Italy. But they were captured and destroyed by Bibulus.[6] At Brundisium, the senior officers were Antony and Quintus Fufius Calenus.[7] Calenus attempted a crossing, but, after receiving word that he would find no safe place to land, returned to port. One of his ships, however, carried on. It was captured by Bibulus, who brutally executed its crew.[8] Not long afterwards Bibulus fell ill and died, but his death did nothing to weaken the Adriatic blockade. Libo, hoping to prevent any reinforcements from reaching Caesar, launched an attack on Brundisium, sealing the harbour and landing soldiers along the coast. The situation quickly became dire. In reaction, Antony staged a cunning ambush. He disguised sixty or so boats with wicker screens and hid them along the shore of the harbour. He also prepared his cavalry for an assault on Libo's land forces. Two triremes were then sent out of the harbour as bait for Libo's fleet. The ruse worked. Four ships pursued the triremes, which rapidly reversed themselves, drawing the enemy vessels into the harbour, where they were set upon by Antony's hidden boats. At just this moment, his cavalry cleared the coast. Libo's force was repulsed and the blockade broken.[9]

Still, it remained difficult to reinforce Caesar, who dispatched increasingly imperious letters demanding that Antony and Calenus attempt a crossing.[10] Recognizing their commander's desperate situation, the two legates launched their ships, probably sometime in April. As their fleet sailed past Dyrrhachium, a Pompeian squadron was sent out against it. But Antony and Calenus succeeded in landing in a harbour three miles north of the Illyrian city Lissus. Here Antony took sole command of the forces who disembarked, four legions and 800 cavalrymen. He quickly took control of Lissus, which welcomed him, and marched to join Caesar, whose camp was nearly 100 miles to his south. Pompey, aware of Antony's arrival, attempted to block him but was unsuccessful.[11] The welcome combination of Antony's with Caesar's army, although it did not bring Caesar's forces into anything like parity with Pompey's, nonetheless rendered them a serious threat to the great man's domination in Greece. Caesar even made so bold as to offer Pompey an opportunity for fighting a decisive battle.[12]

Instead, the two armies positioned themselves over against one another near Dyrrhachium in a mutual siege shaped and strained by an extensive array of fortifications. Attacks and counterattacks were fierce and frequent. Caesar's army, poorly provisioned and unable to import supplies by sea, had the worst of it and the soldiers' morale suffered. In this desultory but dangerous conflict, Antony exhibited both courage and decisive leadership. He was put in command of the Ninth Legion. This appointment was a significant one because this legion, in the previous year, had staged a serious mutiny against Caesar, an uprising he quelled only by way of threats and executions.[13] Antony's assignment clearly reflected Caesar's confidence in his capacity for inspiring soldiers even of this fibre. He did not disappoint. In a ferocious struggle for the possession of a strategic site, Antony led his men uphill amid heavy losses to seize the site from Pompey's troops. In another struggle, when one of Caesar's fortifications was at risk of falling to the enemy, Antony, although outnumbered, rescued his comrades from defeat. Valour like this, however, was inadequate against Pompey's logistical advantages. Caesar was compelled to withdraw and march north.

Dyrrachium was a victory for Pompey. He was now urged by some of his officers to invade Italy, a sensible proposition in view of its vulnerability during Caesar's absence. This plan, however, Pompey rejected largely on political grounds, nor did he wish to leave Caesar uncontained in Greece. Pompey's preferred strategy was to continue exploiting his logistical superiority, isolating his enemy and eroding his resources until he could no longer offer stout resistance. This reasonable policy, however, was nothing short of anathema to his noble officers, senators whose heroic, romantic sensibilities excelled their practical military acumen. Certain Caesar could not win, and jealous of Pompey's supreme authority, they sought an immediate end to the war through a glorious, pitched battle. Pompey, wearied of being dubbed King of Kings and Agamemnon by his captious colleagues, was unable to resist them. This was a serious lapse in judgement.[14] Nonetheless, when the two sides met in Thessaly, near Pharsalus, on 9 August, Pompey's army greatly outnumbered Caesar's and on any reckoning the odds were strongly in his favour.

Pompey, according to Caesar, commanded his left wing, together with Lentulus Crus. The right flank he assigned to Domitius Ahenobarbus, the centre to Metellus Scipio. Facing Pompey on Caesar's right was Publius Sulla, but also Caesar himself.[15] As commander, he needed mobility when the fighting commenced, but it was vital that his troops observe him facing the great man. At Caesar's centre was an ex-consul, Gnaeus Domitius Calvinus, and his left wing was led by Antony in command of a new legion formed by combining Caesar's depleted Ninth and Eighth Legions. Later sources, however, disagree with Caesar's disposition of commanders on the Pompeian side: they put Pompey on his own right wing, and therefore opposite Antony, while Caesar is confronted by his bitter enemy, Domitius. We cannot be certain which order is the true one, but, whatever the array, the significance of Antony's deployment is clear.[16] Of his performance in this battle, however, we know next to nothing, only the predictable notice that he fought with valour. Pompey's forces were routed, and Cicero later complained that, when chasing down his fleeing enemies, Antony was bloodthirsty. Perhaps he was. As for Cicero's allegation that it was Antony who struck down Domitius, this action, notable if true, is attested nowhere else.[17] Striking down an enemy commander in the heat of battle, however, was nothing to be ashamed of, even in a civil war. Caesar's victory at Pharsalus did not end the civil war. It was not even the fiercest battle of the civil war. But it shattered Pompey's image of invincibility and made Caesar master of the eastern Mediterranean world.

Disunity in the West

Italy, in Caesar's absence, remained a volatile, unstable place. The Roman people's economic miseries found little relief in the hasty remedies introduced by Caesar during his brief dictatorship, a grim reality that became increasingly clear soon after he launched his invasion of Greece. Caelius Rufus, praetor in 48, immediately introduced a series of contentious economic measures. He proposed a year's remission on rents, which appealed especially to the masses (the vast majority of poor Romans rented their homes), as well as reductions in interest and a cancellation of some debts, pressing matters among all segments of the public.[18] Caelius' programme brought him into conflict with Gaius Trebonius, also a praetor in 48, and their struggle soon turned violent. Servilius Isauricus, the consul, turned to the senate, where he introduced a motion forbidding Caelius from putting his bills before the people. It was carried by a majority but vetoed by tribunes. Nevertheless, Servilius forcefully intervened by imposing order in the Forum and blocking further action on Caelius' part. The praetor, however, fought back. In reaction to this violence, the senate temporarily suspended him from office.

Caelius was undeterred. He escalated his struggle into a new civil war by opening communications with Titus Annius Milo. This man, taking advantage of the disorder in Italy, was now active in Campania, where, a self-proclaimed champion of Pompey's cause, he was assembling forces and working to dislodge disaffected cities from Caesar's regime. So successful was he that Servilius sent out the praetor, Quintus Pedius, in command of Italy's sole legion.[19] Milo was defeated and fell in battle. As for Caelius, he withdrew to Bruttium, where he attempted to suborn Roman soldiers stationed in Thurii. Unsuccessful, he was put to death. Economic wretchedness, fierce ambition, and political contentiousness animated Caelius' rebellion, which Servilius contained only by way of brute force and an elastic approach to its constitutional application. Even Caesar recognized the seriousness of the insurrections led by Caelius and Milo.[20] Their failure was welcome to the consul and to Caesar, but these episodes were hardly signs of a stable administration or a faction firmly united behind its leader.

Rivalries and quarrels also incited civil war in Spain. After defeating Pompey's legates, Caesar left Aemilius Lepidus governor of Further Spain and assigned Nearer

Spain to the loyal tribune of the *plebs*, Cassius Longinus. Early in 48, however, several units in Cassius' army mutinied, ultimately taking Marcus Claudius Marcellus, Cassius' quaestor, as their leader. Throughout this year Cassius and Marcellus fought a civil war which was sorely destructive to the cities of the province. Each army defended its legitimacy by proclaiming its loyalty to Caesar, but the conflict only intensified and expanded. Foreign forces, including Bogud, the king of Mauretania and a close ally of Caesar, were soon drawn into the struggle. Late in the year, Lepidus left Further Spain in order to settle the conflict. From Rome, Trebonius, doubtless on instructions from Caesar, rushed westwards to supersede both Cassius and Marcellus.[21] Further fighting followed, after which Cassius took flight and drowned while trying to escape from Spain. Only then was order restored.[22] Caesar was so deeply impressed by Lepidus' intervention that he later honoured him with a triumph and a consulship.[23] In Spain as in the city, however, it was obvious how easily the men of Caesar's party could descend into bitter, dangerous conflicts.

Caesar in Egypt

After Pharsalus, probably in late October, Servilius Isauricus, obeying instructions he received from the victor, oversaw Caesar's election as dictator for the second time.[24] Exceptionally, Caesar entered this office while still abroad and in pursuit of Pompey, who was making his way to Egypt. There the great man had strong claims of loyalty on Ptolemy, the teenaged king. Pompey's intention was to exploit Alexandria as the centre of his operations while he prepared for a fresh offensive. When he arrived, however, he was assassinated on the recommendation of Ptolemy's closest advisors. Caesar arrived soon afterwards, at the start of October, but with only a small force. He nonetheless asserted Roman authority over this client kingdom and, to the dismay of many in Alexandria, began extracting moneys owed him by the royal house.[25]

Egypt, when Pompey and Caesar arrived, was also afflicted by civil war. After the death of Ptolemy XII in 51, Cleopatra VII, no more than eighteen, ascended the throne with her brother and husband, Ptolemy XIII, who was about ten. Almost immediately, the two were locked in a contest for supreme power, behind which stood conflicting factions in the court. The queen, destined to find fame and notoriety owing to her elegance and intelligence, demonstrated her political acumen early on: green in judgement, perhaps, but certainly cold in blood. She made herself popular up and down a kingdom troubled by debt, drought, and regional disturbances. In so doing, she quickly eclipsed her brother. Nevertheless, he and his backers remained tenacious rivals, and by 49 it was Ptolemy XIII, not his sister, who dominated Egypt. This development, however, did nothing to usher in stability: civil strife, often erupting in armed violence between the military forces of the two sides, persisted.[26]

When he arrived in Egypt, Caesar arrogated to himself the right to settle this dispute over the throne. As a consequence, he became a belligerent in a vicious civil war. Unexpectedly, he found himself in a difficult position. Seasonal winds made it impossible for him to sail away or for reinforcements to join him by sea, nor could he easily be relieved by land. This Alexandrian War proved so dangerous for the dictator that it was very nearly the end of him, but late in March 47 his situation recovered with the

Fig. 4.1 Cleopatra VII, 1st cent. BCE bust in the Altes Museum Berlin.
Source: Wikimedia Commons.

arrival of allied troops. These forces gave Caesar a welcome advantage and, in the end, he was victorious. Ptolemy perished in the fighting and Cleopatra was installed on the throne, which she now shared with a different, much younger brother, whom she married. By then she was pregnant with Caesar's child—during the war she had become Caesar's mistress—and sometime in the summer bore Caesar a son, whom she called Ptolemy Caesarion. By then, however, Caesar had departed. But he did not return to Italy until late in September.[27]

Master of the Horse

When Caesar became dictator, Antony was designated his *magister equitum*, the master of the horse, a dictator's second-in-command.[28] His appointment was even more irregular than Caesar's inasmuch as he was selected for the post by Caesar before Caesar was actually made a dictator and he may have been formally appointed by the consul, Servilius Isauricus, instead of the dictator Caesar: other anomalies have also been diagnosed. Although these matters raised constitutional hackles in Rome, they were quickly put aside.[29] Later, however, in his *Philippics*, Cicero complained about the anomaly of Antony's elevation.[30] Caesar's master of the horse did not follow him into the east. Instead, Antony returned to Italy as its governor. He arrived in Brundisium in late October or early November. Almost immediately, and certainly by December, he was issuing public decrees.[31]

Antony took charge of a city equipped with very little in the way of traditional government. The plebeian assembly had elected tribunes and plebeian aediles, but Servilius, doubtless on Caesar's instructions, had not conducted consular elections, owing to which there were no regular magistrates for the year. These were not elected until after Caesar returned. For Rome and for Italy, especially after the rebellion of Caelius and Milo, this was hardly reassuring. Still, Antony, after the Pharsalus campaign, was viewed by most as a loyal, capable man, and Caesar was in any case expected to return early in the year. When, however, Caesar failed to appear, Antony's administration was increasingly suffused by an atmosphere of precarity which exacerbated the severity of every fresh problem. This anxiety was also worsened by Caesar's silence: so far as Cicero knew, and he was very keen to know, not a single letter from Caesar reached Italy between December 48 and June 47.[32] During this time, such news as reached Rome appeared to signal a strong resurgence on the part of Caesar's enemies—even after the death of Pompey.[33] Sustaining order amid such disturbing uncertainty constituted a profound challenge.

Settling Caesar's war-wearied troops in temporary quarters was Antony's first chore.[34] He delivered nine legions to Italy. They were billeted on various towns, mostly in Campania, where they awaited their rewards, the donatives and lands promised by their general. These entitlements, however, could only be distributed after the dictator's return. Antony's task, then, was far from easy. These men were tired yet restless, and maintaining discipline tested his strengths as an officer. Furthermore, the soldiers' presence was deeply unwelcome to any municipality burdened with the cost and inconvenience of furnishing them with quarters. For this reason, after his arrival, Antony immediately made a tour of the affected cities, hoping in this way to forestall any strife between soldiers and civilians.

Even amid this highly serious business, however, if Cicero can be believed, Antony travelled in a merry, indulgent style. He alleges Antony was greeted in Brundisium not only by honour guards and dignitaries but also by Cytheris, once again his steady companion.[35] This detail is entirely plausible, indeed likely. The bulk of our ancient evidence elaborates, often in lip-smacking detail, the debaucheries that marked Antony's tenure as master of the horse.[36] That these reports are hostile and exaggerated is obvious. At the same time, we have no reason to exclude that in 47 Antony lived his private life very much as he had done in 49. He was Antony yet. Still, he was also a busy man, especially in the absence of regular magistrates. The demands of Antony's public life were manifold and often exacting. Aware of the importance of instilling in the public something in the way of a feeling of normality, Antony took on the sacred obligations ordinarily performed by the consuls or a dictator, including a celebration of the Latin Festival.[37] His efforts were not unsuccessful: at the beginning of his tenure, according to the usually critical Dio, Antony preserved a healthy degree of civic order.[38]

Under such extraordinary circumstances, however, difficulties were bound to arise. Some stemmed from confusion and lack of communication. Before departing for Egypt, Caesar, fearing that pardoned Pompeians might stir up trouble in Italy, sent Antony a strongly worded letter ordering him to forbid entry to anyone from that camp to whom he had not granted an exemption. On this basis, Antony wrote apologetically to Cicero, who arrived in Brundisium in October 48, that he could not allow him to enter the country. At the same time, as a courtesy to an old friend, he left him unmolested. The orator, however, did in fact have Caesar's permission, something he could certify by way of a letter that Caesar had sent to Dolabella. For Cicero's subsequent security, Antony then issued a decree exempting him (and another Pompeian loyalist) from Caesar's ban. Cicero groused to Atticus that he did not like this explicit notice of Caesar's clemency and Antony's assistance in guaranteeing it.[39] And much later, in his *Second Philippic*, he complained about Antony's bringing up this episode as a specimen of his past helpfulness.[40] Even defeated senators, it is obvious, were difficult to deal with. Problems like these, however, were the least of Antony's worries.

Dolabella's Reforms

Antony's principal task lay in coping with the ambitions and designs of his friend, Cornelius Dolabella. In the previous year, Dolabella transformed himself into an avatar of Clodius Pulcher. He erected a statue to him and, like Clodius, surrendered his patrician status through adoption by a plebeian so that he could stand for the office of tribune of the *plebs*.[41] Elected for 47, he proposed, like Caelius before him, legislation which restructured or even cancelled debts and measures lowering or remitting rents.[42] Amid the economic crisis entrained by the civil war, these bills were naturally very popular with broad segments of the public, but, as Caelius' collapse had demonstrated, economic reforms were dangerously volatile. Dolabella's proposals, although they appealed to many, were not welcomed by everyone—certainly not by creditors or property owners for whom Dolabella's measures would prove costly. There were also adventurous capitalists, like the rich equestrian Gaius Matius, a friend both to Caesar and Cicero, who, because they found ways to profit from the economy's disruption, had little stake in the application of any remedies.[43] Even senators sympathetic to the plight of the poor or who were themselves coping with massive debts could not fail, after their experience of Caelius, to see in Dolabella's programme a brazen, perhaps dangerous vehicle for the tribune's personal advancement. It was on behalf of these constituencies that the tribune, Lucius Trebellius, as well as Asinius Pollio, also possibly a tribune in this year, opposed and obstructed Dolabella's scheme. Demonstrations by both sides quickly escalated into riots.

Dolabella expected Antony's support; indeed, he may have relied on it, but Antony was disinclined to allow any radical reform without Caesar's approval.[44] This was an obvious position to take and did not per se repudiate Dolabella's designs: it merely postponed any final decision about them. Aware of the city's economic problems, Antony, before making up his mind, very likely consulted with Caesar's close advisors, Oppius and Balbus, each of whom was active in Italy.[45] Policy aside, however, and regardless of Antony's personal attitude towards Dolabella, he could hardly tolerate disorder. Like Servilius before him, he turned to the senate, which attempted to pass a decree insisting no changes in the law be made until Caesar returned. That, however, was blocked by Dolabella.[46] Antony then, hopeful of tempering any street fighting, issued an edict forbidding weapons anywhere in the city. This decree, however, was simply ignored. Antony then brought in soldiers, but he did so only after securing a resolution from the senate recognizing his authority to act. This move, although it temporarily suppressed any serious violence, did nothing to resolve the standoff between the tribunes, possibly because the senate's decree, very likely some version of an appeal calling on all officials to look after the best interests of the republic, was so vaguely worded that the tribunes, no less than Antony, could claim their actions also conformed to its directives.[47] In refusing to take Dolabella's side, Antony alienated but did not deter him, and the capital remained in a state of pitched apprehension throughout the spring and into summer.

Mutiny in Campania

In a letter of 19 January, Cicero speaks unhappily of desperate conditions in the capital. In the same letter, he reveals his worry about the loyalty of the troops unwelcomely billeted in Italy.[48] He was right to be concerned. The soldiers in Campania were mostly men of very long and very hard service. Fighting had depleted their numbers, and, since the start of the civil war, they had often gone unpaid. They were promised back wages and generous bonuses, but these were not forthcoming. Impatient and restless, they began to show signs of mutiny, going so far as to plunder their host communities.[49]

Antony rushed south to restore order, but there was little he could do.[50] He had at his disposal only the single legion he had taken over from Pedius, so intimidation was hardly an option. Nor did he have moneys which he could distribute as donatives. We do not know how long Antony was away, or what his methods were. But, although not entirely successful in mollifying the troops, he somehow managed, by dint, perhaps, of his personality and soldierly rapport, to persuade them to accept, however grudgingly, that nothing could be done without Caesar. Some of these men, after all, certainly the men of the Ninth Legion, Antony had commanded during the campaign in Greece: they knew him and were apparently willing to believe him. The soldiers' anger, however, remained undiminished. Cicero mentions their unrest more than once, which indicates that the problem did not go away. At the same time, he never regards the situation as out of hand. Apparently, then, it remained under control, if only barely.

Caesar learned of the soldiers' ill-discipline in July, after leaving Egypt but while he was in Asia. He was concerned not least because he had decided to reactivate these legions for service in Africa. Consequently, he despatched three legates to take charge, but, unlike Antony, they were repulsed, in one instance by stoning.[51] After his return, Caesar sent the historian Sallust, a praetor-designate, who announced generous donatives for all who agreed to follow Caesar into Africa. The man was very nearly lynched, after which the legions marched on the capital.[52] On their way, they murdered two senatorial emissaries of praetorian rank.[53] Only when masterfully confronted by Caesar himself did they relent, and then only after he gave them everything they asked for.[54] In view of its sequel, Antony's rush to Campania must be viewed as a success. He could do no more than contain the crisis, but containment, it is obvious, was by no means an inevitable outcome.

Conflict in the Capital

Before leaving Rome, Antony put his uncle, Lucius Caesar, in charge of the city as urban prefect.[55] It was unclear, however, whether a *magister equitum* possessed the power to make such an appointment, and this dubious position rendered Lucius, although a senior ex-consul, incapable of constraining the conflict between the tribunes. Violence again flared up. When Antony returned, he, too, was unable to put a halt to this struggle. His opposition to Dolabella, he now recognized, was eroding his popularity with the urban masses, while his ineffectuality in calming civic affairs cost him support in the senate.[56] In July, when Rome learned that Caesar had left Egypt, the expectation of his imminent arrival induced greater moderation on everyone's part. Even so, Dolabella remained formidable.[57] Before long, however, it was reported that Caesar was not on his way to Italy but instead was in Asia Minor leading a campaign against Pharnaces of Pontus. Dolabella began once more to push his reforms, now with at least tepid support from Antony. But Antony also strived to stay on good terms with Trebellius and so appeared to stand with neither side.[58] His situation was a difficult one: both men were Caesarians and each was a tribune, which meant that Antony was loath to take harsh measures against either. His policy, now as earlier in the year, was to postpone addressing this controversy until Caesar was in the capital.

Dolabella, however, would not wait. He promulgated his law and set a date for an assembly to vote on it. As the day approached, his supporters occupied the Forum, erecting barriers for keeping out Trebellius and any opponents of the measure. Antony responded with force, perhaps with the authority of a final decree carried by the senate but more likely acting, like Servilius when resisting Caelius, entirely on his own initiative. He led troops into the Forum, cleared it of Dolabella's partisans, and removed the tablets on which Dolabella's proposal had been posted—not without violence which resulted in deaths. The soldiers remained on guard in the Forum and an uneasy peace was imposed.[59] Antony's energetic suppression of Dolabella was doubtless welcome to the senate and the city's capitalists: in his letters to Atticus during this time, Cicero makes it clear how deplorable a view he takes of his son-in-law's policies and is certain Atticus agrees with him.[60] But the masses were outraged. So, too, Romans who continued to take their constitution seriously. The very man the defence of whose tribunate had been the catalyst for civil war was now storming the Forum with soldiers, scattering the people and preventing an assembly from rendering its judgement on a tribunician measure. Antony foiled Dolabella, but Dolabella's tactics did much to undermine Antony's public image. This conflict was more than their friendship could bear.

Unhappy Families

Amid this political strife, according to Plutarch, Antony, having discovered Dolabella was having an affair with his wife, promptly and furiously divorced her.[61] As for Dolabella, Antony now became his implacable enemy, a development which exacerbated the two men's political standoff. In his personal despair Antony found refuge in the affections of Fulvia, whom he soon married. Plutarch's report is almost universally

accepted as accurate. But doubts have rightly been raised, and, as we shall see, it is unlikely that this divorce took place in 47. Cicero, in his *Philippics*, tells a different story.
In his version, Antony, when he divorced Antonia, took the extreme and ungentle-
manly tack of publicly accusing her of adultery, perhaps by way of a legal action for
making a claim on her dowry. The orator also informs us that, during a meeting of the
senate on 1 January 44, Antony threw up Dolabella's fornication with Antonia as the
origin of his hatred for the man. But Cicero holds Antonia blameless. For the orator,
she and Dolabella were mere pretexts: it was Antony who was having an affair, with
Curio's widow Fulvia—a woman, Cicero insinuates, Antony slept with even when she
was married to Clodius.[62] Antony was, Cicero insists, indecently impatient to take a
new wife: the marriage came quickly after the divorce. But Antony, it appears, married
Fulvia in 46.[63] Cicero's account, then, tends to locate its hasty, lustful Antony and his
reprehensible divorce in that year.

The truth of this matter is important for the politics of 47 and for our understanding
of Antony's private life. Our sources, however, are anything but straightforward. In
Plutarch's case, literary considerations may well have led him to locate Antony's divorce in 47.[64] As for Cicero, who does not specify when the divorce took place, he
had tactical reasons for exonerating Antonia: the move aided him in vituperating his
enemy. But we may be able to get round both the *Philippics* and Plutarch's biography
by following the events of Dolabella's marriage to Cicero's daughter, Tullia, in 47 and
in 46, the year in which she divorced him.

That Dolabella was man of dubious character not even his closest friends denied.[65]
During the year of his tribunate, his marriage with Tullia fell under great strain. Tullia
left Rome, joining her father in Brundisium, where he, in correspondence with his
wife, Terentia, and his friend, Atticus, explored with heightened seriousness the possibility of Tullia's divorcing her husband.[66] As for justifications—a moral and political
necessity but not a legal one—Cicero considered Dolabella's objectionable tribunician
reforms as a possibility. He also reminded Atticus that his son-in-law was a serial adulterer. But the only woman Cicero mentions by name in this context is Caecilia Metella,
the daughter of Metellus Celer and Clodia Metelli.[67] Now Cicero mentions Dolabella's
alleged adultery with Caecilia Metella in July. If, prior to this, Antony had sensationally divorced Antonia for committing adultery with Dolabella, Cicero surely would
have mentioned it as an event which provided just the right kind of cover (during this
time, Cicero was straining himself to stay well informed about and on good terms
with Antony).[68] Which seems to exclude Antony's divorcing Antonia during the first
half of the year.[69]

In the end, Tullia did not divorce Dolabella in 47. Cicero instead endeavoured to
salvage his daughter's marriage. Admittedly Dolabella's standing with Caesar was high
at the time and Cicero fretted about his influence. Perhaps this is why, notwithstanding
his affair with Caecilia Metella and his objectionable politics, Cicero decided against a
divorce for Tullia and took steps to improve family relations.[70] But these efforts failed.
Late in 46, although Dolabella remained close to Caesar, Tullia nevertheless divorced
him—even though she was pregnant with his child.[71] Clearly a drastic change in their
personal relationship had taken place. Perhaps this alteration had to do with Antony's
divorce of Antonia. That action, loud with public imprecations against Dolabella, may
have been the last straw for Tullia and her family.[72] Tullia's divorce was settled quietly

and, although Dolabella played the deadbeat by way of negligence in repaying the dowry, Cicero was careful to remain on good terms with him.[73] In January 45 Tullia gave birth to a son. Owing to unfortunate complications in her pregnancy, however, she died in February. Not long afterwards, her son also died.

Admittedly, aligning Tullia's divorce of Dolabella with Antony's divorce of Antonia can only be suggestive. But doing so appears to make better sense of the two events than Plutarch's date for Antony's divorce. If this is right, and Antony divorced her sometime in 46, it was indeed not long afterwards that he married Fulvia, which conforms with the timing of these events preserved by Cicero—not that we need to share his interpretation of them. We must, then, view the clash in 47 between tribune and master of the horse in different terms from the ones animating Plutarch's sexually charged narrative. Antony's friendship with Dolabella was strained, perhaps ruptured, by their political conflict in that year. But it came to a complete and public end only in 46, when Antony denounced the man, perhaps sincerely, for fornication with Antonia, whom he repudiated in an ugly divorce that did no one any credit. He was soon remarried to Fulvia, the widow of his friend Scribonius Curio.

Fulvia

Fulvia merits a section to herself. She was the daughter of Marcus Fulvius Bambalio and Sempronia.[74] We do not know when she was born. Her first marriage probably took place around 62, when Fulvia will have been a teenager, but a finer degree of preciseness is impossible.[75] If Fulvia married at sixteen, which is likely enough, she was born around 78. She was not, then, much younger than Antony. Both her mother and father derived from old, distinguished families. Little, however, is known about Fulvius Bambalio, and it appears he did not have a political career. In his *Philippics*, Cicero dismissed him as stammering and contemptible, but that is unsurprising and hardly probative.[76] In the same speech, Sempronia, the granddaughter of a consul, is derided as the daughter of an oddball, and there may be something real lying behind that imputation.[77] Sempronia's first husband was the patrician Lucius Pinarius Natta and, after the dissolution of her marriage to Bambalio, she married Lucius Licinius Murena, who was consul in 62. There was great wealth here—even Cicero must concede that Fulvia was a very rich woman—and Fulvia enjoyed the kind of pedigree that attracted regard in Roman society.[78] Which explains the high standing of Fulvia's first husband, Publius Clodius Pulcher, scion of Rome's most eminent patrician family. She bore Clodius two children, a son and a daughter.

Fulvia became politically conspicuous after the murder of her husband, when she played a part in inciting the riots which racked the capital in 52. Even before this, she must have been a figure familiar to her husband's followers. Cicero insists the couple were almost inseparable. Her boldness and devotion in the aftermath of Clodius' death will have won her the affection of many in the lower orders. It is less clear, however, that Fulvia, popular though doubtless she remained, somehow assumed Clodius' mantle as a champion of the common people of Rome or was even a potent symbol of his popular ideology.[79] Fulvia's second husband was Scribonius Curio. Of this marriage we know very little.[80] A son was born. He later fought for Antony at the battle of

Actium and afterwards was executed by Octavian.[81] Fulvia's second marriage ended with Curio's death in 49.

Antony was her third husband, and by the time of this marriage she was a notable figure in her own right both by way of her wealth but also her position in Roman high society. Fulvia, as we shall see, was destined to play a prominent role in Antony's political life during his consulship and, more sensationally, when he was triumvir in the east. Like her husband, she possessed fortitude and acumen. And, also like him, she attracted detractors, which makes her story, as again we shall see, a hard one to recover. Antony and Fulvia had two sons together. The first was born probably in 45. He was given the cognomen Antyllus, evocative of Anton, the family's legendary founder and a son of Hercules. A second son was born after Caesar's assassination, late in 44 or in 43. His cognomen was Iullus, in honour of the dictator.

Confiscations

In dark parallel with Caesar's policy of *clementia* or *lenitas* was his programme of confiscations. In 48, Aulus Hirtius, as tribune of the *plebs*, carried a law, the *lex Hirtia*, allowing Caesar to seize and sell the property of selected Pompeians, a harsh punishment that could be extended to their wives.[82] This was not a blanket measure: individuals, it appears, were adjudged separately. The law's purpose, clearly punitive, was also intended to generate profits. Caesar's regime, reliant on its massive army, was expensive, which meant that he needed to chase every possible source of revenue. At the same time, these confiscations and the public auctions they required, because they took place in an atmosphere of insecurity and even fear, furnished Caesar's friends and henchmen with opportunities for enlarging their private holdings at a minimal cost. Caesar was complicit in this sleazy profiteering. Servilia, the mother of Brutus and the dictator's ex-lover, for instance, acquired multiple properties at low prices. Dolabella bought Pompey's villas at Alba and Formiae.[83] As late as 45, Caesar turned to his trove of confiscated holdings in order to reward a supporter, Lucius Minucius Basilus, a praetor to whom he could not offer a province.[84] And there were other beneficiaries.[85] No one, then, was surprised when Antony, exploiting his position as *magister equitum*, enriched himself by way of these auctions. What provoked consternation, however, was the sheer scale of Antony's shopping spree.

Antony's acquisitiveness took an early start. At the beginning of his tenure as master of the horse, he lived in a house appropriated from the Pompeian, Marcus Pupius Piso.[86] Soon, however, he exchanged this residence for Rome's grandest dwelling, the home of Pompey himself. For this property, Antony was the only bidder.[87] He wanted more: Pompey's gardens; Pompey's Tuscan villa; a country estate belonging to the learned Marcus Terentius Varro, an ex-praetor and devoted friend of Pompey; and a villa at Tibur that was once Metellus Scipio's. Antony also purchased numerous urban properties, possibly originally Pompey's and probably *insulae*, large (and profitable) apartment buildings.[88] But Antony was not the only one who purchased parts of Pompey's vast estate. Nor was he the most avid buyer of confiscated properties.

Publius Sulla, restored from exile by Caesar, was so active in making acquisitions that, when he died at the end of 46 or the beginning of 45, Cicero joked how Caesar's auctions would soon grind to a halt.[89]

It was Antony's purchase of Pompey's house in the Carinae district that attracted attention. The atrium of this famous house of a famous man was adorned with the beaks of ships captured during Pompey's brilliant campaign against pirates in 67, spoils of war that commemorated his magnificent third triumph in 61. This atrium Antony now appointed with images and relics of his family, and he boldly reattributed Pompey's triumphal prizes as memorials to his father and grandfather, each of whom led wars against pirates though far less successfully than Pompey. An aristocrat's grand mansion, his *domus*, was not merely a place of residence. It was a concrete expression of his *dignitas*, his prestige, and a tangible symbol of his family's splendour.[90] Antony did not simply move into Pompey's house: he assimilated it and thereby amplified his civic status and public reputation. Which is why Cicero was outraged by this annexation of Pompey's grandeur. The move prompted the orator's lamentations about Antony's desecration of the great man's noble *domus* through drunken orgies. Plutarch records Roman complaints about Antony's tasteless refurbishments.[91] Not everyone, however, will have taken so negative a view: others will have been impressed, possibly even intimidated by Antony's bold asseveration of family pride and personal clout. Nevertheless, Cicero cannot have been the only man in Rome who judged Antony's avid, opportunistic purchases of unfortunate men's properties as something shameless.

Even as Antony was acquiring multiple properties under the *lex Hirtia*, he was also the official responsible for this law's application. Cicero's letters make it clear how frightening Antony's authority was for anyone potentially affected by it.[92] Although he was permitted to remain in Italy, it was unclear whether the orator's property would be confiscated in retaliation for his service under Pompey. Terentia's property was also vulnerable. On Cicero's behalf, Atticus cultivated Antony, Balbus, and Oppius. He also urged Cicero to send them letters seeking their favour in this matter. Cicero did more than that: he and Terentia condescended to seek the assistance of Volumnia, aid which was forthcoming even if it was received ungratefully by Cicero.[93] He remained on tenterhooks so long as Caesar was isolated in Egypt: apparently Antony agreed to do nothing in Cicero's case until it was decided by the dictator. At last, a letter from Egypt delivered Cicero and his wife the complete clemency he so desperately sought.[94]

Antony was accommodating in Cicero's case. Even so, the orator remained fretful, presumably because Antony's judgements regarding other Pompeians were often harsher. In Rome, property was often a complicated matter because family ties were themselves frequently intricate and variegated. In the case of some families, both Pompeians and Caesarians were involved, which rendered the *lex Hirtia* a potentially dangerous measure if its deployment became hostile. It was because Antony, as master of the horse, oversaw all aspects of this law's regulation, restrained only by his respect for the advice of Caesarian operatives like Balbus and Oppius, that his avidity for glamorous properties met with little competition or resistance. Under these circumstances, he cannot have failed to attract envy and resentment.

Caesar's Return to Italy

After he left Egypt, Caesar was made aware of events in Rome and Italy.[95] He was also apprised of the strong Pompeian forces dominating Africa. This, he concluded, was the urgent threat. And to meet it he needed his veteran legions in Campania. Consequently, he sent legates to Italy to settle disturbances among the soldiers and prepare them to shift to Sicily, where Caesar planned to meet them. During this time, Cicero, anxious over his future in the new regime and desperate for a conference with the dictator, strained every fibre in tracking Caesar's movements. His sources made it clear to him that Caesar intended to make his way from Patrae to Sicily and then on to Africa.[96] This has implications for Antony. Whatever concerns Caesar may have entertained about the conflict between Dolabella and Trebellius and the civil unrest it incited, he obviously believed it could be settled by way of letters on his part. In other words, the situation in the capital, in his view, was not a crisis. The matter of elections was also a pressing one: for practical but also propagandistic reasons, Caesar needed to restore something like a traditional government to Rome. He had already made his decision about consuls for 47 (these would be Quintus Fufius Calenus and Publius Vatinius) and for 46 (these would be himself and Lepidus). But the crisis in Africa meant that he could not make his way to the capital and so could not personally conduct elections. Presumably he planned to delegate that responsibility to his master of the horse. Clearly, then, even amid the uncertainty and volatility which continued to prevail, Caesar's confidence in Antony remained high.

Caesar's legates, however, failed to take charge of the legions, who now became increasingly mutinous. In reaction, and unexpectedly, Caesar altered his plans and came to Italy. Arriving in the south, he now made a circuitous tour of various cities, bypassing Campania for the moment, and arrived in Rome sometime in October.[97] He found the Forum secure, patrolled by soldiers from Antony's legion.[98] In the dictator's presence, the tribunician standoff evaporated, and Caesar made it clear that he blamed neither side for its excesses: Dolabella was explicitly pardoned.[99] He also addressed the economic crisis by carrying several laws adjusting debts and remitting rents, measures which did not differ markedly from Dolabella's programme and came at cost to his wealthy supporters, men like Matius.[100] Caesar then held elections. His central task, however, was recovering his authority over his legions. As we have seen, this he managed largely by giving them, or at least promising them, what they asked for. The dictator did not dally. By December he was in Sicily preparing his invasion of Africa.[101] Lepidus, Caesar's consular colleague for 46, did not take office until the start of the new year. Until then, Rome and Italy continued to be governed by Antony, Caesar's master of the horse.

Antony's Exclusion?

By the end of the year, Caesar was waging war in Africa. In April 46, he crushed his enemies at the battle of Thapsus. The suicides of Metellus Scipio and Marcus Cato supervened. In the same month, Caesar was again declared dictator. Lepidus, his colleague in the consulship, was named master of the horse. Caesar returned to Rome in July, where he celebrated four triumphs in recognition of victories in Gaul, Egypt, Pontus, and Africa. He initiated an ambitious programme of legislation, measures ranging from a reform of the calendar to establishing colonies for veterans to reshaping the courts—and so on. Not every proposal had been carried into law, or even promulgated to the public, by the time of his death. He also made preparations for another war in Spain, where the sons of Pompey the Great had assembled a massive army of at least thirteen legions and driven Trebonius, Caesar's governor in Further Spain, out of his province. Late in the year, he again left Rome. Lepidus conducted elections at which Caesar was elected the sole consul for 45. In Spain, Caesar found fierce opposition but ultimately managed to inflict a decisive defeat on his enemies at the battle of Munda in March 45. By July he had returned to northern Italy. In October, he stepped down from his consulship and was replaced by Quintus Fabius Maximus and Trebonius. In the same month, Caesar celebrated a triumph for his victory in Spain. Fabius Maximus, too, entered Rome in triumph on 13 October in recognition of his valour in the same war. In Rome, Caesar continued to legislate intensively and began to accumulate extraordinary honours, including the right to wear triumphal garb on all public occasions, the title Imperator, the title Liberator, the title Father of his Country (*parens patriae*), a golden chair for all public occasions, and the placement of his statues in Roman temples.[102]

Amid these remarkable events, including the wars which at last guaranteed Caesar's mastery of the Roman world, there is no mention of Mark Antony. At the end of 47, he almost completely vanishes from our sources. We are told that in 46 he did *not* serve under Caesar in Africa nor, in the next year, did he fight for Caesar in Spain.[103] Antony resurfaces briefly in the autumn of 46 and by March 45 is again a recurring presence. In July 45 Antony is once more Caesar's favourite and destined to be his consular colleague in the following year.[104] During the years 46 and 45, however, no official position of any kind is attested for Antony—and Cicero explicitly insists he had none. This hiatus in Antony's career is curious and unexpected. Naturally, it provokes conjecture.

Cicero had an explanation: Antony was a selfish, petulant sensualist—and a poltroon—who sulked and cowered in Rome instead of loyally serving his master abroad.[105] In his *Philippics*, the orator claimed the two men had a falling out, a rupture the orator attributed to Antony's belligerent reaction to Caesar's reasonable demand that he pay for the vast holdings of Pompeian properties he acquired under the *lex Hirtia*. Antony, in Cicero's version, was outraged by Caesar's ingratitude. Instead of serving as Caesar's officer, Cicero alleges, Antony went so far as to plot his assassination.[106] In the end, however, their friendship was inexplicably restored: Cicero emphasizes this mystery by saying no more than this took place 'somehow or other'.[107] A variation of Cicero's account is taken up and adapted by Plutarch, who, by way of explaining the two men's reconciliation, adduces the moral tonic provided by Caesar's fatherly reprovals and by Antony's stabilizing marriage to Fulvia.[108] Traces of Cicero's version of events can also be spotted in Dio.[109]

Cicero explains the hiatus by blaming Antony's anger toward Caesar, animosity arising from the extensive debts he incurred through his purchases under the *lex Hirtia*. This is not the explanation favoured by modern historians. They agree that Antony found himself in financial difficulties after Caesar's return from the east, and they take notice of the damage done to Caesar's reputation by Antony's hedonism.[110]

Nonetheless, it is routinely concluded that Antony was dropped by Caesar not for these reasons but because he was so deeply unimpressed by Antony's ineptitude in governing Rome and Italy in his absence.[111] How it was that Antony pulled himself together and returned to Caesar's favour goes largely unexplained.

This view is untenable.[112] Even if one accepts that Caesar was disappointed by Antony's tenure as master of the horse, that hardly negated his qualities as a warrior—and in Africa and Spain what Caesar most needed were valorous officers. Little reason, then, to leave him behind. But Antony, as we have seen, did *not* disappoint, a reality obvious both from Caesar's original design to travel directly to Sicily without looking in on the capital as well as his later decision to leave Antony in charge for the residue of the year when finally he did leave Rome. Nothing, then, indicates that Caesar lost confidence in Antony—nor is there any explicit statement by Cicero, hostile though he is, that he ever did. Nor, on the standard view, is it easy to understand Antony's sudden rehabilitation and elevation in July 45, an expression of Caesar's favour which militates against any explanation of Antony's absence from Caesar's service that is predicated on Caesar's hostility.

Debts and Divorce

So what happened? Let us begin by agreeing that there is no good reason to assume any kind of serious falling out between Antony and Caesar: that is a confection of hostile Ciceronian rhetoric designed to diminish Antony's claim, after the Ides of March, that he was the leading champion of Caesar's legacy. We need not, however, jettison Cicero's emphasis on Antony's financial situation. Although we have little in the way of particulars, we have seen clearly enough how, during the auctions of 47, Antony bought numerous, posh properties. Amid the prevailing economic and political crisis, it is likely that Antony, equipped with the clout of a master of the horse, was never required to offer a price which came close to matching any property's fair market value under normal conditions. Still, because Antony bought so many properties and all at the high end, we can believe Cicero's contention that he became financially overextended.

Now Antony was by no means a poor man, as we have seen, and his service in Syria and Gaul, we can be confident, made him a wealthy one, or wealthy enough to invest in real estate in Rome. But his lavish lifestyle was expensive, constantly consuming a significant proportion of his ready cash, a condition that required Antony, like other aristocrats, to turn frequently to sequences of loans secured by land or other properties.[113] During the civil war, however, credit was either very expensive or unavailable. It was in part owing to this environment that it was possible to buy confiscated properties relatively cheaply. Nonetheless, doing so on a large scale was possible for Antony only by way of extensive loans from financiers who viewed the master of the horse as a good political investment—and by way of hefty promissory notes owed to the republic. It is likely that Antony was prepared to splash out in this way because he, like other purchasers close to Caesar, expected even his low bids to go largely uncollected.[114] But when Caesar returned to Rome in 47 and was confronted both by an ailing economy and by a desperate need for funds with which to satisfy his legions, he made it clear to all his supporters that he expected them to pay in full what they had offered for any properties acquired under the *lex Hirtia*.[115]

Cicero represents this demand as a serious blow to Antony, and we are probably right in believing him. We do not, of course, know how exposed Antony's finances were. We may ignore Cicero's hyperbolic claim that in March 44 Antony had debts totalling 40 million sesterces.[116] Nor can we draw inferences from the senate's decision in 44 to offer Sextus Pompey a sum of 200 million sesterces in compensation for his father's confiscated estate.[117] That estate, as we have seen, was broken up during its sale, and in any case the senate's award will not have reflected an estimation of the properties' actual costs to purchasers in 47. Nevertheless, even in the absence of any kind of reliable figure, we need not doubt that Antony's debt to the republic was steep. It was probably owing to the sheer scale of his obligations that Antony did not believe they could be resolved by long-distance: hence his refusal to rely solely on equestrian agents or household stewards and correspondence to and from a war zone.

For this banal but very serious reason, and not owing to any falling out between them, Antony could not follow Caesar to Africa nor, later, to Spain, at least not in Caesar's company.[118] Restructuring his real estate portfolio by way of refinancing any debts underpinning them and liquidating dispensable assets demanded Antony's immediate and personal attention. Although not the stuff best suited to pique an ancient writer's political or literary interests, Antony's financial repair work must have been complex and exacting. In at least one transaction, the only one we can spy, he was obliged to expend moneys acquired by way of an inheritance, and even that entailed negotiations and delays.[119] When Caesar returned to Rome in July 46, the sorting out of Antony's affairs was still a work in progress. Therefore, when Caesar left Italy for Spain, sometime in autumn, Antony was not yet in a position to follow him. It is at this point, in Cicero's account, that the break between the two men occurred.[120] But the orator's timing of this spat is for dramatic effect. For not long after Caesar's departure, Antony began to make his way to Spain to join Caesar. He travelled so far as Narbo, no more than fifty miles from the border of Hither Spain, at which point he turned back and returned to Rome.

In 46, Antony's financial difficulties were compounded by divorce and remarriage— if we are correct in placing his bitter divorce from Antonia and subsequent marriage to Fulvia in this year. These very personal and undoubtedly emotional affairs also entailed monetary matters. Antonia's dowry will have been a large one, and its return under any circumstances was likely to entail complications. If Antony did not merely accuse his wife of adultery but also took legal action to retain a part of the dowry, the disorderliness of his financial condition may have been further protracted and even intensified—especially since he was obliged to deal with his avaricious uncle. Similarly, Antony's marriage to Fulvia, a welcome union which brought him a fresh and ample dowry, also entailed negotiations, not least over its potential utility in securing his properties. Amid circumstances such as these, in addition to the urgent issue of settling his debts, it is hardly surprising that Antony was preoccupied with private affairs for much of 46.

The way Cicero tells it, these affairs were very personal. In his *Second Philippic*, he regales his reader with a deliciously defamatory sketch of Antony's homecoming from Narbo. Arriving in a town only a few miles outside Rome, Antony spent an entire afternoon guzzling wine in a cheap tavern. At sunset, he leapt onto a two-wheeled chariot and speeded into the capital, arriving under cover of darkness. He made his way home in disguise. There he presented himself as a courier bearing a letter from Antony to Fulvia. He was granted entry and Fulvia read the letter in his presence. It was a love letter, in which he promised to cast off Volumnia and devote himself exclusively and passionately to his wife. Its tenderness brought tears to Fulvia's eyes, at which sight Antony could restrain himself no longer. Revealing himself, he folded her into his arms.

Although a modern reader may be touched by this romantic vignette, or at least some aspects of it, the tale was told only to discredit Antony, a grown man behaving like a teenager—and a public figure ignoring his civic responsibilities. For Cicero goes on to point out how Antony's nocturnal advent incited anxiety so great that a tribune summoned him to speak at a *contio*, where Antony was obliged to reassure the people that his coming to Rome was not an ominous civic matter. He did so, according to Cicero, only by making a fool of himself. Even in this inventive, arresting smear, it is worth noting, Antony remains, crucially, an important man. Indeed, by the time he was enjoying this prank, according to Cicero, he was already Caesar's choice for a consulship in 44. Nevertheless, in Cicero's speech, Antony had no choice but to return to Rome: he was threatened by yet another personal financial crisis.[121]

This entertaining tale was not entirely a fiction. Cicero also refers to Antony's return from Narbo in two contemporary letters.[122] At the time, the orator was away from the city but received news about Antony from multiple letters. Clearly it was a notable event. In each letter Cicero recognizes that Antony was in Rome to deal with his debts. For this reason, he assures Atticus, he is not personally concerned over Antony's presence. Antony's visit, it is clear, incited a degree of agitation in high circles. Balbus and Oppius, at Atticus' urging, also sent Cicero a joint letter about it. This flurry of correspondence furnishes ample evidence that Antony's journey to Rome was motivated by private financial problems. At the same time, these letters make it clear how Antony was deemed by everyone to be a figure whose every movement mattered, presumably because he was an acknowledged agent of Caesar. There is no hint here of estrangement or any suggestion that Antony was out of favour.

It is time to put together the pieces of our conjectural account of Antony's career after 47. In 46, Antony had no real options for military or magisterial service. It was obvious he must remain in the capital in order to settle his debts, which made it impossible for him to join Caesar in Africa. In Rome, government once more was the responsibility of regular magistrates. But it was Lepidus, not Antony, who became consul with Caesar. This hardly constituted a slight against Antony. Lepidus was the senior man and had proved his value in Spain. At the same time, because he had held the position of master of the horse, it was unthinkable that Antony should be asked to serve as a praetor. And in any case Antony was confronted by too many private demands to take on responsibilities of that kind. Instead, Antony was obliged to devote much of 46 to settling his financial difficulties and giving a fresh shape to his personal life by divorcing Antonia, separating from Volumnia, and marrying Fulvia.

During this year, for all his private concerns, Antony will not have abandoned civic life. A former master of the horse and the intimate of Caesar, he must have occupied a distinguished place in the senate, despite never having held a praetorship or consulship. And by way of traditional expressions of aristocratic power—his mansion, his clients, his opinions on legal and political matters—Antony doubtless continued to project a notable public image. Antony's personal problems, although they disrupted his capacity for military service, did nothing to diminish Caesar's confidence in him. At the elections for 45, Caesar was the only consul returned; for that year, Rome's government was handed over to Lepidus in his capacity as master of the horse.[123] Antony had no role to play in this administration because he was expected to serve in Spain, in which direction he followed Caesar in the autumn of 46.

Antony did not travel to Spain without Caesar's invitation, and it is very likely he acted as Caesar's legate even if the title goes unattested. It is even possible, as Cicero indicates, that by time Antony left Rome for Spain it was widely known that he was to be Caesar's consular colleague in 44. Which is why, when he returned to Rome in March 45, his unexpected presence became something of a sensation. As Caesar's man, his return to the city must have disconcerted many, just as Atticus and others expected it to upset Cicero. Soon, however, it was revealed that Antony's business was personal—debts again—and, once it was settled, he once more left Rome for Spain. On the road to the west, however, he met Caesar, now returning to Italy. Caesar welcomed his friend, and during their journey home Antony rode beside Caesar, a signal of the dictator's esteem.

Consul-Designate

In October 45 Caesar entered the city in triumph. In the same month, he conducted elections for 45. Elections for 44 took place afterwards. At these, Antony was created a consul, although he had never held the praetorship and, at the age of thirty-eight, had not yet reached the legal minimum age of forty-two. Even in the unusual circumstances of Caesar's regime, this was a brilliant achievement and an affirmation of his noble heritage. In these same elections, Antony's brothers were also successful: Gaius Antonius became praetor, Lucius Antonius tribune of the *plebs*. In their ensemble, the family presented a formidable array in the government of the coming year.

Additional distinctions enhanced Antony's eminence. By 45 Caesar had begun to relocate and rebuild the Rostra in the Forum, a notable feature of which was the restoration of statues of Sulla and Pompey in a statement of restored political harmony. Caesar now handed this project over to Antony, who, when he assumed his consulship, would be allowed both to dedicate the work and memorialize his deed in a public inscription.[124] This year is also the likeliest time for Caesar's addition of a new sodality of priests for managing the Lupercalia, a popular sacred festival held in February. Hitherto it was administered by two colleges, named for the patrician clans the Quinctii and Fabii. A third, the *Iulii* (or *Iuliani*), now increased their number, and the chief priest, the *magister*, of this sodality was Mark Antony, another signal honour.[125] His status as a grandee was now beyond dispute. Nevertheless, Antony was only one of several leading Caesarians. Fabius Maximus, who was consul in 45, celebrated a triumph.[126] So, too, did Quintus Pedius.[127] Lepidus continued to enjoy high office and an estimable reputation. Antony's enemy, Dolabella, remained highly regarded by the dictator, and Caesar made it known that, when he abdicated his consulship in 44, he intended this man to be his successor. Antony, prominent though he was, held no monopoly on Caesar's favour.

V
The Ides of March

The End of Civil War

After his victory at Munda, Caesar believed the civil war was at an end. Sextus Pompey, the great man's son and leader of the remnant of Caesar's enemies who survived the battle of Munda, remained unvanquished but did not distract the dictator from his administration of Rome. Instead, Caesar devoted himself to a vast array of reforms.[1] These ranged from deeply serious matters of state—new laws regulating taxation, entitlements, the constitution, and civic religion—to the literally pedestrian, laws regulating footpaths, for instance, and the flow of traffic. Foreign policy was to the fore: the status of Deiotarus, the long-standing client king of Galatia, was under review, and Caesar was busy reaffirming Rome's friendship with Judea.[2] Since 46, Cleopatra and her husband had been in residence in the capital, where her presence was essential: Egypt's alliance with Rome and the Ptolemies' debts to Caesar required a final settlement.[3] For Caesar, it appears, there was always more to do: he saw much in Rome that required repair or resolution.

One looks in vain, however, for anything like a coherent programme. Caesar's reforms are a jumble of consequential policies and ad hoc remedies. This is perhaps unsurprising since they represent the work, not of a single genius but instead the partnership of a gifted general and statesman with the talented, diverse figures who constituted his *consilium*. Nobles like Antony and Dolabella or Decimus Brutus and Lepidus were close to Caesar, and each played a part in shaping and executing his plans. So, too, and with equal influence, rising new men like Gaius Vibius Pansa, Aulus Hirtius, and Munatius Plancus. Less visible but no less important or weighty were Caesar's equestrian supporters, figures like Matius, Gaius Rabirius Postumus, Lucius Cornelius Balbus, and Gaius Oppius.[4] Caesar relied extensively on this devoted inner circle. At the same time, he also turned frequently to others in his extensive network of friends and supporters, which included esteemed men who had previously fought against him, like Cassius and Brutus and Cicero. Because Caesar wanted always to expand the operations of his increasingly ambitious government and perform them with greater efficiency, and because he was loyal in rewarding men who had aided him during the civil war, he allowed the senate to swell until it contained something like 900 members. Its ranks now included rich centurions and native provincials. And this body could only grow larger because Caesar so increased the number of magistrates that, by 44, there were 40 quaestors, eight aediles, and fourteen praetors; in the elections for 43, sixteen praetors were returned. Never before had the people of Rome been served by so many officials or so crowded a senate.

On Caesar's ultimate designs for the Roman state, one can only speculate. That he concentrated power in his own hands was hardly inexplicable in the context of a civil war and no proof that he aimed at a permanent autocracy. Cicero, who disliked and distrusted Caesar, believed that, in the fullness of time, he would, like Sulla before him, restore the republic when he could safely do so.[5] Caesar's fondness for unique honours did not discourage this conclusion, nor his flirtations with the divine apparatus of Hellenistic kings, conduct to which we shall recur. True, Caesar was remembered for disparaging the republic as 'nothing, only a word without substance or form' and for denigrating Sulla for demitting the dictatorship by calling it proof he did not even know his ABCs.[6] Declarations like these seem to signal a man intent on clinging to power. But these remarks originate in invective, an angry pamphlet produced by Titus Ampius Balbus, who was a committed follower of Pompey and known to many as 'the trumpet of the civil war'.[7] Balbus reported these utterances without context, nor is their authenticity assured.

The orator, and others in Rome who remained animated by traditional constitutionalist urges, doubtless took it as a hopeful sign that, by the end of 46, Caesar was planning a massive expedition in the east.[8] Its specific goals are not entirely clear to us, but it was known that Caesar intended to wage war against the Dacians and, in a campaign far more glamorous than that, invade Parthia in order to exact vengeance for Crassus' defeat. Caesar planned to be away from Rome for three years, after which time, it was assumed by all, he would return to the capital victorious, a conqueror greater than Pompey or Alexander. A grand triumph awaited him, and many will have believed that this celebration must mark the occasion on which he would restore the traditional constitution, standing aside for a new generation of aristocrats.[9] Indeed, Caesar gave hints that this was his intention. Nor need we doubt that the republic's restoration would have been welcome to many of Caesar's leading supporters, including Antony. Caesar's retirement would render him a leading, independent grandee operating at the highest level of dignity and personal authority. In such an environment, he could look forward to playing a commanding role.

According to Dio, Caesar's war in the east was authorized by a law awarding him an extraordinary, three-year command. This same measure provided funds for his expedition and permitted him to appoint an ample number of legates.[10] Associated with this assignment was a law passed by the tribune Lucius Antonius which granted Caesar the privilege of appointing half the magistrates and tribunes who would serve during his absence.[11] This legislation was all of it otiose, since Caesar had arrogated to himself the power in all these matters to do as he pleased. Nevertheless, its public passage implicated the sovereign people in the operations required for Caesar's campaign, itself a highly popular undertaking and one which, by way of its old-fashioned imperialism, underscored the end of civil wars. These measures are passed over quickly by our sources, but Caesar meant his war in the east to be viewed as a turning-point. For that reason, these laws may have suggested to many that the conclusion of this war would mark a return to normality.

At the time of these enactments, probably December 45, Caesar indicated that he would be satisfied with holding the dictatorship for only two of the three years of his foreign command, at least according to Dio.[12] In 46, Caesar was named dictator for ten years, but in such a way that the office was to be held in annual instalments—which meant that it was within Caesar's discretion to allow his tenure to lapse.[13] If, as it now appeared, he had it in mind to surrender the dictatorship in 41, a year in which consuls of his own selection would hold office in Rome, and if, consequently, he was prepared to return to Rome as a promagistrate, the stage would well and truly be set for a recovery of traditional government—even if a triumphant Caesar was once again elected consul for 40. So much, at least, hopeful contemporaries may have concluded.

Caesar appointed Hirtius and Pansa consuls-designate for 43 and named Decimus Brutus and Munatius Plancus consuls-designate for 42. He did not, however, make an immediate decision about 41. Instead, he put Antonius' law to work as basis for his negotiations with suitable aspirants. More than one passage suggests that he at the very least opened discussions with Marcus Brutus and Cassius regarding consulships in that year, another hopeful gesture. Cicero implies and Plutarch believes that, before the Ides, he actually selected them, but that is far from clear and there are good reasons for concluding that at the time of his assassination Caesar was still weighing his options.[14] If in fact Caesar was entertaining the idea of appointing as consuls men who had been conspicuous figures on Pompey's side during the civil war, and was willing to allow them to hold this office in a year when he was no longer planning to be dictator, these conversations alone must have been profoundly encouraging to anyone who still believed a restoration of the republic was possible. Subsequent events, however, soon dashed these hopes.

Fig. 5.1 Marcus Brutus, a 1st cent. BCE bust often identified as Brutus in the Palazzo Massimo alle Terme in Rome.
Source: Wikimedia Commons.

Antony, Consul and Augur

Antony entered his consulship on 1 January 44, a day marked by fierce, vituperative exchanges with Dolabella.[15] It was Caesar's intention, when he left Rome for the east, to abdicate his consulship in Dolabella's favour. This was a proposition Antony so abominated that he did not merely denounce it but vowed to obstruct it.[16] The enmity between these men, originating in their political contentiousness during 47 and exacerbated by Dolabella's affair with Antonia, remained ferocious. Doubtless Caesar had endeavoured to reconcile his two friends. But he failed, and on the opening day of the year each man heaped savage reproaches on the other. It was perhaps during this session that Antony promised he would vitiate any assembly gathered for Dolabella's election. This announcement, he knew, must displease Caesar. He also knew Caesar was unlikely to withdraw his support from Dolabella. Which is why, instead of trying to carry his point in the senate with arguments deprecating Dolabella's qualifications— true, Dolabella was too young to hold the office nor had he held a praestorship but this was true also of Antony—he turned to the sacred operations regulating the assemblies. Even Caesar, he believed, must think twice before challenging the Romans' divine laws.[17]

We do not know the date set by Caesar for Dolabella's election. The magistrates for 43 and 42 were elected at assemblies held sometime after the Lupercalia (15 February), but there was no reason for Dolabella's election to wait until then.[18] And, for what it is worth, Cicero's hostile account locates this assembly sometime before the Lupercalia. The events of that day resulted in something of a stalemate. Antony succeeded, as we shall see, in impairing Dolabella's election by way of imposing a significant religious liability on the proceedings. Caesar, however, pushed ahead nonetheless and declared Dolabella consul-designate. It is telling that Caesar did not, perhaps could not, easily command Antony to give way. In part, perhaps, he felt obliged to respect his friend's sensibilities, not least because he required a reliable and reliably loyal administration in Rome after he departed for the east. The controversy over Dolabella, and it was an important one, was not easily resolved. Indeed, when the senate met on the Ides of March, the purpose of that session was to decide what must be done in the matter of Dolabella's consulship. Almost certainly, Caesar expected to have it his own way. But Antony gave no sign of yielding.

Antony's strategy, although distorted through the prism of Cicero's invective, remains clear enough. He began by announcing that, as consul, he would, on the eve of any electoral assembly, seek auspices against it by way of *spectio*, an all-night vigil of the sky. A consul possessed the right to look for omens in this way (these sought-for omens the Romans called *auspicia impetrativa*), and, if he discovered them during the night, he could, by reporting them in person before the assembly properly commenced (an action known as *obnuntiatio*), postpone its proceedings until another day.[19] Antony perhaps hoped that his declaration alone would suffice to deter Caesar and Dolabella. If so, he was wrong, and, when it became certain that an electoral assembly would meet even in the teeth of Antony's *spectio*, he reconsidered his position. He knew very well how Caesar, at a controversial legislative assembly in 59, had forcefully prevented Bibulus, his consular colleague, who had spent the previous night in *spectio*, from actually delivering his *obnuntiatio*, thereby frustrating his attempt at obstruction.[20] Antony did not wish to be foiled by Caesar or Dolabella in this way.

And so he changed his tactic. When Antony did *not* announce that he was looking to the heavens in a night devoted to *spectio*, Caesar must have believed he had acquiesced. It was now Caesar's turn to be wrong. On the day of the assembly, Antony was present. He waited until Dolabella had secured enough votes to be elected. Then, in his capacity as augur, he uttered the formula *alio die*, on another day, which ought to have dissolved the assembly immediately. By the terms of augural law, Antony was justified in declaring *alio die* only if he perceived unsought omens, *auspicia oblativa*, in which case an augur's judgement regarding their validity lay outside appeal or contradiction. Sometimes, the Romans knew, an augur only pretended to see omens. Omens of this ilk were described as *auspicia ementita*, but their pronouncement was nonetheless valid and therefore irresistible on the day.[21] Not even Caesar, the presiding magistrate, could ignore an augur's declaration.

If he heard it. Presiding magistrates were not responsible for augural declarations they did not notice. Antony expected Caesar to dissolve the assembly and make plans for summoning it later. This, he believed, would initiate a procedural contest of wills in which he hoped to benefit from the dictator's imminent departure for the east. This, however, is not what happened. It appears that Caesar did *not* dismiss the assembly, or at any rate did not do so until he had declared Dolabella's election. If this is what happened, Dolabella was now a legitimate consul-elect. But Caesar had not yet got round Antony. Owing to his augural pronouncement, Dolabella, it could be claimed, was *vitio creatus*, which is to say he was elected legally but in despite of augural law: therefore his election was vitiated. Should he take office as a vitiated consul, he posed a danger to the *pax deorum*, the sacred and essential alliance between the gods and the republic. A vitiated magistrate was an authentic magistrate: Dolabella, if he entered office, could justly claim to have been a consul and for the residue of his life justly be regarded as a man of consular rank. At the same time, a vitiated magistrate was obliged to abdicate, lest his every act, carrying legislation, say, or waging war, be blighted by his vitiated condition.[22]

Dolabella, from Antony's perspective, was now left with something of an empty honour and, after his abdication, Antony would be able to preside over the election of Dolabella's successor. But Dolabella had not yet entered office and so was not *yet* a vitiated consul, which meant that an immediate decision about his future was not necessary. In Rome, the senate was the ultimate arbiter of religion and the body responsible for regulating the *pax deorum*.[23] It was Caesar's intention on the Ides to turn to the senate for a final judgement on Antony's augural action and its effect on Dolabella's eligibility to hold the consulship. We can be sure of Antony's arguments against doing so: he will have rehearsed the hollowed traditions of augural law, underlined their vital role in sustaining the *pax deorum*, and appealed to the Romans' conservatism and caution in matters of civic religion. We have no idea what defence of Dolabella's position Caesar intended to offer. Indeed, he never got the chance.

Antony's feud with Dolabella and the measures he took in prosecuting it did nothing to disrupt his friendship with Caesar. Even on the Ides of March, Antony's loyalty to the dictator was recognized by the Liberators. And in every other aspect of his consulship, he remained very much Caesar's man. Antony carried a law changing the name of the month Quinctilis to Iulius.[24] This was the month of Caesar's birth, and by renaming it Iulius Antony evoked an honour allegedly paid to Lucius Junius Brutus, the founder of the republic. Although June, Iunius, was likely named for Juno, a parallel tradition claimed its name originated with Brutus, whose liberation of Rome from the tyranny of the Tarquins was commemorated in this way.[25] Antony's law, then, paid homage to Caesar the Liberator. The measure was intensely disliked by Caesar's enemies. In July 44, Cicero and Brutus strove, unsuccessfully, to revive Quinctilis.[26]

Antony also carried legislation adding a fifth day, dedicated to Caesar, to the Roman Games (*Ludi Romani*).[27] This measure has plausibly been associated with a decree establishing a temple for *Concordia Nova*, New Concord, a divinity invented in honour of Caesar's restoration of Rome's social order. This temple was intended to stand in an obvious dialogue with the temple of Concord attributed to the Roman hero, Camillus, who saved Rome both from the Gauls and from civil strife, thereby earning accolades as Rome's second founder—a venerable precedent for Caesar's eminence.[28] The Roman Games originally lasted three days. When Camillus dedicated his temple, however, a fourth was added, or so it was believed.[29] Now, in order to emphasize the significance of *Concordia Nova*, Antony added a fifth day in Caesar's honour.

Caesar's Final Plans

In 44 Caesar began making his final arrangements for campaigning in the east. He planned to leave Rome 18 March.[30] In order to avoid the convulsions of 47, Caesar accelerated his schemes for settling his long-serving Gallic veterans on lands in Italy and the provinces. Allocating properties to these men took time, especially in Italy, where Caesar limited himself to available public land, *ager publicus*, or holdings he confiscated from enemy Pompeians. When neither source sufficed, he made purchases at his own expense.[31] In the spring of 44, there were still thousands of veterans in Rome awaiting their entitlements. As for Caesar's active troops, by the beginning of the year he had transferred sixteen legions and 10,000 cavalrymen into Greece and Macedonia. In Italy only one legion remained, and it was stationed outside Rome.[32] It was vital to Caesar that the east be stable and secure during his campaigns into enemy territories. He planned to assign Macedonia to Antony: he was meant to take over the province in 43 and possibly hold it for the duration of Caesar's campaigns. As for the other eastern provinces, these, too, needed reliable men. What Caesar had in mind is clear from those assignments which took place after his death and in accordance with his acts: He left Vatinius in place as governor of Illyricum and Marcus Acilius Caninus in Greece.[33] Lucius Tillius Cimber was presently to be sent to Bithynia-Pontus to replace Quintus Marcius Crispus.[34] In Asia, Publius Servilius Isaricus was to be superseded by Gaius Trebonius, and in Syria Dolabella (Caesar did not doubt Dolabella would be consul) would relieve Lucius Staius Murcus.[35] Caesar himself, at least through 42, intended to hold command of his army by dint of his dictatorial power. During this campaign, he planned to be assisted by a sequence of masters of the horse: in 44, Marcus Valerius Messala; in 43, Gnaeus Domitius Calvinus; and in 42, his grand-nephew Octavian, the future Augustus, would take the office.[36] By then

Octavian would be twenty-one years old and, after serving under his two seasoned predecessors, adequately experienced for taking up his duties.

It is perhaps a mark of Caesar's inability to detect disloyalty, or to be bothered by lingering resentments, that two of his eastern appointments, Cimber and Trebonius, were among his assassins, and on the Ides Staius Murcus publicly rejoiced in Caesar's death.[37] At the same time, Caesar was hardly a naïf and was certainly aware that there were plots against his life. Nevertheless, at the end of 45 he had dismissed his body-guard and expressed himself satisfied by an oath taken by every senator to defend his life, a duty predicated on the *sacrosanctitas*, the sacred inviolability, which he had been granted.[38] It was not his personal safety but Rome's stability during his absence that most concerned Caesar, especially when he considered the fierce hostility raging be-tween Antony and Dolabella. Perhaps this is why, after delivering so many indications that he intended soon to relinquish the dictatorship, Caesar had himself declared *dictator perpetuo*, dictator in perpetuity, at some point after 26 January and before 15 February.[39] This decision unambiguously reversed any previous indications that the eastern campaign might mark the end of his autocracy. It was now clear that he would *not* surrender his dictatorship while abroad. Instead, as *dictator perpetuo*, Caesar made himself a permanent Roman fixture. Furthermore, he appointed Lepidus *magister equitum perpetuo*, master of the horse in perpetuity, an office he was authorized to hold so long as Caesar held his.[40] Lepidus, unlike Valerius Messala, would remain in Rome, a sober and senior supervisor of Caesar's regime in the west. There he could deliver final judgements on the policies and undertakings of Caesar's magistrates—including Mark Antony.

Lupercalia

The Lupercalia, held on 15 February, was an annual festival of purification and fertility which also celebrated the city's origins, the Lupercal being the site where Romulus and Remus were discovered and rescued after they were exposed on the orders of their wicked uncle, Amulius.[41] The festival, profound in its sacred and historical reso-nances, was also wild and fun, characterized by feasting and drinking: naturally, it was enormously popular. To the sacred colleges which performed the Lupercalia's rituals, the *Luperci Fabii*, who were linked with Remus, and the *Luperci Quinctii*, linked with Romulus, a third, the *Iulii*, had very recently been added—a new feature which, by associating Caesar with the twins, fashioned him into a new founder of Rome. The Lupercalia of 44, then, was like none before it. It marked, by way of civic religion, a new moment in Roman history. Furthermore, if it was not Caesar's first state appear-ance as *dictator perpetuo*, it was certainly among the earliest.

During his dictatorship, Caesar gradually insinuated himself into the traditions of Roman religion by way of a series of deft innovations.[42] After his victory at the battle of Munda, for instance, his statue was placed in the temple of Quirinus, the deified man-ifestation of Romulus, possibly with an inscription reading, *to the unvanquished god*.[43] A temple was also planned for a new divinity, *Clementia Caesaris*, Caesar's Mercy.[44] Other Caesarian qualities, like *Felicitas Caesaris*, Caesar's Divine Success, were like-wise destined to receive cultic honours.[45] We have seen already that the senate decreed a temple for Concordia Nova, a deity associated with Caesar's role in ending civil war. The most remarkable innovation came not long before Caesar's death: a cult was to be established for *Iuppiter Iulius*, the Julian Jupiter. Its worshipful apparatus was to be extensive: a *flamen*, which is to say, a devoted priest like, by way of an intended parallel, the *flamen Dialis*, the sacred priest of Jupiter; a temple to the Julian Jupiter; and a sacred couch for displaying the god's image at public festivals. This transformation of a mortal into a god among men was unparalleled in Rome, although it could not fail to evoke Romulus' transubstantiation into Quirinus. And it was Antony who was designated *flamen Caesaris*.[46] At the time of Caesar's death, however, the senate had not yet acted: the creation of Iuppiter Iulius remained unfinished business.[47]

Caesar's divine pretensions did not in themselves provoke consternation. Cicero, in more than one speech delivered in Caesar's presence, adapted the conceit effortlessly, and in his letters he can even make a joke about it.[48] By the first century, Romans were entirely familiar with the eastern Mediterranean convention of paying divine honours to men of spectacular power, a category that by Caesar's day included not only august figures like Roman governors but also Roman financiers or businessmen who acted as private benefactors.[49] These practices, in a suitable context, were anything but shocking. At the same time, Romans were well aware that, whenever an important man or a generous patron received divine honours, he was being treated like a king, for it was around the institution of Hellenistic kingship that deferential gestures such as these developed. Consequently, although Caesar's divine honours did not perturb the Romans' religious sensibilities, they certainly stirred political worries on the part of anyone who feared Caesar intended to make himself into a Roman version of a Hellenistic king. The *Luperci Iulii*, and their symbolism connecting Caesar with the foundation of Rome and its first king, were very much a part of the dictator's policy of elevating himself, in institutional terms, far beyond his peers. Fun though the Lupercalia was for a majority of Romans, its celebration in 44 was of intense interest to anyone in the aristocracy for whom Caesar's unending domination of the republic rankled.

Antony was the *magister* or the chief priest of the *Iulii*. For this reason, he took an active role in the rites and antics of the day.[50] The festival started at the site of the Lupercal, located near the southwest foot of the Palatine Hill and not far from the Circus Maximus. There the Luperci sacrificed goats and puppies and smeared their foreheads with blood and milk. They then gave a hearty, ritual laugh. The goats' hides were cut up, some turned into loincloths, the only garb worn by the Luperci, others into whips which the Luperci later used to lash celebrants playfully. A feast, with much wine, followed. Then the Luperci ran, sometimes helter-skelter, but mostly following an overall course from the Lupercal to someplace in the Forum where, on this day, Caesar sat on the Rostra awaiting their arrival. As they ran, in a sweaty performance of raw masculinity, the Luperci swung their whips, striking anyone they came near, especially women who were hoping for children. These celebrations, it is obvious, were raucous and jolly, but not for that reason unsolemn. Which is why Caesar, proud on his golden throne, sat wearing honorific purple robes and a garland. His appearance was majestic and suitable to the historic recognition he received in this ancient festival. The majesty of the dictator, however, is no reason to conclude he did not share in the people's good humour.

What happened next is, in a sense, very well known, but only in its outline and not its specifics. Antony produced a diadem, the symbol of Hellenistic kingship and by the late republic also a symbol of monarchy in Rome. He offered it to Caesar, who rejected it. In later versions of the story, Antony repeats his gesture three times, and each time Caesar refuses it. As these theatrics took place, the people roared with approval—or disapproval—of the dictator's unwillingness to accept Antony's token. In the end, Caesar did something decisive but exactly what he did is uncertain. In one version, he ordered the diadem to be taken to the temple of Jupiter on the Capitoline, for this god, he declaimed, is Rome's sole king. He also ordered that his rejection of the diadem be recorded in the *Fasti*, Rome's official calendar.[51] In another, after Caesar's refusal, Antony ordered the diadem placed on a nearby statue of the dictator.[52] A third version is more complicated. Here the diadem is placed on a throne, as if it were a divinity of some kind, perhaps an abstract divinity akin to Caesar's *clementia* or *felicitas*, possibly, in this instance, *victoria Caesaris*, Caesar's victoriousness, or *virtus Caesaris*, Caesar's valour, both qualities intimately connected with the ideology of kingship.[53] Caesar's encounter with the diadem, an episode so pregnant with symbolism, provoked different interpretations at the time—hence the very different recollections of it—but this confusion, amid a festival marked by mirth and hijinks, may have been a part of Caesar's and Antony's strategy. There was never any question of Caesar declaring himself king at the Lupercalia. But something was afoot. Caesar's identification as a new founder of Rome was unambiguous. His relationship to kingship, by contrast, remained real if still unclearly defined.

It is doubtful whether ordinary Romans, even those whose sore heads the next morning let them remember the festivities of the day before, gave this show much further thought. But this was not the first time Caesar had been offered a diadem; his statues had previously been crowned, events that incited controversies which, like the Lupercalia affair, were recorded in versions so diverse that we can no longer know what actually happened, only that reactions were mixed.[54] There were also rumours in circulation that Caesar was imminently to be declared a king, or at the very least king of Rome's foreign subjects, but, once again, these remain unclear to us and were doubtless cloudy and uncorroborated then.[55] Nevertheless, it is certain that a controversial, ill-defined association between Caesar and the symbol of monarchy was in play in Rome before the Lupercalia and, with whatever jollity, was brought to the fore on 15 February. Antony's offer concentrated the attention of the aristocracy.

Cicero, it appears, was disturbed immediately.[56] And yet the true significance of this episode appears not to have been clear even at the time, which is why it spawned such varying traditions. For some, Caesar's conduct, sincere or not, must have seemed restrained. For others, however, his behaviour was surely regarded as outrageous: Antony's offer of the diadem, they will have believed, was arranged by Caesar and this affair was yet another stage in his pushing the Roman people into accepting autocracy. Antony's role was also scrutinized. Was he a toady? an enemy of a free republic? or did he secretly hope to embarrass Caesar by making it obvious to everyone how easily the dictator could become a king? Caesar's assassination and the political struggles it entrained so transformed affairs in Rome that they render any assessment of Antony's motives very difficult.[57] He *may* have acted independently, seeking to exacerbate the resentments stimulated by Caesar's permanent dictatorship. It is likelier, however, that on this day Antony, flushed with wine and enthusiasm, was a happy toady, a posture he willingly adopted in order to advertise his loyalty to Caesar even as he continued to challenge him over Dolabella's consulship.[58]

This was perhaps not Antony's only public exhibition of deference to Caesar. A notable event took place when a grand procession of magistrates and senators approached Caesar as he was sitting in front of his temple to Venus Genetrix and supervising the construction of his forum. This distinguished embassy carried a bundle of highly honorific decrees and its procession was a conspicuous, civic affair, hardly, as some ancient sources suggest, a spontaneous undertaking. Everything, including its setting, was clearly arranged in consultation with the dictator. But when the procession arrived, Caesar did not rise in a traditional expression of courtesy. The dictator's failure to stand offended many, which is why this episode is frequently repeated in our sources, often as proof of his arrogance. Most of our sources appear to date this event to 45. But Nicholas of Damascus sets it just after the Lupercalia, and in his account this procession is led by Antony as consul.[59] If this was the case, it was Antony who presided over the senate's passage of the decrees the embassy bore to Caesar. And it was Antony who collaborated with Caesar in this spectacle concentrating attention on the dictator's unparalleled grandeur. This episode, like the Lupercalia, was provocative and offended many in the senate. In each case, Antony was a willing partner in probing the limits confining Caesar's prestige and authority within the traditional sensibilities of the aristocracy.

Conspiracy

Caesar was now master of the Roman world, a conqueror in every corner of the empire and the architect of a new order. His autocracy did little to deter the adulation of the masses, who remained besotted by the dictator's charisma, exhilarated by his unbroken successes, and grateful for his improvements to the city. A figure without parallel, they adored him and relished his accumulation of novel honours. Nor did they judge him unfit for the divine accoutrements of Hellenistic kings. He was, they believed with all their hearts, destined to conquer Parthia and the Dacians, fearsome enemies fated by Caesar's valour to become Roman subjects. Dashing authoritarians inspire affection, and Caesar was so beloved of the people that for many he, the Liberator, was a greater treasure than the historical freedoms they exercised in elections or assemblies. The identity of Caesar's *dignitas* with Roman *libertas* was now complete.

This idolatry was not limited to the poor and ignorant, even if, for men and women in the upper orders, it was more calculated. Caesar remained popular with the prosperous classes in Rome and throughout Italy so long as his regime guaranteed stability and security, and for this reason they reacted warmly to many of his reforms, even legislation that may have cost them something when collecting debts or renting properties. Caesar's government, marked by an expansion of magisterial colleges and small-fry senators with regional ties throughout Italy, enhanced, for many municipal elites, their access to the centre of influence and executive action in Rome. As for the wealthy financiers and senators who enjoyed a close familiarity with the dictator or at

Fig. 5.2 Gaius Cassius Longinus, an imperial bust known as the Pseudo-Corbulo but usually identified as a bust of Cassius in the Palazzo dei Conservatori of the Capitoline Museums.
Source: Wikimedia Commons.

the very least his inner circle, they recognized the value and profitability of his friendship and endeavoured to sustain it. Caesar's dictatorship meant an end to the civil war and a return to law and order. That appealed to everyone.

Or nearly everyone. By the time the Lupercalia was performed, a senatorial conspiracy existed which was furiously plotting Caesar's assassination. And in the streets of Rome, graffiti, perhaps scribbled by men from the lower orders, lamented the absence of any suitable heir to the legacy of Marcus Brutus, the founder of the republic who expelled the last Tarquinian king of Rome.[60] Caesar was aware that discontent and disgruntlement soured some against him. But opposition was nothing new to Caesar and, whatever pockets of resistance remained in the city, he had fewer enemies now than at any time in his career. Or so he believed. As we have seen, the dictator was entirely satisfied with the security furnished by his *sacrosanctitas*. That proved a fatal error.

The Ides of March

As many as sixty, and perhaps even eighty, senators ultimately joined the conspiracy. We know the names of only twenty.[61] Still, it is clear that they were a disparate group, drawn both from Caesarian loyalists and Pompeian converts. Some were disappointed they had not profited better from their service to the dictator: Ser. Sulpicius Galba, a noble adherent, was bitter he had been denied a consulship when new men like Hirtius, Pansa, and Plancus were preferred. Others, too, had personal complaints against Caesar: Lucius Minucius Basilus, for instance, did not receive a province and, although Caesar tried to compensate him with very generous gifts, he remained unsatisfied. The leaders of the conspiracy did not harbour grievances of this kind: Gaius Trebonius was consul in 45; Decimus Brutus was a consul-designate. As for Marcus Brutus and Gaius Cassius, praetors in 44, they were each of them honoured by Caesar. These men, by their own lights, truly were Liberators. Like Caesar before them, they thought of *libertas* in terms of their own *dignitas*, and each was diminished by the reality of a *dictator perpetuo*. Tradition and philosophy, as we shall see, demanded action. They did not intend a coup d'état—that was Caesar's technique for protecting freedom and prestige—nor did they wish to implicate others in Caesar's tyranny. After all, in the building of his regime, they, too, had dirty hands. A question arose about Mark Antony: big, strong, and brave, and certain to be alongside Caesar at any meeting of the senate, he was a formidable obstacle even to a crowd of men armed with daggers. Could he be spared? Caesar, Brutus insisted, and Caesar alone was tyrant in Rome: he must be the sole target of their conspiracy.

The senate was scheduled to meet in the Curia of Pompey on 15 March in order to debate Dolabella's consulship. The conspirators chose this day, nearly their last chance before Caesar's departure from Rome, for the assassination. Arriving at the senate, the dictator would hardly expect an attack. At the same time, the Liberators would have in their peers the very audience they sought. The Ides of March also marked the festival of Anna Perenna, a goddess celebrated by way of picnicking outside the city, which meant that many citizens would be distracted.[62] Gladiatorial games were also to be produced on this Ides of March in the Theatre of Pompey, a part of the same grand complex as the Curia. This coincidence allowed Decimus Brutus to station a troop of gladiators nearby, who could furnish the Liberators armed security should it be needed.

On the morning of the Ides, Caesar very nearly decided not to attend—his wife, Calpurnia, had experienced frightful dreams, he was not entirely well, and various omens seemed to urge him to remain home—but in the end he was persuaded he could not stay away. As senators assembled, Trebonius, true to the plan, chatted with Antony and kept him outside the Curia after Caesar had entered.[63] Seizing their opportunity, the Liberators struck. Only two senators, Gaius Calvisius Sabinus and Lucius Marcius Censorinus, leapt to the dictator's defence, uncommon loyalty for which they were later rewarded with consulships in 39.[64]

Great Caesar fell. And panic erupted.[65] Marcus Brutus, intending to address the senate and proclaim the restoration of its liberty, stood away from the corpse and prepared to speak.[66] The ghastly sight of this speaker, however, spattered with blood and clutching a dagger, excited disgust and terror. For all anyone knew, they were witnesses to a coup d'état. The dictator and consul lay butchered in the sacred precinct of Pompey's Curia. So monstrous was this murder, and so gruesome the scene before their eyes, that horror was the natural reaction even on the part of senators who disliked Caesar's autocracy. Every man in the chamber, each ignorant of the conspirators' intentions and apprehensive of further violence, rushed to find his escape—even the brave men who had struggled to rescue Caesar.

This pandemonium was exacerbated when stampeding senators collided with fretful crowds streaming out of the nearby Theatre of Pompey, where the gladiatorial show was brought to a halt by cries from the senate house. As spectators emerged, they were confronted by the sight of conspirators still soaked in gore, still clinging to their weapons, and senators in a desperate flight for safety. Brutus now endeavoured to allay their consternation with pleas for calm. Unsurprisingly, he was ignored. Alarmed by blood and steel and by the sight of terrified senators—what sign could be more baleful?—many fled to their homes, where they anxiously awaited events. Others, taking advantage of this sudden collapse, took to looting.[67]

Antony also fled. If Trebonius tried to reassure the consul when the two men heard shouts within the Curia, he failed. Antony's enemies later alleged that he put on the disguise of a slave in order to slope off unnoticed. But that is a familiar, indeed unimaginative trope from ancient escape narratives and it merits no credence. It is never mentioned by Cicero, not even in his *Second Philippic*.[68] That Antony ran away out of fear, however, is hardly to be doubted. He was made of the same stuff as his fellow aristocrats, after all, and like them he found himself in an unexpected, unpredictable, and perilous situation. At home he barricaded himself behind the defences of his mansion on the Carinae. He could not, however, simply wait on events. He was now Rome's sole consul and it was crucial that he act quickly, even decisively. But the way forward was far from clear. Indeed, it could not have been obvious to Antony that he was not also a target.

Honourable Men: The Conspirators' Motives, Methods, Symbols

The origins of the conspiracy against Caesar are no longer recoverable in detail, nor is it clear when it was begun. The story that as early as the summer of 45 Trebonius sounded out Antony on a plot to assassinate Caesar is sometimes taken as an early sign, but, as we have seen, this is a Ciceronian fiction intended to undermine Antony's Caesarian credentials.[69] It is more likely that the conspiracy formed quickly, the catalyst being Caesar's move to make himself *dictator perpetuo*. In acting against Caesar, as we shall see, the conspirators evoked many fine principles ranging from Greek ethical theories to old-fashioned republican imperatives. But prior to 44, none of the men who assassinated Caesar, even those who had fought for Pompey, found in these same principles any motivation adequate for raising a hand against his friend and master. Each of the conspirators, even the most unsatisfied, had done well under Caesar's regime. But they expected him, like Sulla when he was dictator, to step aside at some point and hand the republic back to the aristocracy—the men to whom, in their firm view, the management of Rome properly belonged. Being an influential man under Caesar's regime was not the same thing as being an influential man full stop. Caesar's undisguised and unending grip on power, however, made it clear how vain anyone's aspirations for independent dignity had become. Which is not to say that none of the conspirators was genuinely attached to *libertas* as defined by Greek philosophy or to

Fig. 5.3 Reverse of a denarius minted by Marcus Brutus (*RRC* 508.3): a *pileus* between two daggers, all above EID MAR (Ides of March).
Source: American Numismatic Society.

mos maiorum, ancestral custom. But behind the conspirators' lofty ideals throbbed an obsession with 'privilege and vested interests'.[70]

Our accounts of the conspiracy and its aftermath are all of them tendentious and animated by one of two prevailing perspectives: the conspirators are viewed either as wicked schemers or impractical idealists. This bifurcated reception began at once. Contemporaries who condemned the killing of Caesar abominated his assassins. By contrast, even Cicero, who admired the Liberators, thought their strategy incomplete and its execution inept. As for imperial writers, although many esteemed the integrity of Marcus Brutus, they nonetheless felt obliged to concede that he fell on the wrong side of history: these writers, consequently, tend to represent the conspirators' deeds as ingenuous rather than realistic.[71] The consequences of this approach endure: the prevailing modern habit is to underline the Liberators' naïveté or lionize their devotion to liberty.[72] The conspiracy, however, was a complicated affair. It incited powerful emotions in everyone because its actors, both the Liberators and the Roman people in all its variegation, perceived Caesar's death with starkly contrasting feelings and by way of very different ideological perspectives.

Whatever their other defects, the conspirators were not stupid men. Striking down Caesar, they recognized, was an action so sensational it could only incite a general panic and in many quarters provoke animus. It was basic to Roman nature to find extreme actions disturbing, and a political assassination, especially in an environment freighted with anxieties over autocracy, could only raise fears of a coup d'état.[73] The Liberators were certainly aware of Caesar's popularity with the urban masses. The public, however, they believed could be brought along if they could put before it clear and convincing proof of their commitment to old-fashioned, customary virtue. Like most members of Rome's political aristocracy, the Liberators were confident that in the end the multitude would defer to the leadership of their betters—*if* they gained the backing of their senatorial peers.[74] Winning over the people and the aristocracy, they knew, demanded justifications of more than one kind.

In the beginning, when the leaders of the conspiracy were endeavouring to recruit new members from the senatorial order, they employed philosophical discussion as a medium for intrigue. Tyranny and tyrannicide were familiar topics in Greek ethical theory, and wary Liberators, by examining a fellow senator's commitment to the right kind of philosophical argument—the kind that made tyrannicide a civic virtue— diagnosed his inclination to join or at least acquiesce in their conspiracy. They could do this because, by the time of the late republic, philosophical thinking was a central part of the intellectual and moral apparatus of many in the Roman aristocracy. Philosophy was, however, deployed not only as a kind of code but instead as an assay of a senator's commitment to freedom's imperatives.[75]

The Liberators never doubted that their peers, even the humbler sorts Caesar had recently bunged into his bloated senate, preferred the traditional republic to an unending dictatorship. At the same time, they did not fail to grasp how their violence against Caesar must be viewed by everyone as a terrible violation of their friendship, their *amicitia*, with the man who was also their benefactor. Each of the conspirators professed to be Caesar's friend, and for many of them Caesar's clemency had shackled them with a debt of gratitude they could never hope to repay.[76] For Romans, friendship and gratitude were solemn, profound connections. Which is one of the reasons the Liberators turned to the moral escape clauses supplied by Greek philosophical principles, which often put tyrants outside the obligations of family and friendship and elevated tyrannicide to the category of a lofty virtue. In this way, the assassins found ideological justifications for letting a love of liberty, and one's obligations to a free community, come before Roman constancy and the bonds of friendship. Getting to this view, in some cases, entailed a bit of tortuous reasoning. Nevertheless, it is certain that many of the Liberators were truly committed to precepts of this kind.[77] And these same arguments, the Liberators hoped, would, for many in the aristocracy, furnish a sufficient justification for Caesar's assassination.

Not everyone, they understood, could share that perspective. Every traditionally minded citizen who valued *libertas* also esteemed gratitude, so much so that for Romans of all classes ingratitude induced feelings of disgust and hostility.[78] Nor was every member of the elite disposed to be convinced by syllogisms that dismissed the demands of friendship. An illustration of this is not hard to come by. In a letter to Cicero composed shortly after the assassination, Caesar's intimate associate, Gaius Matius, made short work of Liberators' Hellenizing evasions of the obligations of friendship:

> They account it a failing on my part that I take it hard and am outraged that a man I loved has perished. They say that one's country should come before friendship, as if they had made a clear case that his death was a good thing for the republic. But I do not want to make a clever argument: I confess I have not attained to their level of philosophical competence.... It was not Caesar I followed during our civil strife but a friend. Even when I disapproved, I did not forsake him.[79]

Caesar, he goes on to say, was the truest of friends.[80] The Liberators, by contrast, are beyond arrogant and nothing short of wicked.[81] For Matius, the Ides of March was all machinations, hollowness, treachery. Men like this, the Liberators knew, they could never win over. The best they could hope for was to gain their acquiescence to a fait accompli.

This was not the only moral issue confronting the Liberators. Even graver than censure for betraying Caesar's friendship was the certain accusation of sacrilege. Through legislation enacted by the people, as we have seen, Caesar, like tribunes of the *plebs*, was inviolable, or *sacrosanctus*, protected by a *lex sacrata*, an oath sworn by all citizens to protect his person. This law and this oath rendered anyone who harmed Caesar a *homo sacer*, an abomination to gods and men and a danger to the republic. Indeed, there was a religious imperative to eliminate a *homo sacer*. Consequently, a *homo sacer* could be killed with impunity and his property consecrated.[82] When they slew Caesar, the conspirators unambiguously violated their oath and the *sacrosanctitas* bestowed on Caesar by the Roman people, and it is difficult to exaggerate the importance of this violation. It was fundamental to Roman thinking that the health of the republic depended on the *pax deorum*, the Romans' correct ritual relationship with the gods. As a consequence, they were always animated by strong and serious anxieties over religious propriety.[83] The presence of a *homo sacer* threatened the city and its inhabitants with *contagio*, pollution, and blight.[84] And the anger of the gods.

But the Liberators had a counterargument and a design for conveying it. They intended to appeal to an ideology forged at the very founding of the republic. Lucius Brutus, when he liberated Rome from the tyranny of Tarquin the Proud, obliged the people to swear an oath that they would never again suffer a monarch to reign over the city. So fierce was Brutus in his administration of this oath, Roman traditions insisted, that he ordered the execution of his own sons when their treacherous Tarquinian loyalties were uncovered.[85] And the great hero of the first year of the republic, Valerius Publicola, carried legislation that rendered the life and property of anyone plotting to seize *regnum*, absolute power, forfeit to Jupiter.[86] *Libertas*, the Liberators could correctly claim, was not simply a topic for philosophical debate: it was a traditional Roman obsession lying at the very core of personal and political life. And, as Lucius Brutus had demonstrated, it was worth killing for.[87]

Publicola's ancient law was another *lex sacrata*. Anyone who violated it became a *homo sacer*, which meant that scheming after despotism rendered a man anathema to the republic. His elimination was a sacred obligation, which is why a man who slew a tyrant was explicitly deemed *not* guilty of *parricidium*, the archaic expression for murder.[88] This was an extreme and terrible remedy, which is why the Romans, so they believed, always preferred the operations of justice. Hence the fates of Spurius Cassius in the fifth century and Marcus Manlius Capitolinus in the fourth: each was accused of aiming at *regnum*, tried, condemned, and thrown to his death from the Tarpeian Rock. Cassius' house was razed and Manlius' property became the site of the temple of Juno Moneta on the Capitoline.[89]

The case of Caesar, the Liberators could and doubtless did argue, was different. Already installed in a position of absolute power, he could hardly be dragged into the courts or before an assembly. The apposite *exemplum* for his case was supplied by Gaius Servilius Ahala, a hero who in the fifth century saved Rome from the tyrannical designs of Spurius Maelius by stabbing him to death with a dagger he concealed under his arm (thus his cognomen Ahala, which means *armpit*). Maelius' property was confiscated, his house levelled, its site becoming, so it was believed, the Aequimaelium, an open space on the slope of the Capitoline.[90] It was these precedents that made Brutus so suitable a leader in the conspiracy. He had long asserted his kinship with Ahala as well as his descent from Lucius Brutus.[91]

The legends of Lucius Brutus and Publicola, the fates of Spurius Cassius and Manlius Capitolinus, the story of Ahala's doughty rescue of Roman freedom, these were not recondite or forgotten episodes confined to antiquarian disquisitions. These deeds were visible in the fabric of the city, rehearsed in history and drama, and replayed in oratory.[92] For any Roman at the time of Caesar's death, however, the inescapable precedent for the enforcement of Publicola's *lex sacrata* was Tiberius Gracchus. Tribune of the *plebs* in 133, Tiberius made himself a champion of the poor but came to be perceived by the aristocracy as a menace to the state. The particulars of his tribunate are complicated and need not detain us here. It is enough to observe that a band of senators, acting, so they insisted, in defence of the republic, ignored Tiberius' tribunician *sacrosanctitas* and lynched him.[93] The day of his death was never forgotten. Publius Scipio Nasica, a private citizen, called upon his fellow citizens to join him in rescuing the republic.[94] In doing so, he summoned the force of Brutus' oath and Publicola's *lex sacrata*: Tiberius, Nasica declared, aimed at tyranny and thereby rendered himself *sacer*. His tribunician *sacrosanctitas*, under these extreme circumstances, was no shield.[95] Nasica and his followers attacked Tiberius on the Capitoline in front of the temple of Jupiter Best and Greatest. There the tribune and hundreds of his followers were killed. Their remains were cast into the Tiber.[96]

For many in the aristocracy, Nasica was a hero and a saviour. But the Roman public remained deeply divided over the contention that Tiberius ever posed any threat to liberty.[97] Nor was it agreed by everyone that Nasica's consecration of Tiberius was a righteous one.[98] Harming a tribune of the *plebs*, like aiming at tyranny, was a shocking violation of a *lex sacrata*, and the death of Tiberius pitted two sacred demands against one another.[99] Even at the time there was controversy, but it was soon resolved to the satisfaction of the gods and therefore the people.[100] Indeed, the events surrounding Tiberius' death furnished, for those who needed it, proof that aiming at *regnum* rendered a man *sacer*, even if he possessed *sacrosanctitas*.[101]

There was nothing subtle, then, or far-fetched about the Liberators' evocation of the Romans' sacred duty to save the city from tyranny. This was strong stuff. But it was also risky stuff. They knew speeches would not suffice for convincing the public of the righteousness of their deed, which is why they devised a series of spectacles for demonstrating the reality of Caesar's crime and the necessity of the Liberators' remedy. The first of these, Suetonius tells us, was to be a ceremonious dragging of Caesar's corpse to the Tiber followed by the confiscation of his property, penalties ordained by tradition for punishing a tyrant.[102]

In the event, because they were stymied by a general panic, the Liberators left Caesar's body where it fell. But this was not the only public demonstration they had in mind, and on the basis of their actions on the Ides we can recover much about their original design for winning the people's approval. It is clear that from the beginning they planned a solemn procession through the city and along the Sacred Way towards the Capitoline, during which, on the day, they urged their fellow citizens to recall the oath of Lucius Brutus.[103] They also, on the day, displayed their daggers, the trophies of tyrannicide. All this was planned in advance: through these actions, they hoped to call to mind the venerable statue of Lucius Brutus on the Capitoline, the object of their procession. There the founder of the republic was depicted brandishing this very weapon, a potent symbol of the ferocity with which he defended freedom.[104] The Liberators deployed other symbols, notably, hanging from a spear a *pilleus*, the freedman's cap that was the token of his manumission from slavery. Daggers and the *pilleus*, from the start, were meant to impress on their audience the true meaning of Caesar's assassination. This was symbolism they continued to employ: in 43 or 42, Brutus minted coins stamped with a *pilleus* framed by two daggers and bearing the legend EID MAR, the Ides of March.[105]

By way of a different gesture the Liberators hoped to associate themselves with Scipio Nasica and the death of Tiberius Gracchus. As they advanced through the Forum towards the Capitol, each conspirator wrapped his toga round his left arm. Appian, who supplies this information, goes on to say that this was done for reasons of self-defence, the twisted togas serving as makeshift shields.[106] If so, the action was unplanned. Everyone in Rome, however, remembered how Nasica and his senatorial followers, on the day of Tiberius' death, wrapped the hem of their togas round their left arms when they attacked the tribune.[107] By reprising the aspect of Nasica, the Liberators endeavoured to conjure that day—a precedent they hoped would justify Caesar's assassination in the sacred cause of liberty. But this was not without its risks: Tiberius remained a popular figure among the urban *plebs*.

It was vital to the designs of the Liberators that their actions be viewed as something more elevated than mere murder and certainly nothing suggesting a coup d'état. Confident they may have been, but the Liberators were keenly aware also that Caesar's death could be viewed, even by the sympathetic, as an act of sacrilege. Which is why the sacred as well as the patriotic significance of striking down the man who would be king had to be enacted for all to see.[108] Caesar, such was their claim, was *sacer* and forfeit to Jupiter. Even the day of his assassination was propitious, for the Ides of every month was sacred to Jupiter and a procession to the Capitol and a sacrifice at his temple was a prescribed ritual.[109] Moreover, the Capitol was the city's most profoundly evocative site, centre of the empire and symbolic of law and order. Indeed, it was from the Capitol that Spurius Cassis and Manlius Capitolinus had been cast to their deaths. The site signified the sovereignty of the people, the foundation of the republic, and its precincts were adorned with the trophies of Roman greatness, including the statue of Lucius Brutus.[110] Numerous ceremonial processions ascended the Capital in every year, each civic ritual marking the city's good order and elaborating the integration and consensus, the very *libertas*, enjoyed by Rome's variegated citizenry.[111]

The Liberators' occupation of the Capitoline, it is claimed, 'was a symbolic act, antiquarian and even Hellenic'.[112] Symbolic, certainly, and antiquarian, yes, but the march to the Capitol they planned was hardly a Greek gesture. In that culture, although a city's liberation could indeed be marked by the removal of oppressors from its citadel, seizing the acropolis routinely indicated a coup d'état, typically by forces inimical to popular freedom. Invaders, too, ceremoniously ascended the acropolis of a defeated city in order to worship its gods. Their presence there was always an act of

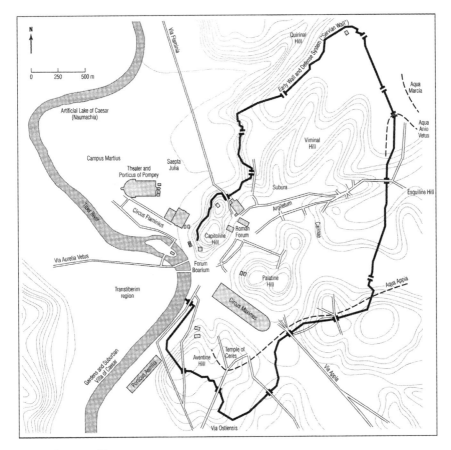

Map 5 The city of Rome

appropriation.[113] These were hardly the implications the Liberators wanted anyone to recognize in their procession. Nor did the Liberators intend anything like the staging of a triumph.[114] Instead, by evoking so many hallowed rituals precious to the city, they hoped to persuade everyone that Caesar's assassination was not an act of revolution but instead a heroic, traditional deed restoring the republic.[115]

Procession to the Capitoline

The events following Caesar's assassination remain difficult to untangle. Our sources are detailed but marred by conflations, compressions, and distortions.[116] Confusion is perhaps the central culprit: matters were muddled at the time, which frustrated subsequent attempts to recover a coherent and honest account of what actually happened. Not that later writers appear to have been deeply concerned with honesty: each of them is, in one way or another, tendentious. Any modern version of the aftermath of Caesar's death can only be provisional. What is obvious, however, is how, for all their careful preparation, the conspirators' plans failed to win over the public as they had hoped. Nor, in the beginning, was the senate's response anything like a favourable one. When Marcus Brutus attempted to address the senate immediately after Caesar's assassination, it was doubtless to denounce Caesar as a tyrant and appeal to his colleagues to join him in dragging the dictator's body to the Tiber. This first of the Liberators' intended performances, however, was frustrated by the terrified reactions of their peers. The conspirators had assumed the righteousness of their action would be grasped instantly and by nearly everyone in the senate. That they got terribly wrong.[117]

Still, these were stalwart men, and despite being abandoned in the Curia and ignored by the panicked crowd fleeing Pompey's theatre, they persevered in making their way through the Forum towards the Capitoline. As they moved through the city, Brutus protested to the people that what had just taken place was a good thing, for a tyrant had been slain.[118] The Liberators, Plutarch tells us, 'welcomed any aristocrats they met'.[119] And they were soon joined by several senators, some of them notable. We do not know the names of everyone, only those who, in the civil strife which followed, came to a bad end.[120] Still, their number included, along with lesser-known figures like Gaius Octavius Balbus and Marcus Aquinius and Quintus Patiscus, the ex-praetors Marcus Favonius and Lucius Staius Murcus. The noble Publius Lentulus Spinther, a quaestor who was son of the consul of 57, also took part. By far the most significant and glamorous attachment was Dolabella, a favourite of Caesar and a darling of the urban masses. His consular regalia, hastily donned, could not fail to attract attention or to lend a substantial degree of authority to the Liberators' procession. When they ascended the Capitoline, Brutus delivered a speech that was well received by those on the spot.[121]

Presently Brutus and Cassius, attended by other members of the conspiracy and the senators who had joined them, returned to the Forum, where again they addressed the people.[122] Not without careful preparation. Appian complains that the Liberators resorted to bribery for the sake of rallying an audience.[123] But the use of payments in the acquisition of a popular following, including wrangling a crowd for a *contio*, was a routine one.[124] Supplying such emoluments required both amassing sufficient cash and the discreet deployment of agents for its distribution, which makes it clear the Liberators had looked ahead to this moment. And they were right to do so. Already signs of public despair were unmistakable. More worrisome for the Liberators' cause, many of Caesar's veterans, angered by their old commander's murder and truly alarmed by any possibility that Caesar's land grants might be cancelled, were stalking the city with increasing menace.[125]

The Liberators and their supporters furnished the people with a striking spectacle: three praetors and a consul of Rome. The collective prestige of the speakers can only have impressed. The details of the speeches delivered on this day, however, are blurred.[126] It is certain that the address by the praetor Lucius Cornelius Cinna, who had once been Caesar's brother-in-law, was met with open hostility. Dolabella, by contrast, commanded greater respect, although the tenor of his speech did not differ significantly from Cinna's. Cassius, it appears, also gave a speech. Brutus certainly did. They exhorted their audience to emulate their ancestors in devotion to liberty, reprising the themes enacted by their earlier procession.[127] They offered reassurances that the assassination did not signal a revolution, and it was perhaps now that Brutus promised the veterans that Rome's promises to them would be kept.[128]

The Liberators staked much on this event. Doubtless they hoped that the message of freedom restored, expressed in pageantry and oratory, would incite popular acclaim sufficient to furnish the residue of the senatorial order, equestrians too, with enough confidence to join their cause openly. Their obvious intention was to persuade the public that they were its champions. But try though they might the Liberators failed to elicit a strong, supportive response from the people. The rhetoric of liberation, for all its ancestral pieties, did not ignite the crowd's enthusiasm. Instead, if Appian is to be believed, a chant rose up for peace.[129] The Liberators had summoned the spirits of the past. The multitude, however, were plagued with anxiety over the immediate future. They sought order and an end to further violence. This was disappointing, but the Liberators' position remained far from hopeless. It soon became clear that their appeals to liberty were beginning to appeal to many in the senate and more than a few in the equestrian order.[130] Among the urban *plebs*, there were different reactions in different quarters, some of them encouraging.[131] Nonetheless, their grand design for liberating Rome had hardly been a conspicuous success. They had paraded to the Capitoline, so they believed, as heroes of the republic. They were now stranded there.

Calpurnia and Antony

While the Liberators urged the citizenry to rally to their cause, Calpurnia directed three slaves to place Caesar's corpse on a litter and bear it home.[132] Curtains were drawn to shield the dead man's modesty, but one arm dangled pathetically from its carriage. Caesar's body was carried through the Forum, and all who saw it were overcome with emotion as the reality of his death became a palpable sensation. For onlookers with no grudge against the dictator, nothing in the Liberators' pageantry could match that. At his home, Caesar's remains were received with wailing and lamentation, doubtless sincere but also performed before an impressionable audience. Calpurnia's recovery of Caesar's corpse constituted a clear challenge to the conspirators' designs. Caesar would not be cast into the Tiber. Instead, his body would receive a proper burial.[133]

Antony turned to Calpurnia with a request for Caesar's papers and any public moneys kept in the dictator's private possession. These were removed and transferred to Antony's house.[134] Calpurnia cooperated fully. Nor was there anything exceptionable in Antony's taking responsibility for his dead colleague's official documents. In fact, Caesar and his scribe, Faberius, in preparation for the dictator's departure, had already begun transferring important papers to Antony, who did not doubt how useful these documents would soon be.[135] Antony's appropriation of Caesar's cash, however, was a less straightforward matter. During his dictatorship Caesar had been entrusted by the senate with absolute authority over Rome's public finances, a duty he exercised mostly by way of public officials. Antony, however, would later insist, at least according to Appian, that in the hurly-burly of Caesar's eventful, busy administration, public funds were occasionally confounded with the dictator's private resources. His death, then, necessitated an audit.[136] The amount involved was a significant one: according to Plutarch and Appian it came to 98 million sesterces, a figure which is far too high but suggestive of the scale, or certainly the perceived scale, of the moneys taken by Antony.

These appropriations later attracted calumny. In Appian we find the claim, attributed to Octavian, that on that night Antony helped himself not just to cash but also a variety of Caesar's possessions, furniture, perhaps, or works of art.[137] This was the kind of complaint raised by Octavian when he clashed with Antony over his inheritance, and Appian's formulation of it appears to borrow elements of Cicero's invective in the *Philippics*.[138] We need not take these aspersions seriously. At the same time, Antony's motives in seizing the funds in Caesar's house were hardly benign. Uncertain how the present crisis would unfold, the consul was determined to have ample supplies of money to hand. It is certain Antony that did not lay his hands on Caesar's war chest. These funds, earmarked for Caesar's invasion of Parthia, were already in Brundisium, where later they fell into the hands of Octavian after he returned to Italy. At the time of Caesar's death, Octavian was in Apollonia, a city across the Adriatic in southern Illyria. Arriving in Brundisium, he apparently made a show of leaving these moneys untouched and returning them to the authorities in Rome.[139] Whether this story is true or not, this cash lay beyond Antony's reach even if he had wanted it.

Antony was later accused of putting his hands on public funds accumulated in the temple of Ops, a goddess of abundance, and this complaint finds its way into modern accounts of the Ides. But this allegation has nothing to do with events following Caesar's assassination. Deposits stored in the temple of Ops constituted an account, swollen by Caesar's confiscations during the civil war, which belonged to the people of Rome but was distinct from the *aerarium*, the public treasury housed in the temple of Saturn.[140] The basis for Caesar's separation of these funds is no longer clear. It is nevertheless certain that these moneys were not the personal property of the dictator. The amount was immense: 700 million sesterces is the figure furnished by our sources. Even if not all this money took the form of hard currency, removing it in a single night would have been physically impossible. And the temple of Ops lay on the Capitoline, where the Liberators were ensconced.[141] But no ancient source alleges that Antony even attempted to do so. Instead, Cicero and others later complain that Antony, Dolabella too, embezzled or misspent the moneys in this account, resulting in its depletion. But that was later and took place over several months.[142]

Emergency Responses

Though confined within the safety of his house, Antony did not remain isolated. In the midst of crisis, communication was essential, and so messengers were dispatched by Antony to his close associates throughout the city—especially to Lepidus who, as Caesar's *magister equitum*, was in command of a legion. In principle, Lepidus' command ought to have evaporated with Caesar's death, but on this day constitutional scruples hardly applied and Antony very much needed Lepidus' cooperation.[143] Throughout the afternoon and evening, agents and emissaries must have crisscrossed the city in profusion, all hoping to extract from the prevailing disorder something in the way of reliable information.[144] But staggered visits by men travelling on foot could do little to furnish anyone with a full account of the current scene. Indeed, these intensive exertions may have added to the muddle. Still, it was crucial for Antony to discover the disposition of the men closest to him and in return convey his determination, as consul, to impose his authority on events.

By evening the Liberators had installed themselves on the Capitol and were receiving friends and relations as visitors and advisors. Cicero was there, urging Brutus, as urban praetor, to summon the senate: only in this way, he argued, could they seize control of events.[145] His view was shared by others.[146] But it was impracticable, not because praetors lacked the capacity to summon the senate but because they could have no opportunity for exercizing it. An immediate emergency session could hardly be assembled before dark, and the day after every Ides was a *dies ater*, a black day unfavourable for so solemn an occasion.[147] Any summons was in any case certain to be countermanded by Antony, whose consular powers gave him precedence in managing the senate. Nevertheless, the orator stubbornly persisted in his view. It was for this reason, when the Liberators asked him to take a leading role in their negotiations with Antony, that he refused. Consequently, this responsibility was assumed by the Liberators' relations and by other, more reliable, friends.[148]

Throughout the evening and into the night, Antony received delegations from multiple parties, including representatives from Caesar's veterans who threatened repercussions should their entitlements be annulled.[149] Friends of the Liberators, including men of consular rank, passed back and forth between Antony's house and the Capitol. Whatever else they had to say, two points were to the fore. In the first place, they urged that all enmities be put aside until stability could be restored to Roman affairs.[150] In addition, and this was the second point, the Liberators wished it to be known that it was outside their intentions to challenge or annul any of Caesar's legal or political dispensations, especially the entitlements arranged for his veterans.[151] The Liberators also invited both Lepidus and Antony to meet with them in the Temple of Jupiter Best and Greatest on the Capitoline. By the time these negotiations had begun, or certainly before they were concluded, Antony had established reliable communications with Lepidus and was in a position to speak for them both.[152] He did not decisively reject the Liberators' request for a truce, not least because he recognized the level of senatorial support on their side. At the same time, he promised them nothing. He must be allowed, and the concession was a fair one, to take council with his own circle of friends. As for his attendance on the Capitoline, that was out of the question. A consul could hardly be expected to condescend to answer a summons issued by praetors, praetors who were also assassins. The very suggestion was insulting.

Lepidus was far too busy for any parley. After mustering his soldiers, he spent the afternoon in deploying them to the Campus Martius. It was a bold action, almost certainly taken on his own authority. Then, during the night, he led his troops into the city, where he occupied the Forum. This move was more forceful still and potentially provocative. On the morning of the sixteenth, Antony reappeared in public, armed and wearing military garb, a clear signal of his approval of Lepidus' manoeuvre.[153] Behind Antony's display, however, was a compromise. Appian makes it clear that, at least originally, Antony opposed introducing soldiers to the city; Dio explains this by alleging that, at this time, Antony was wary of Lepidus' control of the soldiers. Nonetheless, he needed Lepidus' help. Whatever the initial tensions between them, they were soon put aside. Perhaps it was now that Antony promised to secure Lepidus' election as Caesar's successor as pontifex maximus. In any case, by the sixteenth the two men were cooperating closely and very soon it became obvious that Lepidus acknowledged Antony's leadership in dealing with the crisis.

Also on the sixteenth, Antony convened a meeting of advisors, who discussed the Liberators' plea for peace. Lepidus, although Brutus was his brother-in-law, wanted vengeance. So, too, did Balbus. Nothing stood in their way. Although the conspirators had done what they could to fortify a position on the Capitoline, and although they had the protection of a troop of gladiators, they could hardly hold out against Lepidus' soldiers. When Saturninus and his supporters seized the Capitol in 100, Marius, who was consul, forced them down in a matter of hours and with only hastily armed citizens for muscle. The Liberators, attacked by Lepidus' legion, could not hope to fare any better. Hirtius, however, took a different view. He preferred negotiation to bloodshed. This need not imply that he did not wish to see the Liberators punished. It was possible, after all, to establish a special court for trying the assassins, a legal process that would reinforce Caesar's legitimacy and eliminate the Liberators' contagion without deploying soldiers against citizens. Antony agreed with Hirtius.[154]

As consul, Antony had a duty to keep the peace. And perhaps he believed an assault on the Capitol would only provoke retaliation and incite further violence. At the same time, Antony appears to have given no thought to holding trials or bringing anyone to justice. He wanted instead to find a solution that allowed Rome to move forward without dilating on the rights and wrongs of Caesar's dictatorship and without inflicting fresh injuries on anyone. But how to do it? Throughout this day, ideas and proposals passed among Antony and his associates, between Antony and the Liberators and, it is obvious, between Antony and Cicero, still an old friend and a figure whose political acumen and moral stature Antony sought to put to work. In realistic terms, the Liberators were at the mercy of their enemies and Antony was their only hope. They had little choice, if they wanted to survive the crisis they had created, but to accept such terms as they were offered. Antony's difficulty lay in finding a compromise that was acceptable to the people and the senate and did not betray his personal loyalty to Caesar and his legacy. The divergence between the *lex sacrata* protecting Caesar and the *lex sacrata* vindicating the Liberators' deed was total and unbridgeable. But within a single day Antony and Cicero found a workable solution. That night Antony summoned the senate to a meeting on the morning of 17 March.

The Amnesty of 17 March

The senate met on the Liberalia, sacred to Liber, an agricultural god who became a Roman version of Dionysus. But this popular festival went unobserved, a disappointment that exacerbated the people's apprehension. The senate convened in the Temple of Tellus on the Carinae, near Antony's mansion.[155] Antony chose this location, he made clear, for the sake of his personal safety, and on his way to the session as well as afterwards he exhibited to everyone the cuirass he wore beneath his toga. This was a gesture he borrowed from Cicero, who when conjuring the dangers of Catiline had donned the same brand of protection.[156] The temple was also guarded by soldiers, further theatre spotlighting the danger Antony attributed to the conspirators. The consul had ordered the senate to assemble before dawn, another sign of precarity and urgency.

Antony opened the session with a moving speech, admired by Cicero even after they became enemies, in which he extolled the virtue and necessity of political concord. For many in the senate, who had not been privy to the grandees' councils, the moderate tone of Antony's address may have come as a welcome, reassuring surprise. Still, it was far from obvious how harmony could be achieved. On one side, champions of the Liberators condemned Caesar as a tyrant. Senators who rejected this view abominated the Liberators as murderous oath-breakers: a toxic, sacrilegious contagion whose very presence in the city was a danger to the republic. Compromise between these contrarieties was a legal, constitutional, religious, and logical impossibility. Nevertheless, Antony insisted, something in the way of squaring a circle must be done, and although his speech doubtless put forward basic principles for doing so, it remained for the senate to clothe these principles in a workable policy. Antony took the first step when he announced an end to his enmity against Dolabella and recognized him as his colleague in the consulship, a transparent enactment of concord. On the Ides, as we have seen, Dolabella exhibited his sympathy for the Liberators. His consulship, however, was a gift from Caesar, now publicly acknowledged by the consul who had earlier opposed it.

It was proposed that the Liberators be invited to attend the session. Antony agreed at once because, we are told, he knew they would not come. Which was an unattractive look for men who claimed to be defenders of the republic. Nevertheless, from some quarters honours for the Liberators were demanded, most forcibly by Tiberius Claudius Nero, father of the future emperor. This, however, was unacceptable to Caesar's following, and even senators sympathetic to the Liberators' cause had to understand how any decree that officially endorsed Caesar's murder represented a potential threat to men who had been Caesar's staunch supporters: almost by definition they became henchmen. Instead, less passionate senators made a case that, because the Liberators did not seek honours but sought the restoration of the republic, it was enough if they were allowed their place in it. For some on the other side, even this was intolerable. Demands for vengeance, consequently, were vented loudly. But these were rejected by most senators as divisive and destructive. Apart from a ferocious few, it soon became clear, there was little appetite for further violence. Men who had lived through the civil war appreciated the peril of sending so many aristocrats into exile, something as dangerous as it was unseemly: they would soon join Sextus Pompey or strike out on their own. Caesar's murder, most senators were convinced, was an ugly episode which needed to be contained and consigned to the past. This meant the Liberators must somehow be accommodated.

Intervening in the debate, Antony reminded the body of the practical realities of Caesar's regime, which could not be ignored even by the most high-minded of the Liberators. He drew everyone's attention to the implications of declaring Caesar a tyrant or annulling his measures. A majority in the senate, he observed, held their rank owing to Caesar's dispensations and would be obliged to withdraw; doing so would also require the current government to step down and fresh assemblies be held; even Rome's administration of its provinces would, were Caesar's measures cancelled, require immediate revision; the soldiers' entitlements, too, would be revoked. As for Caesar's unfulfilled plans, abrogating these entrained further unwelcome consequences. Decimus Brutus, for example, would no longer be consul-designate, nor would the several Liberators who had been assigned important provinces be eligible to govern them. Nothing, Antony argued, short of disaster loomed if the senate did not affirm the decrees, laws, and regulations of Caesar's administration, his *acta*, including those which had not yet been formally affirmed by the senate or people. Of the seriousness of Antony's point the entirety of the senate were immediately seized.[157]

More than one figure spoke in support of compromise, including Lucius Munatius Plancus. Most important of all was Cicero. In his speech, the orator evoked the famous Athenian amnesty of 403, by means of which Athens avoided social breakdown after the Thirty Tyrants were toppled by civil war. He even used the Greek word for it, *amnēstia*, the forgetting of past wrongs, as a special effect underlining the historical momentousness of the debate.[158] Although on this day Antony was the author of peace, it was Cicero who made the formal motion to the senate.[159] According to its terms, the *acta* of Caesar were recognized as valid and the Liberators were pardoned, both actions taken 'for the sake of the republic'.[160] This formula was by no means an empty one. The issue of the conspirators' sacrilege, all too real because Caesar's constitutional position was not invalidated by the amnesty, must in some way have been addressed by the senate's decree and the debate surrounding it. The senate's formal pardon, qualified as a decision salutary for the state, was apparently believed to serve as a satisfactory shield against divine anger. As for the conspirators themselves, their enemies could console themselves with the traditional conviction that the gods were capable of looking after their own interests and would ultimately visit destruction on Caesar's desecrators.[161]

Other, more immediate concerns preoccupied the body on this day. The veterans and their demands could not go unsatisfied. Strictly speaking, of course, the compromise guaranteed that all Caesar's allocations to these men were secure. Nevertheless, no one wanted to risk any misunderstanding on the veterans' part and therefore a decree was passed for their benefit. A third decree was moved by Lucius Calpurnius Piso, Caesar's father-in-law. It granted Caesar a public funeral. We learn from Cicero that, in the immediate aftermath of the assassination, Atticus had warned the conspirators that a public funeral for Caesar would gravely undermine their position.[162] This was good advice, and the Liberators' friends in the senate must have resisted Piso's motion. Their efforts fell short, however, and the motion was carried.[163] At the end of this day, the Liberators knew the future would not be plain sailing: they must prepare themselves for a public pageant celebrating Caesar's career and mourning his death.

After dissolving the senate, Antony and Lepidus addressed the people.[164] The senate's decisions were announced and justified before a populace some of whom were fearful, some confused, and others outraged. According to Appian, both men made it clear that their sympathies lay against the Liberators. At the same time, they argued for the benefits of restraint and order. Doubtless they made much of their plans for fostering reconciliation: each promised to send his son to the Capitoline as a hostage, and each agreed to welcome an enemy to his table, Lepidus hosting Brutus and Antony Cassius. Soon Antony's infant son, accompanied by nurses and perhaps even by Fulvia, was observed by the citizenry as he was carried to the Liberators. Throughout this day, the Liberators had been made to appear dangerous and aloof.[165] This final action cannot have failed to depict them as outsiders in the centre of their own city and Antony as a consul willing to run risks for the sake of civic concord.

The Restoration of the Republic

From the Ides through 17 March, Antony's was a masterly performance of statesmanship. Amid uncertainty and danger, he tempered his leadership with moderation and calculation, exhibiting amity with Dolabella and cooperation with senatorial grandees like Cicero and Calpurnius Piso. On 17 March he emerged from the senate a champion of concord and the author of peace. On the previous day, there had been no reason to imagine such an outcome. It had seemed far likelier that Rome would descend into further violence, perhaps ending in riots, rebellions by veterans, and a slaughter of the Liberators on the Capitoline. Instead, in a meeting of the senate under Antony's presidency, the first steps were taken towards a restoration of traditional, constitutional government. In a very real sense, the constitution *was* restored. For this achievement, a truly historic success, Antony was rightly praised.

At the same time, in different quarters of the city he remained unappreciated. The public's response to the amnesty could hardly be described as jubilant. True, there was great relief, but that feeling was diluted by a lingering sense of apprehension. As for the Liberators, they had gained what they had asserted they wanted. For these reasons, Antony rightly believed he possessed a strong claim on their gratitude.[166] They saw it differently. At Antony's banquet on 17 March, Cassius was playfully asked by his host whether he was carrying a dagger. Yes, he replied, a large one, in case you, too, try to play the tyrant. Their ingratitude persisted. Cassius argued with Antony over Caesar's will. And although Cicero praised Antony's compromise in his *First Philippic*, his correspondence with Atticus reveals his increasing distaste for a figure he regards as too partial to Caesar's legacy.[167] Trebonius, in a letter, shared with the orator a passage from a satire he was writing, an obscene attack on Antony, a man he describes as disgusting.[168] At the same time, Antony's rescue of Caesar's murderers came at a cost because it disturbed old associates. The dictator's most fervent supporters were certainly disappointed. Men like Oppius and Balbus and Matius remained resentful and profoundly unsatisfied. Matius, Cicero told Atticus, despised the senate's peaceful settlement because he hated the Liberators. Cicero also learned that, although Matius corresponded with Lepidus, he was no longer on close terms with Antony.[169] Hirtius, too, Caesar's friend and a consul-designate for 43, very soon fell out with Antony, though that perhaps had nothing to do with the amnesty. For men like these, Caesar's betrayal was not easily consigned to the past and consequently they dispraised Antony's disinclination towards vengeance.

These extreme sentiments, however, remained minority views among the aristocracy. The bulk of the senate, like most members of the prosperous classes, sought peace and quiet and were grateful to Antony for delivering it. Nonetheless, Antony could not fail to perceive the potential danger of his position: suspended as he was between passionate belligerents, he risked a fall. At the same time, he was aware of his strengths. He possessed Caesar's papers and moneys, and, in view of his long, distinguished service to the dictator, his authenticity as a defender of Caesar's legacy was unimpeachable. The party of Caesar, Antony knew well, perished with his great friend. These Caesarians were men most of whom had been united only by their loyalty to a single leader. The assassination and the senate's response to it had uncovered the tenuousness of their alliance with one another.[170] But the *idea* of Caesar, and the devotion that idea continued to inspire in the public and soldiery as well as among the dictator's old circle of intimates, remained robust. Antony intended to put it to work not only in preserving Caesar's legacy but also in sustaining his suddenly acquired pre-eminence. This, however, would not be easy: the idea of Caesar belonged to everyone, and it remained incendiary.

VI

A consul and an Antony

Antony's Consulship

During his consulship, so Cicero complains in his *Second Philippic*, Mark Antony repeatedly styled himself *et consul et Antonius*, at once a consul and an Antony.[1] We have no reason to doubt it. In the freshly restored republic, Antony naturally luxuriated in the splendour of his nobility and aimed to exercise the authority he possessed as Rome's supreme magistrate. His posture was a traditional one. A noble's advantages, however, because they were real, also incited envy and a persistent suspicion they might be abused.[2] A powerful noble, although a refuge and aid to many, could also act selfishly, treating others with contempt or even cruelty. It is this anxiety that animates Cicero's grumbling about Antony's boast. His tactic was hardly novel: rhetorical instruction urged pupils to exploit their audiences' nervousness about the nobility's bullying and unfair treatment of others, and orators were not hesitant in applying this lesson.[3] A new man like Cicero, when calumniating a noble enemy, was almost certain to advance the claim that it was in his enemy's nature to want to dominate others.[4] That worry, he knew, was an easy one to conjure. Antony's statesmanship on 17 March was inspiring to all. But this admiration did not dispel all apprehensiveness about this noble consul's ambitions.

In the aftermath of the Ides and amid Rome's unsettled turmoil, it may have been reassuring to many that the consuls were each of them men of the nobility. That, from a conservative perspective at least, was what a proper Roman government should look like. And yet neither man was a traditional consul. Too young and improperly credentialed, Antony and Dolabella held Rome's highest office because each had been one of Caesar's most reliable henchmen—and everyone knew it. Although both men must now strain themselves in excelling their peers and installing themselves as permanent senatorial grandees, doing so, in the present, fraught atmosphere, could only provoke a high degree of distrust—among the Liberators, of course, but also on the part of their former Caesarian cronies. The bulk of the senate, too, could only be wary. After Caesar's dictatorship, all were uneasy because they were intensely aware how suddenly old-fashioned political and social eminence could stir conflict and inflict a collapse into individual domination and despotism. Few in Rome could view Antony's actions, even those they welcomed, without questioning his motives.

Caesar's Will

The meeting of 17 March constituted a new beginning for Rome. According to Plutarch, the senate met again on 18 March, when the restored republic began its work. This session is doubted by some scholars, mostly because only Plutarch mentions it and because he indicates that, during this meeting, the senate paid honour to the Liberators, gestures which had been firmly rejected on the previous day.[5] It is impossible to be certain, so great are the chronological confusions in all our sources for the days following the Ides, but there is no obvious reason to doubt the reality of this meeting—even if we need not accept every feature of Plutarch's account of it. Although he furnishes no details, Cicero, too, in his *Philippics*, appears to indicate a meeting on the day following the amnesty.[6] And it would have been rather surprising if the senate had *not* convened: even after the crucial breakthrough of the previous day, the senate still had much to do. Not all of it was purely practical: it was vitally important, for symbolic reasons, that the Liberators join their senatorial peers as soon as possible.

The first order of business was the passage of a celebratory decree commending Antony for rescuing the republic from peril.[7] We are not told who made the original motion—perhaps Plutarch did not know—but Dolabella is a very likely candidate. Practical matters followed. It was agreed that the senate would promptly take up its formal allocation of provincial assignments. True, these had been decided by Caesar and Caesar's *acta* had, on the previous day, been affirmed. On this day, the senate's decision served as a clear signal of the body's fealty to the compromise of 17 March and underlined the Liberators' restored inclusion in Rome's government. For that reason, this agreement may have furnished a basis for Plutarch's conclusion that honours were voted for the assassins, several of whom were destined for provincial commands. The final topic on the agenda concerned Caesar's will. The senate had voted to grant Caesar a public funeral. It was now proposed, possibly by Calpurnius Piso, that his will be read from the Rostra in the presence of the people.[8] The suggestion was strongly opposed by the still contumacious Cassius, but he was fiercely resisted by Antony and soon found himself on the losing side of the debate. Brutus, by contrast, acquiesced, a gracious gesture which hardly mattered: the decree was carried easily.

Probably on the same day, at a *contio* summoned by Antony, Caesar's will was read out.[9] By then its contents were familiar to Piso, Antony, and others. But for the public, avidly interested in anything to do with Caesar, his testament was breaking news. Caesar's principal heirs were Octavian, his great-nephew; Quintus Pedius, a nephew; and Lucius Pinarius Scarpus, another great-nephew. Octavian, the youngest of the three, received three-quarters of Caesar's estate. The residue was to be divided between Pedius and Pinarius, although later each of them made a gift of his inheritance to Octavian.[10] Antony and Decimus Brutus were among Caesar's secondary heirs and were certainly recipients of generous legacies. Other legacies were bequeathed to several of the tyrannicides. The people reacted strongly when these sections of Caesar's will were read: the sheer ingratitude of the Liberators could hardly have been spelled out more clearly. Their animus against the conspirators was intensified further when Caesar's public bequests were announced: his gardens near the Tiber he handed over to the people as a park, and to every male citizen he left a legacy of 300 sesterces.

The reading of the will did its work. It reminded the masses of their affection for the dictator and rekindled their hostility against his assassins. In addition, any Liberator who received a legacy from Caesar was put in a difficult spot: keeping it looked ugly, but rejecting it appeared both ungracious and a repudiation of the compromise of 17 March. But what of Antony? In his *Second Philippic*, Cicero sneers that Antony, before

Caesar's death, was in the habit of boasting he would be the dictator's principal heir and even his adopted son.[11] This is a slur repeated elsewhere, but it originates after Antony fell out with Octavian over executing the terms of Caesar's will. Although Antony was distantly related to Caesar, and although Caesar was childless, it would have been extraordinary had the dictator ignored his nephew and great-nephews when writing his will. Antony cannot have expected him to do so. That Octavian was the principal heir, in view of the favour previously shown him by Caesar, was no surprise to anyone. Caesar treated Antony handsomely in his will, as even Cicero, in his own way, was forced to concede.[12] Antony, in a later speech attacking Cicero, claimed the orator was so unpopular he rarely received legacies, whereas he himself was often a favoured beneficiary. The allegation stung, and in reaction Cicero carefully tabulated the bequests which had come his way; he admitted Antony got more, but that he attributed to the man's bullying and arm-twisting.[13] If in this feud over legacies Cicero had been able to claim Caesar had short-changed Antony, he surely would have done so.

Come I to Speak in Caesar's Funeral

Caesar's funeral took place on 20 March.[14] It was a grand ceremony and the occasion for a funeral oration which, in accordance with tradition, celebrated the deceased's heritage but chiefly recounted the departed's illustrious deeds and their value to the republic.[15] Speeches of this kind were usually delivered by a man's son or a close relation. But Octavian was not yet in Rome—he was making his way from Apollonia— and it appears Pedius and Pinarius, like Calpurnius Piso, were willing to yield their place to Antony, who seized the moment for himself. This was the most important speech of Antony's career, and it remains the most famous. Nevertheless, so divergent are our sources' treatment of it that no reconstruction can be accurate in its details. Cicero describes it as pathetic and deeply moving, not because he deemed it a bad speech but rather because he judged it an oration that was too affecting on behalf of the wrong cause.[16]

Exactly what Antony said is now lost. He may have uttered a refrain of references to Caesar as 'an extraordinary man' and 'an illustrious man'. These were unremarkable expressions in a funeral oration, but it appears they were often repeated and soon became slogans recycled by anyone reproaching the Liberators.[17] Antony's speech also showcased several striking features. He inserted documents, either by way of deploying a herald or by reading them out himself. The senate's decrees honouring Caesar, especially the text of the oath obliging every senator to protect him, were recited. Into each recitation Antony intruded his personal observations, contrasting what actually took place on the Ides with the promises made by the Liberators and indeed the whole of the senate. It was not only the conspirators, Antony made it clear, who ought to feel shame over Caesar's death.[18] Antony also staged several theatrical flourishes—at the very least he displayed Caesar's blood-stained toga—all designed to intensify the public's grief and stir its hostility against the conspirators.[19] His performance was stunningly effective.

The Liberators, as we have seen, were aware of the damage Caesar's state funeral was likely to inflict on their position. Consequently, they took precautions on that day by posting private guards to protect their houses. They were wise to do so: the public revulsion conjured by Antony's speech was nothing short of violent. Caesar's body was cremated in the Forum and angry mobs threw themselves against the houses of the Liberators. So savage did the crowd become, so we are told, that in its madness it fell upon Helvius Cinna, a poet and a friend of Caesar, confusing him with the praetor Cornelius Cinna, one of the conspiracy's sympathizers. This story is almost certainly a fiction, but its origins lie in recollections of the public's outrage after Antony's speech.[20] Antony, however, did not unleash an angry mob and leave its fury unconstrained. He and Lepidus, in order to prevent anything like the rioting and destruction of 52, stationed soldiers where they could protect the city's buildings. The crowd was allowed to express its rage but only up to a point. Soon order was restored in the Forum and assaults on the houses of the Liberators were abandoned.[21] The people, still moved, kept a solemn vigil at Caesar's pyre into the night.

Antony had made his point. He forcefully exhibited his devotion to Caesar's memory. At the same time, by containing and ultimately quelling the violence of the crowd, he displayed to everyone but certainly to the Liberators the very real extent of his personal authority. Antony's funeral oration was intended not only to praise Caesar but more importantly to render as targets of public outrage the men his amnesty had only recently rescued from catastrophe. Friction with Cassius had made clear the ungrateful posture of the Liberators. The perturbation and violence incited by Caesar's funeral now impressed upon all of them how deeply unpopular they were with the masses. The events of the day also made it obvious how dependent they remained on civic order, something that lay beyond their control and could be sustained only by Antony and his allies. If the Liberators and their friends, or even Antony's rivals among the old Caesarian circle, believed his statesmanship on 17 March stemmed from weakness or diffidence, they were now dramatically disabused of that misapprehension.

Antony did not wait long to reinforce for the Liberators the true nature of their vulnerability. This is something we can detect in a letter addressed to Brutus and Cassius by Decimus Brutus.[22] Decimus tells them he has recently been visited by Hirtius, who made it clear that Antony was now unsure whether he could allow Decimus to take up his province. This uncertainty Decimus decries as treacherous bad faith and expects Cassius and Brutus to feel the same way. Hirtius, he further reports, explained to him that Antony, concerned by the public's agitation, was anxious over the Liberators' safety. This anxiety, presumably, constituted Antony's ostensible reason for reconsidering Decimus' governorship.

Decimus' consternation is understandable. The terms of the amnesty guaranteed the execution of Caesar's *acta* and on 18 March the senate confirmed it would ratify Caesar's provincial appointments. Antony was probably not suggesting that he would fail to execute the senate's decree. But any Liberator who, like Decimus, was a *privatus*, a private citizen not holding a magistracy or promagistracy, required, in addition to the senate's formal sanction, further enabling legislation, a *lex curiata de imperio*, before he could take up his command as a provincial governor.[23] In reality, nothing prevented Antony or Dolabella from providing Decimus with the required *lex*, but Antony, it appears, by exaggerating and exploiting Rome's changed atmosphere after Caesar's funeral and underlining the public's hostility against Decimus and men like him, was now expressing doubts over whether he could successfully assemble a curiate assembly. Would the urban *plebs* permit it?

Behind Antony's expressions of concern was an unmistakable threat, which is why his conversation with Hirtius panicked Decimus.[24] In his letter, Decimus tells his fellow Liberators that he fears it is only a matter of time before they are declared public enemies or condemned to exile. Although open to suggestion—Decimus informs Cassius and Brutus that he was urged by Hirtius to seek their views—his letter recommends fleeing to Rhodes or anywhere out of Antony's reach. In the meantime, however, he has requested a public bodyguard for himself and all the Liberators. Very soon after this exchange, however, Decimus' crisis was resolved: in early April he was able to leave Rome to take up his province.[25] In the interval, however, the Liberators were obliged to react both to Antony's pose of phoney concern over their unpopularity and to the fear it instilled in Decimus and others. They were also now obliged, as the weaker party, to negotiate with Antony by way of every expression of aristocratic courtesy and even deference. Which, for Antony, was the motive behind his hesitation over Decimus' province. It was not his purpose to violate the spirit or letter of the amnesty. But it was important for him to furnish everyone with a practical lesson in the reality of his clout and his determination to use it.

Coin of the Realm

It cannot have been long after Caesar's funeral that Antony instructed the moneyer Publius Sepullius Macer to mint a series of denarii on which the consul's head was pictured on the obverse. There Antony was depicted bearded, a sign of mourning, and his head was veiled. To mark his identity as an augur, a *lituus*, the sacred wand employed in taking auspices, was also represented. On the reverse was a *desultor*, an acrobat skilled at leaping from horse to horse in Roman games: this figure was pictured with a palm and a wreath.[26] This coin was modelled on a Caesarian predecessor, one of the dictator's final issues. On the obverse of Caesar's coin, he was portrayed, head veiled, as pontifex maximus; on its reverse this coin bore the *desultor* Antony borrowed for his issue. This *desultor* is very likely a reference to the games in Caesar's honour which were added to the Paralia, a festival which took place on 21 April.[27] Antony will have wanted his coins in circulation before then.

By design, this coin is easy to understand. Here Antony depicts himself as Caesar's devotee but also as a major figure in his own right. This assertion is most obvious in the sheer existence of the coin. Caesar was the first living man whose portrait appeared on a Roman coin. Antony—without sanction from the senate or the people—was now the second. This was a bold move. In this single coin we possess visual evidence of Antony's principal challenge as consul. He must remain loyal to the idea and legacy of Caesar. At the same time, it was vital that he establish his political independence by way of unmistakable individuation within the constraints of his fealty to his old master and friend. Even had he wanted to, Antony could not free himself from his identity as Caesar's champion. And yet it was imperative that he emerge from Caesar's long shadow.[28]

Reconciliation and the Restored Republic

Antony, as have seen, was not slow in putting the multitude's anger to work as a jus-tification for discomfiting Decimus and the other conspirators. Troubling these men by accenting their vulnerability, however, was only a tactic, not a strategy. Antony, like any republican grandee, was intent on excelling his rivals. At the same time, he did not wish to see the Liberators ruined and in the coming weeks impressed even Marcus Brutus with his collegiality.[29] Antony was conscious of the senate's regard for them and, as the author of peace, he had an obligation to forestall destabilizing crises. It was by way of preserving this balance between Caesarian loyalist and republican statesman that, soon after his funeral oration, he introduced in the senate a motion abolishing the office of dictator. He did so in an unusual fashion: he read out the draft of his proposed decree and, without opening a debate, immediately called for a divi-sion. In this way, Antony eliminated any awkwardness likely to be produced by revisit-ing the issues of 17 March and obviated any invective against Caesar.[30] Because it was obvious that eliminating the dictatorship came very close to being an implicit criti-cism of Caesar's regime, Antony could not fail to perceive that his motion would of-fend the dictator's most fervent admirers. Nevertheless, he knew it would enjoy wide popularity in a senate eager to put the past behind it. The decree was carried and in June passed into law.[31]

After Caesar's death, it was necessary to fill the sacred and coveted post of pon-tifex maximus and Antony presided over the assembly at which Lepidus was elected.[32] Collaboration during the Ides and its aftermath had forged a strong friendship be-tween the two men, a relationship they now elevated to a family connection through the betrothal of Antony's daughter to Lepidus' son.[33] By this time Lepidus had demit-ted his position as master of the horse and in compensation was made governor of Narbonese Gaul and Nearer Spain. This was a fresh assignment initiated by Antony: it was Caesar's plan, as we have seen, that Lepidus remain in Italy as perpetual master of the horse. That was no longer possible, and Lepidus' provincial command faced no opposition.

There were good reasons for despatching Lepidus to the west. Pompey's son, Sextus, commanded a hostile army in Spain. To deal with him, Caesar had sent Asinius Pollio out as governor of Further Spain.[34] But Pollio was ineffectual. There was, then, a clear need for a senior figure like Lepidus. His purpose, however, as later events revealed, was not principally to vanquish Sextus but, if possible, persuade him to come to terms with the republic.[35] This was an undertaking worked out privately by Lepidus and Antony, the purpose of which was both to neutralize a military threat and also stage a powerfully symbolic reconciliation in Rome. Sextus was not unreceptive. Before the end of April, it appears, Antony made it known that he intended to introduce a measure restoring Sextus and compensating him for the confiscation of his father's estate. The suggestion was enormously popular with the senate and by summer many were certain that Sextus would accept Antony's offer.[36]

Of more immediate concern were provincial appointments for Liberators awaiting a senatorial decree allowing them to assume their commands. Indeed, by provoking Decimus, Antony had made this matter an urgent one. And so, in early April, on the basis of documents in Caesar's papers, these assignments were formally confirmed

Fig. 6.1 Marcus Aemilius Lepidus on the obverse of a denarius (*RRC* 495): around the image of Lepidus the coin reads: LEPIDUS PONT MAX III V R P C (Lepidus, pontifex maximus, triumvir appointed to set the republic in order).
Source: Wikimedia Commons or CNG.

by the senate. This allowed a much-relieved Decimus Brutus to depart for Cisalpine Gaul and other Liberators, like Tillius Cimber and Trebonius, to take up their provinces. It was likely during this same session that Dolabella's command of Syria and Antony's governorship of Macedonia were ratified.[37] Although Florus and Appian report that Caesar assigned Syria to Cassius and Macedonia to Brutus, this is almost certainly an error.[38] We do not actually know what provinces Caesar had in mind for these men and in any case the senate did not pass a decree allocating provinces to the praetors of 44 until 28 November.[39] By then much had changed in Rome. But in April, the consul and senate cooperated in executing Caesar's *acta* and by doing so restored these Liberators to an active role in the government of the republic, exactly as the amnesty of 17 March prescribed. Little wonder Cicero, in his *First Philippic*, relished this time in Antony's consulship by celebrating how 'one day after another, you did not fail to bring the republic its daily gift'.[40] In private, the orator was, if less effusive, equally sanguine: of Antony he writes, 'my own view is that he thinks harder about dinner parties than about getting up to trouble'.[41]

Gaius Amatius Herophilus

Not long after Caesar's funeral, a mysterious, dangerous figure took possession of the Forum.[42] In a letter to Cicero, composed in 45, this man styled himself Gaius Marius, son of the consul of 82 and grandson of the great Marius. He was, in fact, an imposter, whose name was Gaius Amatius, possibly Gaius Amatius Herophilus, a freedman. When he contacted Cicero, Amatius was in legal difficulty, and soon afterwards Caesar exiled him.[43] After the dictator's death, however, he returned to Italy and in Rome erected an altar and a column on the site of Caesar's cremation. There he offered the dictator divine honours and rallied mass demonstrations against the Liberators. By early April, the capital had become too dangerous for Cassius and Brutus to remain and so they withdrew to the country. Cicero, too, left Rome to visit his estates and take a holiday in Campania. Brutus, because he was urban praetor, needed a special dispensation to leave the city. Antony aided him in getting it, exertions for which Brutus and by extension Cicero were grateful.

Antony and Dolabella now took direct action against Amatius. His altar was demolished. When Amatius led angry riots in reaction, Antony used force to suppress them, arrested Amatius, and put him to death, perhaps on the grounds that he was an exile who had installed himself in the capital illegally. Antony's energy in eliminating Amatius surprised and delighted the senate. Cicero heard of it on 16 April, when he also learned of Brutus' heartfelt approval of the deed. The crowds who had supported Amatius, however, persisted in seditious rampaging. Soldiers were despatched and several demonstrators were killed in the fighting, though we may prefer to doubt some of the sensational details furnished by Appian, slaves crucified, for example, and freedmen hurled from the Tarpeian Rock. Without question, this clash damaged Antony's reputation with some sections of the urban *plebs*. But is far from clear that this episode incited what Appian describes as the public's 'unutterable hatred'. True, Amatius' following was unforgiving. But there will have been many ordinary people in the city, shopkeepers and craftsmen and others active or domiciled in the vicinity of the Forum, who were thankful for an end to Amatius' disturbances. Certainly, the business and trading interests which operated in and around the Forum, and everyone associated with the courts and duties of public officials, were relieved by Amatius' removal.[44]

This was not the end of it, however. Near the end of April, when Antony was away from Rome, remnants of Amatius' movement restored Caesar's altar and revived hostile demonstrations against the Liberators. It was now Dolabella's turn to take action. The site was cleared, the crowd violently dispersed. Again, there were deaths. Cicero was elated and praised Dolabella to the sky, believing his actions augured well for Brutus and Cassius.[45] We learn from a letter to Atticus that Pansa dispraised Dolabella's treatment of the demonstrators. If so, he cannot have approved of Antony's earlier elimination of Amatius. But Pansa, who perhaps was willing to tolerate disorder in the capital if it threatened the Liberators, was no friend of either Antony or Dolabella.

Unfinished Business: Caesar's *Acta*

The amnesty of 17 March affirmed the validity of Caesar's *acta*, including those not already carried into law or enacted by a senatorial decree. Implementing this official policy, however, was an unsimple affair. Practical difficulties derived in part from the condition of Caesar's surviving papers—tablets, notebooks, memoranda, even scribbles to himself—any scrap of which potentially carried the force of law. Problems were also thrown up by the sheer inefficiency of Roman record keeping, the unreliability of Rome's bureaucracy, and endemic miscommunication among the governing class.[46] The predicament facing the consuls and senate is easily illustrated. On 9 February, at a meeting presided over by Caesar, the senate recognized privileges which Rome had previously granted the Jews; on 11 April, the body voted to make an official record of its decree; but at the time of Caesar's death over a month later nothing had been done.[47]

Even Roman insiders found themselves frustrated by misadministration and failures in communication. Caesar selected the city of Buthrotum, a harbour town in Epirus, as the site for a veteran colony and began making arrangements for confiscating its lands. Atticus, however, who possessed extensive holdings in Epirus and a prized estate in Buthrotum, collaborated with Cicero in lobbying Caesar to change his plans. The dictator agreed on the condition that Buthrotum pay a sizeable indemnity, moneys which Atticus furnished on the city's behalf—doubtless in the form of a highly profitable loan to the town. Thus, they believed, the matter was settled.[48] But Caesar was slow in communicating his decision to his subordinates, confusion that led to some friction between the dictator and the wealthy knight, and at the time of his death operations were again underway for installing a colony despite what Atticus, Cicero, and the people of Buthrotum regarded as an act of Caesar. Whether or not they were right in doing so was a matter of enormous consequence for the Buthrotians and for Atticus, whose investment was at risk.

These examples make clear how essential it was to arrange for an orderly review of Caesar's papers, a process that also entailed a close scrutiny of senatorial decisions which remained unregistered. The learned Servius Sulpicius Rufus proposed entrusting this process to the two consuls acting in coordination with a board of advisors, a motion that was carried with Antony's and Dolabella's support.[49] It appears, however, that the consuls did not appoint their advisors until 1 June. During this interval, they instead submitted any measure they deemed a valid act of Caesar to the senate for its consent. On 2 or 3 June Sulpicius' policy was ratified as part of an Antonian law granting Caesar's *acta* the force of law. This procedure for vetting Caesar's papers, although sensible, did not surmount every hazard owing to the unavoidable complexities involved in sorting out Caesar's real intentions from his fancies or, when faced with conflicting documents, difficulties in determining Caesar's final judgement on a matter. Antony's personal possession of Caesar's papers presented another and very serious concern. Since it was possible for him to produce forged documents, he easily fell under the suspicion of corrupt practice. It is on this aspect of the enactment of Caesar's *acta*—Antony's fraudulent behaviour—that Cicero and, consequently, later historians concentrate their attention.[50]

The system devised by Sulpicius went to work immediately. On 11 April, the outstanding matter of privileges for the Jews was settled. There must also have been many other decisions and measures about which we know nothing. Our record of this procedure and its results depends mostly on Cicero, which means we are furnished with a highly selective litany of complaints. Even before he began finding fault with Antony, Cicero detested the validation of Caesar's *acta*. 'The tyrant is dead', he wrote to Atticus on 17 April, 'but tyranny lives on'.[51] In a letter of 22 April, he is expansive in his outrage over a Caesarian law promulgated by Antony—in exchange for a massive bribe, Cicero insists—granting citizenship to the Sicilians. In the same letter he observes that Deiotarus has been confirmed in his kingdom. The monarch's acquittal pleases Cicero but he is certain that getting it involved making under-the-table payments to

Fulvia. Furthermore, Cicero groans, these two cases of corruption are not the only ones. This letter is the first of many Ciceronian fulminations on Antony's sleaze. At the same time, and revealingly, Cicero immediately observes how this is just the kind of behaviour on the consul's part that should render Atticus hopeful in the matter of Buthrotum.[52] In the end, and although he was constrained to make some compromises, the Buthrotum affair was resolved to Atticus' satisfaction. It was settled in a meeting with Antony, after which Atticus described himself as unperturbed by the irregularities he perceived in the consul's operations: 'let us sooner be parted from the commonwealth than from our private wealth', he wrote to Cicero.[53]

In his *Philippics* and letters, Cicero's disapprobation of Antony's corruption, his complaint that Antony accepted bribes and falsified Caesarian laws, is angry and loud. Writing to Cassius in early May, Cicero bemoans the reality that Caesar's despotism lives on after his death. Worse, he laments, Rome is in thrall to fakery: 'we approve measures which that man, had he lived, would never have passed and we do so on the false grounds he was *thinking* about them'.[54] Allegations like these, recycled by Antony's enemies, eventually made their way into the narratives of historians—often as statements of fact. Out of all this noise, however, four measures emerge which attract Cicero's recurring outrage: (1) citizenship for Sicily; (2) the acquittal of Deiotarus and the restoration of his realm; (3) tax exemptions for Crete and an end to the island's provincial status; and (4) a decree restoring exiles.[55] Now we need not reject every feature of Cicero's invective. Forged documents, even senatorial decrees, were real features of Roman public life during Caesar's dictatorship.[56] As for corruption, there was no time in republican history when it was absent from public affairs.[57] Nevertheless, it must also be borne in mind that each of the four measures Cicero objects to was, so far as we can tell, reviewed by both consuls and either put before the senate or, in the case of Cretan independence and possibly the decree on exiles, vetted by the consuls' advisory board. These safeguards by no means rendered bribery or fakery impossible. But it was not the case, as Cicero's complaints imply, that Antony was able to act entirely on his own as a kind of legislating maverick.

Let us begin with citizenship for Sicily. At some point during his dictatorship Caesar extended Latin rights, a legal standing very close to the condition of actual citizenship, to the people of Sicily. In early April Antony announced that Caesar had also intended to grant citizenship to at least some Sicilian cities or perhaps, as Cicero insists Antony claimed, all of them. This law, Antony must have maintained, had not properly been recorded but now, after official scrutiny by the consuls and senate, could be published and enforced. Cicero denounced Antony's action as dishonest and venal, which may of course be true. Nevertheless, Antony managed to persuade the senate otherwise.[58] If the measure was indeed a limited one and not a universal application of citizenship, there is no obvious reason to reject the idea that it reflected Caesar's intentions. The question of the measure's authenticity is distinct from the matter of Antony's willingness to accept gifts from Sicilian cities before bringing it forward. Interested parties in Sicily must have pressed both consuls on this topic, but especially Antony because he controlled Caesar's archive. That these exchanges involved emoluments is indeed likely.

The fate of this law is unclear. We know that in the time of Augustus the whole of Sicily did *not* possess Roman citizenship and for this reason the usual view is that the measure was annulled in 43 along with the rest of Antony's legislation. But that conclusion can hardly be automatic. This law derived from an act of Caesar: was it deemed an Antonian or a Julian law? Antony's law validating Caesar's acts was certainly annulled in 43 but it was promptly replaced by Pansa's law to the same effect and Caesar's acts were later reaffirmed by the triumvirs.[59] Sicilian citizenship, especially if it was confined to a few cities and was recognized as an act of Caesar, may thereby have been restored. During the triumviral period, affairs in Sicily were affected by Sextus Pompey's occupation and by punishments imposed on the island by Octavian after he seized the place for himself. Still, the preponderance of our evidence indicates that citizenship was not universal in Sicily when Octavian became its master but instead was expanded, very slowly, both during the age of Augustus and subsequently.[60] Antony's measure, then, either granted citizenship to the whole of the island and was somehow dropped even after Pansa's law on the grounds that Antony lied about its Caesarian origin or, because in fact only selected cities were rewarded by Caesar or Antony with citizenship, this limited measure subsisted but left most of Sicily dependent on the administration of Augustus for any improvements in its condition.

Deiotarus was the king of Galatia, a large and strategically important kingdom in Anatolia. A friend of Pompey, he fell out of favour with Caesar during the civil war but kept his realm by paying a heavy tribute.[61] In 45, Deiotarus' grandson, Castor II, accused him of plotting against the dictator. Cicero delivered a speech on behalf of the king and Brutus offered his support.[62] At the time of his death, however, Caesar had not announced his decision on the matter. Antony produced evidence that Caesar accepted Deiotarus' innocence and planned to add Armenia Minor, territory the king had recently occupied, to his realm. Caesar's generosity Cicero deems too suspicious to be genuine and he alleges that the king's good fortune owed itself to a bribe—Cicero cites the figure of ten million sesterces—which Fulvia extracted from the endangered monarch.[63] That Deiotarus was willing to offer a large sum to save his throne is unsurprising and the practice was hardly an unfamiliar one as we have seen in the case of Ptolemy Auletes. Corruption, then, seems not unlikely, nor is there any reason to exclude Fulvia's participation even if we reject Cicero's claims that she was in the business of auctioning kingdoms to the highest bidders.[64] At the same time, it is also probably true that Caesar intended to acquit Deiotarus. The man had long been a reliable Roman client and his ability as a monarch was beyond dispute. In making ready for an invasion of Parthia, Caesar could not have intended to install an untried king in a region so strategically important as Galatia. All of which suggests that the decree in Deiotarus' favour was an authentic one, which Antony and Fulvia almost certainly exploited in extruding a hefty bribe from the king.

A law affecting Crete was carried sometime in late summer, after Cassius and Brutus were assigned provinces: Cassius was appointed governor of the Cyrenaica and Brutus of Crete.[65] In his Second Philippic, Cicero complains that by way of abusing Caesar's papers, Antony fabricated this law, which granted tax exemptions to rich cities in Crete and stipulated that, at the conclusion of Brutus' governorship of the island, Crete would cease to be a province. This boon to Crete, so runs the orator's predictable allegation, constituted a highly profitable transaction for the consul. Clear proof of Antony's dishonesty, Cicero gleefully observed, lay in the impossibility of Caesar's knowing Brutus would ever have been governor of Crete.[66] Although Cicero does not belabour the point, he was aware that his readers were familiar with the close and profitable connections between the Antonii and the peoples of Crete, a reality that enhanced the persuasiveness of his aspersion.[67]

Let us begin with the pertinence of Brutus' praetorship. In extracting Caesar's intentions from the documents in his archives, the consuls will not always have found fully drafted decrees but will often have relied on memoranda. On the basis of texts like these, they set about formulating suitable decrees or laws. That a law was issued which employed contemporary references for its implementation, then, is unsurprising and by no means incriminating. And, unless Antony was a complete idiot, this will explain the expiration of Brutus' governorship as the turning point for Crete's status. Whatever Caesar's intentions, Antony will not have wanted to do anything which appeared to interfere with Brutus' term in office. Setting the end of Brutus' administration as the inception of this law's operations had the further advantage of implicating the Liberator in making suitable arrangements for enacting Caesar's law.

But what did this law entail? Grants of immunity from taxation call for little comment. During Caesar's dictatorship, Crete had a good friend in Antony, whose family had long been invested in Cretan affairs. Other important stakeholders in the island included the elite of Capua, an Italian city with extensive public holdings on the island.[68] For Caesar to aid his allies in this way, extending their influence in Crete by way of influence-accruing benefactions, was a perfectly natural operation in Roman provincial administration. But this is quite unlike Cicero's claim that Crete was somehow to be liberated from its provincial status. If that is what this law prescribed, it was indeed nothing short of shocking. Now Brutus did not in fact become governor of Crete in 43—instead he seized control of Macedonia—and another civil war supervened, after which Crete was temporarily administered, on Antony's authority, by a federation of Greek cities. When Antony returned to the east in 39, he united Crete and the Cyrenaica into a single province, an arrangement which was continued after Actium.[69] It is very likely this amalgamation of Crete and the Cyrenaica which Caesar had in mind and which Antony enacted in the summer of 44. Cicero, by way of his habitual deformation of any enemy's legal proposals, misleadingly rendered this measure an abolition of Crete's provincial status.

The restoration of exiles is a policy which we can view only from Cicero's perspective. During Caesar's regime, the dictator pardoned and recalled numerous exiles, and in Caesar's papers Antony discovered further notices which restored various individuals. The recall of one exile became the subject of an exchange of letters between Antony and Cicero. Sextus Cloelius was a scribe who became a close political ally of Clodius Pulcher. In the aftermath of Clodius' assassination in 52, he joined with Fulvia and others in inciting the riots which led to the destruction of the Curia. Consequently, Cloelius was accused of *vis*, political violence, and condemned.[70] The man had influential friends, including Fulvia's husband Antony, and it is no surprise that Caesar was persuaded to recall him. Before executing Caesar's decree, however, Antony took the trouble of writing Cicero, ostensibly seeking his consent but in reality serving him with a polite notice of an unwelcome event. Antony's letter could never be wholly successful—Cicero was certain to be outraged by Cloelius' recall—but, notwithstanding an ample quantity of courteous expression, Antony's missive to the orator was too clumsy even to make a good impression.

Antony ought to have centred his request around Cicero's dignity as well as the influence and gratitude he would garner in exchange for his clemency to a past enemy. Instead, like the author of many an irksome modern memorandum, he began with a reference to how busy he was: true, yes, but always a poor means of winning over the recipient of any communication, then as well as now. Antony afterwards spent too much time underlining that Cloelius' recall had been decided by Caesar, as if Cicero did not grasp that point, and he tastelessly implied that contumaciousness at Cicero's end could result in enmity on the part of Clodius' son, still a child but rich and noble and likely, if perturbed, to become a problem.[71] Better, Antony advises, if he and Cicero can persuade the young Claudius that feuds need not be hereditary, but then he goes on to deliver an unsubtle threat: 'doubtless your future security is proof against any peril, my dear Cicero; nonetheless, I assume you would rather spend your old age in peace and with honour and not racked by anxiety'.[72] Cicero was offended and sent a copy of this letter to Atticus: 'you can easily judge for yourself how clumsily, how disgracefully, and how viciously [he writes to me]'.[73]

Cicero also sent Atticus his reply: 'I have made myself the most easy-going man in the world'.[74] Indeed, Cicero's letter teems with fulsome friendliness, delivered in a manner so over-the-top that Antony could not fail to perceive its insincerity: 'for one reason only', he begins, 'do I wish you had taken this matter up with me in person and not by letter, for then you could have recognized my love for you not only from my words but rather, as the saying goes, in my expression and in my eyes and in my face'. He goes on, at length, saying yes again and again: 'I of course yield to you in this matter, my dear Antony, and I do so with a keen sense of your generosity and courtesy in writing me just as you have done'. He concludes: 'As for me, I shall always and without hesitation and with the utmost zeal do anything which I believe you want done and which advances your position'.[75] Antony wrote again, thanking Cicero for his cooperation.[76] But he did not forget Cicero's nearly sarcastic response to his original request. He kept a copy. And, as we shall see, he later read it to the senate—much to the orator's embarrassment.

Bringing home individuals who were exiled, it is clear, demanded a good deal of social work on the consul's part. As for a law restoring exiles simply and comprehensively, we know less, and Cicero says less, about that.[77] The orator had to tread carefully—he did not wish to offend anyone with an interest in any exile's restoration nor did he wish to appear cruel—but he did not shrink from alleging that the law was manufactured by Antony as part of his illicit trade in favours for cash. Corruption, not tyranny, is the calumny for which this complaint is designed. And yet it can hardly be excluded that Caesar, before launching himself on the east, intended to bring home the residue of men who had petitioned him for pardon.

Cicero's allegations that these four laws were fabricated by Antony become, on close examination, difficult to believe. True, there was little for the orator to gain, and something for him to lose, in complaining about benefactions granted to the Sicilians, who regarded him as a patron; or Deiotarus, who was his friend; or even men languishing in exile. For that reason, perhaps, he believed these were all complaints which would appear credible. Cicero, after all, was a past master at misrepresenting the realities of Roman legislation. The real thrust of Cicero's indictment, however, is not forgery but corruption, an Antonian vice about which he has no personal doubts, as we have seen.[78] Cicero, throughout his invective attacks on Antony, seeks to stir outrage over the man's sleaziness. In his *Fifth Philippic*, for instance, he depicts Antony's mansion as a veritable marketplace in which he and Fulvia have put the entire republic up for sale to the highest bidders.[79] Here, Cicero was certain, Antony was vulnerable: his lavish lifestyle, his indebtedness in 46, the unsavoury reputation of his uncle, his acquisition of Caesar's moneys—all these things lent credibility to Cicero's aspersions of Antonian improbity. And Antony may have been nearly as venal as Cicero's caricature of him. As for these laws, however, it appears that Antony followed the procedures which he and the senate put in place for regulating the recovering of Caesar's unpublished *acta*, however much an outraged Cicero claims otherwise.

During this period of Antony's consulship, it is worth observing, he did not always get his own way. We learn from a passing remark in the *Second Philippic* that Antony recommended holding elections for censors—Cicero claims he urged his uncle to stand for the office—but nothing came of the proposition. The symbolic value of holding a census, solemnity eminently suitable to marking a new beginning for the republic, was obvious and, Antony doubtless assumed, attractive to everyone. But a majority in the senate must have seen it differently. And one can understand why. The political scene remained too fraught for rehabilitating a magistracy invested with the power to stigmatize any citizen's public standing and capable of pruning the senate's membership. Too many senators knew they were vulnerable to exclusion, and the prospect of fresh contentiousness fuelled by bitterness was ultimately deemed too dangerous to allow. Nothing suggests Antony persisted. He knew it was useful occasionally to take no for an answer and perhaps he even agreed with the objections put before him. Or he may have intended from the start only to remind small-fry senators how much they owed to his consulship.[80]

Cicero's criticisms of Antony's exploitation of Caesar's papers and his administration of the city were shared by others. Pansa, we learn, was outraged over Antony's rehabilitation of Deiotarus and Sextus Cloelius—or so he told Cicero, who was clever enough to believe Pansa may only have been saying what the orator wanted to hear.[81] It soon became clear to Cicero that Hirtius' relationship with Antony was also becoming strained. He protested to Cicero that both the Liberators and Antony were dangerous men, and in May expressed fear of Antony's violence. Hirtius also worried that his deteriorating relationship with Antony was damaging his reputation among Caesar's veterans.[82] As for Balbus, he complained to Cicero that he was becoming unpopular in certain quarters and in reaction to this asseverated the depth of his friendship with Antony—in the obvious expectation Cicero would pass the word along to others. Cicero, however, did not believe him. Quite the reverse.[83] He knew how close Balbus and Hirtius had become.[84] What anyone in the aristocracy had to say about Antony outside the presence of Cicero we can rarely recover. But these traces suffice to make it clear how men who had been leading figures during Caesar's regime were increasingly alienated from Antony. This is in some ways unsurprising and must not be attributed entirely to their dissatisfaction over Antony's cordial relationship with the Liberators. Antony, at this time, was going from success to success, and his eminence could only engender envy and contention. Men like Pansa and Hirtius were his rivals and so were cautiously keen to find ways to spike Antony's domination in politics. This Cicero recognized, but he did not intend to take the bait offered him. As he made it clear to Tiro, in a letter composed in late May, he intended to preserve his long-standing friendship with Antony.[85] He made this same point, if more obliquely, to Atticus.[86]

Veterans

In April Antony carried another law, also based on Caesar's *acta*, which favoured the dictator's veterans by making fresh allocations of land and establishing new colonies in Campania. This law, the *lex Antonia de coloniis in agros deducendis*, Cicero later claimed was carried in contravention of the auspices and by way of violence—and in 43 the law was abrogated and replaced by a new law introduced by Pansa.[87] At the time, however, neither Cicero nor anyone else objected. The orator does not include it among the measures he denounces as forgeries. In order to execute the terms of this law, and extract credit for it, Antony left Rome near the end of the month and travelled to Campania. There he supervised the foundation of a colony at Casilinum, even going so far as to plough with his own hand the sacred furrow defining its territory. This was the new home for the Eighth Legion, men Antony commanded at Pharsalus. He also entered Samnium, there to reassure veterans settled in the region, including the Eleventh Legion and the Fifth *Alaudae*, the Larks. Everywhere he went, however, Antony encouraged veterans to remain battle-ready, warning them that their entitlements continued to face political obstacles in Rome.[88]

If we can believe Cicero, Antony's journey to Campania constituted another orgy of graft and sensuality. In his *Second Philippic*, the orator fustigates Antony for lavishly doling out public lands to his cronies, including actors and actresses, his drinking companions, his physician, even his tutor in rhetoric. This reprehensible largesse, Cicero bemoans, was made more disgraceful by Antony's incessant indulging in gluttony and drunkenness—calumnies that can only be described as predictable. Antony, in Cicero's account, is too distracted by his vices to get things right: when establishing colonies, he makes one legal or ceremonial blunder after another. Vituperation of this kind is unremarkable and implausible. What is rather more surprising is that Cicero does not complain or worry about Antony's alleged formation at this time of a bodyguard of perhaps as many as 6,000 men.[89] According to Appian, he was authorized to do this by the senate, but that is unlikely. Nor need we conclude that Antony formally enrolled a personal force composed of veterans. More likely, he was instead rallying men to join him in Rome, where they could support his designs and preserve their rights.

By early May, Cicero had heard rumours that Antony was urging veterans to make their way to the capital. Their presence in the city, he was told, posed a fresh danger to the Liberators and their sympathizers.[90] In reaction, Brutus and Cassius wrote to Antony expressing their surprise over these developments. They, like Cicero, show no awareness that Antony was allowed by the senate to assemble any kind of official unit. Instead, it was obvious to them, Antony was recruiting a personal following the purpose of which was unclear but disconcerting. This was, after all, a very different Antony from the champion of concord and the loyal servant of the senate whose statesmanship in Rome had led them to hope for a stable future. In their letter, consequently, the Liberators expressed disquiet over Antony's reliability: they ask whether Amatius' altar will be restored, whether they can be confident of their safety, and whether Antony shares their commitment to *libertas*. In a long letter, they finally come to the point: why are veterans amassing in the city?[91]

Antony's Programme for 1 June

Antony believed he needed muscle. Before he left Rome, he announced a meeting of the senate for 1 June.[92] On that occasion he intended to introduce two proposals, neither of which relied on Caesar's papers. Instead, each represented an independent legislative initiative. His first proposition called for an agrarian law which Antony planned to promulgate in partnership with Dolabella, the *lex Antonia Cornelia agraria*: this measure established a commission of seven men to oversee new distributions of land to veterans and the urban poor.[93] The second, a *lex de provinciis consularibus*, was a tribunician proposal—or perhaps we have to do with two tribunician proposals—designed to alter the terms of the consuls' provincial assignments. It extended the length of Antony's and Dolabella's provincial commands from two years to five, an extraordinary break from Caesar's standing legislation on provinces; this law also permitted Antony to exchange Macedonia, his original provincial assignment, for Cisalpine Gaul; furthermore, it allowed him to retain command of the legions currently stationed in Macedonia.[94]

It is not difficult to explain the consuls' motives for wanting to carry an agrarian law, which could only enhance their popularity with veterans and the urban *plebs*. It was this measure which Antony employed as a spur in urging Caesar's veterans to come to Rome, almost certainly by making a case that without their presence the law might fail to pass. In their letter to Antony, Brutus and Cassius make it clear they are aware of this claim: they describe it as complete rubbish.[95] And rightly so, since there was little doubt but that the measure would be carried. It was nonetheless an effective ploy. Antony also intended to bring his law affirming Caesar's *acta* to a vote in early June: this, too, was an inducement for the veterans, whose stake in this measure was obvious. He wanted veterans in Rome and in serious numbers because he believed he needed staunch supporters, not for the sake of the agrarian law or the measure on Caesar's *acta*, but because he was certain there would be opposition to the plebiscite awarding him Cisalpine Gaul.

The *lex de provinciis consularibus* was certain to be provocative. It altered Caesar's *acta* by shifting Antony from Macedonia to another province and it furnished both consuls an exemption from Caesar's *lex de provinciis*, which limited governorships for ex-consuls to two years. These aspects of the bill did not render the measure illegitimate: it was a fundamental principle of the republic that the sovereign people could not be constrained by any prior legislation. But it was certain to draw animadversions, especially from Antony's rivals. The attraction of holding an extended command was obvious: each consul thereby received greater scope for winning glory or personal enrichment, and each consul was shielded from prosecution by his enemies for five years. Paramount though he was, Antony was aware of the extent and in some case the intensity of his political opposition, nor did he harbour any illusions regarding the steadfastness of the senate's majority. A five-year command supplied him with valuable protection after he laid down his consulship. The events of recent years, however, had revealed how precarious even legal safeguards could become should a proconsul be attacked by powerful enemies, and by now Antony expected unfriendliness from the consuls of 43. Which is why he preferred nearby Gaul to distant Macedonia.

By joining forces with Dolabella both in the agrarian law and in pushing for these new provincial arrangements, Antony forged a useful alliance. Neither man intended to retire from public life nor was either willing to be dispensed with by Hirtius or Pansa or any future leaders of the senate. Through this law they installed themselves as major figures for the next five years. The *lex de provinciis* was bold, and soon it became central in the complaints of Antony's enemies, but it could not have come as a complete surprise: the atmosphere of Roman politics, efforts at reconciliation notwithstanding, remained dangerously contentious, so much so that it was predictable that Antony and Dolabella would take firm measures for their security. The method they chose was hardly a novel one: extraordinary governorships were familiar features of the late republic.

Antony made no secret of his scheme or the tactics he was prepared to employ in securing its success. Doubtless he hoped to forestall any serious resistance. By late April, his designs were well known but it was not until late May that Cicero began to see any danger in them. Decimus Brutus, he worried, would be unwilling to relinquish his province early, which meant there could be violence.[96] Cicero, however, was more concerned about his own safety should he return to a Rome overrun with veterans, and he continued to fret over Cassius and Brutus. But he was by no means alarmed. Later, true, the orator would condemn this measure as Antony's first step toward tyranny. But in May, although Cicero expressed no enthusiasm for the law, he was not deeply bothered by it. In a letter to Tiro, he dismissed it: speaking of Antony and his law, he writes that 'he may do whatever it is he likes about it'.[97] Not everyone, Antony knew, was so prepared to be complaisant. For that reason, he anticipated widespread opposition from all sides. But he was determined to put up a fight.

Octavian

Octavian, as we shall call him, began life as Gaius Octavius, the son of a rich new man who reached the praetorship before succumbing to illness.[98] His wife, Atia, was the daughter of a modest senator who married a sister of Caesar before Caesar was a great man. This was a heritage any noble might despise. Caesar, however, was not distracted by his grand-nephew's origins, and it is obvious he found much to like in him. Octavian was destined, as we have seen, to hold the office of master of the horse at the age of twenty-one, an appointment which cannot be dismissed as simple nepotism. Sickly and spotty Octavian may have been, but he was also calculating and ruthless, a man directed by steely realism and yet bold to take big risks.[99] He was also, notwithstanding Antony's later calumnies, brave. Imperial writers, however, almost uniformly exaggerate his genius. It is easy, for instance, to forget that Octavian's meteoric rise in politics also interrupted his academic studies: of the two, Antony was, in traditional terms, by far the more cultured man.[100] Octavian, as time would tell, was the luckier man, though in most respects he made his own luck. Of his many notable abilities, the most valuable, perhaps, was an aptitude for titrating, exactly and usually correctly, the reservoirs of his talent. He knew, or learned quickly, what he was good at, when he needed help, and when he did not. Antony, by contrast, big and beautiful and unfailingly confident, rarely doubted that he had the right stuff for any challenge.

Octavian was in Apollonia on the Adriatic when he learned that he was Caesar's heir. By early April he was in Brundisium, where he was warmly greeted. Although only nineteen, he was, by dint of his inheritance, an instantly glamorous figure— and honouring him was a natural expression of esteem for Caesar's memory. From Brundisium he travelled to Puteoli, where he took residence in his stepfather's house next door to Cicero. The orator found him personable but worried he was falling under the influence of men who were hostile to the Liberators but also dead set against the current regime—men like Hirtius, who, as we have seen, distrusted Brutus and Cassius *and* Antony.[101] Sometime in early May, Octavian moved on to Rome, where he appeared before Gaius Antonius, who in Brutus' absence had taken on the responsibilities of the urban praetor. There he formally accepted his inheritance.[102]

According to the terms of Caesar's will, Octavian could receive his share of the estate only on the condition that he accept Caesar's name. This legal requirement, the technical term for which is *condicio nominis ferendi* ('the action of taking a name'), is often—and misleadingly—denominated testamentary adoption. This action, however, must not be confused with actual adoption. When a Roman was adopted, by way of *adoptio* or *adrogatio*, legally he left his family altogether—he abandoned its sacraments, the tribe of his birth, and the like—and was placed under the *patria postestas*, the legal authority, of a new father into whose family he was entirely assimilated. The *condicio nominis ferendi*, however, was something entirely different: the heir did not fall under the *patria potestas* of the testator for the obvious reason that the testator was dead, nor did he enter the testator's family. Nor did he abandon his native tribe or native sacraments. Instead, he simply took on the testator's name, thereby preserving and memorializing it. In other words, a man who inherited by way of *condicio nominis ferendi* did not become the son of the testator.[103]

Octavian, however, claimed otherwise. Gaius Octavius, by way of accepting his inheritance, legally became Gaius Iulius Caesar Octavianus, hence the habit of referring to him as Octavian. But his name was now indeed *Caesar*, a label he deployed to its fullest social and political advantage. But this young Caesar did more than that: he posed as if he were Caesar's son by adoption and referred to the departed dictator as his father—a transparent falsehood for anyone conversant with Roman law. Octavian did not make this misleading assertion because he was unaware of the difference between adoption and the *condicio nominis ferendi*. It was rather because he was certain that ordinary Romans had no notion of this distinction. And why should they? It was not a legal procedure to which the common man was likely to turn. And, so far as we know, Octavian was the first Roman to lie about it. The urban *plebs* and Caesar's veterans accepted his claim without hesitation. Members of Rome's elite knew better, but more than a few of them believed it was in their interests to humour this young Caesar if his popularity as a young Caesar could be exploited in resisting Antony. In the end, as we shall see, even Cicero embraced the fiction. And there can be no underestimating how valuable it became to Octavian not merely to be known as Caesar but deemed

Caesar's son. Dishonest though it was, it was a brilliant stroke. Indeed, it was not long before Antony bitterly complained that Octavian was 'a boy who owed everything to a name'.[104]

As Caesar's heir, Octavian could not fail to be popular, and he sustained his appeal by promising to meet all the terms of his inheritance, including the dictator's gifts to the public. Lucius Antonius, as tribune, invited Octavian to address the people at a *contio*. Cicero, when he heard about it, found the speech upsetting. In it, Octavian doubtless drew attention to his devotion to Caesar, whom he now described as his father, perhaps by pledging himself to exacting vengeance. The Golden Rule did not obtain in Roman society: vengeance, within suitable bounds, was an act of virtue. When undertaken on behalf of one's father, it was the epitome of *pietas*, the profound loyalty every good Roman felt towards his family. A good son should want to punish anyone who had wronged his father, and Octavian was determined to play the part of a good son. In that vein, he also announced that he would sponsor the celebration of the *Ludi Victoriae Caesaris*, the Games in honour of *Victoria Caesaris*, Caesar's Victoriousness, which had been instituted in the previous year. It appears that in this same speech he expressed his gratitude to Matius and Rabirius Postumus, rich knights whose generosity would guarantee the event's splendour.[105] In so doing, Octavian made clear his cooperation with a circle of former Caesarians who were now alienated from Mark Antony.

By the end of the year, Octavian was a major figure in Roman affairs. In the end, his victory over Antony at the battle of Actium made him master of the Roman world. These later realities influence nearly all later accounts of the early months of his career in Rome, in which Octavian is regarded as central to the political events surrounding him. In these narratives we find a recurring dynamic: Octavian acts, Antony reacts. Consequently, even in some modern treatments, this phase of 44 is often viewed almost exclusively as a contest between Antony and Octavian over the political legacy of Caesar. A very different picture emerges from Cicero's correspondence from this period and his first two *Philippics*. There Octavian makes more than one appearance, but always as a person of interest, never as a serious political operator. Admittedly Cicero's letters at this time are less informed regarding events in Rome than we should like—he was away from the capital from 7 April until 31 August—but the orator always strained himself to remain *au courant* and his *Philippics* were composed in Rome and with the benefit of hindsight.[106] As we shall see, Octavian, from the time he arrived in Italy, became deeply involved with prominent men who, although they had been close to Caesar, were now rivals of Antony and, increasingly, his opposition. In Octavian they found a precious focus for expressing a political posture which offered an alternative to Antony and Dolabella. Octavian, by way of his cooperation with this circle, managed to make himself a visible figure in public affairs.[107] But this took time, and it is a mistake to exaggerate Octavian's influence on Antony's actions, even after Caesar's heir put himself at the head of an army.

Soon after his return to Rome, Antony welcomed Octavian within the confines of his gardens on the Campus Martius. We cannot know exactly what passed between them—Appian furnishes each participant with a long, fictitious speech—but it is certain their meeting ended badly and everyone soon knew about it.[108] They disagreed over the condition of Caesar's estate and the extent of Antony's interference in it.

Antony emphasized the need for an audit which could separate out the public funds Caesar had allowed to fall into his private holdings. As for the rest of Octavian's inheritance, that was subject to various legal claims which for obvious reasons had not been advanced during Caesar's dictatorship: Antony was unwilling to offer any assistance in these matters and was later accused of exacerbating Octavian's difficulties.[109] This disaccord is not easy to explain. Gaius and Lucius, after all, had been helpful to Octavian. Why not Antony? It is probably true that Antony and Octavian rubbed each other the wrong way, but each was sophisticated enough to look past that. It is possible that Antony, having seized moneys that Octavian had a right to recover, simply refused to do so, an abuse of his authority as consul and a violation of basic decency. Alternatively, Octavian's claims, however sincere, may have been ungrounded but nonetheless sparked a sharp disagreement. Or, if Octavian was already collaborating with Antony's enemies, the entire affair may have been tactical on his part, a move to justify his joining the resistance against Antony's consulship. At the time, however, this quarrel and its stakes were of minor importance to Antony. For Octavian, by contrast, this confrontation played a significant part in the shaping of his political identity in Rome.

Antony's New Laws

Octavian was not yet central to anyone's concerns.[110] Attention was instead fixed on the meeting of the senate set for 1 June. By late May, Rome was teeming with veterans, all of them out of temper with the Liberators and their sympathizers. Nor were they pleased with anyone who exhibited opposition against Antony—even if they were former officers of Caesar, as Hirtius complained to Cicero.[111] Anxious senators, worried over likely disturbances, decided to leave the capital. Cicero, too, wary of disruption or violence, stayed away.[112] Nor did the consuls-designate attend. Antony, it appears, had originally intended that the senate endorse the proposed *lex de provinciis* as a sign of unity before he took the bill before the people. His supporters in the body came prepared, ready to draw exaggerated attention to the unrest in Gaul precipitated by Caesar's assassination and complain, unfairly, of Decimus' unfitness.[113] Lucius Antonius certainly prepared a speech attacking him.[114] But when the senate was so poorly attended on the day, a clear sign Antony's tactics had alienated many, he abandoned his original design and turned to the staunch support of the veterans.[115] Clearly, he had underestimated the level of senatorial disapproval stimulated by this bill or by his marshalling of veteran muscle.

The *lex de provinciis consularibus* was carried by the plebeian assembly on 3 June, not without violence and not, as events would show, without incurring disapproval in the senate.[116] Cicero later denounced the measure for irregularities in its passage, but at the time he preferred to ignore any of that and instead exploit the law for purposes of his own. Because he wanted to move freely and securely and because he wanted the legal protections enjoyed by anyone away from Rome for the sake of the republic, Cicero immediately asked Dolabella to appoint him his legate. The consul complied, and the orator expressed satisfaction over his possession of this privilege for the next five years.[117] Also on 3 June, Antony's law affirming Caesar's *acta* was carried.[118] Next, but on a different day, came the consuls' agrarian law. Its passage provoked no con-temporary comment, but later, in his *Fifth Philippic*, Cicero thundered against it: it was, he declaimed, passed with violence and amid a tempest, an inauspicious event which permanently vitiated the law. And perhaps the weather was bad on that day, though one is suspicious. In the same speech Cicero makes the same complaint, in nearly the same language, about another Antonian law, his law on juries, which was carried in September but also, if the orator is to be believed, during a raging storm.[119] Both this portent and any attending violence, however, went unremarked at the time. Instead, we learn that Lucius Antonius, who was appointed to lead the Commission of Seven which administered this law, wrote to Cicero assuring him that his properties would not be affected by it.[120]

Antony now turned again to the Liberators. He understood their reluctance to return to the city—indeed, he and his brother had been helpful in making their ab-sence possible—but he was no longer willing to tolerate their presence in Italy, which he viewed as disruptive. Antony was not the only one in Rome who worried about their designs, as we can see in a letter sent to Cicero by Hirtius, and it was in any case unseemly for two praetors to spend their year in office sitting on their hands.[121] The senate met on 5 June and carried a decree which assigned Brutus and Cassius respon-sibility for supervising the city's grain supply during the remainder of this year: Brutus was to look after shipments from Asia, Cassius Sicily. As part of this same decree, they also received provincial assignments for the next year; these were Crete for Brutus and the Cyrenaica for Cassius.[122] For nobles of praetorian rank, everyone recognized, the grain commissions were demeaning. At the same time, even Cicero conceded the Liberators needed to do *something*.[123] The matter became controversial and both men, although willing to accept their provinces, strenuously rejected the commission re-garding the grain supply. Brutus' mother, Servilia, promised to have it removed from the decree.[124] She apparently promised more than she could deliver: it appears this decree was still in effect on 1 August, as we shall see below.

Cicero reacted variously to Antony's *lex de provinciis consularibus*. In writing to Atticus, he foresaw war if Antony attempted to cut short Decimus Brutus' command. To Tiro, however, he expressed indifference, as we have seen: 'he may do whatever it is he likes about it'.[125] After the law was carried, again as we have seen, Cicero was quick to make use of it for his own advantage. Jeremiads went undelivered. Others, however, were much angrier, or at least so it appears: matters are rarely clear during this period when Cicero does not talk about them. Decimus Brutus can only have been outraged at what he must have regarded as ill-treatment. Cassius and Brutus probably shared Decimus' opinion, especially since they believed Antony was now fobbing them off with demeaning chores. It was about this time, according to Appian's admittedly con-fused account of things, that the two Liberators began making contingency plans for an uprising should violence be required.[126] Appian was onto something: by August Antony publicly alleged that both Cassius and Brutus had long been engaged in sub-versive machinations.[127] As for Antony's rivals, they recognized the law on provinces for what it was—and doubtless they worked hard in rousing resentment on the part of others. It was not difficult for them to find an audience: that many in the senate were disturbed by Antony's conduct becomes clear to us in August, when Lucius Piso, by no means an opponent of Antony, delivered a stinging reproach, an event to which we shall return. Sentiments of this kind were clearly circulating in June and afterwards, even if they get no more than the odd notice in our sources. By the end of June, for instance, Cicero learned that his nephew, hitherto an ardent supporter of Antony, had broken with the consul over behaviour he regarded as autocratic.[128]

The *lex de provinciis consularibus*, certainly the exchange of provinces, was overreach and, because it furnished his rivals with a conspicuous focus for their resentment, probably a political error. Not that Antony saw it at the time. Indeed, he must have believed that his recent legislative programme had been a complete success. In a letter composed on 20 June, Cicero puts it to Atticus that Antony is well and truly in charge of Rome. He has reduced politics into two camps, Cicero observes, the weak and the wicked. Right-thinking citizens, he laments, despair of the republic, the Liberators are useless, and for himself he sees little choice but to depart for Greece.[129] We must reject Cicero's reductive binary, but it is instructive for us that, from his perspective, Antony was very strong indeed. He will not have been the only Roman who was certain Antony had attained a dominant, perhaps unassailable role in Roman affairs, a pre-eminence his law now guaranteed to continue over the next five years.

The Games of July

As urban praetor, Brutus was responsible for celebrating the Games of Apollo, the *ludi Apollinares*. Because he refused to come into the city, he had no choice but to leave the presidency of the games, and their administration on the spot, to Gaius Antonius. Nevertheless, Brutus took great pains and went to enormous expense to make them a success. He very much hoped, through these festivities, to win back the admiration of the public. He also intended to use these games to advertise his traditional republicanism. In all notices for the *ludi* he intended to employ *Quinctilis*, the old name for *Iulius*, July, and to underline his commitment to *libertas* he decided to stage Accius' classic historical drama, *Brutus*, a drama which told the story of the founding of the free republic. He was foiled, however, by Gaius, who replaced Brutus' *Quinctilis* with *Iulius* and substituted Accius' *Tereus*, a mythological tragedy, for the *Brutus*. These disappointments aside, the games went off well and his name was much applauded by the audience.[130] Still, he was not so reassured that he resolved to return to Rome.

Soon after this, sometime around 18 July, further friction erupted between Antony and Octavian.[131] The particulars are far from clear. An opening in the tribunate, perhaps owing to the death of the poet Cinna, occasioned an election. Octavian participated in the canvassing as a supporter of a certain Flaminius. Soon, however, it appears there were crowds urging Octavian himself to stand for the office, unlikely if not impossible even for a teenager so ambitious as Caesar's heir. Nevertheless, some later writers believed that he indeed hoped to be made a tribune. Whatever actually took place, this was not a minor event: it prompted a *contio* by Antony. A copy of his speech was later delivered to Cicero, who liked it. He does not say why. Perhaps Antony dilated on constitutional proprieties, perhaps he abominated public disturbances. It is difficult to imagine that Cicero cared one way or another what Antony had to say about Octavian, if he had much at all to say about him. This episode eludes us, unfortunately, but plainly it created a stir and was later viewed as one more factor in the development of hard feelings between Antony and the young Caesar.

In the same month, commencing on 20 July, Octavian produced the *Ludi Victoriae Caesaris*. These games were lavish—Octavian's sponsors were wealthy men—and showcased the young Caesar's claim to be the dictator's adopted son. This year was the first in which these games took place in July, a change doubtless introduced by Caesar in conjunction with Antony's legislation making *Quinctilis* into *Iulius*, timing which only enhanced their significance for Caesar's heir and threw up an unavoidable contrast with the *ludi* produced by the Liberator Brutus.[132] Like Brutus, Octavian did not get everything his own way. He wanted to exhibit Caesar's golden chair, but Antony refused to allow it.[133] This omission, however, did nothing to detract from the games' splendour or their appeal to the public. And it was in this atmosphere, charged with celebration of the dictator's career, that a comet appeared in the sky, an apparition that was subsequently taken as a sign of Caesar's apotheosis.[134]

In his autobiography, Augustus drew attention to the appearance of this comet— in Latin a *sidus crinitum*, a long-haired star—which, he says, was visible for seven days.[135] Ordinarily in Greece and Rome a comet was seen as a bad omen, but in this instance, so Augustus insists, the people spontaneously saw the phenomenon as a sign of Divus Iulius, Julius the god. Perhaps they were strangely affected by residual feelings stirred by Amatius' altar and the divine honours he offered Caesar. Perhaps they were brought round to this belief by evangelical agents of Octavian and his supporters. The young Caesar certainly encouraged this popular interpretation. And he cleverly evaded the adverse implications of a comet by transforming this *sidus crinitum* into the *sidus Iulium*, the star of Caesar. On a statue of the dictator—according to Dio the statue of Caesar in the temple of Venus Genetrix—Octavian placed an image of a star, a feature destined to become a staple of Divus Iulius' iconography.[136] Later, after Divus Iulius was officially established as a god in 42, Octavian consecrated this statue.[137]

Antony and Dolabella had dragged their feet on the matter of instituting Caesar's divinity as part of Rome's civic religion. At first, this was in reaction to the enormities of Amatius. Thereafter, distracted by their own political struggles, they simply did not deem it a priority. The people, it is clear, had not forgotten and now, prodded by heaven and by men both devoted to the dictator's memory and unfriendly to Antony, they warmed to this remarkable manifestation of their new god, Divus Iulius. For some, it was a signal to Antony and Dolabella that they must act. For Octavian, it was an opportunity to be seized. He quickly began to style himself *divi filius*, son of a god. From a technical perspective, this was no truer that his claim to be Caesar's son, but that hardly mattered. Even Cicero, in his *Philippics*, could lambaste Antony for refusing to fulfil Caesar's sacred honours.[138] By then the orator had become Antony's enemy and was consequently working hard to elevate Octavian over Antony as Caesar's true champion; He knew every reference to Caesar's divinity was an oblique advertisement for the *divi filius*. At the time, however, the *sidus Iulium* did not deeply impress members of the senatorial order: for them, Octavian continued to be no more than a sideshow. Among the public, by contrast, including Caesar's veterans, this was a meaningful moment. And that was a development Antony recognized.

Antony was not unaware that Octavian cooperated closely with his principal rivals. But he could see there was little to gain by antagonizing Caesar's increasingly popular

Fig. 6.2 A denarius (*RRC* 540.1), on the obverse of which appears the head of Octavian and the legend: IMP CAESAR DIVI F III VIR ITER R P C (Imperator Caesar, son of a god, for the second time a triumvir appointed to set the republic in order); on the reverse, there is Caesar, pictured as DIVO IUL (Divus Iulius), in his temple; the *sidus Iulium* appears in the temple's pediment.
Source: British Museum.

heir. A reconciliation, he may have hoped, might neutralize Octavian's utility to his opponents. The medium of rapprochement was a circle of veterans, officers close to Antony but also men known to respect Octavian's devotion to Caesar's memory.[139] They delivered Antony's friendly overtures, a gesture Octavian could scarcely rebuff. The pair made a show of their comity by meeting on the Capitol. Thereafter, we are told, Octavian showed Antony every courtesy. Presumably Antony reciprocated. Doubtless he believed his graciousness, which cost him nothing and could not fail to be well-received by the urban *plebs*, was sufficient—for the moment at least—to foil the machinations of his rivals. Whether or not this spectacle blunted the schemes of his rivals, however, it did nothing to alter Octavian's ambitions: polite though he now may have become in his exchanges with the consul, he continued to collaborate with his enemies.[140]

Antony and the Liberators

During July, Cassius and Brutus issued an edict in which they urged, by way of appeals to concord and liberty, the cancellation of their commission for overseeing the grain supply. Servilia's representations on their behalf, it appears, had gone nowhere. Nevertheless, Antony agreed to allow the topic to be debated by the senate in a meeting scheduled for 1 August. This concession spawned a profusion of misapprehension and rumour. The Liberators became convinced that Antony would remove the offending clause from the decree. Even so, they summoned reinforcements, dispatching letters appealing to ex-consuls and ex-praetors to attend and lend support to their cause. This flurry of communication all on its own led many to expect that the first of August would witness a significant change in Antony's policy. Some influential Romans, including leaders of the municipalities, even believed that Antony was now prepared to alter his position on the provinces and renounce his claim to Gaul.[141]

They were wrong. It soon became clear that Antony was in fact offended by the praetors' decree, which he criticized as a provocation or even a betrayal of his collegiality.[142] On the day, whatever the nature of the debate which took place, the senate's decree was not amended. Nor did Antony offer to relinquish Gaul. Perhaps Antony simply overawed any opposition on both points—it cannot have helped the Liberators' cause that they relied on others to make their case for them—or perhaps, after permitting a discussion of these matters, he refused to call a division. Calpurnius Piso, we know, put a motion before the senate, but what he moved we do not know. We do know that he supported it with a speech that was highly critical of Antony. We also learn from Cicero that Piso received little overt support from other senators and none at all from his fellow consulars. At the same time, his performance was a notable one, not least because he was not an opponent of Antony.[143] Piso was proof there were some in the senate, so early as August, who objected to the consul's increasingly heavy-handed and irregular methods, the focus of which was now his *lex de provinciis consularibus*. At the same time, the senate's silence on this occasion revealed Antony's strength. Cicero certainly noticed that. In a letter of 14 August, he made it clear to Atticus that, although he was returning to Rome, he did not intend throw himself into political affairs. There was, he insisted, no point: 'What could possibly be accomplished? No one supported Piso, did he?'[144]

The tenor of the meeting of 1 August, especially Piso's criticisms, stung Antony. And he blamed Brutus and Cassius for it. Immediately he denounced them in an edict and a public letter. We know of these only by way of the Liberators' joint reply, also a public letter, composed on 4 August.[145] In it, they described Antony's edict as harsh and menacing. They rehearsed his serious accusation that both men had secretly been levying troops, suborning armies, and making untoward arrangements in the provinces; indeed, he complained that this was sedition undertaken in preparation for another civil war. In making these complaints, which the Liberators naturally repudiated, Antony was almost certainly correct, as we shall see, and was known to be correct by at least some members of the political class.[146] Antony's edict also—and remarkably—reproached Brutus and Cassius for their role in Caesar's assassination. Never before, the Liberators observed, had Antony upbraided them in this way. And they were correct: even at Caesar's funeral, when Antony manipulated the people's grief in order to intimidate the Liberators, he did not directly traduce them. In August, however, he was taking a radically different tack.

Antony's edict constituted a distinct change in his public posture, but we must be cautious in our interpretation of it. There is no reason to conclude that, by raising the matter of the conspiracy, Antony was now reacting to Octavian and his circle of friends. Nor does anything in the Liberators' letter suggest that the Ides of March was actually central to Antony's attack on them. It was instead a notable new wrinkle in his rhetoric. In depicting Brutus and Cassius as men intent on civil war, Antony, it is probable, calumniated their motives on the Ides of March: domination, not freedom, he now claimed, had been their true goal. Which is why, in their response, Brutus and Cassius were at pains to emphasize their role as true liberators. Antony, they insisted, owed them his freedom. And because they are free men, they underline, they will not deny the claims of their *dignitas* nor be cowed by a consul's threats. They express a longing to see Antony thrive in a republic that is free—*in libera re publica*—but underline what for them remains a fundamental principle: 'we value our freedom far more highly than your friendship', which was exactly the Liberators' attitude toward Caesar when they formed their conspiracy, an implied threat followed by an explicit warning: 'you should think hard not about how long Caesar lived but how briefly he reigned as a despot'.[147]

Antony, as we have seen, accused Brutus and Cassius of making seditious plans. Of their schemes we possess only hints, but they are several. In a letter written sometime in the middle of September, for instance, Cicero tells Cassius that he and Brutus are the republic's only hope and exhorts them to persevere in making plans worthy of the glory they have already garnered.[148] Before August was out, both men departed Italy. Before leaving they issued a final edict in which, unsurprisingly, they professed to prefer exile to conflict and assured the Roman people they would do nothing which could provoke a civil war.[149] But they did not retire into exile, and this exit, punctuated by self-righteousness and high dudgeon, signalled the impossibility of a reconciliation with Antony. The Liberators then sailed away, ostensibly to take up their commissions overseeing the grain supply but in reality, as events would soon show, they aimed at seizing illegitimate authority in the eastern provinces—the base from which they accumulated funds and organized armies as preparation for a civil war.[150]

Power to the People

In August, Antony posted notices for two new laws, which were scheduled to come before the people for ratification in mid-September. One was a measure reforming the composition of Roman juries, the *lex Antonia iudicaria*, the other permitted anyone condemned on charges of political violence, *vis*, or treason, *maiestas*, the right to appeal the verdict before a popular assembly, the *lex Antonia de provocatione*.[151] With these laws, Antony endeavoured to cultivate the affections of the urban *plebs* and the more prosperous classes both in Rome and in the municipalities of Italy. Most of what we know about these measures we know by way of Ciceronian denunciations. Each was later undone when Antony's laws were abrogated in 43 and neither was rehabilitated at the time. The *lex iudicaria*, it appears, was later restored by Antony, after the establishment of the triumvirate.

The *lex de provocatione* invoked a fundamental Roman liberty, the right of appeal, and did so by way of resurrecting the ancient and, by the late republic, nearly obsolete practice of a trial before the people.[152] *Vis* and *maiestas* were crimes against the Roman people, and for that reason, so Antony will have argued, it was appropriate for the Roman people and not the established courts to act as the final judge over any citizen's guilt or innocence. This law, because it empowered the Roman people, was patently populist and therefore was intended to be popular. Cicero disliked it, and doubtless others did as well, but it was unassailable ideologically—the majesty of the Roman people was supreme—and was certain to pass. This law's recognition of popular sovereignty, Antony hoped, would earn its author gratitude from the urban *plebs*.

And doubtless he was right. Had the law not been abrogated, however, it very likely would have become nearly unworkable. Accusations of *vis* and *maiestas* were often politically motivated, and the dynamics involved in any trial before the people could only exacerbate its political aspects.[153] Everyone convicted of either crime would naturally appeal the verdict. Trials before the people, unfortunately, were notoriously susceptible to demagoguery or violence: *contiones* could be packed with supporters or enemies of the appellant and voting in assemblies could be disrupted, preventing or forestalling any final verdict.[154] These unattractive complications were of less concern to Antony, it appears, than the sheer popularity he could acquire by championing the political authority of the *plebs*.

The *lex iudicaria* attracted strong opposition from figures who, like Cicero, were jealous of the privileges enjoyed by senators and equestrians and did not wish to see interlopers intruded into Roman juries. A *lex Aurelia iudicaria* of 70 divided Roman juries into three panels, one drawn from an album of senators, a second composed of equestrians, and a third taken from the ranks of very rich men who remained outside the equestrian centuries and whom Romans denominated *tribuni aerarii*. In 46 Caesar introduced a *lex iudicaria* which eliminated the panel of *tribuni aerarii*.[155] Antony's law once again established a third panel for juries, but now that panel was to be drawn from an album which included men from the First Class. This census class lay just below the equestrian order, and therefore included very wealthy Romans comparable to the *tribuni aerarii*, but its membership also reached down to the level of anyone whose wealth was valued at 40,000 sesterces or more. Some members of the First Class, then, were *much* less wealthy than a knight. Still, even men at the humbler end of this class were prosperous, true even if Cicero can, when addressing the senate, describe all of them in disparaging terms. Collectively, because eighty of the Centuriate Assembly's 193 centuries were populated by the First Class, this slice of Roman society was enormously influential and consequently was assiduously cultivated by Rome's political class.[156] And from the perspective of the bulk of Rome's citizens, all members of the First Class were rich—not rich in the way an Atticus or Cicero was rich but secure enough to be enviable. In philosophical vein, Cicero does not hesitate to deem this class wealthy, or wealthy enough to be on the right side of the social order: in his *On the Republic*, he praises the design of the Centuriate Assembly because 'the greatest number of votes lies in the power not of the multitude but of the rich', by which he means the eighteen equestrian centuries *and* the eighty centuries of the First Class.[157]

By way of his *lex iudicaria*, it has been suggested, Antony sought to pack the courts with men so grateful to him that he and his allies would become almost invulnerable to a conviction. This is what Cicero thought, and Antony certainly did not fail to think about these advantages even if he was, for the next five years, legally immune from prosecution. The orator also claimed that Antony's law aimed at making him popular with the soldiery, and he was right to recognize that many ex-centurions were wealthy enough to be members of the First Class. But Antony's law was more ambitious than that. The *lex iudicaria* conferred a notable new honour on men of the First Class. In Rome, all who made it into the album of jurors gained an important social distinction, in gratitude for which they were expected to become Antony's partisans in elections. Others in the First Class, including men who constituted the elite in the municipalities, shared in the dignity conferred on their kind by Antony's law even if they were not included in the album for jury-selection.

Dignity by way of Antony's law extended beyond Italy. One of Antony's jurors was Lysiades of Athens. He was an eminent man, a former archon in his city, and the son of a famous philosopher. His Roman citizenship is unsurprising, and not even Cicero is critical of the man himself: he objects to his foreignness. He is less kind to another of Antony's eastern friends, Cydas of Crete. He was certainly an Antonian connection and in the aftermath of Philippi, when Cydas held the office of Cretarch, Antony put him to work governing the island.[158] There may have been other distinguished Greeks whom Antony enrolled, which was doubtless a reflex of his Hellenism and an exercise of his patronage wherever he and his family had interests—but it was also a response to the presence in the east of the Liberators. Naturally Cicero has little to say about that. He mentions these men both as a means of exciting the xenophobic tendencies of some in his audience and to distract them from the central focus of Antony's law, the prosperous men in Rome and Italy most senators regarded as sound citizens, the *boni*.

In endeavouring to win over prosperous men up and down the country, Antony operated in close cooperation with his brother Lucius. The tribune, through his administration of the Board of Seven executing Antony's *lex agraria*, had won appreciation from Caesar's veterans: a corps of senior military tribunes erected a statue in his honour.[159] But Lucius also acquired gratitude from municipal property holders whom he shielded from losses, a category of elites which included members of the First Class.[160] Cicero says otherwise: he fustigates Lucius for savage confiscations, comparing his depredations to Hannibal's.[161] But even he must concede the tribune's popularity with the municipalities. In his *Sixth Philippic*, he grumbles that Lucius was awarded a statue, dedicated to him as their patron, by all thirty-five of Rome's tribes. The equestrian order, too, honoured Lucius as its patron. And so did the denizens of the Ianus Medius, the location in the Forum where business transactions were carried out. These financiers, all of them prosperous but not all of them knights, also put up a statue which advertised Lucius as their patron.[162]

For Cicero, these expressions of gratitude rankled, but they reveal the extent of the goodwill won by Lucius from men at more than one social level, including those who, like military tribunes, tribal leaders, and businessmen, were conspicuous in the First Class. That he was honoured by the thirty-five tribes was especially significant: each tribe had its headquarters in Rome, and each tribe had its own officers, most of whom were prosperous men from the municipalities, some of them equestrian, others drawn from the First Class.[163] The tribune's cultivation of men like these was not novel—all Roman politicians did it—but his success was remarkable, which is why Cicero was so bothered by it. It is against this background that Antony's *lex iudicaria* must be viewed. Yes, it gave him clout in the courts, but it was also designed to complement his brother's exertions and add to the Antonian gratitude each had garnered through the operations of the Board of Seven.

Antony's *lex iudicaria* and *lex provocatione* were each of them laws that, notwithstanding the innovations they introduced, relied on highly traditional notions of the relationship between politicians and their public in Rome. Antony sought to win over the urban *plebs*—a predictable move in Roman politics—but he did so not by way of offering financial entitlements of the kind that disturbed Roman elites by rather by enhancing the people's honour. Similarly, his judiciary law conferred dignity on the prosperous classes who fell just outside the ranks of senators and equestrians. The gratitude Antony hoped to gain by these laws could be useful to him only if the normal operations of the republic—elections, for example, or robust activity on the part of the courts—remained efficacious in the future. These were the proposals of a man bent on traditional, republican eminence—not autocracy.

But how many of his contemporaries recognized that? By the time Antony carried these laws, his enemies professed to fear his ambitions and begrudged him any future as governor of Cisalpine Gaul. They failed or refused to recognize that, although his administration had often been heavy-handed, sometimes disconcertingly impulsive, and invariably self-serving, Antony did not aim at absolute power. Cicero, without question, was convinced that Antony posed an existential threat to the Liberators, whose security he increasingly identified with the well-being of the republic. Others in the senate, less alarmed, at the very least eyed Antony suspiciously. Hirtius and Pansa were ambitious men and unfriendly to the Liberators, but they did not excite Cicero's anxiety or anger in the way Antony did. Nor did the young Caesar. All of them were better than Antony in making a good show of expressing esteem for Cicero, respect which stirred and renewed the orator's passion for statesmanship. He was also the Liberators' most influential friend in the senate. These variegated parties had in common their hostility against Antony and in their encouragement of Cicero they found a willing and highly effective ally. Much can depend on personalities. By the end of the summer, Cicero and Antony found little to like in one another. An outbreak of open conflict between them very quickly incited Antony's enemies to flagrancy, even lawlessness, in their amplified opposition against him. Amid these clashes, Antony's restored republic, such as it was, disintegrated.

VII
Civil fury and civil war

Antony's Precarious Predominance

Antony was not unjustified in believing he had rendered valuable services to the diverse constituencies and political factions which contended with one another in the aftermath of Caesar's assassination. The amnesty of 17 March rescued the conspirators and restored them to senatorial society. By abolishing the office of dictator, Antony signalled Rome's repudiation of autocracy—without besmirching the reputation of Caesar, whose *acta* remained the law of the land. Antony's independent legislation furnished material aid to Caesar's veterans and the urban poor and bestowed honour on the Roman people, especially on its prosperous classes. Nor did he doubt his success: he knew he was adept at upsetting and upstaging his opponents. But his primacy was a precarious one. Even senators who were not his enemies, it appears, were displeased by Antony's threats of force when carrying legislation. Nor were they willing to overlook his profiteering instincts. The sleaze and bullying which Cicero complained about should not be exaggerated but nor should these things be ignored. The likes of Hirtius and Pansa did not care for the likes of Cassius and Brutus, nor did Decimus Brutus trust Octavian. But Antony was stronger than any of them because they could not or would not work together. That condition would not last, although Antony could not foresee it. The catalyst for this reaction was an unexpected and unlikely combination of Octavian's revolutionary brazenness with Cicero's influential, authoritative oratory.

Enmity with Cicero and the Unravelling of the Amnesty

Antony summoned a meeting of the senate for 1 September.[1] At the top of the agenda was the award of a supplication, a thanksgiving to the gods, on behalf of Plancus in recognition of his victories in Raetia, where he had been hailed *imperator*. To this straightforward proposition Antony appended a stipulation which he intended to serve as a kind of litmus test for identifying anyone whose loyalties lay with the Liberators in the east instead of the government in Rome.[2] During Caesar's lifetime, the senate had dignified him by decreeing that to every *supplicatio* a day should be added in his honour. Antony proposed to continue this policy, although there was no precedent for thanking the gods in recognition of a dead man.[3] Many in the senate will have assumed this honour lapsed with the dictator's death. Antony, however, by reviving it and rallying senators around this novel dignity for Caesar, sought to impose a consensus which isolated Brutus and Cassius and their contumacious refusal to take up their proper provincial assignments. Only a man more committed to the Liberators than to concord in the capital, Antony believed, which is to say, only someone staunchly opposed to the current administration in Rome, could vote against it. On the day of the senate's meeting, the motion was carried without opposition. Senatorial resistance, however, could be expressed tacitly by a refusal to participate.[4] This was Cicero's tactic. The orator returned to Rome on the last day of August. On the first of September, however, he excused himself from appearing in the senate on the grounds of fatigue. This was far from obviously the case: on the previous day, when he was welcomed into the city, he had been lively enough.[5] Antony did not fail to grasp that Cicero's absence was deliberate and was outraged by it.

We are not told how Antony formulated his criticisms of Cicero—in his *First Philippic* Cicero describes them as acerbic and harsh—but we do know that Antony threatened to punish Cicero by demolishing his mansion, his *domus*. Cicero reports this in terms so literal he can mock them—would not a fine, he suggests, have been a more suitable proposal and easier to execute?—but that is an obvious rhetorical deformation.[6] It is more likely that, in disparaging Cicero, Antony drew unflattering attention to his continuing sympathy for Caesar's assassins and, in doing so, reminded senators of a humiliating episode from Cicero's past: the destruction of his house by the tribune Clodius Pulcher in 58, when the orator was driven into exile for putting citizens to death without a trial. It is not hard to see why Antony might have brought the matter up: Cicero's treatment of the Catilinarians, like the deed of the tyrannicides, was a deadly contest over the real meaning of *libertas*. When Cicero was expelled from the city, a shrine to the goddess Libertas was erected on the site of his ruined house as a commemoration of the orator's punishment for his denial of the Catilinarians' fundamental right to a trial.[7] True, Cicero later regained his citizenship and his property, including his *domus*, but thereafter it remained possible to throw this dark chapter in his face—especially if one wished to discredit the orator's commitment to freedom and to peace. Antony's abuse of Cicero, if in fact he recalled his exile, was harsh indeed.

Antony could easily have accepted Cicero's excuse and overlooked his absence. That he chose not to do so makes it clear how seriously he took Cicero's opposition. That the orator was close to the Liberators presented no difficulty in itself. Antony was sophisticated enough to concede the reality of every aristocrat's complicated network of friendships and attachments. It was Cicero's conspicuous refusal to vote in support of an entirely harmless gesture of devotion to Caesar—a vote transparently designed to do double-duty as an expression of support for Antony's administration—that provoked: Cicero was too important and too influential to be allowed to escape his obligations to the consul who was also his friend. Antony was offended and did nothing to hide his irritation. His criticism now put Cicero in a position in which he must express his loyalties clearly: did his respect for the Liberators trump his friendship with Antony? Cicero responded in a speech which ultimately became his *First Philippic*.

On 2 September, Antony was not present in the senate and the body was presided over by Dolabella. When Cicero rose to speak no one doubted he would react sharply to Antony's remarks on the previous day. His dignity required a response. But many will also have hoped to hear an oration laying out a programme for preserving concord and peace. Instead, Cicero went on the attack. The orator, although he underlined his friendly intentions and conceded the merits of the early months of Antony's administration, nevertheless delivered a scathing review of the consul's recent policies. He pointed to June—specifically the passage of the agrarian law and the *lex de provinciis consularibus*—as a turning point in the year after which followed a flood of noxious legislation.[8]

Cicero expressed consternation over both consuls' motives and interrogated each man by way of an unkind, unfair dilemma: are his actions motivated merely by sleaze and corruption or does he in fact hanker after absolute power?[9] Cicero went on to reject the spirit of the amnesty of 17 March by reminding Antony that Caesar was a man who could be killed not merely with impunity but gloriously, which was another way of insisting that Caesar was indeed a tyrant and the Liberators right in striking him down. In asking Antony whether he preferred to be loved or feared, Cicero evoked sentiments previously expressed in the hostile public letter issued by Brutus and Cassius.[10] He concluded by urging Antony to think about his own future in a republic of men committed to freedom.[11] This was retaliation indeed, in a speech which, putting aside its perfunctory gestures toward comity, was fierce and even threatening. Cicero aligned himself unmistakably with the Liberators against Antony and Dolabella. It was a division that could only be welcome to Antony's rivals in the senate—and it perhaps stimulated a fresh view of Antony on the part of the body's quiet majority. After Cicero's speech, the ex-consul Publius Servilius Isauricus, who was no friend of the Liberators, also spoke out against Antony's recent behaviour.[12]

The senate did not meet again until 19 September—the *Ludi Romani* intervened—at which time Antony delivered his response. Cicero, aware he must be Antony's target on the day, did not attend. We do not possess Antony's speech, but out of Cicero's many reactions to it we can retrieve something of its central features.[13] It was a forceful and effective oration. Cicero's recurring criticisms of it are proof of that. He claims that although Antony invested enormous quantities of time conferring and collaborating with Sextus Clodius, a professional rhetorician, the speech they devised was overworked and poorly delivered: swotted up and vomited out is how Cicero puts it.[14] In many ways, it appears, Antony's oration was standard stuff: it was naturally rife with invective, some of it designed to provoke laughter at Cicero's expense. Antony claimed nobody liked him—even in Pompey's camp the orator's company was avoided because he never stopped prating about the inadequacies of others—and it was owing to this general repugnance, Antony maintained, that Cicero was so rarely remembered in anyone's will. As for Cicero's conceit, that blemish Antony demonstrated by way of citing passages from his speeches and quoting from the epic poem Cicero composed about the achievements of his consulship.

More serious than these barbs was Antony's charge that Cicero betrayed their friendship. Cicero, Antony complained, had long posed as a friend and owing to this pose had received many courtesies and favours. Now, however, and without any legitimate reason for doing so, the orator turned against him. Antony catalogued his past kindnesses. He also read aloud Cicero's letter, written on the topic of Sextus Cloelius' recall from exile, which, as we have seen, was overflowing with fulsome expressions of esteem and affection. All of them were dishonest, Antony protested. In this way, the consul vividly exhibited Cicero's lack of constancy and contempt for the obligations and responsibilities of friendship—the very recriminations to which the Liberators, as we have seen, were vulnerable. Indeed, Antony made Cicero's violation of their friendship both a personal reproach and a political accusation. In this way, Antony aligned him with the conspirators' un-Roman conduct. Which is why Antony also emphasized how Cicero, for all his high-minded speechifying, had made a career of violating the rights of citizens—once again he cited the executions which took place during Cicero's consulship—and Antony went on to argue that, although Cicero could never be so bold as to carry out any deed himself, it was he who was truly responsible for the murder of Clodius Pulcher and the assassination of Caesar.

Antony also reproached the Liberators. Cicero emphasizes that Antony did not actually renounce the amnesty of 17 March in this speech, but the consul certainly rejected the Liberators' claims of innocence. He denied that the *lex sacrata* of Publicola shielded them from a charge of *parricidium*, of murder. Antony evoked Caesar's title *parens patriae*, father of his country, and by deploying the contemporary, visceral sense of *parridicium* he denounced the conspirators—and by extension Cicero—as parricides. In making his case against the so-called Liberators, Antony made much of the moral significance of the title *parens patriae*: because it was a recognition bestowed on a man who preserved the republic's *libertas*, every invocation of Caesar as father of his country was another indictment of the Liberators.[15] The murderers of Caesar, Antony insisted, were *not* liberators because Caesar was not a tyrant. And the abomination of the Ides he now blamed on Cicero.[16] With a flourish, Antony now declared himself Cicero's enemy.[17]

Antony's performance and his open hostility against Cicero were intimidating—and a bold expression of his confidence. The orator responded by boycotting the senate. So, too, did Calpurnius Piso and Servilius Isauricus. But they had few followers. Other consulars preferred to work closely with Antony. Gaius Marcellus, who had been consul in 50, was his ally. The consular Philippus, Octavian's stepfather, also cooperated with the consul.[18] Still, Antony did not cow all opposition. Hirtius and Pansa remained openly defiant, and it would soon become clear that Octavian had not been dormant since his reconciliation with Antony.[19] But the angry consul was not yet worried about these men and in any case preferred to edge them out of public view by directing his energies principally against the Liberators. In public speeches, he pilloried the conspiracy, warned Rome of the dangerous contagion resulting from its sacrilege, and continued to cast Cicero as the author of the crime.[20]

Antony took his case against Cicero and the Liberators before the people. On the Rostra he erected a statue to Caesar on which he inscribed 'deservedly dedicated to the best father' (*parenti optime merito*). Antony will have explained his dedication in a *contio*, but even without knowing what he said Cicero understood the significance of this dedication: the consul was monumentalizing an accusation of *parricidium* against Brutus, Cassius, and even himself. *Parricidium* now became an Antonian catchword for concentrating hostility against the Liberators and undermining their legitimacy—and for calumniating Cicero.[21] According to the orator, Antony now began to speak openly of vengeance.[22] And he began to take official action. He humiliated a legate of Cassius by depriving him of public funds: in doing so, he may even have gone so far as to deprecate Cassius as a public enemy, a *hostis*.[23] Atticus became worried and urged Cicero to arrange an armistice with Antony.[24] The orator rejected this idea nor did he think it feasible. Instead, he remained away from the senate and silent in public. At the same time, he composed his *Second Philippic*, a fictional response to Antony's speech which was read by only a select few before it was more widely published in December.[25] Cicero also embarked on an energetic letter-writing campaign, urging

Brutus and Cassius to take action against Antony and exhorting others to remain ready to defend the republic.[26]

Resistance and Retaliation

While Cicero wrote letters, others among Antony's opponents preferred action of a different kind. Decimus Brutus, after campaigning against various Alpine tribes and receiving an acclamation as *imperator*, applied to the senate for a *supplicatio*. It was only natural for Decimus to seek glory, of course, but by placing this request before the senate he also put the consuls in a spot. They could hardly ignore a victory against foreign foes. Honouring one of the leading Liberators by offering a thanksgiving to the gods, however, clearly ran counter to Antony's strategy of stigmatizing these men as anathema. Decimus did not expect his application to move through the senate smoothly and so wrote to Cicero urging him to return to the body on his behalf. He emphasized that his expedition had made his troops ready to fight in defence of the republic and stressed how, in advancing the case for his *supplicatio*, the orator would be serving the same cause.[27]

Nor was there idleness on the part of Hirtius, Pansa, Octavian, or the members of their circle. On 2 October Antony was summoned to a *contio* convened by Tiberius Cannutius, a tribune of the *plebs* who was among the supporters of the young Caesar. The tribune delivered a blistering attack on the consul—apart from this we know nothing else about his speech—to which Antony reacted by fustigating the Liberators, once more decrying them as parricides and again charging Cicero with responsibility for their crime. Antony even claimed that it was Cicero who incited Cannutius against him, probably by way of remarks which contemptuously dismissed the dignity and independence of this hostile tribune.[28] Only a few days after this, and of much greater moment, there was an attempt on Antony's life, or so Antony alleged.[29] It took place, not in any public setting, but inside his house. The consul suspected Octavian, who naturally denied it.

Because the truth of Antony's allegation eluded all our ancient sources, it eludes us as well. According to Cicero, the masses did not credit Antony's story but many in the aristocracy did: reactions to it varied in accordance with each man's friendliness or hostility towards the consul. The episode disturbed Antony deeply and for good reason. If the assassination attempt was a falsehood put out by the consul as a kind of trial balloon for comparing his popularity with Octavian's, its reception was anything but encouraging. Antony could only be troubled by the public's refusal even to consider Octavian's culpability. Matters were obviously worse for Antony if the attempt on his life was real. That could only be alarming—and it made little difference whether or not Octavian was the man behind it. On 9 October, Antony left Rome for Brundisium.

Intrigue and Sedition

The *lex de provinciis consularibus* assigned Antony the six legions stationed in Macedonia. One of these he despatched to Syria for service under Dolabella. Another he left behind for the protection of the province. The remaining four, however, he summoned to Italy and by October three had arrived at Brundisium; the fourth came later.[30] Octavian and his associates were prepared for this moment. The young Caesar, since his public reconciliation with Antony, had been energetic in cultivating anyone who viewed the consul with suspicion or concern. As early as June he wrote to Cicero assuring him that his antipathy toward Antony was real and his intentions regarding the Liberators benign. Cicero was dubious about the young man's sincerity but saw an advantage in offering him encouragement. He hoped it would be possible to keep him and Antony at a distance from one another.[31] Octavian's exertions were not directed exclusively at distinguished senators. His agents visited veterans in their colonies, where they gauged local interest in standing up for Caesar's heir. Octavian also sent representatives to Brundisium, where they tampered with the troops' loyalty to Antony. The consul was probably not unaware of this. According to Cicero, when Antony left Rome for Brundisium he did so with the expectation that he would have to pay his soldiers for their goodwill.[32]

Even so, Antony appears not to have grasped how thorough and how brazen was Octavian's appeal to the veterans. On the first of November Cicero received a letter from the young Caesar, who informed him he had won over veterans at Casilinum and Calatia. He did so at great expense, offering each man 500 denarii, which is to say 2,000 sesterces, more than two years' salary for an infantryman. He planned to visit more colonies until he had raised an army of 3,000 men. Cicero, writing about this to Atticus, makes no comment on Octavian's criminal behaviour—raising a private army was an act of treason—but instead registers concern over Octavian's youth and ponders the dangerous implications for the Liberators of his open devotion to Caesar.[33] Octavian's movements and his generosity to the veterans were anything but secret and this news soon reached Brundisium, where the troops awaited Antony. They anticipated donatives on a similar scale.

Antony travelled to Brundisium accompanied by Fulvia.[34] Presumably, then, he did not foresee difficulties in collecting his legions. Once in command of an army, he knew he would be too formidable for any enemy in Italy to challenge him. The truly serious contests, he believed, lay ahead: by now word was reaching Rome of the Liberators' seditious movements in the east—neither Brutus nor Cassius had taken up his assigned province but each was instead usurping Roman armies for his own purposes—and closer to home Decimus Brutus, by way of his application for a *supplicatio*, made it plain that he, too, was likely to ignore the law and refuse to yield his province.[35] Dolabella, reacting to the same information, busied himself in making preparations to depart for the east.[36] There he anticipated a struggle against Cassius and Trebonius and Tillius Cimber. Decimus was Antony's problem.

At Brundisium, Antony received a shock. When he offered his legions a bounty of 100 denarii for each man, he was laughed at. Aware of Octavian's liberality, these soldiers expected more than what Antony was offering. Mutinous behaviour supervened and in restoring order the consul felt compelled to turn to executions. This unexpected sedition injured Antony's assurance. He was further disconcerted when he learned of the army of veterans raised by Octavian. The consul was not slow to adapt. Although he insisted on proper military discipline, so he warned his soldiers, he also

Fig. 7.1 Octavian, depicted here as Augustus, a 1st cent. CE bronze in the National
Archaeological Museum of Athens.
Source: Wikimedia Commons.

promised them lavish donatives in the future—and he prepared to make a rapid advance on Rome.[37]

Octavian's Army

'When I was nineteen years old, on my personal initiative and at my private expense,
I raised an army by means of which I restored the republic's freedom at a time when it
was oppressed by the tyranny of a faction'.[38] Thus Augustus in his *Res Gestae*, the record of his achievements which he posted throughout the Roman empire. If the young
Octavian employed the rhetoric of this much later document, then, like Caesar before
him, he put himself forward as a *vindex libertatis*, a restorer of liberty.[39] In raising
a private army Octavian committed a crime. At the same time, and Octavian knew
Romans knew it, there were good republican precedents for taking such an action
amid civil strife. When Sulla returned from the east in order to rescue the republic
by installing himself as dictator, he was aided by Marcus Crassus, Metellus Pius, and
Pompey, still in his early twenties. Each raised an army and each acted unofficially as a
private citizen.[40] The conspirators, too, had acted without an official sanction: their violence against Caesar, they claimed, was legitimated by their personal judgement that

it was only by striking down the dictator that Rome could be liberated. It was into this brand of good citizenship that Octavian now fitted himself. But Octavian's action was different and profoundly cunning. Although his formation of a private army was not in fact a desperate action undertaken to save the republic from tyranny, nonetheless, because it so radically disrupted political affairs and exacerbated the contentiousness prevailing in Rome, it contributed to the creation of the very crisis it ostensibly was designed to repair.

Augustus' later boast does not make it obvious exactly who constituted the faction from whom he liberated the republic. By then it was natural for many readers to take him to mean Antony. An extant Greek translation of the *Res Gestae*, however, perceived a reference to the Liberators.[41] At the time, it appears, Octavian struck more than one pose. In writing to Cicero, he made it clear his purpose was to fight Antony, and later, when he made his first march on Rome, an event discussed below, he attacked Antony in a speech.[42] In rallying Caesar's veterans, however, it is unlikely that Octavian had bad things to say about the consul. Indeed, when he denounced Antony in Rome, many of the veterans expressed their surprise and dissatisfaction.[43] Doubtless, when recruiting veterans, Octavian based his appeal to these men on his status as Caesar's son and *divi filius*, urging them to protect him from his enemies and take up arms in defence of Caesar's legacy. These were sentiments which could not fail to win a welcome response in the colonies. They also furnished a fine moral justification for any veteran who was simply keen to put his hands on the money Octavian was offering him.

It has become unfashionable to draw unflattering attention to the cupidity exhibited by soldiers and veterans during Rome's civil wars.[44] These men, after all, brought to any political conflict the same basic values possessed by other citizens. True, their grasp of constitutional affairs was in many ways limited, but that was a condition they shared with other segments of Roman society. Nevertheless, it is obvious that soldiers were also and unsurprisingly affected by economic motives. An understandable eagerness for bounties and land, rewards for their service which were by no means guaranteed by the state or a priority in the senate, was increasingly evident throughout the first century. During the civil war, Caesar kept his troops' loyalty by way of payments and promises of entitlements, and his relationship with his legions was characterized by a distinctive mixture of discipline and bribery. Antony revived these dynamics, on a small scale, when he recruited veterans to support his *lex de provinciis consularibus*. Octavian now resorted to the wholesale purchase of loyalty by assembling a private, illicit army. Many of Caesar's veterans were keen to join him, and not one of them can have been unaware that Octavian lacked any legal authority for calling him back to action. The events of the next few years, moreover, reveal a striking willingness on the part of the soldiery to take up arms and even intrude themselves into the politics of the day in order to extract some profit out a system in which they had very little leverage apart from the threat of violence.

This was an appetite Octavian exploited. So, too, did his allies in the aristocracy, who furnished him with funds. By putting himself at the head of an army, the young Caesar now made himself important in politics in a way that far transcended his popularity with the urban masses or even his symbolic appeal to men devoted to the idea of Caesar. Suddenly, he was powerful in his own right and could not go overlooked by anyone. Octavian's boldness was in part a reflection of the frayed condition of the re-public in which the young Caesar had learned his political lessons. Octavian had only ever lived in a Rome in which the will to power and wealth was more readily advanced by brazenness and brute force than by observing constitutional conventions. Only a few months before he bought himself an army, Caesar's teenaged heir had been des-tined to become nothing less than master of the horse. The restoration of republican practices under Antony, by contrast, afforded him few opportunities for eminence. That the new order rankled had been the prod employed by Antony's enemies to bring Octavian over to their side. Now, however, he was striking out on his own.

It was only through inciting disruption that Octavian could break open a political space in which he could operate independently and, like Pompey before him, bypass the traditional and legal first steps of a senatorial career. Octavian took an enormous risk in raising an army, and more than once he faltered in trying to deploy it to his ad-vantage. In the end, however, Antony's opponents in the senate—Octavian's friends like Hirtius and Balbus but also allies of the Liberators like Cicero—sanctioned his crime by accepting its ideological claims and by conferring legitimacy on it. In January of 43, the senate bestowed on the teenaged revolutionary an extraordinary command, a grant of *imperium pro praetore*, the military authority of a praetor, along with other high honours. Cicero, we know, for all his praise of Octavian's patriotism, saw him entirely as a club with which to beat Antony. When it was all over, the orator, so it was said, intended to be rid of him: 'this young man must be praised, honoured, dispensed with'.[45] He was hardly the only one of Antony's enemies who felt that way, a reality of which Octavian remained very much aware.

Octavian's March on Rome

Antony directed his legions to march up the Adriatic coast and await him at Ariminum, the city from which he intended to enter Gaul. He then departed for Rome at the head of the Larks, a legion with whom he had a long familiarity.[46] Octavian, in reaction, now led his private army to the capital, where on 10 November he occupied the Forum with troops. This move, however, was no putsch. His aim was to rally the city against Antony and thereby make himself into a hero fighting to protect the capital. Invited to address the people by Cannutius, Octavian warned them that Antony was advancing on Rome and on his way was plundering the municipalities. He proclaimed his alle-giance to Caesar's memory and vowed to prove himself worthy of his father's honours. He then appealed to the senate and people to join him in his defence of the republic. His speech, however, was a failure. It did not stir the masses or inspire the senate. Cicero, who learned of this oration from a distance, was disappointed by Octavian's performance and alarmed by the young man's ominous evocation of Caesar's hon-ours. Worse for Octavian, his abuse of Antony offended the veterans, none of whom had joined the young Caesar because he wanted to take up arms against Caesar's loyal friend and their past benefactor. Some deserted. The residue Octavian led away from the city into Etruria, where he settled at Arretium, a place where his allies, men like Gaius Maecenas, could offer him substantial assistance.[47]

Antony's Consulship: The Last Act

The consul now approached the capital at the head of his forces.[48] He called for a meeting of the senate on 24 November at which he intended to propose declaring Octavian a *hostis*. Antony had to know the motion would be blocked by Cannutius. Nevertheless, he was now free to denounce Caesar's heir without appearing disloyal to Caesar's memory: the young man was seditious and had undertaken to attack him with armed soldiers. By way of contrast with the revolutionary Octavian, Antony perhaps planned to seize this moment for announcing the reconciliation which Lepidus had successfully negotiated with Sextus Pompey. Whereas Octavian came to sow division and renew civil war, the message was clear, Antony's consulship brought an end to the terrible clash between Pompey and Caesar. It was certainly the case that Antony expected to isolate Octavian in the senate—and perhaps thereafter march against him on his own authority. Before any of this could happen, however, disaster struck. Antony learned that Octavian's agents had successfully suborned one of his legions, the *legio Martia*, which now declared for the young Caesar and stationed itself at Alba Fucens, modern Massa d'Albe. Antony had no choice but to cancel the meeting for 24 November. Cicero, in his *Philippics*, explained Antony's change of plans otherwise: the consul, once again, was distracted by drinking and carousing, a riff the orator never tired of.[49] It was, however, a fully sober Antony who dashed to Alba Fucnes in the hope of winning back his legion. But he failed. Soon he learned that another legion, the Fourth, had also gone over to Octavian.

New calculations were now required. Antony no longer saw any profit in trying to push the senate to outlaw Octavian. Nevertheless, he could not resist vituperating his enemy, hurling at him the standard calumnies of youthful unchastity and sneering at his inferior heritage.[50] He also denounced Caesar's heir as a new Spartacus.[51] And although Antony had no respect for Octavian's untested talents as a military leader, because he could no longer trust the loyalty of his remaining legions if he led them against Caesar's open-handed heir, he decided to leave Octavian behind, dangerous though he was, and instead march into Gaul. There Decimus, who was an accomplished general, commanded a host which was bigger than Octavian's and thoroughly battle-tested. He was Antony's more urgent foe. Once Decimus was extruded from the province, preparations could be made for the confrontations which were certain to follow. Antony had underestimated Octavian, but he had long perceived that Hirtius and Pansa—and others—would seek to undermine his position after he resigned his consulship. Consequently, Antony had been assiduous in sustaining his friendship with Lepidus and in trying to draw himself closer to figures like Munatius Plancus and Asinius Pollio, who commanded armies in Gaul and Spain. But it was now imperative that Antony take command of his soldiers in Ariminum and do so as quickly as possible.

Antony made haste slowly. He at once at once furnished his remaining legions with the bounty they desired, a donative of 500 denarii for each man.[52] His agents and officers he put to work recruiting veterans from the colonies and levying fresh recruits.[53] In Rome, he summoned the senate for a meeting on 28 November. Cicero's several depictions of this meeting, on which we must rely, are often contradictory but always hostile and distorting. In one passage, the orator complains that Antony rushed through his agenda, keen to be away from the city; in another, he alleges the senate met at night, and therefore illegally; in still another, innumerable decrees were carried; and so it goes. In presiding over this session, Antony appears not to have been disconcerted: he continued to enjoy support from some quarters of the senate, and with the Larks hovering round the city no one was likely to offer any serious opposition to his agenda.

The first item taken up by the senate was a vote of thanksgiving to Lepidus for concluding a peace with Sextus Pompey. The symbolism of this *supplicatio*, and its usefulness as an expression of Antony's friendship for this crucial ally, are obvious. Nor did Lepidus' honour need any coaxing on Antony's part: it was a major achievement. Antony worried, however, that a debate on the matter might occasion divisive or distracting or merely wasteful rhetoric if any speakers decided to rehearse issues related to the war between Pompey and Caesar. For that reason, as he had done when abolishing the office of dictator, Antony put the question to a vote without calling for speeches from the floor. After the *supplicatio* was carried, the consul turned to the traditional but time-consuming process of allocating provinces for the next year. This traditional exercise in senatorial authority involved drawing lots and passing separate decrees for each province. Some who were allotted provinces preferred not to take them up, which required fresh drawings and lengthened the session. Later, in December, complaints were advanced that Antony's sortition was rigged in such a way that those close to the consul were favoured: his brother Gaius, for instance, received Macedonia as his province. At the time, however, the session passed without controversy, perhaps because it was unexceptionable, perhaps because everyone was wary of the Larks. After the senate rose, Antony prepared to depart for his province.

At Tibur, probably on 29 November, Antony delivered one final performance before leaving Italy.[54] Perhaps he chose this town for setting out against Decimus Brutus on account of its famous sanctuary of Hercules Victor, a legendary ancestor and, so the consul hoped, a good omen.[55] Here Antony mustered the Larks, his veterans, and his new recruits and administered the military oath. Present, too, was a massive delegation of senators and equestrians. They also took an oath of loyalty to Antony. The consul then delivered a speech.[56] For Cicero, the whole affair was sordid, but Appian describes this occasion as a splendid, glorious sendoff—pageantry through which Antony expected to impress his enemies as well as his supporters.[57] He then proceeded towards Ariminum, where his legions awaited him. The time had come for fighting. Antony's officers continued to recruit new men and by early January of the next year he was in command of six legions.[58]

20 December

In Antony's absence, his opposition were anything but idle. Cicero returned to Rome on 9 December. There he conferred with the consuls-elect and held meetings with allies of Decimus Brutus, with whom he corresponded encouragingly. It was crucial, Cicero insisted, that Antony be kept out of Gaul. The Liberator was persuaded and soon issued a decree announcing his refusal to hand his province over to Antony—in defiance of the *lex de provinciis consularibus*.[59] Cicero was not alone in fomenting resistance. There were other schemes afoot. A meeting of the senate was called for 20 December by the new tribunes for 43. They hoped to secure bodyguards for the consuls-elect, a proposition which was openly provocative: its premise—that Hirtius and Pansa were somehow in imminent danger—was an aspersion against Antony. Cicero, sensing an opportunity, made an unexpected appearance at this session. There he delivered his *Third Philippic*, in which speech he defiantly urged the senate to preserve the republic by taking up arms against Antony.[60]

In this speech, and in several of the *Philippics* which followed it, Cicero depicts Antony as an existential threat to republican freedom. He also summons and refits for his own purposes the arguments, philosophical and traditional alike, deployed by the Liberators when they justified resorting to private initiative, including acts of violence, whenever doing so became vital to the defence of *libertas*. Like Lucius Brutus and Scipio Nasica, Cicero insists, Decimus Brutus is right to take an independent stand against tyranny. So, too, Caesar's heir and the soldiers who joined him in safeguarding liberty. This is a theme to which Cicero returns throughout his contest with Antony: later he will argue that, in the east, Brutus and Cassius are right to become their own senates and their own lawgivers. In the teeth of Antony's enormities, the orator insists, any unsanctioned or constitutionally questionable action is legitimate so long as its purpose is to preserve freedom.[61] The incoherence of Cicero's doctrine, that the republic can only be saved by subverting its laws and conventions, is obvious but irrelevant: his speechifying furnished Antony's enemies with the moral cover they needed. And Cicero's passionate, thumping eloquence incited even indifferent senators to cast their votes against Antony.

On this occasion, Cicero persuaded the senate to pass a decree which permitted the consuls-elect to take such actions as they deemed necessary for assuring the senate's security when it assembled again on 1 January. It also commended Decimus Brutus for retaining his province on behalf of the republic. It furthermore instructed Decimus and all provincial governors who held their appointment under Caesar's provincial law to retain their provinces until successors were sent by the senate. And, finally, the senate praised Octavian and his soldiers and promised them rewards and honours in the new year when Hirtius and Pansa were installed as consuls.[62] It now became clear that Antony had been unable to win over a single member in this college of tribunes, which is why there was no one to intercede on his behalf. This is an astonishing failure. Antony more than most knew how vital it was for any provincial governor to have the support of a loyal tribune. The oath sworn at Tibur was no substitute for that. Distracted though he was by mutinous legions, Decimus' contumaciousness, and Octavian's sedition, it is a mark against Antony that no tribune could be persuaded to take his side. This was a lapse which neither Caesar nor Pompey would have committed.

The senate's decree was revolutionary. That the senate should now esteem, and therefore legitimize, Octavian's criminal behaviour against Rome's consul can in part be explained as an unavoidable accommodation: Caesar's heir commanded two legions whom the senate did not wish to alienate. But this decision was also a clear strike against the consul of Rome, whose legions Octavian had suborned. So, too, was the senate's decision to annul the results of the sortition of provinces conducted on 28 November. That action was not illegal—the senate was within its rights to cancel any previous decree—but it was a patent insult to Antony as well as to anyone whose pro-magisterial appointment was now undone. The most remarkable feature of this de-cree, however, lay in its countermanding the *lex de provinciis consularibus*: Dolabella, the senate now decided, was to be denied Syria and Antony Gaul. This action, how-ever, lay beyond the senate's competence. True, a law passed by the Roman people could be annulled by the senate by way of a process known as *abrogatio*, which undid a law carried with violence or in defiance of the auspices.[63] But nothing in Cicero's speech, nor anything in the *Fourth Philippic* which rehearsed before the public the res-olutions taken at this meeting, hints at that. Instead, the senate, in passing this decree, simply and blatantly ignored the constraints of Roman law— apparently for the sake of defending *libertas* against Mark Antony.

According to Cicero, only a single senator, Lucius Varius Cotyla, opposed his mo-tion.[64] Nor, as we have seen, did any of the tribunes support Antony and Dolabella by interposing a veto against the senate's flagrant violation of the *lex de provinciis consul-aribus*, a plebiscite carried by one of their predecessors. Only weeks ago, the senate was carrying decrees on Antony's motion and solemnly saluting him as he departed for Gaul. The same body now honoured his enemies and illegally denied him his prov-ince. After the senate rose, Cicero went before the people: Antony, he declaimed, had been pronounced a public enemy. This was done, he clarified, not by way of applying the label of public enemy—Antony was not declared a *hostis*, not *yet* anyway—but by its actions the senate made it clear that the consul was indeed an enemy of Rome.[65] How can one explain this sudden revulsion? Appian found the senate's reversal baf-fling and believed contemporaries were equally confused: who, men wondered, were those senators who had celebrated Antony when he made his departure?[66]

Cicero, when he recounted this day in a letter to Trebonius, attributed his success to an enormous exertion of tenacity and eloquence. The senate, he says, was inert until he roused it to action.[67] But his success was uneven. As he put it to Cassius, writing to him in February of the next year, there was much wavering on the part of the senate's leadership. Its rank and file, however, remained resolute.[68] This was Cicero's principal audience, and he was undoubtedly effective in stirring its passions. Many senators, it must be remembered, were men willing to listen to advice and follow it if they were convinced it was sound. These men, although they may not have welcomed Octavian's march on Rome, were soon persuaded by the orator that the young Caesar's actions, by frustrating Antony's ambitions, had been a good thing for the republic. This is a conviction the bulk of the senate did not abandon. Cicero recurred again and again to this simple dilemma: if Octavian, and like him Decimus Brutus, were good citizens, then Antony was not; if Antony was not a danger, then Octavian and Decimus were outlaws. But Octavian and Decimus were Cicero's friends: few in the senate could im-agine the orator endorsing a criminal.

Clearly, many in the senate were inclined to believe the worst of Antony. In part, that may reflect intensive lobbying and even the application of pressure by Hirtius and Pansa and other influential men, including friends of the Liberators. It was also the case that, in the aftermath of Caesar's dictatorship, many were more than willing to accept the worst about any powerful figure, not least a consul who deployed vet-erans in securing an advantageous provincial command.[69] That these concerns were so strongly felt, however, is a symptom of Antony's failure to convince the bulk of his peers that his intentions were sound. Cicero could cite and discard Antony's good works—like abolishing the dictatorship—because he realized that in trying to reconcile Caesarians and Liberators Antony had acquired little real gratitude. His graft and overweening manner—both a consul and an Antony—had offended small fry senators in numbers large enough for them to become a useful constituency for Cicero. Neither Dolabella nor Antony had violated the law, unlike Octavian, nor was either man in any obvious way threatening the republic. Yet Cicero, through his eloquence and reputation for integrity, persuaded the senate otherwise: he, they believed, knew a danger to the republic when he saw one. This is not to say Antony lacked friends in the senate. But on this day, apart from the plucky Cotyla, the others, intimidated perhaps, or simply surprised, remained silent.

Standoff at Mutina

Antony collected his legions at Ariminum.[70] From there he sent Decimus Brutus a formal notification that his successor was entering the province and he must begin to unwind his governorship. Predictably, Decimus refused and the two men began to exchange hostile missives. When Antony entered Gaul, Decimus avoided any direct confrontation. This allowed Antony an opportunity to secure the towns, especially the important city of Bononia.[71] Lucius Antonius, now Antony's legate, served as his second-in-command, an appointment that furnished Antony the mobility he needed to move freely in the province, where he installed garrisons in various locations.[72] Decimus, by contrast, after equipping Mutina with supplies sufficient for withstanding a long siege, retreated behind the city's walls. Antony promptly blockaded Mutina by way of circumvallation. But he made no attempt to storm the place. Instead, he prepared to spend the winter besieging his enemy.[73]

In order to mark this early success and to commemorate the terror he inflicted, or at the very least claimed to have inflicted, on Decimus, Antony, it appears, allowed his soldiers to hail him *imperator*. No ancient source accounts for Antony's first acclamation as *imperator*, and yet, by the time he joined Lepidus in April 43 he was minting coins on which he is designated *imperator*.[74] Even before then, he was styling himself *imperator*, something we can gather from a snarky remark by Cicero in his *Thirteenth Philippic*, which he delivered 20 March 43. In the salutation of his public letter to Hirtius and Octavian, discussed more fully below, Antony wrote simply: 'Antony to Hirtius and Caesar'. This casual address was intended to conjure an atmosphere of faux-familiarity and friendliness—the letter is in fact an aggressive piece of political propaganda—and Cicero, who in addressing the senate furnished an almost line-by-line refutation of the epistle, treats it sneeringly: 'He does not call himself *imperator*, nor does he call Hirtius consul, nor Caesar propraetor. That's rather clever: he would rather drop a title that doesn't belong to him than give the others the titles they have right to'.[75]

Antony, then, was already denominating himself *imperator*. And Cicero believes he can score off Antony by impugning his right to do so. Now before his consulship, there was no obvious occasion on which anyone could have hailed Antony as *imperator*: all his prior fighting had taken place under the auspices of Gabinius or Caesar.

Only when marching out against Decimus did Antony lead troops under his own, independent authority. Although frightening Decimus into shutting himself up in Mutina falls short of anything like a true victory, this is nonetheless the likeliest moment for Antony to have been hailed *imperator*.[76] Despite its inappropriateness, the acclamation can only have raised his soldiers' morale, and doubtless it gave Antony an opportunity of promising further bounties to an army whose loyalty he very much needed. By advertising his achievement by way of grandiose titulature, Antony certainly hoped to make an impression on anyone in Rome who remained hesitant over fighting a civil war.

During this time, Antony was a busy correspondent. He remained in frequent contact with his connections in Rome. He also solicited men with armies. Of Lepidus' reliability Antony entertained no doubts. He was less confident, however, of Asinius Pollio in Further Spain or Munatius Plancus in Transalpine Gaul. His relationship with these men was cordial but not conspicuously close. Each was a talented man, but each was also an opportunist. In a long letter to Cicero, Pollio concedes as much. Indeed, Decimus Brutus openly distrusted him. As for Plancus, in his correspondence with Cicero and the senate a reader is furnished with exquisite models of smooth equivocation.[77] Both men were now very important to the struggle between Antony and the senate, as everyone recognized. Cicero wrote to them assiduously. So, too, did Antony, although none of his letters survives. It was crucial to Antony's cause that he convince them that he and Lepidus would prevail. At the same time, Antony could not ignore either man's republican sensibilities. Pollio, self-serving though he was, was also unsympathetic to another stint of one-man rule. So too, we may believe, was Plancus, who looked forward to exercising an independent consulship in 42. It was incumbent on Antony, then, to exhibit not only strength but also a sound political orientation. He had to make it clear he was not the tyrant Cicero made him out to be.

The Senate against Antony

On 1 January, the new consuls convened the senate. Their attitude toward Antony was openly hostile, but by now Antony's supporters—along with cautious statesmen leery of civil war—were prepared to stand up to them and to Cicero. The senate debated its position over four days.[78] Fufius Calenus, Pansa's father-in-law, spoke for moderation, as did Lucius Piso, a past adversary of Antony but now unwilling to see the senate abandon any attempt at finding compromise and a solution to the current crisis. They were not alone. When Cicero demanded Antony be declared a *hostis*, his proposal was vetoed by a tribune named Salvus. His action perhaps represented popular sentiment outside the senate—Appian reports that the public were not in favour of condemning Antony—or perhaps he hoped to avert an outbreak of violence.[79] It is possible Antony succeeded in persuading him to take his side. If so, he was disappointed: Salvus soon lost his nerve and vanished from subsequent debates, a failure that may explain why he was later proscribed by the triumvirs.[80] During the course of these senatorial sessions, Fulvia and Julia led Antony's friends and relations in protests. Dressed in mourning, a powerfully moving expression of victimization in Rome, they visited the houses of senatorial grandees and pursued them on their way to and from the senate.[81] Little wonder the masses became distraught over the government's actions against Antony.

In the end, it was Octavian who gained the most. He received a grant of praetorian *imperium* and was adlected into the senate (an unconstitutional act) with the right to speak among the ex-consuls. He was also permitted to stand for the consulship ten years early. His troops were rewarded with bounties and promises of lands in Italy. These measures were supported not only by Cicero but also by Servius Sulpicius Rufus and Servilius Isauricus, Caesar's colleague in the consulship in 48 who now betrothed his daughter to Octavian. As for Antony, it was decided to send an embassy, consisting of Piso, Marcius Philippus, and Sulpicius Rufus, who would put the senate's demands before the proconsul. This was a disappointment to Cicero but not a surprise: he was aware of negotiations taking place between Antony and leading senators who hoped to solve the standoff in Cisalpine Gaul by shifting Antony's province to Transalpine Gaul.[82] Cicero gained only a single success: Antony's *lex agraria* was abrogated, presently to be replaced by a law put forward by Pansa.[83] Pansa's law almost certainly included specific provisions for Octavian's soldiers, but those measures could have been carried separately. The abrogation of Antony's law was a transparently hostile action which abolished the Board of Seven and potentially opened afresh all its dispositions in the Italian countryside. As for Hirtius, the senate directed him to begin conscripting new troops and to take command of all Roman forces in the field, including Octavian's.

In the senate, it was clear, Antony was at a disadvantage. Although he had influential supporters and although many in the majority may have hoped to avoid a new civil war, there was no appetite whatsoever for revisiting the decree of 20 December and its violation of the *lex de provinciis consularibus*. For all practical purposes, that policy was now the senate's policy. Antony and his supporters could not expect to persuade the body to reverse that decision. Future moves on their part, consequently, must work around that reality. At the same time, no one imagined that Antony would accept the terms for peace delivered by the senate's embassy. The senate demanded that Antony withdraw from Cisalpine Gaul into Italy but remain at least 200 miles from Rome. He must then submit to the authority of the senate and people of Rome, who would decide his fate.[84] In response, Antony issued a counterproposal, which was taken to the capital by the senate's ambassadors and Antony's stalwart, Varius Cotyla, now his legate. This delegation arrived in Rome around 2 February. On the journey home, Sulpicius Rufus fell ill and died, later to be honoured by the senate for his devotion to the republic.[85] Antony now offered to yield Cisalpine Gaul and instead govern Transalpine Gaul, keeping his army for five years—or possibly longer: he made it clear he would not vacate his province until Cassius and Brutus, if they were elected consuls for 41, departed from whatever provinces they were subsequently assigned. Antony also insisted that his *acta* remain valid, and he claimed the same compensation for his legions which the senate had granted to Octavian's.[86]

Word of these terms reached Rome before the embassy did.[87] Cicero denounced them as intolerable. Antony, by contrast, described them as fair, even restrained.[88] From his perspective, it was unthinkable that he should give up his army—he was doomed if he did—and, although Antony demanded another highly strategic province on more or less the same terms as the now discarded *lex de provinciis consularibus*, by conceding the likelihood that Brutus and Cassius would stand and be created consuls, he offered a concession to Cicero and the Liberators' supporters which, he hoped, might create a rift between them and Octavian, Hirtius, and Pansa. It did not. The senate reacted to Antony's offer by passing its final decree, which appealed to the consuls to rescue the republic. The senate did not, however, declare war, *bellum*, against Antony: Lucius Caesar and Pansa prevented that. Instead, a military emergency, a *tumultus*, was declared and citizens were instructed to don the *sagum*, a military cloak. Cicero put one on and wore it defiantly. Antony's soldiers were ordered to lay down their arms by the Ides of March. All his laws were abrogated, although those deemed good for the republic were carried anew by Pansa. A few calls for peace were raised, notably by Fufius Calenus, but these went unheeded. The senate now prepared for battle.[89] For the public, however, patriotism began to clash with daily life: emergency taxes in Rome and financial exactions from the municipalities were enacted, demands that provoked widespread unpopularity.[90] Nevertheless, Hirtius and Octavian began their march into Gaul. By the beginning of February, the consul had seized Claterna and Octavian was encamped at Forum Cornelii.[91]

Civil War in the East

News from the east affirmed the Liberators' usurpation of Illyricum, Greece, and Macedonia, which Brutus now dominated. His control was formally recognized by the senate, which named him proconsul in charge of these regions but urged him to remain focused on the crisis in Italy.[92] Brutus' success affected Antony in a very personal way. When his brother Gaius arrived in the east and attempted to install himself as governor of Macedonia, he was stymied by Brutus, who subsequently took him prisoner.[93] Cicero was soon urging Brutus to put Gaius to death, but the Liberator resisted the orator's cruel advice.[94] Cassius, further away from the capital, was master of Syria, where he commanded a huge army and was busy extruding moneys from subject cities. Asia, however, was in the hands of Dolabella. When Dolabella arrived in the province, he came into conflict with Trebonius, whom he defeated and executed. This was a serious blow both to Brutus and Cassius, not least because Dolabella seized control of Rome's richest province. The senate, when it learned of Trebonius' death, was outraged. On the motion of Fufius Calenus, Dolabella was declared a *hostis*.[95] Hirtius, Pansa, and Octavian, remarkably, shared in the senate's displeasure at the death of one of Caesar's assassins. Although Cicero hoped to persuade the senate to name Cassius proconsul of Syria and assign him the war against Dolabella, he was frustrated by competing claims in Rome: Lucius Caesar proposed an extraordinary command against Dolabella for Servilius Isauricus, while Fufius Calenus moved that the consuls, after relieving Decimus, should both depart for the east and take command of Syria and Asia.[96] Cassius did not wait for the senate to decide: he marched on Dolabella at once.[97]

Mark Antony's Letter

The reality of civil war and its costs introduced hesitation. In late February or early March, Piso and Fufius Calenus proposed a second embassy to Antony. Cicero detested the idea, but it was nonetheless decreed that five consulars—Piso, Fufius Calenus, Lucius Caesar, Servilius Isauricus, and Cicero—should act as ambassadors. This was a weighty assemblage of senatorial prestige and a clear sign of unwillingness on the part of some to allow the standoff in Mutina to break out into open civil war. Servilius and Cicero, however, refused to go and the idea was dropped. Negotiations were now at an end.[98] Pansa, consequently, assumed command of his newly recruited troops and began his march to Gaul. Antony, however, remained a busy correspondent, writing both to his supporters in the senate and to the governors of neighbouring provinces.[99] On 20 March, the senate, under the presidency of the urban praetor, Marcus Caecilius Cornutus, met to discuss two letters, one from Lepidus and another from Plancus. Both urged the senate to make peace with Antony. Lepidus' letter must have made his loyalties clear: Cicero attacks it in his *Thirteenth Philippic*, delivered at this session, and on the same day he composed a terse, unpleasant letter to Lepidus warning him to change his course. Plancus' letter, by contrast, was less decisive. Cicero does not mention it in his speech and in his correspondence remains hopeful of persuading Plancus to take his stand with the senate.[100]

The central focus of Cicero's *Thirteenth Philippic* is its analysis and indictment of a public letter issued by Antony, our only complete specimen of his propaganda during this cold war between himself and his enemies in the senate. In his speech, Cicero dismembers Antony's letter, subjecting each bit of it to an unkind exegesis. In doing so, because he preserves all its parts, Cicero makes it possible for us to reassemble it.[101] Antony's letter was ostensibly addressed to Hirtius and Octavian but intended for a wide audience, doubtless including the soldiers on every side of this conflict. In it, Antony depicts himself as Caesar's avenger, Hirtius and Octavian as hypocrites, and Cicero as the master manipulator who has brought Rome once again into civil war. Antony does not mention his prior exertions at reconciling Liberators and Caesarians. Indeed, this letter utterly repudiates the amnesty of 17 March. The letter poses as an exercise in a very different brand of unification: it urges its addressees to join Antony in fighting for Caesar and concludes by threatening anyone and everyone who refuses to exact punishment from the Liberators, a cause in which, Antony makes it clear, he is willing to offer his life.

Antony does not waste time in his letter making a legal argument over his right to govern Cisalpine Gaul. That issue, he knows, is no longer pertinent. Instead, he opens by rejecting the conspirators' claim to be Liberators. Instead, he righteously insists, they are parricides, an unholy contagion which must be excised from the republic—by violence if necessary. It is on the basis of this principle that he justifies Dolabella's execution of Trebonius, a parricide who has paid a just penalty for his crime.[102] Antony thus decries the senate's decision to declare Dolabella a *hostis*. In this way, Antony associates his senatorial enemies with the cause of the Liberators and chief among them is Cicero: none of these men, according to Antony, acts for the cause of *libertas* but rather, because they champion the conspirators, actually work against it. Caesar's cause, it is implicit but unmistakable in this letter, is the side which favours freedom.

Parricidium, the offence of the men who slew the *Liberator,* is Antony's loudest note in this manifesto.[103]

Antony's letter does not eschew personal vituperation. Hirtius is an upstart. Octavian is 'a boy who owes everything to a name'. Decimus Brutus is a *venefica*, a vile and deadly petticoat poisoner, and it is for the sake of a creature like him that Hirtius and Octavian seek to become liberators (Antony uses the verb *liberare*). Cicero he calumniates as a *lanista*, a trainer of gladiators, and in this letter he is the man responsible for the current spectacle and the carnage to come.[104] This is colourful stuff and pointedly put. However stylish or entertaining, however, these insults remain invective of a fairly predictable order. More interesting, however, is the novel conceit whereby Antony draws attention to the unnatural collaboration with Cicero and the Liberators on the part of Caesar's friend and Caesar's heir: he observes how the conspirator Servius Galba is serving alongside Hirtius and Octavian, still wearing the same dagger with which he murdered Caesar.[105] This obscenity, however, is merely part of a larger perversion of purpose on their part. In Antony's letter, Hirtius and Octavian have devoted themselves no longer to Caesar's memory but instead to restoring the cause of Pompey the Great.

Pompey, or rather his cause, is another central theme of this letter. Antony depicts the current crisis as a replay of the conflict between Caesar and Pompey the Great—he reprises language, imagery, and topics from the rhetoric of that war and its outbreak—and in so doing defines the opposing sides at Mutina as the party of Caesar and the party of Pompey.[106] This is more novel than perhaps it sounds. In Rome a *party*—*partes* is the Latin word for any side in any confrontation—does not refer to anything like a modern political party or any kind of alliance predicated on a common ideology or even loyalty to a family. *Partes* is instead more naturally used for denominating temporary coalitions rallying behind the leadership of a single military or political leader. In republican usage, formulations of this kind are possible only when the leader is alive: after his death, any party, or *partes*, once associated with him ceases to exist.[107] Antony, however, in this letter—and even before he distributed this letter—configured the politics of 43 in terms of *partes*, parties, defined almost in a modern sense by way of reference to two men each of whom was gone: Caesar and Pompey. Cicero found this usage unnatural and too strange to mean anything: 'he keeps banging on about a conflict between parties', Cicero complains in his *Fifth Philippic*, 'but what parties? One has been defeated, the other comes from the midst of those who were the party of Gaius Caesar'.[108] In reaction to this letter, Cicero cries, '*party*, you madman, is what one says in describing sides in speaking in the Forum or voting in the senate'. He comes back to this point: the parties Antony invokes 'no longer exist'.[109] In this matter of usage, however, Cicero was on the wrong side of history. By June, when writing to Pollio, Cicero speaks of Antony and his forces as the party of Caesar, *Caesaris partium*, and in a letter to Brutus he employs Antony's language of parties, but with open distaste: 'as they are called nowadays'.[110] In this letter, Antony supplied contemporaries with the stuff they needed to believe in a party of Caesar. It had little purchase at Mutina, but soon proved useful, as we shall see, when Antony, Lepidus, and Octavian crafted the Triumvirate.

For Antony's purposes, however, the past is present at Mutina. Throughout his letter, it is all Caesarians versus Pompeians—and Hirtius and Octavian are on the wrong side. Cicero, in his speeches, dubbed Brutus and Cassius their own senates. Antony complains to Hirtius and Octavian, 'you are calling Pompey's camp the senate', and he pillories them for supporting the actions of the Liberators in the east.[111] 'Is there anything', he asks, 'which Pompey would do, if he came back to life, which you have *not* approved or done?'[112] The Pompeians lost last time and will lose again, Antony contends, and yet the camp of Hirtius and Octavian teems with Pompeians. And they are each of them subservient to Cicero: he is the *dux*, their leader. He is also, like all Pompeians, subpar: 'you have that loser Cicero as your leader'.[113] Many of the same issues of the old civil war are echoed by Antony in his representation of this new one: friendship, loyalty, dignity, senatorial overreach. Antony promises he will not forsake the party which Pompey hated. Nevertheless, he, like Caesar, prefers to be reasonable. In the past he has offered to resign and withdraw if all his enemies agree to do the same.[114] And he continues to seek to negotiate a just peace: indeed, he is awaiting the senate's second embassy, a pose he knows his readers know is hopeless because the senate has abandoned the project: 'I do not believe the ambassadors are coming'.[115]

Antony's posture does not want aggression. He vows to extirpate Decimus Brutus— if he can, however, he will leave the man's soldiers unharmed. He promises to remain faithful to Caesar's memory and to his friends, Dolabella, Lepidus, and Plancus. By inserting them into this letter as members in good standing of the party of Caesar, Antony makes it clear that he is not alone. Although he urges Hirtius and Octavian to join him, he also makes it clear he will not shrink from fighting to the death anyone who refuses to avenge Caesar's death, into which category Hirtius and Octavian have wrongly placed themselves. Antony's letter is a marvellously inventive and superbly crafted specimen of political propaganda. It did not bring Hirtius or Octavian over to his side at Mutina, but it provoked suspicions on the part of some: by April Cicero was struggling to suppress a general worry that Hirtius and Pansa might go over to Antony.[116] In more general terms, Antony's letter, like Cicero's *Philippics*, exacerbated the atmosphere of crisis in Rome, and it must have given many senators and equestrians—and even some soldiers—second thoughts about the purposes for which Rome was again preparing to fight a civil war. By evoking Pompey and Caesar, Antony at the very least reminded his readers that Mutina was likely to be the beginning and not the end of a painful and perhaps lasting crisis. A replay of the last civil war, Antony's message is clear, is not in anyone's interests.

The Battles of Forum Gallorum and Mutina

The army commanded by Hirtius and Octavian, although its paper strength excelled Antony's, included legions not all of which were fully manned.[117] The ranks of some units, moreover, were filled by men who had only recently been conscripted. Consequently, even as spring arrived, they avoided an open battle. For his part, Antony was content to wait. Decimus was running out of supplies and his capitulation, although it would not end the conflict, would represent a significant success. In April, however, Pansa entered Gaul. He brought four legions. These men were welcome reinforcements but were also fresh recruits. Hoping to exploit their inexperience, Antony decided to launch an offensive. He marched out of camp with two legions and a large force of cavalry. He then prepared a trap near Forum Gallorum where the Via Aemilia passes through land that is mostly marshes. His plan was to shock Pansa's recruits with a sudden attack and cut them down as they scattered in disarray. As a distraction from his movements, Lucius Antonius led several assaults on the camp of Hirtius and Octavian. Hirtius, however, was not deceived by Antony's tactics. He and Octavian dispatched the *legio Martia* and their praetorian cohorts: their mission was to protect Pansa's forces.

On 14 April, battle erupted. It was a sudden, disorganized conflict fought in a difficult terrain broken up by mires and other obstacles. We possess an eyewitness account composed by Sulpicius Galba, the Liberator who, to Antony's horror, still carried the dagger he used in murdering Caesar. One of Hirtius' legates, Galba commanded several cohorts sent out to protect Pansa's army. In a letter to Cicero, he furnished a detailed, vivid account of the fierceness and the panic attending this battle—during the fighting of which Galba came very close to Antony and nearly lost his life in escaping.[118] A similar and far more elaborate version is supplied by Appian. In the end, Antony's forces prevailed and pushed their opponents back to their encampment. Pansa, grievously wounded, had to withdraw from the fighting. Antony first tried unsuccessfully to take the enemy's camp, then elected to lead his exhausted men back to Mutina. But during this march he was bushwhacked by Hirtius, who fell on him with two rested legions and won a stunning success which forced Antony and his troops into a hasty, disorderly retreat. The battle of Forum Gallorum, very nearly a victory for Antony, ended in defeat. On 20 April, the senate, informed of Hirtius' victory, decreed a *supplicatio*. At this same session, however, Cicero could not persuade the senate to declare Antony a public enemy.[119]

Antony's siege of Mutina subsisted. He deployed cavalry to harass and distract Hirtius and Octavian. And he awaited the arrival of Publius Ventidius, who had raised three veteran legions in Italy and was marching towards Gaul. Decimus' situation remained critical, however, even if Antony's enemies were buoyed by their success. Hirtius and Octavian now moved their armies closer to Antony. The able consul detected a vulnerable point in Antony's siege works and on 21 April attacked it. Antony reacted, but Hirtius' soldiers got the best of the fighting. A sortie on the part of Decimus further wrongfooted Antony's men. At that point, Hirtius fell in battle. Octavian did not despair but made a bold show of trying to rally his men. Antony's forces, still confused, were routed and took refuge in their camp. In two successive battles, Antony had been bested by Hirtius. He now decided his position at Mutina was untenable. On the next day, he retreated to the north.[120]

Plutarch depicts Antony's march as a brutal slog during which the general distinguished himself by sharing his men's misfortunes and raising their morale through his heroic example.[121] This is perhaps proleptic of Antony's more famous retreat from Parthia in the thirties. We can be sure Antony's retreat was a brisk one, which means it was an arduous trek. His march to the north was sudden and apparently unexpected by his enemies. Admittedly, Decimus and Octavian were shaken by the death of Hirtius. And on 22 April, the day of Antony's departure, Pansa succumbed to his wound. Nor did Decimus and Octavian trust each other. Only after Pansa's death did Decimus set off in pursuit. Octavian refused to join him and appears to have offered no material support. As for Antony, he moved toward the Alps, intending to cross into

Transalpine Gaul where he could link up with Lepidus and, he hoped, induce Plancus to join them. Decimus, for one, was convinced Lepidus, Plancus, and Pollio would all join Antony.[122]

Before leaving his province, however, Antony allowed his soldiers to pillage Parma, a city already occupied by his brother Lucius.[123] This was a brutal action but one which secured needed supplies and provided plunder sufficient to sustain his soldiers' loyalty. Antony may also have exploited this inglorious offensive as a means of tightening, during this desperate time, the bonds connecting him with his men. After his failure at Mutina, Antony very much needed the devotion of his men, especially as he drew near the military governors in the north. Decimus' certainty notwithstanding, Antony could no longer be entirely confident even of Lepidus' faithfulness. Consequently, he was obliged to do everything possible to preserve his legions' steadfastness. True, he was a man who could outstare the lightning, but at this dire moment even the confident Antony knew that he must draw on his every resource.

VIII
The domination of the triumvirs

The Party of Caesar

In Rome, the senate convened on 27 April.[1] The liberation of Mutina and Antony's defeat were duly and extensively celebrated. But the coalition against Antony was already dissolving. The senate awarded Decimus a triumph but granted Octavian nothing.[2] From the east, Brutus began criticizing Cicero for his friendship with Caesar's heir.[3] So, too, did others in the capital. The senate's antipathy against Antony nevertheless remained focused enough to allow Cicero at last to have him, along with his allies in the field, declared *hostes*, an action which also entailed the confiscation of their property.[4] This decree, although it had little practical effect on Antony, was catastrophic for his family: it impoverished his children and put Fulvia at risk. Almost immediately, she found herself entangled in multiple legal conflicts, during which difficulties Atticus emerged as her only reliable friend.[5] The equestrian's loyalty was not forgotten. Nor was the viciousness of Antony's enemies.

Antony continued his march to the north. He was soon joined by Ventidius—it was alleged that Octavian did nothing to stand in his way—and Antony adroitly eluded Decimus, who constantly failed to catch up with his prey. When Antony reached Transalpine Gaul, near the end of May, he was welcomed by Lepidus, still faithful. Their peaceful reunion, predictably, was credited to the will of the soldiers.[6] This was a crucial turning point for Antony. With Lepidus as his ally, he was again a formidable figure.[7] Decimus entered the region in early June. He turned to Plancus, who was still playing every side. This situation changed, however, when Pollio arrived and declared himself an ally of Antony. Plancus could no longer resist. By the end of summer, he, too, was for Antony and Lepidus.[8] Confronted by Plancus' duplicity, Decimus had little choice but to withdraw. But he was soon deserted by the bulk of his forces, who journeyed south to join Octavian. Taking to flight, he aimed at making his way to the east, where he hoped to join Brutus and Cassius. But he was captured by a Gallic chieftain who, on Antony's behalf, put him to death.[9]

Antony, Lepidus, Pollio, and Plancus constituted a powerful coalition. That they would march on Rome was obvious to everyone, which is why Cicero scribbled letter after letter begging Brutus to return with his forces in order to defend the capital.[10] That, however, was not Brutus' inclination, nor, it appears, did the idea attract many in the senate: instead, legions were summoned from Africa.[11] Later, however, the senate decided to recall Brutus, but he did not come.[12] What Antony's coalition had in mind for Rome when they liberated it from their enemies we do not know. Their soldiers, we can be sure, craved entitlements and may have hoped for an end to citizen slaughter. Their leaders, too, may have preferred peace. But Antony was now publicly committed to fighting the Liberators and their champions, men like Cicero and Octavian. It will have been on those terms that Lepidus and the others joined him. Some application of violence, then, was unavoidable in restoring—yet again—the just operations of the republic, operations that by definition must treat Antony and his allies honourably. And in the east, wars loomed. Brutus and Cassius could no longer be tolerated without shattering the party of Caesar.

In Rome, and contrary to Cicero's wishes, the senate persisted in its neglect of Octavian. Honours and official duties were instead granted to Liberators. Sextus Pompey was named admiral of Rome's naval forces.[13] As for Caesar's heir, he was excluded even from the commission appointed to manage the legions' rewards.[14] In reaction to the new coalition in the north, Lepidus was now proclaimed a public enemy, a moral victory but hardly an action likely to deter his march towards Italy.[15] Cicero was frustrated by the senate's lack of urgency and lack of gratitude towards Octavian. For his part, Octavian was alarmed. He recognized how very disposable the senate now deemed him. Nor did he fail to perceive how many enemies were gradually gathering against him. In the east, there were Brutus and Cassius. Of more immediate concern was Antony and his coalition: he knew he was certain to be a target when they returned to Italy. His position was truly precarious.

The young Caesar remained in Gaul, where he now made an extraordinary proposal. Owing to the deaths of Hirtius and Pansa, two replacement consuls were required, and it was within the senate's competence to arrange it so that only two candidates stood for these offices. Octavian bruited the possibility that he and Cicero, both men who deserved well of the republic, be put forward. This proposition could hardly be rejected on constitutional grounds: the senate had spent the past few months ignoring any laws or conventions it found inconvenient. From Octavian's perspective, the plainly sensible course for the senate at this time lay in securing the loyalty of the only general who stood between Antony and the capital. This overture, however, was dismissed. In July, Octavian, isolated and sensing his peril, now led his army out of Gaul into Italy.[16] Cicero and the senate were soon to learn how wrongly they had judged the character of Antony and consequently of Octavian. The results were catastrophic.

As he advanced towards Rome with eight legions, it became clear to everyone that nothing could be done to stop Octavian from seizing power. A single legion protected the capital, to which were added two more, withdrawn from Africa, which had only recently arrived. But these were no match for Octavian's forces, and all three legions promptly took the side of Caesar's heir. Octavian arrived at Rome by the end of the month or perhaps early August. He scrupulously remained outside the city, where a deputation of distinguished senators went out to meet him. Cicero was one of them. He now had no choice but to face his greatest dread, the return of autocracy, the agent of which, he knew, was in many ways his own creation. He must have been a shattered man. The senate, confronted by an unopposable strongman, now offered bounties to Octavian's troops and the consulship to their general. Although only nineteen, on 19 August he was elected consul. His hand-picked colleague was Quintus Pedius, Caesar's elderly nephew.[17] The symbolism of this Caesarian consular college was clear to everyone. Its most important audience was Antony and his coalition.

The two consuls went to work quickly. Octavian's claim to be the dictator's adopted son was now given legal and sacred reality by the Curiate Assembly.[18] No dissenting views were expressed as Caesar's heir became Caesar's son. The *hostis*-declaration against Dolabella, who by this time had committed suicide after suffering a defeat by Cassius' forces, was formally rescinded.[19] So, too, the *hostis*-declarations against Lepidus and Antony.[20] Texts of these decrees, and others expressing senatorial goodwill, were forwarded to Antony. The admiralty of Sextus Pompey was annulled, and a tribune of the *plebs*, Publius Titius, with the blessing of both consuls, carried a measure which deprived his colleague, Publius Servilius Casca, of his office: Casca was one of Caesar's assassins.[21]

Pedius carried a law, the *lex Pedia*, which established a special court for prosecuting the conspirators.[22] We are poorly informed of this law's specifics, but there is no doubt that it made both killing Caesar and being a party to the plot against him a crime. This second category, however it was formulated, was flexible and capacious, adaptable enough to enable Octavian to secure Sextus Pompey's conviction under its terms.[23] Cicero was doubtless distressed at the possibility that he might suffer the same fate, but, Antony's prior denunciations notwithstanding, he was not indicted. This court did its work quickly, possibly within a single day. All who were accused were also condemned—whether or not they were present in Rome and even if they were serving the republic as officers or officials, something forbidden by law and custom. The punishment was exile.

Thus Octavian fulfilled his promise to avenge the death of Caesar. But not only that: through this hastily drafted measure Octavian marked a formal, legal termination to the amnesty of 17 March. As we have seen, Antony publicly, indeed forcefully discarded this amnesty in his letter to Hirtius and Octavian. The connection between Antony's letter and Pedius' law was anything but accidental. Octavian, although master of the city, was from the very start of his consulship looking ahead to Antony's return. All his actions in Rome, in a sense, represented his answer to Antony's invitation to return to the party of Caesar. Octavian, everyone could see, was vigorously rehabilitating that party and stood unambiguously against the party of Pompey. Clearly, or so he hoped, he was acting as an ally of Mark Antony. He was assiduous in corresponding with Lepidus and Antony, from whom he received conciliatory responses.

The Formation of the Triumvirate

Octavian marched north, returning to Cisalpine Gaul. Soon Antony and Lepidus, at the head of seventeen legions, drew near. By the time they met, both sides had agreed to make peace. The legions approved. Receptive to the idea of the party of Caesar, they were averse to further fighting on the part of its leaders. As for Antony, he was willing to see in the complaisant policies of Octavian's consulship proof enough of his repentance. Meeting in November near the city of Bononia, the three men, over the course of two days, reached a critical, indeed historical, agreement. They decided to seize power, but to articulate their authority by way of legislation grounding it in the will of the people and furnishing it with a divine sanction. Their stated intention was not to establish a permanent junta but instead to assemble an emergency administration capable of restoring the republic to its traditional health. It is notable that Pollio and Plancus were excluded from this emergency administration: presumably they lacked the heft necessary for intruding themselves into the top rank. As always in Rome, this new regime was influenced by precedents. In the fifth century, so it was believed, Rome was temporarily administered by an extraordinary Board of Ten Men who were empowered with consular *imperium* in order to write the laws. More recently Sulla had held absolute power as a dictator appointed to write the laws and set the republic in order.[24] The office of dictator Antony had abolished. Instead, Lepidus, Antony, and Octavian denominated themselves *tresviri rei publicae constituendae*, the Three Men appointed to set the republic in order—in short, the triumvirs. Their purpose was to make it possible for the republic to recur to its traditional operations. In order to achieve this, they committed themselves to putting an end to civil war by way of a final victory and by extirpating the conspirators' unholy contagion.

Not even in the aftermath of the senate's decrees on 20 December did Antony imagine he would soon enter Rome as one of its masters. Nor did Octavian. True, he avidly sought prominence, but there is no reason to believe that, until he was tossed aside by the senate, he aimed at autocracy. As for Antony, before he suffered defeat at Mutina, his ambition lay in seizing his legally allocated province, where he could fortify himself against his enemies. After Mutina, however, it was clear that his only security lay in a march on Rome, and for that he needed Lepidus—who joined him, perhaps owing to loyalty, perhaps owing also to his distrust of the senate and the Liberators in the east. Both Lepidus and Antony had worked hard to put Caesar in power. Now they were prepared to fight for themselves. But this was not by design. It is clear that they, like Octavian, were reacting to events, of which some were of their own making, others the work of their enemies. 'They wished it so', was Caesar's judgement after the battle of Pharsalus. The triumvirs doubtless held this same view now.

After they marched into Rome, the position of the triumvirs was furnished a legal foundation by the tribune Titius. His *lex Titia* was carried on 27 November and the triumvirs entered office immediately. The *lex Titia* invested the triumvirs with supreme *imperium* and an array of special rights. The most important of these was the right of each triumvir to issue edicts carrying the force of law. The triumvirs also possessed the power of life and death over every citizen, an authority uninhibited by *provocatio*, a citizen's right to appeal to the people. Discretionary powers over public funds were also assumed. The stipulations of the *lex Titia* served as clarifications but not limits on the triumvirs' power to act. Indeed, legal and constitutional punctiliousness was only occasionally a feature of Roman government during the triumviral period. Nevertheless, the principle of collegiality rendered the triumvirate a regime less conspicuously despotic than Sulla's dictatorship. Nor was the triumvirate a permanent institution. The triumvirs recognized how Caesar's open declaration of perpetual authority turned the aristocracy violently against him. This was a reaction they sought to avoid by underscoring how the triumvirate was a temporary if harsh necessity. Once the republic was set in order, Rome, they promised, would recur to its traditional government. The *lex Titia* provided a term of five years for repairing the state. That restriction, however, did not entail the evaporation of a triumvir's powers on a certain day: like several other magistracies in Rome, the triumvirate was an office that expired only upon abdication, abrogation by law, or death. Implicit in the triumvirs' appointment was the possibility that their assignment could require more than five years.[25]

The passage of the *lex Titia* came only after the triumvirs reached Rome. Before that, while still in Gaul, they had much to work out among themselves. Octavian, on

Antony's insistence, agreed to resign his consulship. The three men then allocated future magistracies, including consulships, for the next five years. For the remainder of 43, they appointed as consuls Ventidius and later, after the sudden death of the elderly Pedius, Gaius Carrinas. Not much is known about this latter man: his father fought against Sulla, who executed him. Like Ventidius, whose family rebelled against Rome during the Social War, his name resonated with Italian aristocrats. He may have been Octavian's choice: he later served as one of his governors and, after Actium, celebrated a triumph earned under Octavian's auspices.[26] For the next year, Lepidus and Plancus were designated consuls. In 41 the ex-consul Servilius Isauricus would again hold the fasces, with Lucius Antonius as his colleague. Asinius Pollio was destined for a consulship of 40; his colleague would be another deeply loyal Caesarian, the ex-consul Gnaeus Domitius Calvinus. Thereafter they installed friendly figures drawn from the nobility: for 39 the consuls-designate were partisans of Antony—Lucius Marcius Censorinus and Gaius Calvisius Sabinus—whereas in the next year the office fell to men who, by that time in any case, were allies of Octavian, Appius Claudius Pulcher and Gaius Norbanus Flaccus. As for the administration of the empire, the triumvirs arrogated to themselves the administration of all Rome's provinces. Antony took Cisalpine and Transalpine Gaul. Lepidus was allocated Narbonensis Gaul and the two Spains. Octavian got the residue: Africa, where resistance was likely, and the islands Sicily, Sardinia, and Corsica, each of which required defence against Sextus Pompey. The triumvirs assumed the right to administer their provinces through legates, which allowed them mobility should they want it. The eastern provinces, because they were occupied by the Liberators, were not allocated.

The war against Brutus and Cassius was central to the triumvirs' mission, the challenge of which was enormous. The resources of the Liberators were now vast and, owing to their domination of the east, they deprived the capital of the bulk of its income. The triumvirs, consequently, were in desperate need of money, essential if they hoped to sustain the loyalty of their legions. These soldiers were keen to fight Caesar's assassins, but they also sought bounties and properties—and that is what the triumvirs promised them. These commitments, however, came at the expense of the municipalities of Italy. Because they could not, as Caesar had done, purchase the lands required for settling so many men, the triumvirs elected simply to seize them. They designated eighteen prosperous towns, cities like Capua and Nuceria, as sites for colonization by veterans. There the triumvirs intended to appropriate—by edict and without compensation—whatever lands they required.[27] The triumvirs' colonization scheme constituted dispossession on a massive, catastrophic scale. The whole of Italy, and not merely the cities faced with immediate ruin, trembled in reaction.

The triumvirs' soldiers, by contrast, were elated, and they cheered the conclusion of their masters' negotiations. From the legions, or so it was said, came an appeal that Antony and Octavian secure their newly formed friendship through ties of affinity. Antony's daughter, as we have seen, was betrothed to Lepidus' son. Now it was decided that Octavian would break off his betrothal to the daughter of Servilius Isauricus and instead agree to marry Antony's stepdaughter Claudia, the very young daughter of Clodius Pulcher and Fulvia. The announcement of this engagement furnished the army with proof the party of Caesar was truly united against its enemies. The triumvirs then entered Rome. A sequence of three military parades over three successive days exhibited to everyone the real nature of the new regime. The city was occupied with soldiers—the triumvirs made no attempt to disguise their occupation of the city—and on 27 November the *lex Titia* was carried by way of an irregular legislative procedure. But that hardly mattered now.

Proscriptions

On the next day, the triumvirs promulgated an edict announcing proscriptions.[28] In it, they observed how Caesar's clemency had earned him no gratitude and resulted in the sacrilege of his assassination. That was a mistake the triumvirs were determined to avoid. Instead of pardoning their enemies they now preferred to eliminate them. Consequently, they were resurrecting Sulla's policy of proscription. As part of this edict, a list of names was published—over time it was emended and expanded—and anyone included was condemned to death and the subsequent confiscation of his property. Moreover, anyone who aided the proscribed would be punished by proscription. The public were invited to join in exterminating the triumvirs' enemies: large rewards were offered for the heads of the proscribed, which were displayed in the Forum. Informers, too, received a bounty.

More than one motive led the triumvirs to institute the proscriptions. The men on their list were all of them rich and they hoped, by confiscating wealthy estates and putting them up for sale, to fill the public coffers. The triumvirs also intended to terrorize the Roman people: the cruelty and capriciousness of this violent assault on the aristocracy made it clear that no one who stood up to the new regime could be certain of his safety. Most of all, however, the triumvirs wanted revenge. Ancient writers argue over which of the triumvirs was the most bloodthirsty. For Suetonius, it was Octavian. For Dio, it was Antony.[29] It is a pointless calculation: these sanctioned murders were the work of them all. And they were all of them open to suggestion: the triumvirs gladly accommodated their marshals, allowing Pollio and Plancus to add the names of personal enemies to the list of the proscribed.[30] Nonetheless, it was certainly true that the events of the past year had thrown up more offences against Antony than either Lepidus or Octavian. Almost certainly he felt betrayed by many in the senate and others in the equestrian order who backed his rivals. He had old scores to settle—and so did his wife. Fulvia had been abused by many when Antony was declared a *hostis*: she did not forgive.[31]

The triumvirs closed the gates of the city, installed soldiers to guard harbours, and sent patrols through the city in search of the proscribed. Panic was everywhere. We do not have precise or reliable figures for the number of men proscribed: it probably ran to 300 senators and possibly as many as 2,000 equestrians. Our sources are more concerned with moralizing drama, recording tales of courage and cravenness, greed and sacrifice—admirable or despicable actions committed by men and women of every social order, including the enslaved. The sheer horror of this purge, the shock of which transcended the quantity of its victims, was never forgotten. Old ties were sometimes helpful, but sometimes did nothing to guarantee safety. Lepidus proscribed his brother, Antony his uncle Lucius Caesar, while Octavian, as a favour to Antony, added Cicero to the list. Both Antony and Lepidus had advocated reconciliation with Sextus

Pompey. Now, surely at Octavian's insistence, he was proscribed. Lepidus' brother, however, was allowed to escape Italy. Antony's uncle was redeemed when Antony's mother, Julia, demanded it. The rich equestrian Atticus was vulnerable: not only his wealth but his intimacy with Cicero and Brutus rendered him a likely candidate for proscription. But his kindness to Fulvia saved him.[32] Cicero, however, had no advocates. He and his brother and their sons were all of them proscribed. The orator's son was in the east, where he was an officer under Brutus. Only he escaped destruction, surviving the age of the triumvirs and attaining a consulship in 30. As for Cicero, his head and even his hands, we are told, were carried to Antony, who relished the sight. Then, like others, these were nailed to the Rostra, where, according to hostile tradition, Cicero's head was mutilated by Fulvia. Cicero was the only ex-consul who perished in the proscriptions, and his death, for many later writers and historians, marked the spiritual end of the republic.[33]

The proscriptions were a blunder. They added to Rome's misery and incited hatred against the triumvirs. They were also unprofitable: the prosperous classes were too petrified to pay large sums for confiscated properties. Indeed, owing to the panic inspired by the proscriptions, moneys were hidden away and disguised, and throughout Italy credit dried up once again, reprising the financial crisis of the civil war. Apprehension in the city's financial circles was further exacerbated by concern, even fear, over the looming dispossession of property owners in the municipalities.[34] A civil war mentality quickly descended on Rome. As for the trimvirs' enemies, many escaped and joined either the Liberators in the east or Sextus Pompey in the west. For the triumvirs' gratification, only revenge remained.

New and unprecedented taxes were imposed. Everyone resident in Italy whose possessions matched or excelled the equestrian census, whether or not he was a citizen, was obliged to lend the triumvirs two percent of his wealth and to hand over a year's income.[35] Failure to do so risked proscription. An extraordinary tax was also imposed on the estates of 1400 of Rome's wealthiest women, the leaders of whom sought relief by lobbying the wives of Lepidus and Antony. Fulvia, however, refused even to meet with them. This delegation of women, led by Hortensia, daughter of Hortensius Hortalus, the famous orator and consul of 69, confronted the triumvirs directly as they were holding court in the Forum. There she delivered an oration which soon became a classic of Latin literature in a performance that so thoroughly moved the crowd that the triumvirs were forced to compromise. The list of women subject to this tax was reduced to 400.[36] The spectacle of triumvirs berated by women to the applause of the people made clear the new regime's unpopularity—and its clumsiness.

A New Order

In the new year, the deified Caesar, Divus Iulius, was officially consecrated as a god. The young Caesar was now truly *divi filius*, son of a god. Before the dictator's death, Antony had been declared *flamen Caesaris*, the priest of Caesar's sacred cult, whatever shape it finally took.[37] Now he became the new god's *flamen*-designate, although he was not inaugurated until 39. Caesar's deification emphasized the solemn character of the looming war against the parricides, Brutus and Cassius. So, too, did another triumviral measure: the *acta* of Caesar were reaffirmed and every senator took an oath to uphold them. In preparation for the campaign in the east, the triumvirs reallocated their legions.[38] Because Antony and Octavian were to share the command in this war, each was assigned twenty legions. Lepidus kept three. These were deemed sufficient for maintaining order in the capital and in Italy. Lepidus was experienced in such matters, but he was not left on his own. Fufius Calenus, Antony's legate, also remained in Italy, where he commanded an army of eleven legions. Pollio, too, was nearby: he was Antony's governor in Cisalpine Gaul. From these arrangements it is obvious that Antony, clearly the dominant triumvir, planned to maintain his pre-eminence in Italy while he was fighting in the east.[39]

Coins advertised the regime of Rome's new masters, a media blitz that put concord and prosperity to the fore. Already in 43, the triumvirs' coinage emphasized collegiality. Antony, for instance, minted coins with himself on the obverse and either Octavian or Lepidus on the reverse.[40] In the next year the mint in Rome produced a profusion of coins depicting individual triumvirs and their attributes. Lepidus, whose family was the most distinguished of the three, is linked with his famous ancestors. Octavian, unsurprisingly, underlined his Julian heritage and drew attention to his piety towards his father. In the case of Antony, he is associated with Hercules and with Caesar.[41] All three triumvirs, however, are more than once depicted in combination with joined hands, the symbol of concord, and with the cornucopia, a hopeful icon promising a better future. At the same time, the reality of the triumvirs' power remained undisguised: each of them was pictured with Mars.

In a hopeful gesture and as another means of putting the republic in order, censors were elected in 42.[42] One was Antony's uncle, Gaius Antonius. The other was Publius Sulpicius Rufus, a patrician ex-praetor. He had served Caesar with industry and loyalty both in Gaul and during the civil wars and he was married to a Julia.[43] The triumviral suitability of each was obvious. The last census of the republic had taken place in 50. Antony, it appears, had plans for a census in 44, but nothing came of them. After the disruption of civil war, dictatorship, and civic conflict, a fresh census, which in Rome included an assessment of each citizen's wealth and character, was urgent. Regarding the quality of any individual's character the triumvirs may have lacked curiosity, but they very much wanted to know how much wealth he possessed. And for all Romans the censors' assignment of social class was a designation that mattered. The censors were also responsible for the album of senators: doubtless they were instructed to enrol as many of the triumvirs' partisans as they could. From this year forward, the number of Rome's senators balloons.[44] Even with the support of absolute rulers, however, this census did not go smoothly. The censors' final duty, the sacred *lustrum*, a ceremonial purification of the city, was not performed.

Fulvia and Roman Coinage: An Antonian Innovation?

The partnership of Antony and Fulvia was central to the politics of his consulship. Her stature was enhanced when he became triumvir. And a case has been advanced that, during this period and through his coinage, Antony portrayed his wife as a figure of truly international consequence. At Lugdunum, coins were minted that advertised the friendship of Antony and Lepidus. From this same mint, in 43 or 42, came coins the reverse of which signal Antony by name, image, or birthday. On the obverse is a female bust, almost certainly the goddess Victoria. It is often argued, however, that the female bust on these coins is not Victory but rather Fulvia.[45] If so, this would be the first instance of a living Roman woman's representation on a coin minted under Roman authority—and consequently a remarkable innovation on Antony's part. But caution is called for.

It is certainly the case that this Victoria is marked by idiosyncratic features: the coiffure, combining a conspicuous loop of hair on top of the goddess' head with a prominent bun in the back, is highly distinctive, and the goddess' physiognomy strikes some observers as less than divinely ideal. Although Fulvia is not explicitly mentioned on either issue, the case for seeing her portrait in this Victoria is regularly made by adducing two issues from the Anatolian city Eumenea, modern Isilki, on which appears a remarkably similar goddess of victory. These Eumenean coins, it is argued, were minted at a time when the city had changed its name to Fulvia: on this view, the Eumeneans became Fulvians, a change reflected in their coins' claim to be those 'of the Fulvians'. The routine conclusion is that, when Antony was in the east after his victory at Philippi, the citizens of Eumenea endeavoured to curry favour by renaming their city after his wife and, in doing so, borrowed their iconography from Lugdunum, perhaps by way of Antonian advice (the city would not have altered its name without first seeking Antony's permission) or perhaps by way of a Gallic connection between Eumenea and the west.[46]

Now there is no question but that the Lugdunum Victoria and her Anatolian counterpart look very much alike. The Eumeneans' adoption of Fulvia's name, then, ought to suffice to make the case for discerning her presence on the Lugdunum coins. But there is no certain evidence that the Eumenean coins actually mention Fulvia. The legends on these issues are unreadable either in whole or in part and their Fulvian restorations are highly speculative: we find . . . *VIANS* on one issue; the other is entirely unreadable.[47] Nor is the version of Victoria on the coins of Lugdunum and Eumenea limited to the mints of those two cities. There is a third Victoria of this same brand who appears in Rome on an issue which was probably minted in 41.[48] This coin has no obvious connection either to Antony or Fulvia and perhaps suggests that our distinctive and international Victoria must be explained otherwise than by appealing to any specific woman. Fulvia, formidable though she was, was not, on the present state of our evidence, the first Roman woman to appear on a coin. Nor did the Eumeneans rename their city for her. The coins of Lugdunum advertise Antony—but not his wife. Fascinating though they are, these coins are not pathbreaking.[49]

War in the East: Philippi

Antony and Octavian faced formidable opponents.[50] After Cassius defeated Dolabella in July 43, the Liberators were the unchallenged masters of the eastern Mediterranean. By way of extraordinary brutality and rapacity, they accumulated a massive war chest and assembled a vast host. Their fleets dominated the seas. The building of this war machine came at a great cost to Rome's subjects. Moneys were pitilessly extruded from cities and client kingdoms and any act of resistance was mercilessly punished. In 42 the Liberators turned their eyes towards the riches of Rhodes and Lycia. Neither disgorged what the Romans demanded and as a consequence each was conquered in swift, deadly assaults. The province of Asia, utterly cowed, was ordered to furnish ten years' worth of tribute immediately. The Liberators remained aware of developments in the west. When Brutus learned of the proscriptions and the death of Cicero, he ordered the execution of Antony's brother, Gaius. Both Cassius and Brutus expected an invasion by the triumvirs. In mid-summer, they joined forces at Sardis and began marching west.[51]

Early in 42, eight legions under the command of Gaius Norbanus and Lucius Decidius Saxa crossed the Adriatic as the triumvirs' vanguard. Soon, however, the Liberators' fleet, led by Lucius Staius Murcus, a Caesarian officer who, on the Ides of March, took the conspirators' side, and Gnaeus Domitius Ahenobarbus, son of Caesar's fierce enemy, the consul of 54, began to block the triumvirs' way into Greece.[52] At about this same time, Sextus Pompey took complete control of Sicily and began to operate aggressively in the waters west of Italy. He occupied parts of Italy, especially regions near Rhegium. Sicily was Octavian's province, which made Sextus his problem. Quintus Salvidienus Rufus was dispatched. He gained some ground in Italy but was defeated at sea. A truce was achieved only by Octavian's agreeing to exempt Vibo and Rhegium from the triumvirs' colonization scheme.[53] Already a hero to many because he offered sanctuary to the proscribed, Sextus was quickly winning a following in Italy at a cost to Octavian's authority.[54] Inglorious though this settlement was, however, it was sufficient to allow Octavian his chance to join Antony. By midsummer and after considerable difficulty, the triumvirs crossed over into Greece. By then Norbanus and Saxa had advanced into Macedonia. They took up a position on the Via Egnatia near Philippi.

The army of the Liberators soon drew near. By way of an aggressive march and an intelligent exploitation of their total naval superiority, they easily isolated and outflanked Norbanus and Saxa, who withdrew to Amphipolis. Brutus and Cassius then advanced so far as Philippi, where they occupied a strong position, elevated and well-watered.[55] A secure route to nearby Neapolis furnished an excellent supply line: there the Liberators' fleet could import provisions stored on Thasos. They constructed two camps, joined by fortifications which blocked the Via Egnatia. There they awaited their enemy. Antony arrived first. Octavian, who had become gravely ill, fell behind but joined his colleague ten days later. The triumvirs constructed a single camp, but unlike the Liberators' theirs lacked an adequate supply of water. As a consequence, they were obliged to dig wells. Provisioning their camp was also difficult: supplies could not be brought in by sea, so they were forced to extract food and fodder from nearby towns and villages. By now it was autumn and the calendar was working against the triumvirs, who could not maintain their difficult position indefinitely. Their principal hope lay in achieving success in a pitched battle before winter set in. But although Brutus and Cassius routinely arrayed their forces for fighting, they always kept so close to their camps that an attack by the triumvirs would have been reckless.

Antony devised a plan for forcing a fight.[56] He began throwing up fortifications which, if completed, would deny the Liberators easy access to Neapolis. Antony's constructions, however, were detected by Cassius, who began building operations of his own. In this way, he sought to hinder and even neutralize Antony's blockade. Each side laboured furiously to circumvallate the other until Antony, early in October, launched an assault intended to break up the enemy's working parties. Conflict supervened and escalated quickly. Soon Antony attacked Cassius' camp directly. In response, Brutus counter-attacked, but his forces were confronted by Octavian's men, although the young Caesar remained ill and was not in command. A hostile tradition located him in the nearby woods, where he cowered in fear, an unfair slur but one never forgotten by his enemies. As for Octavian's army, it was soon pushed back by Brutus, who routed his enemy and broke into the triumvirs' camp. On his side of the battle, Antony himself led a charge into Cassius' camp, which he captured but could not hold. Cassius, unaware of Brutus' success, concluded instead that his partner, too, had been defeated. Consequently, Cassius committed suicide. As the day came to an end, both armies retired.

The first battle of Philippi was something of a stalemate, and on the following day the triumvirs received the unwelcome news that their reinforcements, while crossing the Adriatic, had been attacked by Staius and Domitius and subsequently captured.[57] It was now too late in the year for them to expect more troops, nor, under their current circumstances, could they expect any improvement in their supply lines. Their position was becoming increasingly difficult, but Antony was loath to withdraw. Instead, he intensified work on the fortifications which threatened to separate Brutus' camp from Neapolis. This instilled a sense of urgency among the Liberators, and although Brutus preferred restraint—he was aware that he still held a logistical edge over the triumvirs—his officers and soldiers were eager for battle. Soon, his subordinates forced him to abandon 'the uninspiring policy of inaction', a catastrophic failure in judgement.[58] On 23 October, Brutus put his legions in battle array and prepared to fight.[59] The combat which followed was, even by Roman standards, ferocious and bloody. Antony's soldiers pushed Brutus' further and further back until they broke and ran. During the retreat, the Liberator managed to reassemble four of his legions. But that, he knew, was not enough to win the war. Like Cassius before him, he took his own life. The second battle of Philippi was an overwhelming victory for Mark Antony.

The Victor at Philippi

The campaign at Philippi was instantly the stuff of legend. Never had Rome fought a single battle so massive or so bloody. The losses on each side can safely be reckoned at around 40,000 men—all of them Romans. International auxiliaries also fell in large numbers.[60] The historic dimensions and political implications of Philippi were weighty. Owing to Antony's victory, the future of Rome belonged to the idea of Caesar and, for the foreseeable future, the regime of the triumvirs. All Rome was profoundly affected. And everyone, Roman and subject alike, was deeply impressed by Antony's triumph. That he was a valorous man and a good officer no one had ever doubted, and not even his defeat at Mutina had seriously tarnished his reputation as a commander. This was commendable but hardly remarkable: other nobles, after all, were brave and capable. Philippi, however, changed everything. Now his dashing exterior was matched by real achievement. Antony was esteemed the sole victor in this most momentous of clashes, and his fame was launched to a new, brilliant level. In the imaginary of his contemporaries, he became, suddenly, a conqueror on a par with Pompey or Caesar. Indeed, in the years that followed Antony was regarded by many as little short of invincible, an intimidating mystique predicated on this single campaign.

For imperial historians, the Liberators' defeat at Philippi, like the assassination of Cicero, marked the death of the free republic. Appian, after describing the final battle, observes how the Romans' constitution was permanently decided on that single day, with which sombre judgement he closes the fourth book of his *Civil War*—an exclamation point. At stake at Philippi, in Dio's view, was Roman liberty, and Brutus' defeat forever settled this matter.[61] Antony's contemporaries need not, indeed probably did not, share this view. For them the battle of Philippi was an important step towards the end of civil war. Not, however, the final step, even after the fall of Brutus and Cassius. Sextus Pompey, Domitius Ahenobarus, and Staius Murcus remained to be dealt with. As for restoring the republic, the conditions for that remained distant. Abused and plundered by the Liberators, the eastern empire was in a dire state. In the west, Italy was still reeling from the terror of the proscriptions, while up and down the peninsula many were frightened, and soon to be impoverished, by the triumvirs' colonization scheme and its extensive, unprecedented appropriation of private property. Philippi was certainly viewed as a great achievement. And yet, for men and women at the time, awestruck though they may have been by Antony's glorious victory, their principal concern lay in the new beginnings it must usher in. Apprehensiveness over an uncertain future now animated Rome and its empire.[62]

First, however, there were lugubrious practicalities. The proof of Antony's victory was carnage on a ghastly scale and the landscape was soon alight with ceaseless funeral pyres. The fate of one corpse attracted special attention. On Antony's instructions, so we are told, the body of Brutus was cremated and his ashes returned to his mother in Rome, perhaps over Octavian's objections.[63] Plutarch tells us, though he does not tell us how he knew it, that even while the battle raged Antony remained unsure how he would treat Brutus should they encounter one another.[64] It was certainly possible, as Octavian apparently preferred, to deny the man burial or send his head back to Rome as proof of vengeance duly applied. Revenge for Caesar's murder, after all, was advertised as chief among the motives animating the triumvirs and their armies. Nor could Antony easily forget that Brutus had ordered the execution of his brother. And yet now he preferred this graceful, humane gesture, reminiscent in some ways of his treatment, when he was a younger man, of the fallen Archelaus after Gabinius' capture of Alexandria.[65] If Plutarch can be believed, Antony, the moment he spied Brutus' body, with a flourish stripped himself of his general's cloak so as to wrap the corpse in suitable dignity.[66]

In Alexandria it had been a sense of decency urged by a past friendship that inspired Antony to find his better nature. Perhaps this was once again the case. He and Brutus had once been friends, and although Antony might hate Brutus for the sake of Gaius, he may yet have esteemed him, as did so many of the man's contemporaries. Indeed, this small kindness was highly likely to pay dividends in Rome, and Antony was certainly capable of making calculations of this kind: in the eyes of the leading men and women in the city, Brutus, even if he was an outlaw, was by no means a monster—he remained one of them. Antony, one senses, perceived this was the moment to become

192 A NOBLE RUIN

a different man from the sanguinary triumvir of the proscriptions. He was now bigger than that. He was the victor at Philippi, a figure grand enough and confident enough to exhibit magnanimity and majesty, as Caesar had done when it suited him. These were traditional Roman qualities, befitting a Roman conqueror.

Our accounts of the aftermath of Philippi are distorted by later propaganda which strained to depict each triumvir as cruel in victory. Octavian's reputation suffers the most. Cowardly evading any real fighting during the conflict, at least in most versions of Philippi, he was, after the battle, reputed to have been remorselessly savage to the defeated. In turn, the vanquished reviled him—but hailed Antony as their conqueror. As for Antony, a hostile tradition accuses him of expressing his inhumanity by putting to death Marcus Lucullus, the son of the consul of 74, and exalting in the execution of Marcus Terentius Varro Gibba.[67] Gibba, with his dying words, prophesied Antony's ruin, a melodramatic element that signals this episode's invention by a later writer. Plutarch includes a more elaborate story. Quintus Hortensius was the proconsul who carried out Brutus' order to execute Gaius Antonius. Captured after Philippi, he was sacrificed by Antony on his brother's tomb. This is a very literary death: slaughtering anyone over the tomb of his enemy is an old story and a recurring trope in Roman invective.[68] This gruesome episode, it appears, was contrived to counter equally false tales about Octavian indulging in human sacrifice after the fall of Perusia.[69]

Which is not to say there was no cruelty after Philippi. Many were put to death: these were men who contumaciously refused to seek the triumvirs' pardon, anyone condemned under the *lex Pedia*, and individuals proscribed by the triumvirs' edict. But the victors were mostly inclined towards clemency whenever it was practical. It was decided that Brutus' men, if they surrendered, would benefit from an amnesty. Pardons, too, were forthcoming for some allied forces, but they had to ask for it and each petition required separate adjudication.[70] The victors required no more than fresh military oaths from the defeated legions, and this same leniency was afforded to many of their officers. Perhaps Antony took the lead in this policy, but his colleague did not demur.[71]

Their mercy extended even to some of the proscribed.[72] Two of Brutus' officers, for instance, Marcus Valerius Messala Corvinus and Lucius Calpurnius Bibulus, each of them on the list of the proscribed, managed to escape to Thasos, where they remained in possession of troops, ships, and treasure. We do not know who initiated negotiations, but very soon Messala and Bibulus agreed to capitulate to Antony and Octavian, who for their part agreed to a general amnesty for the forces at Thasos, including a pardon for both officers. Antony travelled to the island—Octavian was perhaps incapacitated by illness—where he personally accepted their surrender, after which both men entered his service.[73]

This episode initiated a sequence of pardons aimed at reintegrating those members of the resistance who accepted the authority of the triumviral order. When Antony held court in Ephesus during the following year, he pardoned any past officers of Brutus and Cassius who asked for it—with the exception of a certain Petronius, who is otherwise unknown but was one of the senators who murdered Caesar, and Quintus, also a non-entity, alleged to have betrayed Dolabella.[74] Antony later pardoned Cassius' brother Lucius and many others who sought clemency: it was only when dealing with actual conspirators that he remained implacable.[75] At Bithynia,

Antony accepted the surrender of Marcus Appuleius and his forces. Appuleius, too, had been proscribed: he was now pardoned and was destined to become consul in 20, during the reign of Augustus.[76]

The capitulation at Thasos was a welcome event. But there were now far too many men under arms, a vast army that included soldiers who had fought with Caesar in Gaul as well as men who had joined him during the civil war against Pompey. An immediate reorganization was essential. Men whose time had expired were released from service and dispatched to Italy where they could await the lands promised them. Not all elected to go. Some 8,000 men volunteered to remain in service and were formed into praetorian cohorts for the two triumvirs, a mark of honour. The soldiers of Brutus who had surrendered were, as we have seen, incorporated into the triumvirs' legions: according to Appian, these numbered 14,000 men. The troops who fled to Thasos were also enlisted in the new army. In all, it was possible for the triumvirs to field 11 legions at full strength—66,000 Romans under arms.[77]

During the campaign, Antony and Octavian had received disquieting reports regarding Lepidus' loyalty. It was alleged that he was pursuing an independent alliance with Sextus. That Lepidus was entitled to act on his own as the man on the spot in Rome is scarcely to be doubted, and his colleagues were aware that he would very likely be constrained to negotiate with the man, as Octavian had been obliged to do after Salvidienus Rufus' defeat. But Sextus was now a formidable figure. And Lepidus had a personal stake in his rehabilitation: he had previously, before the conflict at Mutina, received a *supplicatio* for securing an armistice with Sextus.[78] It was not unimaginable, however, that the two men could come to terms unwelcome to Lepidus' triumviral colleagues. At the same time, Antony and Octavian did not fail to appreciate the difficulties involved in maintaining communications between east and west, nor were they unaware of the various motivations that impaired their informants' reliability. They decided to keep an open mind. Nevertheless, they took it upon themselves to reallocate the responsibilities of all three triumvirs, an operation in which Lepidus was demoted.[79] This decision was an important development. Diminishing Lepidus was an act which could only appear ungrateful on Antony's part in view of how much, after Mutina, he owed his colleague. Clearly, Antony felt there were reasons to distrust Lepidus. And he now believed it was in his interest to work closely with Octavian. Notwithstanding all the old loathing, and the two men never really liked one another, they now, after campaigning side-by-side, esteemed one another with a respect hardy enough to put Lepidus' standing in the shade.

Italy, as before, because it was not a province, was to be governed jointly by the three triumvirs. And Italy was now enlarged by the addition of Cisalpine Gaul, the provincial status of which was abolished. This was a recommendation put forward by Octavian, and Antony plainly concurred, although it deprived him of one of his own territories. In compensation he received Narbonese Gaul, which previously belonged to Lepidus, and he continued to govern Transalpine Gaul. Lepidus' Spanish provinces were reassigned to Octavian, in compensation for Octavian's loss of Sicily and the other islands. Octavian also remained governor of Africa, although Dio indicates that Octavian and Antony divided Africa between them. This is possible but in any case soon became irrelevant: Lepidus' loyalty to the triumvirate was later affirmed and Africa was re-assigned to him. It is possible that Sardinia remained under the triumvirs' control: if so, that island remained a part of Octavian's allocation.[80] The young Caesar was also assigned the war against Sextus.[81] That, however, would have to wait.

The disposition of veterans and troops was the most urgent business pressing the victors. The favour or hostility of Rome's soldiery had often proved decisive in the political struggles of 44 and 43, and nobody, least of all the triumvirs, was inclined to cross these men now. Before the battle, Antony and Octavian promised each man 5,000 denarii—and considerably more to the centurions and military tribunes.[82] Losses had been heavy, but as many as 80,000 men subsisted who were entitled to donatives, the payment of which demanded a staggering, perhaps impossible quantity of money. Nor was that the end of it. Lands must now be furnished for as many as 50,000 veterans.[83] At Bononia, as we have seen, the triumvirs decided to seize lands by way of proscription, a scheme subsequently enacted into law and, at the time of Philippi, one which was currently being executed under the direction of Lepidus and his fellow consul Plancus.[84] But establishing a veteran colony, even under the best of circumstances, was hardly a simple affair. It entailed surveys, inevitably interrupted by negotiations and pleas for exemptions by any prior landholders who believed they were being unfairly treated, as well as careful assessments of the value of potential allocations in order to ensure the settlement's basic fairness. Making the final dispositions—legal, administrative, and even sacred—of each new settlement was always time-consuming, and the entire enterprise was an expensive one.[85] Colonization on the scale planned by the triumvirs required massive additional funds for its execution. And even if everything went ahead as the triumvirs hoped it could take two or three years before all their veterans were provided with farms, a reality that made the payment of donatives imperative for discharged men in need of money.[86] Every delay in meeting their soldiers' demands incurred a risk more dangerous to the triumvirs' authority than any hatred provoked by confiscating land in Italy or by exacting tax and tribute in the east.

As the senior figure in the triumvirate, Antony was able to deposit the unpleasant business of dispossessing Roman citizens into the hands of his junior colleague. This assignment was, in a sense, a kind of promotion for Octavian: Lepidus was currently in charge in Rome but he would now be replaced, indeed, shunted aside by his younger colleague, who, owing to his duties in Italy, would now play a dominant role in the city.[87] Later, Octavian claimed to have taken on this assignment owing to his poor health, which at the time obliged him to return to Rome instead of taking on any military assignments abroad.[88] Face-saving retrospectives aside, and notwithstanding the opportunity of winning gratitude from Rome's veterans, Octavian's task was plainly an odious one: Dio is explicit in attributing the decision that Antony and not Octavian remain in the east solely to Antony.[89]

Dio observes how the triumvirs eschewed distributing provinces which were in too extreme a state of turmoil for anything like normal administration to be possible. Which is why the eastern provinces go unmentioned in the triumvirs' new allocations. These regions of the empire had been battered by warfare and racked by the ruinous exactions of Brutus and Cassius. And, from the triumvirs' perspective, the local leadership, even if they were obliged by circumstances to side with the Liberators, had taken a political stand against the republic. For these reasons, Antony was assigned the

re-imposition of Rome's legitimate domination in lands that, under the rule of renegades, had been severely convulsed and perhaps rendered disloyal. He also took on
the task of finding in the east the moneys needed in Italy for rewarding the soldiery.[90]

These new arrangements were all set down in writing.[91] This document was not
intended to supply some kind of legal safeguard protecting one triumvir from the
other. Its purpose was instead to aid in promulgating the new order everywhere outside Philippi by way of a clear and accurate communication of its new particulars. The
triumvirate's immediate priorities were laid out for everyone to grasp. Nor could anyone fail to discern in this document the unmistakable signals that Lepidus was now
a second-rate member of the triumvirate—or that Antony was the senior man. He
expected to finish his work in the east by the time Octavian had completed his invidious assignment in Italy. Then the victor at Philippi could return to Rome as its most
eminent leader, bask in the gratitude of the veterans, and perhaps offer succour to any
disadvantaged Italians who resented Octavian's harsh treatment of them.[92] Then, too,
it would perhaps be time to unwind the triumvirate and restore the republic. What is
certain is that, after Philippi, Antony had no plans to remain in the east as its permanent governor: that was *not* his assignment. After the Perusine War and the agreement
reached at Brundisium in 40, true, Antony returned to the east as the region's viceroy,
leaving the management of the western provinces to his colleagues. But that was later,
and by then the nature of the triumvirate was much changed. In 42, Antony did not
begin to imagine he would spend most of the residue of his life outside Rome. Nor did
the eastern provinces suspect they were soon to welcome a permanent overlord.[93]

It was time to allocate the triumvirs' eleven legions. It was decided Antony should
take six, Octavian five. Of that five, however, Octavian handed over two legions to his
colleague in exchange for two legions Antony had left in Italy under the command of
Fufius Calenus. Which meant that Antony, remaining in the east, commanded eight
legions.[94] These he clearly needed in order to parade Roman authority throughout the
eastern Mediterranean and intimidate or suppress any armed resistance he might encounter. Antony also had to take thought for the security of the empire. The Parthians
remained a potential problem and, owing to the region's current instability, Antony was
obliged to consider the defence of Rome's eastern frontier. Furthermore, Macedonia
was under threat from neighbouring tribes, a danger so imminent that Antony left a
considerable portion of his army (how great we do not know) with Lucius Marcius
Censorinus, whom he installed as governor of that province.[95] An impartial observer
might conclude that, in view of the potential hazards of his assignment, Antony's army
was perhaps too small. Still, Antony could have had more legions had he insisted on
them. That he did not suggests a high level of confidence on his part.

The victory at Philippi was marked by the army with magnificent sacrifices and
feasting.[96] Its importance was commemorated by founding a Roman colony, Victrix
Philippensis, *Victory at Philippi*. This colony celebrated the assassins' defeat but was
also proof of the triumvirs' determination to reward their soldiers. To mark the colony's creation, coins were minted in quantities sufficient to advertise the occasion and
provide something in the way of a down payment on promised donatives. Significantly,
this colony was not a joint venture: Antony, and Antony alone, was the founder, a
spectacular exhibition of his primacy and one Octavian did nothing to resist. Caesar's
heir goes unmentioned on the colony's new coins, which are explicit in recording that

Victrix Philippensis was founded 'by order of Antony'.[97] The real work of laying and completing the colony Antony delegated to an officer, Quintus Paquius Rufus, a new man whose activities, also depicted on the colony's coins, could do nothing to obscure Antony's glory.[98] Victrix Philippensis was a monument to Antony's brilliance as the victor at Philippi and his status as the senior figure among the triumvirs. Triple pillar of the world, Antony no longer believed his supremacy could be challenged.

IX
Athens to Alexandria

The Road to Athens

From Philippi, Antony and Octavian travelled together. Although no literary source mentions it, they followed the Via Egnatia to Thessalonica. This city had stoutly resisted the regime of Brutus and Cassius, and such loyalty could hardly go unacknowledged.[1] It was in any case on their way. Numismatic evidence indicates that they were lavishly welcomed. Coins were minted celebrating the city's freedom and commemorating games in the triumvirs' honour.[2] The triumvirs then proceeded to Pella, another city which issued coins marking its regained freedom.[3] Here, too, there will have been festivities. At this point Antony turned south, marching towards Athens. What other cities Antony called in on as he made his way we do not know. He certainly visited Delphi. It was an important, symbolic stop. The Liberators, in their struggle against the triumvirs, claimed the patronage of Apollo, a protector of Roman freedom, often signalling this relationship through the imagery of the Delphic tripod, an icon of the god's oracle.[4] In reaction, even before departing Italy, Antony vowed in the senate that in victory he would restore Apollo's damaged temple, and at Philippi *Apollo* was the triumvirs' watchword.[5] The victor at Philippi, then, could hardly fail to make a pilgrimage. Plutarch records Antony's welcome promise to repair Apollo's temple. He knew Antony never kept this promise but declined to say so.

Antony in Athens

These stages were all a prelude to Antony's winter in Athens. This city, unlike Thessalonica, had not stoutly resisted the Liberators. Quite the contrary. Brutus and Cassius and the cause they stood for had been honoured by the city when bronze statues of the pair were placed alongside those of Harmodius and Aristogeiton, the celebrated, even legendary opponents of tyranny in sixth-century Athens.[6] On Delos, too, the Athenian community paid its respects to Brutus, 'the divine Caepio', which is to say, the divine Brutus.[7] After the defeat of the Liberators, then, the city's position could only be described as compromised. But there was no Roman appetite for punishing Athens, a determination doubtless revealed early on after the triumvirs' victory. Which meant that Athens, like Pella and Thessalonica, could seize the moment of Antony's visit to celebrate its regained freedom.

Athens, by the late first century, was no longer a city of military or economic consequence.[8] Cultural capital was a different matter, however, and Athens continued to preserve, even cultivate, its traditional significance as a centre of Hellenic civilization.[9] Furthermore, because it was host to a large community of Roman aristocrats and businessmen, Athens offered practical attractions to anyone journeying east or west.[10] Which is why, in the aftermath of his victory at Philippi, Mark Antony elected to spend his first winter there. It was not merely that Antony relished the refinements of Greek culture, although of course he did. It was rather that, from Athens he could project his fresh identity as victor at Philippi to eastern provinces and principalities anxiously awaiting his delivery of the new dispensation—including the fresh financial exactions the collection of which constituted Antony's assignment in the east. It was a momentous juncture, and Antony selected a venerable and conspicuous stage on which to play it out.[11]

According to Plutarch, Antony devoted the winter of 42/41, his first official visit to Athens, to lofty if conventional Hellenic pursuits:

> Antony' manner toward the Greeks was friendly, neither immoderate nor irksome, at first anyway, and for pleasure, he took delight in listening to the discussions of scholars, attending the games of the goddess, and being initiated into the mysteries. He was fair in his administration of justice and relished being addressed as a lover of Greece, even more as a lover of Athens: he bestowed many gifts on the city.[12]

In Plutarch's telling, Antony balances his duty as a triumvir with his passion for Greek culture. And there is no obvious reason to doubt it. Antony's philhellenism was a conspicuous feature of the sources consulted by Plutarch, and the biographer was also steeped in the Athenians' oral traditions of the triumviral period.[13]

Antony in Athens was in fact a very busy man. He was, after all, responsible for restoring the geopolitical health of the east even as he bled the region of the wealth necessary to satisfy Rome's soldiers.[14] For this reason, Athens became the focus of all political attention, and Antony will have been deluged by correspondence and emissaries endeavouring to secure their homelands the best possible terms in the new world order. Not only statesmen and ambassadors clamoured for the triumvir's attention. Roman and perhaps also eastern financiers, all eager to find new opportunities in the east's new order, hoped to gain an audience with Antony and his circle. Traders, too, will have been keen to cultivate a relationship with Antony.

Antony and the Athenians

The Athenians had an obvious interest in pleasing Antony, and both the city and the triumvir were familiar with the customary conventions for exhibiting good political relations between subject and master. Plutarch, as we have seen, says nothing about anything the Athenians may have done in the way of congratulatory spectacle or divine honours for Antony. These are aspects of Hellenistic civil life which the biographer deplores. And here, for literary reasons, Plutarch omits them in order to furnish us an Antony who succumbs to eastern flummery of this kind only when he leaves Athens, arrives at Ephesus, and soon afterwards falls in with Cleopatra.[15] Yet it is hard to imagine how the city that was not too shy to denominate Brutus divine and accord him and Cassius legendary honours could neglect to pay its respect to the man who vanquished them. Failure to do so would have been remarkable, not least because by now such gestures had become so very routine. Their omission, under these circumstances, could only be shocking, even offensive.[16] Antony's arrival was too important not to be punctuated by grand ceremonies, and not only for the sake of the triumvir. Greek cities in the Hellenistic period were deeply interconnected with one another and therefore keenly competitive in the international contest for prestige.[17] After games and festivities in honour of the triumvirs in Thessalonica and Pella, Athens could hardly have neglected these brands of flummery: its reputation was at stake. The Athenians, there can be no doubt, hoped to impress.

Nor could Antony refuse such honours, even if Plutarch finds them distasteful. By the first century negotiating political power through an exchange of dignified and respectful gestures was conventional stuff and, for all parties involved, more or less obligatory. Because these ceremonies helped to establish a comprehensible and courteous relationship between ruler and ruled, they remained important elements in sound government. This was the case not merely for kings but also Roman governors—and was certainly the case for Antony, whose authority in the aftermath of Philippi was nothing short of awesome from any Greek perspective.[18] Which is why Plutarch's depiction of Antony as a grandee who ignores all ceremony and spectacle, preferring to behave unpretentiously, is astonishing and unbelievable. A figure of Antony's stature eschewing all pageantry would have been an aberration so extreme that it could only flummox and consequently disconcert not only the Athenians but their international audience as well. In practical terms, Antony, as Plutarch portrays him, would have begun his eastern circuit disastrously for all concerned.

So we must try to fill in the gaps. Antony's advent, for instance. Our sources furnish us a wide inventory of standard ceremonial gestures appropriate for welcoming a distinguished guest. No one pattern dominated, but it is reasonably clear that visits to Athens by kings or Roman officials were routinely greeted by receptions, processions, the opening of temples and sanctuaries, sacrifices, banquets, and an invitation to address the citizenry. Further honours were also possible, including sacred ones.[19] Antony's introduction to the city will not have fallen short of this standard, and it will certainly have been on this occasion that he declared the city's freedom and made clear to its citizenry his beneficent intentions. Fulsome expressions of Athenian gratitude, as a matter of course, could not fail to ensue.

We possess tangible evidence of this gratitude. The Athenians minted bronze coins that honoured Antony's generosity. On one of them, we find the head of Athena on the obverse and, on the reverse, Fulminating Zeus, a figure who by this time was readily viewed in Athens as a reference to Zeus Eleutherios, Zeus the protector of freedom. The message was unmistakable. On another issue we find on the reverse a tripod, clearly the Pythian tripod, a symbol of Apollo's divine presence at Delphi and equally clearly an allusion to Antony's generosity to the sanctuary—and perhaps a reference to the triumvirs' claim to champion the cause of liberty.[20] This coin also suggests a very personal tribute to Antony, if it alludes, as surely it must, to the mythological contest over the Delphic tripod between Heracles and Apollo.[21] Perhaps the Athenians were aware of Antony's recent issues in Rome, which foregrounded his Herculean ancestry.[22]

Antony and the Athenians—Reading
Plutarch Speculatively

Plutarch was aware of the realities of Antony's experience in Athens and, although he is selective, he does not, as we have seen, erase from his account every element of the triumvir's official occupation of the city. His respect for historical truth is too serious for that.[23] With that in mind, a close and careful— and speculative—scrutiny of Plutarch's concise rehearsal of Antony's Athenian pastimes may repay the effort. One sentence will occupy our attention:

> for pleasure, he took delight in listening to the discussions of scholars, attending the games of the goddess, and being initiated into the mysteries.[24]

The immediate impression is a highly conventional one. These are activities one might well expect of any philhellenic Roman visiting Athens. But Plutarch's sentence teems with complications. Antony's presence at lectures presents no difficulties. But his other diversions, his attendance at games and mysteries, must detain us. One feels that Plutarch's sense here should be clear: the games of the goddess must be the Panathenaea.[25] As for the mysteries, in the case of a Roman visitor one naturally recognizes a reference to the Eleusinian Mysteries.[26]

But a simple take on this Plutarchan line will not work. Let us begin with the mysteries. Plutarch cannot mean the Eleusinian Mysteries, which had already been celebrated before Antony arrived.[27] If Antony was ever initiated into the Eleusinian Mysteries, that took place in 39 (that appears to be the only possible year in which he was in Athens at the right time, unless he was initiated as a younger man). Perhaps, however, Plutarch has in in mind the Lesser Mysteries, celebrated in the spring when Antony was still in residence.[28] This event, if it took place, would certainly have suited Antony's image. The Lesser Mysteries, at least according to some versions of their origins, were founded in order to purify Heracles and lead him on to his initiation at Eleusis.[29] The celebration of these rites by Antony would have allowed him to re-enact a sacred episode underscoring his mythological heritage—and marking his new relationship with Athens, since the Lesser Mysteries furnished the solemn means by which a powerful foreigner, Heracles originally, and, in this instance, Antony, was successfully integrated into the religious fabric of Athens. The political fabric too: associated with Heracles' initiation was the tradition that he became an Athenian citizen.[30] It is clear that by 32 and very probably by 39, when he held the office of gymnasiarch, Antony possessed Athenian citizenship. It was a possession he may have acquired on this visit.

We turn now to Plutarch's 'games of the goddess'. This expression has suggested to some that Plutarch has in mind the Panathenaea, but that festival took place during the summer, again at a time when Antony was not in Athens.[31] Which means that, if Antony attended games in honour of Athena, these games were somehow extraordinary in nature. This invites the conclusion that they were games the purpose of which was to celebrate Antony's beneficent presence in the city. Now it is hardly surprising that the Athenians should want to put on games in honour of their powerful Roman guest. Such celebrations were hardly novel, and, as we have seen, Thessalonica had put on games for Antony and Octavian, an occasion the Athenians could hardly ignore.[32]

Still, the question remains. What games? How did the Athenians conjoin games in honour of Antony and 'the goddess'? The most prudent course would be to concede our ignorance, agreeing that they came up with something. But there is a speculative possibility we should not overlook. We know that later, in 39/8, the Athenians celebrated games in Antony's honour called (almost certainly) the Panathenaic Antonia. These games are cited, among others, in a decree of the subsequent year.[33] Two lines of that decree are pertinent to Antony and his games:

> [and he competed in the] games both at the Thesei[a and at the Epitaphios] as well as the Pan[athenaic] Antoneia of the god Antony, New Dionysus, [. . .] on the seventeenth of Anthesterion.[34]

Early on it was suggested that Antony's games absorbed or augmented the Panathenaea itself and for this reason this inscription was sometimes restored to read *Panathenaea of Antony*.[35] But there is no good reason to take this view: the Antoneia, as the inscription shows, was held in spring in the month of Anthesterion, whereas the Panathenaea was held in the summer in a different month (Hekatombaion).[36] This discrepancy cannot be resolved by the suggestion that in 39/8 the Panathenaea, for Antony's sake, was celebrated in spring—a proposal based on an alleged imperial habit whereby the Panathenaea was sometimes held in that season. The evidence gathered for that habit is either faulty or irrelevant.[37] In sum, there is simply no reason to connect the Antoneia with the Panathenaea. Still, the Antoneia, it is clear, was a festival that, in some way celebrated both Athena and Antony. It sounds very much like Plutarch's 'games of the goddess'.

It is because in our inscription Antony is denominated the New Dionysus, an identification he assumed in Athens only in 39/8, that modern scholars assume the Antoneia was inaugurated in that year in celebration of the new god. But this conclusion, although possible, is not inevitable. If, after all, the Antoneia existed before Antony became the New Dionysus, it was only natural that, *after* his assumption of this identity, references to him in any formal Attic inscription would denominate him New Dionysus. In other words, nothing in our inscription requires the conclusion that the invention of the Antoneia was tethered to Antony's manifestation as the New Dionysus. Perhaps, then, the games referred to by Plutarch were in fact the Antoneia, games which the biographer could legitimately if misleadingly describe as 'games of the goddess'. The Athenians had no reason to suppose that in celebrating Antonian games in 41 they were introducing a permanent civic institution. But, when Antony returned to the city in 39/8 as the New Dionysus, it was only to be expected that the Antoneia would then be revived. Hence the reference to New Dionysus in our inscription. Almost certainly, however, in 42/41, when Antony was named in any public document, he was, as in the inscription of 39/30, 'Antony the god'.

Antony and the New Order

Celebrations, receptions, games, and sacred honours—although ceremonial flummery of this kind was unattractive to Plutarchan sensibilities, in the aftermath of Philippi its very conventionality can only have signalled to contemporaries a highly welcome degree of continuity. Performances of this kind were institutions as familiar to the Romans as they were to their eastern subjects, and by the first century they had become indispensable as majestic components of government. Antony in the east, events in Athens made clear to everyone, would be nothing in the way of an aberration, nothing unpredictable. Like other overlords before him, including other Roman grandees, he would remain approachable, even cooperative, and so local agency would continue to matter in the exercise of Roman power. Greek cities could expect, under the government of the triumvirs, to move forward by way of familiar exchanges of dignity and esteem. From our perspective, Antony's conventional posture is unsurprising, but in the east, at a time so charged with anxiety, it could hardly have been expected by everyone that the old imperial patterns would be sustained. After Thessalonica, Pella, Delphi, and especially Athens, however, the east could safely conclude that the new order would be nothing too frightfully new, and this brand of normality could only be reassuring as a prelude to the unwelcome financial impositions that lay ahead.[38]

Athens to Asia

Late in spring 41, Antony left Athens. He marched northwards, regaining the Via Egnatia which he followed through Macedonia and onwards to the Hellespont, where he passed into Asia.[39] This was the obvious route. Antony was not well equipped with naval transport,[40] and this journey furnished an opportunity to make a final assessment of foreign threats along the Macedonian frontier and confirm his arrangements in Thrace. In Macedonia Antony had eight legions, but not all or even most of these followed him into Asia. We do not know how large an army Antony left under Censorinus' command, nor do our sources exhibit any serious interest in subsequent Macedonian affairs. It is nevertheless clear that Censorinus' military requirements were substantial. On the first day of his consulship in 39 he celebrated a triumph, and his successor, Asinius Pollio, was equally engaged in fighting along his province's northern frontier.[41] Antony's legate, Marcus Insteius Tectus, was also busy defending Macedonia during the thirties: his actions earned him an acclamation.[42]

It is highly likely, then, that the bulk of Antony's legions remained in Macedonia. This conclusion is confirmed by events in 40, when the Parthians invaded Syria. Antony's legate in Syria, Lucius Decidius Saxa, was easily routed by the enemy's superior numbers. Many of Saxa's troops were in fact former republican soldiers whom Antony had only recently folded into his own army.[43] It was not only in Syria that Rome had too few soldiers. Antony's legate in Asia, Marcus Turius, also lacked manpower adequate for confronting the Parthians. He soon fled to the islands.[44] During this Parthian incursion, Antony was in Egypt, accompanied only by his praetorian guard.[45] It is apparent, then, that Antony entered Asia with fewer legions, perhaps far fewer, than he left behind in Macedonia.[46] Obviously, he anticipated little resistance.

Antony promulgated his itinerary in advance, so cities could prepare to greet him in an appropriate manner and delegations desiring an audience could know where to find him. And find him they did. Antony's settlement of the east, although it entailed little in the way of fighting, demanded nothing less than prodigious administrative assiduity, often in reaction to local crises. He held court first in Bithynia, probably in Nicomedia, its capital. There he was pressed by embassies from so far away as Judea.[47] Thereafter he made his way to Ephesus, where he delivered the triumvirate's financial demands on Asia. Subsequently he made a grand tour of the east: from Ephesus he travelled northeast to Phrygia, then northwest to Mysia, east again to Galatia, further east to Cappadocia, then south to Cilicia (where, at Tarsus, he encountered Cleopatra), and onwards to Syria and Palestine. Afterwards, notoriously, he wintered in Egypt. Antony could cover so much ground only by moving with haste, a pace that intensified his operations at each city or principality he visited. There was much to negotiate.

Ephesus

Our sources dilate on the assizes held by Antony when he was at Ephesus. This city, which served as the capital of Asia, was a natural setting for the delivery of grave announcements by a Roman general. It was at Ephesus, in the aftermath of the First Mithridatic War, that Sulla proclaimed the heavy costs to be imposed on the province.[48] More recently, Caesar had entered the city after his victory at Pharsalus. He briefly settled in Ephesus, where he decided on regional matters before pressing his pursuit of Pompey.[49] Although sorely in need of funds, Caesar exhibited extraordinary generosity—to cities and states. He was liberal with grants of immunity from taxation, remitted a large slice of the levy imposed on Asia by Pompey, and eliminated some of the operations of the *publicani*. At the same time, his treatment of individuals to whose support of Pompey he took exception was nothing short of punitive. Deiotarus of Galatia, for example, although he kept his kingdom, was fined an enormous sum. Similarly, a heavy portion of the property of Pythodorus of Tralles, a rich friend of Pompey, was confiscated and sold.[50] By focusing his exactions on individuals of ample means, including a king, Caesar was able to secure needed monies without inordinately alienating the cities whose goodwill he knew he may need to rely on. After Zela, however, Caesar was a changed man: he plundered Tyre in punishment for its past support of Pompey, his exactions in Greece were severe. Dio, in recording Caesar's extractions at this time, describes him as 'a complete money-grubber'.[51]

Antony, in his turn, came to Ephesus adorned, one might say, with gay religions full of pomp and gold. For there the triumvir was celebrated as Dionysus the Benefactor and Bringer of Joy in a pageant populated by women dressed as Bacchants, boys and men parading as Pans and satyrs, and musicians.[52] These were not the first of Antony's divine honours, as we have seen, and his glorification here was animated by the same impulses that moved the Athenians. Ephesus—indeed, the province of Asia—endeavoured to appeal to the east's new master by way of a medium he could not decently despise. Caesar, after all, when he visited Ephesus, had been honoured by the Greek cities of the province as 'the descendent of Ares and Aphrodite' and 'a god made manifest'—indeed, as 'the common saviour of humanity'.[53] At Athens, Antony was exalted for his kinship with Heracles, protégé of Athena. In Asia he was esteemed a fresh manifestation of Dionysus, another divine benefactor.

Only Plutarch records Antony's Dionysiac reception at Ephesus. Neither Appian nor Dio—each of whom is keen in reporting Antony's transgressions during his visit to this city—mentions divine honours.[54] By contrast, it is amply attested how Antony, as a matter of policy, took on the role of New Dionysus when he returned to the east in 39.[55] Hence the not unreasonable suggestion that, in relating this episode, Plutarch has displaced Antony's later association with the god to his earlier Asian advent.[56] That Plutarch's evidence is exceptional, however, is no reason for concluding he got it wrong. It is not mere pedantry to point out that, according to Plutarch, Antony was *not* New Dionysus at Ephesus, the version of the god he adopted in 39 and thereafter. Nor should we fail to recognize that in 41 it will have been the Ephesians and not Antony who proposed Dionysiac honours.[57] To be sure, his consent was essential, but his willingness to participate in the Ephesians' pageantry, a conventional specimen of symbolic cooperation between a city and its overlord, must not be confused with any new policy on Antony's part. Antony, after all, did not intend to linger in the east any longer than was necessary. For the cities of Asia, however, his arrival represented a singular opportunity, at a very crucial juncture, for winning his favour. Which makes it a certainty that Antony, like Caesar before him, was accorded divine honours of some kind: such treatment, as we have seen, was *de rigueur*, and Antony, like all Romans, appreciated the importance of displaying authority by way of a clearly understood medium.[58]

The Ephesians, perhaps in the hope of capping previous honours, turned to Dionysiac spectacle. This god, wildly popular in archaic and classical Greek society, was the bringer of wine and release, patron of song and drama, and, as the object of mystery cults, a very present help in any mortal's confrontation with the afterlife. To these attractions were added, in Hellenistic times, facets that focused attention on the merits—and duties—of kings. Dionysus' story was somehow brought into conformity with the career of Alexander the Great and, as a consequence, this god become nothing less than a mighty conqueror of the east and, like Heracles or Alexander, a hero whose valour brought him divinity.[59] Dionysus, it was said, was the inventor of the diadem and, with it, Hellenistic monarchy.[60] Indeed, Dionysiac associations suffused the institution of eastern kingship. 'Dionysus', it has rightly been observed, 'was the Hellenistic god *par excellence*'.[61]

In honouring Antony as Dionysus, the Ephesians signalled the Roman's stature as heir to Alexander as vanquisher of the east—and as heroic benefactor. This, surely, was the point: by according Antony Dionysiac dignities, the Ephesians sought to cast the triumvir in a part made for the expression of an almighty goodwill. And, on the day, they were right to be hopeful. Antony made sacrifice to Artemis and, on this same occasion, announced his intention of doubling the extent of the temple's precinct for offering sanctuary.[62] This became a sacred space which Antony scrupulously observed, except in the case of any tyrannicides he apprehended.[63]

For Antony did not come to Ephesus only to play the part of a regal, eastern god, however much he may have relished the role. He was also—and principally—an avenger of Caesar, and reverently devoted to his great friend's memory. Antony ordered the inscription, in Greek translation, of the legal proposal which created him the *flamen* of Divus Iulius, the new Roman god.[64] This measure, as we have seen, was a facet of the triumvirs' early and urgent legislative agenda in 42.[65] The surviving inscription is highly fragmentary and not entirely free of doubtful points, but, on any reading, it is clear enough that it foregrounds Antony's status in the cultivation of the divine Julius Caesar:

> . . . do you desire and so order that Mark Antony . . . the flaminate of Divus Iulius[66]

The promulgation of this measure—in Ephesus and almost certainly elsewhere in the east—made clear to everyone, in yet another elaboration of the sacred contest between himself and the tyrannicides, the very Roman brand of religious authority which Antony would deploy in punishing enemies of the Caesarian cause. And perhaps he went even further. A speculative but carefully constructed argument advances the intriguing claim that, during this visit to Ephesus, Antony supervised the installation of a cult to Rome and Divus Iulius.[67]

The triumvirs' righteous struggle against the impiety of the Liberators was a theme, struck by Antony again and again, which both justified the campaign at Philippi and also characterized the essential quality of his mission in the east. The centrality of this sacred vengeance is unmistakable even in Antony's communications with Rome's subjects. In a letter to Hyrcanus, the ethnarch of Judea, Antony is expansive on the topic of the Liberators' profanity: they were abominations, transgressed divine ordinances, violated temples, and broke holy oaths.[68] In avenging Caesar, Antony asserts, the triumvirs are now restoring peace to Asia.[69] In another letter, to the Tyrians, in addition to cataloguing the respects in which the Liberators violated the Roman constitution, Antony underscores their sacrilege and, once again, their violation of oaths. Antony also emphasizes the peace which the triumvirs will ensure.[70] These paired themes—vengeance and peace—doubtless recurred in all Antony's correspondence.[71] Not that Antony imagined any of Rome's eastern subjects found their hearts strangely moved by the religious dimensions of Caesar's assassination, but it was his intention to advertise the ideological pretext animating the triumvirs' office and to remind his Roman audience—the substance of these communications certainly will have made their way to the capital—that in his provincial administration he carried on in championing Caesar's cause.

The divine honours which Antony accepted in the east at this time were never intended to serve as any kind of counteraction to Octavian's official status as *divi filius*. His flaminate, however, installed him in a conspicuous and sacred relationship with the new divinity and reinforced his role as Caesar's avenger. At least for now, it remained an aspect of his identity he meant to show off, even in the east.[72] The victor at Philippi, no one could doubt it, was committed to the elimination of the dictator's murderers—as well as anyone else who refused to be reconciled to the new order. The regime of the Liberators was well and truly at an end.

Exactions

Neither the Bringer of Joy nor the Benefactor, Antony's version of Dionysus, as Plutarch put it, was soon revealed as the Devourer.[73] At Ephesus he made it painfully clear how grievously Asia was to be taxed. Although our sources concentrate almost wholly on this one province, it had to be obvious to every delegate in attendance that the Romans' exactions were hardly to be limited to any single region, whether or not other levies were now promulgated.[74] At first the triumvir sought ten years' tribute within a single year—no more, he observed, than had been extorted by the Liberators—but this demand was met with protests so vehement that he eventually reduced it and agreed to be satisfied with the revenues of nine years, which he allowed to be handed over within a period of no more than two years.[75] Even this revised bill was an enormous one.

Whether Antony, like Caesar before him, also confiscated the property of wealthy individuals is less certain. Plutarch cites outrages perpetrated by the triumvir in order to enrich his eastern friends: none of these actions is unthinkable, but, in their ensemble, they suggest an excerpt from anti-Antonian polemic.[76] Accusations of cruelty in provincial administration were commonplace in Roman vituperation, and Antony's behaviour at Ephesus was an episode held against him during his later propaganda contest with Octavian: Marcus Valerius Messalla Corvinus, by then an ally of the young Caesar, attacked Antony with a tract entitled *On the Settlement of Asia's Taxes*.[77] This censure persisted into the reign of Augustus, who, in his *Res Gestae*, boasted of restoring to the temples of Asia the sacred objects Antony had appropriated as his personal property.[78] It is in polemic of this ilk that most complaints of Antonian thefts will have originated and ultimately made their way into Plutarch. Which is not to say that Antony neglected his own interests. He was certainly entitled to confiscate, on Rome's behalf, any lands or other properties belonging to proscribed Romans. At least some of these acquisitions became the triumvir's personal property, a reality reflected in the profusion of Antonii throughout Asia and elsewhere, including rural regions: these are likely to be descendants of Antonian freedmen originally operating on his estates.[79]

According to one likely calculation, the annual tribute from Asia was around 2,500 talents—a significant sum—but this is only a very rough estimate.[80] In any case, we cannot know at what precise figure Antony reckoned Asia's tribute for the purposes of his exactions.[81] But it was probably on the high end of routine expectations—in which case we may believe that Antony insisted on a payment, spread over two years, of perhaps as much as 23,000 talents. Our sources ignore Rome's other provinces, for which, once again, we must turn to other imprecise estimates. It has been proposed that the annual tribute for Cilicia was around 300 talents, for Bithynia and Pontus around 800 talents, and, in the case of wealthy Syria, a figure in the neighbourhood of 5,000 talents.[82] If these provinces, like Asia, were required to furnish Antony with nine years' tribute, their contribution may well have amounted to something like 55,000 talents. Less lucrative were any contributions demanded of Greece, and once again we know very little about the Roman levy there.[83] We know even less about the tribute Rome collected from the Cyrenaica or from Crete. The economy of the former, it appears, was ailing during this time.[84] Crete remained robust but may have benefitted from its close connection with Antony's family. Nevertheless, in view of the triumvirs' current requirements, each region certainly will have been taxed. Antony also imposed on the independent kingdoms and states in Rome's eastern empire, although (once again) we do not know the magnitude of these levies.[85] Antony will also have intended to punish Egypt for its alleged support of the Liberators: he was familiar already with its riches and certainly expected to appropriate a share of them in order to pay the triumvirs' expenses in Italy. Now it must be underlined that the deployment of specific numbers in this paragraph should in no way be confused with anything like quantitative accuracy. Still, we are perhaps not too far wrong in speculating that Antony expected to extract as much as 85,000 talents from the east. This figure, even if it is lowered by, say, as much as 10,000 talents, remains staggering—and it is certain that, out of their own immediate resources, few of the cities or principalities of the east could begin to meet it.[86]

Not every state fell victim to Antony's levy. Before departing Rome for Philippi, Octavian and Antony vowed to rescue Rhodes and the Lycian Federation from Cassius' enormities.[87] In keeping with that promise, Antony freed the Lycians from taxation and may have aided them in rebuilding one of their cities, which had been sacked by Cassius. Immunity from the levy, although it goes unmentioned, must have been one of the benefactions Rhodes received from the triumvir.[88] Laodicea and Tarsus were also spared. There may have been others.[89] Antony also went to the expense of offering relief to at least some of the cities which had suffered during Cassius' tenure in the east.[90] With every act of generosity, however, Antony reduced his overall takings—unless of course he compensated himself through an exercise of severity elsewhere. Immunity from taxation cannot in any case have been a frequent reward.

Confronted by Antony's demands so soon after disgorging the sums exacted by the Liberators, the east had little choice but to borrow.[91] Although numerous states had certainly been impoverished, and although the triumvirs were strapped for funds, great wealth remained in private hands both in Italy and especially in the east.[92] Polities must now turn to *publicani* and other financiers in order to meet their obligations to Rome. This unavoidable expedient was nothing less than dire, as recent provincial history had demonstrated. When, at the conclusion of the First Mithridatic War, Sulla decreed that Asia must immediately pay 20,000 talents (the total he calculated for indemnities he imposed on Asian cities, Rome's military expenses, and the amount of five years' worth of provincial taxes), this sum could be raised only through loans. And these loans could be secured only at high interest. The consequences were devastating: fourteen years later the province's debts had swollen to 120,000 talents, and the region's fiscal misery was cured only by reforms introduced by Licinius Lucullus in 70.[93]

Calamity of a similar order—expensive loans and crushing civic debts—loomed once again, and not only for Asia, which explains the boldness with which Antony's demand was resisted. We do not know what measures, if any, Antony took to regulate the terms offered by lenders. In view of the grim financial landscape left behind by the Liberators as well as the urgency attending Antony's need for funds, he will have been disinclined to put constraints on credit, which, predictably during a time of civil war, remained tight.[94] Nor was Antony likely to put himself or his associates at a disadvantage when it came to profiting from provincial exigency. After all, along with rich and opportunistic *publicani*, investors in the east would now doubtless include some of the men in Antony's entourage—as well as local elites enjoying close ties to Antony or other influential men in Rome.[95] Antony, too, may have supplied loans, like Pompey before him: he, uniquely, was in a position to lend without furnishing any real capital, since no one on the Roman side could call him to account. For obvious reasons, then, this was hardly the time to let future profits go unclaimed, whatever the implications for the subsequent economic health of the east. Antony's programme was interrupted by the Parthians' invasion in the following year, but, after he regained the east, it will have been reimposed. It brought Antony great rewards: by the time of the battle of Actium, Antony's wealth was enormous.[96] Nor is it obvious that the economy of the east in general was at that time in difficult straits. Some cities, however, continued to struggle. After Antony's defeat, Octavian felt obliged to cancel at least some public debts in the Asian provinces, a benefaction that was long remembered.[97] Nor can we doubt that, in 41, Antony's levy was abominated: inhabitants of the island of Arados, to take a single example, went so far as to lynch the tax-collectors he sent to them.[98]

The condition of loans which had previously been arranged by cities or kingdoms struggling to meet the impositions of the Liberators offered fresh ground for negotiation. Antony was in a position to annul these, and it is almost a certainty that, in many cases, he did so. After all, financiers whose investments had enabled enemies of the state could hardly expect gentle treatment.[99] Perhaps there were not so many of these loans: the Liberators preferred to seize and abscond with whatever valuables they could lay their hands on.[100] Still, for any existing loans it was important that Antony exercise a degree of discrimination in assessing them. Sometimes, as Cicero discovered in governing Cilicia, important figures lurked behind complex financial arrangements.[101] And although it is true that, during civil war, Roman leaders rarely hesitated to inflict losses on *publicani*, it was important for Antony, when punishing some capitalists, not to offend those on whose services he and the east were now dependent.[102]

For Antony and Octavian very much needed the cooperation of the financiers, not least because the cities of the east can, at this point, have possessed only modest supplies of cash or precious metals. Antony's immediate requirement was hard currency. Even if he was willing to burden his subjects with the expense of provisioning his army, he needed coined money with which to pay it.[103] Antony also undertook the building of a fleet (by the spring of 40 it was 200 ships strong): although he was in a position to requisition raw materials, Antony needed coinage with which to pay craftsmen and hire sailors.[104] Now it is clear enough that the east was populated with *publicani* holding massive cash reserves—during the civil war against Caesar neither Metellus Scipio nor Pompey scrupled to deprive them of funds—and this meant that Antony could expect some payments in cash either directly from the cities or from their creditors.[105]

The bulk of Antony's proceeds, however, were required in Italy, and while it was not impossible for him physically to shift large quantities of coins or precious metal to Rome, that was not the Romans' preferred approach when transferring funds.[106] It is more likely that Antony employed some sort of paper transactions.[107] Doing so allowed Octavian to gain nearly immediate access to cash already sitting in Rome.[108] Proscriptions, seizures, and harsh taxation had enabled the triumvirs to issue massive quantities of coins in 42.[109] But these funds were expended in the war against the

Liberators. By opening the east to profitable investment Antony and Octavian hoped to find a gentler, indeed positively attractive means of putting their hands on the cash still held back by anxious Italian capitalists. Naturally the cooperation of *publicani* was needed in order to render this operation feasible, a state of affairs that gave them ample leverage when setting the terms of their loans. Antony's brother, Lucius, was popular and well-connected among Rome's financiers.[110] Consequently, the brothers Antonius were in a position to exploit their ties with this important circle in order to promote stability and profit—in the west.

It is routinely concluded that Antony did not come close to extracting the money he demanded of the east, but this is a conclusion that neglects the utility of turning to lenders east and west.[111] And, by constructing loans early on, Antony perhaps avoided the shortfall that supervened upon the Parthian invasion in the next year, after which direct exactions from the bulk of the east became impossible for at least two years. Still, the extraction of 85,000 talents was no small or simple matter, and in executing this policy there must have been disappointments and failures, often serious ones. But even that amount, though large, fell short of the truly gigantic sum which the triumvirs had promised their legions, true even if Antony planned to impose a hefty penalty on Egypt. Perhaps Antony and Octavian grossly overestimated the wealth available in the east. It is more likely, however, that they never expected fully to honour their pledges and instead hoped that most veterans would be satisfied with grants of land and most rankers would, in the end, gladly accept whatever bonus they received. In this they appear to have reckoned rightly. Still, there remained many soldiers who never saw anything in the way of promised rewards: these, too, when they complained, the triumvirs endeavoured to satisfy with allocations of property instead of cash.[112]

A New Dispensation

The restoration of political order was imperative. During the near anarchy of civil war, cities were racked by local perturbations and opportunistic dynasts seized their moment to pursue parochial ambitions.[113] As Antony observed, the east suffered from 'a grave disease', and his administration was to be the remedy.[114] We have nothing in the way of a comprehensive account of Antony's resettlement of the east. Information regarding his arrangements for Greece and the Aegean focuses on Athens and Rhodes. As for the residue of Rome's eastern dominions, our evidence is scanty and uneven, especially when it comes to minor principalities the settlement of which also required Antony's intervention. Antony had much to do, and circumstances required that he work quickly. But he did not, indeed could not, remake the geopolitical conditions of the east from scratch: his resettlement of the east was shaped by prior Roman policies, especially the dispositions imposed in the east by Pompey the Great and by Caesar.

The organization of Rome's eastern empire was principally shaped by Pompey in the aftermath of the Third Mithridatic War (73–63). He annexed regions he deemed easily and profitably governable, or where there was no viable alternative. To the existing provinces of Asia, Bithynia, and Cilicia, Pompey added Syria and (after an intensive programme of urbanization) the region of Pontus. As for those territories regarded by the Romans as uncivilized or too alien to manage without misunderstandings, these he handed over to native kings and dynasts: they knew better than the Romans how to maintain order in their own territories. And by promoting clients Pompey shifted the costs and exertions of government and defence to them.[115] In most cases, Pompey also required tribute, and of course Rome reserved the right to demand any client's resources whenever it required them.[116] This strategy was not without its risks. Each autocrat set his own survival ahead of the interests of the republic. For this reason, every autocrat remained susceptible to the pressures of factions within his realm and was inclined to be suspicious of neighbouring clients (who were personal rivals as much as partners in the Romans' empire).[117] The Romans were fully seized of these realities. Nevertheless, they expected loyalty, and often rewarded it.

It was the Romans' preference, whenever possible, to leave well enough alone. When Caesar imposed a fresh settlement on the east after his victories at Pharsalus and Zela, he preserved, with only a few tweaks, existing arrangements.[118] Loyalists, to be sure, were rewarded. Mithradates of Pergamum, a man valued by Caesar, became king in Bosporus and additionally received a portion of Galatia.[119] A Bithynian noble, Lycomedes, was, as we have seen, installed as Priest in Cappadocian Comana.[120] Caesar's prevailing policy was to pardon even dynasts who had lent Pompey their support. Deiotarus I, although he was heavily fined and deprived of parts of his dominion, remained king of Galatia.[121] Ariobarzanes III of Cappadocia, Antiochus of Commagene, and Tarcondimotus of Heirapolis-Castabala were each of them retained: a grateful Tarcondimotus went so far as to name his daughter Julia.[122] It is clear—and was made clear to all—that Caesar understood the exigencies imposed on Roman subjects by the realities of civil war: even the brother of Ariobarzanes, Ariarathes X, who fought alongside Pompey at Pharsalus, was endowed by Caesar with a principality of his own.[123]

Like Caesar before him, Antony endeavoured to make the best of the political infrastructure he found. But the situation Antony confronted was a grim one. The Liberators had brought Greece, Asia, and Syria nearly to rack and ruin. For the triumvirs, then, it was nothing less than a duty to restore order, and that responsibility lay with Antony.[124] Our sources, however, deliver us an Antony who appears anything but responsible. Once in Asia, we are told, he put kingdoms and principalities up for sale. As a consequence, he was mobbed by monarchs tussling with one another in a contest to offer the highest bid. Queens, too, sought Antony's favour by way of their beauty or accessibility. Such is the tenor of the accounts we find in Plutarch, Appian, and Dio.[125] But here their polemical inclinations are unmistakable. This, after all, is an Antony who carries on the Ciceronian caricature of a debauched noble deploying his authority not as a serious stateman but instead as a womanizing profiteer.[126] Such defamation should not distract us from the reality of Antony's exertions.

And yet there *were* rumours of frivolous, irresponsible behaviour. In Italy, during the strife occasioned by the Perusine War, Octavian could mock Fulvia in obscene verses which drew attention to Antony's affair with Glaphyra, the comely wife of Archelaus, king of Cappadocia—evidence that gossip in Asia soon reached so far as Rome.[127] Even the sober Appian reports that Glaphyra's good looks induced Antony to prefer her son, Sisines, over Ariarethes when the two men contested the Cappadocian throne. But here Appian is confused or misled. Ariarethes X reigned in Cappadocia until 37 or 36, when he was replaced (on Antony's order) by Archelaus, who was indeed Glaphyra's son and just conceivably a Sisines who, when he became king, adopted a fresh regal identity by taking on the name of his father and grandfather.[128] This is not to say that Antony did not seduce Glaphyra in 41—that would hardly be out of character—but it is obvious from Appian's version of events that ancient polemicists told a tale in which a concupiscent Antony was early on manipulated by the Cappadocian queen. That side of the story we can safely reject.[129] As for kings bearing gifts, it was only to be expected that Antony should be receptive to regal generosity: tangible expressions of esteem were an essential dimension of these negotiations.

In putting the east to rights, as we shall see, Antony was a busy man. Nothing could be more misleading than the long-standing judgement that, in making his settlement, Antony 'gives an unfortunate impression of laziness'.[130] Our sources are correct to say that he was mobbed by kings and petitioners, and he was obliged to come to grips with the social and political condition of multiple states and principalities. The principles he employed in making a new settlement were various: in some cases, he punished; in others, he rewarded; in still others, he left matters more or less as he found them. Often, but not always, he looked to Caesar's disposition.

Greece and the Aegean

We begin with Greece and the Aegean. To Rhodes, which had suffered grievously for its resistance to Cassius, Antony awarded the islands Andros, Naxos, Myndos, and Tenos—this last a possession sought unsuccessfully by Athens, whose confidence had clearly been restored by its experience with Antony over the preceding winter. And not without reason: although he denied them Tenos, Antony granted the Athenians Aegina, Ceos, Icos, Sciathos, and Peparaethos. The latter two islands Antony withdrew from Thasos as punishment for its assistance to the Liberators.[131] Eretria and Oropus were perhaps also assigned to Athens.[132] He certainly confirmed the city in its possession of Imbros, Scyros, Delos, and Salamis.[133] Antony's reorganization of this region may have gone beyond these arrangements, but apart from these reports our sources fail us.

Crete, which in 44 had been assigned to Brutus, required attention. It appears, however, that Antony did not immediately install a Roman governor. His personal ties with the island were close and perhaps close enough for him to perceive that, in the short term, the island's consolidation and the Romans' extraction of tribute were tasks best left in local hands. Consequently, he appointed Cydas, perhaps the same man whom he enrolled as a juror in Rome, as Cretarch for overseeing the operations of Crete's federated cities.[134] During his consulship, as we have seen, Antony had pressed for greater autonomy in Crete. But that is no reason to conclude that he now intended this arrangement to be a lasting one. And, indeed, when Antony returned to the east in 39 he appointed a Roman governor to the island. Cretan society enjoyed close connections with the Cyrenaica. This province too, which in 44 became Cassius' responsibility, now needed a governor. Antony presumably furnished one, but we know nothing about him.

Greek cities favoured by Antony were not slow in displaying their gratitude. The Athenians' celebrations of the triumvir we have remarked. The Rhodians, too, expressed thankfulness by way of divine honours. On Naxos the Rhodians dedicated a statue of the triumvir in the island's venerable temple of Dionysus. Antony's Ephesian acclamation as Dionysus clearly resonated, and few places were better suited than Naxos to endorse his connection with this god. By locating Antony's statue in the cella of Dionysus' temple and denominating its subject as divine, Rhodes dignified Antony by establishing a connection with local sacred institutions.

Or so we can safely conclude from this dedication's material remains.[135] What survives is a headless Roman general, clad in a cuirass whose ornamentation includes Dionysus attended by a panther and whose chest plate features both Heracles fighting the Nemean lion—one of the hero's celebrated labours—and the punishment of Dirce. The labour of the Nemean lion, obviously, exhibits Heracles' superhuman service to humanity and registers Antony's descent from this mighty figure. The punishment of Dirce is a perhaps less straightforward depiction of divine justice. Here the sons of Antiope, Amphion and Zethus, bind their mother's tormenter to a bull which will trample her to death. The travails of Antiope were best known in antiquity by way of a celebrated tragedy by Euripides. Impregnated by Zeus and persecuted by her family, Antiope was sorely abused by her uncle's wife, Dirce. When she escaped, she was very nearly murdered by Dirce. This wicked character, leading a band of maenads, women worshipping Dionysus in a state of ecstasy, attempted to recapture Antiope. But Antiope was rescued by her sons, and it is their gruesome punishment of Dirce which is portrayed on the cuirass of the Naxian General. In this scene Dirce is punished for her wrongdoing, and the presence of a bull, a clear reference to Dionysus, signals the god's agency in meting out justice to those falsely pretending to honour him.[136] In the general's outstretched arm, according to the statue's likeliest reconstruction, he held a dancing maenad, a true celebrant.

This statue's base is important to its identification: on it are traces of an earlier inscription, conspicuously erased and replaced by a reattribution: 'to the divine Caesar', that is, to Octavian.[137] The iconography of the statue, however, in its combination of Heraclean and Dionysiac imagery, is strongly suggestive of Antony, even if we admit that both divinities were always entirely pertinent to the projection of regal or imperial power in the Hellenistic east. More decisive is the statue's reattribution: the erasure on its base almost certainly reflects the ostentatious marks of Antony's *damnatio memoriae* and his replacement as just lord of the east by Octavian. That the young Caesar should permit himself to be commemorated in this guise is unsurprising. Legend had it that, at the demise of his career, Antony was abandoned by Dionysus, who preferred his rival's cause, clearly a specimen of Octavian's propaganda.[138] Thereafter Augustus duly appropriated both Hercules and Bacchus, the Roman manifestations of Heracles and Dionysus, an almost predictable manoeuvre in view of the pervasiveness of their symbolic work in the east.[139]

This Rhodian compliment to Antony operates at more than one level. The relief on the cuirass of the Naxian General, it is clear, adapts a freestanding statue: the famous Rhodian punishment of Dirce. This masterpiece, now lost, was later transported to Rome and eventually inspired the Farnese Bull, recovered from the remains of the Baths of Caracalla. The Naxian General's unmistakable iconographic reference to the

Rhodian Dirce reinforces that island's gratitude to Antony for its acquisition of Naxos. It also possible that, on the General's cuirass, a viewer might see in the deed of the twins an expression of gratitude both to Octavian and to Antony—both triumvirs, after all, had vowed to rescue Rhodes—and Antony could hardly object to his junior partner's receiving a cameo appearance here.[140] Now it is possible that Rhodes dedicated this statue only after Antony returned to the east in 39, but it is in the immediate aftermath of the triumvir's benefaction that this gesture appears to fit best. The dedication will certainly have been advertised widely (there is no evidence whatsoever that Antony ever saw it with his own eyes) and it was clearly well known: otherwise Octavian should hardly have taken the trouble of usurping it after Actium.

Antony the Philhellene

As the east's resident master, Antony was ideally placed to indulge his natural philhellenism. Our evidence, however, is sometimes scrappy, sometimes refracted by way of hostile defamation.[141] The favouritism he showed his artistic friends during his stay in Ephesus attracted Plutarch's opprobrium.[142] The biographer complains that the property of private persons was seized in order to reward skilled dancers and musicians—even a gifted chef. Underlying this obvious defamation rests Antony's fondness for Greek performances and the virtuosos whose talents made them possible. True, connections of this kind could be adduced by detractors as disgraceful owing to the vast discrepancy in rank between a senator and any singer or actor or musician. Still, men like Sulla and Caesar were unashamed to number Greek performers among their friends.[143] And aspiring politicians in Rome often had to make it their business to win over distinguished artists for the sake of the games and festivals they were obliged to produce for the public.[144] Outside politics, the elite, not least Roman grandees, exhibited their wealth and culture by way of sumptuous, private banquets, the glamour of which depended on dramatic and musical entertainments. That an impression of pre-eminence could be made by such rich and refined affairs was a lesson the Romans had learned from Hellenistic kings and their courts. And it was a practice which Roman leaders could and did employ when cutting a commanding figure in their eastern empire.[145] Antony was no exception.[146] Lavish and dazzling personal pageantry was, for the triumvir, an instinctual, thoroughly Roman exhibition of his primacy.

So, too, Antony's generosity towards Greek cultural institutions. A papyrus reveals that he reaffirmed the privileges of a body known as the Synod of Worldwide Wreathed Winners in the Sacred Games—and granted new ones besides.[147] This document, a letter sent by Antony to the Federation of the Greeks in Asia, credits Antony's friend and athletic trainer, Marcus Antonius Artemidorus, as well as Charopeinus, an Ephesian who was an official of the Synod, with drawing the Winners' circumstances to his attention. In this same letter Antony further agrees to Artemidorus' request that a bronze plaque commemorating the Synod's honours be engraved and dedicated. This is our first historical encounter with the Wreathed Winners. Although the nature of their society remains debatable, the likeliest conclusion, admittedly provisional, is that the Wreathed Winners were an organization of athletes.[148] Now the importance of athletic competition in Greek civic life hardly needs expansion here, but Antony's bestowal of privileges was not limited to the Wreathed Winners: he also favoured distinguished learned societies, including travelling grammarians, rhetoricians, and physicians.[149] Antony's benefactions were obviously meant to endear him with the eastern public, in the hope, perhaps, of proving he was something more than Rome's most recent tax-collector.

In another gesture of philhellenic generosity, Antony endowed a gymnasium, or perhaps sponsored the office of gymnasiarch, in Tarsus, a city he exempted from his eastern levy. Antony's friend, the poet and orator Boethius, filled this position, from which post and by way of Antony's patronage he made himself master of the city.[150] We learn of this benefaction only en passant, but Antony's gesture was nothing short of grand. The centrality of the gymnasium in any Greek city during the Hellenistic period is well established.[151] This institution was so important that it was frequently a site for exhibiting regal honours, even ruler-cult. Early in the second century, Titus Quinctius Flamininus, celebrated as a liberator of Greece, was honoured by Chalcis when that city's gymnasium was dedicated to the Roman and the god Heracles.[152]

Romans living abroad, especially Romans who had been educated there, were intimately familiar with the social capital Greeks invested in the gymnasium.[153] In Chios, for instance, at some time in the late second or early first century, a wealthy Roman businessman, Lucius Nassius, dedicated statues of his sons in the city's gymnasium.[154] Some Roman grandees shared Nassius' sensibility. In Sicily Marcus Claudius Marcellus donated a gymnasium to Catana, and Scipio Africanus dedicated a statue of Hermes in the gymnasium of Tyndaris. Even the disreputable Verres grasped the idea: he allowed the city of Leontini to erect his statue in its gymnasium.[155] Romans, certainly Romans with Hellenic inclinations, recognized clearly how, by in some way endowing or at the very least adorning a city's gymnasium, they could win prestige in Greek communities. Antony's benefaction to Tarsus carries on this practice. It is possible, of course, that Antony's philanthropy in Ephesus or Tarsus or elsewhere was performed only in reaction to strategic requests by opportunistic locals. Even so, such petitions required his personal involvement in community affairs. And his dispensations, plainly, were designed both to enhance his prestige widely and also, in the case of places like Tarsus, impose lasting and local personal clout.

Rome's Eastern Empire

When it came to settling Rome's eastern clients, Antony preferred, when he could, to retain what he found. Predictably, he respected arrangements put in place by Caesar. Consequently, Antiochus I remained king in Commagene.[156] So, too, other dynasts: Lycomedes in Pontica Comana; Iamblichus in Emesa; Tarcondimotus in Hierapolis-Castabala; Malichus, king of the Nabatean Arabs.[157] In the case of cities, too, Antony often preserved Caesar's dispensations. Laodicea in Syria and Antioch by Daphne were again proclaimed free. In recognition of Cassius' harsh occupation of Laodicea, Antony now bestowed immunity from taxation.[158] He did not, however, simply rubber-stamp Caesar's arrangements: he adapted his dispensation to its new circumstances. Although Caesar had granted freedom to the city of Amisus, Antony now subjected it to a king.[159] Asander, king in Bosporus, was disliked by Caesar, who encouraged Mithridates of Pergamum to wage a war against him. But Mithridates was repulsed by Asander. This success made it clear to Antony that, however unpopular the man had been with Caesar, he possessed the competence required for maintaining order in a highly strategic part of the east (grain from the regions of the Black Sea was a vital resource). Consequently, he left Asander undisturbed.[160]

Other figures, too, whose ability or tenacity impressed, were permitted to retain their position. Alba was continued at Olba, where ultimately she became a favourite of both Cleopatra and Antony. Among the Ituraeans, Ptolemy, son of Mennaeus, was the chief figure. From his capital, Chalcis, he dominated the plain of Massyas. This man had survived Pompey and all subsequent Roman authorities. Now this man was no friend of Antony's friend, Antipater's son Herod. Nonetheless, Antony kept this energetic dynast on.[161] Adiatorix, a Galatian tetrarch as early as 50 (and so obviously a ruler kept on by Caesar), attracted Antony's favour: he saw his domains increased by the addition of Heraclea Pontica. Deeply loyal to Antony, he was ultimately executed by Octavian.[162]

Antony proclaimed the freedom of many cities: Syrian Apamea, for example, in gratitude for which benefaction an Antonian era was introduced.[163] In some cases Antony's action must imply a change of government. In others, however, his proclamation constituted a reassuring signal of continuity. Antony's actions are only occasionally mentioned explicitly. More often we must rely on inferences drawn from the later treatment of individual cities at the hands of Augustus or his successors. On this basis, it is clear that nearly twenty-five cities were declared free by Antony—and perhaps there were more.[164] Freedom, admittedly precious, did not in itself entail immunity from taxation, though sometimes both privileges were granted, as in the case of Cnidus.[165] Even on its own, however, a grant of freedom, because it exhibited respect for local elites, fostered their loyalty to Rome.[166]

Elsewhere Antony was more disruptive. In many Syrian cities, tyrants installed by Cassius remained in power.[167] These men had to go, and, after Antony removed them, several fled to Parthia.[168] One of these expelled tyrants was Marion of Tyre, who, after his installation, had waged war against Judea and against Antony's friend Herod. A letter by Antony, addressed to Tyre, indicates his extrusion from power.[169] The promotion of new regimes, then, was also a facet of Antony's resettlement of Syria. It is possible that in some instances Antony simply replaced one autocrat with another. In others, however, he doubtless preferred to work with an oligarchy.[170] Interventions of this kind may have taken place in other regions. It appears that Antony concentrated on rooting out Cassius' men. Channaeus, a dynast in northern Syria whose duplicity and simplicity Ventidius succeeded in exploiting during his campaign against the Parthians, was certainly not the only local potentate Antony left undisturbed.[171]

In the regions of Bithynia and Pontus, Antony's interventions were also stark. Numerous cities were deprived of their freedom: Amaseia and Megalopolis, it appears, were handed over to dynasts; at Zela the traditional authority of its priests was restored; the region of Caranitis was entrusted to a Galatian dynast named Ateporix; the city of Amisus, as we have seen, was handed over to a king, perhaps to the figure later removed by Augustus, a certain Strato.[172] The city of Prusias, also known as Cius, was subjected to the authority of a queen, Orsoberis Musa.[173] It was probably at this time that Antony deprived Neapolis and Pompeiopolis of their freedom and transferred both cities to the dominion of Galatia.[174] It is not immediately obvious why Antony intervened so intensively in this part of the east. Perhaps these cities had been too accommodating to the Liberators' cause. Or perhaps, after so much abuse by way of warfare and Roman exactions, the populations in these places were too restless to entrust them to anything but an autocracy. It was a Roman habit to rescind the freedom of polities roiled by internal faction, and this kind of perturbation may have been especially acute in Pontus. It appears that from the beginning Antony was less than convinced by Pompey's arrangements in this region. Later, in 39, the triumvir entirely abandoned the attempt to make Pontus into a proper Roman province and handed its administration over to kings and dynasts.[175]

The king of Paphlagonia, Attalus, had been installed by Pompey.[176] Neighbouring Galatia was the realm of the durable Deiotarus.[177] Both men died in 41, leaving a vacuum of leadership in a crucial region.[178] In view of the strategic importance of these regions, this was perhaps the most consequential single appointment made by Antony during his resettlement. He placed Deiotarus' grandson, Castor II, on the throne of Galatia. He also set him in charge of Paphlagonia.[179] Castor was well-known in Roman circles. In 45—at Rome—he accused Deiotarus of plotting against Caesar, who personally adjudicated the matter. Cicero spoke on behalf of the king—we possess his speech—and naturally Castor comes in for a good deal of abuse in it.[180] Other prominent Romans, like Brutus, were also the king's close friends.[181] Castor, then, must have made enemies in the capital.

Caesar did not reach a verdict on Deiotarus' loyalty before his assassination. Antony, however, during his consulship, published a decree, allegedly drawn from the dictator's unpublished acts, which confirmed Deiotarus in possession of all his domains, including territory he had only recently reacquired. Cicero, in a letter to Atticus, expresses outrage, and in his *Second Philippic* heaps scorn on the very idea that Caesar could ever have favoured this king in terms so generous as Antony's edict. The inevitable imputation of bribery circulated, in this instance a complaint that Fulvia had extracted a massive sum from the Galatian monarch.[182] That Deiotarus purchased Antony's support, with or without the mediation of Fulvia, one can easily believe. Caesar endured but never embraced Deiotarus, and his hesitation in condemning the man was probably owing to his deference to the king's eminent Roman supporters. In this instance, Cicero's incredulity at Antony's decree was a fair reaction. Antony's willingness to be bribed by Deiotarus, however, does not in itself number him among the king's friends. Quite the contrary: if they were in any way close, the consul would hardly have squeezed so much cash out of the king.[183]

Still, this episode does nothing to suggest that Antony was Castor's friend. Why, then, did Antony elevate him? Perhaps he had come to like the man or at the very least to respect him. In this matter, he was very likely advised by Deiotarus' secretary, Amyntas, whom Antony esteemed. When the king sent forces to fight for Brutus at Philippi, he appointed Amyntas their commander. Amyntas, however, soon perceived the likely outcome of this struggle. Consequently, he and his soldiers defected to Antony.[184] Which left him in an excellent position to furnish advice on Galatian affairs in the aftermath of Deiotarus' demise. It may have been Amyntas' recommendation that won over the triumvir. Castor was in any case the obvious choice if Antony wished to extend Deiotarus' regal line. Clearly Antony had confidence in him: he made him king both of Galatia and Paphlagonia. Castor proved a good choice. He weathered the Parthians' invasion during the subsequent year and retained his domains until his death in 36.[185]

Antony and Judea

Although Antony's political authority was irresistible, it is a mistake to imagine that he could manage the east simply by issuing decrees. Roman provincial administration, as we have seen, always entailed councils and deliberation, consultation with friends and contacts at Rome. Even a pretence of justice—and the perception of justice was important to the Romans—required opportunities for all invested parties to submit claims and counterclaims before any final decision could be rendered by the triumvir. Which is not to say that it was routinely Antony's choice to insert himself deeply into local political conflicts. Far from it: the Roman habit was, so far as possible, to grant subject cities administrative liberty and intrude only when civic discord required it.[186] As for kings, it was Antony's expressed view that those who confer regal authority on a man should leave him free to exercise it.[187] Nevertheless, in the aftermath of the triumvirs' regime change, there was much to settle, as we have seen. Our informants for these activities, unfortunately, are few and random: ancient writers were distracted by Antony's assizes in Ephesus and his surreal encounter with Cleopatra in Tarsus. These episodes very nearly eclipse everything else. We can, however, gain a sense of Antony's finely focused diplomatic and administrative work from Josephus' account of his management of Judean affairs. It reveals much about the challenges confronting Antony.

The triumvir knew Judea well, and as consul he had been instrumental in executing Caesar's policy for the region.[188] Because Caesar was grateful for the assistance furnished by Antipater and Hyrcanus during the Alexandrian War—they led relief forces into Egypt when the dictator was isolated there during his struggle with Ptolemy XIII and on his behalf they rallied the Jewish community in Alexandria—he confirmed Hyrcanus as High Priest and designated him ethnarch of Judea.[189] In addition, he appointed Antony's friend, Antipater, Judea's procurator (*epitropos*), a post of significant authority.[190] Caesar's arrangements, however, remained unregistered at the time of his murder, which prompted an anxious Hyrcanus to send an embassy to Rome seeking a final settlement. Antony and Dolabella, as consuls, secured a senatorial decree assuring the complete implementation of Caesar's dispensation.[191]

Antipater appointed Phaesel, his elder son, superintendent (*strategos*) of Jerusalem and Herod, his younger son, superintendent of Galilee. Their administration was unable to resolve Judea's recurring civic strife, however, and was put in peril by the arrival of Cassius. Ever nimble, Antipater very quickly found favour with Cassius. But when Cassius removed himself from the region, Judea once again collapsed into civil war. Antipater perished—poison was the alleged cause—and soon Antigonus, the son of Aristobulus II, re-emerged as a menace to Hyrcanus and the sons of Antipater. With the support of Marion, tyrant of Tyre, and a certain Fabius, a Roman commander in Damascus whom he was able to suborn, Antigonus invaded Judea. Herod, however, quickly gained the upper hand. Such was the condition of Judea in the aftermath of Philippi.[192]

When Antony came to Bithynia, among the delegations greeting him was one which included representatives of Judea. They brought complaints against Phaesel and Herod. Doubtless they hoped that, owing to their cooperation with Cassius, the brothers had alienated Antony, notwithstanding the Roman's long-standing friendship with Antipater. They were soon disappointed. Antony was fully committed to a Judean dispensation resting on Caesar's authority and his own policy as consul: indeed, he had delivered a speech in the senate in support of Hyrcanus and Antipater. Antony was thus disinclined to distrust Phaesel or Herod, an attitude Herod encouraged through his personal generosity to the triumvir. In the end, Antony refused the Judean embassy even a formal audience.[193]

At Ephesus a delegation sent by the grateful Hyrcanus presented Antony with a golden crown. He also submitted a petition seeking both the liberation of Judeans enslaved during Cassius' regime and the return of any territories subtracted from Judea when the Liberator was in command of the region. Predictably, Antony acceded to both requests.[194] Owing to Josephus, we possess a record of Antony's letter to Hyrcanus, in which, after expounding in some detail the wickedness of the Liberators and the nature of his current mission in the east, he granted the ethnarch's petition.[195] Josephus also preserves Antony's letter to Tyre, which again rehearsed the iniquities of the past regime and the ambitions of the current one, along with a text of Antony's decree, which he required the Tyrians to display in Latin and in Greek.[196]

These letters did not simply register administrative decisions. They also made a case against the legitimacy of the Liberators. In doing so, as a mark of the triumvir's engagement in the matter, Antony did not neglect stylistic considerations. In his letter to Hyrcanus, for example, although some expressions are perhaps conventional and unsurprising—disease, for instance, is deployed as a metaphor for civil strife, which offered a reader nothing novel—others are more arresting. Antony claims that, appalled by the Liberators' foul crime against Caesar, the sun reversed its course, a conceit going back to Sophoclean tragedy: the sun reacted in this same way when Thyestes, deceived by his malicious brother Atreus, devoured his own children in a ghoulish banquet.[197] Antony's application of it here equates the Liberators' *parricidium* with the abomination of Atreus' disgusting crime, a forceful Greek expression for Antony's thoroughly Roman objection to his enemies.[198] Now much of Antony's rhetoric was doubtless redeployed in his many and various administrative missives. As the same time, it is clear in the case of this letter that Antony took the trouble to include local, distinctive elements. In railing against the Liberators' universal lawlessness, for instance, he includes a complaint against their transgressions—*anomēmata*—of divine ordinances.[199] Hyrcanus and his court were clearly expected to recognize Antony's selection of a word used more than once in the Septuagint's version of the Torah for indicating the wickedness of violating sacred law. Now there is no reason to suppose Antony personally pored over Jewish scriptures. Perhaps he picked up the phrase from his friends in Judea. More likely its presence in this letter reflects close consultation with local connections. However Antony came to the expression, its inclusion here registered a high degree of painstaking courtesy.

The meeting at Ephesus was hardly the end of Antony's involvement in Judean affairs. At Daphne, a city near Antioch in Syria, Antony was visited by another Judean embassy hostile to Phaesel and Herod. On the assumption that sheer bulk must count for something, this delegation numbered one hundred delegates, and they succeeded in securing a formal hearing. The brothers were defended by Hyrcanus, who also travelled to Daphne, and by Marcus Valerius Messalla. In his final judgement Antony did not merely take the brothers' side: he elevated both Phaesel and Herod to the office of tetrarch. He also arrested fifteen of the hostile delegates, making it clear he regarded their activities as subversive.[200] Or so he doubtless hoped. Yet when Antony made his way to Tyre he was confronted by still another embassy, this time one composed of one thousand delegates, assembled to lodge further complaints against Judea's new tetrarchs. From Antony's perspective, this was intolerable: Judea's affairs had been settled and there were to be no further negotiations, a determination he punctuated with violence and executions.[201] This was hardly personal brutality. As the exemplary Pliny the Younger would later put it, when governing Bithynia and Pontus, punishment is owed to the stubbornness and unyielding obstinacy of any subjects who reject the pronouncement of a Roman official.[202] Antony's harshness here reflected conventional Roman sentiments about magisterial authority abroad.

For no other of Antony's regional arrangements are we so fully informed as we are in the case of Judea, and perhaps not every principality was so divided or so recalcitrant in the face of triumviral administration. At the same time, Antony was more knowledgeable in Judean affairs—and better connected to members of its governing class—than elsewhere in the east, which means that in other situations he must have been less certain of the personal qualities or political acumen of the men whose status he had to confirm or adjust. It is a fair surmise that, in making even straightforward decisions about cities or dynasts, Antony, in learning the lie of each land, routinely confronted complications sufficient to require protracted investigations of the local scene. The triumvir was a very busy man.

Cleopatra

More than once, and with some urgency, Antony summoned Cleopatra.[203] Her intimacy with Caesar brought Egypt no immunity from the triumvirs' emergency exactions, and Antony was unconvinced of the queen's loyalty to the Caesarian cause. In 43 the triumvirs had recognized Cleopatra's son as king in Egypt in appreciation for her willingness to give assistance to Dolabella. But the four Roman legions which Caesar had stationed in Alexandria ultimately fought under Cassius' command. Furthermore, Cleopatra's governor in Cyprus, Serapion, had openly collaborated with the Liberators. Cleopatra could and did protest that she had handed Caesar's legions over to one of Dolabella's officers who subsequently lost them to Cassius, that she had attempted, unsuccessfully, to support Dolabella by sea, and that, had she not been stymied by storms, she would personally have reinforced the triumvirs at Philippi.[204] Antony remained unpersuaded.

The queen, consequently, temporized, a strategy which could hardly safeguard her position for very long. Antony, after all, had to hand Arsinoe IV, Cleopatra's formidable sister, who was a privileged refugee in Ephesus. And in Arados there was a pretender insisting he was Ptolemy XIII.[205] It cannot have escaped Cleopatra's calculations that,

Fig. 9.1 Lawrence Alma-Tadema, The Meeting of Antony and Cleopatra (1885), currently in a private collection.
Source: Lawrence Alma-Tadema, Wikimedia Commons

with so many rivals in the vicinity, she was dispensable. At the same time, Antony was unwilling to be distracted by an invasion of Egypt, at least for now. His irritation with the queen, however, must have been obvious from his letters: Antony knew how to be brusque and even bullying in his correspondence, as Cicero rightly complained.[206] Hence Cleopatra's hesitation.

Amid extreme adversities, as Horace would later observe, one needs a level head.[207] And Antony knew the very man to ease tensions between Egypt and Rome. He dispatched the nimble Quintus Dellius, who quickly won Cleopatra's confidence. Now Dellius must have put Antony's complaints before the queen, and doubtless the matter of tribute was raised. And yet Dellius also succeeded in convincing Cleopatra that Antony was a Roman susceptible to oriental splendour and a man likely to be charmed by her personal attractions. Dellius did not describe an Antony who was entirely unfamiliar to the Egyptian queen. We may discount the tale of Antony's infatuation with the fourteen-year-old princess when he helped to restore Ptolemy XII.[208] But it is probable that Antony, who in 55 made so fine an impression on Alexandrian society, kept up any Egyptian connections he then collected, so that at the very least Cleopatra knew of Antony's reputation in her own kingdom.[209] And their paths must have crossed during the queen's visit to Rome. A hostile story defamed Antony for suddenly and publicly shirking his consular responsibilities so that he could walk alongside Cleopatra's litter.[210] Conduct like that could hardly incite apprehension on the part of the queen, but this calumny was conceived only much later, when Octavian was stirring the senate to fear Cleopatra and detest her paramour. As for their actual intercourse, we can only imagine. It is entirely possible that, at that time, Cleopatra, instead of stimulating passion, somehow irked Antony as much as she disgruntled Cicero.[211] Whatever the nature of their previous encounters, however, and however leery of the triumvir the queen had become since Philippi, encouraged by Dellius she agreed to meet Antony in Tarsus.

Cleopatra's appearance in this city—her spectacular sailing up the river Cydnus and her fabulous entertainments—was preserved by more than one ancient writer, and Shakespeare's description, reprising a truly purple passage in Plutarch, keeps it a fixture of our contemporary literary equipment.[212] This most triumphant lady, advancing on a glamorous cruiser amid pageantry fashioned into scenes of otherworldly luxury and sensuality—all of it saturated with heady aromas—entered Tarsus so sensationally that she may indeed have pursed up Antony's heart. At the very least the triumvir recognized in Cleopatra's theatricality a solemn and expensive show of regal deference to Rome.

Cleopatra exhibited herself as Aphrodite, a pose on the part of their queens that was central to regal ideology in Egypt.[213] Her majestic performance, then, was a familiar one for the people and grandees in Tarsus, who at once took in its significance. Whether or not Antony and his Roman circle at first recognized the Ptolemaic implications of Cleopatra's show, they were soon initiated. What they cannot have failed to register, however, is how this splendid pageant evoked an earlier action by Caesar, when he placed a golden statue of the Egyptian queen in his temple of Venus Genetrix.[214] Caesar's location of this statue is often misunderstood. Cleopatra, goddess though she was in Egypt, did not thereby become a divine fixture in the sacred architecture of Rome.[215] Her presence in Caesar's temple, owing to her identity as Egypt's queen, was instead one of several remarkable Roman signals of Caesar's eastern conquests. Which is not to say that Caesar's gesture was demeaning to the queen. On the contrary, this concrete specimen of deference to Caesar and therefore to Roman authority, in which transaction Cleopatra certainly cooperated, memorialized her suitability and reliability as a friend and ally of the republic.[216] This statue was soon widely known in Italy.[217] That Cleopatra should want to register her Caesarian bona fides is entirely unsurprising in view of the accusations she was confronted with. Polyvalent though the queen's procession was, then, its splendid and carefully orchestrated performance of dignified submission could hardly be missed. And in order to make matters as clear as she could, when the queen entered the city and addressed the public, she announced that Aphrodite had come to Tarsus, where she could greet Dionysus and ensure the happiness of Asia.[218] Expensive gifts, for the triumvir and his Roman associates, soon followed.

More is sometimes made of this episode: it is argued that Antony and Cleopatra, in their guises as Dionysus and Aphrodite, enacted a sacred marriage (*hieros gamos*) which thereby designated Egypt and its queen as Rome's principal partner in the east and certainly the paramount power in that part of the world. This performance, and its implications for geo-political clout, were, it is maintained, the price Antony was obliged to pay in order to win Egyptian support for his expedition against Parthia.[219] But invading Parthia was not yet an Antonian priority, nor was Cleopatra in a position to bargain with the triumvir. As Appian makes clear, amid so much flummery there were also hard negotiations, in which the queen was put under some pressure.[220] Cleopatra did not travel to Tarsus to issue demands or even command parity with Rome but to win Antony's favour.[221] And she succeeded operatically.

Antony, in Plutarch's telling of it, was *ravished* by Cleopatra. Certainly there was no longer any doubting the queen's loyalty. Any Egyptian assistance to the Liberators was now blamed on Serapion's renegade policy. Consequently, this governor was handed over to Cleopatra for punishment. As for the queen's rivals, Arsinoe and the pretender in Arados, each was eliminated.[222] This is not to say that Egypt was relieved of its responsibility to contribute towards the triumvirs' expenses. But for the queen that will have been a small price to pay for a secure realm. Grateful, and doubtless hopeful, Cleopatra invited Antony to spend his winter in Alexandria.

Parthia and Palmyra

As we have seen, when Antony crossed into Asia he left behind the bulk of his army. Perhaps he should have been more cautious. Not that he need fear any of Rome's dependants who had rallied to the Liberators: any state that opposed the triumvirs at Philippi could be expected to truckle to its new masters. Nor was there any reason to worry over the remnants of Cassius' forces in the east. These were soldiers who could be expected to await Antony's pardon and continue in his service. In Parthia, however, lay a very real danger.

It is widely assumed that Antony's eastern settlement was in large part predicated on securing the east against Parthian aggression—perhaps even designed round an impeding invasion of Rome's formidable neighbour.[223] It is an assumption prompted by any reasonable assessment of the eastern scene, by retrospective insight sparked by Parthia's invasion in 40, and by evidence supplied en passant in Plutarch's description of Antony's encounter with Cleopatra.[224] As early as 46, after all, Parthia injected itself into the eastern theatre of Rome's civil war by adding manpower to the republican insurgency of Quintus Caecilius Bassus.[225] In 43, when Cassius arrived in Syria, he absorbed, in addition to other armies, Bassus' forces.[226] Parthian cavalry also took part in Cassius' brief campaign against Dolabella.[227] And before he joined Brutus, Cassius dispatched Quintus Labienus to the court of Orodes to seek Parthian help in the war against the triumvirs.[228] Although no fresh reinforcements accrued from this appeal—the collapse of Brutus and Cassius came too quickly for Orodes to make a difference—it appears that Parthian troops were among the auxiliaries fighting for the Liberators at Philippi.[229]

Why the Parthians should assist the republican cause is far from clear. Before his confrontation with Caesar at Pharsalus, Pompey sent an embassy, led by his cousin, Gaius Lucilius Hirrus, to Orodes. Its purpose remains unknown, but a dubious Dio relates that Hirrus was sent to ask Parthia for military aid—in vain, because the senator was humiliated by the king, who went on to demand Syria as the price of his cooperation.[230] This story, admittedly outlandish as it stands, suffices nonetheless to make it clear that, at least at the start of the civil war, the Parthians were inclined to remain neutral. Whatever the realities of Orodes' demurral, however, Pompey continued to consider Parthia a potential ally even after his defeat at Pharsalus.[231] It was only in the aftermath of Caesar's victories in the east, however, that Parthia became involved in Roman affairs.

Perhaps Orodes sought to stir and thereby sustain instability on the Roman side of his frontier. By meddling in Roman affairs, he might keep his western rival too distracted to contemplate an invasion, a policy that could only appear a sensible one once Caesar's Parthian designs became widely known. After Caesar's death, the rapid rise in the east of Brutus and Cassius changed things and may well have persuaded Orodes that the Liberators, who from his perspective must have appeared redoubtable, were likely to prevail. A judgement along these lines perhaps lies behind Appian's claim that it was Cassius' formidable reputation in the east that brought the Parthians over to his side.[232] If so, Orodes may have hoped that by rendering assistance to the Liberators he might secure his western frontier. The victory at Philippi of Caesar's heir and Caesar's favourite can only have unsettled the Parthian king, who now had to reckon with the very real possibility of a reprise of Caesar's imperialist designs. On the Roman side, Antony must have been aware of Parthia's recent military support of the triumvirs' enemies and its implications for the current relationship between the two superpowers. At the very least, he could not ignore the presence of Labienus in the court of Orodes.[233]

And yet we hear nothing of any diplomatic overtures towards Parthia on Antony's part. Nor do his arrangements for the winter of 41 suggest any concern over Parthian intentions. If Antony believed Rome's allies in the region, still reeling from the Liberators' regime and struggling now to cope with Antony's settlement, were stout enough to forestall any Parthian attack, then his insouciance can hardly speak to his credit. Nor should he have counted on his Roman forces as a deterrent, if we can believe Dio's report that, when settling into winter quarters, Antony's soldiers were demoralized, degraded, and in a state of near mutiny.[234] Admittedly this view is ascribed to Labienus, who advanced the claim when he was endeavouring to persuade Orodes to launch an invasion. But it is far from incredible.

At some point after departing Tarsus, possibly in late summer, Antony undertook a military expedition against Palmyra, a rich, independent trading centre in Syria. Appian is our only source for this, and his account throws up numerous difficulties.[235] Appian did not know the formal basis for Antony's campaign, nor did he believe it was anything other than a pretext for plundering. Nothing suggests that Antony intended a show of force in the region, nor that this incursion constituted any kind of aggression towards the Parthians.[236] It is far more likely that this invasion represented an effort on Antony's part to integrate into his existing forces the troops he had recently taken over from the Liberators and to reward all his soldiers with booty. He hoped that, by way of actual fighting against a foreign foe, he might instil esprit de corps sufficient to foster a fresh sense of soldierly community. Antony was doubtless aware that the morale of his rankers was low,[237] and he, like all Roman commanders, knew how joint service in combat contributed to any unit's cohesion.[238] A bit of plunder, too, could only be gratifying. Antony's design, however, was foiled. The raid appears to have returned little in the way of profit, and it failed to earn him the loyalties of the men who had served under Brutus and Cassius: in the spring of the next year Antony would learn how many of these soldiers, when confronted by Labienus, deserted to the enemy's side.[239] But that was later. After returning from Palmyra, Antony distributed his troops into their winter quarters. Lucius Decidius Saxa was put in charge of Syria.[240] Antony then proceeded to Egypt, accompanied only by his praetorian guard. He was convinced, it is obvious, that the east was now settled.

Winter in Alexandria

Perhaps it was wiser for Antony to winter in Syria. This region was perpetually beset by local strife, and in the immediate sequel to Antony's expulsion of numerous strong-men and autocrats it was natural to expect fresh efforts on their part at returning to power. Nor, as events would later prove, were Antony's troops, many only recently appropriated from the remnants of the Liberators' forces, entirely reconciled to their new conditions, notwithstanding any profits from Palmyran plunder.[241] A different commander might have sensed this and taken the trouble to remain inspiringly or intimidatingly close at hand. Antony, however, was sanguine, confident in his dis-position of the east and in the competence of the reliable Decidius Saxa.[242] He left Syria behind and made his way to Alexandria, a miscalculation—reprehended in antiquity—that is possibly more revealing of his personality than his liaison with the Egyptian queen.[243]

That Antony should desire a return to Alexandria is hardly surprising. No city in the Mediterranean could match its splendour.[244] Its population remembered Antony and esteemed him, affection he now enhanced by entering the city with minimal military dignity—he was accompanied only by his praetorian guard—in order not to provoke anxieties about a Roman occupation.[245] Antagonism lay outside Antony's designs. Whatever financial exactions he imposed on Egypt had been settled at Tarsus. Antony knew he was by no means remote from the business of the world: he remained acces-sible to Rome's eastern subjects, nor, he believed, was he out of reach from the capital, not least because Alexandria was home to a robust community of Roman traders.[246] His stay in Alexandria would not be a long one: he intended to return to Italy in the spring, dripping with success. Since the Ides of March, however, Antony's life had been an ordeal marked by perpetual and precarious labour. In the winter of 41, he was primed for a holiday.

We possess more than one portrait of Antony's winter in Alexandria. In Appian's version, Antony conducts himself like a perfect philhellene, partaking in Alexandria's cultural attractions, its lectures and gymnasia—the Antony we saw in Athens. Still, there is a reproachful tone: Antony abandons his Roman responsibilities and is wholly devoted to Cleopatra.[247] Dio furnishes a very different and far less attractive figure: his Antony simply surrenders to drunken passion and oriental luxury.[248] Plutarch gives us the most lavish and nuanced account.[249] His Antony, as we have seen, is ravished (Plutarch's word) by the queen, and, as a consequence, he is all ineptitude. Although he is a distinguished man in the prime of life, Antony reverts to the less reputable habits of a youngster: he relishes the pleasures of feasting, luxury, and violent pranks—and inti-macy with an exotic woman—all of which corresponds to stereotypical kinds of venial misbehaviour moralizing Romans often attributed to aristocratic youth. Boys, it was agreed—certainly sons of the Roman elite—will be boys, and youthful indiscretions or excesses were deemed tolerable enough so long as, when their salad days were over, Roman men put aside childish ways.[250]

Antony's 'childish amusements', as Plutarch describes them, are catalogued by the biographer in order to register disapprobation: Antony, because he is not acting his age, is being ridiculous. His adolescent pastimes, Plutarch complains, involved dicing and drinking—and going about at night dressed as a slave, making a nuisance of himself, and sometimes brawling.[251] The Alexandrian public found it all delightful, but Antony was a Roman triumvir, not a clown. In a remarkable episode, reported by Plutarch, Antony, unsuccessful at fishing and therefore embarrassed in front of the queen, orders fishermen to dive beneath the water where they attach to his line samples of their fresh catch. Cleopatra, discerning his ruse, arranges for one of her servants to fasten instead a salted fish imported from the Black Sea. When Antony pulls it in, hilarity ensues. But Plutarch deploys this silly story to make a serious point, for here it is the Egyptian Cleopatra who admonishes Antony to get on with his Roman duties: 'conquering general', she says, 'you should surrender your fishing tackle to the rulers of Pharos and Canopus; cities and kingdoms and continents are your proper prey'.[252] This elegant reprimand excels anything in Dio's raw denunciation.

It also reminds us that, for Cleopatra, Antony's visit could never be simply a matter of fun and games. Although she had acquitted herself of any accusations of disloyalty during the war with the Liberators and had persuaded Antony to eliminate rival claimants to her throne, Cleopatra naturally hoped to solidify her and her son's relationship with Rome and to enhance her international influence throughout the east. These were serious topics which entailed earnest, perhaps in some instances fraught, negotiations with the triumvir and his advisors. Domestic politics were also a concern: it was vital that Cleopatra seize this opportunity to exhibit her close relationship with Antony in order to intimidate any recalcitrant or hostile factions in her court, a matter that was perhaps especially urgent in the aftermath of the arrangements made at Tarsus. Which meant that the court's decorum and her personal majesty must remain paramount among her occupations.[253] And there was the issue of securing succession to the throne. Caesarion was her heir, true, but, owing to the realities of ancient demography and the dangers of court intrigue, more than one potential heir was required by a Ptolemaic monarch. Yet Cleopatra was disinclined to marry. Antony offered her a solution: like Caesar before him, he was a grand and powerful figure, entirely suitable for fathering an Egyptian royal whose future, even if fostered by his Roman father, would remain Cleopatra's concern. Intimacy, if only a diversion for Antony—after the winter of 41 he did not see Cleopatra again for nearly four years—was central to the queen's designs.[254] When Antony departed in the spring, Cleopatra was pregnant with his twins, Alexander and Cleopatra. Caesarion was no longer her only child. It was perhaps now that Cleopatra, in an attempt to bind Antony closely to the best interests of their children, bestowed on him vast estates in the Fayum.[255]

It is from this perspective that we must view Plutarch's reports of Antony's grand and glamorous feasting and revelling. The triumvir's banquets were not always crowded affairs, but they were invariably expensive because Antony, who indulged in extended, friendly conversations with his privileged guests, insisted on instant and impeccable service whenever he finally decided to dine (a protocol which required costly overpreparation in the kitchen).[256] Antony and Cleopatra formed an exclusive club, the Guild of the Inimitable Lifestyle, the members of which feasted one another extravagantly.[257] A society of this kind, decidedly roisterous, was also sacred: membership marked a special relationship with the monarch and monarchical power.[258] Now there is no reason to deny the sheer pleasure associated with these remarkable occasions. At the same time, banquets and drinking parties were central to court life in Hellenistic kingdoms. The exhibition of wealth and wit like the display of personal prowess at the table—a king was expected to be a big eater and a big drinker—these were among the chief majestic parts of any monarch's administration. And feasting was a natural setting for negotiating and displaying individual status and therefore personal influence.[259] However delightful, and however susceptible to moralizing deformation, these entertainments were an inescapable duty for the queen of Egypt—and for her distinguished guest. During his time in Alexandria, not least by way of his immersion into courtly practices, Antony was shaping himself into a formidable feature of Egyptian politics: his presence both exalted the queen and stylishly signalled the reality of Roman hegemony in the very person of the triumvir. For Antony, an extensive network of personal connections in wealthy Alexandria was an obvious attraction: he did not yet imagine that the triumvirate would become Rome's conventional government, but he was certainly aware of the value of eastern friendships. None of this was an Antonian innovation. Caesar, too, when establishing himself in Alexandria, hosted late-night dinner parties, and Rome's aristocracy were entirely au fait with this dimension of Hellenistic courts.[260]

Still, there is no good reason to go so far in rehabilitating the Alexandrian Antony that the sheer enormity of his exuberance gets lost. That Antony failed to manage a suitable balance between the elegant pastimes of court society and the dutifulness of a Roman magistrate is a fair conclusion: it was not so long ago, after all, that, as Master of the Horse, he went too far in indulging himself—even in opinion of a Roman so fond of him as Caesar. Nor can we overlook what appears to be a not insignificant degree of sluggishness in his reaction to affairs in Italy or in the east. By the spring of 40, after all, his brother, who was waging a civil war against his colleague, had humiliatingly surrendered at Perusia, while in the very vicinity of Egypt Parthian forces had begun to overrun Syria. Bad luck can explain only so much, and when our sources, for all their variety, agree in complaining that, while wintering in Alexandria, Antony ignored important responsibilities, it is far from obvious that they are wrong. Naturally, ancient writers prefer to blame Antony's lapses on Cleopatra.[261] That, however, cannot in any meaningful way be right. Caesar did not think it amiss to tumble in the bed of Ptolemy, nor did his affair with the Egyptian queen distract him from the realities of imposing his power at home or abroad. In pursuing a sexual relationship with Cleopatra, Antony followed where his old master had led him, a parallel that doubtless added a certain agonistic frisson to this brief romance. But, as we have seen, Cleopatra sought to profit from Antony's strength. It was not in her interests that he should stumble. If the winter of 41 resulted in a setback for the triumvir, the fault was entirely his.

While settling Syria, as we have seen, Antony was kept reasonably aware of developments in Italy. During his time in Alexandria, he must have become informed of their calamitous decline: a fresh outbreak of civil war, the destruction of Sentinum, and the confinement of his brother in Perusia. And yet, so far as we can tell, Antony did nothing even to try resolve these extreme, destructive conflicts. An embassy that reached him in Alexandria he detained until the spring.[262] Winter, to be sure, made communications even more than usually difficult, and perhaps Antony simply concluded that, by this point, he could only wait on events. He must also have concluded that nothing in the perturbations afflicting Italy could truly damage his preeminent standing. But if that was Antony's sole calculation it hardly speaks to his credit.

Of greater consequence were movements in the east, where Parthia was making ready to invade Syria. The logistical preliminaries required by Parthia's strategy could hardly take place in complete secrecy. Nor could the Parthians' unavoidable groundwork in espionage and private exchanges entirely escape detection. That the Parthians, perhaps by exploiting a deep dissatisfaction with Rome's financial exactions, were able to persuade some governments installed by Antony to acquiesce in a change of hegemon is apparent from subsequent events. So, too, Labienus' capacity for winning over too many of Antony's troops. None of this happened instantly and without preparation. Cicero, when he governed Cilicia, did not fail to perceive how the Romans' harsh rule had rendered some allies disaffected.[263] Antony, because he possessed an abundance of important contacts in Syria, should have remained aware even of any rumours flitting about. The ever-acute Herod, to adduce the most obvious informant, whose station depended on Roman authority, could hardly have failed to register and report any untoward signs of Parthian aggression or even interference in Syrian affairs.[264] And yet there is no indication whatsoever that Antony, if he was made aware of the clouds gathering in the east, bestirred himself. The distraction of Cleopatra will not explain this aloofness. Perhaps Antony did not credit the intelligence he received. Perhaps he assumed that his eastern settlement was stout enough to deter any Parthian invasion. He had, after all, energetically immersed himself in reorganizing the east, and doubtless he was confident in his appointments. Romans, we have noted, were not in the habit of micromanaging their subjects. Perhaps, too, he believed that, even if an enemy should make so bold as to invade Rome's domain, there would be ample time for mobilizing his legions and auxiliaries after spring arrived. Whatever Antony's reasoning, and however deep his optimism, subsequent events revealed him to be unwise.

X
My brother's keeper

Italy in the Absence of Antony

But what of Italy? Although suspicions between them subsisted, Antony and Octavian, through the pact they concluded after Philippi, signalled their friendship to the Roman world. Nor had rumours from the west deterred either from seeking to preserve a relationship with Lepidus. Clearly, then, Antony remained fully invested in the triumvirate and its commission to restore the republic. The triumvirs' colonization scheme was central to that mission: it was vital that Rome's veterans be settled into civilian life, rewarded for their service, and neutralized, so it was hoped, as a factor in fomenting future civil strife. At the same time, the dispossession of Roman citizens entailed by this scheme could only provoke profound unpopularity with everyone outside the ranks of the soldiery. This was unpleasantness Antony naturally preferred to avoid, which is why he was content to leave the administration of Italy to his colleague.

He knew he had little to lose by his absence: Octavian could not expect, by dint of his personal supervision of the veterans' settlements, to acquire undiluted appreciation even from these men. Antony's loyal friends, not least his brother, the consul Lucius Antonius, would see to it that his interests were suitably protected. In the same way, if conditions should be improved by any liberalization of capital associated with the loans structured by Antony or by the transfer of hard cash from the east, Antony's allies would herald his role in restoring Italy's prosperity and do so by way of invidious contrast with Octavian's unwelcome measures at home. Tensions, then, even contentiousness, between Antony's adherents and Octavian were inevitable. And perhaps even desirable. When he returned to Italy in the spring of 40, the victor at Philippi, friend alike to Octavian and Octavian's rivals, anticipated, by way of his unassailable prestige and the profits he had extracted from the east, to furnish the triumvirate with the authority it needed to rally Rome round the task of defeating Sextus Pompey and eliminating or assimilating any remaining resistance to the new regime—with Lepidus and Octavian taking distinguished but subordinate roles. Only then could the triumvirs, like Sulla before them, set in order a freshly established republic—with Antony as its first citizen.

But this was not how events played out. The social and therefore the political fabric of Italy was roughly frayed. Outrage in the municipalities, anxiety and avidity on the part of an exhausted soldiery, and sheer dread amongst the aristocracy blighted Octavian's administration and incited Antony's brother to challenge him again and again. Contentiousness between the two led to strife and open revolt. The resulting conflict, the Perusine War, was unsought and unexpected by consul and triumvir alike.[1] But matters moved far too quickly for either man to manage them as he wished, and the outbreak of another civil war in Italy profoundly altered the triumvirate and, with it, Antony's ambitions.

According to the prevailing view, the Perusine War was a violent, ideological twitch, in which the traditional values of the aristocracy, in Rome and in the municipalities, stood up, unsuccessfully, against the domination of the triumvirate. Lucius Antonius, motivated by firm republican principles, openly challenged Octavian's triumviral excesses. In doing so, he roused Rome's subjugated senators and emerged as the champion of Italy's downtrodden cities, many of which rebelled in a final enactment of the rancour animating the Social War.[2] That a case can be made for this interpretation of events is clear enough. Appian is unambiguous in his depiction of Lucius as a fierce republican. In his account, Lucius denounces the triumvirate as an illegal office, an incipient tyranny, and a threat to Roman freedom. Appian's Lucius is prepared even to confront his brother should Antony refuse to repudiate the triumvirate. And there is no question but that freedom—*libertas*—was a rallying cry in the municipalities resisting Octavian.[3] Nevertheless, this is an approach to the events leading up to the siege at Perusia that fails to appreciate adequately how the rhetoric in which they were cast tends (and tended) to obscure the practical obsessions of their twists and turns. To be sure, life moved fast in the summer and fall of 41, but even in our profoundly problematic evidence there appears to be more going on in the way of stimulus-response politics than is credited by any account that is strongly ideological in its reckoning. A fresh approach to the Perusine War, then, may illuminate some of its complexities and contradictions and help us in locating Antony's role in its unfolding.[4]

Crucial though the antecedents of the Perusine War are, they remain difficult to recover—not least because, in its immediate aftermath, the realities of this conflict were obscured by the misleading, even dishonest, revisionism required in conciliating Octavian and Mark Antony.[5] Consequently, the actions and especially the motives of the principal figures elude. To what purpose did Lucius oppose Octavian? Was he affected by ideology or opportunism—or by the designs of his brother? Or all these things—and, if so, in what combination? What role was played by Antony's wife, Fulvia? This formidable woman unsurprisingly sought to advance the interests of her children and her husband. The degree of her independence, however, became material for political propaganda early on. Much of this disinformation is easy enough to identify: Fulvia was hardly motivated, as hostile sources insist, by sexual jealousy (a recurring mendacity attributes her opposition to Octavian to the desire to extrude Antony from the affections of Glaphyra or Cleopatra). Her role in rousing veterans to serve under Lucius is less fanciful, even if we must discount the canard of her cross-dressing in armour and playing the part of a captain.[6] As for her hostility against Octavian, that is patent.[7] When she died, soon after the fall of Perusia, all sides found relief in blaming her for the conflict, with obvious consequences for our historical record.[8] Even more indistinct is the part played by Manius, mentioned only by Appian, where he is denominated Antony's procurator.[9] A Manius served as a cavalry officer under Antony's father, and it is a fair surmise that this man was the procurator's father. A figure of equestrian rank, then, and a friend of long standing. His personality was strong enough to persuade Fulvia to cooperate closely with Lucius, and he is said to have delivered a highly influential speech denouncing Octavian. In the aftermath of the Perusine war, Antony ordered his execution, but that action only stimulates curiosity over whether he acted on secret instructions from Antony or independently of his friend's counsel. Mysteries proliferate, nor is there any agreement on the extent to which the schemes of Lucius, Fulvia, and Manius were coordinated, collectively or individually, with Antony's nearby generals. As for the primary controversy—how closely, if at all, were these three guided by the absent Antony?—that was a question, immediately after the fall of Perusia, Octavian desperately wanted an answer for, even if he was soon persuaded that there was nothing to be gained even by asking it.[10]

The Acquirement, or Communication, of Truth

The crisis of the Perusine was exacerbated by the Romans' primitive means of communicating over long distances, a reality which drove events by adding to everyone's uncertainty over Antony's stake in the conflict. Amid his many diverse and distracting duties in the east, Antony continued to follow affairs in Italy. Cornelius Nepos draws attention to Antony's letters to Atticus at this time, incessant even when he was abroad, but the triumvir's attentions were hardly limited to the eminent equestrian. Roman aristocrats were industrious epistolists: correspondence was essential both to the utilitarian operations of business and social networking but also the crucial work of sustaining a suitably distinguished public identity for the consumption of senatorial and equestrian society.[11] And it was mostly by way of information conveyed in letters that anyone away from Rome could remain tolerably informed of events in the capital. Impediments obtruded: Rome had no formal postal services and therefore correspondence depended on the movements of friends and acquaintances or even connections of a quite distant nature.[12] The realities of ancient travel meant letters moved slowly, especially in winter, and often they never reached their destinations. Particulars are few. Still, we see that, when Cicero was governor in Cilicia, correspondence from Rome reached him only after forty-six days—and, in at least one instance, only after sixty days.[13] Lags like these meant that information moving between Rome and the provinces was always fragmentary and less than certain.

Even when communications ought to have been unproblematic, it was not always easy to make oneself clear, especially if one decided on a change of policy. We can detect this very clearly in the humdrum case of Publius Sestius. Quaestor in 63 and assigned to Gaius Antonius, he duly followed his master to Macedonia in 62 but, before departing, pressed his friends, including Cicero, to work hard in preventing any protraction of his tenure. After reaching his province, however, he preferred to remain. Immediately he began to convey his new decision to Rome. Cicero was not easily convinced. Although informed by Sestius' freedman, Decius, Cicero was disinclined to credit the report. Subsequently, Sestius' wife conferred with Terentia, which prompted Cicero to discuss the matter further with yet another of Sestius' connections. At last Cicero became confident Sestius had indeed changed his mind. He then exerted himself in persuading others in the senate, who were also dubious because earlier they had received letters from Sestius asking them to bring him home: should they trust the man's letters or Cicero's advice? In the end, Sestius got his way.[14] But if even a communication so simple and straightforward as this one could prove knotty, how much greater the difficulty when trying to remain well informed of distant complexities. Or when trying to influence them. Even in urgency decision-making could be hampered by conflicting sources: on the same day in December 50, when Rome's eastern empire was threatened by Parthia, senators listened to contradictory reports sent by Gaius Cassius and Cicero, each including information that was by then out-of-date.[15] Nevertheless, despite these impediments, Romans could hardly evade the reality that frequently they must react to far-flung events although they remained poorly informed. This was a haze which never cleared, and its effect on the events of the Perusine war was consequential.

Colonization in Italy

Affairs in Italy were dominated by the appropriation of land for veteran colonies. It was for this purpose that the triumvirs, united at Bononia, resolved to seize lands in eighteen cities.[16] These confiscations, like all confiscations during the republic, will have been justified by way of a rhetoric (now lost) emphasizing either the fundamental rightness of the republic's actions or the exigencies required in order to preserve the health of the state.[17] Such sentiments, however, could scarcely disguise the unfortunate, pitiless reality. When Appian describes the triumvirs' treatment of the Italian cities singled out for colonization, he resorts to disturbing language: 'it was just as if these cities had been captured by the spear from an enemy'.[18] His simile conjures the misfortunes of a conquered city, and it is true that, in the distant past, Rome sometimes exploited victories in Italy by appropriating land for the installation of colonies.[19]

But here the significant and baleful precedent is Sulla. After his violent invasion of Italy in 83, culminating in victory and dictatorship in the subsequent year, Sulla rewarded his legions by confiscating lands on a massive scale. He singled out for dispossession those communities which had opposed him during the civil war.[20] In the forties, by contrast, the triumvirs could not point to political hostility on the part of their unlucky victims. Perhaps this distinction did not matter, since it was clearly the case that the men who were disentitled were evicted as if they were enemies of Rome. In a speech supplied him by Appian, a distant Antony, with steely candour, describes Octavian's mission in Italy as nothing less than the violent imposition of dispossession on a massive scale.[21] This policy, it is rightly observed, entrained 'an agrarian and social disaster', long bemoaned even by Augustan loyalists.[22] It was only natural that this abuse of triumviral power activated fear—and hostility—throughout the cities of Italy, even in places not directly affected by colonization.

The grim business of expelling citizens from their lands was taken up immediately. As early as 42 this activity was under the direction of Lepidus and his fellow consul, Plancus.[23] There was much work to be done: in the aftermath of Philippi the triumvirs were obliged to furnish lands to as many as 50,000 veterans.[24] Under the best of circumstances the creation of a colony was a complicated matter: it entailed surveys, close assessments of the quality of the plots to be allocated, and constitutional arrangements for each colony's local government. This cost time and money.[25] But the triumvirs' colonization programme did not take place under the best of circumstances. They did not seize lands from conquered or rebellious peoples, but from

Romans dwelling in Italy. These men lost their lands and any possessions that could be put to work in farming.[26] Nor was there any refuge or recourse for the many small farmers for whom dispossession spelt calamity: they were reduced to the rigours of tenancy or became refugees within their own country.[27]

At Philippi Octavian accepted the responsibility of managing the triumvirs' colonization project. And almost immediately he became an object of nearly universal loathing.[28] From the start, and for obvious reasons, the holdings of veterans were exempted from confiscation.[29] By grim contrast, the properties of senators were not. Nor were men of equestrian rank spared. The poet Virgil, for instance: although no threat to the regime, he, too, suffered when the triumvirs' appropriations were extended from Cremona to his native Mantua.[30] Indeed, many men of this class will have been reduced to penury by what they can only have viewed as a hateful theft of property, one instilling fear in municipal aristocracies up and down the peninsula. As for humbler Romans in the countryside, these men were simply cast out and left to fend for themselves. In despair, many made their way to Rome, where they were pitied even by the impoverished inhabitants of the capital. Some turned to crime and banditry.[31] The veterans, avid for their rewards, remained restless, complained of any delays, and were often unsatisfied with the properties they finally received.[32] The favour or hostility of such men had proved decisive in the political struggles of 44 and 43, and nobody, least of all the triumvirs, was inclined to cross these men now.[33]

Octavian, although he was responsible for the colonization scheme, was nevertheless well aware that, in operations so dear to the legions, his authority could hardly remain unimpeded. As we have seen, the work of colonization had begun in 42, which meant that prominent figures, certainly Lepidus and Plancus, already had a stake in some of the new settlements. By the time Octavian reached Italy, in January 41, it is highly likely that Lucius Antonius, who was consul and also a man deeply experienced in the business of setting up colonies, was also involved. So, too, Asinius Pollio, who continued to supervise colonization in Cisalpine Gaul. Doubtless other associates of Antony were also at work.[34] Octavian brought with him copies of the pact decided at Philippi, which made clear his new and pre-eminent role. It was perfectly natural and appropriate, in view of this agreement, that Octavian should now exert himself in taking charge and in so doing involve his supporters. Disputes, consequently, were inevitable.

Resistance

Predomination in pleasing the legions and their veterans rapidly became a focus of competition and conflict—an entirely predictable development. As Octavian assumed his legitimate role, allies of Antony complained about his management style. Octavian, they objected, had gone so far as to add six legions to the colonists' numbers. Worse, he was trying to elbow out any Antonians.[35] Antony's brother, in sharp retaliation, demanded that colonization be suspended until the return of Octavian's colleague: he even went so far as to parade Antony's wife and children before the armies while lamenting Octavian's mistreatment of the victor at Philippi. Octavian, enfeebled by illness, preferred compromise to further confrontation.[36] In the end, the number of colonies installed under Antonian supervision exceeded Octavian's.[37] But that was hardly the end of it. All parties persisted in competing for the soldiers' favour. Colonists were indulged even when they trampled on their neighbours' rights, and expropriations were expanded until as many as forty cities were affected.[38]

None of this was good for anyone but the colonists. Still, this brand of political infighting was, in itself, unremarkable. Robust aristocratic contentiousness, even amid abnormal circumstances, was the very stuff of public life: men like these simply could not fail to challenge their rivals. But fierce competition of this old-fashioned kind could only be unnatural and even dangerous in the highly fraught atmosphere of this year. The horrors of the proscriptions abided, an atmosphere that rendered senators and equestrians not merely anxious but truly frightened of the new regime. The cities of Italy, and not only those affected by colonization, remained insecure. They feared the government in Rome—and they feared that government's enemies. In Sicily, Sextus Pompey was entrenched and, along the eastern coast of Italy, Domitius Ahenobarbus raided with impunity. Disruption, and scarcity of grain, intensified Italy's precarity[39]

Most worrisome of all, however, was the palpable distrust between Antony and Octavian, their formal friendship notwithstanding. As Octavian endeavoured to manage affairs in Italy, he knew he was closely observed by Antony's military men. In central Italy, Plancus, in command of at least three legions, was engaged in colonization in the vicinity of Beneventum. In the north, Pollio was similarly occupied in the Transpadane, where he commanded an army twice the size of Plancus'. North of him, beyond the Alps, lay Publius Ventidius Bassus in charge of three legions and Quintus Fufius Calenus with eleven. Other Antonian commanders, too, are known to have been active in these regions.[40] Octavian did not need reminding that his primacy in Italy was anything but unqualified. This reality was underlined when he was ignored by Calenus, who refused to hand over the two legions he owed Octavian under the terms agreed at Philippi.[41]

There was little that could be done for the lower orders in Rome, whose plight worsened with the passage of time and the continuous influx of dispossessed refugees. The circumstances of Italian municipalities, especially those which likewise attracted impoverished immigrants, also deteriorated. Curators of the grain supply were appointed by senatorial decree, but even in the matter of supplying basic necessities these authorities continued to favour veterans and soldiers.[42] As a consequence, instances of violence between rankers and civilians multiplied. In Rome an increasingly angry populace shuttered its shops in protest, and vigorous demonstrations went so far as to drive away magistrates when they attempted to conduct public business.[43] Actions such as these, in the teeth of a regime by no means averse to the application of lethal force, unmistakeably signalled desperation.

Popular Desperation

In ordinary times, humble citizens in the countryside would have turned for assistance to local notables, the decurions who governed the municipalities. For their part, these men, the Italian aristocracy, would have sought remedies through their

Fig. 10.1 Sextus Pompey on the obverse of an aureus (*RRC* 511.1); around Pompey's image is the legend MAG PIUS IMP ITER ([Sextus Pompey] the Great, Loyal to his Father's Memory, *imperator* for the second time).
Source: Wikimedia Commons.

connections with members of the senate, perhaps by appealing to municipal patrons but also by appealing to individuals who counted as acquaintances or friends.[44] Prosperous Italians carried weight in tribal associations, which also furnished avenues of approach to the political class in Rome.[45] These relationships were deemed vital and consequently were keenly cultivated by the decurionial order. As Cicero's brother observes in his *Handbook on Electioneering*, senators were a vital personal resource for men of property outside Rome:

> Now, men from the municipalities and from the countryside consider themselves our friends if they are simply known to us by name. If, in addition, they believe they are acquiring a bit of protection for themselves, they do not lose any opportunity of making themselves worthy of it.[46]

Protection was certainly a thing to be desired by Italians with something to lose, for whom there remained, long after the Social War, a degree of estrangement from their senatorial superiors. For Italians were all too frequently confronted by an unequal application of justice that put them at a disadvantage when they contended with the elite in Rome, unless they could help themselves by gaining favour from a senator who would take their part.[47]

This very real estrangement between senators and decurions, however, was mitigated, again in ordinary times, by the latter's outsized role in the selection of praetors and consuls. In order to harness the electoral clout of the prosperous classes in the countryside, prospective candidates were obliged to pursue relationships, often quite close, with the municipal aristocracy.[48] These contacts were paraded both at the polls but especially during the pageantry of canvassing, annual public rituals which enacted and reinforced the reciprocal bonds integrating Rome's various social orders. The social work of elections and the canvassing that preceded them was vital in sustaining the inevitably unequal balance between Roman grandees and the propertied classes of Italy—and for identifying in Rome's magistrates and its senate a leadership whose eminence was validated by the people's will and its loyalty.[49]

Municipal notables shared the same values which thrummed in the ideology of the Roman senate. Nevertheless, and above all else, they sought security and stability, aspirations that rendered many in the municipalities less rigid in their political thinking than their counterparts in the capital. Cicero, for instance, was well-known for his extensive Italian connections, and yet, at the start of the civil war between Pompey and Caesar, complained bitterly about their priorities:

> I'm absolutely certain that if Caesar takes no one's life and deprives no one of any property, then he will become positively adored by those who positively dreaded him. The people in the municipalities and the people in the countryside all speak with me a great deal. But they think of absolutely nothing else but their lands, their precious farmhouses, and their precious money.[50]

Cicero's outrage was motivated by what he viewed as a failure of integrity. Yet even the esteemed Atticus could write to Cicero, when justifying, on one occasion, his preference for profit over political principle, 'let us sooner be parted from the commonwealth than from our private wealth.'[51] Perhaps these prosperous men would argue that it was the duty of the republic and its leadership to preserve them in their possessions. In any case, as Cicero begrudgingly recognized, the relationship between the Italian aristocracy and its senatorial betters was fundamentally an instrumental one: because even the rich among them were vulnerable, men in the countryside were inclined to follow a leader who could and would protect them.

The practical and ideological efficacy of the networks which fastened the urban and Italian elites, however, was dashed by the operations of the triumvirate. In the aftermath of the proscriptions, senators who did not flee the city were quailed and thereby rendered of little value to Italians in need of influential friends. And because the triumvirs arrogated to themselves the selection of magistrates, canvassing was eliminated or, if elections subsisted in some tenuous form, became irrelevant and therefore no basis for accruing any kind of magisterial gratitude. There remained no environment for any meaningful expression of popular sovereignty or for the social and political exchanges that, in ordinary circumstances, benefitted senators and decurions alike. Instead, there was only a civic void cleared by the enormity of triumviral power. This collapse of instrumental connections was perhaps not immediately apparent even amid the terror of the proscriptions. Near the end of 43, after the passage of the *lex Titia*, Antony, in his role as triumvir, presided over elections, and it is securely attested that these elections were preceded by canvassing. But very soon, even if the formality of elections continued, their traditional essence evaporated. And this stark alteration in political life made it clear to everyone how, in the new regime, the triumvirs and their lackeys were now the only figures in Rome worth waiting on.[52]

The Rise of Antony's Brother

Hence an opportunity for Lucius Antonius, who had recently assumed (we do not know when) the unusual cognomen Pietas in order to signal his deep fraternal devotion. Consul in 41, Lucius commenced his year in office by celebrating a triumph. Not, it appears, without at least some opposition, which was overcome (we do not know how) through the influence of Antony's wife, Fulvia. Her aid, however, was not spontaneous—Lucius had to ask for it—which perhaps indicates some coldness between the two.[53] Nonetheless, as we have seen, they were soon cooperating in advancing Antony's interests in the colonization scheme. And each was willing to stand up to Octavian.

Lucius' importance was enhanced by his brother's prestige. At the same time, his personal clout was formidable. During his tribunate in 44, in the aftermath of Caesar's assassination, Lucius had been recognized as patron of the thirty-five tribes, an honour reflecting his influence not only in Rome but also in the municipalities. Moreover, he was declared patron by the equestrian order and by the city's financial consortia.[54] These extraordinary declarations demonstrated the depth of Lucius' associations with many of the richest men in the republic. Amid the perturbations of 41, when, as we have seen, the absolute authority of the triumvirs subverted any traditional networks linking the wealthy in Italy to the centres of political power, Lucius can only have appeared a welcome and present help to anyone rebuffed or ignored by Octavian. During past crises, Lucius had stood on their side, and now he was conspicuous, both a consul and an Antonius. Because he was Antony's brother, it was believed, he was, perhaps uniquely, in a position to persuade Octavian to take actions aimed at mitigating the harshness of the triumvirs' administration of Italy. No one, after all, and least of all Octavian, wanted to cross Antony. Antonius Pietas, as a consequence, appeared untouchable. Naturally, then, he received appeals for succour from multiple constituencies, from senators and equestrians, and from the decurional orders throughout Italy—all seeking some limit to the triumvirs' brutal shake-down.[55]

It is probably a mistake to confuse this confluence of desperate and disparate parties with anything in the way of a coherent social movement or the recrudescence of a deeply old-fashioned republican ideology.[56] Those who aligned themselves with Lucius were men seeking immediate relief, if not actual restitution for their losses, and they very much hoped he was the man to deliver it. For the consul, this opportunity to extend his influence—his *gratia*—could hardly be spurned. By exercising his office and clout in more or less traditional ways, he could, so he believed, enhance his personal status without affecting his brother's renown, and by standing up to Octavian on behalf of the municipalities, he could expect to garner lasting gratitude which would pay dividends when the triumvirate lapsed and the republic was restored. To be fair, this was unquestionably thinking of a republican kind insofar as it was transactional along familiar, even traditional, lines. But Lucius' relationship with his variegated constituency, at this point certainly, was predicated, not on a philosophical repudiation of the triumvirate so much as on the public's deep dissatisfaction over its failure to be helpful to injured parties.

Appian, however, and Appian alone, insists that Lucius was hostile to the institution of the triumvirate owing to deep-seated republican sensibilities.[57] The historian goes so far as to depict the consul declaiming how he would wage war even against Antony if his brother stood against republican freedom.[58] And it is clear enough, as we shall see, that, in differentiating himself from Octavian, Lucius employed a fiercely republican, down-with-the-triumvirate rhetoric in order to rally his supporters.[59] Appian's portrait has been highly influential. But we must be wary.[60] Traditional slogans were easy to exploit and more or less unavoidable when taking any kind of public stance: what other discourse, apart from the vocabulary of ancestral custom—*mos maiorum*—was available to a Roman? Lucius did nothing to reach out to Sextus or Domitius. Nor, so far as we know, did he undertake to make use of any traditional constitutional machinery in advancing his cause. Instead, he advanced new policies for rewarding the triumvirs' legions at Philippi—and he complained about Octavian's emasculation of the consulship. Even this, one must observe, was enough to render Lucius attractive to Romans of staunchly republican leanings: Tiberius Claudius Nero, for instance, fought for him at Perusia.[61] For men like this, however, unless they retreated from Italy, Lucius, such as he was, was their only hope.

Freedom indeed became the rallying cry for Lucius and his adherents. That honest citizens ought to be secure in the possession of private property, especially of land, was a conspicuous element in the Romans' basic notion of *libertas*. Sustaining this security was a fundamental responsibility of any good state and a hallmark of sound republican practice.[62] From this perspective, the triumvirs' appropriations were depredations amounting to an abuse of magisterial power. It was a consul's duty no less than a tribune's to safeguard the freedom of Rome's citizenry.[63] Hence the centrality in Lucius' politics of the role of the consulship. And Appian may well be right that, owing to the dispossession of innocent Italians, many in Rome, and not only in Rome, became convinced that the republic was indeed being overthrown, not restored, by the triumvirs and the veterans whose interests they served.[64]

Lucius' New Deal

Lucius' newly independent posture involved two gestures. First, he made a show of his receptiveness to the pleas of the dispossessed or anyone fearing dispossession. These will have been mostly persons of some property—senators, equestrians, municipal decurions—but the symbolism of Lucius' comity can only have rallied the hopes of the desperate orders. Lucius, it appears, began to promote an alternative, less arbitrary approach to rewarding the veterans at Philippi. Instead of simply seizing more and more lands solely for the sake of creating colonies, a policy which could only punish more and more innocent citizens, he proposed that veterans should henceforth receive lands and moneys out of the residue of the proscriptions; further expropriations, which he conceded would be required, should be visited only on the properties of those who fought for the Liberators or collaborated with Sextus or Domitius. As for future colonies, because the municipalities had suffered enough, Lucius urged that these be established in the rich province of Asia.

Here Lucius struck a very Caesarian pose. The dictator had confiscated the property of intransigent Pompeians but had resolutely and explicitly refused to imitate Sulla in the way of dispossessing property owners. Lucius' policy, conservative and clearly intended to be viewed as a return to Caesar's programme, promised that hereafter it would be enemies of the state, not loyal Romans, who paid the price for restoring the republic.[65] The triumvirs could hardly object to that. Nothing in Lucius' designs, the point must be underlined, was intended to undo the triumvirs' existing colonies. Otherwise, Lucius could not have sustained, as patently he did, the loyalty of the soldiery. Veterans too. No city was more loyal to Lucius than Nursia, where an Antonian colony had already been imposed: there, as events would prove, *libertas* and hostility to Octavian's excesses remained stirring values.[66] Rome, Lucius argued, could balance loyalty to the legions with the property rights of Roman citizens in Italy.[67]

Lucius' other gesture was directed towards ideological concerns. The triumvirate, he complained, enfeebled and therefore disgraced the consulship. He demanded its restoration. Here Lucius defended a principle championed by his brother: when he was consul, he was prepared to challenge Caesar himself on the matter of the consulship's integrity, as we have seen in the controversy over Dolabella's elevation to the office.[68] In making his case for the traditional status of the consulship, Lucius somehow stoked fears on the part of some that the triumvirs might refuse to relinquish their office when it expired, that Lepidus and Octavian, if not Antony, sought to maintain their junta at the expense of a republic they had no intention of restoring.[69] In order to highlight the personal risk he was running by championing property rights and the hereditary republic, and at the same time to signal his closeness to Antony, Lucius organized a personal bodyguard composed of his brother's veterans.[70] But this move only incited Octavian, a past master of exploiting veteran bodyguards. He could not fail to see aggression in Lucius' action.

Lucius' stance provoked surprise and, at first, resistance. Antony's legions were startled and sensed betrayal: Octavian exerted himself in insisting that Lucius' policy posed a danger to their landholdings.[71] Antony's wife, according to Appian, likewise blamed Lucius for exciting instability and taking a stand that did nothing to advance Antony's interests.[72] If that report is true, it suggests that at this point Lucius acted independently of his brother. At the very least, Antony had not yet recommended Lucius' scheme to every member of his inner circle in Italy. Fulvia, however, was quickly brought round, even if we must reject Appian's sexist and anachronistic explanation for her change of mind: he insists that Fulvia was convinced that stirring up trouble in Italy was the only way to distract Antony from Cleopatra. But Antony was not yet involved with Cleopatra nor, obviously, was Fulvia the sexist caricature Appian posits here.[73] Lucius and his associates must have made a strong case for their policy and its potential for further enhancing Antony's stature. As for the legions, they were soon persuaded that Lucius' policy was not to their disadvantage.[74] Predictably, the enthusiasm of the senate and propertied classes was palpable.[75] In its beginning, then, Lucius' new programme won him new adherents and successfully exacerbated Octavian's unpopularity.

Octavian, consequently, was obliged, again, to yield. He insisted, probably rightly, that proceeds from the proscriptions were mostly expended and inadequate for meeting the remaining veterans' needs. It does not follow, however, that the public, including the soldiers, were convinced of that. In any case, if he had not already begun to do so, Octavian turned to confiscating the lands of men who had fought for the Liberators at Philippi. The poet Horace is a famous example: after serving as a tribune in Brutus' army, he returned to Rome to face, not outright ruin, but certainly the loss of his estates.[76] At the same time, Octavian introduced important concessions in the matter of appropriating land. He now exempted the properties of senators.[77] He also excluded anyone whose tiny farm was smaller than a veteran's allocation—probably to be reckoned at 50 *iugera* (approximated 12.5 hectares).[78] It was owing to this dispensation that Octavian was later celebrated in Virgil's *First Eclogue*: there the humble Tityrus, spared dispossession, honours his benefactor as a god. This exemption, however, although a welcome relief for some, was not extended to everyone—a reality also depicted in the *First Eclogue* (as Meliboeus puts it at *Ecl.* 1.34–5: 'I am an exile from my native land, while you, Tityrus, are at ease'). These concessions, however, were unwelcome to the veterans, who expressed their displeasure so forcefully that Octavian also exempted any Italian lands belonging to the veterans' relations.[79] Virgil's Tityrus may sing of Octavian, and strictly speaking it was under the triumvir's direction that these more generous dispensations were introduced. At the time, however, the justice of these reforms was credited to Lucius.[80]

Contentiousness

Octavian's accommodation did nothing to deactivate Lucius' antagonism. As a consequence, the triumvir was forced to push back, and he did so by drawing adverse attention to Lucius' defence of the consulship. Octavian, depicting Lucius as an inveterate enemy of the triumvirate, emphasized to the veterans that their land holdings remained secure only by dint of that office's legitimacy. Lucius' hostility to the institution, he alleged, put their rights at risk, a state of affairs, he also claimed, as unwelcome to Antony as it was to himself.[81] Events would ultimately prove that, in pushing this point, Octavian had found an effective wedge issue. But that came later: for now Lucius remained too attentive to the veterans' interests and too close to his brother to be viewed as a threat. Octavian remained frustrated.

At about this time, Octavian divorced Fulvia's daughter, Claudia. In doing so, he went to great pains in assuring everyone that his act did not signal any kind of rupture between himself and the brothers Antonius.[82] Instead, for public consumption, he endeavoured to locate the tensions between himself and Lucius in the person of Fulvia, a figure who, not least owing to her gender, Octavian hoped would constitute a more congenial target for the soldiers' ire. Doubtless he expected some members of the public to appreciate his situation. After all, although Fulvia was naturally expected to look after her husband's interests, she was also expected to look after her daughter's, and this entailed exhibiting something in the way of solidarity with her son-in-law.[83] Instead, she cooperated with his rivals. Octavian did what he could to concentrate attention on Fulvia. Consequently, he emphasized Claudia's blamelessness. He even went so far as to affirm by way of a public oath that her virginity remained intact, testimony that preserved his ex-wife's reputation and did nothing to diminish her future prospects. This was a notable declaration, not least because Octavian's confession left *him* open to insinuations of inadequacy or depravity—or objectionable political calculation.[84] On any view, this was a very clumsy action, susceptible to more than one parsing, and evidence of Octavian' difficulties in finding his way forward. Without question the divorce increased rather than diminished tensions in Italy. Antony, when the news reached him, cannot have been pleased.

An alarming episode now took place. Quintus Salvidienus Rufus was leading six legions to Octavian's Spanish province. When they reached Placentia, the troops mutinied, apparently demanding a donative or, perhaps, in protest that their pay was in arrears. Discipline was restored only through the grim expedient of imposing financial exactions on local communities.[85] Now the extrusion of funds from unfortunate cities was nothing new in triumviral Italy. It was the policy of all the triumvirs—the severity of Pollio's exactions on Antony's behalf were long remembered—but this incident, occurring amid Lucius' exertions on behalf of the municipalities, was especially embarrassing to Octavian.[86] The triumvir, it appeared to some, could not sustain his military authority without oppressing innocent citizens. Asinius Pollio, with the cooperation of Ventidius and Fufuis Calenus, took actions to prevent Salvidienus from advancing out of Italy, thereby protracting this unpleasant situation.[87] Boxing in Salvidienus was too immediate a response to reflect consultation with Antony. If the idea was not Pollio's, then it must be attributed to Lucius. It was certainly Lucius who later agreed to allow Salvidienus to depart. Octavian was profoundly alarmed. He backed away from his hostility toward Fulvia and Lucius. Instead, and awkwardly, he now strained at reconciliation.[88] But without success.

Subversion

Lucius, emboldened by Octavian's vulnerability, began to interfere in his provinces. He encouraged, so it was alleged, Bogud of Mauretania to make strikes against Gaius Carrinas, Octavian's commander in Spain.[89] He also stirred up trouble in Africa. Earlier in the year, in accordance with the triumvirs' agreement at Philippi, Lucius had written to Titus Sextius, the proconsul, instructing him to hand Africa to Gaius Fuficius Fango, one of Octavian's officers. Now he wrote again, urging Sextius to remain in the province and take it back. The inevitable standoff erupted into open violence, resolved only in the following year when Fango was defeated and committed suicide. Sextius was subsequently succeeded by Lepidus, who, according to Dio, believed the man had acted on Antony's behalf.[90] Which may be true, in a sense: in the aftermath of Lucius' capitulation at Perusia, when Octavian and Antony came dangerously close to civil war, Antony can have had little interest in allowing Africa to slip out of his hands. That reality, however, does nothing to render Antony the prime mover in Lucius' communications with Sextius. Nevertheless, these disruptions were dangerous, and Octavian was fully justified in feeling threatened.

The Agreement at Teanum

The peril posed by these circumstances was not lost on the troops or their officers, who once again intervened, proof that neither side had alienated the armies—nor entirely won them over. They arranged a conference, which took place in Teanum in Campania.[91] This environment might have been thought to favour Octavian inasmuch as, at the time, his representatives were installing a veteran colony there.[92] But Teanum was notorious as the site of an outrageous abuse of authority. Sometime in the second century, a consul, angry when his wife was offended by insufficiently scrubbed baths, ordered the local magistrate stripped and beaten in the forum. This abuse became widely known, was rehearsed in the oratory of Gaius Gracchus, and remained infamous during the empire.[93] The venue of this conference, then, can only have ignited the Italians' historical sensibilities regarding Roman arrogance, circumstances that can have escaped neither party.[94]

Lucius now agreed to allow Salvidienus an unimpeded march to Spain. He also conceded that Calenus should at last disgorge the two Antonian legions owed to Octavian.[95] In making these concessions, Lucius did no more than grant Octavian what was rightfully his, a transaction which can only have been humiliating for the triumvir. In addition to these issues, arrangements for compensating the veterans were further refined. Octavian, for his part, vowed to honour the traditional prerogatives of the consulship, and, on this basis, Lucius dismissed his bodyguard. For Lucius, the conference at Teanum was a political triumph. Octavian's submission to negotiations was, in and of itself, a win, and throughout this confrontation the consul managed to rally the support of constituencies opposed to Octavian without foregoing his personal standing with the armies or the veterans. Octavian, by contrast, emerged a diminished figure.[96]

What Antony made of these events goes unrecorded, as Appian complains.[97] Lucius and Fulvia, immediately following the conference, sent him letters and representatives.[98] So, too, did Octavian. On his behalf, the senator Lucius Cocceius Nerva and a certain Caecina travelled to Phoenicia, where they found the triumvir. Cocceius remained, but Caecina returned with letters for Octavian which Antony later characterized as friendly.[99] By this point, then, he was fully informed of Lucius' policies regarding colonization and the rehabilitation of the consulship, but nothing suggests he took sides with either Lucius or Octavian.[100] Nor was there any reason for him to insert himself now that, in principle, the two parties had reached an understanding. Doubtless he considered affairs in Italy more or less settled.

In reality, the conference at Teanum did nothing to restore concord. The consul, taking a victory lap, toured several municipalities, advancing his claim that the Philippi agreement was no longer operative because the consulship had been restored. This can only be viewed as a wilful misrepresentation of Octavian's position. In promising to respect the consulship, Octavian made a concession, arguably a humiliating concession, designed to conciliate Lucius. But he certainly did not intend to surrender his superior legal authority as a triumvir. Nor did he intend to cancel the agreement arranged at Philippi. Octavian had already demonstrated his willingness to cooperate in the matter of colonization, and at Teanum he once again and very publicly collaborated with Lucius in the matter of compensating the veterans. But the Philippi agreement, a dispensation signed and endorsed by Mark Antony, was too central to his primacy in Italy for him to allow anyone, even Antony's brother, to tear it up. Yet Lucius advanced this very claim. In doing so, he succeeded in alienating many Italian cities from Octavian, whom they viewed as a menace held in abeyance only by the consul. And, for that reason, the municipalities began to expect tangible reforms from the consul, including an end to Octavian's taxes and exactions. Indeed, many in the cities may now have felt safe in rejecting Octavian's mandates.[101]

Fulvia, too, struck an aggressive posture. She alleged that Octavian was a threat to her children's safety and therefore removed herself to Praeneste, where she grandly received equestrian and senatorial visitors.[102] Lucius followed her lead. Complaining that Octavian was also plotting against him, he joined his sister-in-law. Like Teanum, Praeneste was not a random choice. During the civil war of 83 this city was the site of a horrific slaughter by the victorious Sulla. The episode was gruesomely punctuated by its spectacle of favouring Romans over Italians. Sulla divided his prisoners into three groups: Romans, Samnites, and Praenestines. The Romans he spared. The rest he annihilated.[103] The city was subsequently sacked and colonized for Sulla's veterans.[104] Although by Lucius' day most of the region was in the hands of the wealthy and few traces remained of the colonists' holdings, the infamy of the executions endured.[105] The parade of dignitaries to Praeneste, from Rome and from the municipalities, demonstrated unmistakably how central Lucius and Fulvia had become to the dynamics of political power. Furthermore, the symbolism of their physical separation from the capital marked Octavian out as a danger to the health of Italy. Once more, Octavian sought to conciliate the consul by way of various intermediaries. Again, his efforts were rebuffed: clearly Lucius believed he held the advantage.[106]

The agreement at Teanum, it was obvious, had done nothing to resolve the antagonism between Octavian and Lucius. Nor were all its terms respected, and soon the pact was recognized as a failure.[107] The soldiery, anxious for peace, demanded another conference, this time at Gabii, midway between Praeneste and Rome. In the end, however, Lucius refused to appear, perhaps because his advance guard was ambushed by Octavian's men, perhaps, as Octavian claimed, because the consul disdained submitting to the authority of the veterans.[108] This failure provoked further, increasingly desperate, attempts at mediation, but nothing, it appeared, could suspend the suspicion and hostility prevailing on each side.

The absent Antony remained at the centre of every complaint or justification. Lucius and Fulvia stressed their roles as Antony's agents.[109] And yet neither of them could brandish a letter from Antony, somewhere in Syria, or produce an emissary from the east, affirming his support for their policy of opposing Octavian. By contrast, Octavian could at least hold up a text of Antony's agreement at Philippi.[110] In a speech reported by Appian, Manius now denounced Octavian for comprehensive ineptitude and for undermining Antony's influence in Italy.[111] He even flourished a letter from Antony which instructed his friends to fight for his prestige. Appian believed this letter a forgery, probably wrongly: the sentiment was a generic one, after all, and entirely unsurprising. More likely Manius' letter simply did not apply to its immediate circumstances, which is why no one was impressed by it. In the presence of the senate, Octavian responded by defending both his competence and his collegiality. The implacable Lucius, he insisted, was provocateur in this crisis, which was now hastening towards a fresh outbreak of civil war. Octavian pleaded with Antony's friends to send letters affirming his loyalty, and, in order to demonstrate Lucius' deceitfulness, sent a delegation of senators to Praeneste to ask in just what particulars he had diminished Antony's reputation.[112] This was strong stuff, but it did nothing to damage Lucius' standing: he continued to attract broad support among the aristocracy.[113]

Civil War

Both sides now braced for the prospect of war, even if neither party truly expected to come to blows. Octavian ordered Salvidienus Rufus to return.[114] Lucius began to raise legions in Italy. Nothing indicates that he sought senatorial authorization.[115] We must not make the mistake of viewing Lucius' army primarily as an Italian bulwark against colonization. Lucius' men also included veterans from the colonies, men recalled to active service by appeals to their devotion to Mark Antony and doubtless by reminding them of Lucius' role in establishing Antonian colonies.[116] The consul's cause was, by awkward turns, a defence of Antony against Octavian's aggression *and* a defence of Roman freedom against triumviral excess. Lucius managed to raise six legions. Even if none of them was at full strength, this was nevertheless a force of significant size.[117] Antony's nearby legions constituted further assets.

It is likely that Lucius intended nothing more at this stage than a further heightening of his rivalry with Octavian, a conflict in which he continued to maintain an advantage. His designs, however, were shattered by local leaders in some of the cities of Italy, for whom waiting for Antony was no longer a satisfactory strategy. Lucius' Italian supporters decided the time had come to put their leader to the test. As we have seen, municipalities which had been spared colonization had nonetheless been subjected to severe taxation and other harsh exactions. These communities, relying now on Lucius' protection, rose up: Octavian's agents were violently expelled or, in some instances, put to death.[118] This was contrary to Lucius' expectations and reveals discrepancies between the consul's agenda and the aspirations of his municipal allies. Open rebellion in Italian cities, intolerable to Octavian and therefore certain to be punished, left Lucius with no choice but to take a decisive stand. He could hardly desert his allies, which meant that he must now deploy his legions in their defence.

Lucius responded adroitly. The Sabine city of Nursia, a flashpoint of this rebellion, he at once protected by dispatching a force led by Tisienius Gallus.[119] Lucius also directed Gaius Furnius to occupy Sentinum, a town of strategic value owing to its position on the Via Flaminia. This was the principal route through the Apennines and onward to the Gallic provinces: Lucius hoped, by holding this city, to impede any incursion from the north by Salvidienus and, by the same action, to facilitate the movement of any reinforcements sent by Antony's legates.[120] The security of Italy's cities, central to Lucius' claim on their loyalties, was necessarily his primary concern. Undeterred, Octavian marched on Nursia. But he was unable to dislodge Gallus, who repulsed him. He then advanced northwards against Sentinum, where, again, he suffered defeat. This city, however, because it was too important to abandon, he besieged. Octavian did not fail to grasp the gravity of his increasingly difficult and embarrassing situation. It was perhaps now that Octavian sent another embassy to Antony, this time a delegation of veterans, in order to make it clear to his colleague that he was resorting to arms only under compulsion.[121]

Lucius turned toward Rome. The city was defended by two legions under Lepidus' command. These Lucius quickly defeated, for which victory he was hailed *imperator*. The consul entered the city and addressed the people. He denounced the triumvirate, reproaching Lepidus and Octavian but not his brother: Antony, too, Lucius insisted, repudiated the triumvirate and its excesses. Lucius promised to bring this baleful institution to its end and restore the republic—immediately. The consul then convoked the senate, which obligingly declared Octavian a *hostis*. Lepidus too, perhaps. The senate's decree was immediately promulgated before an approving populace.[122] Lucius was now openly at war with Octavian.

The senate's decree did not annul the *lex Titia*, nor did it declare Octavian *hostis* on the grounds that he operated as a triumvir. Otherwise Antony, too, must have been declared an enemy of the state. Octavian must have been outlawed for tyranny or treason or some confection of offences. Clearly there was broad senatorial agreement, unimpeded by constitutional hair-splitting and fortified by the presence of Lucius' legions, that even a triumvir could go too far in his treatment of Roman citizens. Whatever the arguments used on the day, Lucius' actions placed Antony in a difficult, unwelcome position: his very public friendship with Lepidus and Octavian will have obliged him to resist the militancy of his brother, whom *pietas* demanded he support—nor can there be any doubt that Antony, although he doubtless intended to resign his office when the triumvirate elapsed, intended to do so on his own terms and not those dictated by his brother or anyone else. Antony would not learn of Lucius' march on Rome perhaps for weeks—by this time he was very likely campaigning in Palmyra—but its announcement could only throw his plans for a masterful return to Italy into utter disarray.

Lucius, mindful of Salvidienus Rufus' imminent return, sought to augment his ranks by calling up even more veterans loyal to Antony.[123] At this same time, Octavian abandoned his siege of Sentinum in order to regain control of Rome. Lucius had foolishly left the city unguarded, which allowed Octavian to enter without resistance.[124] The triumvir quickly summoned the senate so the conscript fathers could annul their previous decree in order to declare Lucius an enemy of the state.[125] Octavian now remained in Rome, entrusting the prosecution of the war to his generals.[126] That his situation was precarious he fully grasped: Lucius was formidable, and if he was joined by Antony's marshals he would almost certainly be unbeatable. He must also consider the possibility that Lucius acted on Antony's orders. With that in mind, he dispatched a legion to Brundisium to guard against reinforcements arriving from the east.[127]

Antony's Quaestor

It was at just this apprehensive moment that Antony's quaestor, Marcus Barbatius Pollio, arrived in Italy. He was interrogated, almost certainly at Rome, in an expectation of uncovering the unvarnished views of his master.[128] Barbatius, it is clear from the coins he minted in the east, was held in high esteem by Antony: he enjoyed the position of *quaestor pro praetore* and was a colleague of the noble Lucius Gellius Publicola and the rising star Marcus Cocceius Nerva.[129] These men were destined to become consuls in 36.[130] Barbatius was not made of the same stuff. He had made his way into Antony's favour through long-standing service to the Caesarian cause. A *novus homo*, he was disdained by Cicero as one of Caesar's desperate and inconsequential hangers-on whose loyalty, after the Ides of March, was transferred to Antony.[131] This attachment led to his service at Philippi and, thereafter, to responsible duties on Antony's eastern staff. Not without success. The Carian city of Caunus designated Barbatius its

Fig. 10.2 Antony and Octavian on a denarius minted by Marcus Barbatius Pollio (*RRC* 517.2): the obverse shows Antony with the legend M ANT IM AU III VIR R P C M BARBAT Q P (Mark Antony, *imperator*, augur, triumvir appointed to set the republic in order—Marcus Barbatius, quaestor *pro praetore*); the reverse depicts Octavian with the legend CAESAR IMP PONT III VIR R P C (Caesar, pontiff, triumvir appointed to set the republic in order), reproduced with the permission of the Classics Museum of Victoria University of Wellington.

patron and benefactor, honouring him with a golden crown and a bronze statue. On the inscription recording these dignities, Barbatius is labelled *quaestor pro praetore* and aedile-designate.[132]

In Italy, at this crucial juncture, Barbatius played a notable if enigmatic role in the stand-off between Lucius and Octavian. This episode is reported by Appian:

> Barbatius, Antony's quaestor, had returned owing to some disagreement with him. When he was asked, he answered that Antony was displeased by those who were fighting with Octavian and thereby damaging their joint authority. Some, because they did not perceive Barbatius' deception, changed sides, deserting Lucius for Octavian.

In Appian's account, Barbatius is misleading because he is disgruntled and so seeks to work against Antony's and therefore Lucius' interests: owing to his recent return and his former trusted position, he manages to influence a segment of Lucius' supporters, who change sides. This episode, as Appian tells it, is an awkward one. And it appears odd when set beside our epigraphic and numismatic evidence.

Key to Barbatius' credibility, on any reading of Appian, is his quaestorship. By convention, the relationship between quaestor and commander was deemed a close and enduring one, any violation of which attracted disapprobation. Nor was it suitable for a quaestor to remove himself from provincial service without the permission (if not, admittedly, always the goodwill) of his commander.[133] If Barbatius' presence in Italy resulted from a collapse in his relationship with Antony, this alienation could hardly have been kept secret. Such an estrangement might not render Barbatius entirely useless as an informant but would unquestionably undermine his credibility—that, after all, is Appian's point—especially in any attempt to alter public opinion.

But Barbatius *did* alter public opinion. The insistence on the part of some that he and Antony had fallen out, although it persuaded Appian (or his source), did not prove persuasive at this contentious moment.[134] Perhaps this was because Barbatius had not returned in a state of high dudgeon, as Appian's account suggests, but instead in order to take up his aedileship. And inasmuch as he was bound to return to Italy, he was just the man to perform one final, and important, quaestorian duty. In the east, Barbatius was responsible for issuing gold coins, aurei, which recorded his relationship with Antony as well as, and more importantly, Antony's collegial bond with Octavian. He also issued silver coins, denarii, on the obverse of which, again, he paired himself with his commander, while on the reverse the consulship of Lucius Antonius was celebrated.[135] These coins were not purely for eastern consumption. It was Antony's mission, as we have seen, to raise crucially needed funds and to do so rapidly. By late summer 41 he should have been in a position to send to Italy a first and welcome instalment of hard cash, some specimens of which signalled his partnership with Octavian while others commemorated the consulship of his brother. The delivery of these moneys, the security of which was protected by a fleet of five warships, was a task suitable for a quaestor.[136] And this quaestor, it was natural to assume, would also bring home important communications from the triumvir in the east.

If Barbatius returned to Italy in this role, it is easy to see how the views of an Antonian aedile-designate, freshly returned from the east, must stimulate the curiosity of all parties. It is also easy to see how anyone dissatisfied with his answers might try to discredit him. Why, the captious or disappointed might ask, was this man deemed dispensable, apt for shipping home? Insinuations like that may even have made an impression on some. But clearly not on everyone. And yet there can have been little prospect of Barbatius, whatever the circumstances of his return, answering his interrogators in any other way than he did. He was, like Antony, publicly committed, if only by way of their joint coinage, to harmony between the triumvirs *and* solidarity with Lucius—one could hold the proof in one's hands— and Barbatius' were not the only coins communicating this message to anyone who bothered to look.[137]

Rebellion against triumviral authority was not an official stand anyone outside Lucius' most ardent supporters could easily take, and that included Barbatius—and apparently Antony, even if we can be confident that Antony, when he despatched Barbatius, was unaware of the violent collapse taking place in Italy when the quaestor arrived. Barbatius' testimony simply reinforced Antony's unsurprising commitment to the existing government. At the same time, this episode, for all the puzzles it presents, makes it obvious that no one in Italy possessed anything in the way of information from Antony that unambiguously took Lucius' side or clearly authorized Octavian to do whatever was necessary in order to preserve the triumvirate. Again, this is entirely to be expected in view of the rapidity with which events in Italy were taking place. Nevertheless, and this is equally obvious, everyone, especially the soldiers, was desperate for any indication of Antony's preferences.

Antony's unrelenting taciturnity provoked consternation in antiquity, as we have seen, nor have modern scholars penetrated his silence. Ancient moralists insisted that a debauched Antony was so deeply in thrall to Cleopatra that nothing else could occupy his attention.[138] That, clearly, is nonsense. Alternative explanations ascribe Antony greater agency. It has been proposed that Antony truly sought his colleague's overthrow but left it to his brother so that he could preserve a degree of plausible deniability.[139] This argument demands much in the way of personal hazard and self-sacrifice from Lucius. Which is not to say that Octavian's failure would have been unwelcome to Antony, but that is not the same thing as believing he was actively plotting against his fellow triumvir. A better argument implicates Antony in the alleged republicanism of his brother.[140] But it has been urged here that too much in the way of an ideological motivation on the part of Lucius has been inferred from his championing of the consulship or his defence of property rights. And, if one accepts that view, there is also no basis for insisting instead that Antony and his brother were at principled odds during the Perusine crisis.[141] A still different approach proposes that Antony relished, if he did not actually foment, perturbation at home because distress there distracted attention from his failure in the east to acquire funds adequate to resolve social tensions in Italy.[142] This does not persuade, not least because there is no reason to believe that Antony believed he had failed in the east.

We must bear in mind that, even once Antony became aware that war had broken out in Italy, he lacked the particulars he required for formulating a policy capable of balancing the competing interests of his brother and his colleague, each of whom, we should conclude, acted in his own interests while endeavouring to preserve a good relationship with Antony.[143] Loyalty to his wife and to his brother, *pietas*, was a moral imperative. So, too, loyalty of a different brand, *constantia*, which demanded that he observe the terms of his very public agreement at Philippi. Until he could return to Italy, he had no choice but to rely on the judgement of his deputies on the scene. Octavian, to his credit, had hedged his aggression: true, he had divorced Claudia and fallen out with Fulvia, but he had subsequently taken conspicuous steps to be reconciled with her and with Lucius—and to preserve his partnership with Antony. Lucius, whose sudden eminence in 41 was mostly a function of his resistance to the unpopular Octavian, ultimately found himself driven into open conflict by Italian decurions fiercely hostile to the triumvir. The early stages of their rivalry will not have been uncongenial to Antony. Outright violence, by contrast, he cannot have welcomed. Not that even these conflicts were damaging to Antony's status, but order in Italy was a triumviral imperative. Nor did Antony wish to see his brother or wife endangered or even embarrassed.

Possibly, had Antony's generals inserted themselves, they could have restored an uncomfortable peace. But owing to personal rivalries, perhaps, or a lack of fortitude, they seized upon the absence of explicit instructions from their master as an excuse for inaction. They may have believed that, in the end, Lucius and Octavian could sort things out for themselves, and they, like Antony in the east, remained certain that even in extreme circumstances Octavian would treat Lucius humanely out of respect for his brother. In a sense, this is what happened, but only after the bitter siege of Perusia intervened. This entire episode, pervaded by fear and suffering in Italy and in Rome, underlines a serious failure of judgement and leadership by all parties. In the case of Antony, his aloofness, intended from the start to respect the authority of Lucius and Octavian alike—and, perhaps, to demonstrate Italy's very real need for the commanding presence of the victor at Philippi—ultimately allowed Italian affairs to collapse too quickly for him to do anything in the way of propping them up.[144]

With Barbatius' appearance, the dynamics of Lucius' contest with Octavian were seriously altered.[145] Not everyone was willing to back the consul against the triumvir unless Antony's support for his brother's insurrection was unambiguous. Lucius was deserted by some who were now disinclined to take sides and by others who judged the triumvirate the stronger if not the better cause. It is perhaps at this point that at least some in the soldiery, influenced by the gap between Barbatius' message of harmony and Lucius' militancy, became willing to be convinced by Octavian's claims that the consul's support for the Italians represented a threat to their material interests.[146] And it was at about this time that Salvidienus returned to Italy. His forces had been shadowed, but in no way impeded, by Ventidius and Asinius Pollio.[147] He promptly captured Sentinum, which he plundered and burned, a lesson that was not lost on Nursia. This city soon capitulated, only to be ruined later by Octavian's vengeful taxes and tolls.[148] The struggle for primacy in Italy had now turned destructive.

The Siege of Perusia

Lucius now intended to spend the winter revising his plans for dealing with Octavian in the spring and preparing for his brother's return. He marched north in order to form a secure combination with Ventidius and Pollio. But he was foiled by Marcus Agrippa, who, in staging an attack on Sutrium, an ally in the consul's cause, created a diversion. Constancy obliged Lucius to turn to the city's defence, but in so doing he found himself trapped amid forces led by Agrippa, Salvidienus, and Octavian, who had again entered operations. Ensnared, Lucius hurled himself into the stoutly fortified city of Perusia. His arrival was unexpected, but he was welcomed: later events make it clear that the town's leaders were hostile to Octavian.[149] The consul was now isolated.

Lucius sought relief from Ventidius, to whom he dispatched Manius. He also deployed a cavalry force under the command of Tisienus: its mission was to harass and distract Octavian. He then made preparations for wintering in Perusia.[150] This season, he must have believed, would now be spent in a stand-off with Octavian, one which he could address and sustain by way of fresh negotiations. Owing to the menace of Antony's commanders and pressure from aristocrats up and down Italy, Lucius could assume, Octavian would remain satisfied with his immediate advantage and endeavour, as previously he had done, to find an accommodation with Antony's brother. But Octavian was no longer willing to tolerate insolence and rebellion on the part of Italian cities—his treatment of Sentinum made that clear—or on the part of his colleague's renegade brother. Aware that Perusia was entirely unprepared, Octavian laid siege. In doing so, he ran the risk of waging war against Antony's marshals if they chose to fight. But, although no source even hints at it, he must somehow have indicated to them and to Lucius that all hostilities would cease once the consul acquiesced—unambiguously—in the triumvir's authority.[151] Harming Lucius was not in Octavian's interest, but nor could he allow this man to continue to rally Italian cities against him. His siege of Perusia, then, was a political statement as well as a military tactic. And it was bold.

Fulvia did not fail her brother-in-law. She wrote Antony's commanders—Ventidius, Pollio, and Quintus Fufius Calenus—urging them to rush to Lucius' aid. Ventidius and Pollio complied, at first anyway, by advancing to the south. As for Calenus, he remained unmoved. Destined to die early in the next year, he was perhaps already too ill to act. By putting her enormous personal influence to work, Fulvia also managed to raise fresh troops for Plancus. With these reinforcements, he annihilated one of Octavian's legions near Rome.[152] The soul of assiduity, Fulvia even began a correspondence with Sextus Pompey, whom she pressed to take advantage of this opportunity to strike.[153] In the end, however, none of her exertions mattered. Octavian's forces were quick in blocking the advances of Ventidius and Pollio, nor could Plancus distract and dislodge Octavian. Lucius' cause was not helped by the reality that these Antonian generals disliked and distrusted one another. Although action was now required, Ventidius alone was bold: Pollio remained cautious, and Plancus was ultimately persuasive in making a case to the others that they should wait on events.[154]

Propaganda played its part during this crisis, a reality visible on surviving sling bullets that were cast by troops on both sides.[155] Soldierly esprit was stimulated by inscribing designations of legions or the names of esteemed commanders—or by etching in abuse of the enemy.[156] 'Lucius Antonius, baldy, you are doomed', reads one. Others ridicule Octavian—he is always denominated *Octavian* or even *Octavius* and never *Caesar* by Lucius' men—in fiercely obscene terms. Fulvia, too, attracted scurrility.[157] It hardly mattered that she was elsewhere. For the Romans, insults against women very often came by way of collateral damage in conflicts between men, and this is obviously the case here.[158] Brickbats hurled at Fulvia implied that she, not Lucius, was the central figure, a conceit that degraded the consul and fashioned any opposition to the triumvir as something perverse and unnatural. This was a strategy that owned Octavian's approval. An epigram attributed to him[159] defines the Perusine War as the consequence of Fulvia's jealousy and sexual appetite:

> Because Antony fucks Glaphyra, Fulvia sentences me to this punishment: I must fuck her too. I fuck Fulvia? What if Manius begged me to sodomise him? Would I do it? I don't think so, not if I have any taste. 'Fuck me or fight me', says she. Well, isn't my dick dearer to me than my very life? Let the trumpets sound![160]

Here Octavian belittles Lucius' campaign by humiliating Manius and Fulvia—all by way of a robust and vulgar sexism (and a witty allusion to Caesar's claim in his *Civil War* that his dignity was dearer to him than his life).[161]

It may be owing to this strategy of trivializing Lucius that the consul is mocked as *calvus*. He may, of course, actually have been bald. But baldness was a disfigurement Romans often took as evidence of sexual incontinence: even Caesar was needled by his soldiers as a *moechus calvus*, a bald adulterer.[162] During the empire, the semiotics of baldness, because it marked a man for his carnal excesses, could also signal an emperor's tyrannical tendencies.[163] Consequently, it has been suggested that these sling bullets launch a similar slur against Lucius.[164] But not everything is about sex, and it is perhaps more likely that here Octavian's soldiers refer to a familiar figure from popular mimes, one of the public's favourite forms of entertainment. The Stupid Bald Man, the butt of ridicule in multiple mimes, was a stock character who, because he was hopeless, hapless, and stupid, 'was deceived and disappointed in all that he did'.[165] This is an insult that works very neatly with complaints about Fulvia's masterful manliness. Lucius got the point. He, too, ventilated vilification: in pamphlets or in verse he reproached Octavian for surrendering his chastity to Caesar and to Aulus Hirtius.[166]

We must ask: does Octavian's epigram against Fulvia deprecate Antony? An affair with Glaphyra, if one took place, while not exactly a specimen of sterling behaviour, was by no means profoundly immoral or even objectionable conduct for a Roman husband. Its inclusion here hardly constitutes calumny. By contrast, any sexual advance outside marriage was absolutely disgraceful on the part of a Roman matron.[167] In this poem, Fulvia is irredeemably bad, and Antony is, if anything, unfortunate in the choice of his wife. Octavian's feud, this poem makes clear, is with the irrational and reprobate Fulvia—and so by unmistakeable implication with the non-entity Lucius. Not, however, at least not strictly speaking, with Antony. Some of the sling bullets cast by Lucius' soldiers are inscribed with Antony's name and underline his victory at Philippi: the great man's prestige was clearly a rallying cry inside Perusia.[168] Nothing in the way of a contradiction ever fell from the other side. Lucius and Fulvia were targets of abuse in this conflict, but never Antony.[169]

Inside Perusia's walls, deprivation soon led to starvation—and desperation. More than once, Lucius attempted to break out, but without success. In the end, he was forced to capitulate.[170] Lucius was not merely pardoned by Octavian but offered a command in his Spanish province. Under the circumstances, he could hardly refuse. He is not mentioned again: presumably he died not long afterwards. Lucius' officers and staff, including his senatorial and equestrian supporters, were likewise pardoned, although some preferred flight. Tisienus joined Sextus Pompey. Claudius Nero, after staging another unsuccessful rebellion in Campania, also made his way to Sicily, taking with him his wife, Livia, and their son, the future emperor, Tiberius.[171] Perhaps this was wise: a very few aristocrats, Octavian's bitterest enemies, were executed. As for Lucius' soldiers, they were added to Octavian's. And the townsfolk of Perusia were spared. The leading men of the city were not so fortunate. With a single exception, a man who had served on the jury which condemned the Liberators, the town's council were put to death. The city itself was wrecked, perhaps by Octavian's pillaging troops, perhaps by arson.[172] Perusia's grim fate was later memorably lamented in the poetry of Propertius. And, in the months prior to Actium, Octavian's cruelty at Perusia, including allegations of human sacrifice, animated Antonian propaganda.[173] In time the city was restored, as Perusia Augusta, and once more it thrived.[174] But in the winter of 40 its ruin, and the execution of its decurions, made it clear to the whole of Italy that rebellion against Octavian would not be tolerated.

Coda

For Octavian, this was intended to be the end of the matter. His conflict with Lucius was now concluded. So, too, any further resistance from the municipalities. Lucius insisted to Octavian that his brother played no part in his rebellion and Octavian, whether or not he was convinced, deemed it prudent to take him at his word.[175] Antony, he hoped, would likewise be prepared to move forward. Fulvia, to whom Plancus granted an honour guard of 3,000 cavalrymen, travelled east to join her husband. Plancus accompanied her. Octavian took no action to deter them. Nor did he impede Antony's mother, Julia, when she departed Rome for Sicily, from which island she, too, headed east to meet her son.[176] Her movements must have worried Octavian. Still, he took no action to hinder her. Ventidius moved, without opposition, to southern Italy, where he took command of Antony's legions in the region, apart from two which elected to serve under Agrippa. Asinius Pollio, now consul, shifted his forces to Venetia. There he commenced negotiations with Domitius Ahenobarbus. Once again, there was no intervention by Octavian, who, anxious over Antony's reaction to the Perusine crisis, was instead endeavouring to relax tensions between himself and Antony's partisans.[177] From the east, there was still no word.

XI

Enforce no further the griefs between ye

Rude Awakening

Very early in the spring of 40, Parthian armies, led by Labienus and Pacorus, the king's son, invaded Syria.[1] Owing to its political instability, even after Antony's settlement, a fact of Syrian life familiar to the Parthian court, this region was vulnerable. Nor was Decidius Saxa, Antony's legate in the province, in a position to repulse his attackers: he lacked sufficient troops and many of his soldiers remained discontented men. He did what he could, but after more than one defeat was driven into Cilicia.[2] Some of his soldiers deserted him, preferring the victorious Labienus.[3] When Antony learned of this disaster, he reacted at once. He sailed to Tyre, which, divided by water from the mainland, remained secure.[4] By then, however, Syria had been lost. Labienus was making his way into Cilicia. Pacorus turned toward Palestine. Antony then sailed toward Asia Minor.[5]

Antony was alarmed but undaunted. His immediate plans are fathomable enough. He could not summon legions from Macedonia, where Marcius Censorinus, its governor, needed every man in defending the province from incursions by northern tribes. Consequently, it would be necessary to import troops from Italy. Lucius and Octavian, Antony would insist, must put aside their conflict for the sake of the empire. Until reinforcements arrived, Antony must rally such Roman resistance as he could and deploy auxiliaries supplied by client kings. The situation was grim but far from unsalvageable. True, Antony could not repel the enemy straightaway, but he could confront it stoutly enough to reassure Rome's subjects and, before the end of the summer, launch his counterattack.

None of these things happened. When Antony learned of the fall of Perusia, he turned his attention fully toward Italy, still the centre of any Roman's political universe. What to make of matters there remained far from obvious, but Antony was soon briefed by trusted informants. He travelled to Greece, where he met Fulvia and Plancus. Manius was also there.[6] Antony's mother, Julia, soon joined them. She was accompanied by a highly distinguished delegation from Sextus Pompey, including Lucius Scribonius Libo, Sextus' able and cunning father-in-law, who sought an alliance.[7] Their collective account of Octavian's conduct and current disposition will not have been a balanced one, nor was its tenor intended to reassure. Lucius' failure they portrayed as the consequence of Octavian's aggression against Antony.

We do not know what was said or how at first these disturbing reports were received by Antony. Later revisionism required an Antony who was furious with his brother, his procurator, and especially his wife, whose health broke down under her husband's reproaches. But this thread in the story must be unpicked. If Antony's temper was now raised, it was owing to allegations of Octavian's cruelty and menace. Julia certainly did not blame her younger son for the Perusine crisis. Indeed, it is highly plausible that it was Julia, abetted by Fulvia's earlier correspondence, who persuaded Sextus to seize this opportunity to seek an alliance with Antony. What part, if any, was played by the embassy of veterans who had spent the winter in Alexandria with Antony, we do not know.[8] But even if they spoke up for Octavian, Antony had no reason to prefer them to his closest family and advisors. Or his own political instincts. It was not so long ago, after all, that Antony had been a victim of Octavian's aggressive, opportunistic antagonism. And when news reached him from Asinius Pollio that Domitius Ahenobarbus, like Sextus, was seeking his friendship, he must have concluded that these parties, like his wife and mother, now saw Octavian as his enemy.[9] The old animosity was rekindled. Parthia would have to wait.[10]

And so Antony left the east to fend for itself. Decidius Saxa was subsequently routed in Cilicia, captured, and executed.[11] Labienus proudly minted coins on which he styled himself Q. *Labienus Parthicus imperator*, Quintus Labienus Parthicus, conquering general. Pacorus invaded Judea, toppling the government of Hyrcanus and Herod and installing Antigonus, the son of Aristobulus II, as king. Herod fled to Rome. Soon Parthian domination extended from Nabatea in the south into Anatolia in the north, where Labienus marched westwards into Caria.[12] Antony's legate in Asia, Marcus Turius, evacuated.[13] Coastal regions managed to remain in touch with Roman authority. Inland, some of Rome's client kings and a few determined cities, hopeful of a Roman counterattack, struggled loyally if not always effectually against Parthian hegemony. In the Phrygian city of Laodicea, for instance, Zeno the Rhetorician and his son, Polemo, led a heroic struggle against Labienus.[14] Laodicea was not unique: resistance was also exerted in Aphrodisias, Alabanda, Miletus, Mylasa, and Stratonicea.[15] But these were exceptions. Unaided by Rome, polities too weak to maintain their independence had little choice but to accommodate their new masters. Antony's departure was striking. It signals his conviction that Octavian was now truly his enemy, and it marks Antony's determination to prevail even if that meant misery for Rome's eastern subjects. Neither Sulla nor Caesar, although each strained everything in his quest for political domination, abandoned the east as Antony did. Only a year ago Antony had entered Rome's eastern possessions by way of a splendid, confident parade of triumviral authority. He now withdrew, leaving behind a shambles.

War in the West

Fighting yet another civil war held no attractions for Antony, but nor was he inclined to flinch from it if Octavian refused to submit to his authority.[16] It was with this possibility in mind that he accepted an alliance of some kind (we cannot be more specific than that) with both Domitius and with Sextus Pompey.[17] Antony gathered his ample fleet and a modest force of soldiers, probably little more than his praetorian guard. For troops, he realized, he must rely on his legions in Italy and the two legions under Domitius' command.[18] Sextus, too, had infantry. Antony believed he held at least twenty-four legions in or around Italy, but at what strength he could not be sure. He was certainly outmanned by Octavian, who soon improved his advantage: by the time Antony reached Italy, Fufius Calenus, Antony's governor in Transalpine Gaul, had died and Octavian had usurped his eleven legions, an extraordinary and provocative action.[19] But Caesar's heir, however much he may have hoped Perusia could be relegated to the past, remained too astute not to prepare for the worst. Even he was shocked by the news that Sextus had begun negotiations with Antony. His colleague's protracted silence—not a single signal of comity arrived from the east even after Lucius' surrender—can only have provoked graver consternation.[20] So he naturally seized every resource: retaliation, he was certain, was on its way. Antony's coalition with Sextus and Domitius was proof of that.

This renewal of hostility against Octavian stimulated an adjustment in Antony's public posture. Amid the conflicts of 44, as we have seen, Antony was obliged to repudiate the amnesty of 17 March. Since that time, he had campaigned as a fierce avenger of Julius Caesar, openly despising his enemies as the 'party of Pompey'. Even after Philippi, during his reorganization of the east, he persisted in condemning, at every chance, the Liberators' pollution and treachery. Constancy counted for much among the aristocracy. How, then, could Antony justify his new coalition against Caesar's heir? For he was now allied with Domitius Ahenobarbus, nephew of Cato and a resolute enemy of the dictator. This man, almost certainly involved in the conspiracy to assassinate Caesar, had been condemned by the Pedian law.[21] Even more incongruous to his earlier policy, Antony was also attached to Sextus Pompey.

Antony made use of the resources offered by Domitius and Sextus because he believed he needed them. That much is obvious. But there is something more. He also believed that he *could* make use of Domitius and Sextus without suffering any significant ill-will in Italy. He was convinced that, as the victor at Philippi, he need no longer be defined solely as a Caesarian or even as the leading Caesarian. His loyalty to that cause could hardly be impugned, but now his personal stature was ample enough for him to move ahead by forming a distinctive, Antonian political identity. The soldiery and the citizenry of Italy, knowing he had crushed the Liberators, must trust him in his decision to cooperate with Domitius and Sextus. It was a bold gamble, but also an expression of Antony's confidence and optimism, undeterred even by a Parthian invasion and violent conflict at home.[22]

This new posture Antony scaffolded with a new policy, or rather, by recurring to the programme of reconciliation that had animated his consulship in the aftermath of the Ides. Antony complained of Octavian's failures as a colleague, and he denounced his unrelenting propensity for strife. By contrast, Antony emphasized his preference for harmony and concord among the aristocracy. We can see this, at least obliquely, in Appian's distillation of Antony's agreement with Sextus: he promised to regard Sextus as an ally in war but only if Octavian proved to be his enemy. If, however, Octavian remained a loyal colleague, Antony promised to do what he could to repair the breach between Caesar's heir and Pompey's son.[23] Similarly, he endeavoured to bring Domitius home to the republic. In Appian's account, these are negotiations Antony handed over to his diplomatic friend, Lucius Cocceius Nerva, who folded Domitius' restoration into a more general triumviral policy of making peace even with men who in the past had been sympathetic to the Liberators' cause: with the Liberators now removed, Cocceius insisted, this shift was necessary if the triumvirs did not wish to remain the enemies of nearly everyone.[24] As for Domitius specifically, it was now claimed he was never actually one of assassins, and although he may have approved the deed, it was now necessary that he, like any others who had fought on the wrong side at Philippi, be regained by the republic for the sake of the republic.[25] Who better to make this claim than the victor at Philippi and his supporters? Clearly Cocceius and Antony had in mind the multitude of distinguished refugees who had fled Italy for safety with Sextus. And it is clear how all this sounds very much like the Antony of 44, who preferred amnesty to revenge. By way of these principles, then, which he hoped would appeal to many, Antony publicly justified his deployment of the forces of Domitius and Sextus.

Antony departed Athens accompanied by his wife and mother. Almost immediately, however, as they were rounding the Peloponnese, Fulvia fell ill. Because the expedition could not delay, she was settled in Sicyon. Antony then sailed for Italy, along the way combining his forces with the fleet of Domitius.[26] But when he arrived at Brundisium, the city refused him entry, frightened, it was alleged, by Domitius' presence. Antony, as triumvir, could not legitimately be barred from Italy. For him, this exclusion from Brundisium was sufficient proof of Octavian's enmity.[27] At once he laid siege to the place. It was perhaps soon afterwards that he learned he had lost Fufius Calenus' legions. Consequently, he took the extreme step of summoning troops from Macedonia. The stakes in Italy had become too high to leave them where they belonged.[28] Antony also unleashed Sextus, who seized Sardinia and launched multiple attacks against Italy, while the navies of Antony and Domitius struck at cities on the peninsula's eastern coast. By capturing the harbour-town of Sipontum, Antony soon found a satisfactory substitute for Brundisium.[29]

On land Antony faced a real fight if he hoped to defeat Octavian. But he dominated the seas. Which meant that, by combining embargo with pillaging, he was in a position to inflict harm on a scale that could only put intense pressure on Octavian's government in Rome. Under such conditions, Octavian's troops might find themselves famished or forced to plunder, and the peoples of Italy were certain to suffer deprivation or even violence. Admittedly Antony ran the risk of appearing an invader, but he was certain it was Octavian who would be blamed for any misery his coalition inflicted on Rome and Italy. Octavian, however, tried to turn Italy's woes against Antony by denouncing any common cause with his father's murderer or the followers of Sextus Pompey, men he claimed were Italy's mortal enemies.[30] Octavian worked hard to kindle concern among the soldiers and veterans by recycling propaganda he had previously put to work against Lucius: Octavian warned that, because Antony meant to restore the enemies of the Caesarian cause, they must all of them expect to lose their properties and donatives. These men, however, remained unconvinced: the esteem in which they held the victor of Philippi would not allow them even to consider the possibility that Antony could betray them.[31]

Octavian, sensing the difficulty of his position, now sought an alliance with Libo, notwithstanding his position in Sextus' camp. He made an offer of marriage to Scribonia, Libo's sister. Twice married previously, to men of consular rank, this woman was wealthy, splendid, and older than Octavian.[32] Through this connection, Octavian hoped to gain some credibility and influence with the aristocracy-in-exile serving under Sextus.[33] Octavian's offer was accepted—the forward-thinking Libo perceived an advantage in this unexpected alliance—but the betrothal did nothing to deter Sextus' attacks.[34] Nor, after the couple were married, did they get along.[35] Octavian's flash of dynastic inspiration, in short, achieved nothing. Nor did it instil confidence in his inner circle. Quite the reverse. Lepidus refused to remain in Italy: he preferred to take up his African province.[36] More serious by far, Salvidienus Rufus, sensing his master's imminent defeat, began secret negotiations with Antony. He offered to desert to Antony, bringing his army with him. If, as seems likely, Salvidienus was now in command of Fufius Calenus' legions, this was a betrayal certain to turn the conflict decisively in Antony's favour.[37] In the end, it never transpired, but this covert affair makes it obvious how, even among Octavian's most trusted men, Antony's position appeared strong. For his part, Antony continued to work very hard in appealing to Italy's veterans.[38]

On the back foot he may have been, but Octavian was hardly finished. He dispatched Agrippa against Sipontum. On the march, this talented general amplified his legions by recruiting veterans from the colonies. These men, however, believed they had been activated for the defence of Italy against Sextus. When they learned it was Antony's forces they were called on to fight, they refused. This mutiny, a notable event, dispirited Octavian. But not Agrippa, who, relying on his regular legions, succeeded in recapturing Sipontum. In the south, at about this same time, Sextus suffered a significant reverse. By now, however, Antony had completed his siege engines and was preparing a major, perhaps the final, assault on Brundisium. Octavian advanced south in the hope of relieving the city. Because the situation was urgent, he sent ahead a large cavalry force under the command of Publius Servilius Rullus.[39]

Antony now seized an opportunity for making an almost theatrical display of his courage. Taking personal command of a small contingent, he rode out to confront Octavian's advance force, which was camped at Hyria, modern Oria. He then led a risky night raid against the town, and, by surprising Servilius, captured both him and his cavalry. The victorious Antony made a splendid public show of delivering the prisoners to his camp at Brundisium.[40] This dashing adventure, of no real military consequence, nevertheless proved decisive. By flourishing an old-fashioned, heroic, even inspiring kind of valour, Antony dazzled soldiers on both sides of the conflict, not least the veterans among Octavian's forces who were already disinclined to take up arms against him. Octavian's officers now made it clear that they wanted an armistice. Antony's men were likewise keen to end any fighting.[41] Even if the soldiery did not express their views in terms of concord or harmony, their position conformed neatly with Antony's current policy, which emphasized reconciliation for the sake of the republic. Nor, for different reasons, was the soldiers' demand unwelcome to Octavian. Both triumvirs seized this opportunity to halt hostilities by way of an expression of solidarity with their armies.

This resolution was made easier when Italy learned of the death of Fulvia.[42] Presumably she succumbed to her illness. That is the clear impression given by Plutarch, although Appian prefers to attribute her end to heartbreak owing to her husband's anger and his liaison with Cleopatra. Antony grieved her loss, as well he might: the partner of his labours since their marriage in 47, she had borne him two sons and boldly championed his interests during his absence from Italy; after Perusia, she, with Julia, played a crucial part in opening negotiations between Antony and Sextus Pompey, a combination from which he had clearly profited. A vital, formidable, and keenly intelligent figure, why should Antony not mourn her? That he was an unfaithful husband must not be viewed as marking any absence of affection. And yet

Antony, even in his grief, acquiesced to a version of history, originating in Octavian's propaganda, in which Fulvia, a virago, betrayed his interests by rousing Lucius against the legitimate government of the triumvirs. The violent rift between the triumvirs, it was now decided, was all her doing, and with her death all parties could be reconciled without further recriminations. A not so noble lie, but it became the foundation for the fresh arrangements settled on at Brundisium. Antony deeply regretted, so we are told, his mistreatment of Fulvia.[43] Perhaps so, and perhaps it was this episode which inculcated his sense of remorse. Nevertheless, confronted by calamity in the east and a political crisis in Italy, he did not hesitate to betray Fulvia's memory.[44]

The Pact at Brundisium

The triumvirate and its dilapidating government, it was obvious, required restructuring, reforms that demanded intelligent, resourceful negotiations. The principal figures in these crucial deliberations, at least initially, were Lucius Cocceius Nerva and Antony's mother, Julia, who, acting as Octavian's correspondent, helped to persuade her son to yield to his colleague in delicate matters. Gaius Maecenas and Asinius Pollio, too, played significant parts, as did delegations from the armies. Lepidus, now in Africa, was naturally excluded. His absence was his own fault, after all, and in any case it was understood that, so long as his circumstances remained undiminished, he would agree to any arrangements made by his colleagues. Delay was in any case intolerable, and by September it was agreed to draw a bold line in history by way of an amnesty separating the present moment from all recent conflicts, including the Perusine war. As for the future, that would now be defined by a solid, stable friendship between Octavian and Antony. This new relationship, it was widely urged, should be cemented by a marriage between Antony and Octavia, Octavian's sister, recently widowed by the death of a noble ex-consul, Gaius Claudius Marcellus. In a public display of restored comity, the triumvirs embraced in the presence of the armies.[45]

Antony's restored friendship with his colleague did not come without a cost. Octavian still nursed wounds he had received from Manius' lacerating oratory. In a perverse act of triumviral loyalty, Antony gave the man up. Although an Antonian connection of long standing, Manius was summarily executed. At the same time, Antony refused to abandon his new allies. Domitius Ahenobarbus, rehabilitated in the pact of Brundisium, was appointed by Antony as governor of Bithynia and Pontus, a position he retained until his consulship in 32. Accommodating Sextus, by contrast, presented more serious difficulties, not all of which are visible to us. It seems clear enough that Octavian despised him, and, unlike Domitius, Sextus refused to join in the machinery of triumviral government: he insisted on joining the junta only on terms that rendered him more or less an equivalent to Lepidus, if not actually a peer of Octavian or Antony.[46] This was unacceptable to Octavian, whatever the preferences of his colleague.[47] A compromise was reached whereby the door to an arrangement with Sextus remained open. According to Appian, it was agreed that Octavian was free to wage war against Sextus 'unless an agreement could be reached between them'. Rome's conflict with Sextus was now entirely and explicitly Octavian's responsibility.[48] Antony had done what he could to broker a comprehensive peace.

Dio, however, reports that Antony agreed to join forces with Octavian in the fight against Sextus. This is an observation he introduces principally in order to find fault with Antony for his treachery: 'they cooperated in waging war on Sextus, although Antony had, through intermediaries, sworn oaths to side with him against Caesar'.[49] Presently, in Dio's account, Sextus is confronted by the shocking reality of Antony's betrayal.[50] This is a very different story from the one we read in Appian and it derives from later polemic in which Octavian and his apologists condemned Antony's cruelty and disloyalty to Sextus, a recurring leitmotif in Dio's treatment of Antony.[51] We need not be distracted here. In 40, Antony, true to his word, though he could not win over Octavian and bring about a reconciliation, nonetheless held himself aloof from his colleague's belligerence.

Provincial assignments were reallocated. Lepidus kept Africa. Antony, however, relinquished his western provinces in exchange for the eastern ones. That Antony should return to the east was by no means inevitable. But he knew the advantages of that part of the world—in wealth, prestige, and high culture—and was unwilling to give them up. Nor could he bear allowing anyone else to rescue the region from the blunders of his recent tenure. Antony's central mission in the east was defined as avenging Crassus' defeat by the Parthians at Carrhae. This was a tactful formulation for Antony's real job there: recovering those parts of Rome's domain he had lost to Labienus and Pacorus. Thereafter, he had license to punish the Parthians. Reestablishing Roman primacy in the east, necessary for reviving its payment of taxes and tribute and interest, was unquestionably indispensable to any restoration of the republic. And it was likely to be glorious. For his part, Octavian assumed control of the west, apart from Africa, an assignment that for practical reasons included Illyricum. Scodra, on the Adriatic, henceforth divided the triumvirs' provincial authority. Because Italy was not a province, all three triumvirs shared in its administration, though it was recognized that Octavian, soon to be the sole triumvir on the scene, would bear the brunt of that duty.[52]

The triumvirs' tripartite division of the world did not impose borders which sealed off their territories from traditional lines of social or political contact or influence. Our most illuminating evidence for this comes from Aphrodisias, an eastern city favoured by Julius Caesar, Lucius Antonius, Antony, and Octavian.[53] Inscriptions preserved in this city reveal how, during Antony's administration, Octavian won local appreciation when he acted as its patron. He recommended the city's privileges to Antony and, in correspondence with other cities in the region, urged them to respect the Aphrodisians' rights.[54] It was only natural that Octavian, as Caesar's heir, should act as Aphrodisias' benefactor, and, because he also owned property there, he could properly represent the place through a traditional exercise of neighbourliness (what the Romans called *vicinitas*), a vital relationship between an individual and the communities in which he was, by way of residence or ownership, a member.[55] Octavian's collaboration with the Aphrodisians could not, and did not, offend Antony, who was also intimately implicated in this city's society. Antony, whose patronage and properties extended to cities in Italy and possibly elsewhere in the west, will have acted likewise.[56] As did other senators who were patrons and property-holders, though doubtless they lobbied the senate and triumvirs with greater circumspection than did Octavian or Antony. Even during the empire, certainly under the Julio-Claudian emperors, senators were allowed and even expected to champion the interests of provincial cities.[57] This was an aristocratic habit the triumvirs had no interest in closing down. Quite the reverse, for they now sought to lessen some of the social anxieties stirring up aristocratic opposition to their administration.

Slouching Towards Rome

After concluding their pact, each triumvir was hailed *imperator* by his troops. They then returned to Rome, where each celebrated an ovation—not for winning a victory but for making peace with his colleague: Octavian, according to the *Fasti Triumphales*, 'because he made peace (*pax*) with Mark Antony'; Antony, 'because he made peace' with Octavian.[58] The acclamation of *imperator*, the celebration of an *ovatio*, even the boast of making peace, all of this, from any Roman perspective, connoted victory or, at the very least, capitulation by one's opponent.[59] In this remarkable double pageant, however, although both men paraded themselves as victors, there was no loser. The message the triumvirs hoped to convey was that the republic itself was the true winner, and in the celebration of twin ovations they sought to inspire popular confidence in the restored triumvirate.

Antony's highly publicized marriage to Octavian's sister was meant to signal the same optimism. First, however, these nuptials required an official intervention by the senate. Octavia was born around 69. Previously married to Gaius Claudius Marcellus, she was already the mother of three children, a son and two daughters.[60] Recently widowed, she was obliged to observe a ten-month interval before marrying again, a legal and social obligation the purpose of which was to lend clarity to the paternity of any offspring a woman's deceased husband may have fathered. The senate decreed an exemption from this requirement, a clear mark of this wedding's importance to the republic. Dio tells us that Octavia was pregnant when she married Antony. If so, the identity of this child's father must have been officially defined in the senate's decree (a widow who actually gave birth was released from any impediment to remarrying).[61] No child of Marcellus is known to have been born, however, and Octavia was very soon pregnant by Antony. Perhaps there was a miscarriage. If so, this was a sombre start for a new family.

It is in the nature of our sources that we learn nothing about Octavia's feelings or agency in making this match. Because this union was the product of political calculations aimed at salvaging the republic, she could not properly resist doing her patriotic duty, welcome or not.[62] Octavia is praised by Plutarch for her beauty and wisdom, and his moralism extends to recording the hope on the part of Antony's contemporaries that a woman of her calibre could win his love and restore him to sound Roman sensibilities. Here the biographer makes her a foil for Cleopatra in a struggle over Antony's character. But Plutarch's Octavia is not a complete fiction: her future career makes clear how able and astute she was. And she knew what was expected of her, as, in this instance, did Antony. The pair presented themselves to the Romans as the loyally married couple everyone desperately wanted them to be. Soon they were awaiting their first child, who was born in 39.

Early in that same year, Antony issued coins commemorating the union: his head, identified by the legend *M. Antony, imperator, triumvir for restoring the republic,* appeared on the obverse; the reverse featured the head of Octavia, without a legend. Her identity was obvious.[63] This was an extraordinary event: for the first time, a living woman was portrayed on a Roman coin—unmistakable testimony to the sheer importance to the republic of the marriage of Octavia and Antony. At this same time, Antony also minted coins marking the renewal of good relations between the triumvirs.[64] Octavian did likewise.[65] His coins portrayed the goddess Concordia and the triumvirs' hands clasped in friendship. A few supporters in the municipalities, encouraged, perhaps, by connections in the capital, also celebrated Antony's reconciliation with Octavian.[66] By advertising their friendship and kinship in parades, games and festivities, and through coinage, the triumvirs urged all Romans to relish the restoration of harmony and the felicity of the new order.

They did not succeed. Soldiers and veterans, whatever their relief that civil war had been averted, now demanded the discharge of unpaid bounties. Their impatience was understandable, but, with the east in disarray, immediate payments were out of the question. The triumvirs instead promised to make good on their commitments as soon as they could.[67] The Roman people, too, were aggrieved—by deprivation.[68] And the cities of Italy were afflicted by renewed exactions.[69] Furious at his exclusion from the pact of Brundisium, Sextus assailed Italy's coast and launched attacks from his garrisons. Worse, he intensified his embargo so fiercely that no one outside Italy was willing even to attempt to provision the capital. Grain became scarce, prices soared, and a famine-stricken population turned to protests and demonstrations, all demanding peace with Sextus. In Rome, demonstrations soon turned into riots. In one incident, Octavian, confronted by an angry mob, was nearly stoned to death. Antony rushed to his aid. At first the crowd did not stone him because it was well known how he, unlike his colleague, preferred an accommodation with Sextus. Still, he could extricate Octavian only be unleashing soldiers who did not hesitate in cutting down recalcitrant civilians. Antony thus rescued his brother-in-law in a bloody spectacle of affinity and authority. The populace was quelled, but their hatred for the triumvirs, especially Octavian, subsisted.[70]

Poetic Interlude

Virgil's *Fourth Eclogue*, profoundly beautiful and devotedly studied, commemorates the consulship of Asinius Pollio, Virgil's friend and literary patron, as a turning point in Roman, indeed, human history. It opens in a mood bright with confidence:

> O Muses of Sicily, let us sing of greater things.
> Orchards and tamarisks do not delight everyone.
> If we sing of woodlands, let them be woodlands worthy of a consul.

> * * *

> Now a new generation comes down from high heaven.
> You, chaste Lucinia, must favour the birth of a boy

on account of whom the iron age shall at last come to its end
and a golden race rise up throughout the world. Your beloved Apollo is now king.
And this marvelous age shall begin when you are consul,
Pollio, and the mighty months shall begin their march
with you as their leader.[71]

Past is the violence of civil strife. Ahead lies a golden age of civic harmony, the advent
of which is marked by the birth of a boy—a *puer*—whose maturity will precipitate this
new and better order. Nearly every modern commentator associates this poem with
the Treaty of Brundisium, in the negotiations of which the consul Pollio played an important part.[72] The blessed boy in this eclogue, on that reading, is routinely taken to
be the anticipated child of Antony and Octavia, a son (it was hoped) whose line would
combine the legacies of the two triumvirs.[73] And perhaps this is right. The attractions
of this interpretation are clear. But doubts obtrude. Certainly not everyone in antiquity read the *Fourth Eclogue* this way. Gaius Asinius Gallus, Pollio's son born in
41, was fond of boasting that he was the prophesied child. He was not dismissed as a
crank. Quite the contrary: the learned Asconius deemed his view worth recording.[74]
    The dramatic date of Virgil's poem is 40. Readers who detect in it a reaction to the
Treaty of Brundisium conclude that the poem was in fact composed at some time after
September and rather late in Pollio's consulship, or even after his consulship, since
he and his colleague abdicated soon after the triumvirs returned to Rome.[75] That the
poem's appearance, on this view, perhaps post-dated Pollio's actual tenure as consul,
though odd—the poem emphasizes the commencement of Pollio's office in lines 11
and 13 (*te consule . . . te duce*)—need not disturb readers for whom the true focus of
the *Fourth Eclogue* rests not on Pollio but on the benefits of the triumvirs' agreement
and on Antony's hoped-for son. But other readings are possible. It is far from obvious
why the *puer* cannot instead be read symbolically, a metaphor and not a specific baby,
and indeed some critics do.[76] In late antiquity, when this poem was still read with
fasciation, the birth of this *puer* was identified with the birth of Christ, an interpretation which secured Virgil an honoured place in Christian thought and literature.[77]
Although the particulars of this poem may perplex, it is nonetheless clear that, around
the time of Brundisium, the occasion of fresh affinity and harmony between the triumvirs, Virgil elected to celebrate a hopeful new beginning.
    At roughly the same time as Virgil's poem, Horace, in his *Epodes*, offered readers a
very different appraisal of Rome and its future. In *Epode* 7, the poet cries out:

Where, where are you rushing—to your ruin!—you wicked men? Why are your
hands again grasping swords from their sheaths?[78]

Horace grieves because Roman civil war is the answer to the Parthians' prayers and
fears the city is fated to labour forever under the fratricidal curse of Romulus and
Remus. The dramatic date of this poem is usually located in 39 or 38, but nothing in
this epode fails to fit the circumstances of 40.[79] Nor is this poem Horace's only protest
against current events. *Epode* 16, a complex and in many ways subversive response
to the *Fourth Eclogue*, beseeches the Roman people to abandon all hope, forsake the
city, and seek the Iles of the Blest somewhere in the distant west. To remain, Horace

insists, means certain doom.[80] This bleak poem, which fiercely demands something better from Rome's feuding ruling class, reflects more truly than Virgil's masterpiece the despair, anxiety, and anger animating Rome and Italy even after the treaty of Brundisium.

New Management

Amid volatile conditions, the triumvirs pushed on. In order to signal a fresh start, the consuls and praetors abdicated and were replaced by new magistrates.[81] At once this refurbished government faced a grim, orchestrated crisis in which they were obliged to register their loyalty to the triumvirs. After their reconciliation at Brundisium, Antony revealed to Octavian the treachery of Salvidienus Rufus. Octavian was unforgiving: he summoned the man to Rome, denounced him as an enemy of the state, and turned to the senate for guidance. The body revived the *senatus consultum ultimum* and appealed to the triumvirs to preserve the republic. Salvidienus was put to death and his legions handed over to Antony. Salvidienus' dramatic fall from power was long remembered, but this emergency, with all its constitutional trappings, did nothing to distract the public from its unremitting ills.[82]

Which is why Antony remained in Rome. Although by now he could have left Italy to take up his provinces, doing so, he recognized, would only exacerbate instability in the west, perhaps ruinously. He did not, however, ignore the turmoil in the east. Domitius had already been directed to Bithynia, doubtless in command of the two legions he previously furnished Antony. Now Antony sent Pollio to Macedonia, where he replaced Censorinus, destined to be consul in 39.[83] More important than these appointments was Asia, which went to Plancus.[84] Each governor was responsible for protecting Roman interests from any Parthian menace, but command of that war, along with the province of Syria, Antony entrusted to Ventidius. He left immediately, initially, it appears, with an army which was somewhat modest for its critical mission.[85] But the Romans could not wait any longer before attempting to reverse their losses, a decision that imposed a weighty responsibility on Ventidius, now faced with a major campaign against Labienus and Pacorus.

Antony made further assignments, not all of which are recoverable by us, and some of which suggest haste. In Cyprus, for instance, instead of a fellow senator he put in charge a trusted freedman of Julius Caesar, Demetrius. It was he who later arrested Labienus after he was defeated by Ventidius.[86] Antony also took measures to ensure the prosperity of Rome's client rulers. The tyrant of Cos was the learned, literary Nicias, a figure well-known in Roman circles. Sometime in 40 or 39, Antony secured significant tax and trade benefits for important individuals on the island, measures that may also have furnished a fillip for the economy in Asia. This action in Rome can only have elevated Nicias' authority—his Antonian connection was proof of his clout—and it instilled local loyalty amid the instability incited by the Parthian invasion.[87]

Eastern embassies, we can be sure, came to Rome. One of them became a focus of very public attention. When Antigonus, backed by the Parthians, overthrew the regime of Hyrcanus, Herod escaped to Rome. He arrived late in 40. Relying on his long-standing friendship with Antony and appealing to Octavian's gratitude for

Antipater's services to Caesar, he sought their aid. The decision was made to recognize him as king of Judea in place of the usurper Antigonus. Again, the triumvirs turned to the senate. Octavian, as triumvir, summoned the body. Herod was introduced and praised by Valerius Messalla, who had previously spoken on his behalf at Daphne, and by Sempronius Atratinus. Antony also spoke, making the case that Herod would be a vital ally in the war against Parthia. After the senate declared Herod king, a procession of triumvirs and monarch, led by the consuls and magistrates, ascended the Capitol to make sacrifice to Jupiter Best and Greatest. This impressive ceremony was followed by a banquet in Herod's honour hosted by Antony.[88] Thereafter he dispatched Dellius with instructions for Ventidius to take on the task of installing Judea's new king. The busy Ventidius handed this assignment on to Quintus Poppaedius Silo, a legate.[89]

The new year began with Censorinus' triumph, celebrated on the first day of his consulship. In this way the triumvirs exhibited to the citizenry how Roman power in the eastern provinces remained secure.[90] Censorinus, and his colleague Calvisius Sabinus, also a triumphator, signalled Caesarian reconciliation. These men—and in the senate these men only—had struggled on the Ides to defend the dictator from his assassins.[91] That Censorinus was Antony's man will have been overlooked by no one. The triumvirs generously expanded the senate's membership, and this augmented body obediently ratified all their acts since taking up their extraordinary office, a resolution which, by way of constitutional affectation, underlined the reality of triumvirs' absolute control of Roman affairs. New, unwelcome taxes supervened.[92] No degree of flummery, however, nor making patriotic noises about punishing the Parthians, could win over a public beset by famine and fear for the future.

The Pact of Misenum

During a long and miserable winter, Antony exhorted Octavian to come to terms with Sextus or defeat him, something he knew lay beyond his colleague's capacity.[93] Whenever it was possible, the people cried out for peace, sometimes, even now, in violent demonstrations.[94] No settlement, however, could come easily. It was not only that Octavian and Sextus loathed one another. Within Sextus' coalition, competing strategies were advocated by leading figures, some of whom pressed for staying the course of starving the triumvirs out. Sextus, however, remained open to an accommodation. Perceiving an opportunity, Antony began to press Libo to come to Italy under the pretext of celebrating his alliance with Octavian, who could hardly refuse his relation safe passage. In this way Antony urged both sides to begin negotiations. Libo came to Aenaria in spring of 39. Octavian consented to preliminary discussions.[95]

Notwithstanding the urgency of reaching an agreement with Sextus and his party, progress was slow, consuming most of the summer. In these diplomatic exchanges, it became necessary to activate the influence of Mucia, Sextus' mother. In the end, it was Octavian who acquiesced. The triumvirs offered Sextus an eminent position. Although he must remain, strictly speaking, a subordinate, Sextus would administer independently a province including Sicily, Sardinia, Corsica, and the Peloponnese— territories in the east as well as the west—and his authority would last until the conclusion of the triumvirate. This proposal, which Sextus accepted thereby ushering in a real chance for peace and stability, was a diplomatic success for Antony.

The parties met near Misenum, in the Bay of Naples, and reached a comprehensive agreement whereby Sextus agreed, in exchange for his new office, to evacuate his forces from Italy and drop his embargo. In addition to his extensive province, Sextus was designated consul for 33, received his father's augurate, and was reimbursed for the loss of his father's estate through a grant of seventy million sesterces. Furthermore, the Romans who had joined Sextus in exile, apart from anyone who had been condemned for the murder of Caesar, were allowed to return to the city and regain their properties. Men who had been proscribed were pardoned and received a quarter of their old wealth. Magistracies would be awarded to men of senatorial standing who had, by joining Sextus, missed their chances in Rome: in the next year, sixty-seven men held the praetorship, and others were awarded coveted magisterial dignities in lieu of actually holding an office. Finally, there were rewards for the slaves and freedmen who had served under Sextus, and his soldiers became eligible for the same rewards as the troops of the triumvirs. This agreement, the pact of Misenum, was signed by all parties, probably sometime in August, and its sentiments were sealed by betrothing Sextus' daughter to Marcellus, Octavia's son and Antony's stepson.[96] Each was a small child at the time, and their wedding never took place.

The Triumvirate after Misenum

Our sources expatiate on the profound emotions inspired by the return of Sextus' refugees.[97] This, everyone knew, marked the end of the baleful proscriptions. Rome's aristocracy, it was deeply felt, was again made whole. Jubilation that could only be orchestrated in the aftermath of the pact of Brundisium was now spontaneous and impassioned. This was a clear triumph for Sextus.[98] Antony, too, received credit for the amnesty, and soon more than a few restored nobles exhibited their willingness to lend him their support.[99] As for Octavian, whose consent at Misenum was clearly coerced, the new coalition presented fresh challenges and it was perhaps at his insistence that, as part of the arrangement made at Misenum, it was agreed that the triumvirate be prolonged.

Amid such joy, both triumvirs remained cautious. Which is why Antony could easily be persuaded by Octavian not to abdicate his position at the end of 38 but instead to agree to extend the triumvirate for a further five years. Nothing stood in their way: so long as they refused to demit office or unless new legislation abolished it, the triumvirs could not be prevented from perpetuating their commands. In order to furnish a degree of definition to their extended terms, the triumvirs now designated magistrates through the year 33, when the two men would be consuls for the third time before finally restoring constitutional government to Rome.[100] It was obvious that Antony could neither recover the east nor punish the Parthians unless his tenure was prolonged. Nor could affairs in Italy soon be set in order. The domestic scene was rendered more complicated still by the return of Sextus' refugees. Happy though this event was, any restoration of dishonoured or deprived citizens, especially one likely to incite conflicts over property, was potentially destabilizing. As tribune,

Antony carried legislation enabling Caesar to recall exiles and rehabilitate the sons of the proscribed.[101] He knew well the revolutionary potential of such enactments—as did all Romans of the governing class.[102] No one could be sure how the arrangements at Misenum would alter the dynamics of politics in Rome, especially when the circumstances of Italy remained fraught. The republic, the triumvirs could reasonably insist, was not yet ripe for restoration.

Matters, as we know, did not work out as planned. Consequently, the decisions made at Misenum concerning the triumvirate and magistrates-designate are obfuscated (for us) by later formalities enacted in the pact of Tarentum.[103] In that agreement, the triumvirs once again extended their tenure—down to 31: at Tarentum in 37 Antony and Octavian declared a continuation of the triumvirate for five years, from 36 through 32, and (it appears) amended their prior magisterial designations so that, instead of holding consulships in 33, the two would hold the office in 31, when at last the triumvirate would give way to traditional, constitutional government.[104] This proclamation, as we shall see, played a part in repudiating the pact of Misenum and in preparing Romans for military campaigns against Sextus and against the Parthians.[105] That, however, came later. At Misenum, even as they celebrated a renewal of political concord and the end of Sextus' blockade, the triumvirs announced this extension of their supreme authority, the promulgation of which, whatever its justifications, can only have confirmed the worst suspicions of many in Italy, who had not forgotten the Perusine war.

Immediately after peace was restored at Misenum, Antony was inaugurated as *flamen Caesaris*.[106] As we have seen, Antony advertised his flaminate in the east.[107] Why he was not yet inaugurated we do not know, not least because we know so little about the legislation through which the people granted him his office. During his early conflict with Octavian, there were obvious political reasons to dispute Caesar's divinization. But these evaporated after the formation of the triumvirate. Perhaps by then there was simply too little time. Now, however, by way of Antony's formal inauguration, the establishment of Divus Iulius in Rome's civic religion was complete. Plans for a temple could and did commence.[108] In this renewed emphasis on Divus Iulius, the triumvirs signalled to their new allies—Sextus and the restored refugees—that in making concessions to former foes they were in no way abandoning their devotion to Julius Caesar and his memory. Doubtless this was one of Octavian's unnegotiable conditions.[109]

Antony, His Wife, and His Connections

Sometime in 39, Octavia gave birth to Antonia. This moment should not be passed over lightly. It was widely assumed by Romans, nor is the sentiment exotic to modern sensibilities, that the birth of a child stimulated tender feelings in a married couple and among their wider kin.[110] Octavia's marriage to Antony was a political one. But with Antonia's birth, perhaps, their relationship began to transcend simple duty to the republic: our ancient sources certainly underline Antony's affection for Octavia and this should not be credited entirely to the moralizing and literary motives which induced them repeatedly to emphasize her competition with Cleopatra. Not even so calculating a personality as Octavian's, one suspects, could remain entirely immune to the warm feelings surrounding the arrival of his niece.

By now Antony's family affairs were extensive. Presumably he kept up his connection with Fulvia's children by Clodius. To act otherwise could be deemed unseemly.[111] His immediate circle was a large one: a daughter by his first wife; two sons by Fulvia; stepchildren—two daughters and a son—through his marriage to Octavia; and an infant daughter. All these children were quite young. Plutarch dilates on Octavia's devotion to all Antony's children.[112] Antony intended, after leaving Italy, to settle in Athens and from there administer his eastern provinces. Which raises a question: how many of his children travelled east with their father? Nothing prevented Antony from taking them along, especially as he expected to remain abroad for several years. Residence in Athens was by no means an unattractive prospect and Antony's recent experience had perhaps suggested the usefulness of keeping one's family close. Our sources are mostly obsessed with politics and warfare, so naturally we are uninformed regarding these domestic matters. Still, Antony's household in Athens may well have been substantial, marking his resolution to concentrate on the affairs of the east.[113]

It may not have been until 39 that Antony received the news that Cleopatra had borne him twins, Alexander Helios and Cleopatra Selene. These were foreign children to whom he was in no way obliged. At the same time, they constituted a connection between the triumvir and the Egyptian queen which Antony did not repudiate. Whether or not this report was welcomed in Roman circles, there was no one, certainly not his wife, who harboured any illusions about Antony's past: 'he did not deny his relationship with Cleopatra', as Plutarch underlines when narrating Antony's marriage to Octavia.[114] In Cleopatra's court Antony had, in some ways, played the part of a second Caesar: among his rivals, not least Octavian, that may have rankled. What Octavia thought of it is lost to us. Perhaps, however, with the birth of Antonia, nothing that had happened in Alexandria was any longer regarded as significant.

After Misenum, Antony's position was a strong one. And as the year advanced, he received welcome reports from the east, where Ventidius, exhibiting extraordinary tactical brilliance, inflicted defeat after defeat on the Parthians. Labienus he eliminated in 39, and in the following year, at the battle of Gindarus, the Parthian army, commanded by Pacorus, was crushed and the Parthian prince fell fighting. The east was secure.[115] By contrast, conditions in Italy remained unpleasant for many and were sometimes desperate. The end of Sextus' embargo, to be sure, improved the basic quality of everyone's daily lives: the people no longer feared famine. But other pressures persisted. Despite Ventidius' successes, revenues from the east were not yet accessible to Rome. Consequently, Octavian could not abandon the triumvirs' policy of extortionate taxation. In 38, after Antony's departure, the public reacted so violently against his exactions that Octavian was forced to deploy soldiers to enforce payment.[116] As for the western provinces, even before the pact of Misenum was finalized there was unrest and rebellion in Spain and Gaul. So unstable was the situation in Gaul that Agrippa was dispatched to cope with it. And, before the end of 39, Octavian joined him there.[117] In the east Antony was now the sole authority. Roman power in the west, however, was divided among three independent chiefs, two of whom distrusted and detested one another. That Antony failed to grasp his advantage over Octavian, Sextus, and Lepidus is unimaginable. Each was in any case an ally, Octavian a relation. For the foreseeable future, Roman affairs were settled—in principle. Should any one of his colleagues, however, prove antagonistic, Antony saw no reason for fear.

Goodbye to All That

Antony now departed. But not without theatre. His governor in Macedonia, the reliable Pollio, had secured a handful of victories over the Parthini, a rebellious tribe in the region of Dyrrachium. This man, whose steady offices in a time of crisis had reconciled Antony with Domitius Ahenobarbus and both men with Octavian, merited a reward. Antony now elevated Pollio's successes into a brilliant victory over a fearsome, foreign foe. Pollio was summoned home, where on 25 October he was accorded the dignity of a triumph—proof of the new Rome's reversion from civil to just war and testimony to Antony's deserved fame as a commander of men and guarantor of Roman security.[118] Antony, we know, was still in Rome in early October.[119] It is highly unlikely that he quit the city before his friend's dazzling celebration. This event, we can be certain, was the work of Antony. The Parthini were hardly subdued by Pollio: almost immediately upon his return to Greece, it was necessary for Antony to organize another expedition against them.[120] But that hardly mattered. Antony's leadership—and his loyalty—were, in the person of Pollio, paraded before an admiring public. That occasion, and his ceremonial departure for the east, were Antony's final performances in the capital.

Athens Again

In November Antony returned to Greece. Our principal sources are, in different ways, so preoccupied in assessing Antony's deportment in Athens, the city where he settled for the winter, that they ignore, distort, or displace other matters. For Plutarch, Antony is once again an exemplary philhellene. In Appian's version, Antony's winter with Octavia reprises his cultured but irresponsible holiday with Cleopatra in Alexandria. As for Dio, his account seethes with censure and vituperation: this Antony is un-Roman, uncultured, and unabashedly greedy.[121] The literary and moralizing agenda of each writer is an impediment frustrating any attempt at recovering a detailed or even clear account of events. At the same time, the importance of this Athenian winter, like Antony's previous visit to the city in the aftermath of Philippi, is undeniable: there could be no better opportunity for the triumvir to define and exhibit his new political identity. From that perspective, Plutarch, Appian, and Dio got it right: what happened in Athens did not stay in Athens. The city remained highly visible internationally and was now teeming with embassies from throughout the east, all keen to congratulate their new master and negotiate a place in the new regime. The Athenians, too, aimed to please, and it was perhaps now that the city's colossal statues of Eumenes II and Attalus I, kings of Pergamum and generous benefactors of Attic society, were reattributed to Antony.[122] In the whole of the east, there was no doubt, Antony's return constituted a new beginning.[123]

Administration

But first, provincial administration and regional security. Even before winter set in, Antony deployed Roman forces against the Parthini and the Dardanii, tribes which threatened Macedonia's security. These campaigns were intended to extend into the next year. Troops were also stationed in Epirus.[124] Presumably the supervision of these operations was entrusted to Gaius Cocceius Balbus if he was in fact Pollio's successor as governor of Macedonia.[125] By now Marcus Cocceius Nerva was selected as Plancus' relief in Asia.[126] One other administrative change is observable: dissatisfied with Silo's slow progress in restoring Herod in Judea, Antony dispatched the energetic Gaius Sosius. Appointed governor of Syria and Cilicia, he was now in charge of that campaign.[127] Ventidius, so brilliantly successful in driving the Parrthians from Asia and destined for a triumph in Rome, Antony did not seek to distract with problems in Palestine.

Executing arrangements for the transfer of Achaea to the authority of Sextus Pompey, a provision of the pact of Misenum, was another likely assignment for Balbus, unless Antony delegated this responsibility to Lucius Sempronius Atratinus, his legate who was certainly active in the Peloponnese at this time.[128] Dio claims that Antony sought first to plunder this region before surrendering it, political polemic derived from later propaganda aimed at blaming Antony for the outbreak of Octavian's war against Sextus. An alternative version, however, and no more credible, blamed Octavian for interfering in Greece.[129] Antony's congenital cupidity is hardly to be denied, but here we may safely lay aside the assertion that he abused the cities of Achaea. It is nevertheless likely that handing over Achaea involved legitimate complexities: to whom, for instance, were back-taxes owed?[130] Sextus will have had agents on the spot who were ready to act on his behalf. But how much time was spent in these negotiations, we cannot know.

The region was certainly restless. Factionalism in Sparta provoked Roman intervention. Lachares, a prominent figure, was put to death on Antony's instructions. In reaction, this man's son, Eurycles, hated Antony and later brought Sparta into the conflict at Actium as an ally of Octavian.[131] In the end, of course, Sextus never acquired Achaea. Under Antony's jurisdiction his friends and allies became powerful figures in this region's cities. We can detect, for instance, the importance in Corinth of Antony's procurator, Marcus Antonius Theophilus, as well as his friend, the poet and rhetorician Marcus Antonius Aristocrates.[132] Spartan resentments notwithstanding, Antony's administration of Achaea was highly efficient: after Actium the system of taxation and tribute Antony employed there was maintained by Octavian.[133] So, too, were many leaders from Antony's circle.[134]

New Dionysus

At Athens Antony proclaimed himself the New Dionysus. During his previous tour of the east, as we have seen, Antony more than once accepted the formal, almost routine courtesy of divine honours, including his identification with Dionysus by the Ephesians and others. Now, however, Antony's divinity became an official triumviral policy.[135] At Athens it was welcomed with theatrical celebrations and sensational pageantry.[136] Games in Antony's honour, the Antoneia, at which he was hailed New Dionysus, were either reprised or established.[137] Antony, who now assumed the important Athenian liturgy of gymnasiarch, doubtless presided.[138] By doing so, he registered not only his enduring philhellenism but also his personal involvement in promulgating his new eastern identity. This policy was comprehensive: the Athenians even minted coins depicting a youthful Dionysus.[139]

Octavia, too, showcased her philhellenism and enjoyed the company of philosophers and writers.[140] She received divine honours in conjunction with her husband: an inscription describes the couple as *theoi euergetai*, beneficent gods, a phrase recalling the sacred propaganda of Hellenistic kings and queens.[141] This, too, was Antonian policy: dignities of this kind, as we have seen, were familiar to inhabitants of the east; they were so closely associated with the imagery of monarchy that they constituted an easily recognizable medium for projections of power and civic expressions of respect. Antony's Attic signals were intended for a wide audience. At Ephesus he produced coins portraying himself and Octavia in an environment rich with suitable Dionysiac symbols.[142]

Octavia, it is clear, had a significant role to play in Antony's programme. Our sources comment on their appearances together and their obvious affection for one another: Antony, as Appian puts it, 'was gushingly devoted to her'.[143] There is no reason to doubt it. At the same time, their devotion to one another was a crucial element in the triumvirate's policy of projecting political stability—desperately important to everyone both in the west and the east. In Athens, consequently, Octavia was a beneficent goddess and Antony's conspicuous partner in the majesty of cult. This collocation was hardly limited to our single inscription.[144]

In Rome, as we have seen, Octavia appeared with Antony on his coinage, where her extraordinary presence as his wife signalled Antony's affinity with his colleague, Octavian. In the east, too, she modelled triumviral stability. In his so-called Fleet Coinage, a profusion of low denomination coins produced in Achaea and intended for everyday use by Greeks and Romans alike, we find coins the obverse of which show jugate busts of Antony and Octavian looking at a bust of Octavia.[145] The message on these coins is obvious, but their artistic vocabulary is striking. Jugate busts were very rare on Roman coins: we know of one republican issue which portrays the Dioscuri, the divine brothers Castor and Pollux, in jugate busts.[146] Nor did many Roman coins depict busts of individuals looking at one another: Sextus Pompey minted coins on which his elder brother met the eyes of his father; in imitation, Octavian struck the same pose on coins he issued which represented him with his divine father.[147] From a Roman perspective, then, a numismatic canon figuring profound family unity, *pietas*, was emerging during the triumviral period: in his coins Antony puts this conceit to work in a novel way underlining his solidarity with his brother-in-law, Octavian. Not that any of this background was needed to get the point: Antony and Octavian in jugate could only indicate unity and the reality that their relationship relied on Octavia was hardly to be missed. More intriguing are the issues on which appear only Antony and Octavia gazing at one another, a declaration of unity the focus of which remains fixed on the wedded couple.[148]

The Fleet Coinage was issued for the use of all social classes in Achaea and by Greeks and Romans alike. For many Romans in the east, doubtless, and certainly for any Greek, the most notable series are the coins on which jugate busts of Antony and Octavia appear on the obverse.[149] These coins, like the others, communicate stability, but they also evoke, remarkably in a Roman context, the familiar regal imagery of Hellenistic queens and kings. Jugate royal portraits on coins were emblems reaching back to the Ptolemies but by Antony's day suffused the Hellenistic world.[150] It was a signature pose for royal power couples but by way of an iconography entirely alien to Rome. Although the Fleet Coinage remained local coinage in Achaea, its imagery was extensive. The Dionysiac coins of Ephesus portray Antony (in the guise of Dionysus) and Octavia as a jugate pair.[151] That this imagery recurs in coinage in various locations, minted for different purposes, suggests that it was more widespread than our current evidence indicates.[152]

As we have seen, it was a thoroughly Roman practice for officials in the east to appropriate the imagery and postures employed by Hellenistic kings in projecting their authority. Roman governors had been doing it for years. Nothing, then, was truly revolutionary in Antony's innovative deployment of Octavia in coinage or in cult. Still, Antony's pose as New Dionysus along with his widely promoted presentation of himself and Octavia by way of regal iconography could only suggest to viewers that their joint authority matched that of a royal couple. At the same time, Antony, his majestic station notwithstanding, made it clear to the Athenians how much he enjoyed activities like attending lectures and wrestling in the gymnasium.[153] In doing so, Antony introduced a new, programmatic dimension to what previously had been localized, ad hoc Roman reactions to eastern honorifics. He also made it obvious in the east that his position there was unlike that of any Roman administration they had known before.

Antony's Dionysiac pose provoked nothing in the way of animadversion in Rome. And why should it? Eastern conventions like these were entirely familiar in the west. Even in so populist a genre as Roman comedy, paying a man divine honours was a recurring, unsurprising motif.[154] Later, however, when all things Antonian were subject to deformation in Octavian's propaganda, his identity with Dionysus furnished abundant material for invective—but not owing to Antony's divine pretensions. Instead of the god of culture and conquest, Dionysiac Antony was then pilloried for drunkenness, effeminacy, and luxury.[155] That came later. But one allegation of Antony's divine perversity must occupy us now. A hostile tradition, preserved by the Elder Seneca and Dio, related how the Athenians, in a debased attempt to curry favour, proposed a divine marriage between the New Dionysus and Athena. Antony agreed but exploited this footling gesture by extorting an obscenely large dowry. This report, although sometimes given credence, is an obvious fabrication.[156] Any marriage for Athena is a patent impossibility and early on in Greek literature the very idea became a formula for expressing hubris.[157] It is pertinent that this moralizing trope had been applied to Demetrius Poliorcetes, one of many outrages committed during this debauched king's residence in Athens.[158] Its application to Antony, then, was a natural move in vituperating his activities in the same city. Perhaps this tale originated in Octavian's propaganda or perhaps emerged later in Augustan declamation schools. In any case, it is a transparent fiction.

Fig. 11.1 A cistophorus from the east (*RPC* 1.2202) the obverse of which displays a jugate portrait of Antony and Octavia with the legend M ANTONIUS IMP COS DESIG ITER ET TERT (Mark Antony, *imperator*, consul designate for the second and third time); the reverse exhibits Dionysus between twisted serpents with the legend III VIR R P C (triumvir appointed to set the republic in order).
Source: Wikimedia Commons.

Reshaping the East

By the time Antony arrived in Athens, Ventidius had successfully repulsed the Parthians' invasion and was busily pacifying pockets of active, often fierce, resistance in Asia and Syria. Welcome though this military solution obviously was, the return of robust, engaged Roman government was now an urgent imperative. Antony had begun consolidating alliances and planning a reorganization of the east while still in the capital. By way of senatorial decrees, he rewarded cities whose loyalty had withstood Parthian pressure or actively supported Rome: Stratonicea, Aphrodisias, and Miletus certainly, and very likely Rhodes, Lycia, Laodicea, and Tarsus as well.[159] Steadfast allies, like Castor II, will also have been recognized. Heroic individuals were also recognized by Antony. Our information is hardly comprehensive, but we know about the installation of Ateporix as ruler in Caranitis, Nicias in Cos, Strato in Amisus, Hybreas in Mylasa, even the obscure Cleon, an adventurer who stood up against the Parthians and was made into a petty dynast in Gordium by a grateful Antony.[160] There were two men in the east who impressed Antony profoundly. Polemo, the son of Zeno, defended his native Laodicea stoutly. He was now granted a principality in Lycaonia, centred in the city of Iconium.[161] The actions of Amyntas, the able official of Deiotarus who now served that man's son, Castor II, go unreported, but they were doughty enough to earn Antony's esteem. This man now became a ruler in his own right, receiving Pisidia and a part of Lycaonia as his domain.[162]

In creating these principalities in Lycaonia, Antony carved out parts of the Roman province of Cilicia. This was a reflex of Antony's sweeping reform of Rome's provincial arrangements. Asia and Bithynia remained intact, but Antony now began dismantling Cilicia and Pontus. He also consolidated Crete and the Cyrenaica into a single province. As a consequence of these changes, Rome's client kings were assigned a much greater role in the administration of the east than had been the case under Pompey's arrangements, which, as we have seen, were largely preserved by Caesar and, after Philippi, by Antony. These reforms were not completed instantly—as always it was necessary to react to local circumstances—and much about the chronology of this settlement remains unclear. Undoing annexation and handing administrative duties over to client kings, it should be underlined, was hardly un-Roman, nor did these reforms in any way diminish Roman authority in these regions. As we have seen, the Romans' conception of their empire included its subject cities and principalities: power, not provinces, was the main thing.[163]

Cilicia was simply taken apart. This province, established early in the first century in reaction against regional threats by pirates and other marauders, was from its beginning 'a counsel of despair', as it has rightly been assessed.[164] Always unwieldy, it could no longer be justified by military necessity. Clearly Antony thought it best to leave its difficult administration to others—if the idea originated with him: it has been proposed that Cilicia's elimination was one of Caesar's unfulfilled ambitions.[165] Parts of Cilicia, as we have seen, were handed over to Polemo and Amyntas. Tarcondimotus also benefited; the Cilician king declared himself *Philantonius*, Antony's friend.[166] Other territories were assigned to Egypt, as was Cyprus. Because this island was administered by the governor of Cilicia, its reassignment was necessitated by Antony's abolition of the province. In the aftermath of the Parthians' invasion, as we have seen, Antony had dispatched a freedman, Demetrius, to manage Cypriot affairs.[167] That was an emergency arrangement which could not be prolonged. Caesar had granted Cleopatra control of a portion of Cyprus. Antony, it appears, now allocated her its residue.[168]

Cyprus had long been a property of the Ptolemies. Now Cleopatra would manage it on Rome's behalf. This decision, it must be underlined, was a practical one. Egypt's gains here are not to be explained by Antony's affair with Cleopatra, though the episode can hardly have damaged her prospects. Nor was this apportionment an inducement made by Antony with an eye toward exploiting Egypt's wealth when equipping himself for his forthcoming Parthian expedition. Egypt was a client state and Antony could demand of it whatever resources he required whenever he required them. Antony's generous treatment of Egypt is instead a reflection of the kingdom's reliability as an ally. Polemo and Amyntas, good men though they were, had not yet proven themselves as rulers on a big scale. Tarcondimotus, whose loyalty was total, was not meant for greater things, or so Antony apparently believed. Nor did he think Cyprus ripe for self-government. As for Cleopatra, Antony could realistically expect competence and stability in her administration of these new territories.[169] She was a rational choice.

Had Antony been held in thrall by Cleopatra, he might now have handed over the Cyrenaica or Crete. But he did not. Although it is often asserted that Crete and the Cyrenaica were governed by the Romans as one province after the island's annexation in the sixties, there is no certain evidence of it before Antony's reforms in 39. Social commerce between the two regions is clear enough, but that dynamic, a reflex of past Ptolemaic administration, existed before the Romans came on the scene. In the aftermath of Philippi, as we have observed, Antony entrusted Crete to Cydas the Cretarch, who managed the island's affairs by way of the federation of Cretan cities. How the Cyrenaica was then governed we do not know. Now Antony united the two regions into a single province, the governor of which continued to work closely with the Cretan federation: this much is clear from our numismatic evidence.[170] Antony's close personal ties to Crete doubtless played an important part in shaping his views on how best to empower local leadership. So, too, lobbying by Capua, whose financial stake in Crete was significant.[171] If, as has been argued, the Cyrenaica was undergoing economic difficulties at this time, and was therefore less than entirely viable as a stand-alone province, that fact may also have contributed to Antony's decision.[172] In uniting the two regions into a single province, Antony acknowledged the long-standing ties between them. This disposition, then, must have been a welcome one, and the arrangement worked well: after Actium Rome continued to govern Crete and the Cyrenaica as a single province.[173]

Antony resurrected the kingdom of Pontus, disestablishing the Roman province.[174] He selected as its king Darius, son of the Pharnaces defeated by Caesar at Zela.[175] By 37, however, Darius was dead or possibly had been deposed. Polemo, whom Antony had installed as a dynast in Cilicia, was then elevated to this throne.[176] At about this same time, Castor II died. His vast domains were now divided. His son, Deiotarus IV Philadelphus, became king of Paphlagonia (the borders of which Antony somewhat adjusted).[177] Galatia, however, Antony handed over to the highly favoured Amyntas.[178] These were significant changes and in making them, it is clear, Antony was more concerned with personal competence than local traditions. Although Philadelphus inherited his realm, neither Polemo nor Amyntas was thrown up by dynastic recommendations. Antony, however, perceived in each man the right stuff for reigning as a client king. And it is clear he got it right, as events showed. Soon after Polemo's installation, another son of Pharnaces, Arsaces, seized control of Phazemontis, a region of Pontus.[179] Polemo reacted instantly. Joined by Lycomedes, the Priest of Pontic Comana appointed by Caesar, he dislodged Arsaces, captured him, and put him to death—a restoration of order that required no expense or effort of any kind by Antony or Rome.[180] Afterwards Polemo was rewarded by an increase to his kingdom.[181] Lycomedes, too, or so it appears from a brief notice in Strabo.[182]

Antony's preference for client kings is conspicuous. His approach was by no means untraditional or controversial. On the contrary, the advantages of exploiting client kings in the east, as we have seen, had long been recognized in Rome. And the establishment or affirmation of every throne came at a price: Antony demanded exactions from Rome's client kings and fixed new levels of tribute for each principality—levies from which not even Egypt was excluded.[183] Antony, in managing the east so that Rome could recover the best possible return by way of its vassals, was simply perpetuating a long-standing practice. Pompey's experiment in Pontus he now judged a failure, and by ridding the empire of the difficulty of directly managing Cilicia he introduced a useful economy to Rome's imperialist enterprise. There was also an immediate dividend. Antony's reforms released Roman resources and legions for deployment against Parthia.[184]

Sordid factors, too, played into Antony's calculations. The intimate relationship between power and profiteering in the provinces we have observed more than once. It
was simply easier, in legal and moral terms, for financiers to get their way in client
kingdoms than when they were subject to the scrutiny of a Roman governor. Antony's
disposition in the east was expedient for Rome's *publicani* and therefore useful in sustaining his clout within their influential circles. For investors and businessmen in the
capital, Antony, though absent, remained a highly valuable connection. Nor will the
triumvir have neglected any opportunities for cashing in—or for abetting his close
allies when they tried to cash in. Sleaze of this kind was also, in its own way, traditional. Information on matters like this rarely reaches us, but there is no reason to
doubt it: Pompey had led the way.[185]

An enticing scrap of papyrus, illegible in all the wrong places, can nevertheless
offer us a glimpse into the Romans' opportunistic operations in Antony's east. This
papyrus, published in 2000 and soon famous because it appeared to bear Cleopatra's
actual autograph (disappointingly, this seems not to be the case), records a generous,
very profitable tax-break granted by Egypt (in the thirties) to a Roman (the name
of whom is poorly preserved), who owned land in the kingdom.[186] This Roman
was first identified as Publius Canidius Crassus, who was consul in 40 and one of
Antony's most trusted officers; he was a figure whose loyalty, according to Plutarch,
Cleopatra, on the eve of Actium, endeavoured to purchase.[187] Closer analysis of the
papyrus, however, renders that reading unlikely. Instead, he appears to be a Quintus
Cascellius, who is not otherwise known.[188] Now an Aulus Cascellius was praetor
during the late forties. He was remembered for his legal learning, his bold refusal
to confer legitimacy on triumviral excesses, and his lifelong outspokenness against
authority—the sort of man, perhaps, likely to be drawn to Lucius Antonius.[189]
Earlier republican Cascellii, none of them senators, can also be detected.[190] In the
Julio-Claudian period, sometime late in Augustus' or early in Tiberius' reign, a
Quintus Cascellius, clearly not a senator, is honoured by the Egyptian city of Caunus
as a patron and a saviour.[191] The beneficiary of Cleopatra's mandate is almost certainly a kinsman of this man and a member of the larger clan of Cascellii, animated
by ambitions both political and commercial, which aimed at acquiring prominent
connections both in the capital and the eastern provinces. We cannot exclude that
our Cascellius, in gaining this royal favour, owed nothing to the triumvir. But it is
hard to imagine any Roman doing business in Egypt in the thirties and failing to
solicit Antony—not even a distant relation of the headstrong praetor. In any case,
Cascellius' Egyptian boondoggle typifies the unearned profits available in a client
kingdom even for a Roman aristocrat who was not exactly a grandee. Cascellius'
was by no means the only sweetheart deal of its kind in Egypt or elsewhere in the
east, and key players in Rome or in Antony's eastern circle could doubtless do even
better out of their relationship with the triumvir. Which is why Antony's organization of the east, including his expansion of the role of client kings, was not deemed a
surrender of Roman power or property. Quite the contrary: for many Romans at or
near the top, or enjoying ties with these circles, Antony's reforms came as a welcome
opportunity.

Italy

During this winter, Octavian's attitude toward Sextus hardened into open hostility and he resolved to abandon the pact of Misenum. There was nothing secret in his change of heart: he divorced Scribonia, the mother of his only daughter, thereby severing his tie with the family of Sextus, and married the pregnant Livia, who remained his wife for the rest of his life. When he divorced Claudia, Octavian held her blameless. In divorcing Scribonia, by contrast, he complained of her character.[192] The action was undisguised in its aggression, and its publicity was underlined by Octavian's appeal to the pontiffs for permission to marry a woman when she was pregnant with another man's child.[193] Octavian's loathing of Sextus we have observed, nor can this man's will-to-power ever be discounted. So long as Sextus dominated Sicily and the seas round Rome his power was too formidable for Octavian to accommodate it without tension or worry. But all that was true when the pact of Misenum was agreed. Why Octavian should seek to act now, however, is unclear and was unclear in antiquity, as Appian complains.[194] There was evidence of faction in Sextus' camp, to be sure, which revealed weaknesses an enemy could exploit. In public, however, Octavian objected to Sextus' bad faith in his dealings with Antony over the administration of the Peloponnese, a pretence designed to project concord with his brother-in-law and neutralize suspicions that the triumvirate was imperilled by Octavian's enmity with Sextus. Octavian also alleged that Sextus had not halted his attacks on Italy but now deployed pirates as raiders on his behalf. On the basis of these grievances, Octavian summoned Antony and Lepidus to Italy, where they could reconsider their alliance with Sextus. Lepidus remained in Africa, but Antony, at the start of spring, travelled to Brundisium. Octavian, however, was absent. Antony did not wait long. Before departing, he dispatched a letter to Octavian urging him to respect the terms of the pact of Misenum.[195]

This episode is mysterious. Octavian later faulted Antony for his hasty return.[196] But it can hardly have mattered that the two did not meet. It is obvious how, since Antony left Italy, he and Octavian had taken pains to remain in contact with one another. When Octavian complained to Antony about Sextus, he will have sent not only letters but also agents entrusted with supplying his colleague anything he needed in the way of exegesis. And when Antony arrived at Brundisium, Octavian's representatives will have been there to greet him and brief him on Octavian's immediate designs. Antony must have been convinced that he knew enough. Almost certainly he knew that Octavian intended, on flimsy grounds, to launch a war against Sextus. This was an unwelcome development, but Antony, as events would show, had no desire to fall out with his brother-in-law over Sextus. Nor, however, did he wish to appear faithless when he knew many in Rome would recall that it was he who had championed the triumviral policy which became the basis of the pact of Misenum. Constancy, then, demanded he keep to its terms. A meeting and a joint decree might have furnished Antony with enough institutional cover to satisfy his critics and persuade Octavian's that they were not witnessing a replay of the Perusine crisis, which is why Antony could be bothered to return to Italy. But Octavian, for whatever reason, failed to appear. The consequences of this failure were likely to be more serious for him than for Antony.

Nevertheless, Antony drafted and dispatched a more or less public letter to Octavian. Its predictable and perhaps vague sentiments were hardly intended to remain private. Octavian doubtless hoped for something more, hence his complaint that Antony left too soon. At the same time, he was also aware that Antony harboured no objections to his plans so profound that their friendship could be shattered if took up arms against Sextus. And that was enough. Indeed, soon after he attacked Sextus, Octavian insisted to his Roman audience that he enjoyed Antony's endorsement, a performance recalling Lucius and Fulvia during the Perusine conflict and one that perhaps garnered more or less the same credibility.[197] As for Antony, having met the minimal expectations of his brother-in-law in Rome and his ally in Sicily, he returned to his provinces—aware that a conflict in Italy was a certainty, something he must watch with care.

Antony in the East

At last Antony could march eastwards, inspect the operations of his officers, and refresh his authority with the legions he planned to lead against Parthia. At this point, Syria remained embroiled in conflict, especially in Judea, where Antigonus continued to occupy Jerusalem. Other cities, too, like the island fortress of Arad, were holding out against Rome. Ventidius was now encamped at Samosata, the capital of Commagene. Its king, Antiochus, had yielded to Parthia during its invasion and was now harbouring Parthian refugees. When Ventidius demanded he yield and surrender these Parthians, Antiochus refused. Possibly his recalcitrance was owing to uncertainty regarding his future: Ventidius, he knew, was not in a position to guarantee his throne, nor, it appears, had Antony revealed his intentions.

Antony marched first to Samosata. What happened next remains controversial. Two very different traditions subsist. In one, preserved in Plutarch and Dio, Ventidius' command is undermined by a jealous Antony. In this version, Antiochus offers Ventidius, Rome's general on the scene, a rich tribute in exchange for his throne and the safety of his city. When he arrives, however, Antony rejects this offer, avidly demands a bigger one, and extends the siege. But he fails to take the city. In the end, the triumvir must accept an embarrassingly small price in exchange for Antiochus' formal acquiescence and his continued tenure as king.[198] It is a humiliation. The other tradition, the traces of which were once in Livy and remain in Orosius and are also found in Josephus, cannot furnish us anything like a full narrative. Enough comes through, however, to make it clear that in this account Antony's forces, although they did not overrun the city, inflicted enough damage on it to compel Antiochus' surrender.[199]

Now it cannot be excluded that at Samosata Antony botched the job. Indeed, most modern historians believe he did.[200] The fact that at Rome Antony's campaigning during this year received public praise and thanksgivings is no impediment to that conclusion: Octavian was in duty bound to celebrate his brother-in-law.[201] But in this instance, our principal sources seem less than credible. The claim that Antony was invidious and unfairly sought credit for Ventidius' achievements was a commonplace of Octavian's later propaganda. So, too, the recurring recrimination that he was avaricious.[202] These motifs are very likely operative here and are put to work for their own purposes both by the hostile Dio and the more sympathetic Plutarch.[203]

One cannot be certain, of course, but it is difficult to imagine Antony's simply swallowing so severe a disgrace at Samosata as Plutarch and Dio report. Doing so could only have undermined his authority at a time when he was busy handing over vital administrative responsibilities to other eastern kings, who could hardly fail to notice an episode like this one, and at a time when he very much needed this region's confidence and respect if he hoped to launch a Parthian invasion from it.[204] A wilful, Parthian-friendly Antiochus whose recalcitrance was so extraordinarily successful as we find in this version of events could only be intolerable. Rome's reputation, as well as Antony's, was at stake. At the very least, we must conclude that Antiochus, when he yielded, did so in in a manner that unambiguously signalled the triumvir's superiority to everyone. A possible proof of Antiochus' complete and abject acquiescence may be spied in the outrage his gesture incited in Parthia—if he is the Antiochus assassinated by Phraates when he became Parthia's king in the next year.[205] Or perhaps we should consider the old proposal that Antony, after he accepted the city's surrender, removed Antiochus from his throne, replacing him with his son Mithridates.[206] There is no questioning that man's loyalty to Antony: he remained faithful even at Actium and on that account may have been put to death by Octavian.[207] We do not know enough to dispel every uncertainty. Nevertheless, there is no reason to doubt that at Samosata, notwithstanding a hostile version that made its way into Plutarch and Dio, Antony established the authority of Rome in Commagene in a manner that bolstered his reputation in the region.

Antony now moved on to Syria. He was joined by Sosius, his governor, and by Herod, who had assisted at Samosata. To Sosius Antony assigned operations at Jerusalem. He took charge of the offensive against Arad.[208] This city, fearful of Roman repercussions, refused to surrender and took refuge behind its formidable defences. A siege was organized, but Arad held out. In autumn Antony departed for Athens, leaving the region and its pacification under Sosius' authority. He was well-equipped: Antony left him in charge of eleven legions.[209] Doubtless Antony expected to return, but instead, early in the next year, he once again travelled to Italy. Syrian and Judean affairs then fell entirely to Sosius. In Athens, Antony honoured the victorious Ventidius, who at last returned to Rome. There, in November, he celebrated a triumph over the Parthians—the only Parthian triumph ever celebrated by a Roman. This was a pageant that justly marked Ventidius' military brilliance. It also advertised the success of Ventidius' commander.[210] Indeed, at Rome Octavian led public thanksgivings for Antony's achievements in the east.[211]

Events at Rome

By then Octavian was desperate for something to celebrate. After Antony's return to Greece in the spring, war had broken out in Italy—perhaps sooner than Octavian had anticipated. There was unrest in Gaul and outright rebellion in Aquitania, events so dangerous that he was obliged to dispatch Agrippa. Indeed, he, too, had travelled there in order to make a personal inspection.[212] Octavian was not too distracted, however, to fail to probe any indications of faction or disloyalty on Sextus' side. Thus he found Menodorus, Sextus' trusted admiral. This man went over to Octavian, bringing along a fleet, three legions, and Sardinia and Corsica.[213] For Sextus, this was a serious and intolerable blow. He launched attacks on Campania and began marauding up and down the coast. Octavian fought back, but with disastrous results. In successive sea battles he suffered crushing defeats.[214] This violation of the pact of Misenum outraged the public and consternated the soldiery. Octavian insisted that he acted on behalf of Antony as well as himself. Few were persuaded. Perturbation in the capital gave way to violence, and all of Italy despaired.[215] The perfidious Menodorus, sensing he had chosen the wrong side, began negotiating his return to Sextus.[216] Maecenas now rushed to find Antony. In late autumn he found him in Athens, where it required all his charm and ingenuity to convince Antony to give aid to his brother-in-law. Antony agreed, but there were conditions, unknown to us, which Maecenas was to carry back to Rome.[217] Perhaps he returned in the company of Ventidius. In Rome there was at last good news. Agrippa had been victorious in Aquitania. Octavian awarded him a triumph, which he refused.[218] Our sources insist that Agrippa acted in deference to his master, whose multiple failures he did not wish to underline by way of parading his own glory. But Agrippa's glory was Octavian's glory, and its celebration should have been a tonic for the triumvir. Instead, Rome, rocked by Octavian's defeats, ignored his Aquitanian victory in order to lavish greater honour on Ventidius and Antony. This was symbolism Octavian very much hoped Antony, when he learned of it, would appreciate, for he very much needed his brother-in-law's goodwill and cooperation.

Wars in the East

After the victories of Ventidius and the restoration of Roman authority, the moment was right for Antony to fulfil his mission in the east by avenging Crassus' defeat at Carrhae. The invasion of Parthia was, after all, central to Antonius' triumviral duty. In the spring of 37, Sosius and his legions were again at work pacifying Syria and Judea. During this year, Sosius succeeded in taking Jerusalem and restoring Herod, for which achievements he was hailed *imperator* and later celebrated a triumph.[219] Arad, too, was captured, though only after fierce fighting.[220] In this same year, Antony's marshal, Publius Canidius Crassus, invaded Armenia in command of four legions. There was no resistance: Armenia's king, Artavasdes, submitted at once. Canidius then continued into Iberia and Albania. Kings there were more stalwart and Canidius encountered strenuous resistance. He campaigned for the remainder of the year: only in spring of 36 did these regions accept Roman hegemony.[221] The operations of Sosius and Canidius were each of them important preludes to Antony's Parthian invasion, whatever route he chose to follow. It is not clear to us whether Antony had yet arrived at a final strategy. Caesar's plan of attack, we are told, was to march east by way of lesser Armenia. When governor of Syria, however, Gabinius entered Parthia by crossing the Euphrates into Mesopotamia.[222] Antony, both an intimate of Caesar and an officer in Gabinius' command, was familiar with the difficulties and advantages of both approaches, and the campaigns of 37 kept both options open to him. In each theatre of war there was glory to be won. Surely Antony ought to have been in Syria, imposing peace, if not in the north extending Rome's dominion into Iberia and Albania. Instead, he sailed to Italy.

Standoff at Tarentum

In spring Antony returned once more to Italy, where he met Octavian on the river Tara between Tarentum and Metapontum.[223] From the start, their negotiations were uneasy and protracted. Indeed, it was perhaps so late in the year as August before Antony could depart again for the east. This episode, and its resolution in the pact of Tarentum, was a significant moment in the relationship between Octavian and Antony. The pact of Misenum was discarded and superseded by a new dispensation. Antony and Octavian, although they preserved their partnership, emerged from this encounter as allies, true, but, extravagant displays of concord notwithstanding, were less truly united than in the aftermath of the pact of Brundisium. What took place before and during the conference at Tarentum and any specifics of the triumvirs' transactions there are mostly lost or concealed in sources which rely, as they must, on competing, contradictory, and distorting versions of this affair—propaganda and spin already vigorous as events were unfolding.[224] A palpable obscurity, then, the mystery of which signals its importance.

In autumn of the previous year, as we have seen, Antony acquiesced to Octavian's demand for a war against Sextus. He even agreed to aid him in this conflict. Antony's assistance and endorsement were sorely needed after Octavian's multiple failures and in view of his increasingly deep unpopularity in Italy. For Antony, the decision cannot have been a simple one. Antony was the architect of the triumvirs' policy of political reconciliation which had been codified at Misenum. Taking Octavian's side against Sextus was nothing less than a repudiation of that agreement, a political solecism that rendered him vulnerable to denunciations of inconstancy. Octavian's unyielding bellicosity came at a high cost to his brother-in-law. At the same time, Antony's relationship with Octavian, cemented by his marriage with Octavia, was now central to his public identity in the east and west alike. Central, too, perhaps, to his private sentiments, if our sources are right in observing Antony's matrimonial happiness. Maecenas' diplomacy, there can be no doubting it, was amplified by Octavia's interventions on her brother's behalf. In the end, Antony gave way and elected to discard Sextus. But he was Antony yet—and will have wanted something in return.

Octavian needed ships and their crews. And he needed Antony's full-throated endorsement of his war against Sextus. None of this, however, required Antony's presence in Italy. It was enough for Antony to dispatch a fleet led by competent, trusted admirals—which, in the end, was what he supplied: 130 ships commanded by Antonian officers like Lucius Sempronius Atratinus, Lucius Calpurnius Bibulus, and Marcus Oppius Capito. Public letters and trusted personal emissaries would have sufficed to make his position on Sextus clear to everyone in Rome. But Antony did not simply send ships, statements, and ambassadors. Instead, he sailed to Italy at the head of an armada of 300 ships. Plutarch records consternation and confusion in Italy; hostile intentions were attributed to Antony. It is hard to imagine, however, that Antony had not made his purposes, whatever they were, clear to Octavian, perhaps so early as in his dealings with Maecenas. Which is not to say Octavian was highly motivated to dispel Italian anxieties. Clearly he found Antony's arrival unwelcome. It is possible that Brundisium refused to admit him, and equally possible that it refused in the hope of pleasing Octavian. If so, it hardly mattered: Antony's destination was Tarentum.

But why had he come? Doing so kept him out of Syria and far from his invasion of Armenia. And why was his coming marked by controversy or even disconcertment? Plutarch describes Antony as inflamed with rage: his account hints at an invasion only just averted by Octavia's intervention. Dio is briefer, but he likewise perceives malice lying in the background, the triumvir's profession of good intentions notwithstanding. Appian tells a different story. In his version, Antony came bringing Octavian the reinforcements he had asked for, but Octavian now made a conspicuous and inexplicable show of rejecting this aid. He had changed his mind, Appian suggests, or 'was once more finding fault with Antony over something'.[225] Appian's reader, too, can only find this recalcitrance baffling: it was neither prudent under the circumstances nor remotely collegial. It was true that, since his return from Aquitania, Agrippa had busied himself in preparing a fleet. But his forces were by no means ready for an attack on Sextus. And in any case, there was little sense in rebuffing Antony's generosity, especially when it was Octavian who had sought it in the first place. Appian's Octavia, like Plutarch's, acts as a mediator, bringing the triumvirs to an agreement. None of these versions, it is obvious, is remotely satisfactory. And each writer knew it: hence their frequent recourse to imprecise generalities like 'various slanders' or 'mutual grievances' and the like. There is nothing left for us, then, but conjecture.

Perhaps it was not ships or crews that Octavian rejected but rather the terms under which they were offered and delivered. Antony did not come simply to deposit a fleet or trade ships for infantry, although that is what happened in the end. These things, as we have seen, could have been arranged by intermediaries. When Antony sailed to Italy, he brought along his wife and family: he intended to remain in the west for some time. Dio, intriguingly, reports that, as his pretext for returning to Italy, Antony claimed he intended to take part in the war against Sextus on account of Octavian's prior misfortunes.[226] Dio introduces Antony's claim, which he deems an honourable one, only to reject it on the grounds that his purposes must have been sinister. But it can hardly be excluded that this is exactly why Antony came to Italy.

Let us consider the possibility that Antony came to fight Sextus alongside his brother-in-law, to join with him in settling affairs in Italy but, owing to his superior martial stature and his abundant fleet, thereby to take the lion's share of the credit for restoring peace. Octavian could have his mead of glory, to be sure, but, in the new dispensation that must follow Sextus' suppression, Antony's primacy would again be the focus of Italian celebrations. If this, or something like this, was the condition Antony put to Maecenas, Octavian was ready for it. Naturally he rejected Antony's imposition: it was more than he bargained for. Antony's friendly invasion of Italy, if we are right in believing he came to fight alongside Octavian, was patently a highly aggressive move. Which is why Octavian allowed the circulation of rival claims asserting that Antony's motives were untoward, perhaps dangerous, even if, technically, Italy lay open to all three triumvirs and its protection was the duty of them all. Although this reconstruction can only be speculative, it is otherwise difficult to make sense of Antony's unnecessary return to Italy or Octavian's protracted, unexpected resistance to his brother-in-law's compliance with his original request.[227] Without question the two men were at loggerheads and without question they were at pains to disguise the nature and seriousness of their disagreement.

Hence their extended standoff. It appears that Antony, even if he anticipated Octavian's initial reluctance, did not expect him defiantly to refuse taking the junior post in their joint campaign against Sextus. His excessive confidence and Octavian's stubbornness provoked a political crisis. Much time was now wasted and heavy diplomacy was called for. Perhaps Antony, even if he had nothing else in the way of an alternative strategy, expected Octavia's mediation to be decisive on his behalf. If so, he was disappointed. Despite the undeniable weakness of his position, a resolute Octavian would not budge. And Antony, as Octavian hoped, had no stomach for severing ties with his brother-in-law at this time. Each triumvir knew his soldiers would not tolerate open conflict, nor was either man ready to rupture the relationship each had worked so hard, against the grain of their personalities, to cultivate. In the end, Octavian prevailed, and it now became necessary to find a way for Antony to depart with dignity, his failure hidden behind expressions of mutual goodwill and Octavian's gratitude for his brother-in-law's generous support.

Our sources dilate on the pageantry with which Antony and Octavian exhibited their friendship and mutual trust before both their troops and the wider public. It was agreed that the triumvirs would make an exchange, ships for soldiers, and the campaign against Sextus would be delayed until the next year. Lepidus, not Antony, would join Octavian in this campaign, perhaps owing to a proposal by Antony: in this way, the credit for defeating Sextus would not belong to Octavian alone.[228] Even these details are somewhat muddled in our sources, but in our most credible account Antony handed over 120 warships and ten skiffs while Octavian gave his brother-in-law 1,000 elite troops and a promise of 20,000 legionnaires, or four legions, to follow. These legions were never delivered, and Antony never counted on them, but that was less important at the time than the publicity of Octavian's promise.[229] This arrangement permitted everyone to recognize the triumvirs' cooperation and goodwill— and it did nothing to damage Antony's international standing. Family ties were now deployed in order to define, advertise, and bolster the triumvirs' newly restored comity. Perhaps in an attempt to salvage at least a part of his reputation as an advocate of reconciliation, Antony betrothed his daughter by Octavia, the Elder Antonia, to the son of Domitius Ahenobarbus. In this way, Domitius became a connection of both triumvirs.[230] Though children at the time, Antonia and Domitius were wed after Actium: they became the grandparents of the future emperor Nero. Of far greater significance, Octavian's daughter Julia was engaged to Antony's eldest son, Antyllus, who was still just a boy.[231] That marriage, however, would never take place: indeed, after Actium, Antyllus was put to death on Octavian's order.

The Pact of Tarentum

It was now necessary to abrogate the pact of Misenum. Although this decision was effectively made by Octavian and Antony, Lepidus' participation was at the very least a formal necessity. Remaining in Africa, he expressed his inevitable assent by

way of his personal representatives in Italy.[232] The triumvirs did not simply revert to
the terms of the pact of Brundisium. New conditions for restoring the republic were
introduced, and the triumvirs' tenure in office was extended. It was decided that the
triumvirate should now extend until 31, in which year Antony and Octavian would
be consuls and in which year the republic would be fully restored.[233] This decision
entailed some reshuffling of previous consular appointments, but only one man was
now extruded: Sextus Pompey. He was stripped of his consulship, his augurate, and
his property: almost certainly he was formally declared an enemy of the state. For
this new edition of the triumvirate, previous provincial allocations were affirmed—
with a highly likely new provision entrusting Sicily to Octavian. All this lay within the
powers of the triumvirs. Nevertheless, and probably at Antony's insistence, this reorganization of the triumvirate was subsequently passed into law by the people.[234] In
this way, the whole of Rome was implicated in the triumvirs' abandonment of the pact
of Misenum: that Sextus was an outlaw was thus rendered an official and universally
accepted policy.

Inflection Point?

The standoff at Tarentum was a crisis. Amid the delicate and difficult negotiations
required in resolving it, Octavia clearly played a central role. Her exertions in reconciling brother and husband, because they were later elaborated by our sources with a
high degree of melodrama, make it obvious how the episode at Tarentum, although
principally a political contest, was also a family dispute fraught with intense and competing loyalties. Of this matter, unfortunately, we know so few of the facts that we
will never plumb its psychology. Nevertheless, it is as clear as such things can be that
Antony's relationship with Octavia was deeply altered by events at Tarentum. In 31
January 36, Octavia gave birth to her second daughter by Antony, Antonia the mother
of the future emperor Claudius.[235] By way of a simple calculation, we can locate
Antonia's conception at some time in May 37, when tensions between Antony and
Octavian were fierce. This rivalry, it appears, had not yet poisoned all tender affections
between Octavia and Antony.

What of Octavia's deportment thereafter? In Plutarch and Appian she is her husband's loyal advocate, although her gains on his behalf are minimal. That, however, reflects the image-making of later propaganda which presented Octavia as an
ideal but unappreciated and long-suffering spouse. Whatever positions she actually
espoused in these negotiations, the final result was unfavourable to Antony. Which
is why one cannot fail to notice that, when he left Italy, Antony left Octavia and his
children behind. In Dio's account, this decision is made on the return voyage, when
Antony halted at Corcyra in order to send Octavia and his children back to Italy. The
ostensible reason for this melodramatic gesture was Antony's wish that his wife and
family not be exposed to the risks of the Parthian war. But that was nonsense: they
resided in Athens. It was their final encounter: Octavia and Antony never again saw
one another.

In the aftermath of the crisis at Tarentum, one has the very strong sense of breathing
a new air. This encounter, for all its ostensibly harmonious conclusion, marked a new

phase in the triumvirate and a new stage in the relationship between Antony and his wife and brother-in-law.[236] Not that any conspicuous estrangement comes immediately into view—under the circumstances one would hardly expect to find that—nor, thereafter, was any party undutiful in observing the obligations of alliance or affinity. Octavian honoured his brother-in-law even after his disappointing campaign in Parthia. Octavia remained a devoted wife. Still, for Octavian, Antony's friendly invasion, his rash attempt to take charge of the war against Sextus, must have introduced a new variable to his political calculus—even after Antony was persuaded to step back: this man, he could sensibly conclude, even when bound by alliances, was bold and dangerous and ambitious for primacy. As for Antony, he could not fail to recognize his brother-in-law's steely resolution, his lack of principle, or the devotion he inspired in his sister. The war against Sextus Antony now left to Octavian and Lepidus. Antony's concentration he now fixed determinedly on the east. And, for the last time in his life, he departed Italy.

XII
Fierce wars and faithful loves

Antony in Antioch

Leaving Italy, Antony travelled directly to Syria and to its capital, Antioch. During his absence, Sosius had achieved victory in Judea and pacified the region. Antony now imposed a final settlement. Herod was installed in Jerusalem. His rival, the pertinacious Antigonus, was publicly executed, grim proof of the eradication of Parthian influence within Roman domains and a clear if frightening signal to the kingdom that Herod was there to stay.[1] The stability of Syria and its surrounding principalities was a crucial prerequisite to Antony's invasion of Parthia. For this reason, Lysanias, the ruler of Chalcis who had cooperated with the Parthians and supported Antigonus, was deposed and executed. His kingdom, however, was not added to Herod's. Instead, Antony entrusted it to Cleopatra, who administered it through a vassal, a certain Zenodorus, possibly Lysanias' son.[2] This assignment was only one part of an extensive allocation of cities and territories to Egyptian suzerainty. Much of the Phoenician coast was also handed over to the queen, along with rich, fertile portions of the interior.[3] Although it is all too easy to attribute this dispensation to Antony's fondness for Cleopatra, it is necessary to recognize the importance of this region to Rome's strategic interests in the east. No local figure was obviously up to the task of ensuring order during Antony's expedition. Not even Herod: for all his promise, recent events had brought to the fore his almost total reliance on Roman support. Egypt and its queen offered Rome a more seasoned, more reliable administration.[4] Too often it is asserted that Antony acted as he did because he needed Cleopatra's money. That, however, was his for the taking. What Antony required was the queen's indisputable talent as a monarch.

Antony dispatched Gaius Fonteius Capito to Alexandria to fetch the queen.[5] We need not doubt the splendour of the entertainments which greeted her in Antioch, even if our sources in this instance pass them over. A regal reception and ceremonies suitable for marking this significant increase in Egypt's possessions were incumbent on the triumvir. Nor should we discount the affections rekindled by their reunion. Cleopatra introduced Antony to his twin children, whose paternity he publicly acknowledged.[6] Perhaps, as Plutarch reports, he did so by evoking his Herculean heritage: the great hero fathered children throughout the world, so Plutarch's Antony observes, thereby furnishing the genesis of many races and cities; leaving behind a race of kings, he declaimed, likewise fitted Roman greatness—and his own nobility. This gesture, doubtless part of a public pageant, did nothing to render the twins Roman citizens. But it elevated their importance in Egypt. Indeed, the transactions at Antioch—the expansion of Cleopatra's domains, the recognition of her children by Antony—were events that, for the queen, ushered in a new age: the year 37 officially became the year 1 as Egypt looked to its future.[7] As for Antony, these occasions once again registered throughout the east his recurring claim that he was no ordinary Roman governor, a conspicuous element of his administration since he became the New Dionysus. Not everything was purely for show however. Spending the winter together, Antony and Cleopatra renewed their sexual relationship—intimacy that was perhaps especially welcome after his disappointments at Tarentum—and by the new year the queen was pregnant with Antony's child. In 36 she bore him a son, Ptolemy Philadelphus.[8]

However voluptuous or playful he may have been in Cleopatra's company, at Antioch Antony was a busy man. It was now that he finished off the details of his reorganization of the provinces and client kingdoms in the east. Amid these negotiations, Cleopatra perhaps acquired control of some cities in Crete. Perhaps, too, she also hoped to make gains in the Cyrenaica, but this region, along with the bulk of Crete, remained a Roman province.[9] Cleopatra made further requests for territories along the Levant, but these, too, Antony refused.[10] Fond of her though he plainly was, an efficient and tolerable administration came first—and in any case it was useful for Antony to sustain a healthy rivalry among Rome's subject states.

Plutarch and Dio alike insist that Antony's relationship with Cleopatra elicited strong disapproval in Rome.[11] This is unlikely. As we have seen, their diplomatic intercourse was an act of prudence: Egypt was the obvious choice for securing stability in this part of the east. By the time news of his conduct at Antioch became known in Italy, Antony was leading Roman legions into Parthia, hardly, in the eyes of anyone who was not already his enemy, the conduct of a disloyal or unsound citizen. Gossip, perhaps malicious gossip, there may have been. Disapprobation, too, by anyone so prudish as to be upset by Antony's uninhibited womanizing. But serious complaints about Cleopatra came later.

Marriage with Cleopatra, Part One

And yet it has often been claimed, and the claim remains a pervasive one, that, at Antioch, Antony married Cleopatra, an action certain to provoke reproaches, even outrage, in Rome.[12] This assertion requires clarification. Because Cleopatra was not a Roman citizen, she and Antony lacked the capacity to make a marriage in accordance with Roman law.[13] Antony divorced Octavia in 32, but until then he remained, from any Roman perspective, a married man, and in Rome polygamy was impossible: Cleopatra, if she was anything, was Antony's mistress. Egyptian law, however, was something different, nor did Hellenistic custom forbid a sovereign from marrying as she pleased, especially if her marriage advanced the fortunes of her realm. The sensibilities of a Roman noble, by contrast, discouraged stepping outside Roman law and taking a foreign wife. Caesar, who knew something about Egyptian romance, took it as a mark of Alexandrian depravity that Roman soldiers serving in Egypt abandoned 'the name and moral order of the Roman people' in order to take local wives and with them father children.[14] Clearly he distinguished between his affair with Cleopatra, which was man of the world stuff, and anyone's settling down in an illicit, alien union, which was disgraceful. Did Antony?

Complaints over Cleopatra's seduction of Antony, central to Octavian's rhetoric of outrage when he was mobilizing Italy for the war at Actium, stimulated contemptuous allegations that she was his foreign wife, an oxymoron deployed to portray Octavia as a woman wronged and Antony as beyond the Roman pale.[15] In the *Aeneid*, Cleopatra is *Aegyptia coniunx*—an Egyptian wife—and the poet has no words for such an abomination: *nefas* he calls it, ineffably evil.[16] Some historians, by contrast, shied away from the word. Livy, it appears, preferred to say that Antony began to behave towards Cleopatra *as if* she were his wife; Strabo employs similar language. Velleius deprecates Antony as Cleopatra's love-slave, not her husband.[17] And Dio, although ever so capacious a depository of Antonian inculpation, never censures him for marrying the queen. Plutarch has it both ways. For him, Cleopatra is usually Antony's mistress, but, in his *Comparison of Demetrius and Antony*, she becomes his wife.[18]

The Elder Seneca, by contrast, is straightforward. He cites a humorous, bilingual graffito scrawled in Athens: 'Octavia and Athena to Antony: consider yourself divorced'. This inscription is clearly a fiction generated by the false story of Antony's sacred marriage to Athena. Seneca, who believes in its authenticity, explains it (and somewhat spoils the joke) by way of observing that, while he was married to Octavia, Antony also took Cleopatra as his wife.[19] Seneca's credulity over Antony's sacred marriage is beside the point here. His certainty that Antony and Cleopatra were married is unambiguous. But Seneca is cataloguing instances of eloquence and cleverness: he is not writing as a historian. Other imperial writers, like Seneca, including some commentators and historians, also take it for granted that Antony and Cleopatra were married.[20]

Part of the problem for ancient writers lies in an uncertainty felt by some of them over applying the vocabulary of marriage, and even for modern historians the controversy can easily descend into quibbling about semantics. This was true even when Antony and Octavian were exchanging unkindly misinformation and distorting calumny. In a public letter penned in 33, lobbed at Octavian amid their propaganda war, Antony makes it clear that he grasped what was at stake in the Roman reception of his relationship with the Egyptian queen.[21] For this reason, he clothes it in formulations appealing to the coarse but nevertheless pervasive sensibilities of Roman men of his class:

> What has changed you? The fact that I am entering the queen? Is she my wife? Have I just begun this or has it been going on for nine years? As for you, is it only Drusilla you enter? You would be doing well if it's the case that, when you read this letter, you haven't just entered Tertullia or Terentilla or Rufilla or Salvia or Titisenia—or the lot. Does it matter to you in whom you insert your engorged cock or where you do it?

This letter, like any specimen of Roman invective, is designed to say bad things about its victim and, at the same time, portray its author in a plausibly positive light.[22] Here Antony sets an epistolary scene in which he and Octavian are two men whose sex lives are not confined to their home lives. As we have seen before, such conduct, if perhaps less than sterling, was unobjectionable in Rome—nor uncommon. Antony does not attempt to portray himself as a paragon of marital fidelity: indeed, to do so would be ridiculous for a man who had paraded about Italy with Cytheris in tow. He admits at once to a sexual relationship with Cleopatra, an affair hardly unknown to Octavian when he arranged his sister's marriage: hence the precise indication of the liaison's long-standing nature and his complaint that Octavian lacks constancy ('What has changed you?'). But Antony's affair with Cleopatra—he is explicit on this point—is *not* a marriage.[23] How could it be when he is married to Octavia?

Antony's Latin makes it clear that he does not even *make love* with Cleopatra: he *enters* her, an activity in which Octavian also engages with several women whom Antony lists. This verb, *inire*, is a word more often applied to animals than people.[24] And when it is used of women and men, it is cold and utilitarian and devoid of anything even hinting at sentimentality or affection. We see this starkly put in Ovid's *Remedia Amoris*, the *Cure for Love*, in a passage where the poet is giving his pupil (this poem takes the shape of an instruction manual) frank advice on how to prepare for a tryst.[25] A young man, advises Ovid, in order to avoid premature orgasm in the arms of his beloved, should procure prior gratification:

> I recommend you enter (*inire* is the verb) somebody else first.
> Simply find anyone in whom your first moment of pleasure
> may expend itself.

It is obvious that Ovid has in mind a slave or prostitute—anyone to hand, really. And the very word he uses to communicate this brand of sexual exploitation is *inire*.

In this letter, then, there is nothing un-Roman in Antony's attitude towards Cleopatra. By contrast, Octavian's serial seductions are depicted as shocking. Here he is a man who cannot resist debauching aristocratic, *Roman* women. Not sexually satisfied with Drusilla, that is, with his wife Livia, Octavian also enters a string of women the identity of whom eludes but whose status is unquestionably distinguished. It is not that Octavian is an indiscriminate adulterer strictly speaking. It is rather that Octavian has only one standard: his women must be of the right class—and therefore women who are out of all bounds in legal and moral terms. Despite their elevated social standing, however, Octavian treats them as if they were slaves or foreigners (*inire* again). Sexual depredations of this kind, Antony need hardly spell it out, are outrages typical of a tyrant.[26] Romans could hardly forget the rape of Lucretia or the dreadful fate of Verginia.[27] Octavian, readers of this letter are warned, is coming for your wives and daughters.

Antony makes it clear he is not that kind of triumvir. Here he is too fine a gentleman even to embarrass the aristocracy by naming names. Amid so much coarseness in this letter, its author reveals a sound social delicacy. Modern historians sometimes complain that Antony uses only *cognomina* (nicknames) and refuses to name *nomina* (clan names), which renders it impossible to identify the women he has in mind here.[28] That, of course, was precisely the point. Antony sleeps with the queen of Egypt. He has been doing so for several years and so it can hardly stand as a legitimate reason for changing one's view of him. And his sexual relationship with Cleopatra, like his past sexual relationship with Fadia or with Cytheris, is merely a matter of harmless utility. It is Octavian who is dangerously lubricious.

As late as 33, then, Antony could publicly declare himself not married to Cleopatra—at least to a Roman audience. And it also to an audience of Roman men that he portrays his relationship with Cleopatra in terms that are, for her, debasing. Now the queen of Egypt was too astute to fail to grasp the politics of Roman invective. She knew, as do we, that this letter is a performance. But it tells us that nothing at Antioch or later at Alexandria could unambiguously be denominated a marriage. Antony's very real intimacy with Cleopatra, however it was understood by the two of them or perceived by others, soon became an unsimple affair which, in the years after this winter in Antioch, developed in sudden, unexpected ways. When Antony presided over the Donations of Alexandria, which took place in 34, their relationship as parents and partners became implicated in geopolitical aspirations affecting nearly the whole of eastern Mediterranean and therefore fair game for attacks by his political enemies. At the same time, as we have seen, Antony could insist that Cleopatra was not his wife. And in Cleopatra's Egypt, no document denominates Antony the queen's consort.[29] Nonetheless, something marvellous, or perhaps alarming, certainly unprecedented, had, by the time of the Donations, come into the world. To that we shall recur.

Evidence for a marriage, or something very much like it, occurring at Antioch is sometimes seen in three issues of tetradrachms produced in Syria.[30] These coins carry, on one side, a portrait of Cleopatra, denominated in Greek 'Queen Cleopatra, the Newer Goddess', and, on the other, Antony, who is (in Greek) 'Antony, thrice imperator, triumvir'.[31] The exact site of their minting is uncertain, and it has been proposed that more than one mint was involved in their production. One likely source, however, is Antioch.[32] On the prevailing view, these coins began to be issued in 36 and were closely connected with Antony's promotion of Cleopatra.

Now, if these coins are so early as 36, they are indeed so extraordinary that one must conclude they signal a momentous development in Antony's relationship with Cleopatra, even if one need not deem it a marriage. Instead of sharing a coin with another Roman magistrate or with his wife, Antony here, unprecedentedly and uniquely, shares it with a foreign monarch. That was indeed a gesture likely to stimulate consternation in Rome, nor could it go unnoticed in the east, where it must designate Cleopatra's superiority over any rival potentate. For these reasons alone, however, this issue could only complicate rather than stabilize conditions in the east or in Rome at just the moment when Antony was planning to march into Parthia. Now there are several other issues depicting Antony and Cleopatra on the same coin, but these come later and under political circumstances that, as we shall see, render them not less remarkable but readily comprehensible. Our tetradrachms, by contrast, are distinct and highly significant outliers—if they appeared in 36.

In fact, however, this dating is highly provisional.[33] There is no question but that these coins were in circulation by 33: one of them was reused and restamped in that year by the Parthian king Phraates.[34] But there certainty ends. Antony's arrangements at Antioch, so clearly designed to impose order and security during his absence, are inadequate as a justification for tethering these unquestionably provocative coins to 36. It is far more likely that they belong closer to the other issues portraying Antony and Cleopatra together, which is to say, sometime around late 35 or 34.[35] Nonetheless, there is no denying these coins possess a kind of pushmi-pullyu quality: *if* there was a marriage, they make a kind of sense in 36, their brazenness notwithstanding, but they only make a kind of sense at that time if there was a marriage. For that very reason, however, on the question of whether a marriage actually took place at Antioch, they cannot be probative.

At Antioch Antony recognized his Egyptian children, very probably in a public ceremony. He expanded Cleopatra's realm, so much so that it justified the inauguration of a new age for Egypt. That these actions were significant ones is undeniable. But Antony then marched away and there is no reason for us to believe he had specific plans ever to return to Cleopatra. His expedition into Parthia was intended to consume more than one year, perhaps as many as three. And, after winning victory there, Antony knew he would be confronted with whatever contests and challenges were thrown up in winding down the triumvirate and restoring the republic. We may, then, safely lay aside any suggestion that, in any sense of the word, Antony and Cleopatra were married at Antioch.

War with Parthia

It was at Antioch that Antony received the formal submission of Armenia's king, Artavasdes. Canidius' forceful acquisition of Armenia and this kingdom's return to an alliance with Rome were commemorated by Antony on a denarius the reverse of which exhibited an Armenian tiara amid titulature noting Antony's status as a conqueror.[36] An Armenian embassy to Antioch conveyed the king's renewed enthusiasm for Rome and his urgent advice that Antony march into Parthia by way of his kingdom.[37] Other eastern monarchs, too, were consulted about the war with Parthia.[38] This expedition, and its strategy, were Antony's central concern during his winter in Antioch.

During this same winter, a Parthian nobleman, Monaeses, came to Antony as a political refugee.[39] Sometime in late 38 or 37, the Parthian king, Orodes, abdicated in favour of his son Phraates. The new monarch proceeded to purge the kingdom of his enemies, real or perceived, including his unfortunate father. Kinsmen and estranged or suspected nobles were assassinated. Numerous notables fled abroad. Monaeses, an important figure in Parthia, was one of them. He made a strong impression on Antony, who took him in and promised to establish him as an overlord of several cities at the extreme east of Rome's empire. At Antioch, a plan was hatched whereby Antony would invade Mesopotamia in a bid to install Monaeses on the Parthian throne. This was a reprise of Gabinius' plan for invading Parthia in 56, when Antony was his officer.

In the end, however, nothing came of the idea. Monaeses was invited to return home by Phraates and subsequently released by Antony, who nonetheless maintained a close connection with the Parthian noble. The triumvir now sent an embassy to Phraates requesting the return of Parthia's Roman prisoners and the standards lost by Crassus at Carrhae.[40] In this way, even before he invaded, Antony presented Phraates with a diplomatic solution to their imminent conflict: surrendering Rome's standards at the right moment could bring the war to an honourable conclusion. Antony's expedition, it will have been clear to the Parthian king, was not aimed at total conquest: slices of Parthia might be seized, but Roman revenge required an act of submission. Throughout the later campaign, Phraates rejected this idea. But later, during the reign of Augustus, a transaction of just this kind—Phraates swapped his Roman eagles in exchange for the safe return of his son—constituted the basis of Augustus' boast that he compelled Parthia to submit to Roman authority.[41] In the spring of 36, however, Antony did not wait for Phraates' reply. He began a march towards Zeugma.

Antecedents

In 55, Aulus Gabinius crossed the Euphrates in an invasion of Parthia designed to place Mithridates, a brother of the king, on the throne. This undertaking, however, was soon aborted, Gabinius preferring the profits of dynastic intervention in Egypt.[42] In 54, Marcus Crassus superseded Gabinius in Syria, from which province he, too, marched into Parthia. This was a major operation: Crassus commanded seven legions and aimed at seizing a significant slab of territory from Rome's formidable neighbour. The ruler of Armenia, our Artavasdes, sided with Crassus. The king urged him to attack the Parthians from the north, by way of Armenia. Instead, Crassus entered Mesopotamia, where he aimed at capturing Ctesiphon. Near Carrhae he was defeated, slain, and his forces almost entirely annihilated.[43] A remnant, led by his quaestor, Cassius Longinus, made its way back to Syria, where for the next two years and with only a few troops he guarded Rome's border.[44] But Parthia did not retaliate until 51. Their incursions at that time, although they amounted to little, contributed nonetheless to regional anxieties about a superpower rivalry that was now dangerous to the security of the lesser states caught between them.[45]

During the civil war between Pompey and Caesar, Parthian intervention remained a very real possibility. After he became master of Rome, Caesar decided that in 44 he would march east, where he intended to vanquish Dacia and conquer Parthia, or so it was said. Caesar's actual designs remain controversial, and it is unclear whether he planned to overrun the kingdom or rather to target specific, less ambitious gains. There is, however, no doubt that he meant to invade Parthia—this time through Lesser Armenia—and his preparations for doing so entailed, it appears, assembling a force so large as 16 legions and 10,000 cavalrymen.[46] But great Caesar fell, and the east's subsequent exploitation by the Liberators created geopolitical fractures into which Parthian influence intruded. As we have seen, this condition was not adequately corrected by Antony's first organization of the east in 41, which in the following year led to a major invasion of Rome's dominion by Labienus and Pacorus. Ventidius drove them out, by way of perceptive, innovative tactics and with vigorous fighting. He defeated Labienus in 39 and in the 38 his decisive victory at Gindarus brought this campaign to a quick conclusion, an efficient development that perhaps encouraged Romans to believe the Parthians were less formidable than they had feared. It was through the prism of this slice of recent history that Antony and his advisors, during the winter at Antioch, weighed competing strategies. Their brief collusion with Monaeses suggests that, even at the start of 36, the Romans had not yet reached a final decision on their line of attack.[47] But the time had now come for embracing a single strategy.

Mobilization

Antony's invasion, as we have seen, required preliminary operations in two the-atres: Canidius' march into Armenia, Iberia, and Albania secured a northern route, while Sosius' pacification of Syria and Judea left it possible to enter Parthia by way of Mesopotamia. With Antony and the bulk of his army away, these two regions were also presently to become vulnerable to potential counterattacks or political disruption. In Syria, Antony's reorganization, punctuated by executions, was designed to instil order. A similar purpose animated Canidius' campaign.

At the start of 36, Antony's forces were divided. In the north, Candidius had four legions. Sosius commanded eleven. Antony also assembled additional forces, including an abundance of auxiliaries. Crassus' defeat had made clear the lethal effectiveness of Parthian cataphracts and mounted bowmen. For this reason, Antony mustered (as Caesar had planned to do) a formidable cavalry, 10,000 riders from Gaul and Iberia, the largest cavalry force any Roman army had ever assembled.[48] Our sources disagree on the specific size but not the scale of Antony's infantry. It was a big army. In total, it certainly included 16 and possibly as many as 18 legions; its auxiliary forces amounted to 30,000 men. In addition to Antony's Gallic and Iberian cavalry, Artavasdes added 6,000 Armenian riders.[49] Other client kings also contributed men.[50] This army, far larger than Crassus', very likely excelled the host Caesar intended to employ in his invasion. Aware of the aridity of Parthian terrain, Antony also arranged for the construction of siege equipment, some of it massive, which he carried with him in a wagon train. Like Caesar, perhaps, Antony envisioned a campaign lasting so long as three years. Magnificent and awful, Antony's army began its march near the end of spring.

Sources

We have, in Plutarch and Dio, two extended narratives of Antony's campaign, and we possess traces of others.[51] The subject attracted readers, especially in the aftermath of Actium, when it furnished grim proof of noble Antony's failures even as a military leader. Livy, a contemporary, drafted an account that, so far as we can tell, was mostly hostile. His rendering was rehearsed and adapted by many, including Dio. Plutarch's account, often sympathetic and inclined to approbate Antony's affection for his soldiers and the devotion they returned, is nonetheless also highly critical. Enamoured of Cleopatra and keen to return to her embraces, in Plutarch's telling, Antony possessed too little patience and discipline: 'he conducted the whole of his campaign in a confused, agitated manner'.[52]

All of these writers had at their disposal a history of this war composed by a distinguished participant, Quintus Dellius.[53] We have met him before: it was he who persuaded Cleopatra to travel to Tarsus. Amid the hazards of civil war, Dellius was a highly successful survivor. He offered his talents to Dolabella, then to Dolabella's enemy Cassius, after whose collapse he joined Antony. On the eve of Actium, he took Octavian's side. He was highly esteemed in the new regime, distinction reflected in the Horatian ode dedicated to him.[54] A man so eager to be of service could not escape detraction: enemies alleged he had been Antony's catamite.[55] Dellius' political versatility prompted Messala Corvinus, also a figure remarkable for changing sides at the right moments, to dub him the *desultor bellorum civilium*, the horse-vaulting acrobat of the civil wars.[56] Dellius also enjoyed a literary reputation. After Actium, he composed a (now lost) work, *Dirty Letters to Cleopatra* (*Epistulae ad Cleopatram Lascivae*), in which he entertained readers by luridly smearing the memory of the Egyptian queen, perhaps in the voice of Antony.

More important was his work as a historian. He wrote an account of the Parthian campaign, in which he served as a legate. Plutarch read it, and it is probably owing to Dellius that his account includes so many dramatic features: confusing night combats, diverting episodes of fraternization between enemy soldiers, the Parthians' awed silence when confronted by the legions' disciplined manoeuvres, Parthian shouts of appreciation for the Romans' valour, a colourful guide who appears out of nowhere and at just the right moment; a mysterious diplomat, who also finds Antony just when Antony needs him.[57] Dellius, clearly, was a delightful read. But, although he was obliged to celebrate the mettle of his fellow Romans, he did not hesitate to impugn the leadership and character of their general. Hence, in this unfriendly work, Dellius offered readers, more than once, justifications for his deserting to the better side.[58]

Plutarch cites Dellius more than once, and throughout his treatment of the campaign finds uses for Dellius' criticisms of Antony. At the same time, Plutarch's account is by no means a simple reproduction of Dellius. Plutarch's Antony, notwithstanding his natural vices, is capable, again and again, of rising to meet his most serious challenges.[59] Though addled by his shameful love for Cleopatra, Antony is nonetheless constantly valiant. And, during the Romans' retreat from Medea Atropatene, as Plutarch tells the story, he reprises the heroism, adaptiveness, and leadership exhibited by the highly admired Greeks celebrated in Xenophon's *Anabasis*, a connection made clear by way of allusion and explicit quotation.[60] The sheer literariness of our sources, it is undeniable, each trying to tell us something significant, usually something bad, about Antony's character, throws up grave obstacles against any recovery of the events of his campaign. And, as we shall see, matters are made still worse by the politicism and dishonest publicity that shaped reports of Antony's expedition throughout the east and in Rome in its immediate aftermath, years before denigration of Antony's eastern career became orthodoxy. Consequently, no account of Antony's campaign can be more than a provisional one.

Antony Invades

Cleopatra returned to Alexandria. Antony and his vast host began their march.[61] Unlike Crassus, Antony allowed himself to be persuaded by Artavasdes and aimed at entering Parthia by way of Armenia, which was also Caesar's intended route. The king's advice was hardly disinterested. This line of attack would launch the Roman invasion into Media Atropatene, Armenia's local and bitter rival.[62] The fall of this kingdom could only work to Armenia's advantage: hence his earlier recommendation to Crassus. But neither Caesar nor Antony preferred this approach for Armenia's sake. Crassus' fate convinced them that advancing from the north was a sounder tactic. The aim of Antony's first campaign season, then, was the subjection of Media Atropatene. His target was its capital, Phraaspa. Here resided the king's family and his central treasury. In taking this city, Antony was certain, he would detach the kingdom from Parthian hegemony—and, by way of plunder, gratify his legions.

Antony's further ambitions we do not know. He may have expected that Phraates, after losing Media Atropatene, would be willing to hand over Crassus' standards and Rome would thereby be avenged. He could then, having conquered the Mede and humbled the Parthian, claim glory that excelled even Caesar's. If, however, the king was recalcitrant, Antony could, in his second season and operating from an advanced base in Phraaspa, penetrate further into Parthia, perhaps so far as a royal city like Ecbatana.

These, of course, were optimal expectations. Romans knew well that few campaigns avoided serious reversals, and Antony's campaign was certain to be especially hazardous. Its challenges were formidable. He was presently to lead an enormous army, with its vast array of sutlers, into a hostile kingdom defended by a powerful army in a terrain entirely alien to him and his officers. True, he had the advice of client kings, and Antony did what he could to extract intelligence from the other side. And he was prudent enough to carry with him equipment and supplies he could not easily acquire when he marched into Media Atropatene. Roman warriors did not shrink from adversity. Nonetheless, Antony's expedition called for something more than outright boldness: it needed resolution tinged with sober caution.

Antony directed a part of his army towards Zeugma, where he hoped to cross the Euphrates—not in order to invade Mesopotamia but because crossing here afforded him the most direct route to Armenia. Doubtless he anticipated the presence of a Parthian garrison, which he could easily surmount. Instead, however, the Romans found forces ample enough to offer stout resistance. Phraates had, moreover, concentrated his army in Mesopotamia and that was a confrontation Antony had no intention of meeting under the same conditions that ruined Crassus. Antony cannot have been entirely surprised by this: after Crassus' invasion and in view of the presence in Syria of a large Roman army, the Parthians naturally expected a crossing at Zeugma. Still, the direct approach to Armenia was too attractive for Antony not to investigate it.[63] Disappointed, he now took the very long and roundabout march through Commagene, entering Armenia from the west and joining up with Canidius at Artaxata.[64] It was now late June or even late July.

A chorus of ancient sources censures Antony for failing to spend the winter in Armenia, postponing his invasion to the following spring.[65] Doing so would have given the Romans, in the subsequent year, a full fighting season during which to overrun Media Atropatene. But it was not too late in July to undertake operations, and Antony trusted in his mighty host and his military acumen. Furthermore, he had received reports that the Parthian army remained in the south, a posture which rendered Media Atropatene vulnerable to attack. This information was inaccurate, as Antony would soon discover, but at the time he deemed it reliable. After provisioning his army, he advanced along the Araxes valley. This route furnished protection from the Parthian cavalry, should the enemy make an unexpected appearance, and facilitated the passage of his cumbersome baggage train. Owing to the bulk of his siege equipment—it was carried by 300 wagons—he was compelled to move excruciatingly slowly.[66] Antony stayed with the river until he was well advanced into Media Atropatene. He then marched into the flatlands, 'a treeless plain', as Plutarch describes it, on his way to Phraaspa, wherever, exactly, it lay.[67] Antony's order of march put his wagon train near the rear, protected by two legions assigned to Oppius Statianus. Following these were auxiliary forces, including a contingent led by King Polemo and the Armenian cavalry commanded by Artavasdes. The new terrain did nothing to accelerate the army's progress, hampered as it remained by its onerous but vital baggage.

Now, at last, Antony could unleash his soldiers. As they advanced, the Romans despoiled Media Atropatene.[68] Villages and settlements, perhaps even prosperous towns, were attacked. Nor was this kingdom without its treasure towers.[69] And the army, as it passed through the region, was able to replenish its provisions. Despite all the destruction the Romans now inflicted, there was no opposition on the part of the Parthians, an absence that encouraged Antony to believe the enemy were indeed elsewhere. For this reason, he thought it safe enough to leave behind his baggage train, advance rapidly to Phraaspa, and commence siege operations. If the city did not capitulate—Dio claims Antony hoped to take Phraaspa 'without striking a blow'—or fall quickly, the arrival of his siege equipment would soon finish the job.[70] The Romans could then winter in the defeated capital.

This was a mistake. The Parthians, no longer in the south but instead near their Roman enemy, seized this moment to attack Antony's baggage train. Perhaps this was not part of a grand design but instead the Parthians' forces arrived just in time to make a strike. In any case, they caught the Romans unaware and fell on them in overwhelming numbers. Statianus' legions were annihilated, the auxiliaries routed. Artavasdes and his cavalry retreated to Armenia.[71] Polemo was taken prisoner. This ambush, it appears, was led by the king of Media Atropatene, whose name, unhelpfully for us, was also Artavasdes. This king took as his reward the standards of the two Roman legions he had slaughtered and a prized royal captive.[72] Antony's siege equipment was burned. When the Parthians first struck, Statianus managed to send word of it to Antony—the baggage train, clearly, had come very close to arriving at Phraaspa— who hastened to the rescue.[73] But he arrived too late. On his return, his party, too, was pounced on by Parthians. Antony repulsed them but was unable to follow up this success. He returned to Phraaspa.[74] The destruction of his wagon train cost Antony the bulk of his provisions and all his siege equipment. These losses, more even than the loss of two legions or his Armenian cavalry, constituted a severe blow. Capturing Phraaspa was not now an outright impossibility. But it could only be a daunting task, especially because the Romans were certain to be harassed and impeded by Parthian forces.

Antony's overconfidence was now tempered by this reversal. For the next two months or so, the Romans struggled to take Phraaspa, improvising siege machinery in a treeless terrain by throwing up towering mounds and probing the city for weaknesses. It had none. Well garrisoned, Phraaspa's soldiers fought back fiercely, lashing out in bold, often destructive, sallies. For its part, the Parthian army harassed the Romans constantly but were incapable of dislodging them. It could, however, prey on Roman foraging parties, inflicting severe losses. The Romans fought back, and both sides suffered greatly. Antony, in an attempt to draw the Parthians into a decisive, pitched battle, led the bulk of his legions on a major foraging expedition. Dellius provided his readers with an elaborate account of the Romans' tactics, including impressive feats of infantry discipline that left the enemy awed if not shocked. A clash ensued, the Romans were successful, but could not pursue the Parthians effectively. Consequently, too few Parthians fell for the battle to be counted a significant victory. For Dellius, as well as Plutarch and Dio, who adapt his account of this battle, Roman tactics and Parthian casualties are the only aspects of this episode that matter. They neglect the mission's other purpose, which was to acquire supplies on a scale that minimized the Romans' need to deploy smaller, more vulnerable foraging parties.

Even so, the Romans' position at Phraaspa was deteriorating. There was little chance of capturing the city. And wintering under canvass in so harsh a climate was unfeasible. By autumn, then, it was clear that retreat was unavoidable. The Parthians, too, endured much hardship, sustained painful losses, and were eager to see an end to their defence of the Median capital. Indeed, the various contingents of the king's army were already making preparations for their departure into winter quarters.[75] Phraates initiated a parley, during which Antony's representatives, in the teeth of the king's intimidating posture, refused to abandon the Romans' earlier demand that he restore the standards of Crassus' legions. Dellius furnished a vivid scene of the Parthian king on his golden throne, menacingly twanging the string of his bow. These negotiations collapsed without a result. In November Antony prepared to march back to Armenia. This action, too, presented challenges: retreating entailed fresh technical and tactical difficulties, nor was there any possibility that the Parthians would allow them a safe passage out of the country. For reasons of his own, Phraates needed a victory over the Romans.

Antony did not go back the way he came in. Instead, heeding the advice of local guides, not least a mysterious Mardian who enters our ancient narratives suddenly and on cue, the Romans took a more direct route which led them through hill country, where they could expect to pass near villages accessible for trade or plundering.[76] This terrain, although it hardly insulated the Romans from Parthian attacks, nonetheless helped to neutralize the potency of their cavalry tactics and enabled Antony to deploy slingers and javelin throwers effectively. Antony also acquired valuable intelligence from the other side. An agent of Monaeses, a cousin named Mithridates, furnished Antony with information regarding the Parthian king's plans. In our sources, this figure is another timely apparition.[77] In reality, his aid must derive from an ongoing but covert relationship between Antony and Monaeses which began in Antioch. Still, it is hard to imagine Monaeses assisting Antony solely for friendship's sake: he must have been impressed by the Romans' campaign, notwithstanding the severity of its setbacks, and he must have been convinced that Antony would return. Better, then, to sustain a degree of comity. Monaeses' double-dealing, welcome to Antony, constitutes evidence that, on the Parthian side, not everyone felt the war had gone entirely their way—even if the Romans were now withdrawing.

Plutarch embellishes Antony's retreat with allusions and references that reprise Xenophon's *Anabasis*. This fourth-century Athenian classic told the tale of a Greek army which, isolated inside the Persian empire, succeeded, amid much adversity, in retreating to the sea and to safety—an achievement owed to the men's virtue but especially to the talents of their leaders, one of whom was Xenophon. Plutarch's adaptation is an impressive purple passage, and in it the biographer more than once gives elo-quent expression to Antony's devotion to the welfare of his soldiers and their gratitude for his generous humanity: his men trust and respect him still. In Plutarch's telling, Antony plays the part of the historiography's ideal general.[78]

Now Plutarch's literariness need not disqualify his basic claim: Antony, in retreat, remained an effective leader of men. At a more practical level, Antony quickly adapted his tactics to the demands of this new terrain and the methods now employed by the Parthians. The Romans experienced attack after attack, which they repulsed—nearly always with heavy losses on the Parthian side. On the fifth day of the march, however, disaster struck. Owing to the indiscipline of a certain Flavius Gallus, one of Antony's officers, the Parthians managed to isolate and cut down a large detachment of cav-alry and light-armed troops. This struggle soon drew in the legions and a catastrophic defeat loomed. Antony, however, managed to bring reinforcements, rescuing the bulk of his force but at the cost of 3,000 dead and nearly twice that number wounded. This rally, however, must have inflicted even greater damages on the enemy, because Antony's troops saw it as a great victory: they even hailed Antony *imperator*, according to Plutarch. This, however, must be a literary flourish: Antony 'paradoxically wins . . . acclamation through his magnificence in defeat', as an eminent critic has put it.[79] The triumvir's coins, by contrast, make it clear to us that he never commemorated a saluta-tion from this campaign.[80] He did, however, seize this occasion to deliver an inspiring speech to his men. Before doing so, he went so far as to take advice on the costume most suitable for winning their affection: he finally appeared in his general's cloak, but only after deliberating whether to come dressed in mourning.[81]

The remainder of the retreat was punctuated with furious, often desperate fighting. But the Romans continued to get the better of it: in all, the Romans defeated the Parthians in eighteen battles. Now, however, famine and thirst—and disease—became more dangerous to the Romans than Parthian attacks. Matters appeared so hopeless, Plutarch claims, that Antony braced himself for suicide, although that, too, is perhaps a literary flourish. After 27 days of hard, sanguinary slogging over nearly 500 km, the Romans at last reached the River Araxes and the security of Armenia. Because the Armenian king's loyalty was now suspect, Antony evinced nothing in the way of anger or even disapproval of his earlier withdrawal. Instead, he paid him every formal cour-tesy, and the king dutifully offered the Romans his assistance.

It was now the height of winter and during their march through Cappadocia on the way towards Syria the legions were buffeted by snowstorms.[82] Even more men, Plutarch says 8,000, perished on this march. Antony again looked to his men's welfare. He sent urgent couriers to Cleopatra demanding emergency supplies for the troops. He made similar demands on the cities, on Herod, and on other regional allies.[83] But our sources are more interested in Cleopatra. So, too, was Antony. Leaving the army in the care of Canidius and Domitius, he advanced to the Syrian coast where he awaited her arrival. She came promptly. When the legions arrived, in whatever cities they were quartered, they were amply furnished with fresh clothing and other provi-sions. Antony also paid the troops a generous donative in recognition of their valour. According to Dio, each legionnaire received 400 sesterces, the equivalent of nearly half a year's regular pay.

No Substitute for Victory?

Historians vary in their assessment of Antony's Parthian campaign. For some, 'it was a defeat, but not a rout or a disaster'.[84] Others, however, believe this episode so severely tarnished Antony's reputation that it constituted a turning point in his career.[85] Whatever it was, the expedition was not a success. Antony did not capture Phraaspa nor did he defeat Phraates in a decisive engagement. Either achievement would have furnished glory sufficient to sustain Antony's aura of invincibility and preserve his unquestioned Roman predominance. Critics have not failed to observe, correctly, how Antony underestimated the defences and resolve of the Median capital and misjudged the skill and pertinacity exhibited by the Parthians in protecting their kingdom from invaders. Still, fierce though they were, the Parthians could not drive the Romans away from Phraaspa. The siege failed owing to the Romans' loss of the equipment and supplies they carried in their baggage train, a disaster attributable to Antony's overconfidence and impatience. Nevertheless, even after these losses, the Romans inflicted multiple defeats on the Parthians, even if a decisive victory eluded. Unfriendly to Antony though our sources are, they report that, on their return march, the Romans bested the Parthians no fewer than eighteen times. But no retreat, however courageous, can be truly glorious.

In his correspondence with Rome, Antony could honestly rehearse his personal heroics and dilate on the punishment his army inflicted on the enemy: never before, he could correctly observe, had Romans marched into Parthian territories and performed so valiantly. These claims may not impress us. But we must ask how credible or persuasive they were from a Roman perspective. What was the likely Roman response—at least for men who were not already hostile to Antony? It might seem intuitive to us that, in a society so bellicose as Rome, defeat was indubitably disgraceful, indeed, intolerable. Certainly, it was no recommendation. Yet it is clear to us that the Roman view of commanders who suffered military setbacks was complicated by the very real influence of what was then a widely held 'myth of universal aristocratic competence', a popular predisposition that operated even more strongly in favour of the nobility.[86] An unambiguous loss on the battlefield did not obviously diminish the prestige of a noble who fought bravely. This was a judgement, our evidence makes clear, which Romans were all the more likely to reach when it was possible to point to failings on the part of insubordinates or the perfidy of allies, not least when these failings contrasted with a general's energy and valour. Furthermore, it was a Roman habit of mind to look at each defeat as a setback that was no more than a single step along their path towards ultimate victory.[87] Antony, the whole world knew, outstared the lightning after his reverse at Mutina. The world expected him to do so again.

The Roman view of Antony's campaign was not the only view. During the winter, he received an embassy from Artavasdes, the king of Media Atropatene, who now sought an alliance with Rome. Dio asserts that Artavasdes had fallen out with Phraates in a conflict over the distribution of spoil captured from the Romans.[88] That seems unlikely, since there cannot have been enough in the way of booty seized from the Romans to motivate any serious squabble. But it is not at all surprising that the Romans' invasion, and Phraates' inability to crush it, created tension between the king and his vassals—especially the vassal whose realm had been ravaged and was certain to be the target of Rome's next expedition. On the other side of this war, what Artavasdes saw of the Antony's army must have made a profound impression, so much so that he was willing to break with Phraates in order to become a Roman ally. His chief emissary was Antony's friend, King Polemo, whom Artavasdes now released in a gesture of goodwill.[89] Diplomacy now brought Media Atropatene over to Rome, and later, upon the final conclusion of their agreement, the Median restored the standards Antony had lost during the expedition. The king's friendship was durable: Artavasdes' daughter was later betrothed to Alexander Helios and the Median king fought for Antony at Actium.[90]

For Antony this overture was welcome indeed. He gained a valuable ally in the region, useful against Armenia and Parthia alike. He could also now legitimately claim that, through his expedition, he had overawed Armenia, subdued Iberia and Albania, and won Media Atropatene for Rome. Doubtless Antony portrayed the Median king as a suppliant, frightened of Roman arms, appalled by Parthian weakness and treachery, and beseeching the republic for its friendship. A great and wealthy kingdom, Antony could and certainly did declare, had been added to the empire. Suddenly the invasion of Parthia was not such a disappointment after all.

Rome awaited news of Antony's campaign. Winter will have delayed the arrival of his emissaries, but certainly by spring Octavian and the senate had received Antony's report. Dio describes it as an exercise in self-praise, and doubtless it was. Both Velleius and Florus complain that Antony deported himself as if he had been victorious.[91] But even Antony's enemies, however much it pained them, could not deny the significance of detaching Media Atropatene from Parthia and adding it to the dominion of Rome. Octavian certainly did not deny it. Indeed, he dutifully celebrated his brother-in-law's achievement with public thanksgivings and festivals. These festivities made a lasting impression, which were not entirely dispelled by Octavian's later propaganda campaign nor even by Augustus' later suppression of Antony's reputation.[92] Virgil, in his *Aeneid*, introduces Antony as 'conqueror of the peoples of the dawn'—*victor ab Aurorae populis*—an expression the later commentator Servius explains with the note, 'because he had previously conquered the Parthians', making it clear to us how the line was generally taken.[93] Still, the less attractive aspects of Antony's campaign also eventually became known in Rome, certainly to men in the political class, and some, even some without partisan inclinations, will have been disconcerted by them.[94] After all, the Roman disposition to trust in the martial valour of the nobility, however prevalent, was probably not a universal instinct. For most Romans, however, and so far as Italy knew, Antony's campaign, though costly, had been a success. Parthia had been punished. And would again be punished.

The human cost of this campaign had been great. Many had fallen to Parthian arms. Just as many to disease and complications from wounds. Even approximate casualty figures, however, are difficult to determine. The numbers in our sources are exaggerated and almost certainly derive from Dellius, whose attitude towards Antony was unfriendly. Nonetheless, at least two legions perished in the Parthians' initial attack and thousands more must have joined them before the Romans reached their winter quarters. As is regularly the case, auxiliary losses go unmentioned. These, too, were certainly severe. Probably a quarter of Antony's army, and perhaps as much as a third, was lost.[95] Antony, who was close to his men, felt these losses deeply. Nor, however triumphant his posture, could he ignore the implications of so major a setback in his campaign against Parthia. While his soldiers recuperated in their winter quarters, Antony joined Cleopatra and travelled with her to Alexandria.[96] There, once again, the disappointed triumvir took comfort in her company and counsel. They had much to talk about.

War against Sextus

In early September 36, Octavian and Lepidus, buoyed by the skilful admiralty of Agrippa, defeated Sextus Pompey, whose navy was crushed in the battle of Naulochus. Sextus fled to the east with what was left of his forces.[97] Octavian returned to Rome, where he celebrated an ovation for his victory and accepted fresh honours from the senate.[98] To the Roman people he proclaimed an end to civil war, an achievement he commemorated by erecting in the Forum an elevated statue of himself with an inscription Appian records as 'peace, long disturbed by civil strife, he restored on land and at sea'.[99] The triumvirate's conclusion was nigh, he insisted, because the menace of Sextus had been eliminated. Octavian then began—ostentatiously—to entrust the city's magistrates with greater responsibility and the authority to exercise it, a shift towards traditional constitutional government punctuated by a return to law-and-order in the Italian countryside and the remission of at least some of the triumvirate's emergency exactions.[100]

The story of the war against Sextus, however, was not so simple. Before Naulochus, Octavian's forces were subjected to more than one serious defeat. Throughout the campaign there was unrest in Rome, where Sextus enjoyed popularity, and in Italy, where Octavian did not.[101] Indeed, the triumvir's concentration of all Rome's resources on vanquishing Sextus only exacerbated miseries in the capital and the municipalities. It was vital, therefore, that the people of Rome be convinced it was all worth it: hence Octavian's very welcome proclamations of peace and an imminent return to customary government. In order to allay anxieties among the aristocracy, Octavian also made a show of destroying any and all correspondence recovered from Sextus' Sicily.[102] Like his brother-in-law, Octavian made it plain, he now embraced a policy of reconciliation suitable to an end of civil war. The public, though it welcomed an end to armed struggle, was not immediately won over, however many honours the triumvir extracted from the senate. Unrest persisted, even among the legions: Octavian was confronted with open mutiny, a challenge that can only have disconcerted a population hoping for a real end to civil war.[103] Indeed, the captious could observe that this civil war was not yet over: Octavian had allowed Sextus to escape.[104]

The Fall of Lepidus

That Octavian was perceived to be vulnerable is clear from Lepidus' attempt to challenge him. In the immediate aftermath of the victory over Sextus, Lepidus tried to seize control of Sicily. Octavian, in reaction to this unexpected aggression, managed, by combining personal boldness with shameless bribery, to win over his rival's legions.

Lepidus was subsequently stripped of his triumviral authority, but kept his property, his senatorial status, and his position as pontifex maximus. He was, however, confined, for the rest of his life, to the resort town of Circeii, on the Italian coast.[105]

Naturally there was no possibility of consulting Antony during this final crisis, and it was important to Octavian that Lepidus' demotion be rendered an irreversible fait accompli before his brother-in-law could react to it. Possibly, Octavian permitted Lepidus to resign his office.[106] Or he may have turned to the senate, which traditionally possessed the authority to annul a part of any existing legislation and could therefore rescind Lepidus' position without abolishing Antony's or Octavian's offices.[107] Triumphant after Sextus' defeat, Octavian was unlikely to confront serious senatorial resistance on Lepidus' behalf, and this ostensibly constitutional approach allowed him to implicate the whole of the order, including Antony's allies, in the final decision. Whether he abdicated or was deprived of his office by the senate, Lepidus' removal was executed by way of an official act that could not easily be reversed. As for his internal exile, that probably reflected an informal agreement between himself and Octavian. No contemporary outcry over Lepidus' fate is known to us. Nevertheless, the reality that resentment over Lepidus' overthrow persisted is evidenced by a conspiracy against Octavian, led by Lepidus' son and uncovered in 30 during the aftermath of Actium.[108]

Octavian, then, even after his success in Sicily, very much needed his brother-in-law's support. If Antony should take Lepidus' part, or forge a fresh alliance with Sextus, it was hardly obvious that, for all his senatorial honours, Octavian could manage to retain Italy's loyalty in the teeth of an eastern invasion. It is no surprise, then, even to the most cynical, that Octavian celebrated Antony's Parthian campaign so generously. Nor that, when making promises to restore the republic, he reminded Rome that the triumvirs could not resign before Antony had exacted vengeance from Parthia. If only for reasons of self-interest, concord and comity were clearly to the fore in Octavian's public attitude towards Antony. His communications with his colleague will have conveyed the same hopeful sentiments. Antony did not disappoint.

Altered States

Perhaps even before he settled into Alexandria, Antony began to receive letters and emissaries from Octavian. The two men had much to explain to one another, little of it straightforward, and each, for reasons of his own, was hopeful of the other's loyalty. Circumstances in Rome were much changed since Antony's march into Parthia, altered by events heavily freighted with political and military consequences for both triumvirs. Lepidus, Antony learned, had been stripped of his magistracy. This must have come as a shock. Nor was Sextus any longer master of Sicily. That cannot have been entirely unexpected, but Antony also learned the man was in the east, bringing with him a continuation of the civil war the conclusion of which Octavian was celebrating in Rome. Sextus was now Antony's problem, hardly a congenial development for a man determined to return to an eastern campaign. How Antony would react to Lepidus' fall or Sextus' extrusion from the west were matters of serious concern in

Rome, not least for Antony's brother-in-law. Even before spring, embassies and correspondence between the two triumvirs crossed frequently. So, too, communications between Antony and his friends in Rome.[109]

Antony and Lepidus

Antony did not demur to his brother-in-law's discarding of Lepidus, although he owed the man so much, perhaps because, since Philippi, Lepidus had become almost embarrassingly dispensable. Later, when vituperating Octavian's character, Antony animadverted on his treachery in corrupting Lepidus' soldiers.[110] In the spring of 35, however, Antony was compliant. Indeed, he may have made his position clear by way of a very public divorce. In 44, Antony's eldest child, his daughter by Antonia, was betrothed to Lepidus' son. In 38 Antony was busily making preparations to give her away.[111] There is no reason to doubt he soon did so. In 30, however, this young Lepidus was discovered plotting against Octavian. The man was summarily executed and his wife, admired for her loyalty to her husband, committed suicide.[112] This woman was a Servilia. Now it is possible that Servilia's way to marrying Lepidus was cleared by Antonia's death. If that was not the case, Antonia and Lepidus must have divorced. The disgrace of Lepidus senior was an appropriate moment for Antony to divide the couple, thereby signalling his family's support of Octavian's actions.

What became of Antony's daughter after this divorce? The prevailing view is that she married Pythodorus of Tralles, a fabulously rich statesman. An inscription from Smyrna records, in a singular manner, an Antonia Euergetes who is identified as the mother of Pythodoris Philomater, the queen of Antony's favourite Polemo, king of Pontus. Since Pythodorus of Tralles was Pythodris' father and Polemo's father-in-law, it is often concluded that Antonia Euergetes is Antony's daughter, Antonia. This identification is, at best, circumstantial. On the inscription, Pythodorus goes unremarked and instead it is Antonia who receives pride of place, a striking feature. This oddity has been explained by proposing that Antonia Eueregetes is foregrounded at the expense of her husband because she is the triumvir's daughter. In other words, after her divorce, she was married off to the very rich and Roman-friendly Pythodorus by her philhellenic and acquisitive father.[113]

But there are good reasons for doubting this. A marriage between the daughter of a triumvir and a provincial subject can only have been explosively controversial, however expansive the man's wealth. And in view of Octavian's later complaints that, in the east, Antony was corrupted by his going native, it is astonishing we hear nothing of Antonia's marriage. It probably never took place. In view of what has been described as 'the pullulation of Antonii among the Greek citizenry of the East', the odds are actually against any identification of Antonia Euergetes with the daughter of Antony.[114] Moreover, our evidence (mostly epigraphic) for Polemo's descendants, on the basis of its most recent analysis, is also against it.[115] Better, then, to abandon the idea. Antonia, we can be confident, married Lepidus' son. If she was alive when Lepidus fell from power, the two were divorced, a signal that Antony repudiated his longstanding ally. Thereafter she vanishes from history.

Antony and Sextus

During the winter, Sextus established himself in Mytilene. He came in the hope of reactivating, at least in some quarters, the old fealty to his father, a vestigial loyalty that perhaps proved sufficient for adding something to his resources in men and money. By spring he managed to raise three legions, hardly a mighty host but an army dangerous enough to threaten cities or villages and lean enough to be reasonably mobile when deployed in Asia. Negotiations with Antony, a plea for an alliance, were commenced. True, after Tarentum, Antony was committed to the view that Sextus was a public enemy. But Antony, Sextus knew all too well, had changed his mind in the past. This time he did not. Instead, he mobilized a fleet, which he placed under the command of Marcus Titius. Titius was a nephew of Plancus and a battle-tested officer who had served as Antony's quaestor during the Parthian campaign. And he had a prior relationship with Sextus: during the proscriptions, Sextus had rescued Titius' father; he had also, at a later time, spared the life of Titius himself. Titius now acted as chief of Antony's operations against Sextus, and his selection suggests that, in the beginning, Antony perhaps sought Sextus' honourable but unconditional surrender. Once acquired, the man could then be shipped back to Octavian. But Antony was taking no chances: he also activated Gaius Furnius, the governor of Asia, and Domitius Ahenobarbus, installed once again in Bithynia. King Amyntas, too, was summoned.[116]

Sextus was disinclined to capitulate. He distrusted Titius and refused to deal with him. Antony had miscalculated there. Sextus, ever energetic, endeavoured to win support by suborning officers on Antony's side—he succeeded in the case of Curius, a legate of Domitius—and he managed to take control of the city of Lampsacus, where he recruited cavalry and added veteran colonists to the ranks of his legions. Furnius he defeated in more than one engagement, and he kept the loyalty of his soldiers through pillaging. But Titius' fleet soon forced Sextus to abandon the coast. Consequently, he made for Parthia, where, like Labienus before him, he hoped to be welcomed: Phraates, anticipating another Roman invasion, needed reinforcements. Antony's forces, however, soon boxed him in, and he was forsaken even by his closest allies, including Libo, his father-in-law. At Midaeum, Sextus was finally captured. His legions were joined to Antony's.

What happened next is not entirely clear. Sextus was taken to Miletus and there was put to death, possibly on the order of Titius, who supervised the execution. Or, possibly, on the order of Plancus, or even Antony. A melodramatic fiction furnished readers a dithering triumvir who sent instructions ordering Sextus' execution, then thought better of it and dispatched a pardon—only for his letters to arrive at their destination in the wrong sequence.[117] Sextus' death, as we have seen, later became an issue during the propaganda war between Antony and Octavian.[118] Hence, in our sources, so much finger pointing. At the time, however, Sextus was a public enemy whose violence in Asia fully justified, by Roman standards, his elimination. There can be no doubt that, after Sextus initially refused to surrender, Antony had decided to put him to death. It was not a bold decision. Sextus was not unpopular in Rome, as we have seen, but with that constituency, if he concerned himself with it at all, Antony enjoyed the cover provided by the conduct of Libo and the rest of Sextus' inner circle, who freely entrusted themselves to the triumvir. Although it was necessary, even prudent, to spare Lepidus, Sextus was simply too dangerous—on practical and symbolic grounds—to let live. With his death the triumvirs' civil war at last came to its end. Caesar, by every possible measure, was avenged.

Antony's suppression of Sextus Pompey was duly honoured in Rome. In celebration of Antony's achievement, Caesar's heir held elaborate games in the circus. A chariot, set up in front of the Rostra, was dedicated to Antony, and, with obvious symbolic significance, his statue was placed in the temple of Concord. The senate also, as a lasting commemoration of the triumvir's achievement, granted Antony and Octavia and their children the right to hold annual banquets in that temple on the anniversary of Antony's victory.[119] In the restoration of peace by land and by sea, Octavian was determined to share its glory with his brother-in-law.

The fall of Lepidus and the flight of Sextus were each of them events which easily might have ruptured the affinity between Antony and Octavian, turning them into open enemies. That did not happen because each remained true to the friendship established between them at Brundisium, even after it was put to the test at Tarentum. The quality of their partnership, during the opening months of 35, was obvious to all. Octavian celebrated Antony's eastern campaign and his victory over Sextus. Antony, for his part, accepted Lepidus' demotion and refused Sextus' advances. Nor did Antony fail to furnish proof of his devotion to their common cause.[120] When, early in the year, Octavian began planning a campaign against hostile tribes in Illyricum, Antony promised his full cooperation, even going so far as to offer a contribution from his own forces.[121] This was a gesture of solidarity, he knew, Octavian was unlikely to accept. But that was hardly the point. The triumvirs' continued comity, despite their natural distaste for one another and even amid the potential crises thrown up by Lepidus and Sextus, augured well for the republic, something recognizable to everyone. The Roman people, at last, had good reasons to be hopeful. And yet this was the end of it: these were the final acts of cooperation between Antony and Octavian.

The End of Comity

What happened? What changed? In our ancient sources it is simply take it for granted that open conflict between Antony and Octavian was unavoidable. Not without reason: the two men disliked one another intensely, and their relationship, from its inception, was characterized by a rivalry that was often very bitter. At Mutina they fought on opposite sides, and it was only owing to opportunism or compulsion that they formed alliances and an affinity. The battle of Actium, from that perspective alone, could hardly come as a surprise. As for the catalyst which ignited the violence, ancient writers inevitably point to Antony's corruption by Cleopatra. Nor do they ignore Octavian's ambition. Modern historians have largely shared this approach.

And yet, from the establishment of the triumvirate, it is remarkable how earnestly Octavian and Antony endeavoured to sustain their uneasy, transactional, highly formal friendship. Even during the Perusine war, Octavian strained himself in avoiding any permanent rupture with Antony, and after the pact of Brundisium Antony remained conspicuously loyal to his brother-in-law, even when provoked, as he was at

Tarentum. Self-interest played an unmistakable part in all their calculations, naturally, but it is far from obvious that from the start either man was absolutely determined to replace Julius Caesar as undisputed master of Rome. Both Antony and Octavian sought to be a dominating figure in the new republic, whatever form it took—that much is patent—but it is unsafe to assume either had clear, firm designs, or that their plans, whatever they were, required the other's destruction.

'No war', as A.J.P. Taylor famously put it, 'is inevitable until it breaks out'.[122] Precarity pervaded all dealings between Antony and Octavian, and yet, again and again, their arrangements held. The events of early 35 had, once again, exhibited the two men's determination to sustain their friendship in circumstances under which everything could easily have fallen apart. And yet, by the end of this year, it is clear, Antony's attitude towards Octavian and Octavian's sister changed markedly. Octavian, too, began to appear hostile. Because our sources insist it was bound to happen, they exhibit little interest in trying to explain this untowards development—apart, of course, from observing, again and again, the baleful influence of Cleopatra.

Antony in 35

Antony's physical movements in 35, even during the campaign against Sextus Pompey, are anything but clear to us. As for Cleopatra, we can be sure that she remained in Egypt.[123] According to Dio, when Antony left Alexandria, he began a march towards Armenia: he pretended he was undertaking a fresh invasion of Parthia, but in reality intended to capture the Armenian king; indeed, he tried more than once to get his clutches on the man through deceit. He was interrupted, however, by the advent of Octavia, who travelled east to meet him. Plutarch's Antony is not on the march but is looking forward to invading Armenia and then renewing the war against Parthia. He, too, is interrupted by Octavia's visit. Appian, by contrast, concentrates at considerable length on Antony's negotiations with Sextus and the coordinated exertions of his officers in capturing him. His Antony could be nearly anywhere: after Sextus' death, Appian observes tersely, Antony invaded Armenia, but there he does not refer specifically to actions taking place in 35: at that point, Appian is condensing his narrative as he wraps up what for us is the final book of his *Civil War*.[124] Plutarch and Dio are each of them concise because each is keen to rush through the events of this year: they are far more interested in the next one, when Antony captures Armenia and, returning to Alexandria, celebrates his victory with grand, controversial pageantry.

Antony did not invade Armenia in 35. Very likely, he had no plans to do so. During this year, as we shall see below, Octavia came to the east to see her husband and spend the coming winter with him in Athens. She did not expect Antony to depart on an invasion of Armenia at this time. Dio's Antony, true, is a general on the march, but Dio's opening description of Antony's actions in this year is something of a doublet with his introduction to the triumvir's operations in the *next* one and is very likely an instance of chronological displacement, a common enough feature in Dio's narratives.[125] In 35, we may believe, Antony was busy making ready not simply for an attack on Armenia but rather a second invasion of Parthia, as Plutarch reports: for this expedition he now had a valuable ally in Atravasdes, the king of Media Atropatene, a development which, however welcome, could only complicate the logistics of his expedition.

But there was no reason to rush. Antony was now fully seized of the hazards of being too hasty, and an undertaking on this order demanded ample preparations. In the spring of 35 he was not yet ready. He had Sextus to squelch, a problem he could not leave unresolved when he marched east for more than one year. Nor was Sextus his only worry. In Judea, Herod plotted against his kinsmen, who, in reaction, turned to Cleopatra, whose hatred of Herod and intimacy with Antony they hoped to deploy for their protection. Josephus' account of this clash is melodramatic, shocking, and, at times, goatish.[126] Nonetheless, the episode reveals a real risk of instability in this always volatile kingdom. And Josephus makes it clear how, in scheming against his rivals, Herod was prepared to go so far as to make diplomatic contacts with Phraates, not a disloyal act, one can be certain, but bold enough to demand Roman attention. These Judean perturbations rendered Herod vulnerable to Cleopatra's complaints against him. Antony duly summoned the king to join him in Laodicea, where he was obliged to explain himself. In the end, he did so successfully. In this matter, and against Cleopatra's interests, Antony took the king's part. Defeating Sextus and managing tensions between client kingdoms came on top of the business of touring his provinces, inspecting his troops, and securing their provisions. Keen Antony doubtless was to renew his war against Parthia, but, before any expedition could commence, there was much to occupy his energies.

Octavia

More important than Sextus, Herod, Armenia, or Parthia—at least so far as Plutarch and Dio are concerned—was Octavia.[127] Early in the year, perhaps when he was still in Alexandria, Antony learned that Octavia was travelling to Athens. She brought valuable presents with her, some of them furnished by her brother, including money, clothing for Antony's troops, pack animals for his expedition, gifts for his officers, cavalry, and a select corps of 2,000 men to serve as his praetorian guard. She may have arrived in Athens before spring, and she almost certainly expected to remain through the winter.[128] There she was met by letters from her husband. In them he explained in detail the plans for his forthcoming expedition. He also instructed her to remain where she was, sensible advice in view of the danger posed by Sextus. As for her gifts, Antony accepted them and called for the cavalry, if not also the praetorians, to join him immediately.

A number of ancient writers regarded Octavia's visit with suspicion, as if it laid a kind of trap for Antony: according to Plutarch, it was the opinion of many—'most people say' is how he puts it—that Octavian allowed his sister to visit the east only because he hoped thereby to contrive a pretext for war should Antony somehow neglect or insult her. Plutarch, and the writers he relies on, apparently believed that Octavian expected Antony to humiliate his sister by making clear his preference for Cleopatra, an action which would justify a break in their relationship.[129] For modern historians, it is Octavia's presents for Antony that attract attention. Much is made over Octavian's unfulfilled promise, made at Tarentum, to furnish his colleague with

20,000 legionaries. In the aftermath of Naulochus, Antony received what was left of his fleet but not the legions he was owed. Instead, he was offered cavalry and a praetorian guard. The standard verdict on Octavia's gifts declares them a trap for Antony: should he accept these gifts, he thereby submitted to Octavian's violation of their agreement, but if he refused them, he insulted his wife and his brother-in-law. In short, he was confronted with a cunning and debilitating dilemma.[130]

That Octavia should wish to visit her husband during this interval between Parthian campaigns could hardly be deemed provocative. After the Lepidus affair and amid the ongoing struggle with Sextus, Octavian may have wanted to be sure of his brother-in-law's loyalty. Politics aside, Octavia may also have missed Antony's company. Admittedly there must have been a certain awkwardness when Antony's wife and his mistress were even remotely proximate, but Antony was experienced in this sort of thing, as was Cleopatra, and Octavia was no naïf. Relations between Octavia and Antony, it has been suggested in an earlier chapter, were strained when they separated in 37. Since that time, however, we can be sure communications remained regular, whatever the register in which they were conveyed. Antony needed to know about domestic affairs, and during his absence Octavia played an active role in looking after Antony's business and political affairs, tending on her husband's behalf to the needs of his friends and dependents.[131] For his part, Antony was obliged to answer with something more than mere stimulus-response missives: Roman society, as Antony knew, expected a wife to remain au fait with the views of her husband. Their marriage, each of them was aware, was important still to the health of the republic, and Octavia's journey to Athens furnished an opportunity for them to signal to the world, and possibly convey to one another, that harmony prevailed.

Let us turn now to Octavia's gifts. It is true that Octavian's undelivered legions became an element of later Antonian invective. But that is not a reason for concluding that at this time Antony was resentful of Octavian's tardiness in furnishing them. He was aware how Octavian was confronted by mutiny and urgent demands from veterans, all at a time when he was assembling soldiers for his campaign in Illyricum. Antony in fact offered Octavian military assistance, not the act of a man desperate for legions or angry with his brother-in-law. Octavia brought clothing, pack animals, and other supplies—at what scale we do not know—and these provisions were doubtless welcome as Antony continued in making arrangements for an eastern campaign. So, too, the cavalry provided by Octavian. As for Octavian's gift of a praetorian guard, that was clearly a gesture of respect. Antony accepted everything at once. Doing so, and doing so graciously, did nothing to absolve Octavian of his debt of the legions. That, however, was a payment that could wait. Nothing about Octavia's gifts set Antony on the horns of a political dilemma.

It is clear, then, what ought to have happened. Antony, after vanquishing Sextus and relishing the honour he was paid in Rome for doing so, and after completing his preparations for renewing the campaign against Parthia, ought to have wintered in Athens with his wife, thereby assuring himself of Octavian's loyalty and conveying to the wider world, especially the world of Roman politics, that triumviral comity subsisted. Thereafter he could march east, fulfilling, by avenging Crassus, the final condition of the republic's restoration. Then it would be time to settle Antony's and Octavian's place in Rome's new dispensation. None of this meant Antony could never again cheat with Cleopatra or enjoy the company of his Ptolemaic children. But they would have to wait. Duty demanded that he defer these pleasures.

The Winter of 35

But that is not what took place. Antony did not join his wife in Athens. Instead, he spent the winter with Cleopatra in Alexandria. In this turn of events, Plutarch makes much of Cleopatra's agency. In his account, Antony dutifully instructs Octavia to await him in Athens, a notice to which the queen reacts with desperate, pathetic performances designed to stimulate Antony's sympathy as much as his desire. Her courtiers, too, play strongly on Antony's emotions. In the end, he succumbs, a surrender that is all the more humiliating for Octavia.[132] That, however, is Plutarchan artistry. It is more likely that, as Dio reports, Antony, before winter set in, ordered his wife to return to Rome.[133] This decision certainly came late in the year, after Antony had accepted Octavia's gifts, defeated Sextus, and been honoured in Rome by Octavian and the senate.[134]

Antony's snub was unexpected and unwelcome, both to Octavia and her brother. When she returned to the capital, her brother urged her to divorce. Octavian, to be sure, had in the past failed to grasp completely the political subtleties of aristocratic divorce, but by now he could hardly fail to understand that an end to Octavia's marriage to Antony must result in renewed animosities between himself and his colleague. At the same time, he was, as we have seen, not yet prepared for a real conflict, the overly cynical calculations of Plutarch's 'most writers' notwithstanding. His advice to Octavia, then, is proof something had gone very wrong. Perhaps he viewed Antony's behaviour towards Octavia as a prelude to divorce and was therefore determined to try somehow to turn what he perceived as Antony's aggression to some advantage. When Octavia refused to divorce her husband—apparently her feelings for him survived even this humiliation—Octavian soon began offering up his sister's fidelity and dutifulness as evidence of Antony's depravity.[135] This did not remain Octavian's only reproach, nor was Antony unwilling to respond with complaints and calumnies of his own. In the next year, recriminations and outright vituperation between the triumvirs became increasingly intensive as relations between the two men eroded ever further.

Octavian fulminated over his sister's ill treatment. About Antony our sources have little to say apart from melodramatic reproofs of his passion for Cleopatra. We nonetheless possess clear traces of a fundamental change on Antony's part in his political policy. The evidence lies in his coinage. After 35, Antony no longer minted coins depicting Octavia—or Octavian. Their place, notably, was taken by Cleopatra, a replacement begun perhaps by the end of 35 and certainly by 34—and lasting until Actium.[136] This was a grave, consequential development. The appearance of a foreign monarch on a Roman coin, even provincial coins minted for regional consumption, could hardly go unnoticed, or fail to be scrutinized. The Egyptian queen, because she shared a Roman coin with a Roman triumvir, was unmistakably elevated above any eastern rival, thus marking a new phase in Antony's organization of the east. On these coins, Cleopatra's regal status is conspicuous: she sports a diadem and is often explicitly identified as queen and even a goddess. At the same time, the same coins convey Roman authority, even when Antony is not identified as triumvir. We find, for instance, no certain jugate portraits of the kind we saw for Octavian and Antony, which might in the case of Cleopatra signal something in the way of Ptolemaic dynastic pretensions. Instead, Antony and Cleopatra appear on opposite sides of the same coin, by now a familiar Roman convention. And Cleopatra's portrait, when she shares a coin with Antony, is altered. On her own currency, when she appears without Antony, she is youthful and idealized, an image natural to Hellenistic regal representations. On Antony's coins, by contrast, Cleopatra is mature and distinctly less idealized, conforming to Roman canons of representation. Cleopatra, for all that she remains a queen, is thus Romanized and is therefore pro-Roman.[137] The hybridity characterizing these coins is arresting even now, and it was no less striking at the time of their minting.[138] The depiction of Antony and Cleopatra in these coins, in an apt formulation, 'does not indicate a joint reign . . . but a jointness of reign'.[139] Nonetheless, issuing these coins was a provocative action. They were a symptom of a profound transformation in Antony's relationship with Rome's client kings in the east. More importantly, they expressed an altered relationship with his wife and brother-in-law in the capital. It was by no means unreasonable for Romans to wonder what it meant for the future of the republic and Antony's place in it.

Antony's coins we can see for ourselves. It is only by report, none of it dispassionate, that we learn of paintings and statue groups exhibiting Antony and Cleopatra together and in sacred guise, Antony as the Egyptian god Osiris or as Dionysus, Cleopatra taking the part of the Egyptian Isis or Selene, goddess of the moon.[140] These notices tend to be delivered amid later reproaches, abuse in some instances perhaps derived from Valerius Messala's polemical pamphlet, *On Antony's Statues*.[141] According to Dio, portraits of this kind were numerous and ultimately included statues installed on Athens' acropolis.[142] There is no obvious reason to doubt the existence of artwork like this, or its increasing presence outside Egypt, and its production very likely commenced in 34. During that year, statues of Antony certainly began to appear in Alexandria. By the time the city fell to Octavian, they were present in some quantity.[143]

We lack a narrative into which to fit this evidence, nor, apart from anti-Antonian defamation, has any kind of explanation been preserved for what is distinctly a new approach for Antony's government of the east. Whatever his reasons or justifications, which he must have had and must have promulgated among his supporters, they are lost to us. This change, consequently, puzzles. Just as Octavian had nothing to gain by alienating Antony at this point, nor did any obvious advantage for Antony lie in disturbing Roman sensibilities by elevating Cleopatra beyond any reasonable the horizon of expectations. Our sources see Octavia's journey to Athens as a turning point, but by way of interpretation they have nothing to offer but a reductive, retrospective view of Octavian's ambition and sustained denunciations of Antony's seduction by Cleopatra. It is nevertheless obvious that *something* changed at this time. Antony's coins and his appearances in artwork are proof of that. His relationship with Cleopatra was now exhibited to the world in a new and extraordinary way. It is little wonder that his contemporaries struggled to understand the transformation.

Love, Actually

In Octavian's propaganda, and hence Augustan ideology, Cleopatra became the ultimate threat to Rome—*fatale monstrum*, the apocalyptic abomination.[144] A woman and an Egyptian, paired slurs appealing to Roman sexism and nationalism, Cleopatra was condemned for seeking to seize possession of the Capitoline and scheming to relocate the centre of Mediterranean power to Alexandria.[145] A very present danger, this version of Cleopatra is mighty but her might relies on her sexual mastery of Mark Antony, 'her dupe and her agent'.[146] Octavia was her constant rival.[147] But she was no match for the Egyptian: Cleopatra, Roman polemic lamented, seduced Antony, whose lubriciousness Octavian had little need to exaggerate, by way of voluptuousness and a courtesan's deceitful tricks.[148] She also applied magic and philtres, rendering the man mad.[149] He neglected his duties to pore over her love letters.[150] At a public banquet, he dropped to his knees to wash and anoint her feet.[151] He addressed Cleopatra as queen—and master.[152] He became her love-slave.

Nobody now believes any of this. It is too patently over the top, a conclusion one would certainly reach even if unfamiliar with the tropes and techniques of Roman vituperation: 'the enslaved sensualist belongs to popular and edifying literature'.[153] Antony's protection of Herod against Cleopatra's designs, in this very year, demonstrates the triumvir's independence. But we need not resile from Octavian's defamation of Antony so violently that we conclude the man lacked a deep affection for Cleopatra. True, at Tarsus he was by no means ravished. Although he caroused with the queen in Alexandria, and left her pregnant, it is clear that she enjoyed no real claim on his affections. Nor did he wed Cleopatra at Antioch, despite his amplification of her domains. Before 35, nothing in Antony's political and sexual relationship with Cleopatra suggests anything but Antonian opportunism, in every sense of the word. By the time he reached this year, however, Antony had spent two consecutive winters with Cleopatra. Each time, and especially after his retreat from the Parthian campaign, Antony was a man suffering from serious disappointment. A pattern had begun to emerge: Cleopatra was his solace and diversion, and a trusted advisor.

As another winter drew closer, the opulence and glamour of Alexandria attracted Antony. So, too, the versatile, electric, and deeply intelligent personality of its queen. We are right in ignoring our sources' stories of lurid or romantic enamoration. But there is no good reason to doubt that Antony had feelings or that by 35 his feelings for Cleopatra were deep ones. Indeed, his actions are very difficult to explain otherwise. This is not to say that he was uninterested in remaining Octavia's husband. He was too astute a politician, and too much a Roman noble, to fail to recognize the importance of their marriage. He simply had no wish to spend this winter with his wife, a decision he may have expected Octavia to tolerate. And, in a sense, Octavia did tolerate it. Her brother, however, could not bear it. And he made his position clear to everyone when he urged Octavia to divorce Antony.

Did Antony anticipate this? Was his treatment of Octavia an early move signalling his claim to be the dominant figure in the new version of the triumvirate? That cannot be discounted. Or was it something simpler and more personal, out of which later spilled, for the remainder of his tenure in the east, a new policy regarding Cleopatra, reflected in his coinage and art? In either case, Octavia's dismissal from the east was an

Fig. 12.1 A denarius, the obverse of which exhibits Antony in front of an Armenian tiara with the legend ANTONI ARMENIA DEVICTA (Antony—Armenia conquered); on the reverse is Cleopatra with the legend CLEOPATRAE REGINAE REGUM FILIORUM REGUM (Cleopatra, queen of kings and of kings who are her sons).
Source: Wikimedia Commons.

event which could only instil uncertainty and anxiety in Roman politics. If its origin lay in urges that were distinctly personal, it represents selfishness on Antony's part and, in a Roman stateman, a grave failing.

War with Armenia

On the first day of 34, Antony assumed his second consulship, with what ceremony we do not know. He immediately abdicated in favour of Lucius Sempronius Atratinus, a loyal officer who had been seconded to Octavian during the naval campaign against Sextus and was now in Rome.[154] Antony's honour was not an empty one: it marked his importance in capital affairs. There his friends and supporters could fill his absence with reminders that Antony was again waging war on Rome's behalf against Parthia and its allies, campaigns that in the public's imagination contrasted favourably with any expedition against Illyrian tribesmen. Everyone in Rome was soon aware that Antony was again marching east. His destination was Armenia, the first phase of a renewed war against Parthia.

It was a major expedition, involving at least sixteen legions and undertaken in close cooperation with Polemo and the Median king Atravasdes.[155] Antony's Armenian war later became a focus of fierce Octavian defamation, polemic so successful that it suffuses and distorts all our sources. The central charge complains of Antony's unmanly treachery, what Tacitus dubs 'Antony's villainy'. Unwilling to face the Armenian king in honest combat, so we are told, Antony, more than once, endeavoured to lure him outside his defences by making a pretence of friendship. In the end, and again by way of this deceit, he ensnared his man. Only later, owing to the valour of the king's subjects, was Antony obliged to fight for control of the country. The likely source of these tales is, once again, Dellius. Antony put him to work as his ambassador to Armenia and it was doubtless he who later claimed Antony sent him with a dishonest proposal of an alliance, the marriage of his son, Alexander, to Atravasdes' daughter.[156] That Antony dispatched Dellius to Armenia we can believe. But his mission was not to bamboozle the king but rather to demand his capitulation.

Antony's attack on Armenia was something a blitzkrieg. By the start of spring, his army had reached Nicopolis in Lesser Armenia. Again, he demanded the king's surrender, but without waiting for his answer Antony advanced rapidly towards Artaxata, the Armenian capital. We are not told about the operations of the Median king, but presumably he, like Polemo, took part in this campaign. The Armenian king's position was hopeless. His advisors urged him to come to terms, which Artavasdes endeavoured to do by offering Antony a tribute so massive it incited his nobles to open rebellion. They chose a new king, Atravasdes' son Artaxes, who rallied the army against Rome. But he was quickly defeated and fled, making his way to Phraates. Antony now firmly imposed Roman control over the whole of the kingdom, parts of which he handed over to his soldiers for plunder. Artavasdes he made his prisoner, elegantly binding him in silver chains. Antony's soldiers hailed him *imperator*.[157]

Antony's arrangements for Armenia could not be implemented instantly and were not finalized until the next year, when he returned to the region for a conference with Artavasdes of Media Atropatene and Polemo. Lesser Armenia he added to Polemo's realm. A slab of Armenia was awarded to Atravasdes. Antony's young son, Alexander, who was no more than six, was named king of Armenia. Atravasdes' daughter, Iotape, also a child, was betrothed to Alexander and destined to become his queen. It was also decided that, while awaiting her ascension, she would live in the palace at Alexandria, a hostage to Atravasdes' continued good intentions. Until Alexander was capable of governing in his own right, the administration of Armenia would remain with Antony: no thought was given to making the kingdom into a Roman province.[158] In order to enforce these extensive changes, unwelcome to the Armenians, Antony installed sixteen legions, some of whom he deployed in Media Atropatene in case Parthia should attempt to restore Artaxes to his kingdom.[159]

Some of these decisions Antony may have made only after seizing control of Armenia. That he invaded in order to exact vengeance is hardly to be doubted. It is also clear that, in punishing Atravasdes, he planned to deprive him of territories and exact a very steep fine. Whether it was a part of his design to depose him is a different matter, and it cannot be excluded that Atravasdes' fall owed itself as much to the actions of the Armenian nobility and his son, Atraxes, as it did to Antony's conquest. Once Antony recognized that Artavasdes had lost the support of his nobility, however, there was no reason to keep him on the throne. Instead of replacing him with another of his sons, Tigranes or Atravasdes, who were also now Rome's prisoners, Antony decided to make the kingdom into something very much like his personal property by handing it over to his Ptolemaic child.[160] This was an extraordinary development. It was also very unpopular in Armenia, so much so that Armenian hostility towards Rome on account of Antony's occupation lasted for many years.[161] It was owing to the Armenians' palpable resistance to their new circumstances and the threat of Parthian intervention that Antony left behind so large an army: they were needed to enforce the terms of the kingdom's new dispensation. Armenia's complete pacification was a prerequisite to Antony's invasion of Parthia.

From Armenia Antony extracted an enormous quantity of plunder. Financial urgency was not his motive. Antony was already a very wealthy man, almost certainly, at this point, the wealthiest man in the Roman world. Pompey the Great, during the Third Mithridatic War, by way of booty and the acquisition of properties, but especially through investments—lending on his own account and cooperating closely with Rome's *publicani*—had excelled his contemporaries in riches.[162] As master of the east, Antony employed the same methods as Pompey but on a grander scale. Nor was he unwilling to enrich others, both his officers in the east and interested parties in Rome. As we have seen, for Rome's financiers Antony's preference for client kingdoms was an attractive feature of his administration. Wealthy Armenia, under Roman occupation, presented another highly profitable opportunity, and we can be sure this was the message sent abroad by Antony to his friends among Rome's business classes.

This is not the kind of activity ancient writers find interesting. Nonetheless, we can be sure that Roman investors seized this new opportunity. For their presence in the kingdom we have an oblique, and very grim, report. In 32, when Antony was mustering his forces for the conflict at Actium, he withdrew his troops from Armenia and Media Atropatene. Soon afterwards, Atraxes, with Parthian support, regained his kingdom. One of his first measures was the execution of the Romans who remained in Armenia. These men, it has long been suggested, were Roman traders and financiers, figures whose exploitation of Armenia rendered their eradication a very popular action for the new king to take.[163] These Romans were there to reap profits, and it was Antony who had made that possible. In 34 and 33, investing in Roman-controlled Armenia was very appealing, and Antony expected this boondoggle to keep him in the good books of his wealthy Roman associates. By opening up Armenia to Roman investment, Antony reminded Italy, should Italy need reminding in the rising din of Octavian's propaganda, of his basic soundness: he remained a valuable proponent of Rome's real interests in the east. Indeed, he had now expanded them.

This goodwill was important to Antony, not least because, as Antony was aware, Octavian's attitude towards his brother-in-law was growing increasingly inimical. In Rome, Octavian elevated the status of Livia and Octavia through grants of legal autonomy (freedom from the institution of *tutela*, or formal legal guardianship, a condition of all Roman women apart from Vestal Virgins) and *sacrosanctitas*. He also erected statues in their honour.[164] These were extraordinary privileges. On the surface, because Octavian awarded them both to his wife and the wife of his colleague, they were politically unexceptionable. But they came in an environment in which Octavian was drawing unfavourable attention to the contrast between Octavia's loyalty to her husband and Antony's callousness in cavorting with Cleopatra.[165]

Antony was not so concerned by Octavian's complaints that he intended to forego his expedition against Parthia. At the same time, he was not so ingenuous as to make no preparations whatsoever. He knew Octavian's character and therefore could not ignore the possibility that Octavian might amplify his current hostility into outright belligerence. It was for this reason that he extruded so much wealth from Armenia. His native acquisitiveness aside, Antony was accumulating a war-chest.

The Donations of Alexandria

When Antony elected to spend the winter of 35 with Cleopatra instead of Octavia, it marked an unmistakable divagation from the script everyone expected the triumvir to follow. Indeed, he had previously distinguished Athens as an important seat of his government by settling there with his wife, and filled the east with evidence of his divine, almost regal partnership with Octavia. Antony's refusal to join her in Athens was nothing short of notable, even if its motivations were largely personal. We are not told how Antony and Cleopatra spent their time in Alexandria. Much of it, presumably, was lavished on the routine pastimes of the court, such as feasting and drinking. Much, too, on the inescapable burdens of administration. Central to their deliberations, however, was the campaign against Armenia. Antony had little doubt he would prevail. Canidius, after all, had overawed the country with an army of only four legions. Antony took at least sixteen and deployed the auxiliary forces of Polemo and the Median king. What should come in the aftermath of victory, however, required extensive planning.

The subjugation and despoilation of Armenia were Antony's immediate objectives, achievements he and Cleopatra were determined to celebrate in Alexandria by way of majestic, Ptolemaic ceremonies. Pageantry on such a scale required enormous expense, meticulous organization, and ample time for recruiting an international audience. Antony's so-called Alexandrian triumph and the Donations of Alexandria were not reactive or spur-of-the-moment events. They were the culmination of a grand design that displayed Antony's predomination in the east and Cleopatra's preeminent place within Rome's eastern dominions. Juxtaposed, however, with Antony's snub of Octavia, these same exhibitions were susceptible of more than one interpretation by Octavian and by Antony's enemies in Rome. This was a hazard that provoked no disquiet in the east.

Antony entered Alexandria in great pomp.[166] A lavish, celebratory parade commemorated his return to the city, pageantry predictably dispraised in later Octavian propaganda as a disrespectful travesty of a Roman triumph. Octavian's calumny pervades our sources, and for this reason we cannot be confident in the particulars they furnish. Still, we can believe Antony appeared riding a chariot and resplendent in his guise as New Dionysus, conqueror of the east. As proof of his victory, he exhibited captives, Artavasdes and his family, and plunder in abundance. He was greeted by Cleopatra. She accepted the royal prisoners, who were subsequently confined to the palace.[167] Sacrifices and banquets followed, and doubtless there were also games, as was the habit at Hellenistic festivities of this kind. This occasion will have attracted, indeed required, ambassadors from the Greek cities and Rome's subject principalities. That, after all, was the point: to display by way of Alexandrian splendour, and the striking procession of Rome's victorious legions, the sheer power of the triumvir.[168]

Antony was not the first Roman victor who staged a celebration of his success while abroad. In the aftermath of the Third Macedonian War, Lucius Aemilius Paullus won fame in the east for his magnificent, Greek-style festivities, splendid and costly demonstrations of Roman might in the Mediterranean's new world order.[169] Other Roman generals, too, paraded their victories outside Rome. Their enemies were not slow in deploying such pageants against them, mostly by stressing the logical impossibility of observing a Roman triumph in a foreign land. These complaints were sometimes effective.[170] Deformation of this kind affects our accounts of Antony's Alexandrian parade, an event that was clearly intended to impress upon the east, in a symbolic language it understood, the reality of Roman supremacy. True, Cleopatra played a role a Roman audience would not readily welcome. But no one in the west not already disposed to dislike Antony could fail to grasp the significance of this display of Roman power and personal authority. Senators and equestrians were au fait with ceremony of this kind, a familiarity that was both practical and theoretical. Many had been to the east, nearly all had close ties there. And reading about this kind of pageantry, in the Hellenistic poet Theocritus for instance, was a part of each man's claim to high culture.[171]

The culmination of these festivities was a pageant conducted in Alexandria's monumental gymnasium, an elegant and much-admired structure. There Alexander and Cleopatra sat on golden thrones resting on a silver dais. Cleopatra's children also sat in state. The triumvir now proclaimed Cleopatra Queen of Kings and Queen of Kings who are Her Sons.[172] Her kingdom, he announced, took in Egypt, Cyprus, and parts of Syria, all regions she currently governed. Caesarion was decreed King of Kings and Cleopatra's co-ruler, a position he had long held in Egypt. Antony's children by Cleopatra he designated monarchs in their own right. Cleopatra Selene became ruler of Cyrene, her brother king of Armenia and all the lands east of the Euphrates so far as India, an allocation that included Parthia. Young Ptolemy, not yet two, he made lord of Syria and every western principality between the Euphrates and the Hellespont. Thus, the empire of Alexander the Great was now the domain of the family of Antony and Cleopatra, at least in theory.[173]

This ceremony was elaborate and highly theatrical—Cleopatra appeared as Isis and Antony almost certainly as New Dionysus—and it was destined to be reprehended in Rome. But, like Antony's procession into Alexandria, the Donations at Alexandria were a grand, readily comprehensible performance enacting the ideology of Hellenistic monarchy—under the authoritative auspices of a Roman magistrate. The specific donations, it is often observed, were over the top and untethered to geopolitical realities: no actual changes were introduced to Antony's administrative arrangements in the east. Grandiosity of this kind, however, was routine in the majestic and magical theatre of Hellenistic kings, whose claims to greatness sometimes involved even cosmic pretensions. This kind of regal mythmaking was meant to impress observers in ways that transcended the banality of life's stubborn facts. An eastern audience could not fail to grasp its claims: Ptolemaic renaissance, yes, but Roman power first and foremost, formulated in a cultural grammar that easily made sense in the east, where Antony sought to put a strong seal on his predominance.

As was the Roman habit, the triumvir's authority, an expression of the capital's power, was expressed in Alexandria in a local vernacular. There was nothing remarkable in that apart, perhaps, from the sheer scale and glamour of the celebrations, which dazzled the east and helped to win the affections of Alexandria's populace. This event was widely advertised. Antony minted coins which, on one side, commemorated his conquest (these coins exhibited his head and the inscription

Armenia Devincta, Armenia Vanquished) and, on the other, Cleopatra's elevation on his authority (they showed a bust of Cleopatra, wearing a diadem, denominated in Latin as 'Cleopatra Queen of Kings and of Kings who are her Sons').[174] The brilliance of Antony's Alexandrian pageants made clear to the world his absolute control of the east—they showcased his power, the enthusiasm of his clients, and the consequences of betrayal—a claim to personal superiority that no one in Rome could fail to recognize.

Not every Antonian vaunt was centred round Alexandria. During this year, Antony minted more than one issue of a golden aureus commemorating his relationship with his eldest son, Antyllus.[175] Although no more than eleven, Antyllus appeared on the reverse of coins the front of which pictured his father surrounded by his Roman titles and honours. The two, it is obvious, were by now reunited (we do not know when Antyllus left Rome for the east) and Antyllus was therefore an honoured guest at his father's celebrations in Egypt. His presence, the Roman son of his Roman father, could only aid the triumvir in demarcating the hybrid quality of the Donations. That Antony was making much of Antyllus is obvious from his coins. Octavian had shared coins with Caesar, true, but never before had a living son shared a coin with his living father. This was a notable distinction for Antyllus. Nor would it be unfair to see here a dynastic assertion. Still, there was nothing un-Roman about celebrating familial grandeur, and it was a highly customary point of pride in Rome to be a father of sons.[176] Nor was this an innovation Octavian could complain about: Antyllus was betrothed to his daughter, Julia. Affinity, then, forbade grumbling, even if Antony's boast represented a claim to personal vitality that must distinguish the two triumvirs in patently traditional terms.

Marriage with Cleopatra, Part Two

The Donations of Alexandria were soon denounced by Octavian, who did what he could to distort its meaning by exaggerating Cleopatra's menace and Antony's descent into eastern delusions. He also refused to honour Antony in Rome for his victory in Armenia, a highly aggressive action, or perhaps, a reaction. Not everything about the ceremonies in Alexandria were anodyne. In honouring Cleopatra and Caesarion, Antony described the queen as Julius Caesar's *woman*, by which he clearly meant *wife*, and Caesarion as Caesar's son. He went on to evoke his esteem for Caesar as the true stimulus for his elevation of Cleopatra and Caesarion. It was as if, an observer might conclude, Caesar had actually married Cleopatra, which, of course, he had not done and never intended to do. But in this ceremony Antony was hardly operating at a level cluttered by historical or even legal realities. Our sources make much of Antony's assertion that Caesarion was Caesar's natural son. But there was nothing new in that, and an Egyptian bastard was no threat whatsoever to Octavian's standing in the capital or his status as Caesar's Roman son, *divi filius*. In casting Cleopatra as Caesar's wife, however, and by doing so in a pageant that also and dramatically advertised the regal destiny of *his* children by Cleopatra, Antony, by analogy, conjured a discernible if inconcrete justification for his intimate personal relationship with the queen. They were not husband and wife, strictly speaking, but they were something so very much like it that no one could doubt the depth and decisiveness, personal as well as political, of their union.

The Donations of Alexandria were not a wedding, nor is there any indication that Antony and Cleopatra ever underwent marriage rites of any kind.[177] But by underscoring the predominance of their family and drawing attention to its likeness to what Antony now designated as Cleopatra's marriage to Caesar, the Donations gave a provocative, very public shape to their private, intimate partnership. Antony, as we have seen, could, for tactical reasons, draw attention in a public letter to the reality that he was not actually married to Cleopatra. But this legal distinction, although undeniably true, was rapidly becoming a disingenuous one in terms of his lived-life and the implications of that lived-life for his behaviour as a triumvir. For Caesar, notoriously, the republic was merely a name, without substance or shape.[178] For Antony, it appears, marriage was a concept he could reduce to a matter of semantics when confronted with the political difficulties of finding a satisfactory definition for a relationship yoking a Ptolemaic queen with a Roman triumvir.[179] This was new ground. Their complex, novel connection was unlikely to offend eastern sensibilities, even if in some quarters it sparked resentment of Egypt's good fortune. In Rome, however, the relationship between Antony and Cleopatra, because it was becoming difficult to translate into Latin, was a disconcerting, indeed provocative, perhaps for some a genuinely troubling development. Foreign flings the Romans understood and knew how to talk about, true even among those who disapproved of them. Antony's liaison with Cleopatra, by contrast, was now something very different—and difficult to explain. That alone rendered it objectionable.

Fig. 12.2 Tetradrachm minted in Syria (*RPC* 1.4094), on the obverse of which is Cleopatra and (in Greek) the legend: Queen Cleopatra, the Newer Goddess; on the reverse is Antony with the legend (in Greek): Antony, thrice *imperator*, triumvir.
Source: Wikimedia Commons.

Antony in Alexandria

Winter in Alexandria, once again, was marked by a familiar mingling of serious politics with elegant recreations. Life in the city was no less agreeable than it had been during Antony's first winter with Cleopatra in 41. The Guild of the Inimitable Lifestyle, established during that visit, continued to thrive. Soon after the Donations, a statue of Antony was erected by one of his fellow members. The statue is lost but its surviving inscription reads: *Antony the Great, inimitable in the ways of Aphrodite; Parasitos to his god and benefactor; 28 December 34*. This dedication is sometimes viewed as an expensive, sophisticated joke.[180] The name of the dedicator is a well-attested one, but the same Greek word also commonly refers to a stock character in comedy, a humorous, fulsome hanger-on, a parasite. If the name is a pseudonym, the dedicator strikes a pose which casts an ironic penumbra over the inscription's otherwise unremarkable language of divinity and philanthropy. So, too, its description of Antony as the Great, an appellation that in Alexandria must conjure the city's founder and his conquest of the east. In religious contexts, however—or perhaps, *moreover*—a parasite was a sacred officiant.[181] It cannot be excluded that, in the learned circles of Cleopatra's court, this title subsisted and was held by members of the Guild. Be it witty or earnest, however, this dedication is clearly honorific: it depicts Antony as a god, a conqueror, and its introduction of Aphrodite, a figure associated with Ptolemaic queens, pairs him intimately with Cleopatra. This statue, distinctive though it clearly is, was by no means the only statue of Antony in Alexandria.[182] Nor, it appears, was it the only Alexandrian feature marking Antony out as a god. The Suda reports that Cleopatra dedicated a large temple to the triumvir, the very building, perhaps, which later housed the city's cult to Augustus.[183]

Antony was indeed a benefactor in the Egyptian capital. His celebrations dazzled, and he was diligent in removing to Alexandria prized artworks from throughout the eastern Mediterranean.[184] If only owing to these adornments, alongside the grand temple devoted to his honour, no Alexandrian resident could any longer view Antony's recurring presence in the city as merely a sequence of temporary or casual visits. It was probably during the year of the Donations that Antony constructed a personal residence. Near the temple to Poseidon, on a mole extending into the Royal Harbour, he built a palace. In our sources, to be sure, Antony erects this edifice only after his failure at Actium: this was where he sulked, for which reason, it was said, he dubbed his home the Timonium, an allusion to Timon the Athenian, known as the Misanthrope.[185] This story is an arresting one, but too fit for its pathetic purpose to be entirely credible (the legend offers up a strikingly appalling combination of shame with grandiosity). Perhaps even from the beginning Antony's residence was cheekily denominated the Timonium simply because it was his place of withdrawal from the publicity of the Egyptian court. Perhaps the name came later. In any case, this palace signalled the Roman's permanent and prominent installation in the city's royal precinct. Although neither king nor consort, Antony was now a fixture in Alexandrian society.[186]

XIII
Dissolution

Now or Never

Antony, by way of dispatches and emissaries, informed the senate and people of Rome of his conquest of Armenia.[1] Little imagination is required regarding the tone of his communication: it accentuated Antony's glory and the majesty of the republic, to the domains of which a fabulously wealthy kingdom had been joined. Antony's decision to place his son on the Armenian throne—an action unparalleled by any Roman general or magistrate—he will have reported in an expectation of stimulating admiration from the citizenry and envy from his peers. He will also have made it clear how, until Ptolemy reached his maturity, Armenia would remain a Roman protectorate. As a consequence, the kingdom, like all Antony's east, was open for business. Nor is there any reason to believe Antony failed to describe his fabulous Alexandrian celebrations—even the Donations, a ceremony he will have represented as yet another performance displaying Rome's mastery of the east and the triumvir's personal authority in the region. But Antony had no intention of abandoning his orientation towards Roman values: after the Armenian victory, his troops hailed him *imperator*. Antony now formally requested a triumph, the traditional next step. And he proposed that the time was right for him and Octavian to abdicate the triumvirate and restore the republic. The senate, and Octavian, were required to render a judgement.

Octavian spent little of the winter of 34/33 in Rome. At the conclusion of his second campaign in Illyricum, he returned to take up his second consulship on 1 January 33, an office he, like Antony in the previous year, demitted on the same day. Soon thereafter, certainly before spring, he returned to the war.[2] The Illyricum campaign was a crucial operation for Octavian. During his first expedition, in 35, he cleared the Adriatic of hostile marauders and brought order to Illyricum's coastal regions. In this second season of the war, he invaded Dalmatia. There the fighting was fiercer. Octavian was wounded in combat and now, in the scars he suffered, carried proof of his valour. Under these adverse conditions, discipline in the ranks broke down. Octavian responded with traditional severity, including the grim punishment of decimation.[3] The Dalmatians' pacification remained incomplete, but Octavian succeeded in recovering the standards Rome had previously lost when Aulus Gabinius' forces were ambushed in Illyricum in 47.[4] At the end of the year, as we have seen, he returned to Rome, handing operations over to a trusted general, Titus Statilius Taurus.[5] At this stage, the outcome of the struggle was scarcely in doubt, and by the middle of 33, when Octavian concluded his war against the Dalmatians, the senate duly awarded him a triumph, the celebration of which he deferred.[6] Octavian's exploits, without question, were all the stuff of good, Roman imperialism, but his accomplishments, well-received though they were, could not begin to compare in the public's imagination with Antony's Armenian victory. The senate and the city will have been keen, perhaps even anxious, to learn his official reaction to events in the east and to Antony's submission regarding the triumvirate.

It is a safe assumption that on 1 January 33 Octavian, as consul, addressed the senate on the condition of the republic, a traditional topic.[7] In this way, he could lay out his public response to Antony's official communications. Antony's reports, we are told, provoked consternation and resistance, even on the part of his allies. But what we are told is misleading. In a story preserved by Dio, Antony's friends, Domitius Ahenobarbus and Gaius Sosius endeavoured, during the year 32, when they were consuls, to suppress, for fear of the outrage they would provoke, dispatches from Antony in which he related his Alexandrian festivities.[8] This is a patent absurdity. Information moved slowly in the ancient world, but not *that* slowly, nor were events in Alexandria anything likely to offend a Roman audience. We are also told that Octavian suppressed even the official reports of Antony's victory in Armenia. This, too, is unlikely. For Octavian to refuse to allow any despatch from Antony to be read aloud in the senate would constitute aggression that was too blunt for the moment and too likely to rally Antony's numerous supporters.

Antony's eastern glories, to be sure, were a threat to Octavian's standing. That Antony's Alexandrian ceremonies made a strong and positive impression in Rome is suggested by an opinion expressed by Dio, no friend of Antony. According to him, Octavian's hostility toward Antony's achievements in Armenia was predicated on jealousy: 'he envied Antony his victory celebrations'.[9] Octavian, by contrast, had not yet achieved a final victory in Illyricum. He was, at this time, too unprepared for words or actions amounting to a virtual declaration of war. This is not to say that he could not find ways to depreciate his colleague's claims. Antony's request for a triumph was doubtless approved by a senatorial decree carried under Octavian's presidency. If only for practical reasons, the award will have allowed Antony the right to defer its execution. Octavian, in putting this proposal before the house, may have made the indisputable point that delay was unavoidable inasmuch as a triumph could be celebrated only in Rome, a discourse that permitted more than one invidious comparison between the capital and Alexandria.

It was perhaps in anticipation of Antony's victory in Armenia that as early as 34 Octavian began packing Rome's festive schedule with triumphs. In that year, Antony's lieutenant Sosius celebrated a triumph for his achievement in Judea, and he did so on the anniversary of the battle of Naulochus. But the city's calendar was otherwise dominated by a series of triumphs by Octavian's commanders—Gaius Norbanus Flaccus and Statilius Taurus in 34 and, in 33, Lucius Marcius Philippus as well as, very probably, Appius Claudius Pulcher and Lucius Cornificius.[10] These generals, by parading through Rome, underscored for the citizenry the security and order Octavian's administration brought to the western empire. What Octavian's achievements lacked in glamour he made up for in sheer quantity.

And in tangible benefits for the city, because with triumphs came public building. It was a tradition in Rome for conquering generals to devote their spoils to the adornment or improvement of the city by building or repairing its public works, constructions like temples, porticoes, or aqueducts.[11] Sosius, Antony's loyal officer, distinguished himself by restoring an ancient temple of Apollo. But he was an Antonian exception: all the city's big public works at this time were sponsored by men who promoted Octavian. Cornificius restored the temple of Diana on the Aventine; Philippus the temple of Hercules of the Muses, which he embellished with a portico. Statilius Taurus constructed a new amphitheatre on the Campus Martius. In 33, Octavian, although he did not celebrate a triumph, dedicated the spoils from his campaign to restoring the Octavian Portico, in which structure he deposited the standards he wrested from the Dalmatians. None of these victors, however, including Octavian, did more for the urban fabric than did Agrippa in 33, when he took on the office of aedile. Under the triumvirs, as we have seen, this magistracy was shunned: its costs were high and its political rewards, when there were no elections to contest, meagre. Agrippa, an ex-consul and Octavian's chief marshal, undertook a massive programme of repairs and fresh building, including the completion of the Aqua Iulia, a new aqueduct, the restoration of the Aqua Marcia, and salutary repairs to the Cloaca Maxima, the vital centre of Rome's drainage and sewerage system.[12]

Investments in infrastructure on this scale both improved the conditions of the capital and injected welcome jobs and contracts into the economy of Rome and Italy. It was a very popular, highly traditional, business. Antony's absence from this facet of civic life is something of a mystery. Nothing prevented his participation, nor was he unaware of the political gains associated with monumental building in Rome. This was simply part of the mental equipment of every Roman: when Cicero speaks even casually of public buildings, he does so in terms registering their importance for acquiring clout and glory.[13] It has been proposed that Antony did in fact contribute to Rome's public building during the triumvirate, but after Actium all traces were vigorously erased by Octavian and the Augustan tradition.[14] This is not impossible. It is perhaps more likely, however, that, whatever Antony's designs along these lines, he intended to implement them after celebrating his Roman triumph, whenever that should take place. Julius Caesar, looking forward to his Gallic triumph, began making plans and purchasing land in Rome as early as 54, well before construction began.[15] Antony's approach may have been similar: he could not know he would never return to Rome.

The exuberance with which Octavian's faction invested in civic construction in 34 and 33 was designed to underline Rome's prosperity under Octavian's government and furnish the citizenry with its tangible rewards. Antony's administration of the east, as we have seen, abetted the interests of traders and financiers. Ordinary Romans in the Forum, however, although they doubtless admired Antony's conquests, did not benefit from them materially. In this respect, then, Octavian hoped to gain an advantage over his rival. As for the celebration of multiple triumphs, these he deployed in an endeavour to dilute Antony's glory. Dio was unimpressed by the sequence of Roman triumphs celebrated in 34 and 33.[16] Contemporaries, however, were unlikely to be so jaundiced.

More significant in important respects than Alexandrian flummery or Octavian's reaction to it was Antony's proposal that he and Octavian now resign office and restore the republic.[17] This was perhaps unexpected. The triumvirate, according to the pact of Tarentum, was not due to expire until the end of 32.[18] True, Octavian had urged this same action after defeating Sextus and stripping Lepidus of power, but with the qualification that he must wait until Antony had punished Parthia.[19] That punishment, Antony must have indicated, was now accomplished by depriving the Parthians of Armenia and Media Atropatene, achievements he had glorified in Alexandrian splendour and intended to celebrate in his triumph. Antony's return to Rome, the case was surely made, constituted the right moment for declaring the republic repaired. Antony's critics, chief among them Octavian, could not fail to complain about his unsubtle redefinition of Roman vengeance—and doing so may have allowed further deprecation of Antony's boasts and eastern celebrations—but the sheer attraction of bringing the triumvirate to an end must have appealed to many, whatever they thought of the Donations of Alexandria.

Nor is there any reason for us to believe Antony's offer was disingenuous. At this juncture, Antony was exceedingly rich, possessed vast eastern estates, and enjoyed profound international influence. Whatever shape the new republic took, and naturally everyone expected it eventually to look like the old republic, Antony would be its leading figure, far excelling, say, Pompey in the fifties. Octavian, too, would be a great man—but not so great as Antony. Antony had much to gain by bringing back the republic and doing so would avoid further civil war. The dynamic of Antony's proposal was not a new one. Caesar had presented Pompey and his allies with a similar offer, and it proved very popular with the senate.[20] In the events prior to the war at Mutina, Antony had suggested a similar resolution.[21] Antony's offer, then, was ostensibly a prayer for peace. Dio thought it bold, and one may wonder whether Antony truly expected Octavian to accept it. Nonetheless, his offer put pressure on Octavian. If he concurred, he conceded much to Antony. If he refused, he risked not only darkening his reputation in Italy but also sending a signal that the worrying tensions between himself and his colleague were irreconcilable. In short, Antony's proposition, genuine or not, operated as a conspicuous political trial balloon. We do not know how he formulated or justified his decision, but Octavian preferred to demur. Thereafter, Octavian's refusal to resign the triumvirate became a focus of Antony's political invective.[22] Nor did he now hesitate in making preparations for war.

Consolidation for War

Early in 33 Antony set out for Armenia and Media Atropatene. It was imperative that he conclude arrangements in his Armenian protectorate and finalize affairs with his Median ally. They settled on a mutual defence pact, Atravasdes promising his support against Octavian, Antony pledging Roman protection against Parthia. Thereafter, Antony ordered his legions to march westwards in preparation for war with Octavian. The time had come, and Antony was making the first moves. He now turned to Ephesus, the capital of Roman Asia. Cleopatra was waiting for him there. We can do little to fix the chronology of these actions. We know Antony was in the distant east on 1 May, when his officer, Lucius Flavius, became consul. The man's elevation had long before been decided by the triumvirs, but it was with Antony's army that he both accepted and demitted the office, doubtless with impressive ceremony. How long Antony remained in Armenia, however, we cannot say, but his troops must have left this region in time to settle into winter quarters by late autumn.[23]

Although we are not told so, Antony's procession through the east, and certainly his residence in Ephesus, involved intensive communications between himself and Rome's clients. All were loyal or indebted to him, to be sure, but now was not a time for taking anything for granted: Antony wanted a united east. And he wanted soldiers. Throughout this year he enlisted men, many of them native easterners, in order to complement his legions.[24] Cleopatra, too, will have played her part in rallying the kingdoms of the east. Along the coast, she and Antony began assembling a great fleet of warships and transports. Their belligerent intentions were intentionally obvious. Nor did Antony ignore Italy: his agents were active up and down the peninsula both as reassuring diplomats and as generous bestowers of Antonian largesse. Only in the next year, according to Dio, did Octavian discover the extent of Antony's efforts at buying supporters in the west: the revelation was an unwelcome one, and required countermeasures.[25]

As for Octavian, after returning to Dalmatia he was very quick to declare victory. He was back in Rome before the end of summer, where he basked in the credit of Agrippa's aedileship and the glory of his marshals' triumphs.[26] More crucially, he also began preparations against Antony. These go unreported, but Octavian was not unaware of Antony's eastern movements. It will have been now that Octavian devised, or perhaps even began implementing, a severe scheme of emergency taxation required for raising the funds needed for financing a war against Antony: on the property of wealthy freedmen he levied a tax of 12.5%; the property of free men he taxed at 25%.[27] The mobilization of soldiers and ships also required advanced planning. That Antony enjoyed real advantages in wealth and allies Octavian was all too aware. It was vital, then, that Antony, who was making loud noises about ending the triumvirate, not take on the appearance of Italy's liberator. Consequently, Octavian and his proxies engaged in full-throated denunciations of their opponents.

Heaped Calumny after Calumny

Romans were very good at saying bad things about one another. Indeed, they learned it in school. Vituperation was an essential element in forensic discourse, in senatorial arguments, in public debate, even in canvassing for office, which meant that young aristocrats were taught its basic principles, along with grammar, diction, and prose rhythm. It was owing to this strain in Roman high culture that, in all contentious public situations, adversaries routinely vilified one another as avaricious and cruel, base-born murderers and fornicators, perverts and child-molesters, and, oddly anticlimactic to us perhaps but no less earnest for them, bad with money and poor literary stylists.[28] Restraint was out of the question: 'in the allegation of disgusting immorality, degrading pursuits, and ignoble origin the Roman politician knew no compunction or limit'.[29] But ranting and raving, merely spewing slander, that was entirely unsatisfactory. Abuse demanded flair and just the right compounding of the particular with the conventional. Indeed, its delivery said as much about the deprecator as it did about the object of his spleen. In other words, it was the mark of a gentleman to sling mud with a sound sense of its suitability to circumstances and without getting any of the stuff on himself. Censorious though they were by nature, Romans were also very good at spotting those who were not very good at saying bad things: in Rome one always ran the risk, when abusing others, of revealing a flaw in one's own character, and while it was the height of elegance to target others' blemishes, it was nothing short of stupidity to allow blemishes to be observed in oneself.[30] This was no idle worry. Cicero, a master of derogation, made it his habit to dismantle and thereby debilitate his opponents' efforts at invective. By drawing attention to the vituperative failures of his rivals, he discovered a forceful, effective tool for discrediting their smears.[31]

The clash between Antony and Octavian was the final great propaganda contest of the republic.[32] Some of it centred round specific complaints intended to demonstrate the other leader's political bad faith. Antony faulted his rival for mistreating Lepidus, for failing to keep his promises, and for refusing to share provinces and troops he usurped from both Lepidus and Sextus. He also accused Octavian of refusing to furnish lands for his soldiers. On the other side, Octavian blamed Antony for Sextus' death and complained that he treated Egypt and Armenia as if they were his personal properties. As for Rome's eastern veterans, Octavian suggested Antony settle them in Media, or perhaps—a clear dig—in Parthia.[33] These recriminations, much like modern talking points, did nothing to frame the terms for genuine negotiations. Instead, they merely furnished an ostensibly legalistic scaffolding for the searing invective which soon dominated political discourse. It is difficult for modern historians, but nonetheless vital, to grasp the operations of the triumvirs' invective, not least because it was instrumental in driving the conflict between them.

Both parties enthusiastically remixed the oldies from the forties. Cicero's Antony was lubricious, luxurious, sensual, stupid, and a drunkard. And an enemy of the republic. So, now, was Octavian's Antony. In retaliation, Antony again drew renewed attention to Octavian's inferior birth, alleged that sexual deviance which was the only way he could win Caesar's affection, and complained about his cowardice. To this Antony added cruelty: stories of Octavian's viciousness after Philippi and Perusia— the site, it was claimed, of human sacrifice to Divus Iulius—were all so thrillingly told they were soon sewn into the fabric of later historical narratives.[34] Both parties deployed public letters and edicts, pamphleteering and rumour-mongering, any form of communication which could animate, intimidate, or possibly persuade the multiple constituencies of Italy. Octavian's supporters did not fail him: Valerius Messala composed multiple tracts attacking his old master: *On Antony's Statues*; *Against Antony's Letters*; *On the Settlement of Asia's Taxes*. We learn from the elder Pliny that in one of these—he does not say which—Messala revealed how the luxuriate Antony, surpassing Cleopatra in shamelessness, made it his practice to defecate into golden vessels, an anecdote combining an array of un-Roman vices into a single vivid image. Pollio, too, although he styled himself a political independent, took up his pen on Octavian's behalf: he wrote a work known as *Against Antony's Insults*.[35]

As for Antony, we know that he, too, had a stable of propagandists, but the only volume we learn of is a piece attributed to him, *On His Drunkenness*. The elder Pliny gleefully reports how Antony 'vomited up this book' before the battle of Actium. Little of its contents, however, are uncovered by his terse account of it. What he reports suggests an essay on the glories of drinking, which seems inapt.[36] Perhaps Antony composed a satire on the lampoons launched against him. It has also been suggested that, in this piece, Antony attempted to explain to man the ways of the eastern god Dionysus. It is more likely, however, that this work was a specimen of pseudepigrapha, a literary performance of Antony's excesses by an enemy. It seems not to have mattered very much. Antony's letters, by contrast, were important, incisive, and widely read—hence Messala's riposte—and they remained in circulation even during the empire. Octavian, in the aftermath of Actium, publicized a selection of them which, he felt, supported his case against his enemy's personality and character.[37] This intensive exchange of propaganda left traces and more than traces in subsequent historical accounts. In some instances, its effects are obvious. No one, for example, believes Antony's allegation that Octavian attempted to betroth his daughter to Cotiso, king of the Getae; at the same time, we are safe in detecting in this accusation the reality that the betrothal between Julia and Antyllus was broken off, which we would have inferred in any case.[38] In others instances, however, it is less obvious whether a feature of an ancient narrative derives from fact or propaganda.

Amid so much angry noise, however, a single, forceful cause predominated on each side. For Octavian, it was rescuing Italy from an evil, foreign power, a motif which evoked freedom but did so by provoking the public's fear and prejudice. Octavian's mission, as he proclaimed it, was nothing less than his country's salvation. An Egyptian queen aimed at conquering Rome and reigning from the Capitoline, and it was every citizen's duty to repulse her. Not for the first time, Octavian exploited the Romans' ample capacity for crude sexism. During the Perusine crisis, as we saw, he did not hesitate to distort Fulvia's masterliness or denounce Lucius Antonius' submission to it. This was a familiar invective move. In the Hellenistic world, Greeks complained when kings were enslaved and their administration distorted by ambitious concubines.[39] The trope shifted easily into Roman vituperation: Roman officials were routinely faulted for falling under the influence of courtesans.[40] Antony, Octavian lamented, had succumbed to Cleopatra's sexual inducements and abandoned his Roman responsibilities, preferring his lover to his fatherland. Antony's case, however, although common enough in its basic pattern, was dangerously distinctive because Cleopatra, however lewd or sensual her behaviour was made out to be, was plainly no courtesan. Indeed, the arresting novelty of Octavian's application of this typical motif in smearing Antony and Cleopatra lay in its exploitation of the very real power of the queen of Egypt, the baleful implications of which Octavian hugely amplified.

Misogyny, then, was a prejudice Octavian could aggravate with nationalism and xenophobia. Romans, aware of their society's multicultural origins, ordinarily welcomed or at least accommodated outsiders.[41] At the same time, they rarely doubted their culture's superiority and, especially in moments of elevated social tensions, chauvinism, even jingoism, erupted. It was an appeal to these baser instincts that was central to Octavian's programme against Cleopatra. Hence Agrippa's action as aedile, whereby he expelled astrologers and magicians—foreigners all—from the capital.[42] As early as 33, Octavian was laying the groundwork for suspiciousness and worry regarding eastern imports. Fierce nativist passions and belligerent alien anxieties were soon to follow.

The conflict between Octavian and Cleopatra remained a foundation myth of the Augustan age, and the flavour of its propaganda is perhaps best perceived in its literary recapitulation by the leading poets of the time. Horace returns to Egypt's vile menace more than once:

A frenzied queen raised an army for bringing ruin on the Capitol and destruction on our empire, an army of men fouled by the pollution of the queen's perverted ruck, an incontinent queen so drunk on good fortune as to hope for everything.[43]

Alas, a Roman soldier serves as a slave to withered eunuchs, and amid the legions' standards the sun shines on a disgraceful mosquito-net.[44]

In describing the shield of Aeneas in an ecphrasis depicting the history of Rome through its culmination in Octavian's triumph over Antony and Cleopatra, Virgil elaborates the antagonists' frightening contrasts in this way:

There is Caesar Augustus, with the senate and people of Rome and the gods of Roman households and the city's great gods, leading the Italians into battle.... There is Antony, rich in barbarian wealth and leading a motley force . . . he brings Egypt and powers of the east and even distant Bactria, and his Egyptian wife (unspeakable!) follows.... Every kind of monstrous god and barking Anubis wield weapons against Neptune and Venus and Minerva.[45]

More extreme examples of orientalist othering one would be hard pressed to find. The same themes resonate in later histories: Dio furnishes Octavian with a speech in which he laments how low Antony has fallen, once a mighty *imperator*, now a sad figure who has abandoned the customs of his ancestors in order to embrace eastern barbarism and grovel before Cleopatra as her love slave.[46] Octavian's message was as loud as it was clear: only a resolutely Italian strong man could stand between Rome and the Egyptian queen, an oriental hedonist abetted by the concupiscent, besotted stooge, Mark Antony.

Antony's propaganda, although concentrated on Roman sensibilities, did not ignore Hellenistic civilization or his eastern allies. He staged elaborate festivals and ceremonies, on Samos and in Athens, which, by once again employing the regal grammar of Hellenistic majesty, instilled confidence in his overlordship. He also rallied support by way of oaths.[47] Proud of his philhellenism, Antony rejected Octavian's crude xenophobia. But there was nothing anti-Roman in his eastern posture.[48] His enemy was Octavian, and when appealing to his Italian audience, Antony made it clear that his conflict with Octavian was political, not cultural. His rallying cause, for obvious reasons, receives little elaboration in our sources. It is nevertheless clear how he, again and again, demanded an end to the triumvirate and the restoration of the republic.[49] It is not unreasonable to conclude that *libertas* was once again his slogan, and he may again have resorted to the language of parties and factions, casting Octavian and his cronies as an outfit obsessed with clinging to absolute power. Octavian tried to frighten Romans with a queen. For Antony, the threat was *regnum*, un-Roman autocracy. In a speech Dio composed for Antony, the triumvir declares it his aim 'to confer liberty on our enemies as well as ourselves', and he contrasts himself with Octavian.[50] We should not doubt that Antony's programme was well received in Italy, even if Octavian's patriotic pageantry obscures it in our sources. Antony's following in Rome remained anything but inconsequential, even on the eve of Actium. Perhaps many were inclined to believe that Antony was sincere in seeking a return to traditional government.

Octavian, as we have seen, also championed freedom—freedom from Cleopatra—even if subsequent history revealed his unwillingness to restore the republic in anything but nominal terms or in a compromised version. As for Antony, we can never know exactly what he had in mind for Rome had he been victorious, but we cannot exclude the possibility that he was prepared to bring back elections, autonomous magistrates, and a deliberative senate. Fabulously wealthy and deeply, even happily implicated in the society of the east, Antony may not have relished the idea of resettling in Rome or shouldering the work demanded by despotism. But could a man like him find satisfaction in a complete return to private life? In triumph, he might expect a gratefully restored republic to install him as a permanent or near-permanent governor of the east, a responsibility he could responsibly accept and from which position he could, if need be, look after the republic as it made its first independent steps. Or perhaps, at the peak of his glory, he may have preferred a dignified retirement, like Sulla, and a life of privilege and influence amid the splendours of Alexandria. Each was a future which may have enticed far more than the hazards and burdens of autocracy in Rome. Doubtless Antony pondered these things. But all that, he knew, must come later, and of course it never came at all. In his contest with Octavian, it was unnecessary for Antony to promulgate a detailed or far-reaching programme. For the moment, his cause was simple, straightforward if unimaginative, and highly traditional: liberty.

Hearts and Minds

The effect of the antagonists' propaganda is not easy to gauge. Intense and intensive, it was undeniably arresting and often highly entertaining. Did it make a difference? It is widely concluded that nothing mattered more: 'Created belief turned the scale of history', is the standard view, 'Propaganda outweighed arms in the contests of the Triumviral period'.[51] Now there can be no question but that many Italians were at least somewhat affected by what they heard, if not by the screeds repeated by partisan hacks then from friends and family who, convinced by one claim or another, ventilated the same opinions within their circle. For some, there was no need for persuasion: agit-prop will have articulated exactly what they wanted to hear and galvanized them as they convinced, or intimidated, others. By attacking one another, each triumvir hoped to instil in the public a vivid if reductively simple perception of his own identity and his true aspirations for Rome. Mostly they drowned one another out, but that does not mean the noise was entirely pointless. At the very least, by way of propaganda they rallied supporters and supplied anyone dragged into the fray with a welcome sense that his participation was not unjustified. In the case of veterans and soldiers, it was especially important for Octavian that he furnish them with legitimate reasons to abandon any residual loyalty or affection for Antony.

Throughout this conflict, defections by aristocrats went both ways, and Antony retained the support even of senators notable for their old-fashioned, republican dispositions.[52] As for the masses, lurid vituperation, jingoism, and appeals to liberty doubtless defined their familiarity and engagement with the issues at stake: these were the men and women who preferred stability to ideology and were so weary of civil war that they were resigned to living under either victor if it meant an end to strife and conflict. These Italians were probably more perturbed by Octavian's severe regimen of emergency taxes, and the violence with which he extracted them, than by stories about Antony's goatish habits or fantasies about Cleopatra. Their resistance and rioting constituted a real and recurring danger for Octavian.[53] As for their expectations, a story told by Macrobius reflects their keenness for any end to the perturbations which blighted their lives. Returning to Italy after his victory over Antony, Octavian was greeted by a man with a raven he had taught to say, 'Greetings to Caesar, our victor and *imperator*!'. Delighted, Octavian bought the bird for an enormous price. A jealous neighbour, however, prodded him to ask to see the man's other bird. This raven, too, was produced: it knew how to say, 'Greetings to our victor and *imperator*, Antony'. Octavian knew the public's true feelings. He was not offended.[54]

Confrontation and Flight

The consuls for 32 were Domitius and Sosius, able men and Antonian loyalists. The year began quietly, too quietly for some. Dio tells us that the consuls managed to suppress a despatch from Antony to the senate in which he demanded ratification of his eastern arrangements in terms that could only alienate the body. Octavian pressed them to divulge it, but they refused.[55] This is clearly a fiction designed to portray Antony as arrogant, delusional, and entirely out of touch with Roman sensibilities, exactly the representation of Antony that animated Octavian's propaganda. It was easy then, as it is now, to allege an outrageous but unfulfilled intention on the part of one's opponent—vile even if never actually put into action—and for proof of it to cite the absence of any actual evidence.[56] Still, we may believe Dio when he tells us that Domitius, during his month presiding over the senate, aimed at propriety and order: he had no intention of leading the senate to a crisis.[57]

Sosius was more energetic. In February, when it was his turn to preside over the body, he delivered a fiery speech glorifying Antony and lacerating Octavian.[58] His oration and its tenor were not unexpected, and for this reason Octavian had withdrawn from the city. Speechifying alone Octavian could perhaps tolerate, but Sosius went further. He introduced a motion, the contents of which were unfavourable to Octavian. It is possible Sosius sought a senatorial decree censuring Octavian, but it is more likely that his motion revived something of the dynamics of the struggle between Pompey and Caesar by proposing that both triumvirs immediately resign their positions and surrender their armies and provinces. This proposition was too appealing for the senate to reject, but too dangerous for it to carry. Consequently, the tribune Nonius Balbus imposed his veto.[59] That one of the tribunes would prevent a division of the house was a certainty. Sosius' speech, however, and its ferocious demand for an end to the current crisis on terms that were clearly to Antony's advantage—geography alone meant he would hang onto power and continue to command his legions far longer than Octavian could do so, and he would return to Italy far the more formidable figure—were obviously intended to intensify the contentious atmosphere affecting Rome. It was practical, efficacious theatre. And it was almost certainly a tactic designed by Antony, who knew very well how to bring a senatorial conflict of this kind to a decisive, constitutional crisis. He had played a leading role in furnishing Caesar with a principled justification—the cause of *libertas*—for his invasion of Italy.

Octavian did not disappoint. He entered the city with his praetorian guard, convened the senate, where he sat between the consuls, and excoriated both Sosius and Antony. He then ordered the senate to return on a date at which he would promulgate documentary evidence of Antony's crimes against the republic, perhaps a suggestive reference to the allegedly suppressed dispatch from the east. So acrimonious was this session that no one doubted Octavian intended the next one to mark the outbreak of irremediable hostilities. In reaction, the consuls fled the city, denouncing Octavian's tactics as an unconstitutional putsch. They were joined by hundreds of senators.[60] Their conspicuous flight signalled an appeal to Antony to rescue Italy from Octavian's tyranny. And in its sheer bulk, this exodus made Antony's Roman clout very clear to everyone.

Octavian, as we have seen, convened this sitting of the senate and presided over it.[61] On what constitutional basis remains controversial. The pact of Tarentum, it is forcefully and intelligently (and in my judgement correctly) argued, extended the triumvirate through the end of 32.[62] Octavian, therefore, acted by way of his triumviral powers. In his *Res Gestae*, however, Augustus insists that he was triumvir only for ten consecutive years, a reckoning which, if true, indicates his tenure of office lasted until the end of 33.[63] Till the very end, Antony continued to style himself a triumvir. After 33, however, Octavian no longer did so, at least so far as we can tell. Most modern historians have (more or less) taken Augustus at his word.[64] Some confront the implications of his claim directly and accept that in 32 he held no legal authority to command public affairs. Instead, they maintain, his actions in 32 depended on a *coup d'état*, the ugly particulars of which drove out the consuls and a large portion of the senate but thereafter were largely erased by irresistible Augustan traditions.[65] Others, although they insist the triumvirate's mandate expired at the end of 33, recognize that neither triumvir could be forced to abdicate—unless the senate annulled the *lex Titia* which established the office.[66] This the senate did not do. There is no reason, so the argument runs, to believe Octavian demitted the office. Quite the contrary: Antony, for one, complained constantly that he refused to do so.[67] On this view, then, the triumvirate duly expired at the end of 33 but, so long as the triumvirs refused to resign, they continued to hold the powers conferred on them by the *lex Titia*. No matter how one views it, then, the evidence of the *Res Gestae* is anything but transparent. Even readers who believe Augustus is an honest man on the topic of the triumvirate's term limits are nonetheless obliged to conclude that he resorts to obfuscation or distraction when it comes to his very real retention of triumviral powers after 33. The expiration date of the triumvirate is a problem unlikely ever to be resolved to everyone's satisfaction. Still, it is as certain as such matters can be that in 32 both Octavian and Antony held the powers of a triumvir, even if neither did so in accordance with the prescriptions in the pact of Tarentum. In 31 Octavian was consul. Nothing, however, indicates he laid down his triumvirate at that time.

The Senate in Ephesus

It was at Ephesus that Antony greeted the consuls and senators who fled to him. And there he set up a counter-senate, a body which symbolized Antony's Roman legitimacy and signalled to the west the grave emergency precipitated by Octavian's fierce ambition.[68] Antony was now, at least for his supporters, the true defender of *libertas*. It was a brilliant political coup, but one that introduced fresh difficulties. Till this time, Cleopatra's importance in Antony's deliberations and policy had not, at least so far as we know, provoked any significant controversy among Antony's Roman officers. Domitius, we are told, consistently made a point of addressing the queen by name and not by title, but that was no more than a suitable expression of Roman dignity.[69] Now, however, serious questions over Cleopatra's role in the looming civil war were thrown up. Reports over this debate naturally focus on the leading figures. But the sudden presence in the east of hundreds of Roman senators, all deporting themselves as Roman statesmen serving the republic, defines the environment in which Cleopatra became a focus of contention. In part, this was a result of Octavian's propaganda. Not that Antony's loyalists were influenced by it, but they were very aware of its effectiveness in certain quarters in Italy. Consequently, they fretted over the dubious optics of an Egyptian queen accompanying a Roman triumvir into battle: better, many were certain, that his international forces be led by Roman generals and the anti-senate. Nor, perhaps, were all their concerns about Cleopatra confined to politics. Cicero, we know, detested the queen. He found both her and her courtiers insufferably arrogant.[70] And Cicero was a man Caesar could describe as marvellously long-suffering.[71] One must wonder how many senators, dealing for the first time with Cleopatra and her Ptolemaic officials, soon felt the same way.[72]

Domitius and several other of Antony's closest advisors urged him to deposit the queen in Alexandria. Like Polemo and Herod, she could be entrusted with steadying the east during the Romans' campaign. They made a strong case and, at first, Antony was convinced by it.[73] This was a decision, however, which the queen found intolerable, and she had forceful allies. The marshal Canidius, commander of Antony's infantry, took Cleopatra's side, arguing that her contribution to the war, in ships and treasure, excelled anyone else's. Moreover, Canidius pointed out, she was too intelligent to exclude from future war councils. Persuaded, Antony reversed himself.[74] But the controversy did not abate. Before the year was out, Plancus and Titius defected to Octavian. In justification they adduced their alienation from Cleopatra. There is no good reason to disbelieve them.[75] One should not exaggerate the significance of Antony's decision to include Cleopatra in his march against Octavian. But it was not a wise one. Her continued presence distracted from the advantage he enjoyed by way of the backing of a numerous and distinguished senate-in-exile. More importantly, it introduced a new and unnecessary dissonance into his inner circle. And it furnished Octavian with an increasingly plausible target for vituperation and jingoism.

Samos and Athens

The essential chores at Ephesus were logistic. Antony's army was enormous: in the end he commanded at least nineteen legions and a vast, allied array, in total a force possibly as large as 100,000 infantry and 12,000 cavalry. These men required constant provisioning. It was also necessary, in wave after wave, to carry them by sea to Greece. For this task he deployed 300 transports. Antony also assembled an armada of 500 warships.[76] Demanding though these tasks were, none demanded Antony's personal supervision. He, Cleopatra, and their inner circle instead moved west in comfortable stages. In April or May, they departed Asia for Samos. There Antony had previously scheduled an international, Pan-Hellenic festival, attended by kings and ambassadors from throughout the east, many of whom were destined to fight in the war against Octavian. Sacrifices and contests, especially literary and musical contests, rallied Antony's allies by way of suitable Hellenistic glamour. Grand gestures of generosity also exhibited Antony's majesty, thereby expressing and instilling confidence. One of these we know about, his gift of Priene to the so-called Artists of Dionysus.[77]

By the end of May, Antony was in Athens. Once more there were elaborate ceremonies and festivities. At one of these, Antony, as a citizen of Athens, welcomed Cleopatra to the city.[78] Here, too, in this conspicuous, Hellenic centre, Antony sought to inspire and give courage to his eastern adherents. It was now that Antony sent a notice of divorce to Octavia. Plutarch tells us she grieved at the news and, even after she left Antony's home, continued to care for all his children, a supererogatory burden for a divorced wife in Rome.[79] By divorcing Octavia, Antony freed her from an obvious conflict of loyalties, and perhaps he was glad to do her this small favour. The principal and public purpose of the divorce, however, was to make it universally clear that his relationship with Octavian was now irremediably severed. No longer could Octavia rescue the triumvirs' relationship. For Antony and his allies, and certainly for Cleopatra, this moment was the culmination of the celebrations on Samos and in Athens.

Antony's Last Will and Testament

It was about this time that Plancus and his nephew, Titius, broke with Antony and returned to Rome, possibly in the same company as the agents bearing Antony's notice of divorce to Octavia.[80] Because Plancus was a central figure in Antony's inner circle, his defection was nothing short of sensational. His tergiversation won him few plaudits in the senate but earned him Octavian's enduring gratitude.[81] Plancus wasted no time: in serving his new master he proved no less energetic than he had shown himself as an officer of Antony. He brought valuable information regarding Antony's movements and strategy. And, cunning man that he was, he encouraged Octavian to consider prying into the contents of Antony's will. Plancus, one of its witnesses, persuaded Octavian that some of its provisions were deeply and usefully discreditable. Antony's will was deposited with the Vestal Virgins. When Octavian demanded its delivery, the Vestals refused. Undeterred, he personally took possession of it, broke its seal, and studied its text carefully, excerpting any clauses he deemed provocative. He then publicized Antony's damning last wishes, reading the offending passages before a crowded session of the senate. According to Dio, he also read these same excerpts to an assembly of the people.[82]

In Roman society, one's will was not merely a legal instrument but a solemn, final communication of one's feelings with the world one left behind.[83] Naturally, property was passed down to heirs and legatees. So, too, were judgements delivered, sometimes generous, sometimes harsh. A will was a private document, but testators often shared sections of it with friends and family, and the making of a will, because it required witnesses, often entailed a public ceremony. One man may in his time play many parts, all Romans appreciated, but in his will he expressed his authentic self. 'The will is a mirror of a man's true character', is how the younger Pliny puts it.[84] Lucian's Nigrinus is blunter: 'Romans tell the truth only once in their lives—in their will'.[85] It was for these reasons that the reading of a deceased's will was a notable occasion. Romans listened keenly for any revelation of a man's honest feelings: whom did he honour? whom did he abuse? whom did he ignore? Sulla, for instance, notoriously failed to include Pompey in his will: the slight was nothing short of a scandal.[86] In the senate, Cicero taunted Clodius when he was excluded from an in-law's list of legatees.[87] Cicero in turn was so shaken when Antony alleged nobody ever left him anything that he felt obliged to make and promulgate a tabulation of the total sum of his bequests.[88] This was the testamentary paradigm which governed the interpretation and therefore the composition of every will. Which is why Antony's will—and the illegal disclosure of its contents—was such combustible stuff.

It was unprecedented, outrageous, even abominable to seize another man's will and divulge its contents. And doing so violated a law of Sulla.[89] The Vestals were uncooperative but could not stand in Octavian's way. Nevertheless, when Octavian read passages from Antony's will to the senate, he did not escape opprobrium. Even men disturbed by the contents of Antony's will reproached Octavian for his uncivilized behaviour. Still, however disapproving of this transaction, no one could remain uninterested or unaffected by the sheer frisson stimulated by this shocking infringement and its transfixing revelation into Antony's innermost sentiments. Unsurprisingly, it has been suggested by some modern historians that the will was a forgery. It defies belief, however, that Octavian would have incurred such severe strictures in order to promulgate a fake will, especially since doing so could only run the risk that either the Vestals or Antony's Roman intimates would have revealed his ruse.[90] The will's authenticity was not, so far as we know, challenged by anyone in Antony's camp, and Roman senators were very good at detecting or alleging forgery when confronted by documents they found politically awkward or unlikely.[91] Accepting this will's authenticity, however, is not the same thing as accepting that its terms have been precisely preserved. Propaganda simplifies and exaggerates, and historians rewrite sensational stuff to suit their immediate literary needs. Refracted through media such as these, we can be sure, the objectionable features of Antony's will have been at least somewhat distorted. Nonetheless, because the importance of this will lay in the construction critics imposed on its content, these distortions may have mattered most of all.

What did the public learn from Antony's will? The triumvir, we are told, wanted his remains to be interred in Alexandria. Plutarch relates that Antony requested a state funeral in Rome, after which he his ashes were to be sent to Cleopatra. According to Dio, and only Dio, Antony asked that he be entombed with Cleopatra. Dio also reports that Antony again recognized Caesarion as Caesar's son. More importantly, he left generous gifts to his children by Cleopatra. That is the one stipulation of the will which Suetonius records: Antony named his Ptolemaic children as heirs.

For Octavian, these provisions proved beyond doubt that—in the private confines of his heart—Antony was emotionally entangled with Cleopatra and her children. And he expected many in the senate to share his disapproving judgement. In Antony's testament, one could scarcely avoid detecting a relationship between a Roman and an Egyptian of the very kind that provoked Caesar's disgust. And, if only owing to societal expectations, these revelations must have incited in many a kind of revulsion, something more reproachful than prim disapprovals of open womanizing. In his propaganda, as we have seen, Antony portrayed his affair as the ruthless operation of a confirmed roué: Cleopatra, he insisted, was merely a sex object.[92] By shocking contrast, the Antony of this will now looked very much like the ridiculous, indeed dangerous figure outlined in Octavian's calumny. This was love of a disturbingly different order.

What did Antony's will actually say? It is rightly pointed out that Antony's foreign children were legally incapable of acting as heirs or recipients of legacies.[93] If Antony's will stipulated them in these capacities, it was ineptly constructed. Indeed, it has been intelligently observed that it could be just this legal solecism which stimulated the learned Suetonius' judgement that the will helped to demonstrate how Antony no longer knew how to act like a Roman citizen.[94] But it is not necessary for us to conclude that Antony got his will wrong. What Octavian found objectionable, and hoped others would also deprecate, was the fact that Antony sought to leave a portion of his estate, of the inheritance of his Roman children, to foreign bastards. These were gifts Antony was able to incorporate into his will by way of a *fideicommissum*, a testamentary commission entrusted to a proper heir for its execution.[95] Presumably, this is what Antony's will stipulated. And this is what Octavian read aloud in the senate. But the particulars were too complicated for subsequent animadversions and in any case irrelevant to the basic point: Antony was handing over to foreigners a slice of his legitimate children's legacy. Only a perverse relationship with Cleopatra, Octavian will have maintained, could explain that.

In a sense, Octavian was right. Antony's provision for his Ptolemaic children cannot be separated from his relationship with Cleopatra. In Alexandria and in the east generally, it was important for the queen that all her children bask in the prestige of their Roman origins. An inheritance from Antony would help to ensure his children's status in the Alexandrian court. It was probably by way of looking after their security that Antony also elected to leave a portion for Caesarion, in the text of which commission he apparently indicated his reasons for doing so by identifying the boy as Caesar's son. Accommodating Caesarion alongside his children was clearly an expression of esteem for Cleopatra as well as Caesar. And doubtless Antony hoped it would add a degree of harmony to what he knew would again become, after his death, a contentious, potentially deadly, Ptolemaic court. All of this demonstrates Antony's thorough grasp of Alexandrian politics. It also exhibits the importance of Cleopatra in his final judgements.

Antony asked to be buried in Alexandria. Octavian, as we have seen, claimed Antony and Cleopatra aimed at making Alexandria the capital of their new empire: this clause, he could assert, proved it. Even Romans who could not stretch that far could agree that Antony's request was nonetheless proof of un-Roman sensibilities. The conclusion was not entirely an unfair one. We have seen how, during the last years of his life, Antony relished becoming a fixture in Alexandrian society. Perhaps by now he truly preferred the place to Rome. And perhaps he sentimentally hoped to be buried by Cleopatra's side. There is no obvious reason to exclude it. That, we can be sure, was the construction Octavian put on this clause of Antony's will.

But there may be more to the question of Antony's final resting place. Dio tells us that that at the time of his death, there was in Alexandria a *heroon*, a hero's shrine, dedicated to Antony.[96] Now the living gods who were Hellenistic monarchs tended to eschew heroic cult.[97] But Antony was not a Hellenistic monarch. A *heroon* for Antony during his lifetime was not an impossibility—living men could be denominated heroes and receive heroic honours—but it is more likely that, if Antony was indeed erecting his own *heroon*, he was also planning to play a sacred role in Alexandrian society after his death.[98] For this there was good Antonian precedent: his ancestor, Hercules, was worshipped throughout the eastern Mediterranean both as a god and a hero.[99] Antony's divine aspirations may have aimed at a similar exaltation. If so, the Alexandrian shrine for this cult was a natural place for interring his physical remains. His cult at a *heroon* would set his commemoration apart from that of Cleopatra's deified Ptolemaic ancestors, the worship of whom took a very different form. Still, Antony's enduring, sacred presence will have been useful to the ambitions of Cleopatra and her children. Alexander the Great claimed descent from Heracles, true, but by also evoking Antony's Roman heritage as a descendent of Hercules, this cult, had it come about, would have exhibited something of the cultural hybridity which marked so many aspects of Antony's eastern career. At the same time, a hero cult for Antony, like any hero cult, celebrated an intimate relationship between the hero and the place at which he was commemorated: it would have been an Alexandrian, not a Roman, fixture. This will have mattered more to Antony's critics than any compensating bicultural facets of the *heroon*. This, however, is the stuff of speculation: even for the possibility of this cult we have only a single word in Dio. And in any case, Antony's cult, if it existed, need not have been discussed in his will. Nor, if it was, was it likely to have been nearly so disturbing to those who distrusted Antony than the reality that, even in death, he preferred Cleopatra's Alexandria to his fatherland.

Proof of Antony's un-Roman devotion to Cleopatra was the incriminating truth which Octavian endeavoured to excerpt from his enemy's will. It is, however, worth pausing for a moment to observe how little else in the way of deplorable content Octavian was able to extract. Whenever this will was composed, and Romans were obliged to keep their wills up-to-date, it was deposited with the Vestals before Antony divorced his wife. And yet Octavian could not complain in the senate that *he* had been ignored or ill-treated by his former brother-in-law. Even silence on Antony's part would have provoked an objection. Presumably, then, Antony's will paid Octavian every courtesy and furnished him an appropriate legacy. Nor could Octavian fault Antony's will for abusing his sister. Again, Antony must have supplied suitable remarks and a seemly legacy. In all other respects too, we must assume, his will was a sound one. Antony, it is clear to us if not to his contemporaries, did not, by falling in love with Cleopatra, intend to cast off his Roman responsibilities. His eastern career, flamboyant though it was, did not erode his traditional sensibilities.

Such boring conventionality, however, was hardly the stuff of propaganda for either side. Owing to the profound cultural significance of Roman wills, no one in Rome could now doubt the nature of Antony's feelings for Cleopatra. For Octavian, the will was proof of her baleful mastery of her Roman lover. Octavian's partisans at once embraced this same conclusion. Nor could uncommitted Romans be unaffected by these revelations, especially when Octavian continued to beat the drums of Italian jingoism. That Antony was in love with Cleopatra was now a fact of political life. Still, it is far from clear how many Romans were converted to Octavian's cause or alienated from Antony by the publication of his will. Revulsion at Antony's un-Roman relationship with Cleopatra, however serious, need not entrain the conviction that he intended to hand the capital over to the queen. Antony's programme centred round *libertas*, and he remained surrounded by senators who believed he was the Roman to deliver it. However distasteful they found his Egyptian family, many Romans may have continued to hope that in the end Antony might restore the republic they were certain a victorious Octavian would dispense with.

War

In disclosing the disconcerning contents of Antony's will, Plancus delivered Octavian very welcome information. Less welcome, however, were his reports of Antony's preparations. The scale and the pace of his enemy's westward advance exceeded Octavian's expectations.[100] Even the possibility of an invasion could no longer be discounted. An assault on Italy would be dangerous for Antony, true, but the man had previously exhibited impatience and recklessness when commanding a great army. The situation in Italy, tense, even precarious, could, Octavian had to fear, collapse if Antony managed to arrive on its shores. Octavian reacted with predictable efficiency and rigour, assembling men and money. He could not possibly match Antony's financial resources, a condition which forced him to impose further and heavy emergency taxes. These impositions incited political perturbation throughout Italy, but Octavian did not hesitate to employ violence in restoring order.[101] But these were actions which could only lend credence to Antony's allegations of Octavian's tyranny.

Octavian now took drastic action. The senate deprived Antony of the consulship he was destined to hold in 31. It also removed him from power, somehow annulling the provisions of the *lex Titia* on which Antony's triumviral office relied, or perhaps by way of a simple and unconstitutional decree: Dio's Antony later claimed he was stripped of power illegally, 'neither by the people or the senate'.[102] Naturally, Antony dismissed these actions as invalid: the true senate, in his view, was no longer the body in Rome but the assembly of conscript fathers who joined him. The possibility of declaring Antony a *hostis* was apparently mooted but rejected, a postponement which permitted another sitting devoted to vituperating Antony and taking official action against him. In the end, a decree proclaiming Antony a *hostis* was duly passed: only one man, a certain Sergius whom Antony had rescued during the proscriptions, voted against the declaration.[103]

By late summer, the moment arrived for a formal declaration of war—against Egypt.[104] For this, Octavian revived or perhaps invented (or modified) an ancient pageant, the *ius fetiale*, the ritual enacted by an archaic priesthood, the *fetialies*, for ensuring that every Roman war was a just war, a *bellum iustum*. Various sacred and legal formulas were recited, a patch of land in front of the temple of the war-goddess Bellona was rendered a specimen of Egyptian soil, and the priest, under the observation of at least three citizens, cast a spear of cornel-wood into the enemy's land, calling on the gods and the republic as witnesses.[105] For this occasion, Octavian may have enrolled himself as a *fetialis* and cast the spear himself.[106] Through this pageantry, it is obvious, Octavian emphasized in Italy the defensive nature of his war with Antony and underlined the clash of cultures animating their struggle. These were undeniably powerful incentives, even if everyone knew this *bellum iustum* was yet another version of civil war.[107]

Tota Italia

The looming war, as we have seen, was drawn by Octavian as an existential struggle between virtuous Rome and a mob of debased Orientals. He now resorted to bolder lines:

> The whole of Italy—*tota Italia*—voluntarily swore an oath of allegiance to me and demanded I lead as general in the war at Actium, where I was victorious. The Gallic and Spanish provinces, Africa, Sicily, and Sardinia all swore the same oath.[108]

Italy in the first century contained multiple and highly variegated societies, notwithstanding its common Roman citizenship or the close ties between its municipal elites and the affairs of the capital.[109] When it was expedient, however, a Roman statesmen could claim that all Italy shared a single sentiment and he was its spokesman. Not so long ago, Cicero, in his *Philippics*, deploying the expression *consensus Italiae*, claimed Italy agreed with him in detesting Antony: *tota Italia*, he declaimed, cried out for *libertas*.[110] Octavian's conceptual unification of Italy as a bulwark against the east, however, was an innovation and a denial of the highly international character of many Italian cities. But through his oath he introduced starkly nativist associations by conjuring the traditional features of a *tumultus*, the desperate, emergency levy that in the past had offered Rome its only means of surviving an enemy's invasion.[111] The preservation of Roman freedom was now entirely embrangled in the war against Egypt and its alien aggression. City by city men swore loyalty to Octavian, the peerless leader who constituted their only hope. He conspicuously allowed Antony's traditional clients to abstain, a move which, ostensibly generous, emphasized their isolation from 'the whole of Italy'. Very soon they, too, were bullied into joining Octavian's cause.[112] We may doubt, then, the voluntary nature of this oath. But we cannot ignore its effectiveness. Different the peoples of Italy may have been: Octavian united them in jingoism and devotion to his personal leadership.

Winter in Greece

By autumn Antony's forces were in Greece. In order to inspect his arrangements along the coast, he sailed west so far as Corcyra.[113] The bulk of his fleet rested in the harbour at Actium, but Antony also stationed ships and men elsewhere, in cities like Methone, Leucas, and Taenarum.[114] Satisfied with the distribution and readiness of his men, he returned to Patrae, where he and Cleopatra intended to spend the winter.[115] Even now, Octavian and Antony continued to exchange hostile public letters.[116] Patrae honoured Cleopatra by minting a coin bearing her image and title, Queen Cleopatra, on the obverse and, on the reverse, the headdress of Isis. This issue is remarkable and has been variously explained, sometimes as a statement of opposition to Rome, which is highly unlikely, sometimes as a gesture of support for Antony, making it clear that Patrae took his side in Octavian's war on Egypt.[117] The coin was intended only for local use, which means its geo-political message was limited. At the same time, it is a surviving token of the lengths to which this city went in celebrating its eminent residents. All the familiar solemnities and festivities were once again rolled out. For the last time, Antony was the darling of Greece.

The Battle of Actium

On the first of January in 31, Octavian became consul. Instead of Antony, his colleague was Valerius Messalla, a man whom Antony had salvaged in the aftermath of Philippi.[118] In Italy and Greece, fear and dread prevailed. The end of winter meant the beginning of war on a terrifying scale. In the west, Octavian mustered an army approaching 80,000 men. The troops in Antony's alliance stood at nearly 100,000. Each side fielded approximately 12,000 cavalrymen. Antony enjoyed only a moderate advantage in ships. Ancient estimates vary, but it appears Octavian had a fleet of at least 400. In addition to its transports, Antony's navy numbered around 500.[119] For now, the Adriatic separated their armies, but everyone was keenly aware that, once again, a conflict fought in Greece would decide the government of Rome. In the west, the exaltation of jingoism will have begun to wane. On Antony's side, too, there was worry or at least uncertainty. Philippi and Pharsalus had been bloody affairs, and not even Roman legionnaires, on the eve of such a struggle as loomed before them, were immune from anxiety or unease. On all sides, trepidation was unavoidable.

Antony, by contrast, was all confidence. Unlike his campaign in Parthia, this conflict would be fought out on very familiar turf. Antony served under Caesar on the march to Pharsalus and commanded the armies which were victorious at Philippi. He was certain there could be no significant surprises. Sulla had once successfully invaded Italy, but Antony knew any attack on Brundisium or Tarentum was unlikely to succeed. Octavian's forces were too numerous and his security too strong for that. Instead, Antony readied himself for the predictable sequence of engagements he reckoned would play out in Greece. During its first phase, he assumed, this war would be waged in the Adriatic as he impeded or harassed Octavian's crossing, thereby eroding his assets and possibly his soldiers' morale. Still, he knew that, in the end, his enemy would make a landing and gain a foothold. In that phase of the war, relying on his

Map 6 Actium

superior logistic resources—his ample treasury and well-organized supply lines—
Antony would clash with Octavian in a series of minor engagements leading up to
a decisive, pitched battle. The final theatre of war, he would make sure of it, would be
one of his own choosing. Getting there might take time and require a good deal of tactical manoeuvring. But time was on Antony's side, whereas Octavian would struggle
to provision his army and sustain control of Italy. In the end, Antony believed, he

would have Octavian exactly where he wanted him. For now, however, there was nothing to do but wait for spring.[120]

Agrippa did not wait. Before winter ended, he sailed south and made a sudden attack on Methone (modern Mithoni), far removed from Antony's expectations of any naval assault.[121] Antony expected Octavian to take his chances along the northern coast of the Adriatic. Sailing to Methone, even in the absence of Antonian patrols, was, at this time of year, extremely hazardous. But Agrippa knew the strength of Antony's forces and believed this blitzkrieg was worth the risk. Nor did he fail. The city was taken by surprise. With Methone as his base of operations, Agrippa preceded to launch further attacks along the coast, reaching so far as Corcyra. Antony's forces were thrown into confusion. Before they could recover or gain any grasp on the situation, Octavian crossed the Adriatic north of Corcyra and landed an army at Panormus. Antony's navy did little to hinder his crossing—perhaps it was busy elsewhere trying to repulse Agrippa—and Octavian, moving south, soon took possession of the island. He continued his southwards march, aiming at Actium, where lay the bulk of Antony's fleet. He soon established himself on a site (modern Mikalizi) on the Bay of Gomaros overlooking, from the northwest, the Gulf of Ambracia. This place was not an ideal harbour, but it offered him excellent, elevated terrain for an encampment and easy access to the river Louros.

Antony and Cleopatra rushed to Actium. There he took possession first of the southern promontory overlooking the entrance of the Gulf of Ambracia (modern Punta), gaining complete control of the passage. As more of his army arrived, he established a new camp on the northern side of the entrance (near modern Preveza). The enemies were now divided only by an open plain. Antony deployed his troops in battle array, but Octavian, who possessed fewer men but a superior position, refused to fight. Frustrated, Antony now threw himself into cutting Octavian off from the Louros. By depriving him of ample, fresh water, he hoped to compel Octavian to fight or withdraw. This was the right tactic, and its successful execution would have altered the outcome of this conflict radically. But it failed: Antony's cavalry, defeated more than once by Octavian's horse, were unable to protect his soldiers who were trying to construct the fortifications necessary for isolating Octavian's camp. Antony did not abandon his plan, however, and this struggle persisted into the summer. By that time, however, the disadvantages of Antony's camp near Preveza were becoming obvious. It was low-lying, wet, and increasingly unhealthy. Illness became rife and ultimately Antony had to withdraw again to Punta.

Agrippa then struck another, serious blow. He defeated Antony's forces on Leucas and seized control of the island. It now became much easier for Octavian to provision his camp—and more difficult for Antony to feed his soldiers. Matters became far worse when Agrippa raided Patrae and Corinth. It is unclear whether these cities were captured by Octavian's forces or simply attacked and disrupted.[122] In either case, Antony appeared increasingly helpless at sea. Even if Octavian was unable to impose a strict naval blockade, he managed to deter most ships from carrying supplies to his enemy. Antony was increasingly isolated, nor could he provoke Octavian to the hazard of a pitched battle. A sense of Antony's desperation can be recovered from a story recorded by Plutarch: his great-grandfather used to relate the miseries of his home city, Chaeronea, when, during the struggle at Actium, Antony's soldiers requisitioned its stores of grain; owing to the urgency felt in Antony's camp, the city's citizens were dragooned into lugging sacks of grain and whipped whenever they dallied. In Antony's camp, morale began to collapse.[123] Allied kings, including the able and favoured Amyntas, went over to Octavian. So, too, did distinguished Romans. Domitius Ahenobarbus had had enough. Dellius also defected. They were not alone. Antony reacted violently: a disloyal senator and an unfaithful client king were executed. Antony's situation, it was clear to everyone, had become untenable. By late summer it was time to withdraw.

Councils of war were convened at which a variety of opinions was ventilated.[124] The central controversy concerned the roles to be played by Antony and Cleopatra. It was obvious that the infantry must march inland. It was equally obvious that the fleet must attempt to break out of the Gulf of Ambracia. Of these two actions, the naval engagement was by far the more daunting task: Octavian's navy now had every advantage, and Agrippa's admiralship was intimidating. Canidius urged Antony to take command of his legions, winter in Greece or Macedonia, and prepare to do battle by land in the new year. Cleopatra, he proposed, should be conveyed with the fleet to Egypt. From there, she or Antony's officers could make plans for restoring lines of supply or possibly confronting Octavian's navy in the spring. He rightly recognized that so long as Antony retained the loyalty of his legions, the war was far from over.

This was a view Cleopatra opposed. Our sources attribute her position to cowardice: she had, they report, already begun scheming to flee home to Egypt. That we cannot exclude, but nor should we doubt that the queen had cogent arguments. The sea battle was the riskier venture, she could insist, and so that was the place for Antony's valour. The legions, she doubtless submitted, were accustomed to serving under Canidius. He was capable of leading them to safety, their obedience could be counted on, and in the new year the infantry and navy could again collaborate in fighting Octavian. Other, unspoken factors may also have affected this debate. Cleopatra without Antony, under these extreme circumstances, would become something anomalous and hard to manage. If Antony marched away with his troops, Cleopatra, an Egyptian leader amid Antony's Roman officers in a time of war, would possess an authority that was unclear and difficult to spell out in a way satisfactory to Ptolemaic and Roman sensibilities. The dynamics of that situation could easily incite friction. Earlier anxieties about Cleopatra's presence in this campaign were now proving perspicacious.

Antony's duty, and his only chance of victory, lay with the legions. Any other decision was ignoble and impractical. In the circumstances of this war, animated now more than ever by a dangerous, electric tension, the loyalty of the infantry was vital. And Antony was a general well able to sustain the devotion of his soldiers. Canidius, good man though he was, could not hold the army together after it witnessed its general sailing into the distance with Cleopatra. If Antony's Roman legions went over to Octavian, the auxiliaries would follow. So, too, Greece and the residue of the east. Only arrogance or obtuseness can explain any failure on Antony's part to apprehend this inescapable reality. A naval battle was feasible only if it resulted in an unambiguous victory allowing Antony's forces to retain its position at Actium. That outcome, however, was anything but certain: it was far better to entrust the fleet's extraction to

Sosius or another of Antony's marshals, while Antony led his legions. Canidius, there can be no doubting it, got this right.

And Antony got it wrong. He decided that he and Cleopatra would salvage what they could of the fleet, rescue the treasury, and return to Alexandria in order to plan the next year's campaign. Canidius was instructed to organize the infantry's retreat. Antony would resume command in the spring. His confidence in the loyalty of his soldiers and allies was total. On 2 September, Antony's fleet emerged from the Gulf of Ambracia.[125] The treasure-chest was entrusted to Cleopatra and her Egyptian squadron. Her ships and many of Antony's carried sails, an indication they were prepared for flight once they fought their way past Octavian's navy. Antony may well have hoped for a decisive victory at sea, but his preparations suggest he did not believe that likely. The battle began in the afternoon and soon Antony's ships succeeded in opening up gaps in the enemy's line. Through one of these Cleopatra's squadron, suddenly hoisting its sails, made its escape. Antony and a few warships followed. Most of Antony's fleet was left behind. Fighting did not continue for long after his departure. Many of Antony's ships simply returned to the gulf.[126] The battle was over.

A general policy of clemency supervened, and for seven days Octavian negotiated with Antony's legions. In exchange for very generous terms, they transferred their loyalty to him, as Canidius had known they would.[127] He, however, did not go over to Octavian's side. Instead, he made his way to Egypt. The actual battle of Actium has been scorned as 'a shabby affair'.[128] It was certainly nothing like the heroic contest so fabulously depicted by imperial poets and historians. Actium quickly became the stuff of legend and a foundation myth of the Augustan Age. Literary elaboration aside, however, the battle of Actium was unquestionably the moment of greatest consequence in the conflict between Antony and Octavian. In taking flight, Antony betrayed himself and the men who fought for him. It was an irredeemable failure, and it destroyed him.[129]

After his victory, Octavian hurried to Athens. There, like Antony before him, he could, by way of civic celebrations, communicate to the east the disposition of its new master. From Athens, he moved, first to Samos, then to Ephesus, retracing the final footsteps of Antony and Cleopatra. In each setting, he will have been welcomed, honoured, and mobbed by embassies—all the old obligatory spanieling played out on a magnificent scale.[130] Agrippa he sent to Italy, where he, in partnership with Maecenas, endeavoured to bolster an increasingly insecure order. There were grave difficulties: Maecenas uncovered and eliminated a conspiracy against Octavian led by Lepidus' son, and the legions were dangerously angry. It was winter when Octavian received these reports. He did not delay. He made a rapid journey to Brundisium. There he was greeted by the senate, representatives of the equestrian order, and the mutinous legions. With astonishing efficiency, he satisfied them all.[131] He remained for less than a fortnight, then returned to the east.[132]

The Defence of Alexandria

Cleopatra and Antony travelled together so far at the Peloponnese.[133] There they parted. The queen led her Egyptian squadrons to Alexandria. Dio tells us she adorned

Fig. 13.1 Pompeo Batoni, *Death of Marc Antony* (1763), in Musée des Beaux-Arts, Brest.
Source: Wikimedia Commons.

her ships with garlands, a signal of victory. Upon returning, she purged the court of anyone suspected of disloyalty. Antony sailed to Paraetonium (modern Mersah Matrûh). There he planned to take possession of four legions he had left behind in Cyrene. Antony believed his army was marching into Greece under Canidius' command, but after the reversal at Actium every soldier counted and these legions would be valuable in reassuring or intimidating his eastern allies. Hence the shock when Lucius Pinarius Scarpus, his officer in charge, refused to hand the legions over and declared for Octavian. By now Scarpus must have heard enough of events abroad to believe Antony's cause was a lost one. According to Dio, not all his officers were convinced, but Pinarius quickly eliminated dissonant voices.[134] Antony had no choice but to withdraw to Alexandria. Soon Canidius arrived bringing the disastrous news that the army had gone over to Octavian. Eastern allies, too, were shifting their loyalty from the victor at Philippi to the victor at Actium, as Antony learned from report after report reaching Alexandria.[135]

Events now become extremely difficult to recover, even by the standards of ancient history. Antony and Cleopatra's Liebestod is our sources' chief interest, and this was a tale which was early on elaborated with melodrama on an operatic scale. Theatrics of this kind attracted the talents of writers, excited the curiosity of readers, and suited Octavian's political interests: that Antony was man ruined by deep passions remained the basic justification for fighting and defeating him.[136] Teasing out the truth of any particular, however, is often impossible. We are told, for instance, how, when he returned to Alexandria, Antony collapsed into despair, removing himself to his private residence, dubbed by all the Timoneion, a name recalling Timon of Athens, the legendary misanthrope. In Plutarch's version of this story, however, Antony withdrew not because he hated humanity but because *he* had been abandoned by his friends. In this account, only Cleopatra remains loyal, and she, by contrast, is all action. In the end, of course, Antony recovers himself and returns to his queen and her society. His devotion to her never again wavers.[137] This is stagey stuff, but not for that reason untrue. It can hardly be excluded that Antony was psychologically devasted, at least temporarily, by his entirely unexpected failure—it simply never occurred to him that his soldiers would ever desert him—but whether his disappointment played itself out in an episode of the kind our sources preserve is a different matter.

Whether or not Antony wasted a bit of time sulking in his residence, he was very soon once more in command. Survival, not victory, became the new imperative. Over the winter and into the new year, Antony and Cleopatra contemplated escape, perhaps to Spain, where they might enlist soldiers and rally opposition to Octavian, perhaps to India.[138] All hopes of sailing east, however, were scuppered when Didius, sent by Octavian to take charge of Syria, torched the Egyptian fleet on the Red Sea.[139] Nor did Spain offer good prospects: the man who executed Sextus Pompey was unlikely to forge a republican stronghold there. Instead, Antony and Cleopatra applied themselves to bolstering the kingdom's defences. Naturally they sought support from regional allies, but the rulers Antony installed in the east were all too competent and cunning to fail to join his victorious foe. The only aberration was a revolt in Cyzicus by a fierce band of gladiators, if they were gladiators and not the forces of an unidentified leader still loyal to Antony: these men fought their way through Syria in the hope of reaching Egypt, but the able Didius defeated them.[140] No other reinforcements were even imaginable: Egypt was obliged to fight on its own. Consequently, a levy was conducted, enrolling native Egyptians into the army's ranks, and a fleet was readied for defending the harbour.[141]

Amid even these extremities, Antony continued to join Cleopatra in the ceremonies and festivities which remained essential political operations in Alexandria's regal court. In the city, and especially in its high society, it was vital that Egypt remain something worth fighting for, and it was by way of civic pageantry and palace occasions that the grandeur and culture of the Ptolemies were marked and appreciated. Nor is there any reason to doubt that, when banqueting and parading himself before the people, Antony enjoyed himself. He did not despair of the day simply because it must be numbered among his last. Family affairs were celebrated with great pomp: Caesarion was formally enrolled as an ephebe, a young man eligible for military and civic service; Antyllus donned the toga of manhood.[142] The fabulous Guild of the Inimitable Lifestyle was dissolved. In its place, Cleopatra and Antony assembled the Partners in Death. Every bit as elegant and fashionable as its predecessor, this circle was united by a commitment to end their lives together. But this was by no means an exercise in pessimism. *Partners in Death* was the title of a comedy by the Attic writer Diphilus, a play which by Antony's day was also a Roman classic: Plautus adapted it and Terence famously pilfered one of its scenes.[143] Neither Diphilus' nor Plautus' play survives, but in comedies of their kind there is always a happy ending: the friends or perhaps lovers of the title will have been willing to die for one another but, before the final curtain fell, escaped this fate owing, as always in a new comedy, to a combination of good luck and intelligence. This was the hopeful atmosphere Cleopatra and Antony fostered in Alexandria.

Antony was acutely aware of the strengths and vulnerabilities in Egypt's defences.[144] Which meant that he knew he could not keep Octavian out permanently. Instead, he hoped that, by rendering the invasion protracted and difficult, he might persuade his enemy to prefer negotiating the terms of Alexandria's surrender. Hence the embassies, there were at least three of them, sent to Octavian by Antony and Cleopatra. Capitulation, they accepted, was inevitable. So, too, disgorging their treasure. Octavian, they reckoned, would, in exchange, value a prompt and easy Egyptian conquest. With that on offer, they proposed that Cleopatra be allowed to retain her throne as Rome's client and Antony carry on in Egypt as an exile. When these terms were rejected, they asked that one of Cleopatra's children ascend the throne in her place. As for Antony, he suggested exile in Athens. He was confident Octavian did not want to provoke ill-feeling in Rome by putting him to death. Lepidus, after all, had been allowed to live and even remain a senator.

But Antony was no Lepidus. The latter, even after his son's conspiracy, could remain safely put away in Circeii. For Octavian's security, however, Antony had to die. At the same time, just as Antony surmised, Octavian did not wish to finish his great victory as Antony's executioner. For this reason, he made it clear that Cleopatra could expect favourable treatment for her children if she did away with her lover, giving Antony an end evocative of Pompey's. Ideally, of course, Octavian hoped Antony would fall fighting in some skirmish he could subsequently amplify into a great battle—or take his own life. Leaving Cleopatra on the throne, however, was out of the question, even if Antony committed suicide: that much Octavian made clear.[145]

Cornelius Gallus took command of the Roman troops in Cyrene and in late spring began advancing on Egypt from the west. Relying on the fortifications at Pelusium to impede Octavian on his other front, Antony led a significant force of ships and infantry against Gallus. An early success, he hoped, would incite defections and furnish him with four fresh legions. But he did not succeed.[146] Frustrated by more than one early reversal, Antony prepared for a protracted conflict only to learn that Pelusium had surrendered to Octavian. Later rumours attributed the city's capitulation to Cleopatra but the real culprit was the commander on the scene, a certain Seleucus. He paid a heavy price for his treachery: Antony executed the man's wife and family. Now Antony rushed eastwards to defend Alexandria. In an early skirmish, Antony, relying on a cavalry charge, managed to win the day. In the city there were celebrations, but this momentary victory was anything but decisive. Nor did it render Octavian open to renewed diplomacy. Plutarch reports that Antony went so far as to challenge Octavian to a duel. He received a withering response: surely Antony could find many other ways to end his life.[147]

Gallus continued to march on Egypt from the west. Octavian's forces soon reached the vicinity of Alexandria. There was now little hope. In Plutarch's telling of it, Antony, on the final night of his life, enjoyed a lavish banquet, acutely aware that his next battle must be his last. When day came, Octavian launched an attack by sea and by land. There was little Antony could do. His fleet deserted him. Soon, his cavalry followed. And his infantry, no match for Octavian's, was quickly defeated. Antony retreated to Alexandria. In the palace, he fell on his sword. We cannot confidently say anything more than that. The circumstances and details of his end are richly elaborated in our sources, but they are all of them suspect. More than one story circulated in antiquity. In the one preferred by Dio, Cleopatra, secretly disloyal as Antony fought in defence of Alexandria, exploited his affection for her and by feigning her death tricked him into taking his own life—all in the hope of gaining some advantage from Octavian. This Antony—the lovesick Roman—and this Cleopatra—the monstrous Egyptian—are very much the creatures of Octavian's propaganda, and accounts of this kind, congenial to Augustan sensibilities, must have been commonplace.[148]

Plutarch gives us our most extended and detailed version of events, an emotive, theatrical account wonderfully refashioned into English drama by Shakespeare and now inescapably impressed on the modern reception of Antony's death. Unlike Dio's account, its narrative focus is concentrated on Antony, not Cleopatra. Here as in Dio, betrayal is in the air. Believing Cleopatra is the cause of his soldiers' disloyalty, Antony is enraged. The queen, who is innocent but in terror of her life, flees to her tomb, ordering her slaves give Antony a false report her death. In his grief, Antony's anger is melted. Bereft now of his beloved, he is resolved to die. He orders his slave, the suggestively named Eros, to strike him down. This man loves Antony too much, however, and takes his own life instead. Antony then stabs himself, but the wound is not immediately fatal. He lies suffering on his bed. When Cleopatra is made aware of this, she desires to see him, something that can be accomplished only by depositing the dying Antony on a pallet and hoisting him into Cleopatra's tomb. United for one last moment, the lovers are desperately tender toward one another. Antony calls for a final goblet of wine before urging Cleopatra to do what she can to save herself and forbidding her to grieve his tragic reversal of fortune. His final sentence, in his biographer's account, reprises his Roman sensibilities: 'there is nothing ignoble when a Roman is defeated by a Roman'. Shakespeare, for Antony's final scene, lifted and expanded the sentiments he found in Plutarch:

> The miserable change now at my end
> Lament nor sorrow at, but please your thoughts
> In feeding them with those my former fortunes,
> Wherein I lived the greatest prince o'th' world,
> The noblest; and do now not basely die,
> Not cowardly put off my helmet to
> My countryman—a Roman by a Roman
> Valiantly vanquished.[149]

Plutarch's elaborate account, sympathetic and arresting, is, like Dio's, a confection of different stories, some of which may be true or true enough. Antony, as we have seen, loved Cleopatra and we need not doubt a final interview before his suicide. Nor is it impossible or even unlikely he died in her arms. Even if one believes the queen was all calculation in her dealings with Antony, there was nothing to be gained by failing him at the end. Romans were very good at delivering suitable, sometimes moving parting words. Antony, we can be sure, had something final to say. That he said anything complimentary about Octavian, however, is unthinkable. On the last day of his life, Antony was a defeated man. But not a humbled one. The precise date of Antony's death is unknown, but Octavian celebrated his conquest of Alexandria on 1 August.[150] Antony was fifty-three years old.

XIV
Ending

After the death of Antony, Octavian entered Alexandria without resistance.[1] Anecdotes illustrating the Roman's chauvinism—he could not condescend to view the tombs of the Ptolemies or venerate native Egyptian gods—were crafted for consumption in Rome. In fact, Octavian delivered a public address which emphasized reconciliation and peace.[2] Mercy for the kingdom, however, did not entail pity for the family or supporters of Antony and Cleopatra. Canidius, Antony's loyal commander, was put to death. So, too, was Quintus Ovinius, a senator who had enriched himself by taking charge of Egypt's textile industry.[3] Antony's elder son, Antyllus, and Cleopatra's elder son, Caesarion, were also executed before Octavian returned to Rome. Neither boy, each endowed with an evocative name, could be allowed to become the centre of any future resistance in Rome or in Alexandria, a dangerous political dynamic Octavian understood all too well. The treasury was seized and royal lands were appropriated.

Cleopatra was now a prisoner. She negotiated fiercely for the survival of her children, something that was only possible if she agreed to the humiliation of appearing in Octavian's triumph. This she was unwilling to do. On 10 August in 30 BCE, at the age of 39, the queen committed suicide. How we do not know, but nor is there any compelling reason to accept or reject the popular tale that she ended her life by submitting to the bite of an asp. She was granted a royal funeral and buried alongside Antony. Nothing was done to remove her statues or eliminate her memory in Egypt. On her death, Caesarion became king, officially but only briefly. On 29 August, the first day of the Egyptian new year, Octavian became pharaoh of Egypt. And although it is inaccurate to say that Egypt became his personal property, Octavian gathered the kingdom to himself in such a way that thereafter it remained different from any other Roman province. As pharaoh, the Roman owned or dominated much of the country, and his household soon took possession of vast, extensive estates. Senators and distinguished equestrians were barred from the kingdom without Octavian's permission. He supervised Egypt by way of an imperial prefect—Gaius Cornelius Gallus was the first—and in this way took control of the region's vital agricultural resources as well as its extraordinary wealth. As Tacitus later put it, Octavian *isolated* Egypt, turning it into one of the hidden tools of imperial absolutism.[4]

Cleopatra's children by Antony were destined for Octavian's triumph, which took place in 29.[5] All three were transported to Rome, but death overtook the youngest, Ptolemy Philadelphus, before he could join in the procession. Alexander Helios and Cleopatra Selene, however, were paraded before the populace, along with an effigy of their mother. Alexander died soon afterwards, but the young Cleopatra grew up in the imperial household and was ultimately married to Juba II. The couple were installed as king and queen of Mauretania, where they established a glamorous, Alexandrian-style court. Their son, named Ptolemy, was Juba's successor. His reign ended, however, when he was put to death by Caligula. It is far from obvious that, had Ptolemy or

Fig. 14.1 Juan Luna, *Cleopatra* (1881), in the Museo Nacional del Prado.
Source: Art Resource.

Alexander, Cleopatra's sons, survived, Octavian would have found regal assignments for them. Still, after Actium and the fall of Alexandria, when Rome's new master settled the affairs of his client kings, he did very little to alter Antony's arrangements.[6] Partly this was because Antony, like Pompey before him, had organized the east so ably. At the same time, Octavian was no longer afraid. Although he had orchestrated a great war against Egypt, he did not doubt the docility of the eastern monarchies.

Antony's surviving son by Fulvia, Iullus Antonius, became an attractive, talented man who was much favoured by Octavian. He was married to Marcella, a daughter of Octavia by her first husband, and she bore him a son. Iullus is celebrated by Horace for his poetry. He was also advanced to a consulship in the year 10 BCE and was governor of Asia. In 2 BCE, however, Iullus fell, implicated in a scandal centred round Octavian's daughter, Julia. Ostensibly, the crime was adultery, but almost certainly that disgrace was put forward to mask an extensive conspiracy within the imperial house. Julia was exiled to an island. Four nobles, alleged paramours, suffered relegation. Iullus, possibly the leading figure in the plot, was put to death.[7] His young son was left unharmed but was thereafter confined to life in Massillia, where he was an ardent student of Greek subjects. When he died, in 25 CE, he was, by decree of the senate, buried with high honours.[8] Antony's two daughters by Octavia wed distinguished nobles. The elder married Lucius Domitius Ahenobarbus and was the grandmother of the emperor Nero. The younger married Nero Claudius Drusus, Tiberius' brother. Caligula was her grandson, Claudius her son. 'Antony's descendants', it has aptly been observed, 'become Octavian's successors'.[9]

In Rome, Mark Antony's disgrace began soon after his failure at Actium. The date of his birth, as we have seen, was declared Rome's sole *dies vitiosus*—a depraved and inauspicious day—and his family was forbidden from ever again using the praenomen *Marcus*.[10] The erasure of his name from public monuments, what modern scholars call *damnatio memoriae*, the condemnation of an individual's memory, was soon imposed in the capital, in the provinces, and in subject cities in the east. But *damnatio* of this kind did not remain Octavian's policy. Antony's family, including his Egyptian children, joined the imperial household, as we have seen, and there Octavia, who never remarried, was their chief advocate. The name *Marcus* was dropped by his descendants, but Antony himself was restored to public inscriptions in Rome. In the provinces, too, at least in most instances, Antony's name remained unerased. In part this reflects Octavian's policy of restoring at least an appearance of harmony to Roman affairs, but it is also possible that Antony's partial rehabilitation was owing to the wishes of Octavia. Whatever her feelings about the husband who abandoned her, she recognized that it was hardly in her daughters' interests for every trace of their father to be expunged.[11]

After Antony's defeat, Octavian concentrated his energies on sustaining his predomination of Rome—with unparalleled success. As an old man, he looked back on the moment when he fulfilled his mission as triumvir: 'in my sixth and seventh consulships, after I had extinguished civil war, at a time when, in accordance with the consent of everyone I was master of everything, I handed over the republic from my power to the will of the senate and people of Rome. For this service on my part, I was named Augustus by a decree of the senate'.[12] Octavian's seventh consulship came in 27, by which time, he declared, there was no further need for absolutism. His restoration of the republic was duly celebrated, and Octavian, on a proposal made in the senate by Munatius Plancus, became Augustus, a name so potent and intimidating in its implications that it remains impossible to translate out of Latin. Thereafter, or so Augustus insisted, he influenced public affairs only by way of his prestige and the offices imposed on him by the senate and people of Rome.[13]

Whatever else he did, Octavian did *not* restore the traditional republic.[14] Instead, he imposed on Roman society a novel species of autocracy. His power reposed on the armies but also on the almost slavish devotion of a population desperate for security and stability. They were naturally grateful because he gave them what they wanted most:

> As he bewitched the army with donatives, the public with cheap grain, everyone with the sweetness of peace, he gradually rose to pre-eminence. He gathered to himself the operations of the senate, the magistrates, the laws.[15]

His indispensability he reinforced by way of an intrusive cult of personality exceeding anything the ancient Mediterranean had previously known. At the same time, there was room at the top for compliant aristocrats to win glory, garner prestige, and enjoy influence—especially in the provinces. Property rights were ensured and the courts operated with as much, perhaps more integrity than they had done in living memory. Everyone felt free, or free enough, and they believed they had Octavian to thank for it.

Which they did by honouring him as Augustus and Father of his Country in ceaseless sequences of panegyric.

We cannot know what Rome would have been like had Antony won. It is far from inconceivable that, like Sulla, he would have handed the republic back to the senate and the assemblies. Relishing his wealth and prestige from a distance, perhaps even from Alexandria, he could exercise influence without dominating affairs and changing the fundamental nature of the republic. Or, like Caesar, Antony may have held on to power and carried on, taking a stimulus-response approach to governing, accumulating honours or even waging wars of foreign conquest—leaving it to another generation to fight it out for Rome's future. True, had Antony chosen to dominate affairs from Alexandria, the character of Rome would have changed in important ways—but only by accident and not by design. It is hard to imagine Antony's ushering in a new world order.

Antony was an adaptable, even a creative man, but he was no visionary. For most of his life, he liked the world as he found it. This is unsurprising: he was nobly born, handsomely endowed, and fitted into a place in society where he enjoyed advantages excelling even most of his peers. When challenges arose, he routinely surmounted them, and by the time he had become a grandee he no longer harboured any doubts about his capacity for overcoming others. The greatest shock of Antony's life, without question, was his failure at Actium: that he could lose to Octavian simply never occurred to him, which is why the possibility that his legions might desert him when he sailed away with Cleopatra never entered his calculations. Antony was a towering figure in his day. After Caesar's death, he led the republic. Thereafter, he led the triumvirate. Then, suddenly, he was gone, remembered chiefly for the danger he and his kind posed to Octavian's version of the republic.

But what a legacy! Passion, sensuality, hedonism, vigorous masculinity—all these thrumming in a personality also capable of reasoned senatorial debate, statesmanship, diplomacy, and military discipline. And a doomed love affair with a glamorous, powerful Egyptian queen. The figure of Mark Antony animates much in Latin love poetry, anonymously of course, nor, in a later age, could the moralizing Plutarch resist his fabulously tragic story: he so much wants to reprobate the man, and he does, but he is also strangely drawn to him.[16] It is Antony and Cleopatra—not Octavian, not even Augustus—who captivate poets and playwrights and filmmakers. And for one very obvious reason: Antony was and is a kind of guilty pleasure.

That, however, is a reflex of art, much of it originally Plutarch's art. For the historian, Antony is something different: a Roman aristocrat who, although he lasted longer than men like Scribonius Curio or Cornelius Dolabella or even Decimus Brutus and Cassius Longinus—was not fundamentally unlike them. They shared a common view of what it meant to be a Roman noble seeking a preeminent place in Rome's state and society. Even after Caesar's assassination, when so many ambitious men struggled to stay at the top, each of them—including Antony—contended with his rivals within the confines of republican expectations and possibilities. Fiercely competitive with all of them, Antony was nonetheless made of the same stuff as Hirtius and Pansa, the Liberators, even Cicero. He was not, however, made of the same stuff as Octavian. In the contest between them, that difference did not always give Octavian the edge. But, when victory came, when he was master of everything, because he was *not* fundamentally like Mark Antony, Octavian altered Roman society profoundly and permanently. The Roman republic—not entirely gone, certainly not forgotten—was truly over.

Notes

Preface

1 *Capital*. Faber & Faber, London 2012, 58.

CHAPTER I

1 Senators are *optimi*: Festus 290L.
2 On the controversies associated with the definition of *nobilitas*, see Burckhardt 1990.
3 Hölkeskamp 1988 is fundamental on cultural sensibilities animating the Romans' concept of *nobilitas*.
4 Earl 1967, 21; cf. McDonnell 2006; Balmaceda 2017.
5 Aristocratic values in Roman society: Syme 1939, 10–27; Earl 1967; Meier 1980; Hölkeskamp 2004; Tatum 2015; Mouritsen 2017, 95–104; Beck 2020; Hölkeskamp 2020 (each with further references).
6 Goldbeck 2010; Tatum 2018, 248–9 (with bibliography).
7 Q. Cic. *Comm. Pet.* 45–8; cf. Tatum 2018, 270–5.
8 Plaut. *Trin.* 651; Polyb. 31.23.10–12; 31.29.8; Cic. *Mur.* 23–9; *Acad.* 2.1.
9 What is *rich* in Rome? Romans employed coins in a variety of weights but tended to reckon prices and values in terms of the sesterce (sestertius) and denarius (worth four sesterces). Our sources tend to equate a Greek drachma with a denarius. And a talent is ordinarily understood to be 6,000 drachmas (and therefore 6,000 denarii). It is rarely useful to convert ancient currency into modern equivalents owing to deep differences between their economic system and our own. It may be helpful, however, to observe that in Antony's day an ordinary labourer scraped by on wages of three to six sesterces for a day's work. Soldiers earned an annual salary of 1,200 sesterces. Members of the prosperous First Class had to be worth at least 40,000 sesterces; an equestrian could not possess less than 400,000 sesterces. Senators were expected to be worth at least a million sesterces, and many were richer than that.
10 Sall. *Iug.* 85.4.
11 Cic. *Off.* 1.47; 2.21–2; 2.63; cf. Jacotot 2013; Tatum 2018, 179–80 (with further references).
12 Plin. *NH* 7.139: Quintus was consul in 206, his father in 251. On the importance of intelligence as an assertion of aristocratic excellence, see Jehne 2011; Hölkeskamp 2020, 43–62.
13 Cic. *Att.* 4.8a.2 (Lucius was consul in 54); cf. Wiseman 1971, 107–16.
14 Sall. *Iug.* 85.4; cf. 29; Cic. *Pis.* 2.
15 Sall. *Iug.* 85.10–11; cf. Blösel 2011.
16 Sall. *Cat.* 11.2–6; *Iug.* 85.37; 85.41.
17 Cic. *Fam.* 2.18.2: Lucius is *adulescens potens et nobilis*.
18 Sall. *Iug.* 64.1; 85.38; Romans often associated arrogance (*superbia*) with nobility: Hellegouarc'h 1963, 439–41.
19 *Rhet. Her.* 1.8.
20 Badian 1990.
21 Sall. *Cat.* 23.6; *Iug.* 63.7. On new men, aspersions against them, and their critique of the nobility, see Wiseman 1971; Dugan 2005; Tatum 2018, 166–7 (with extensive bibliography).

22 See, e.g., Cic. *Fam* 1.7.8; cf. Wiseman 1971, 100–105.

23 Plin. *NH* 14.147.

24 Hopkins 1983, 31–119; Broughton 1991; Konrad 1996; Farney 2004.

25 Meier 1980, 175; Hellegouarc'h 1963, 248–54; McDonnell 2006, 335–78.

26 Suet. *Aug.* 2.3; cf. Wardle 2014, 85–7.

27 On the Roman constitution, see Lintott 1999. For various perspectives on the relationship in Rome between the popular principle and the aristocratic one, see, e.g., Morstein-Marx 2004; North 2006; Tatum 2009; Hölkeskamp 2010; Brennan 2014; Tatum 2015; Mouritsen 2017 (all with further references).

28 Cic. *Leg. Agr.* 2.17.

29 On *imperium*, see Beck 2011 (with further references).

30 Cic. *Cat.* 4.21; *Phil.* 2.20; 8.30.

31 Jehne 2011.

32 Nicolet 1966; Brunt 1988, 144–93; Davenport 2019.

33 Brunt 1988, 148.

34 Tribes: Taylor 1960. Tribal organizations, affiliations, and neighbourliness (*vicinitas*): Tatum 2018, 225–7. Antony's tribe: *MAMA* 6.104.

35 Nomenclature in Rome: Salway 1994 (with ample bibliography).

36 Common *praenomina* and their abbreviations include: A. (Aulus); C. (Gaius); Cn. (Gnaeus); D. (Decimus); L. (Lucius); M. (Marcus); M'. (Manius); P. (Publius); Q. (Quinctus); Ser. (Servius); Sex. (Sextus); T. (Titus); Ti. (Tiberius).

37 Anton: Plut. *Ant.* 4.2; cf. 36.7; 60.5; cf. Ijalba Pérez 2009. The name is attested exclusively by Plutarch, if, indeed, that is what he wrote: *Anton*, the widely accepted 19th-century emendation of the manuscripts' *Antaeon* or *Anteon*, is rejected by Huttner 1995, 104. Divine genealogies appeared early in Rome and retained their attraction: Wiseman 1987, 208–9; Smith 2006a, 43–4; see further Syme 1986, 76–8; Hölkeskamp 2004, 199–217. The Fabii: Festus 77L; Plut. *Fab.* 1.2 (the story recurs in Latin poetry). Münzer 1909, 1739–40, argues that the Fabian connection with Hercules did not come into existence before the Augustan period. Other Roman figures fathered by Hercules left no sons: e.g., Pallas and Latinus (Dion. Hal. *Ant. Rom.* 1.43.1). Although the Pinarii were associated with Hercules' worship, they did not claim descent from the hero (Festus 270L; Liv. 1.7.12–13; Dion. Hal. *Ant. Rom.* 1.40.4).

38 Patricians and plebeians: Roman society divided itself unequally between *patricians*, a very small number of ancient families who prevailed in the government of early Rome, and *plebeians*, who were everybody else. Elite plebeian families eventually overcame the patricians' original advantages and, by Antony's day, plebeian families dominated the nobility. Patrician and plebeian status were each a condition of birth, but in the context of ancient Rome neither adjective carries the connotations of their equivalents in modern society; cf. Smith 2006a, 80.

39 M. Antonius, tr. pl. 167: *MRR* 1.433. Other early Antonii include Q. Antonius, who served under the praetor L. Aemilius Regillus and helped to negotiate the surrender of Phocea in 190 BC during Rome's war against Antiochus the Great (Liv. 37.32.8); A. Antonius, who in 168 at the close of the Third Macedonian War was part of an embassy sent to Samothrace by L. Aemilius Paullus in a vain attempt to negotiate the surrender of Perseus, the defeated and fugitive king of Macedon (Liv. 45.4.7). Less certainly historical (and less easily linked to Antony) is the M. Antonius who was briefly master of the horse (*magister equitum*) in 334 or 33 (Liv. 8.17.3); cf. Drummond 1989, 174 and 194; Oakley 1997, 45. An even less certain figure must be mentioned: according to Valerius Maximus, the censors of 307 expelled from the senate a man named either L. Annius or L. Antonius (the correct reading of the text is uncertain); see Val. Max. 2.9.2.

40 Scepticism enters as early as Niebuhr 1830, 364; cf. Ładoń 2016.

41 T. Antonius Merenda: *MRR* 1.46–7; on his patrician status, see Dion. Hal. *Ant. Rom.* 10.58.4. Q. Antonius Merenda: *MRR* 1.69. First plebeian military tribune with consular power in 400 BC: Liv. 5.12.9; 6.38.8—but it has been suggested that Livy is wrong here: Ogilvie 1965, 652–3; Oakley 1997, 372–3; 682.

42 Ranouil 1975; Tatum 1999, 91–5; Smith 2006a, 213–5.

43 See Drummond 1989, 175–6; Cornell 1995, 252–5. Merenda was a cognomen which these Antonii shared with the patrician Cornelii: Liv. 22.35.1; 34.42.4; see Kajanto 1965, 91.

44 False genealogies in Rome: Cic. *Brut.* 62; *Fam.* 15.20.1; Plin. *NH* 35.8. Blurring lines of descent by way of filching a cognomen was not uncommon in the late republic: Badian 1988. So, too, were false claims that a family had once been patrician but changed its status to plebeian: Tatum 1999, 92–3. Revealingly, the late republican Antonii employed neither tactic.

45 Drumann-Groebe 1899, 44–5; Scholz 1963. Sources assembled at *ORF*[4] 221–37; *MRR* 1.563, 539, 576, 568, 572; 2.16–7; 3.19. Antonius' oratorical skill: Hall 2014, 18–20 and 141–44.

46 See De Souza 1999, 102–8 (citing previous scholarship on Antonius' command).

47 *MRR* 2.52. On the importance of the augurate, see Linderski 1986; Driediger-Murphy 2018a; see also ch. III.4.

48 Blom 2010, 226–30.

49 Cic. *Brut.* 139.

50 Cic. *Brut.* 138.

51 Cic. *De or.* 3–5.

52 On the Social War and its consequences, see Gabba 1994, 104–128; Bispham 2007; Steel 2013, 80–120 (each providing sources and previous scholarship).

53 On the career of Marius, see Carney 1961 and Evans 1994. On Sulla, see Keaveney 2005. On the events of 88, see Tatum 2022.

54 On these events, see Seager 1994, 165–73; Steel 2013, 87–95.

55 Hinard 1985, 67–143; Seager 1994, 173–207; Steel 2013, 95–117.

56 Antonius was slain by the military tribune P. Annius: *MRR* 2.49. For concise and intelligent surveys of the conflict between Marius and Sulla, see Seager 1994, 165–97 and Steel 2013, 87–97 (with further literature).

57 C. Antonius was a cavalry prefect under Sulla not later than the year 84 (see *MRR* 2.61–2). Unless he fled to Sulla after his father's death, he can be assumed to have joined Sulla's command from its beginning.

58 Badian 1964, 46–50; cf. Gruen 1965.

59 Cic. *Brut.* 168; *de Or.* 2.2; cf. *Leg.* 3.36; *MRR* 1.569. Another Gratidius was Marius' officer in 88 BC (Val. Max. 9.7b.1), while yet another was legate to Cicero's brother Quintus when he was governor of Asia. On the family ties binding Cicerones, Gratidii, and Marii, see Carney 1961, 77, and Nicolet 1974, 907–8.

60 The Cornelian tribe: Taylor 1960, 272. The original home of the Cornelian tribe remains unknown (Taylor 1960, 362). M. Antonius' tribe was, presumably, the same as his grandson's. On significance of neighbourliness (*vicinitas*), see Tatum 2018, 226–7 (with further references).

61 The centrality of tribes in Roman society: Taylor 1960; Lintott 1999, 50–5; Smith 2006a, 236–50.

62 On the appropriate age for standing for the quaestorship, see Astin 1958, 31–45; Beck 2005, 58–9.

63 Badian 1964, 216.

64 *MRR* 2.126–7, 141, 151–2, 531; 3.18; Drumann-Groebe 1899, 390–96; Ferriès 2007, 388–9; Tatum 2018, 188–96.

65 Tatum 2018, 191–3, assembles evidence and scholarship.

66 Owing to an old and improbable emendation of Q. Cic. *Comm. Pet.* 8, it is sometimes inferred that Antonius, after his praetorship, undertook a mission to Cappadocia, possibly in cooperation with Pompey the Great. But this is incorrect; for a fuller account, see Tatum 2018, 196.

67 On the Catilinarian conspiracy, see p. 21.

68 Linderski 1995, 436–43, is an important corrective to the orthodox view of Marcus; see also S. Day 2017.

69 Plut. *Ant.* 1.1–3; Sall. *Hist.* 3.3McG.

70 Pelling 1988, 117; Pelling 2002, 96–102.

71 During the proscriptions of 43, for instance, Julia saved the life of her brother, L. Julius Caesar (cos. 69): Plut. *Ant.* 20.5–6; App. *B.Civ.* 4.37, and she was an important advisor of Antony in the aftermath of Perusia: see Ch. X, pp. 251–2; and Ch. XI, pp. 253–54, 257–58.

72 *MRR* 2.101–2.

73 Seager 1994, 215–222; Konrad 199; Q. Metellus Pius was a Sullan stalwart who held a consulship in 80.

74 Sherwin-White 1994, 233–48; Kallet-Marx 1995, 291–304; Steel 2013, 140–2. Lucullus' intrigues: Plut. *Luc.* 6–7.

75 De Souza 1999, 142–6. Piratical depredations also endangered Rome's grain supply: Kallet-Marx 1995, 306.

76 On Marcus' command, see (with sources and further literature), De Souza 1999, 141–8; Brennan 2000, 406–7.

77 Ps.-Asc. 259St.

78 The point of Vell. 2.31.4, observing that Marcus' appointment did not incite anxiety on the part of the senatorial elite (as did Pompey the Great's command against the pirates in 67), is not that Marcus was a non-entity but rather that he (unlike Pompey) was not suspected of wanting to seize power.

79 The evidence for Caesar's service under Creticus is the mention of a C. Iulius in *SIG*[3] 748, but the identification is not certain: *MRR* 3.105.

80 The significance of Marcus' campaign against the pirates is demonstrated by the importance of its narrative in the structure of Sallust's *Historiae*: see McGushin 1994, 64–72.

81 In addition to Lucullus' forces, M. Cotta was in command of a fleet whose purpose was to protect Bithynia from Mithridates (*MRR* 2.101).

82 Cic. *Div. Caec.* 55; *Verr.* 2.2.8; 2.3.213–7; *SIG*[3] 748 = *IG* 5.1.146.

83 Sall. *Hist.* 3.2McG; Ps.-Asc. 202 and 259St; Dio 36.23.

84 Antonii in Crete: e.g., Bowsky 2001; see also ch. XI, pp. 273–74.

85 The sources for Marcus' campaign are assembled at *MRR* 2.111, 117, 123; see also Kallet-Marx 1995, 304–11; De Souza 1999, 141–8; Brennan 2000, 406–7.

86 Linderski 1995, 436–43, remains fundamental on Creticus' campaign in Crete.

87 The problem of piracy persisted. Consequently, Q. Metellus (cos. 69) was assigned a command against Cretan pirates (*MRR* 2.131) and in 67 the *lex Gabinia* installed Pompey as commander in a war of vast proportions against all Mediterranean piracy (*MRR* 2.144–5); see De Souza 1999, 159–72.

88 EJ 45; cf. Linderski 2007, 518–9.

89 Plut. *Ant.* 86.8; App. *B. Civ.* 5.8. Young Mark Antony: Drumann-Grobe 1899, 46–7; Rossi 1959, 5–13; Bengston 1977, 11–30; Huzar 1978, 12–26; Chamoux 1986, 13–31; Dettenhofer 1992, 63–5; Halfmann 2011, 13–34; Goldsworthy 2010, 52–95; Southern 2012, 24–43.

90 Sumner 1971, 363; *RRC* 489.

91 Cic. *Vat.* 28–9; Schol. Bob. 149 St.

92 Gowing 1992; Lintott 1997; Pelling 2002; Duff 2004; Stadter 2015, 45–55; 119–29; 215–302; Brenk 2017, 131–266; *FRHist*, vol. 1, 424–5; 430–45; 454–62.
93 Cic. *Phil.* 2.44–5.
94 Sussman 1998; Ramsey 2003, 227–8.
95 Pelling 1988, 118. Antony's father 'not very rich': Plut. *Ant.* 1.2.
96 Plut. *Ant.* 2.4–8; cf. Cic. *Cael.* 30 and see, further, below.
97 Syme 1939, 149. Invective: Süss 1920; Merrill 1975; Corbeil 2002; Craig 2004; Arena 2007. Invective in rhetorical education: Cic. *Inv.* 1.34–6; 2.28–31; 2.177–8; *Rhet. Her.* 3.10–15.
98 Cic *Cael.* 6; Quint. 5.10.26.
99 Schulz 1951, 214; Pakter 1994; Ioannatou 2006, 14–5.
100 Q. Cic. *Comm. Pet.* 8; Asc. 84C; cf. Tatum 2018, 191–4.
101 Dio 46.14.3–4.
102 Jehne 2016, 195–201.
103 Pelling 2002, 301–38.
104 Plut. *Ant.* 1.1–2.3; cf. Pelling 1988, 117–8.
105 Plut. *Ant.* 2.8.
106 See, e.g., Bonner 1977; Rawson 1985; Moatti 1997; Hutchinson 1998; Hall 2009; Scholz 2011, 317–29; Volk 2021.
107 Cic. *Att.* 14.7.2.
108 Caesar: Garcea 2012. Quintus: Cic. *Q.Fr.* 3.5.7. Brutus: Plut. *Brut.* 4.6–8.
109 Cic. *Off.* 1.222; 2.46–7; *Amic.* 1; *Sen.* 10; *Phil.* 2.3; *Fam.* 13.10.2; Plut. *Cat. mai.* 3.4; cf. Scholz 2011.
110 Polyb. 31.29.8; Cic. *Acad.* 2.1; Plut. *Luc.* 1.2; Quint. 12.7.3; cf. Tatum 2018, 22–3. Testimonia for Atratinus' prosecution of Caelius: Alexander 1990, 134; Atratinus reached the consulship in 34.
111 Cic. *Cael.* 28; cf. Laes and Strubbe 2014, 137–40. Youthful indiscretions are venial: e.g., Cic. *Inv.* 2.37; *Cael.* 30; 42; Suet. *Ner.* 26; cf. Austin 1960, 84 and 102; Tatum 2011, 169–70; Dyck 2013, 129 (assembling further evidence).
112 Cic. *Phil.* 2.3; 3.17; 13.23; *Att.* 16.11.1.
113 Cicero previously calumniated Gellius Publicola, an equestrian noble, for marrying a freedwoman, 'not in order to satisfy his lust by to exhibit his solidarity with the common man' (*Sest.* 110); cf. Tatum 1999, 115–6; Kaster 2006, 336–8. Invective attacks on the breeding of an opponent's loved ones: Süss 1920, 247–9; Lausberg 1990, 204–6.
114 Most (not all) biographies accept the idea. So, too, specialist accounts like Rizzelli 2006. This allegation, however, is rejected by, i.a., Ramsey 2003, 165, and Manuwald 2007, 385 (who assembles previous scholarship).
115 On Plutarch's omission, see, more fully, Tatum 2020d.
116 Treggiari 1981, 75. On Roman concubinage, see also *Dig.* 25.7.1–3; Rawson 1974; McGinn 1991; Evans Grubbs 1995, 294–300. Concubines called wives, esp. among the lower orders: Tramunto 2009, esp. 73–85.
117 Suet. *Vesp.* 3.
118 August. *Conf.* 4.2; 6.12–15; cf. O'Donnell 1992, 207; 383–5.
119 Plut. *Ant.* 1.2–2.1; cf. Caesar's mother, Aurelia: Tac. *Dial.* 28.6; Plut. *Caes.* 9.3.
120 Physiognomy in Plutarch: Tatum 1996. Physiognomic theories in Greco-Roman antiquity: Swain 2007.
121 Cic. *Phil.* 2.63; Plut. *Ant.* 4.1–2. Dio 45.30.3 adapts Cicero. Caesar's famous remark, comparing Antony and Dolabella with Cassius and Brutus, that he preferred 'fat, sleek-headed men' to anyone with 'a lean and hungry look', reported by Plutarch more than once, puts Antony in a different light; *fat*, in that expression, signals slow-wits, and sleek-headedness

is a mark of effeminacy: Plut. *Ant.* 11.6; *Caes.* 62.10; *Brut.* 8.2; *Mor.* 206F14; cf. Pelling 1988, 143–4.

122 Smith 1988.

123 Antony's coins are catalogued in *RRC* and *RPC* (with photographs).

124 See, e.g., Draycott 2012.

125 Cairo Egyptian Museum: inv. 42.891; Budapest Museum of Fine Arts: inv. 4807; Narbonne Musée Archéologie Muncipal: inv. 879-1-170; Museum of Thasos: inv. 2434; Centrale Montemartini: inv. 2432; Kingston Lacy Estate: NT 1257603. Antony as New Dionysus: see ch. XI, pp. 269–71.

126 Otto 1962; Michel 1967; Holtzman and Salviat 1981; Smith 1988, 136–7; Kleiner 1992, 46–7 (these works include photographs of these busts).

127 Saller 1994, 181–203.

128 Cic. *Phil.* 4.13; *Phil.* 2.14; 8.1–2; Plut. *Ant.* 2.1.

129 Lentulus' career: *MRR* 2.121; 126–7; 166.

130 On Catiline, see Levick 2015.

131 On this election, see Tatum 2018, 97–105.

132 Debt: Frederiksen 1966; Kay 2014, 257–9. Urban unrest: Cic. *Leg. agr.* 2.8; cf. Manuwald 2018, x–xii; 201–3. Etruria: Rosenstein 2008. Gaul: Sall. *Cat.* 40.1; 49.2.

133 On the Catilinarian conspiracy, see Wiseman 1994a, 346–58; Steel 2013, 150–59; Levick 2015.

134 Gelzer 1969, 71–104; Tempest 2011, 85–100.

135 *MRR* 2.175.

136 Cic. *Phil.* 2.17; Plut. *Ant.* 2.1–3 (Cicero withheld none of the bodies of the executed Catilinarians).

137 Cic. *Cat.* 4.13.

138 Polyb. 6.19.4; cf. Harris 1979, 10–41; Rosenstein 2020.

139 Cic. *Off.* 2.45.

140 Cicero during the Social War: Plut. *Cic.* 3.2; Cic. *Lig.* 21: *Div.* 1.72; 2.65; *Phil.* 12.27; *Q.Fr.* 1.3.10.

141 Cic. *Mur.* 24.

142 Val Max 3.1.1; cf. *RRC* 443.

143 Cic. *Off.* 2.45.

144 Suet. *Iul.* 2.

145 Q. Metellus Macedonicus (cos. 143), for instance, after his victory in the Fourth Macedonian War, was defeated twice in consular elections (*MRR* 1.467; Broughton 1991, 8–9). Metellus' was not a unique case: see, further, Tatum 2018, 21–2.

146 Brunt 1971, 95–6; 253–65; 391–415.

147 E.g., Liv. 39.9.2; 39.19.304; *Lex Rep.* (= *RS* 1).77–8; *Lex Mun. Tarent.* (= *RS* 8).4, 9.

148 Blösel 2011.

149 On the role of *publicani* in provincial administration, see ch. II, pp. 00.

150 Q. Cic. *Comm. Pet.* 8; Asc. 84C; Plut. *Caes.* 4.2–3; cf. *MRR* 2.61–2; Tatum 2018, 191–2.

151 *MRR* 2.80.

152 Potency: Cic. *Verr.* 2.3.28–30; 39; 54–5; 68–9; 155–9. Corruption: Cic. *Verr.* 2.3.84–93.

153 Cic. *Verr.* 2.3.134.

154 Memmius' governorship of Bithynia and Pontus (*MRR* 2.203) took place in 57, the same year in which Gabinius took up his position in Syria (see below). On Catullus' disappointment, see Cat. 10; 28; cf. Tatum 2008, 344–6. Even the frustrated Catullus claims to have made close friends among the tent-mates of Memmius: Cat. 46.9.

155 Cic. *Fam.* 7.5.

156 The excellent suggestion of Rossi 1959, 9–10.

157 *MRR* 2.175–6; 180; 184. Trial: Alexander 1990, 119–20. Thrace, in Roman times, was a region bordered in its north by the Balkans, consisting of the easternmost parts of modern Greece, south-east Bulgaria, and north-west Turkey. Its border with Rome was a site of frequent warfare between Rome and various Thracian kingdoms and tribes.

158 Gaius did not return to Rome from Macedonia until the end of 60: Cic. *Att.* 2.2.3. On events pertinent to the formation of the First Triumvirate, see Gelzer 1968, 71–101; Seager 2002, 86–100; Steel 2013, 163–69; Fezzi 2019, 97–112; Morstein-Marx 2021, 117–119.

159 Morstein-Marx 2021, 264.

160 See further pp. 210–11.

161 Whereas the triumvirate composed of Antony, Lepidus, and Octavian (see ch. VIII, pp. 183–186), sometimes called the Second Triumvirate, was a legally constituted office, this First Triumvirate was an informal alliance of friends: historians often feel the need to emphasize this difference either by avoiding the expression or by qualifying it.

162 *MRR* 2.190. Vatinius and Antonia were certainly married by 57, when Cicero delivered his *In Vatinium*.

163 *MRR* 2.193–4.

164 Tatum 1999, 90–108.

165 Alexander 1990, 119–20; there is some uncertainty over the exact charge against Gaius.

166 Cic. *Dom.* 41; *Sest.* 116; *Prov. cons.* 42; cf. Suet. *Iul.* 20.4; App. *B. Civ.* 2.14; Dio 38.10.1; cf. Tatum 1999, 103–4.

167 Clodius' legislative programme: Tatum 1999, 114–38.

168 Tatum 1999, 139–49.

169 Alexander 1990, 125–6; Tatum 1999, 140–1.

170 Cic. *Phil.* 2.48; Plut. *Ant.* 2.7.

171 Tatum 1999, 152–66.

172 *MRR* 2.199–200.

173 Cic. *Q. Fr.* 1.3.7.

174 Rawson 1985, 6–13.

175 On Antony's style, see Huzar 1982; Mahy 2013; Blom 2016, 248–79.

176 Cic. *Fam.* 2.18.2 (litotes for emphasis in Latin: H-S 777–9); Plut. *Ant.* 40.8, cf. Blom 2016, 250–1.

177 Wisse 1995 assembles the ancient evidence and examines modern discussions of this Roman controversy. On Atticism versus Asianism in Plutarch's time, see Kim 2017.

178 Plut. *Ant.* 2.8; cf. Pelling 1988, 119–20; Calboli 1997.

179 Suet. *Aug.* 86.2.

180 Suet. *Aug.* 86.3; cf. Wardle 2014, 488.

181 Cic. *Phil.* 3.22; cf. Manuwald 2007, 403–7.

182 Style and character: Gleason 1995, 103–21; Connolly 2007; Möller 2004; Borgies 2016, 219–20.

183 Plut. *Ant.* 78.2.

184 Cic. *Phil.* 13.43.

185 Cicero: Keil, *Gramm. Lat.*, vol. 5, 154 (= *fr. epist.* 17.3 Watt).

186 Style in the propaganda contest between Antony and Octavian: Borgies 2016, 220–45. Antony's letters: Ov. *Pont.* 1.1.23; Tac. *Ann.* 4.34.5; Suet. *Aug.* 7.1; 16.2; 63.2; 69.2; Plut. *Ant.* 78.3; cf. Cugusi 1970, 236–69.

CHAPTER II

1 Gabinius' background: Badian 1959; Konrad 1984. His tribunate: *MRR* 2.144–5; cf. Seager 2002, 40–52; Fezzi 2019, 63–70. Service under Pompey: *MRR* 2.156, 160. Consulship: *MRR* 2.193–4.

2 Gabinius' appointment: *MRR* 2.203; 210–11; 218; Tatum 1999, 153; 298–9. Trebonius' law: *MRR* 2.217. Syria rich: Cic. *Sest.* 93; cf. Heichelheim 1938.

3 Lintott 1993, 50–2; Richardson 1994, 580–4; Schulz 1997, 93–199; Braund 1998.

4 On A. Gabinius (q. 101), see *IGRP* 4.116; *MRR* 1.572–3; 3.97; Badian 1959; Konrad 1984. One need hardly posit a role for Clodius Pulcher in introducing Antony to Gabinius, as does Chamoux 1986, 32.

5 As suggested by, i.a., Bengtson 1977, 30–8, and Pasquali 2009, 44–5.

6 Friendship and alliances: Brunt 1988, 443–502. Antony aids Cicero: Cic. *Q. Fr.* 1.3.7.

7 Plut. *Ant.* 3.1: τῶν ἱππέων ἄρχων (which is to say, *praefectus equitum*). On this post, see Suolahti 1955, 198–213; McCall 2002.

8 McCall 2002, esp. 100–113.

9 Suolahti 1955, 213–79; Blösel 2011.

10 Young Crassus: Caes. *B. Gall.* 1.52.7; Cicero's son: Cic. *Off.* 2.45.

11 McCall 2002, 114–36; Rosenstein 2006; Blösel 2011.

12 Wiseman 1971, 176–8.

13 Q. Cic. *Comm. Pet.* 8; Asc. 84C; Plut. *Caes.* 4.2–3.

14 Cic. *De or.* 2.269.

15 Nep. *Att.* 6.4.

16 Antony's career with Gabinius: Drumann-Grobe 1899, 47; Rossi 1959, 13–14; Bengston 1977, 30–8; Huzar 1978, 27–33; Chamoux 1986, 31–41; Dettenhofer 1992, 65; Pasquali 2009, 43–7; Goldsworthy 2010, 99–104; Halfmann 2011, 33–6; Southern 2012, 41–8.

17 See, especially, ch. IX.

18 *StrR* 3.1.645–715; Badian 1968; Lintott 1993, 16–42; Beness and Hillard 2013; Harris 2016, esp. 34–7.

19 Polyb. 1.1.5; 3.4.3; see, further, Kallet-Marx 1995, 22–29; Baronowski 2011.

20 App. *Ib.* 44; cf. Richardson 2000, 142.

21 The fullest discussion of this inscription is Nörr 1989, but see especially Linderski 2007, 53–5. A similar formulation occurs in *ILLRP* 514.

22 This point is made explicitly at Str. 17.3.24–5. Roman practice: instances are abundant; see, e.g., Cic. *Verr.* 2.3.207; 2.5.168; *Agr.* 1.8; 1.11; 2.15; 2.39; 2.98; *Dom.* 90; Sall. *Hist.* 1.55.13M (=1.48.13McG); 2.47.14M (=2.44.14McG); 3.52.6M (=3.34.6McG); *B. Alex.* 34; Suet. *Aug.* 48.

23 Lintott 1993, 22–32; Richardson 1994, 564–80; Kallet-Marx 1995, 11–122.

24 *MRR* 2.163–4; Rostovtzeff, 1941, 980–1; Will 1982, 508–15; Sherwin-White 1983, 206–13; Sartre 2005, 37–44.

25 Liv. 34.41.6.

26 Bernhardt 1985; Lintott 1993, 168–74; Richardson 1994, 591–3; Ando 2000, 58–62; Eilers 2002; Cebeillac-Gervasoni and Lamoine 2003; Dmitriev 2005, esp. 308–12; Santangelo 2007; Fournier 2010; Varga and Rusu-Voulindet 2016; Dench 2018, 29–46; 87–95; 105–133.

27 Cic. *Q. Fr.* 1.1.34.

28 Rostovtzeff 1941, 968–89; Badian 1972, esp. 67–81; Lintott 1993, 86–96; Cottier et al. 2008; Kay 2014, 59–83; Tan 2017, 40–67.

29 Cicero praises the *publicani*: e.g., *Leg. Man.* 17–18; *Agr.* 1.22–7; 2.102; *Planc.* 23; *Att.* 6.1.16; 6.3.3. Cicero's animadversions: e.g., Cic. *Att.* 2.1.8; *Q. Fr.* 1.1.6–7, 32–6; *Off.* 1.150. Cicero's

criticisms were not unique to him: e.g., Cic. *Planc.* 23–4; Val. Max. 6.9.7–8; Plut. *Mar.* 3. On the political activities and the clout of *publicani*, see Badian 1972, esp. 82–118; Brunt 1988, 148–62; Schulz 1997, 197–9; 239–46; Rollinger 2009, 87–101.

30 Cic. *Q. Fr.* 1.1.35.

31 Cic. *Q. Fr.* 2.12.2.

32 Ando 2000; Lintott 1993, 43–69; Richardson 1994, 572–85; Schulz 1997, 93–8.

33 Cic. *Q. Fr.* 1.1.22.

34 Populated by businessmen: Caes. *B. Civ.* 3.102.6; Str. 16.4.21.

35 Cic. *Q. Fr.* 1.1; see, e.g., Badian 1958, 154–67; Badian 1972; Schulz 1997, 93–8; Eilers 2002; Lintott 2008, 81–125.

36 Badian 1972, esp. 105–6; 113–4; Brunt 1990, 354–432; Andreau 1999, 9–29; Schulz 1997, 197–9; 239–46; Ando 2000, 58–62; Rollinger 2009, 117–20; Fournier 2010, 314–23; Kay 2014, 235–64; Morrell 2017, 153–76.

37 *SIG*³ 748 = *IG* 5.1.1146; cf. Sherk 1984, 93–4; Fournier 2010, 316.

38 Cic. *Att.* 6.1.3; *Fam.* 13.56; cf. Badian 1968, 82–4; Morrell 2017, 82–4.

39 Cic. *Att.* 6.1.6.

40 Cic. *Att.* 5.21.10–13; 6.1.5–7; 6.2.7–9; cf. Fournier 2010, 315–6; Tempest 2017, 45–9. On the question of whether Brutus' associates, M. Scaptius and P. Matinius, were equestrians, see Nicolet 1974, 947; 1014–5.

41 Cic. *Att.* 6.1.5; 6.2.7; 6.3.5.

42 Cic. *Att.* 7.1.6; *Fam.* 2.17.4; 5.20.9.

43 Morrell 2017 discusses the Romans' efforts to correct injustices in provincial administration.

44 Will 1982, 508–15; Sherwin-White 1983, 206–18; Sartre 2005, 37–44; Sharon 2017, 59–99.

45 Joseph *AJ* 14.5; 14.5.1; *BJ* 1.8.1; App. *Syr.* 51. Syria's two legions: Joseph *AJ* 14.79.

46 Joseph *AJ* 14.37; cf. *BJ* 1.128. M. Aemelius Scaurus (pr. 56) was Pompey's principal legate in Judea. Gabinius, after subduing enemy resistance in southern Armenia, was dispatched to assist him (Dio 37.5.2–6).

47 *MRR* 2.170; Sherwin-White 1983, 212–8. On the political disorder afflicting Syria, see Sherwin-White 1983, 212.

48 A vast sum: on what counted for riches in Rome, see ch. I, footnote 9.

49 Sources assembled at *MRR* 2.203; 210–1; 218. Cicero's reconciliation with Gabinius: Cic. *Rab. Post.* 19–21; 32–3; Val. Max. 4.2.5; cf. Siani-Davies 2001, 191–2.

50 Joseph *AJ* 14.82–91; *BJ* 160–70; cf. Sherwin-White 1983, 274–5; Sartre 2005, 46–8; Sharon 2017, 100–5.

51 Joseph *BJ* 170.

52 Joseph *AJ* 14.92–97; *BJ* 171–74; cf. Sherwin-White 1983, 274–5; Sartre 2005, 46–8; Sharon 2017, 105–7 (there is no reason to take seriously the view, repeated by Sharon, that Aristobulus' escape was facilitated by Gabinius' enemies in Rome).

53 Joseph *AJ* 14.100–103; *BJ* 1.176–78; cf. Sherwin-White 1983, 274–5; Sartre 2005, 46–8; Sharon 2017, 107–9.

54 Joseph *BJ* 178; cf. *AJ* 14.10.

55 Joseph *AJ* 14.137–9; *BJ* 1.193–4.

56 Joseph *AJ* 14.325; *BJ* 1.244. Joint military service was an important medium for the establishment of friendship between Romans and foreigners: Prag 2015. By 44 Antony employed a bodyguard of Ituraeans, or so Cicero complained (*Phil.* 2.19; 2.112; 13.18): he is likely to have acquired them by way his relationship with Antipater and his family. On the use of bodyguards by Roman aristocrats, a perfectly normal practice in Rome, see Tatum 2020b, which assembles previous scholarship.

57 Tetrarch: Joseph *AJ* 14.325; *BJ* 1.244. King: Joseph *AJ* 14.381–85; *BJ* 1.282–5; Str. 16.2.46; Tac. *Hist.* 5.9.2; App. *B. Civ.* 5.75. See Sharon 2017, 147–55, assembling earlier discussions.

58 Joseph *BJ* 1.162; 1.65; cf. *Ant.* 14.84; 14.92 (Josephus' treatment of Antony in the *Antiquities* is distinctly more muted than in his *Jewish War*).

59 Joseph *BJ* 1.165.

60 Plut. *Ant.* 3.1–3; cf. Pelling 1988, 121–2, who catalogues the stereotypical features of Plutarch's depiction.

61 Josephus' sources are discussed, with ample references to earlier work, by Mason 2016; Schwartz 2016. Another possible source for Gabinius' campaigns are Herod the Great's (lost) memoirs: Joseph *Ant.* 15.174.

62 Toher 2017 is now fundamental on Nicolaus.

63 In his biography of Augustus, predictably enough, Nicolaus' representation of Antony is less approving.

64 Joseph *BJ* 1.388; 1.391–2; *Ant.* 15.193; 15.198; cf. Richardson 1992, 226–34.

65 Murphey-O'Connor 2012, 37–52, furnishes a through discussion of the Antonia.

66 Cic. *Pis.* 44.

67 Cic. *Q. Fr.* 2.7.1; *Prov. cons.* 14–5; *Pis.* 41; *Phil.* 13.24.

68 Cic. *Prov. cons.* 9; *Sest.* 71; *Pis.* 41.

69 On this speech and its circumstances, see Grillo 2015.

70 Cic. *Q. Fr.* 2.7.1.

71 Cic. *Pis.* 41.

72 Cic. *Prov. cons.* 10. Further Ciceronian abuse: *Prov. cons.* 9–11; *Pis.* 41–3; 48–52; *Sest.* 93.

73 Rostovtzeff 1941, 981–3; Badian 1972, 109–10; Sherwin-White 1983, 276–7; Sartre 2005, 456; Morrell 2017, 81–2.

74 Claudian links to Syria: Rawson 1991, 116–7 (Ap. Claudius); Tatum 1999, 51–2 (Clodius). Gabinius' clash with Clodius: Tatum 1999, 170–2. Ap. Claudius' attack on Gabinius: Cic. *Q. Fr.* 3.2.3.

75 Cic. *Q. Fr.* 3.2.3; cf. Dio 39.60.3.

76 Loans: Cic. *Att.* 5.21.12; cf. *Straf.* 885–6; this measure revived an abortive proposal by C. Cornelius (tr. pl. 67): Asc. 57–8C. Embassies in February: Cic. *Q. Fr.* 2.12.3; cf. Cic. *Verr.* 2.2.76 (on senatorial exploitation of ambassadors). Although it is now generally agreed that Gabinius was the author of these laws, disagreement remains over whether he carried them while tribune, praetor, or consul; cf. *MMR* 3.97–8; Morrell 2017, 54–5.

77 Cic. *Att.* 5.21.12; on senatorial exemptions, see Asc. 58–9C.

78 E.g., Cic. *Leg. agr.* 2.19; Asc. 79–80 (Cn. Domitius Ahenobarbus, tr. pl. 104, cos. 96); cf. Tatum 1999, 13–4.

79 Cic. *Sest.* 93; *Pis.* 48; Dio 39.56.1.

80 The *publicani* angry with Gabinius are designated *Syriaci publicani* at Cic. *Q. Fr.* 1.12.2.

81 Schulz 1997, 171–84.

82 Str. 12.3.24. Sources for this episode: *MRR* 2.211; discussion: Sherwin-White 1983, 272–3; Sartre 2005, 47–8. The idea that Clodius' legislation appointing Gabinius to Syria included a mandate to invade Parthia reposes too much weight on Cic. *Dom.* 60, which is after-the-fact hyperbole.

83 Plut. *Luc.* 8.4; App. *Mithr.* 17–8; 32; 40–5; 49–50; 64. *Amicus et socius populi Romani*: Plut. *Sul.* 23.4.

84 Str. 12.3.34; App. *Mithr.* 114.

85 Plut. *Ant.* 3.10–11.

86 Str. 12.3.34.

87 Str. 12.3.24; 17.1.11; Dio 39.56–8; cf. Siani-Davies 2001, 23. Gabinius also prevented Philip II Barypous from travelling to Egypt as a suitor to Berenice: Euseb. *Chron.* 1.40.25–7.

88 Cic. *Leg. agr.* 1.1; Plut. *Crass.* 13.1–2; Suet. *Iul* 11.

89 *MRR* 2.188.

90   Cic. *Fam.* 1.1.1; *Rab. Post.* 6; Str. 17.1.11; Dio 39.12–15. On Ptolemy and Roman politics during the fifties, see Will 1982, 519–25; Shatzman 1971; Höbl 2001, 227–9; Siani-Davies 2001, 1–38; Seager 2002, 111–15; Roller 2010, 17–22; Westall 2010; Morrell 2019.

91   Cic. *Cael.* 23–4; 51; 54; *Har. Resp.* 34; Str. 17.1.11; Dio 39.13.1.

92   *MRR* 2.210.

93   Cic. *Fam.* 1.1.1–2; 1.4.1; 1.5A.3–4; 1.7.3–5; *Q. Fr.* 2.2.3; 2.4.5; Plut. *Pomp.* 49.6; Dio 39.16.1–2.

94   Cic. *Fam.* 1.1.1–3; 1.4.2; 1.7.4; *Q. Fr.* 1.2.15; 2.2.3–4; 2.3.2; *Har. resp.* 1–7; 17; Dio 39.15.1.

95   Tatum 1999, 199–205; Seager 2002, 111–15.

96   Cic. *Att.* 15.15.2; *Fam.* 1.1.1; *Har. resp.* 28; Dio 39.16.3; 39.55.1.

97   Plut. *Pomp.* 51; *Caes.* 21; *Crass.* 14; *Cat. min.* 41; Suet. *Iul.* 24.1; App. *B. Civ.* 2.17.

98   Cic. *Pis.* 49; *Rab. Post.* 9–21; Joseph. *AJ* 14.98; 14.103; *BJ* 1.175; 1.178; Str. 12.3.34; App. *Syr.* 51; Plut. *Ant.* 3.2–5; Dio 39.55.3.

99   Among the soldiers left in Egypt by Gabinius were 500 Gauls and Germans: Caes. *B. Civ.* 3.4.

100 Cic. *Rab. Post.* 21; 30–1; *Fam.* 1.7; Plut. *Ant.* 3.1–2.

101 *MRR* 2.75 (*lex Cornelia*); *MRR* 2.188 (*lex Iulia*); cf. Harries 2007, 72–85; Morrell 135–7.

102 Cic. *Rab. Post.* 20; cf. Joseph. *AJ* 14.101–4; *BJ* 1.176–8.

103 Schulz 1997, 171–84.

104 Plut. *Ant.* 3.4 (hesitation); Dio 39.56.3 (royal generosity to the army). When in 88 Nicomedes III was restored to his throne in Bithynia, he enriched the promagistrate responsible (C. Cassius (pr. 90)) and his officers: App. *Mithr.* 11.

105 E.g., Cic. *Verr.* 2.3.84–93.

106 Plut. *Ant.* 3.5.

107 Cic. *Phil.* 2.48: Antony acted *contra senatus auctoritatem, contra rem publicam et religiones.*

108 Schulz 1997, 191–3, speculates that Antipater may also have been an advisor of Gabinius and urged him to invade Egypt.

109 Plut. *Ant.* 3.6–9 (with Pelling 1988, 121–2); Joseph. *Ant.* 14.98–9; *BJ* 1.175; Dio 39.58.1–3.

110 Plut. *Ant.* 3.10; Str. 12.3.34; Joseph. *AJ* 14.101–4; *BJ* 1.176–8; Dio 39.56.6; 39.58.1–3.

111 Plut. *Ant.* 3.11; Str. 17.1.11; Dio 39.58.3.

112 Caes. *B. Civ.* 3.104.1; 3.110.1–6; Plut. *Pomp.* 80.3; App. *B. Civ.* 2.49; Dio 42.38.1.

113 Cic. *Rab. Post.* 22; 28; 39; Dio 39.60.4. Rabirius' unpopularity in Egypt: *P. Med. Inv.* 68.53 (see Siani-Davies 2001, 33–4).

114 App. *B. Civ.* 5.8.

115 Joseph. *AJ* 14.101–104; *BJ* 1.176–78.

116 Gabinius' trials: *MRR* 2.218; cf. Alexander 1990, 296; 303–4; Siani-Davies 2001, 65–73; Seager 2002, 128–30; Fezzi 2019, 137–40; Alexander 2002,110–118; Morrell 2017, 164–72. The brothers Antonius: Cic. *Q. Fr.* 3.2.1 (they are not mentioned by Cicero at *Q. Fr.* 3.1.15 and so were latecomers in putting themselves forward).

117 E.g., Cic. *Verr.* 2.1.44 (Catiline); *Div. Caec.* 32; 61–3 (Q. Caecilius Niger and others); cf. Pina Polo and Díaz Fernández 2019, 175–6.

118 Fantham 1975, 436. Cicero believed *praevaricatio* perhaps played a role in Gabinius' acquittal in his trial *de maiestate* (Cic. *Att.* 4.18.1).

119 Plut. *Ant.* 4.4–5; cf. Pelling 1988, 124–5 on Plutarch's appropriation of familiar Greek tropes for describing a dynamic commander.

120 Antony's family, after the eastern careers of the consul of 99 and his sons, was well connected in that part of the world, from Greece to Cilicia (*pace* Marasco 1987, 10): naturally Antony endeavoured to build on this network of relationships.

121 Cic. *Phil.* 2.48.

CHAPTER III

1 Cic. *Phil.* 2.48.
2 Str. 10.2.13; cf. Shatzman 1975, 295–9.
3 Treggiari 1991, 83–124; Rohr Vio 2019, 19–28.
4 Cic. *Phil.* 2.99; Plut. *Ant.* 9.1; cf. Ferriès 2007, 40–2.
5 Treggiari 1991, 38; 108–19; 401. The importance of family affinities in Roman politics: Harders 2017 (assembling previous scholarship). Limitations on the political grip of these affinities: Brunt 1988, 443–58.
6 Val. Max. 4.2.6.
7 Gruen 1974, 313–4.
8 *MRR* 2.395.
9 Antonius owned a mansion in the city: Q. Cic. *Comm. Pet.* 9.
10 Preparations for their marriage took place in 38: App. *B. Civ.* 5.93.
11 Rohr Vio 2019, 22. Southern 2010, 35, prefers a much earlier date (around 63).
12 The evidence for Caesar's service under Creticus is the mention of a C. Iulius in SIG^3 748, but the identification is not certain: *MRR* 3.105.
13 Cicero's recommendations to Caesar: *Fam.* 7.5; *Q. Fr.* 2.14.3.
14 Caesar's legates: *MRR* 2.231–2; 238–9.
15 Caes. *B. Gall.* 7.81.6.
16 Scrupulously, Caesar does not here anticipate Antony's title (hence he is a legate). In 51, Antony is denominated quaestor by Hirtius: *B. Gall.* 8.2.1; 8.24.2; 8.38.1. In 50, although it would not have been inappropriate to continue designating Antony quaestor, Hirtius reverts to legate (*B. Gall.* 8.46.4).
17 Cic. *Att.* 6.6.4; 7.8.5; *Fam.* 2.15.4; *Phil.* 2.49–50; 71; *Mil.* 40; *MRR* 2.236; Pina Polo and Díaz Fernández 2019, 215; cf. Drumann-Groebe 1899, 48; Rossi 1959, 11–2; Gelzer 1968, 146–89; Gruen 1974, 337–47; Bengtson 1977, 43–5; Huzar 1978, 36–8; Chamoux 1986, 50–3; Dettenhofer 1992, 66–8; Wiseman 1994b, 403–12; Linderski 1995, 251–61; Seager 2002, 133–7; Cristofoli 2008, 24–5; 27–31; Lintott 2008, 243–5; 249–52; Billows 2009, 179–85; Pasquali 2009, 47–50; Goldsworthy 2010, 109–13; Southern 2010, 54–6; Halfmann 2011, 39–40; Steel 2013, 182–6; Morrell 2017, 204–9; Fezzi 2019, 137–51; Drogula 2019, 207–19.
18 Pina Polo and Díaz Fernández 2019, 51–63.
19 The qualities of a suitable candidate for office: Tatum 2018, 20–9.
20 Cic. *Phil.* 2.49.
21 Cicero and the Antonii: see ch. I, pp. 29–30. Aiding Antonius' praetorian canvass: Asc. 85C. Antony's loan: Cic. *Q. Fr.* 1.3.7.
22 *Att.* 10.13.2.
23 The social and political dynamics of canvassing: Tatum 2018, 19–49.
24 Cic. *Att.* 4.15.7; 4.16.6; 4.17.2–3; 4.18.1; *Q. Fr.* 2.15.4; 2.16.2–3; 3.1.6; 3.3.2; 3.4.1; 3.6.4–6; cf. Gruen 1974, 148–9; Tatum 1999, 231–3.
25 Clodius and Pompey were reconciled in autumn of 56, after the so-called Conference at Luca which resulted in a re-alignment of loyalties on the part of the Claudii Pulchri: see Tatum 1999, 214–5.
26 Metellus Scipio's daughter was married to P. Licinius Crassus, son of Marcus Crassus; he perished at Carrhae, leaving her a widow. Pompey married her in 52 after his election as consul: Plut. *Pomp.* 55.1. On Q. Scipio, see Linderski 2007, 130–74.
27 Asc. 25C; 30C; 34C; 35C; 53–4C; Cic. *Mil.* (passim); *Flacc.* 20; *Fam.* 1.1.3; 2.6.3; *Q. Fr.* 3.6.6; 3.7.2; Schol. Bob. 100St.; cf. Tatum 1999, 234–9.
28 Schol. Bob. 169St. Invective a staple of canvassing: Tatum 2018, 186–8.

29 Cic. *Mil.* 24; 34; 41; 43; Asc. 30–1C; 48C; Plut. *Caes.* 28.3–4; *Cat. min.* 47.1; Liv. *Per.* 107; Dio 40.46.3; 40.48.2; Schol. Bob. 169St; 172St; cf. Tatum 1999, 234–9.

30 Because elections in the *concilium plebis* proceeded independently of elections in the centuriate or tribal assemblies (*StR.* 1.585–6), Clodius, by blocking consular elections, did not thereby prevent the election of plebeian aediles. But in 52, when the senate passed its final decree (see below), it appealed only to tribunes and the *interrex* (and Pompey)—not plebeian aediles.

31 Cic. *Mil.* 40.

32 Cic. *Phil.* 2.21; 2.49.

33 Aigner 1976; on urban violence, see Tatum 2020b.

34 Linderski 1986; Beard, North, and Price 1998a, 21–4; 103–6; Rüpke 2012, 137–42; Rüpke 2018, 119–26; 152–7; Driediger-Murphy 2018a.

35 Linderski 1995, 241–3; Linderski 2007, 620–1. Ryan 2003 (followed by Raaflaub and Ramsey 2017, 69) believes the *comitia sacerdotum* took place before magisterial elections commenced.

36 *MRR* 2.233.

37 Linderski 1995, 190–9.

38 Cic. *Phil.* 2.4.

39 On Fulvia's actions after Clodius' death, see now Schultz 2021, 40–8.

40 Although an *interrex* possesses *imperium* (Vervaet 2014, 329), his putting it to any practical use was out of the question.

41 Asc. 30–3C; 35–6C; 42C; 49C; Cic. *Mil.* 12–3; 27–9; 31; 37; 61; 67–8; 70; 91; Caes. *B. Gall.* 7.1.2–3; Liv. *Per.* 107; Plut. *Caes.* 28.7–29.1; *Cat. min.* 47.2–3; *Pomp.* 54.5–8; App. *B. Civ.* 2.21–3; Dio 40.48.1–50.5.; *MRR* 2.234–7.

42 Sulla: *MRR* 2.66. Public outcry for Pompey to be named dictator: Cic. *Fam.* 8.4.3; Asc. 35C; Plut. *Pomp.* 54.2; App. *B. Civ.* 2.23; Dio 40.50.3.

43 Drogula 2019, 212–7.

44 *MRR* 2.233–4; on the particulars and politics of this proposal, see Ramsey 2016.

45 Suet. *Iul.* 26; Plut. *Pomp.* 56.1–3; App. *B. Civ.* 2.25.

46 Cic. *Att.* 7.1.4.

47 *MRR* 2.236.; cf. Morstein-Marx 2021, 259–69. Cato's opposition: Caes. *B. Gall.* 1.32.3; Plut. *Pomp.* 56.3; Liv. *Per.* 107; cf. Drogula 2019, 219–20. It was necessary to persuade Caelius Rufus, who was tr. pl. in 52, not to impose a veto, persuasion effected by Cicero (Cic. *Att.* 7.1.4).

48 Caes. *B. Gall.* 7.6.1.

49 Decree: Asc. 44C; cf. Schol. Bob. 116St. Pompey's *lex de vi*: *MRR* 2.234. Asc. 36C makes it clear Pompey's law was hostile to Milo (Cic. *Mil.* 13–4 is tendentious); Morrell 2018 takes a different view.

50 On Antony's campaign for the quaestorship, Linderski 1995, 201–23 remains fundamental.

51 Cic. *Fam.* 2.18.2 with Shackleton Bailey 1977, 455. Gaius, too, was elected quaestor for 51.

52 Trial of Milo: Alexander 1990, 151–2.

53 Blom 2016, 254–5; on the role of speechifying in raising one's profile in elections, see Tatum 2013; Tatum 2018, 23; 168–9.

54 Cic. *Phil.* 2.50, but contrast Cic. *Att.* 6.6.4; *Fam.* 2.15.4; cf. Linderski 1995, 219–22.

55 For events down to 49, see Gelzer 1968, 189–223; Gruen 1974, 451–60; Wiseman 1994b, 412–5; Seager 2002, 140–8; Lintott 2008, 267–80; Billows 2009, 184–91; Steel 2013, 189–94; Stevenson 2015, 109–22; Morrell 2017, 209–38; Fezzi 2019, 155–61; Drogula 2019, 218–29; Morstein-Marx 2021, 258–69.

56 Suet. *Iul.* 27.1; cf. Gruen 1974, 453; Seager 2002, 131–2.

57 A sound list of Caesar's fiercest enemies in the senate is furnished by Morstein-Marx 2021, 295.

58 Plut. *Cat. min.* 7.1–3; cf. Gruen 1974, 151–2; Morrell 2017, 208–9; Drogula 2019, 32–3.

59 Plut. *Cat. min.* 48.2. Magisterial *consilia*: StR. 1.307–10.

60 Date: Gell. 10.1.7. Pompey's theatre and its divine values: Clark 2007a, 225–34.

61 Pelling 2011, 281–2.

62 The *lex Pompeia de iure magistratuum* (also referred to by modern historians as the *lex Pompeia de provinciis*): on the particulars of this *lex Pompeia* and the controversies raised by our evidence, see (with ample citation of previous scholarship), Steel 2012; Morrell 2017, 210–36; Morstein-Marx 2021, 265–8.

63 *MRR* 21.514.

64 It is this slow and gradual unwinding of provincial responsibilities that Suetonius has in mind when he describes the Law of Ten Tribunes as enabling Caesar to stand *in absentia* 'whenever the execution of his term as governor should begin to come to its conclusion' (*quandoque imperii tempus expleri coepisset*: Suet. *Iul.* 26.1). On the business of putting together a provincial administration and taking it abroad, see Lintott 1993, 43–54; Schulz 1997, 93–103.

65 *Lex Pompeia Licinia*: *MRR* 2.215. Nearly everything in this uncomplicated paragraph is controversial and has been hotly contested over the past century and a half. Important discussions, some including lengthy doxographies, are furnished by Balsdon 1939; Gruen 1974, 455–90; Lintott 2008, 433–6; Pelling 2011, 285–93; Morstein-Marx 2021, 259–68.

66 *MRR* 2.241.

67 Marcellus' moves: *MRR* 2.241.

68 Scipio's motion: Cic. *Fam.* 8.9.5.

69 *MRR* 2.247–8.

70 *MRR* 2.249; cf. Dettenhofer 1992, 34–63; Pelling 2011, 296–312.

71 Schultz 2021, 49–51.

72 Unexpected volte-face: Cic. *Fam.* 8.6.5.

73 Morstein-Marx 2021, 264; cf. *MRR* 2.185; Wiseman 1994b, 365–6; Pelling 2011, 186–8.

74 *MRR* 1.558 (Marius' triumph on the opening day of his consulship in 104).

75 Pompey returned from his victory in the Mithridatic War in 62 (*MRR* 2.176) but did not celebrate his triumph until months later in 61 (*MRR* 2.181).

76 Cic. *Fam.* 8.14.3.

77 Suet. *Iul.* 30.3–4; Plut. *Caes.* 46.1–3; cf. Raaflaub 1974, 143–7; Pelling 2011, 369–70; *FRHist*, vol. 3, 522–3; Morstein-Marx 2021, 259–63; 622–4.

78 Cic. *Fam.* 8.7.3 (*plane timet*).

79 Cic. *Fam.* 8.8.9.

80 Caes. *B. Civ.* 1.9.2.

81 Cic. *Fam.* 8.14.2; Hirt. *B. Gall.* 8.52.4; Vell. 2.48.1; App. *B. Civ.* 2.27–8; Did 40.62.3–4. Curio probably first offered his proposal during the summer; cf. Morstein-Marx 2021, 630.

82 Cic. *Fam.* 8.14.4.

83 Cic *Att.*7.8.4.

84 Hirt. *B. Gall.* 8.50.4.

85 *MRR* 2.257–8.

86 Cassius: *MRR* 2.259; the Caesarian was *frater*, brother or cousin, to the tyrannicide: Cic. *Att.* 5.21.2. Antony: *MRR* 2.254; 258; Plutarch's account of Antony's tribunate at *Ant.* 5.2–10 sometimes conflates events from his tribunate with Curio's: Pelling 1988, 126–9; cf. Drumann-Groebe 1899, 49; Rossi 1959, 12–3; Gruen 1974, 460–89; Bengston 1977, 45–7; Huzar 1978, 42–7; Chamoux 1986, 53–5; Dettenhofer 1992, 68–70; Wiseman 1994b,

415–22; Linderski 1995, 251–61; Yakobson 1999, 155–6; 176–7; Seager 2002, 137–40; Cristofoli 2008, 31–2; 35–9; Lintott 2008, 249–52; 435–6; Billows 2009, 207–12; Pasquali 2009, 50; Goldsworthy 2010, 130–2; Southern 2010, 58–60; Halfmann 2011, 40–2; Steel 2013, 185–9; Fezzi 2019, 161–73; Drogula 2019, 230–63; Morstein-Marx 2021, 269–303.

87 Cic. *Fam.* 8.4.2.
88 Hirt. *B. Gall.* 8.50.1–3; Cic. *Fam.* 8.14.1; *Phil.* 2.4; Plut. *Ant.* 5.1.
89 Caesar: Hirt. *B. Gall.* 8.50.1–3; the long-recognized influence of Cisalpine Gaul in Roman elections: Cic. *Att.* 1.1.2; *Phil.* 2.76; *Q. Fr.* 2.3.4; cf. Tatum 2018, 98. Curio: Cic. *Phil.* 2.4; Plut. *Ant.* 5.2. Caelius: *Fam.* 8.14.1.
90 Cic. *Fam.* 8.13.2.
91 Lucius' legateship: *MRR* 2.252.
92 Carlsen 2006, 53–68.
93 Cic. *Fam.* 8.14.1.
94 This is the order reported by Plutarch (*Ant.* 5.1). There is no reason to doubt it. The schedule for electing tribunes was independent of the schedule for regular magistracies; if there was a rule for priority in the late republic, we cannot detect it: *StR.* 1.585–6.
95 The order of elections: Linderski 1995, 241–3; Linderski 2007, 620–1. Ryan 2003 (followed by Raaflaub and Ramsey 2017, 69) believes the *comitia sacerdotum* took place before magisterial elections commenced.
96 Caelius reports a single accusation *de vi* (Cic. *Fam.* 8.14.1), which probably resulted in a conviction. Cicero's claim at *Phil.* 2.4 that there were multiple convictions *de vi*, an obvious rhetorical exaggeration, need not be taken seriously. That this election was disrupted by violence, however, is clear enough; cf. Gruen 1974, 555–6; 484–5.
97 Lintott 1999, 84–5; cf. Pina Polo 2011, 65; 301; 315.
98 Cic. *Fam.* 8.11.3.
99 Caes. *B. Gall.* 8.55.1; App. *B. Civ.* 2.31; Dio 40.64.4; cf. Morstein-Marx 2021, 292–4.
100 Plut. *Ant.* 5.4; cf. Pelling 1988, 128. Curio's complaints: App. *B. Civ.* 2.31; Dio 40.66.4.
101 Cic. *Att.* 7.8.5.; Plut. *Ant.* 5.5; cf. Caes. *B. Civ.* 1.9.3; Plut. *Pomp.* 59.3; *Caes.* 30.3.
102 Cic. *Att.* 7.8.5; cf. Blom 2016, 256. On Antony's expression *terror armorum* (fear of war and the threat of war—*not* threats of war), see Morstein-Marx 2021, 300, n. 173. Pompey *adulescentulus carnifex*: Val. Max. 6.2.8.
103 Cic. *Att.* 7.9.1–2.
104 Cic. *Phil.* 2.53.
105 Cic. *Phil.* 2.55.
106 Plut. *Ant.* 6.1.
107 Cic. *Fam.* 16.11.2; Caes. *B. Civ.* 1.1.1; App. *B. Civ.* 2.32; Dio 41.1.1–4. According to Plutarch (*Caes.* 30–1; *Ant.* 5; contrast *Pomp.* 58–9) and Dio (41.2.1–2), Antony on this day repeated Curio's tactic of requiring votes on Pompey's resignation, Caesar's resignation, and on resignation by both (see above). This, however, is a literary doublet without historical foundation: see Pelling 2002, 107–8; *contra* Raaflaub 1974, 307.
108 Cic. *Fam.* 16.11.2.
109 Cic. *Fam.* 16.11.2; Caes. *B. Civ.* 1.1.1–4.4; Suet. *Iul.* 29.2; Plut. *Pomp.* 50.5; *Caes.* 30.1–31.1.
110 Cic. *Fam.* 8.17.1; 16.11.2; Caes. *B. Civ.* 1.5.1–5; Plut. *Caes.* 31.2; *Ant.* 5.9–10; App. *B. Civ.* 2.33; Dio 41.3.2–3.
111 Caes. *B. Civ.* 1.22.5.
112 Raaflaub 1974, 149–52; Brunt 1988, 328; Morstein-Marx 2009.
113 App. *B. Civ.* 1.157; cf. Caes. *B. Afr.* 22.2 (describing Pompey's actions during that war).
114 *Dig.* 6.1.1.2; Gai. *Inst.* 1.134; cf. Kaser 1971, 114–5.
115 Dio 43.44.1; cf. Weinstock 1971, 142–5.
116 Cic. *Att.* 7.9.4; 7.20.2; Suet. *Iul.* 30.5; App. *B. Civ.* 2.30; 2.40; Dio 41.57.1–3; Raaflaub 2003.

117 The spectrum is wide, ranging from Syme 1939, 155 ('political fraud') and Wirszubski 1950, 100–106 ('hackneyed') to views locating Caesar in the very centre of a robust popular ideology, e.g., Wiseman 2009, esp. 211–37; Morstein-Marx 2021; see Brunt 1988, 281–50; Arena 2012; Sigmund 2014.

118 Frier 1985, esp. 52–98; Stewart 1995, 74–5; Paterson 2006a; Lomas 2012; Santangelo 2016; Tatum 2018, 244.

119 Cic. *Att.* 8.13.2.

120 Cic. *Att.* 7.7.5.

121 Sall. *Hist.* 3.48.14–27 M = 3.34.14–28 McG. Sallust inserts this sentiment into a speech by C. Licinius Macer (tr. pl. 73).

122 Political activism on the part of the Roman masses, sometimes spontaneous, sometimes ideologically driven, nonetheless often required a combination of moral and practical incentives, including gifts or payments; cf. Tatum 2020b, esp. 406–11.

123 Caelius: Cic. *Fam.* 8.14.3. Pollio: Cic. *Fam.* 10.31.3.

124 Cic. *Att.* 10.8a.1; cf. C. Matius at Cic. *Fam.* 11.28.2.

125 This is discussed below in ch. III, pp. 76–77.

126 On *partes* in the context of the civil war, see Tatum 2020c, 200–204. On Caesar's coalition, see Bane 1971; Jehne 1987, 392–406; cf. Brunt 1988, 492–3; 501; Morstein-Marx 2021, 352–64.

127 Tempest 2017, 59–62.

128 Cic. *Att.* 9.6.4.

129 Q. Ligurius, in Africa when the war broke out, found himself serving with forces in a province which declared for Pompey: Cic. *Lig.* 4–5; similarly, T. Antistius (q. 50) was in Macedonia when Pompey and his forces arrived: Cic. *Fam.* 13.29.3.

130 Civil war in 49: Gelzer 1968, 195–223; Gelzer 1969, 53–5; Rawson 1994a, 424–32; Seager 2002, 152–65; Lintott 2008, 281–300; Welch 2012, 43–62; Steel 2013, 195–7; Stevenson 2015, 123–7; Fezzi 2019, 173–223.

131 Welch 2012, 43–57.

132 Cic. *Att.* 8.11.2; 8.16.2; 9.6.7; 9.7.4; outrage at its implications for Italy: *Att.* 9.9.2.

133 *MRR* 2.261–2.

134 Caes. *B. Civ.* 1.11.4; Florus 2.13.19.

135 Cic. *Att.* 8.4.4; Caes. *B. Civ.* 1.18.2–5.

136 *Lenitas:* Caes. *B. Civ.* 1.74.7; Cic. *Att.* 9.7c.1; cf. Grillo 2012, 78–104.

137 Curio: Cic. *Att.* 10.4.8. Caelius: Cic. *Att.* 10.9a.1.

138 Caes. *B. Civ.* 1.32–3; Dio 41.15.2–17.3.

139 Cic. *Att.* 10.4.8; cf. App. *B. Civ.* 2.41.

140 Cic. *Att.* 9.9.3 (citing Antony as one of Caesar's men in the augural college); 9.15.2.

141 Cic. *Att.* 10.4.9: Curio tells Cicero, 'now more than ever he [viz. Caesar] hates the senate' (*nunc magis odit senatum*).

142 Dio 41.16.1.

143 Cic. *Att.* 10.4.9; Caes. *B. Civ.* 1.30.2.

144 *MRR* 2.266. L. Antonius was in Asia, where he was *proquaestor pro praetore* (*MRR* 2.260).

145 *MRR* 2.267.

146 *MRR* 2.257.

147 Cic. *Att.* 10.8b (Caesar); *Att.* 9.7a (Balbus and Oppius); *Att.* 9.7b (Balbus); *Att.* 10.9a (Caelius); *Att.* 10.8a (Antony).

148 Cic. *Att.* 10.8a.1: 'I have been all the keener to act because I believe the harder role is mine owing to some objection that has come between us, far more a matter of my rivalry with you than any wrong you have done (*atque eo feci studiosius quod iudicabam duriores*

partes mihi impositas esse ab offensione nostra, quae magis a ζηλοτυπίᾳ *quam ab iniuria tua nata est)*.

149 Tatum 2017, 64–6.
150 Cic. *Att.* 10.10.1–3; there is no good reason to reject the manuscripts' τυρανινικῶς at *Att.* 10.10.1, *pace* Shackleton Bailey 1968, 414, closely following Tyrrell and Purser 1894, 186; on Antony's letter and Cicero's response, see Tatum 2017, 66–7.
151 Cic. *Att.* 10.13.2.
152 Cic. *Att.* 10.15.3.
153 Cic. *Att.* 10.10.5; 10.16.5.
154 Cic. *Phil.* 2.57–8; Plut. *Ant.* 9.5–9.
155 Nicolet 1974, 1082–3; Ferriès 2007, 491.
156 Strong 2016, 71–7; Schultz 2021, 63–7.
157 Ser. ad Verg. *Buc.* 10.1 and 10.6; cf. Hollis 2007, 219–52.
158 *Vir. Ill.* 82.2.
159 Cic. *Fam.* 9.26.
160 Cic. *Fam.* 9.26.2.
161 In the aftermath of Pharsalus, when Cicero, on the losing side, was trying to return to Italy, it appears Volumnia furnished important assistance to the orator and his wife (Cic. *Fam.* 14.6), perhaps by way of intervening on his behalf with Antony.
162 Treggiari 1991, 299–309; Laes and Strubbe 2014, 137–40; Strong 2016.
163 McCoy 2006, 178–81; Strong 2016, 62–96.
164 Sergius the mime-actor was an acquaintance of Antony and, according to Plutarch, travelled with Cytheris (Cic. *Phil.* 2.62; Plut. *Ant.* 9.7). Private theatrical ensembles: Csapo 2010, 179–82. Qualms about musicians: Wille 1967, 326–7; 332–6. Objections to theatrical friends: e.g., Plut. *Sull.* 2.4; 33.3; 36.102 (Sulla); Q. Cic. *Comm. Pet.* 10 (Catiline); cf. Tatum 2018, 207–8.
165 Cic. *Att.* 10.13.1.
166 Plut. *Ant.* 6.6, probably relying on this episode in Cicero, reports that the whole of Antony's administration was marked by laziness and ineptitude.
167 Cic. *Phil.* 2.58.
168 *MRR* 2.266.
169 *MRR* 2.266.
170 *MRR* 2.263–4.
171 *MRR* 2.262.
172 Frederiksen 1966; Crawford 1985, 193–4; Verboven 1997; Verboven 2003; Woytek 2003, esp. 392–412; Ioannatou 2006, 72–94; Rollinger 2009, 177–85; Woytek 2016; Harris 2019, esp. 168–9; 175–80.
173 On the Latin Festival, see Scullard 1981, 111–5; on its political and cultural importance, see Marco Simon 2011.
174 *MRR* 2.256–7.
175 Antony's tribunician legislation: *MRR* 2.258.
176 Gruen 1974, 414–6.
177 Pompey's law: *MRR* 2.234; cf. Gruen 1974, 233–9; Morrell 2017, 210–4.
178 Cic. *Att.* 10.13.1. Cicero, in his *Philippics*, faults Antony for not recalling Gaius Antonius (*Phil.* 2.56), but he was not condemned under Pompey's law and therefore was ineligible. Antonius was restored later, certainly by 44 (*Phil.* 2.99), and doubtless owing to Antony's influence.
179 As observed by Syme 1980.
180 Sh. *JC* 2.1.54–64.
181 Cic. *Att.* 10.8a.1 (*excepto Caesare meo*).

CHAPTER IV

1 *MRR* 2.280; Drumann-Groebe 1899, 51–2; Rossi 1959, 17–18; Gelzer 1968, 223–41; Bengtson 1977, 56–9; Huzar 1978, 56–62; Chamoux 1986, 65–70; Dettenhofer 1992, 166–7; Rawson 1994a, 432–3; Seager 2002, 164–7; Cristofoli 2008, 65–83; Billows 2009, 215–22; Goldsworthy 2010, 158–66; Southern 2010, 68–72; Halfmann 2011, 47; Welch 2012, 62–72; Steel 2013, 197–8; Stevenson 2015, 127–31; Drogula 2019, 283–8; Fezzi 2019, 212–54.

2 *MRR* 2.263.

3 Caes. *B. Civ.* 3.5.3; App. *B. Civ.* 2.47; Dio 41.46.50; *MRR* 2.267; 2.269.

4 *MRR* 2.261; 2.275.

5 Caes. *B. Civ.* 3.2.2; 3.6.2; cf. *MRR* 2.272.

6 Caes. *B. Civ.* 3.8.3; Dio 41.44.3–4.

7 Plut. *Ant.* 7.2–3 and App. *B. Civ.* 2.58–59 appear mistaken in mentioning Gabinius' presence in Brundisium at this time; cf. *MRR* 2.281.

8 Caes. *B. Civ.* 3.14.1–2.

9 Caes. *B. Civ.* 3.23–24; Dio 41.48.1–4.

10 Caes. *B. Civ.* 3.25.3; Dio 41.46.1.

11 Caes. *B. Civ.* 26–30; Plut. *Ant.* 7.3–6; App. *B. Civ.* 2.59; Dio 41.48.1; cf. *MRR* 2.280.

12 Caes. *B. Civ.* 3.41.1.

13 Suet. *Iul.* 69; App. *B. Civ.* 2.47–8; Dio 41.26–36; cf. Plut. *Caes.* 37.5–9.

14 Plut. *Caes.* 41.2; *Pomp.* 67.5; App. *B. Civ.* 2.67.

15 Caes. *B. Civ.* 3.89.2; 3.99.4; App. *B. Civ.* 2.76. This Sulla was either the consul-designate of 65 (the standard view; cf. *MRR* 2.281) or his son (cf. Berry 1996, 12–3).

16 Caes. *B. Civ.* 3.88.2; 3.89.3–4; Plut. *Ant.* 8.3; *Caes.* 44.2–4; *Pomp.* 69.1; App. *B. Civ.* 2.76; cf. Pelling 2011, 365.

17 Cic. *Phil.* 2.71.

18 So popular and necessary was a partial remission of rents that it was eventually imposed by Caesar: Suet. *Iul.* 38.2; Dio 42.51.1.

19 Caes. *B. Alex.* 42.2; cf. Brunt 1971, 475.

20 Cic. *Fam.* 8.17.2; Caes. *B. Civ.* 3.20.1–3.22.4; Vell. 2.68.1–3; Dio 42.22.1–42.23.3; *MRR* 2.273; cf. Simelon 1985; Dettenhofer 1992, 158–65; Ioannatou 2006, 77–8; Steel 2013, 201–2; Courrier 2014, 818–9.

21 *MRR* 2.273.

22 Caes. *B. Alex.* 57–64; Dio 43.1.2–3; *MRR* 275.

23 Dio 43.1.2; cf. Allély 2004, 48–52.

24 *MRR* 2.272. Although his initial appointment was for one year, he did not abdicate before the end of 47.

25 Volkmann 1953, 60–73; Gelzer 1968, 246–52; Rawson 1994a, 433–4; Höbl 2001, 231–9; Seager 2002, 167–8; Billows 2009, 223–7; Roller 2010, 53–67; Steel 2013, 201; Stevenson 2015, 131–3; Sartre 2018, 69–104; Fezzi 2019, 255–62.

26 Roller 2010, 53–60; Sartre 2018, 51–68.

27 *MRR* 2.286.

28 *MRR* 2.272; cf. Jehne 1987, 15–38; Lintott 1999, 109–13.

29 Appointment by a consul: Dio 42.21.1; see the excellent discussion by Konrad 2022, 131–47.

30 Dio 42.21.1–2; cf. Cic. *Phil.* 2.62.

31 Cic. *Att.* 11.7.2; cf. Drumann-Groebe 1899, 52–4; Rossi 1959, 20–21; Gelzer 1968, 253–4; 261–2; Bengtson 1977, 59–64; Huzar 1978, 63–8; Chamoux 1986, 70–83; Dettenhofer 1992, 167–75; Cristofoli 2008, 85–103; Goldsworthy 2010, 182–8; Southern 2010, 64–6; Halfmann 2011, 48–51; Steel 2013, 202.

32 Cic. *Att.* 11.17a.3.
33 Cic. *Att.* 11.10.2; 11.15.1; 11.16.1; 11.18.1.
34 Caes. *B. Afr.* 54; Cic. *Phil.* 2.59; App. *B. Civ.* 2.92; Dio 42.52.1; cf. Chrissanthos 2001.
35 Cic. *Phil.* 2.60.
36 Cic. *Phil.* 2.60; 2.77–7; Plut. *Ant.* 9.5–9; 10.3; *Caes.* 51.2; Dio 45.28.1–4.
37 Dio 42.27.3–4; cf. Pina Polo 2011, 21–57 (religious duties of the consuls); Scullard 1981,
     111–15 (the Latin Festival). On the political and cultural importance of the Latin Festival,
     see Marco Simon 2011.
38 Dio 42.27.1–2.
39 Cic. *Att.* 1.17.1–2.
40 Cic. *Phil.* 2.5.
41 Statue: Cic. *Att.* 11.23.3. Clodius' and Dolabella's adoption by a plebeian: Tatum
     1999, 104–8.
42 *MRR* 2.287; cf. Simelon 1985; Dettenhofer 1992, 165–83; Ioannatou 2006, 78–9; Pelling
     2011, 397–8; Courrier 2014, 819–20.
43 Plut. *Caes.* 51.3.
44 Plut. *Ant.* 9.1.
45 Cic. *Att.* 11.9.1; 11.17A.2; 11.18.2.
46 Dio 42.29.2. According to Dio a decree was passed, but any resolution along these lines will
     have been vetoed by Dolabella.
47 Dio 42.29.2–3; 46.16.12; cf. Lintott 1968, 152. There is no suggestion that either Dolabella
     or Trebellius opposed the senate's decree.
48 Cic. *Att.* 11.10.2; cf. *Att.* 11.16.1.
49 Caes. *B. Afr.* 54.
50 Plut. *Ant.* 10.1; Dio 42.30.1–3; cf. Chrissanthos 2001, 71–2.
51 Caes. *B. Alex.* 65; Cic. *Att.* 11.20.2; 11.22.2.
52 App. *B. Civ.* 2.92; Dio 42.52.2.
53 Plut. *Caes.* 51.2; App. *B. Civ.* 2.92; Dio 42.52.2.
54 Suet. *Iul.* 70; Plut. *Caes.* 51.2; App. *B. Civ.* 2.93–4; Dio 42.53–5; cf. Chrissanthos 2001, 73–5;
     Keaveney 2007, 83–4.
55 Dio 42.30.1–2.
56 Dio 2.31.1–2; cf. Plut. *Ant.* 9.3.
57 Cic. *Fam.* 14.13.
58 Dio 42.31.3.
59 App. *B. Civ.* 2.92; Dio 42.32.1–3.
60 Cic. *Att.* 11.24.2 (March); 11.14.2 (April); 11.23.3 (July).
61 Plut. *Ant.* 9.2.
62 Cic. *Phil.* 2.21; 2.48–9; 2.99; cf. Ramsey 2003, 306; Treggiari 1991, 461–5.
63 Plut. *Ant.* 10.5 dates the marriage to sometime after April 46 (when Caesar is consul for the
     third time and Antony is no longer master of the horse); Cic. *Phil.* 2.77 says only that it took
     place sometime before March 45.
64 It is far from obvious how Plutarch could know when Antony's divorce took place (his
     principal source for this phase of Antony's life, Cicero, does not tell us). The timing
     of the divorce, however, is highly dramatic in its context and moves the reader along
     to Plutarch's elaborate and thematically important account of Antony's marriage to
     Fulvia: Plut. *Ant.* 9.2–10.6 (a highly telescoped passage which includes more than one
     chronological inaccuracy); cf. Pelling 1988, 141–2; Beneker 2012, 173–8. On Plutarch's
     literary techniques in composing episodes of this kind, see Pelling 1988, 137; Pelling
     2002, 92–6.
65 Cic. *Fam.* 8.13.1.

66 Treggiari 2007, 122–8 (assembling the evidence); Cicero frets over Dolabella's clout: Cic. *Fam.* 14.13.

67 Cic. *Att.* 11.23.3.

68 Cic. *Att.* 11.18.2; cf. 11.9.1.

69 Plutarch locates the divorce in the first half of the year, while Caesar remains outside Rome: Plut. *Ant.* 9.9.

70 Cic. *Fam.* 14.13.

71 Treggiari 2007, 131.

72 The family was under severe stress: Cicero's marriage with Terentia was also falling apart at this time; cf. Treggiari 2007, 128–31.

73 Ioannatou 2006, 390–2; 426–7; Treggiari 2007, 139–40.

74 Fischer 1999, 7–63; Rohr Vio 2019, 77–9; 84–6; 110–3; 121–6; 202–6; Schultz 2021.

75 Tatum 1999, 60–1.

76 Cic. *Phil.* 3.16; the cognomen Bambalio, like many cognomina, denotes a blemish or flaw: the name derives from a Greek verb meaning *stutter*.

77 Cic. *Phil.* 3.16; cf. *Acad.* 2.89.

78 Cic. *Phil.* 3.16.

79 Fulvia in 52: see ch. III, p. 62. Clodius and Fulvia inseparable: Cic. *Mil.* 28; 55. Fulvia a symbol in popular politics: Welch 1995; Schultz 2021, 50–1; 67.

80 The only attestation of this marriage is Cic. *Phil.* 2.11.

81 Dio 51.2.5.

82 Cic. *Phil.* 13.32; Dio 42.20.1–2; Cic. *Att.* 11.9.3 (Terentia's property, as well as Cicero's, liable to confiscation). Also attesting to Caesar's confiscations: Cic. *Fam.* 9.10.3; 9.17.1; 13.4.1–4; 13.5.2; 13.29.5; 15.17.2; Suet. *Iul.* 38.1; App. *B. Civ.* 2.94; 2.140; Dio 42.50.1–5. See also Woytek 2003, 201–7; Ferriès 2016.

83 Cic. *Phil.* 13.11.

84 Suet. *Iul.* 50.2 (Servilia); Dio 43.47.5 (Minucius).

85 Cic. *Phil.* 11–12.

86 Cic. *Phil.* 2.62; cf. Ramsey 2003, 251. Piso was later pardoned by Caesar and reconciled with Antony, whose close friend he became (Cic. *Phil.* 3.25).

87 Cic. *Phil.* 2.64.

88 Pompey's properties (including *insulae*): Cic. *Phil.* 2.71–4; 13.11–12; Plut. *Ant.* 10.3; 21.2–3. Varro: Cic. *Phil.* 2.103–5. Metellus Scipio: Cic. *Phil.* 2.42; 5.19. Antony also acquired a house on the Palatine hill (Dio 53.27.5), but when and from whom we do not know.

89 Cic. *Fam.* 9.10.3; 15.17.2; 15.19.3; *Off.* 2.29; cf. Berry 1996, 13.

90 Wallace-Hadrill 1994; Potter 2011; Hölkeskamp 2014; Tatum 2018, 251–2 (with further literature).

91 Cic. *Phil.* 2.64–9; cf. Plut. *Ant.* 21.2–3; *Caes.* 51.3.

92 Cic. *Att.* 11.9.3; 11.12.4; 11.18.1; 11.24.4.

93 Cic. *Fam.* 14.16.

94 Cic. *Lig.* 7.

95 Caes. *B. Alex.* 65.

96 Cic. *Att.* 11.20.2; 11.21.2.

97 Cic. *Att.* 11.22.2: *ergo ille huc veniet, quod non putabant*. A different account is preserved by Dio, who says Caesar went to Italy instead of Africa owing to his worries about disturbances in the capital (Dio 42.50.1; cf. 45.29.3–4).

98 App. *B. Civ.* 2.92.

99 Dio 49.33.1–3.

100   Cic. *Fam.* 11.28.2. On Caesar's economic measures, see Frederiksen 1966; Crawford 1985, 193–4; Verboven 1997; Verboven 2003; Woytek 2003, esp. 392–412; Ioannatou 2006, 72–94; Rollinger 2009, 177–85; Woytek 2016; Harris 2019, esp. 168–9; 175–80.

101   Caes. *B. Afr.* 1.

102   *MRR* 2.286; 2.305–6; cf. Gelzer 1968, 264–99; Rawson 1994a, 435–8; Billows 2009, 230–5; Steel 2013, 202–5; Stevenson 2015, 134–6.

103   Cic. *Phil.* 2.75–6; Plut. *Ant.* 10.3.

104   Cic. *Att.* 12.18a.1; 12.19.1; *Phil.* 2.23; 2.74–78; Plut. *Ant.* 10.3; 11.1.

105   Cic. *Phil.* 2.71–4.

106   Cic. *Phil.* 2.34; 2.74; cf. Plut. *Ant.* 13.1–2.

107   Cic. *Phil.* 2.78: *nescio quo modo.*

108   Plut. *Ant.* 10.4–5; cf. Beneker 2012, 173–79.

109   Dio 42.50.5; 45.28.1–4.

110   Plut. *Ant.* 10.3; *Caes.* 51.2; Dio 42.27.3–4.

111   Drumann-Groebe 1899, 54–60; Rossi 1959, 21–4; Gelzer 1968, 262; Bengston 1977, 64–9; Huzar 1978, 68–72; Chamoux 1986, 83–90; Dettenhofer 1992, 176–8; Cristofoli 2008, 107–28; Goldsworthy 2010, 189–91; Southern 2010, 76–80; Halfmann 2011, 51–9.

112   Ramsey 2004 is fundamental.

113   Andreau 1999; Ioannatou 2006; Jehne 2016.

114   There was a precedent for this assumption: Sulla had exempted some in his circle from paying what they owed for purchases of confiscated properties: Gell. 18.4.4 (= Sall. *Hist.* 4.1 McG).

115   Cic. *Phil.* 2.72; Plut. *Ant.* 10.3; Dio 42.50.5; 45.28.1–4. Caesar's desperate need for funds: Dio 42.50.1–4.

116   Cic. *Phil.* 2.35; 2.93.

117   Cic. *Phil.* 13.12; App. *B. Civ.* 3.4; Dio 48.36.5.

118   Ramsey 2004 offers a very different reconstruction in which Antony operates on Caesar's behalf (almost like a shell corporation) in order to facilitate a profitable liquidation of Pompey's estate; cf. Cristofoli 2008, 116–8.

119   Cic. *Phil.* 2.74; cf. Shatzman 1975, 298–9.

120   Cic. *Phil.* 2.71–2. By contrast, Plutarch, looking for a different literary effect, puts the falling out in 47, before Caesar departs for Africa (*Ant.* 10.3).

121   Cic. *Phil.* 77–78; cf. Plut. *Ant.* 10.7–10. Antony's coming consulship: Cic. *Phil.* 2.76; cf. 2.79.

122   Cic. *Att.* 12.18a.1; 12.19.1.

123   *MRR* 2.306; 2.313.

124   Dio 43.49.1–2; Suet. *Iul.* 75.4; cf. *LTUR* 2.325–7.

125   Cic. *Phil.* 13.31; Suet. *Iul.* 76.1; Dio 44.6.2; 45.30.2; cf. Weinstock 1971, 332–3; Scullard 1981, 76–8.

126   *MRR* 2.304; Fabius died suddenly on the last day of the year.

127   *MRR* 2.309.

CHAPTER V

1   *MRR* 2.305–4; cf. Gelzer 1968, 287–90; 309–15; Yavetz 1983; Rawson 1994a, 438–58; Billows 2009, 241–6; Stevens 2015, 140–5.

2   Deiotarus: Lintott 2008, 335–8. Judea: Jos. *AJ* 14.221.

3   Sut. *Iul.* 52.1; Dio 43.27.3; cf. Roller 2010, 71–4; Sartre 2018, 146–53.

4   Matius: Nicolet 1974, 947–9. Rabirius: Siani-Davies 2001, 38–65; Balbus (who later entered the senate and became consul in 40): Nicolet 1974, 853–5. Oppius: Nicolet 1974, 964.

5   Cic. *Att.* 13.40.1; *Fam.* 4.4.3; 4.5.3; 6.1.6; 6.2.2; 9.17.2; 13.68.2; *Marc.* 26–32; cf. Gelzer 1968, 79; Brunt 1988, 499.

6   Suet. *Iul.* 77. The dig at Sulla is a play on the word *dictator*, which, in addition to referring to the political office, can also evoke the verb *dictare*, to dictate or to express oneself in writing; cf. Henderson 1999, 269. Distinguishing between the denomination and reality of the republic was something of a trope among the disaffected in Rome: Moatti 2018, 166–7.

7   Cic. *Fam.* 6.12.3: *illi appellant tubam belli civilis* (they—viz. Caesar's friends—call you the trumpet of the civil war), and indeed there was much resistance against allowing Caesar to pardon Ampius in 46.

8   *Fam.* 12.19.2 (planning underway in December 46); Caesar's eastern expedition: Cic. *Att.* 13.27.1; 13.31.3; Nic. Dam. 41; Suet. *Iul.* 44.3; *Aug.* 8.2; Plut. *Caes.* 58.6–7; App. *B. Civ.* 2.110; 2.114; 3.77; Dio 43.51.1–9; 44.46.3; Malitz 1984; Syme 1999, 174–92; Pelling 2011, 436–8; Wijlick 2021, 65–8.

9   In a letter written after Caesar's death, Cicero indicates he doubted Caesar would have lived long enough to return from his campaign (*Att.* 15.4.3); others may have harboured similar expectations.

10 Dio 43.51.1–2.

11 Dio 43.51.3; cf. Cic. *Phil.* 7.16; Nic. Dam. 67; Suet. *Iul.* 41.2.

12 Dio 43.51.7.

13 *MRR* 2.294–5.

14 Decisions made for 43 and 42 only: Cic. *Att.* 14.6.2; Nic. Dam. 77; Dio 43.51.6–7. Plans for Brutus and Cassius: Vell. 2.56.3; Plut. *Caes.* 58.1; 62.4; cf. Syme 1939, 95; Gelzer 1968, 304; Dettenhofer 1992, 233–4; 249–50; Manuwald 2007, 1014–5; Pelling 2011, 432–3; 461–2; Tempest 2017, 76; 93.

15 *MRR* 2.315; Drumann-Groebe 1899, 56; Bengtson 1977, 56–9; Huzar 1978, 68–9; Chamoux 1986, 93–4; Dettenhofer 1992, 178–82; Cristofoli 2008, 132–4; Goldsworthy 2010, 199; Southern 2010, 81; Halfmann 2011, 59–60.

16 Cic. *Phil.* 2.79–84; 2.88; 3.7; 5.9; cf. Linderski 1986, 2198; Santangelo 2013, 273–8; Driediger-Murphy 2018a, 138–43.

17 The seriousness with which Romans took their religion and its implications for the health of the republic cannot be overestimated: Polyb. 6.56.615; Linderski 1986; Morgan 1990, esp. 30–1; Beard 1994; Beard, North, and Price 1998a; Rüpke 2014; Driediger-Murphy 2018a.

18 Nic. Dam. 77; Dio 44.11.4.

19 Linderski 1986, 2197–8; Tatum 1999, 125–33; Driediger-Murphy 2018a, 136–54.

20 *MRR* 2.187–8; cf. Tatum 1999, 129–30.

21 Linderski 1986, 2197–8; 2214–5; Driediger-Murphy 2018b. According to Cicero (*Phil.* 2.79), Antony did not even think of *spectio* but instead clumsily announced that he would, as augur, observe unsought omens (*auspicia oblativa*) when the assembly met, a claim that allows Cicero to deliver a patronizing lesson in augural law. Antony, however, was not stupid enough, when contending with Caesar, to discredit his augural declaration by announcing it in advance: his early assertion that he would obstruct proceedings must have come in the context of announcing his consular *spectio*, an action he never carried out.

22 Linderski 1986, 2162–4; at *Phil.* 5.9, Cicero insists Dolabella remained vitiated throughout his consulship.

23 Linderski 1986, 2161–2; Beard 1990; Linderski 1995, 505–6.

24 *MRR* 2.315.

25 Macr. 1.12.31; cf. Weinstock 1971, 152–8.

26 Cic. *Att.* 16.1.1; 16.4.1.

27 Cic. *Phil.* 2.110.

28 Dio 44.4.5 with the important discussion by Weinstock 1971, 264–6. Camillus and the temple of Concord: Momigliano 1942.

29 Liv. 6.42.12; Plut. *Cam.* 42.6.

30 Caesar's Parthian designs: see ch. XII, pp. 291.

31 Brunt 1971, 319–26; Keppie 1983, 49–52. Caesar's rejection of Sulla's policy of appropriating land for veterans: App. *B. Civ.* 2.94. His provincial colonies; *MRR* 2.294 (esp. Suet. *Iul.* 42.1); cf. Brunt 1971, 255–9; 589–601; Jehne 1987, 139–52; 343–7.

32 Brunt 1971, 477–80.

33 Vatinius: *MRR* 2.330–1. Acilius: *MRR* 2.326.

34 *MRR* 2.330.

35 Trebonius: *MRR* 2.330. Staius Murcus: *MRR* 2.327; 331 (on the Ides Staius was presently to be dispatched to Syria to replace C. Anstituius Vetus (cos. 30), who was managing the province as *quaestor pro praetore*).

36 For Domitius Calvinus and Octavian, see *MRR* 2.319. Valerius Messalla's appointment is attested only by a recently uncovered fragment of the *Fasti Privernates*; cf. Zevi 2016, 295–301; Zevi 2017, 12–3.

37 Murcus on the Ides: App. *B. Civ.* 2.119.

38 Caesar dismisses his bodyguard: Vell. 2.57.1; Suet. *Iul.* 84.2; 86.1; Plut. *Caes.* 57.7–8; App. *B. Civ.* 2.124; 2.145; Dio 44.7.4. Caesar's *sacrosanctitas*: Nic. Dam. 80; Liv. *Per.* 116; App. *B.Civ.* 2.106; 2.44; Dio 44.5.3; 50.1; cf. Mommsen *StR* 2.872; Weinstock 1971, 220–1. Oath: Suet. *Iul.* 84.2; 86.1; App. *B.Civ.* 2.145; Dio 44.7.4; cf. Cic. *Marcell.* 32.

39 *MRR* 2.317–8.

40 The nature of Lepidus' appointment is known only from the *Fasti Privernates*. The relevant lines read: C. Iulius Caesar IV dict(ator) abdic(avit) ut perpet(uo) [——] / M. Aemilius Lepid(us) II mag(ister) eq(uitum) abd(icavit) ut perpet(uo) [——] / quoad (?) dict(ator) Caesar esset (C. Julius Caesar, dictator for the fourth time, abdicated so that in perpetuity . . . M. Aemilius Lepidus, master of the horse for the second time, abdicated so that in perpetuity . . . so long as Caesar should be dictator); cf. Zevi 2016, 295–8; Zevi 2017, 11–2; Konrad 2022, 112–4.

41 North 2008 is essential; cf. Latte 1960, 84–7; Scullard 1981, 76–8; Wiseman 1995; Vuković 2018. Antony and the Lupercalia: *MRR* 2.315; Drumann-Groebe 1899, 56–7; Rossi 1959, 44–9; Gelzer 1968, 316–22; Bengtson 1977, 69–71; Huzar 1978, 76–8; Chamoux 1986, 95–9; Dettenhofer 1992, 182–3; Rawson 1994a, 462–5; Cristofoli 2008, 140–52; Billows 2009, 246–8; Wiseman 2009, 170–5; Goldsworthy 2010, 197–8; Southern 2010, 81–4; Halfmann 2011, 60–1; Sigmund 2014, 174–82; Stevenson 2015, 145–51; Tempest 2017, 80–2.

42 The topic is a dense one: Weinstock 1971; Gradel 2004, 54–72; Clark 2007a; Wardle 2009; Koortbojian 2013.

43 Cic. *Att.* 12.48.1; 13.28.3; Dio 43.42.3; 43.45.2–3.

44 Plut. *Caes.* 57.4; App. *B. Civ.* 2.106; Dio 44.6.4; *RRC* 480.21; cf. Clark 2007a, 229–34; 247–50.

45 Dio 44.5.2; cf. Cic. *Att.* 13.42; Clark 2007a, 229–30.

46 *MRR* 2.318.

47 *MRR* 2.358; cf. Koortbojian 2013, 21–39.

48 Cic. *Marc.* 8; Lig. 37; *Att.* 12.45.2; Cole 2013, 111–34. At the outbreak of the civil war, some municipalities accorded Caesar divine honours: Cic. *Att.* 8.16.1–2: *municipia vero deum, nec simulant* (towns are honouring him like a god, and they mean it).

49 Cic. *Q. Frat.* 1.1.26; *Att.* 5.21.7; Suet. *Aug.* 52.1. Evidence is assembled by Cerfaux and Tondriau 1957, 279–85; Bowersock 1965, 150–1; Tuchelt 1979, 45–118; Price 1884, 42–3; Sigmund 2014; Frija 2017; see ch. IX, pp. 00.

50 Cic. *Phil.* 2.84–7; Nic. Dam. 71–5; Vell. 2.56.4; Suet. *Iul.* 79.2; Plut. *Ant.* 12.1–7; *Caes.* 61.1–7; App. *B. Civ.* 2.109; Dio 44.11.1–3; 45.31.3–4. Pelling 2011, 450–5; Toher 2017, 301–3; Vé 2016; Ferriès 2009.

51 Cic. *Phil.* 2.87; Nic. Dam. 77; Suet. *Iul.* 79.2; Dio 44.11.2; 45.31.4.

52 Nic. Dam. 72; 75.

53 Liv. *Per.* 116. The regal virtues in Hellenistic ideology: Goodenough 1928; Walbank 1984; Smith 1988, 46–53.

54 Cic. *Phil.* 13.31; Nic. Dam. 69–70; Vell. 2.68.4–5; Suet. *Iul.* 79.1; 80.3; Plut. *Ant.* 12.7; *Caes.* 61.8–10; App. *B. Civ.* 2.108; 2.122; 4.93; Dio 44.9.2–10.4; 46.49.2; cf. Pelling 2011, 455–9; Toher 2017, 292–3.

55 Cic. *Div.* 2.110; Suet. *Caes.* 79.3–4; Plut. *Caes.* 64.3; App. *B. Civ.* 2.110; Dio 44.9.2; 44.14.3.

56 Quint. 9.3.61; cf. North 2008, 146.

57 In the account furnished by Nic. Dam. 71–2, more than one figure, including Cassius, is involved in offering Caesar a diadem: Cassius hopes simultaneously to discredit Caesar and disguise his private schemes; this version is taken seriously by Bessone 2012.

58 Cicero abuses Antony for his subservience toward Caesar: *Phil.* 2.82; 13.18.

59 Nic. Dam. 78–9; cf. Toher 2017, 318–9. This event is also recorded by Suet. *Iul.* 78.1–2; Plut. *Caes.* 60.4–8; App. *B. Civ.* 2.107; Dio 44.8.1–4.

60 Morstein-Marx 2012; Rosillio-López 2017, 144–6; Tempest 2017, 86–7.

61 Suet. *Caes.* 80.4; Eutr. 6.25; Oros. 6.17.2 (sixty plus); Nic. Dam. 59 (eighty). App. *B. Civ.* 2.111 names fifteen conspirators; for a list of known conspirators, see Klotz 1919, 255.

62 As observed by Drumann-Groebe 1899, 57.

63 Plut. *Brut.* 17.2; App. *B. Civ.* 2.117; 3.26; Dio 44.19.1. At *Caes.* 66.4 Plutarch incorrectly names D. Brutus as the conspirator who delayed Antony; cf. *Ant.* 13.4 ('some of the conspirators').

64 Nic. Dam. 96; cf. Cic. *Div* 2.23; Plut. *Caes.* 66.9 (each of whom says no one came to Caesar's aid).

65 Nic. Dam. 91–7; App. *B. Civ.* 118–25; Suet. *Iul.* 82.3–4; Plut. *Brut* 18; *Caes.* 67.1–7; *Ant.* 14.1–2; Dio 44.20–1; Dettenhofer 1992, 262–80; Morstein-Marx 2004, 150–9; Wiseman 2009, 211–21; Pelling 2011, 484–91; Tempest 2017, 106–13; Toher 2017, 345–70.

66 Cic. *Phil.* 2.28; 30 (Antony claims that Brutus addressed Cicero, who does not demur to the allegation); App. *B. Civ.* 2.119; Plut. *Brut.* 18.1; *Caes.* 67.1.

67 Looting: App. *B. Civ.* 2.118.

68 Cic. *Phil.* 2.88 (Antony makes his way home without attracting notice); App. *B. Civ.* 2.118; Plut. *Ant.* 14.1; *Brut.* 18.6; *Caes.* 67.2; Dio 44.22.2; see Pelling 1988, 151.

69 Cic. *Phil.* 2.34; Plut. *Ant.* 13.1–2; see ch. IV, pp. 96–7.

70 Syme 1939, 59.

71 Wrong side of history: Rawson 1991, 488–507; Swain 1996, 151–61; Pelling 2010, 252–4.

72 Conspiracy and aftermath: *MRR* 2.315–6; 320–2; cf. Drumann-Groebe 1899, 57–73; Rossi 1959, 49–56; Bengtson 1977, 72–81; Huzar 1978, 79–84; Chamoux 1986, 99–109; Dettenhofer 1992, 231–80; Rawson 1994b, 468–71; Matijević 2006, 39–48; Ferriès 2007, 63–89; Cristofoli 2008, 153–88; Lintott 2008, 339–41; Pasquali 2009, 61–70; Wiseman 2009, 178–228; Goldsworthy 2010, 201–9; Southern 2010, 84–93; Halfmann 2011, 62–7; Welch 2012, 120–5; Moles 2017, 185–213; Tempest 2017, 78–113.

73 Roman hostility to extremes: Veyne 1983.

74 On the people's deference to its magistrates and senate, see Meier 1980, 45–63; Hölkeskamp 2010, 45 and 52.

75 Plut. *Brut.* 12.3–4; Sedley 1997; Tatum 2008, 154–64; Sigmund 2014, 183–93; Tempest 2017, 94–7.

76 See, for instance, Cic. *Mar.* 33–4; cf. Syme 1939, 61–77; Tatum 2008, 153–5; Flamerie de Lachapelle 2011, 45–119.

77 Cicero pressed points of this kind in his philosophical works: e.g., *Am.* 36; *Off.* 3.19.

78 Cic. *Off.* 2.63; Sen. *Ben.* 3.1.1; cf. Verboven 2002, 37–48 (and passim); Griffin 2013, 103–24; Jacotot 2013, 376–82; Rollinger 2014, 101–21.

79 Cic. *Fam.* 11.28.2.

80 *Fam.* 11.28.6.

81 *Fam.* 11.28.3: *o superbiam inauditam!*

82 Fest. 422L; Marc. *Sat.* 3.7.5–8; *Strafr.* 550–5; Liou-Gille 1997, esp. 75–81.

83 Polyb. 6.56.615; Linderski 1986; Morgan 1990, esp. 30–1; Beard 1994; Beard, North, and Price 1998a; Rüpke 2014; Driediger-Murphy 2018a.

84 Linderski 2007, 114; Lennon 2012.

85 Polyb. 6.54; Liv. 2.5.8; Dion. Hal. *Rom. Ant.* 5.7–8; Plut. *Popl.* 6.2–6.

86 Oath: Liv. 2.1.9; Dion. Hal. *Rom. Ant.* 5.1.3; Plut. *Popl.* 2.2. Law: Liv. 2.8.2 (cf. 3.55.7); Dion. Hal. *Rom. Ant.* 5.19.4; Plut. *Popl.* 11.2; 12.1; Dig. 1.2.2.16 and 23; Mommsen *StR* 2.15–6; Ogilvie 1965, 252. Discussion: Liou-Gille 1997, 71–5. Whatever degree of legend that must be associated with this law, by the first century it had become rooted in Roman sensibilities.

87 On *libertas* see, with further references, Wirzubski 1950; Brunt 1988, 281–350; Arena 2012.

88 Fest. 422L; Marc. *Sat.* 3.7.5–8; *Strafr.* 550–5; Liou-Gille 1997. Archaic sense of *parricidium*: Magdelain 1984; *Roman Statutes* 702–3; Tatum 2020c, 191.

89 Cassius: *MRR* 1.20. Manlius: Liv. 6.11–20; Diod. 15.35.3; Plut. *Cam.* 36.1–9; Zon. 7.23.10. See Lintott 1970; Oakley 1997, 476–93; Smith 2006b.

90 Ahala and Maelius: *MRR* 1.56. See Lintott 1970; Smith 2006b.

91 Cic. *Att.* 2.4.2–3; 13.40.1; *Brut.* 331; *Phil.* 2.26; *RRC* 455–6; Clark 2007a, 150–3; Tempest 2017, 41–2.

92 Dunkle 1967; Lintott 1968, 52–7; Weinstock 1971, 145–8; Pina Polo 2006; Sigmund 2014, 22–103; 169–94; Wiseman 2014; Martin 2015; Baraz 2018.

93 *MRR* 1.493–4; Earl 1963; Lintott 1994, 62–77; Steel 2013, 15–20.

94 Val. Max. 3.2.17; cf. Cic. *Tusc.* 4.51; Vell. Pat. 2.3; App. *B. Civ.* 1.68; Plut. *Ti. Gracch.* 19.3.

95 Linderski 2007, esp. 113–4; cf. Badian 2004; Flower 2006, 70–6; Clark 2007b; Várhelyi 2011. Wiseman 2009, 185–7 emphasizes the recollection of the oath of Brutus.

96 On the punishments inflicted on Gracchus and his followers, see Beness 2000.

97 Although Cicero routinely adduces Nasica in highly laudatory terms, he could, when addressing the people, say nice things about Tiberius, a reflection of popular sentiments: e.g., Cic. *Agr.* 2.10–1; see Béranger 1972; Bücher 2009; Blom 2010, 119–20; Arena 2012, 124–68; Manuwald 2018, 168. Other orators professed a positive view of Tiberius, as evidenced by *Rhet. Her.* 4.7; 4.31; 4.38; 4.42. On these conflicting traditions, see Flower 2006, 76–81; Wiseman 2009, 177–89; Blom 2010, 105–6; Lapryionok 2010; Martin 2015, 449. On Tiberius in Latin literature generally, see Rieger 1991.

98 Clark 2007b; Várhelyi 2011, 126–8.

99 Liv. 2.33.1; 3.55.6–7; Fest. 422L; Ogilvie 500–2; Liou-Gille 1997, 75–81; Lintott 1999, 123–6 (each with further references).

100 Cic. *Rep.* 1.3.6; Val. Max. 5.3.2e; Plut. *Ti. Gracch.* 21; *ILS* 8886. Placating the gods: Cic. *Verr.* 2.4.108; Val. Max. 1.1.1; cf. Spaeth 1996, 73–9.

101 Lintott 1970; Flower 2006, 44–51.

102 Suet. *Iul.* 82.4. By the first century, casting Caesar's corpse into the Tiber would have marked him out as a political criminal and a failed tyrant; see App. *B. Civ.* 2.128; 2.134; 3.18; Le Gall 1953, 88–92.

103 App. *B.Civ.* 2.119; cf. Nic. Dam. 92.

104   The statue of Lucius Brutus brandishing a dagger: Plut. *Brut.* 1.1. Brutus' dagger may
        have been inspired by representations of the Athenian tyrannicides Harmodius and
        Aristogeiton, even if Brutus overthrew and did not assassinate Tarquinius; see Weinstock
        1971, 145–6. By the late republic there was a statue of the Athenian tyrannicides on the
        Capitol, probably in the temple of Fides; its origins are unclear: see Flower 2006, 109–10;
        Pina Polo 2006, 88–92. The precise location of Brutus' statue on the Capitoline is uncer-
        tain. App. *B. Civ.* 1.16 places it in front of the temple of Jupiter Best and Greatest. See, fur-
        ther, Evans 1990.
105   *RRC* 518. On the symbolism of the *pilleus*, see Clark 2007a, 141–50.
106   App. *B.Civ.* 2.119.
107   Vell. 2.3.1; Val. Max. 3.2.17; Plut. *Ti. Gracch.* 19.3–4. See the discussion by Clark 2007b.
108   Tempest 2017, 107: 'a demonstrable act of piety'; contrast the cynical appraisal at Dio
        44.21.2 ('they ascended the Capitol on the pretext of offering thanks to the gods'.
109   Ov. *Fast.* 1.56; 1.587–8; Macrob. *Sat.* 1.15.14–8; cf. Wissowa 1902, 100–101 (who assem-
        bles further evidence).
110   The significance of the Capitoline: Wissowa 1902, 110–3; Edwards 1996, 70–2; 82–8;
        Hölkeskamp 2004, 137–68; Clark 2007a, 117–23; Bradley 2012; Russell 2016a, 105–10;
        Hölkeskamp 2020, 181–9.
111   See the evidence assembled by Wissowa 1902, 445 n. 3. Processions register con-
        sensus: Hölkeskamp 2010, 55–61 (and references cited there). On the symbolism of
        Roman processions, see Flaig 2003, 32–68; Flower 2014; Bell 2004, 34–7; Sumi 2005, 16–
        47; Hölkeskamp 2017, 189–236; Rosillio-López 2017, 42–64.
112   Syme 1939, 99; cf. Huzar 1978, 81.
113   Mark of liberation: e.g., the ejection of Cleomenes in 508/7 (Hdt. 5.72); cf. Pelling 2011,
        487; Moles 2017, 192–3. Coup d'état: Simonton 2017, 163–7. Appropriation: Parker
        1998, 24–6. In Aristophanes' *Lysistrata*, the women's seizure of the acropolis is likened
        to Hippias' tyranny (*Lys.* 619) and Cleomenes' coup (*Lys.* 271–85); on the implications of
        the acropolis in that play, see Loraux 1980/81. Syme did not view the occupation of the
        Capitoline as a symbol of liberation: 'Rome was not a Greek city, to be mastered from its
        citadel' (Syme 1939, 99).
114   The Liberators' procession to the Capitol was not intended to mark 'a warrior's simple
        pride in having killed a rival' and was certainly not 'like a gladiator's victory lap in the
        arena', the suggestions of Strauss 2015, 146.
115   One civic ritual evokes another: Hölkeskamp 2017, 227–30; Tatum 2018, 32–7.
116   Gowing 1992, 33–8; Pelling 2011, 477–8; 484–6; Toher 2017, 345–7; Moles 2017, 186–206.
117   On this revealing misapprehension on the part of the Liberators, see Dettenhofer
        1992, 264.
118   Nic. Dam. 92.
119   Plut. *Caes.* 67.3–5.
120   App. *B. Civ.* 2.119; Plut. *Caes.* 67.4–6; cf. Dio 47.49.4.
121   Plut. *Brut.* 18.9–10; cf. Moles 2017, 194–5.
122   Nic. Dam. 99; App. *B. Civ.* 2.122; Plut. *Brut.* 18.9–10; *Caes.* 67.7.
123   App. *B. Civ.* 120.
124   Morstein-Marx 2004, 132–3; 152–5; cf. Tatum 1999, 180–1; 198–9; 203; Tatum 2018,
        259–60. Wiseman 2009, 202, regards any payments to the populace as unhistorical on the
        grounds that there was no opportunity for the Liberators to organize the distribution of
        payments.
125   Cic. *Att.* 14.14.2; Nic. Dam. 94; 103; Flor. 2.17.2; App. *B. Civ.* 2.119–20; Dio 44.34.2–6; cf.
        Botermann 1968, 1–8.

126 Nic. Dam. 49; 99–101; App. *B. Civ.* 2.120–2; Plut. *Brut.* 18.12–3; *Caes.* 67.7; Dio 4.20–21.1. None of these accounts is satisfactory. A useful attempt at sorting out their difficulties is Moles 2017, 198–206.

127 The theme of L. Brutus persisted in the rhetoric of the Liberators: e.g., Cic. *Fam.* 12.22.2; *Phil.* 1.13; cf. Sumi 2005, 84.

128 App. *B. Civ.* 2.141; cf. Plut. *Brut.* 18.11.

129 App. *B. Civ.* 2.121.

130 Nep. *Att.* 8.3–4; Cic. *Att.* 14.6.2.

131 Morstein-Marx 2004, 150–8; Pelling 2011, 484–5; Tempest 2017, 109; Knopf 2018, 53–78, esp. 64. *Libertas* was seen differently from different social stations: Brunt 1988, 327–34; Arena 2012, 45–72.

132 Nic. Dam. 97; Suet. *Iul.* 82.3.

133 Tempest 2017, 108, correctly emphasizes the importance of this event.

134 Cic. *Phil.* 2.35; 2.109; Suet. *Iul.* 83.2; Plut. *Cic.* 43.8; *Ant.* 15.1; App. *B. Civ.* 2.125; 3.17; 3.20.

135 App. *B. Civ.* 3.5.

136 App. *B.Civ.* 3.20.

137 App. *B.Civ.* 3.17; Dio 43.45.2; cf. Jehne 1987, 68–79.

138 Cic. *Phil.* 2.35; 2.109.

139 Nic. Dam. 55; App. *B.Civ.* 3.11; Dio 45.3.2.

140 Cic. *Phil.* 1.93; 2.25; 2.93; Nic. Dam. 110; Jehne 1987, 76–8.

141 Richardson 1992, 227; *LTUR* 3.362–4.

142 Cic. *Phil.* 1.17; 2.93; 4.14; 5.11; 5.15; 8.26; 12.12; *Att.* 14.14.5; 14.18.1; Vell. 2.60.4; Dio 45.24.1; see Manuwald 2007, 431.

143 Although a *magister equituum* can continue in office after the death or abdication of his dictator, Lepidus' tenure was explicitly limited: *quoad dict(ator) Caesar esset*; cf. Konrad 2022, 112–4.

144 App. *B.Civ.* 2.125, referring specifically to the night of the sixteenth.

145 Cic. *Att.* 14.10.1; 15.11.2; *Phil.* 2.89.

146 Cic. *Att.* 15.11.2.

147 Undertaking anything new was forbidden on a black day: Varro, *Ling.* 6.29; Liv. 6.1.12; Gell. *NA* 5.17.1. But an emergency meeting of the senate was not thereby prohibited, and one could insist that, in settling the issue of Caesar's assassination, no new business was being undertaken—all points doubtless raised by Cicero at the time.

148 Nic. Dam. 101; Cic. *Phil.* 2.89; App. *B. Civ.* 2.123–4.

149 App. *B. Civ.* 1.125.

150 App. *B. Civ.* 2.124.

151 Nic. Dam. 101.

152 This is the natural implication of the narrative at Nic. Dam. 101.

153 Lepidus: Nic. Dam. 103; 106; App. *B. Civ.* 2.119; 2.125; Dio 44.20.3; 44.22.2. Antony: Nic. Dam. 103. App. *B. Civ.* 2.126 indicates that Antony claimed he was opposed to introducing soldiers to the city, which may have been his original view. It is in any case clear that he acquiesced in Lepidus' action.

154 Nic. Dam. 103; 106; cf. App. *B. Civ.* 2.123–4; cf. Rosillo-López 2022, 225 and 231–2.

155 Cic. *Phil.* 1.1–4; 1.31–2; 2.89–90; *Att.* 14.11.1; 14.2; Vell. 2.58.3–4; Plut. *Brut.* 19.1; *Cic.* 42.3; *Ant.* 14.3; App. *B. Civ.* 2.126–35 (Appian makes no mention of Cicero); Dio 44.22.3–34.6. Plutarch, Appian, and Dio all collapse the events of 16–20 March, one effect of which is their common misdating of this meeting of the senate to 16 March: cf. Moles 2017, 198–206.

156 Cic. *Mur.* 52; Plut. *Cic.* 14.7–8; Dio 37.29.4.

157 The senate had previously sworn to execute Caesar's *acta*: App. *B. Civ.* 2.106.

158 Cic. *Phil.* 1.1; cf. Ramsey 2003, 86, for other possibilities for Cicero's Greek word.

159 Vell. 2.58.3–4: Antony *pacis auctor.*

160 App. *B. Civ.* 2.135.

161 Cic. *Leg.* 2.19: *deus ipse vindex erit.*

162 Cic. *Att.* 14.10.1.

163 According to Appian (*B. Civ.* 2.136), it was after the senate's sessions ended that Piso demanded the body reconvene to address his motion, but this is almost certainly unhistorical, *pace* Rosillo-López 2022, 232–4; Piso's motion, despite Appian's dramatic retelling, will have come during the senate's single sitting for the day.

164 App. *B. Civ.* 2.130–2 locates this *contio* during an intermission in the senate's sitting. A break in the session would have been, so far as we know, unprecedented (*if* it took place, Antony presumably handed presidency over to Dolabella). Despite the extraordinary circumstances of 17 March, it is almost certainly unhistorical and a symptom of the chronological compression afflicting Appian's narrative (in Appian's account, the consuls do not furnish the people with a report of this meeting until the next day: *B. Civ.* 2.142); it is far more likely Antony and Lepidus addressed the people after the meeting's conclusion. On the problems in Appian's chronology at this point in his narrative, see Moles 2017, 201–4.

165 At App. *B. Civ.* 2.137–41, Brutus summons the public to the Capitol for a self-justificatory *contio*, but here Appian almost certainly has in mind the *contio* Brutus delivered on 16 March (a speech which, immediately afterwards, Brutus asked Cicero to edit for subsequent publication: Cic. *Att.* 15.1a.2); this confusion stems from Appian's incorrect dating of the senate's meeting to 16 March; cf. Moles 2017, 201–4.

166 App. *B. Civ.* 2.132.

167 Cic. *Phil.* 1.2–3.

168 Cic. *Fam.* 12.16.3.

169 Cic. *Att.* 14.1.1; 14.2.3; at *Fam.* 11.28.7, a letter designed to burnish his image, Matius insists that he does in fact routinely visit Antony. On the reactions among Caesarians to the amnesty of 17 March, see Ferriès 2007, 64–80.

170 Brunt 1988, 492–3; Ferriès 2007, 63–89; Matijević 2014; Tatum 2020c, 200–204. On Caesar's senate, see Jehne 1987, 392–406.

CHAPTER VI

1 Cic. *Phil.* 2.70. It has been suggested that this expression occurred several times within a single speech given by Antony, certainly to underline his nobility and perhaps to score off Cicero's *novitas*: Ramsey 2003, 260.

2 Epstein 1987, 56–8; Kaster 2005, 84–103.

3 Instances include: *Rhet. Her.* 1.8; Cic. *Inv.* 1.22; *Parad.* 46; *Caec.* 57; *Clu.* 94.

4 Dugan 2005; Blom 2010, 35–59; Dench 2013, 130–4; Yakobson 2017; Tatum 2018, 166–9.

5 Plut. *Brut.* 19.4–20.1; cf. Moles 2017, 210–1. The historicity of this meeting is doubted by, i.a., Pelling 2002, 37 n. 90; Ramsey 2003, 144.

6 Cic. *Phil.* 1.32.

7 Honours and praise for Antony after 17 March: Cic. *Phil.* 1.2; 1.31; 2.90; Plut. *Ant.* 14.3.

8 Plutarch includes both the funeral and the will in his account of this meeting; all our sources tend to blur the two events; cf. Wiseman 2009, 229.

9 Wiseman 2009, 228. Sources for Caesar's will assembled at Champlin 1991, 190.

10 App. *B. Civ.* 3.22; 3.23.

11 Cic. *Phil.* 2.71; cf. Nic. Dam. 74.

12 Flor. 2.15.1; Dio 44.35.2; 44.36.2.

13 Cic. *Phil.* 2.40. On the Romans' social expectations regarding wills, see Champlin 1991; see also ch. XIII, pp. 331–3.

14 The date can only be approximate, but the case for dating Caesar's funeral to 17 March advanced by Carotta and Eickenberg 2011 is unpersuasive. Our principal sources are: Cic. *Phil.* 2.90–2; Nic. Dam. 48–50; Suet. *Iul.* 84.1–5; Plut. *Ant.* 14.6–8; *Brut.* 20.2–7; App. *B. Civ.* 1.143–7; Dio 44.35–51; cf. Drumann-Groebe 1899, 73–6; Bengtson 1977, 81–4; Huzar 1978, 84–5; Chamoux 1986, 110–5; Pelling 1988, 153–5; Matijević 2006, 96–104; Wiseman 2009, 228–30; Goldsworthy 2010, 209–11; Southern 2010, 93–6; Halfmann 2011, 67–8; Welch 2012, 125–6; Mahy 2013, 39–40; Blom 2016, 264–7; Moles 2017, 217–23; Tempest 2017, 118–9.

15 Flower 1996, 91–158; Hölkeskamp 2017, 218–21.

16 Cic. *Att.* 14.10.1.

17 Cic. *Att.* 14.11.1 (*tantus vir* and *clarissimus vir*); 14.22.1 (slogan); 15.20.2 (*clarissimus vir*).

18 Suet. *Iul.* 84.2; App. *B. Civ.* 2.144–5.

19 Many of the theatrical details in Appian's account are probably fictitious: Hall 2014, 134–40.

20 Wiseman 2009, 232–3.

21 App. *B. Civ.* 147; Dio 44.50.1–51.1.

22 Cic. *Fam.* 11.1. Controversy attends the correct dating of this letter. Numerous, perceptive historians assign it to a time between the assassination and the meeting of the senate on 17 March (e.g., Lintott 2008, 340–1). On balance, however, a date after Caesar's funeral appears more likely: Shackleton Bailey 1977, 463–4. A close reading of this letter is provided by Rosillo-López 2022, 150–3.

23 Vervaet 2014, 332–40; 346–9. Trebonius, also a *privatus*, was in a similar circumstance and doubtless received a similar notice from Antony.

24 In the view of Matijević 2014, 47–9, Hirtius makes this (false) report to Decimus in order to provoke a division between Antony and the Liberators.

25 Matters were certainly settled by mid-April: Cic. *Att.* 14.10.1 (Trebonius); 14.13.2 (Decimus); App. *B. Civ.* 3.6; cf. *MRR* 2.328.

26 *RRC* 480.22; cf. Newman 1990, 52–3; Rowan 2019, 57–9.

27 The suggestion of Crawford in *RRC*, p. 495; cf. Cic. *Att.* 14.14.1; 14.19.2; Dio 34.42.3. Caesar and Antony at the Paralia: Weinstock 1971, 184–7; Matijević 2006, 105–10. Although it was Caesar the dictator who was first to put his image on Roman coins, the Liberators, like Antony and Octavian, later took up the practice.

28 Ferriès 2012.

29 Cic. *Att.* 14.6.1; 14.8.1. For events taking place between Caesar's funeral and 1 September, see Drumann-Groebe 1899, 76–122; Holmes 1928, 4–23; Charlesworth 1934, 1–10; Syme 1939, 103–22; Frisch 1946, 63–118; Rossi 1959, 66–87; Bengtson 1977, 84–94; Huzar 1978, 85–97; Chamoux 1986, 115–27; Dettenhofer 1992, 278–87; Rawson 1994b, 471–7; Gotter 1996, 29–86; Kienast 1999, 21–9; Matijević 2006, 105–60; Osgood 2006, 28–43; Manuwald 2007, 10–9; Pasquali 2009, 68–83; Goldsworthy 2010, 212–7; Southern 2010, 95–101; Halfmann 2011, 67–75; Welch 2012, 126–30; Tempest 2017, 113–41.

30 Ramsey 2003, 89.

31 Cic. *Phil.* 1.3; 2.91; 5.10; App. *B. Civ.* 3.25; Dio 44.51.2.

32 *MRR* 2.333.

33 Dio 44.53.6; App. *B. Civ.* 5.93; cf. Allély 2004, 82–7.

34 *MRR* 2.327.

35 *MRR* 2.326; cf. Allély 2004, 82–7; Welch 2012, 130–1.

36 App. *B. Civ.* 3.2; cf. Cic. *Att.* 15.22; 15.29.1; 16.1.4; cf. Allély 2004, 89–92; Welch 2012, 130–4.

37 Cic. *Att.* 14.9.3; 14.10.1; 14.13.2; App. *B. Civ.* 3.2.

38 Flor. 2.17.4; App. *B. Civ.* 3.2; cf. Magnino 1984, 122–3.

39 Praetorian provinces were assigned by lot on 28 November (Cic. *Phil.* 3.20; 3.24–6); Brutus and Cassius appear to have been assigned provinces earlier (Cic. *Att.* 15.9.1; cf. *MRR* 2.320–1).
40 Cic. *Phil.* 1.32.
41 Cic. *Att.* 14.3.2, written 9 April.
42 Cic. *Att.* 14.6.1; 14.7.1; 14.8.1; *Phil.* 1.5; Val. Max. 9.15.1; Suet. *Iul.* 85; App. *B. Civ.* 3.2–4; cf. Nic. Dam. 31–3.
43 Cic. *Att.* 12.49.1. Exile: Cic. *Att.* 14.6.1; Val. Max. 9.15.1.
44 Rome's auction halls, for instance, were located near the Forum: *LTUR* 1.132; Andreau 1999, 38–9; 48–9; Hinard 2011, 431–44.
45 Cic. *Att.* 14.15.1; 14.16.2; 14.17a; 14.19.1–2; *Fam.* 12.1.1; *Phil.* 1.30.
46 Culham 1989; Meyer 2004.
47 Jos. *AJ* 14.217–22.
48 The Buthrotum affair: Cic. *Att.* 12.6a.2; 14.10.3; 14.14.6; 15.1.2; 15.12.1; 15.14.2–3; 15.15.1; 16.16a–f; 15.18.1; 15.29.3; 16.1.2; 16.3.1; 16.4.3; cf. Deniaux 1988; Rosillo-López 2022, 226–8. Atticus's properties: Marshall 1999, 59–60.
49 Cic. *Phil.* 1.3.
50 The principal sources for the policy of enacting Caesar's unpublished designs are Cic. *Phil.* 1.3; 2.91; 2.100; *Att.* 16.16b.1; 16.16c.1; *Fam.* 12.1.1; Dio 44.53.2–5; 45.23.7–8. Other references are assembled at *MRR* 2.316. The best discussion of this decree and its implementation remains Ramsey 1994, which survives objections raised by Matijević 2006 and Cristofoli 2019.
51 Cic. *Att.* 14.9.2.
52 Cic. *Att.* 14.12.1.
53 Cic. *Att.* 16.3.1 (July 44): *deseremur ocius a re publica quam a re familiari.*
54 Cic. *Fam.* 12.1.1.
55 This is Cicero's preferred order even when he is succinct: *Phil.* 2.92–8; 5.11.
56 Fezzi 2003.
57 Rosillo-López 2010.
58 Cic. *Att.* 14.12.1; *Phil.* 1.24; 2.92; 3.30; 5.12; 7.15.
59 Cic. *Phil.* 5.10; 10.17. Caesar's acts reaffirmed by the triumvirs: *MRR* 2.358.
60 Soraci 2018 (assembling evidence and previous scholarship). For a very different view, see Sherwin-White 1973, 230 and 341.
61 *B. Alex.* 67–8.
62 Cic. *Deit.* Brutus' friendship with Deiotarus: Cic. *Att.* 14.1.2; *Brut.* 5.21; Tac. *Dial.* 21.6; Plut. *Brut.* 6.6; Dio 47.24.3.
63 Cic. *Att.* 14.12.1; *Phil.* 2.93–5; cf. Schultz 2021, 86.
64 Cic. *Phil.* 3.10; 5.11.
65 Provinces for Cassius and Brutus: *MRR* 2.320–1.
66 Cic. *Phil.* 2.97 (cf. *Phil.* 7.15); Dio 45.32.4; 46.23.2 (Dio merely recycles Cicero).
67 Antonii in Crete: e.g., Bowsky 2001; see also ch. XI, pp. 212–20.
68 Capua: Rigsby 1976; España-Chamorro 2012.
69 Bowsky 2002; Pałuchowski 2005; Chevrollier 2016.
70 Cic. *Mil.* 33; 90; Asc. 33; 55–6C; Tatum 1990; Damon 1992; Tatum 1999, 115–7.
71 Clodius' son: Wiseman 1987, 42–56.
72 Cic. *Att.* 14.13a.1–3; cf. Tatum 2017, 67–9; by contrast Hall 2009, 93–9 discerns greater politeness on Antony's part.
73 Cic. *Att.* 14.13.6.
74 Cic. *Att.* 14.13.6.
75 Cic. *Att.* 14.13b.1–5.

76 Cic. *Att.* 14.19.2.
77 Cic. *Phil.* 1.24; 2.98; 5.11; Dio 45.25.2; 46.15.1 (recycling Cicero).
78 Cic. *Att.* 14.12.1; *Fam.* 12.1.1.
79 Cic. *Phil.* 5.11; cf. 2.95.
80 Cic. *Phil.* 2.98. The census: Lintott 1999, 115–20; Clemente 2022 (with further references).
81 Cic. *Att.* 14.19.2.
82 Cic. *Att.* 15.1.3; 15.5.2; 15.8.1.
83 Cic. *Att.* 14.21.2.
84 Cic. *Att.* 14.20.4.
85 Cic. *Fam.* 16.23.2.
86 Cic. *Att.* 15.5.2.
87 Cic. *Phil.* 5.3; 5.10; 5.44; 13.31; App. *B. Civ.* 2.135.
88 Cic. *Att.* 14.20.2; 14.21.2; *Phil.* 2.100–2; cf. Keppie 1983, 52–3.
89 App. *B. Civ.* 3.5.
90 Cic. *Att.* 14.21.2; 14.22.2.
91 Cic. *Fam.* 11.2.1–3.
92 Cic. *Att.* 14.14.4; cf. 15.4.1; 15.5.2; *Fam.* 11.2.1–3; *Phil.* 1.6; 2.10.
93 *MRR* 2.316; 2.332–3.
94 Cic. *Att.* 14.4.1; 15.4.1; 15.11.4; *Phil.* 1.25; 2.6; 2.42; 2.109; 5.7–8; 8.28; Vell. 2.60.5; App. *B. Civ.* 3.27–30; Dio 45.9.3; cf. Jordan 2017. The law on provinces is also denominated in our sources the *lex de permutation provinciarum*. Caesar's *lex provinciis*: *MRR* 2.294.
95 Cic. *Fam.* 11.2.3: *valde leve est ac nugatorium*.
96 Cic. *Att.* 14.14.4; 15.4.1. As an ex-praetor, Decimus was entitled to govern his province for no more than a single year, but the terms of the *lex de provinciis consularibus* cut short even that brief tenure.
97 Cic. *Fam.* 16.23.1.
98 Wiseman 1971, 246.
99 Octavian's appearance and constitution are described by Suetonius at *Aug.* 79–81; not every particular should be taken literally: cf. Wardle 2014, 470–81.
100 A typical take on Octavian's genius: Nic. Dam. 4–36. More balanced is Suet. *Aug.* 84–9, esp. 84.1–2 and 89.1; the entire section, however, includes much special pleading; cf. Wardle 2014, 481–97.
101 Cic. *Att.* 14.11.3; 14.12.2.
102 Octavian's early movements are known only approximately. Toher 2004 proposes that Octavian, after arriving in Italy in April, went directly to Rome, later to Campania, finally returning to the capital in May, but this is sufficiently refuted by Wardle 2018 (with ample references). Octavian appears before Gaius: App. *B. Civ.* 3.14.
103 Schmitthenner 1973, 39–90; Syme 1982; Konrad 1996, 124–7; Linderski 2007, 133–40; Lindsay 2009, 79–86; Scuderi 2015, 495–6.
104 Cic. *Phil.* 13.24–5. On Octavian's exploitation of the name *Caesar*, see now Scuderi 2015 (assembling sources and scholarship). It is perhaps worth observing that opportunistic politicians had previously been less than honest in the matter of adoption: Clodius Pulcher, Cornelius Dolabella, and others had ignored the full legal implications of their politically motivated adoptions; cf. Tatum 1999, 104–8.
105 Octavian's speech: Cic. *Att.* 14.20.5; 15.2.3; cf. *Fam.* 11.27.8; 11.28.6. On the *Ludi Victoriae Caesaris*, see Weinstock 1971, 111–2. Octavian as avenger: Havener 151–92, with further references.
106 Rawson 1994b, 472; Matijević 2006, 125.
107 Antony's rivals and their cultivation of Octavian: Gotter 1996, 61–2; Matijević 2006, 111–29; Welch 2012, 122; Matijević 2014.

108 Vell. 2.60.3; Plut. *Ant.* 16.2; App. *B. Civ.* 3.14–20; Dio 45.5.3.

109 App. *B. Civ.* 3.21–2; cf. Magnino 1984, 140–1.

110 Dio 45.9.1 incorrectly claims that Antony's agrarian law was concocted in reaction to Octavian's popularity.

111 Cic. *Att.* 15.4.1; 15.4.4; 15.5.3; 15.8.1; 15.6.2.

112 Cic. *Att.* 15.3.1; 15.5.3; *Phil.* 1.6; 2.108–9.

113 Unrest in Gaul: Cic. *Att.* 14.1.1; 14.5.1; 14.6.1; 18.8.1. After arriving in Gaul, Decimus undertook campaigns against various Alpine tribes, for which campaign he was, by early September, hailed *imperator*: Cic. *Fam.* 11.4; cf. *MRR* 2.328.

114 Cic. *Att.* 15.5.3.

115 Poor attendance: Cic. *Phil.* 1.6; App. *B. Civ.* 3.27; 3.30; Dio 45.9.1–3.

116 For the date, see Cic. *Att.* 15.11.4.

117 Cic. *Att.* 14.11.4.

118 Cic. *Att.* 16.16c.2.

119 Stormy weather: Cic. *Phil.* 5.7 (*lex agraria*); *Phil.* 5.15 (*lex iudiciaria*).

120 Cic. *Att.* 15.12.2.

121 Cic. *Att.* 15.6.2–3.

122 Frisch 1946, 103–4.

123 Cic. *Att.* 15.9.1.

124 Cic. *Att.* 15.11.1–2.

125 Cic. *Att.* 15.4.1; *Fam.* 16.23.1.

126 App. *B. Civ.* 3.6; cf. Magnino 1984, 126–3.

127 Cic. *Fam.* 11.3.4; cf. Tempest 2017, 136–7.

128 Cic. *Att.* 15.21.1.

129 Cic. *Att.* 15.20.1–3 (*media enim tollit Antonius. Illa infirma, haec nefaria*).

130 Sources at *MRR* 2.319 (under the entry for C. Antonius).

131 Suet. *Aug.* 10.2; Plut. *Ant.* 16.2; App. *B. Civ.* 3.31; Dio 45.6.3; cf. Ramsey 2001, 261–5 (decisive on the approximate date); Wardle 2014, 120–2; Blom 2016, 268.

132 Ramsey and Licht 1997 is now fundamental, assembling all the evidence and including doxographies covering every controversy. Celebration in July: Ramsey and Licht 1997, 44–7 argue that it was Octavian and his supporters who arranged for these games to be celebrated in July.

133 Nic. Dam. 108; App. *B. Civ.* 3.28.

134 On the appearance of the comet, see Ramsey and Licht 1997, 61–117.

135 Aug. *Vita Sua* fr. 1 *FRHist.*

136 Aug. *Vita Sua* fr. 1 *FRHist*; Suet. *Iul.* 88.1; Dio 45.7.1; Koortbojian 2013, 27–8.

137 It is often concluded, on the basis of Aug. *Vita Sua* fr. 1 *FRHist*, that this statue's consecration followed more or less immediately on its decoration, but that is not what Augustus says: *quo nomine id insigne simulacro captis eius, quod mox in foro consecravimus, adiectum est* ('for this reason, that symbol was attached to the head of a statue which I subsequently (*mox*) consecrated in the Forum'); the word *mox* emphasizes a sequence of events but in no way implies immediacy; cf. Rose 1927.

138 Cic. *Phil.* 2.110.

139 Nic. Dam. 115–9; Plut. *Ant.* 16.6; App. *B. Civ.* 29–39; Dio 45.8.1–4; cf. Magnino 1984, 147–8; 154; Toher 2017, 393–4. The evidence is highly problematic: Appian furnishes two reconciliations, the second very likely a doublet of the first. In our sources, the veterans are the prime movers instead of intermediaries, but see Halfmann 2011, 74–5. For this episode, the sources are each of them sympathetic to Octavian and impute political calculation to Antony.

140 Dio 45.11.1.

141   Cic. *Att.* 16.7.1; *Phil.* 1.8; cf. Ramsey 2001; Tempest 2017, 139–40.

142   Cic. *Fam.* 11.3.1.

143   Cic. *Att.* 16.7.5; *Phil.* 1.10; 1.14–5.

144   Cic. *Att.* 16.7.7.

145   Cic. *Fam.* 11.3.

146   Tempest 2017, 135–9.

147   Cic. *Fam.* 11.3.4.

148   Cic. *Fam.* 12.2.3; Tempest 2017, 135–9 assembles and assesses the evidence.

149   Vell. 2.62.3.

150   Brutus' departure: Nic. Dam. 135; Cic. *Att.* 16.5.3; 16.7.5; *Phil.* 1.9; 10.8; Vell. 2.62.3; Plut. *Brut.* 23.1; App. *B. Civ.* 3.24; Dio 47.20.3. Cassius was probably not far behind, but that remains controversial; cf. Moles 2017, 245–7.

151   *Lex iudicaria*: Cic. *Phil.* 1.19–20; 5.8; 13.3–5; cf. Ramsey 2005 (fundamental). *Lex de provocatione*: *Phil.* 1.21; 13.5; Dio 46.36.2; cf. Greenidge 1901, 516–9. On Antony's strategy, Deniaux 2005 remains useful.

152   Greenidge 1901, 344–66.

153   Alexander 1993; Rigsby 1999, 79–119.

154   Morstein-Marx 2004; Mouritsen 2017, 72–94.

155   Caesar's law: *MRR* 2.294. What became of the *tribunii aerarii* is not entirely clear. Perhaps they were assigned other judicial duties outside the criminal courts; perhaps many of them became proper equestrians (by promoting large numbers of equestrians into the senate, Caesar created openings in the equestrian centuries): *StR.* 3.192; 489; 535; Nicolet 1966, 623–5; Ramsey 2005, 33–4.

156   Tatum 2018, 9–11; 16–9.

157   Cic. *Rep.* 2.39.

158   Cic. *Phil.* 5.12–4. Lysiades' father was Phaedrus, an expert Epicurean whom Cicero admired (Cic. *Fam.* 13.1.2; *Fin* 1.16). On Cydas, see ch. IX, pp. 212; XI, pp. 211.

159   Cic. *Phil.* 6.14; cf. Manuwald 2007, 796–8.

160   Roddaz 1988, 328–30.

161   Cic. *Phil.* 5.20; 14.8–10.

162   Cic. *Phil.* 6.13–5; cf. Manuwald 2007, 801–2.

163   Nicolet 1985; Tatum 2018, 174–6; 225–8; 230–1; 240; 242–4.

CHAPTER VII

1   From 1 September until the outbreak of tensions over Mutina, see Drumann-Groebe 1899, 140–55; Holmes 1928, 23–37; Charlesworth 1934, 1–13; Syme 1939, 162–71; Frisch 1946, 119–59; Rossi 1959, 87–90; Bengtson 1977, 94–100; Huzar 1978, 97–105; Chamoux 1986, 110–5; Kienast 1999, 29–31; Matijević 2006, 213–37; Osgood 2006, 47–50; Lintott 2008, 374–85; Pasquali 2009, 99–121; Goldsworthy 2010, 218–21; Southern 2010, 102–6; Halfmann 2011, 75–80.

2   *MRR* 2.329; Cic. *Fam.* 10.1; 11.2; cf. Lintott 2008, 375.

3   Decree: Dio 43.44.6; 45.7.2; cf. Ferrary 1999. The decree's anomalous quality: Cic. *Phil.* 1.13.

4   Failing to attend a meeting of the senate need not signal resistance, but, on any day on which a major or controversial issue was to be raised, absences were noticed: Bonnefound-Coudry 1989, 364–6. Plancus, it is clear, was offended by Cicero's failure to attend: Cic. *Fam.* 10.2.1.

5   Plut. *Cic.* 43.5–6 dates Cicero's return to 31 August. Cic. *Fam.* 12.2.1 suggests that he returned on 1 September, but Cicero's letter can be taken in more than one way: Shackleton Bailey 1977, 514. The public jubilation Plutarch attributes to Cicero's entry into the capital

is clearly exaggerated, but there is no reason to doubt that the distinguished consular was well-received by his loyal constituencies.

6   Cic. *Phil.* 1.11–3; Plut. *Cic.* 43.7–8; cf. Ramsey 2003, 110–1; Blom 2016, 268–9.
7   On this episode, see Tatum 1999, 153–66.
8   Cic. *Phil.* 1.19–26.
9   Cic. *Phil.* 1.18; 1.29; 1.33.
10 Cic. *Fam.* 11.3.
11 Cic. *Phil.* 1.33–5; 1.38.
12 Cic. *Fam.* 12.2.1.
13 Useful reconstructions by Frisch 1946, 133–5; Blom 2016, 269–71.
14 Cic. *Fam.* 12.2.1; *Phil.* 5.19–20. The allegation of relying on a ghostwriter was an unoriginal invective move: cf. Suet. *Gramm.* 26.2.
15 Caesar as *parens patriae* and its significance: Weinstock 1971, 200–5; Stevenson 2015, 139–52. *Parens patriae* and *libertas*: Cic. *Rab. perd.* 27; *Dom.* 94; *Rep.* 1.64; 2.47; cf. Tatum 2020c, 198–9. Caesar as *parens patriae* on coinage: *RRC* 480.19 and 22.
16 Cic. *Phil.* 2.30–2; cf. Tatum 2020c, 196–7.
17 Open enemies: Cic. *Phil.* 5.19.
18 Cic. *Fam.* 12.2.1–2.
19 Cic. *Fam.* 12.22.2.
20 Cic. *Fam.* 12.2.1; 12.3.1–2; 12.22.1; 12.23.3.
21 Welch 2015, 280–5; Tatum 2020c, 196–200.
22 Cic. *Fam.* 12.3.2.
23 Cic. *Fam.* 12.3.2.
24 Cic. *Att.* 15.13.2: Atticus used the word *indutiae*.
25 Ramsey 2003, 157–9.
26 Cic. *Fam.* 12.2.3; 12.22; 12.23.
27 Cic. *Fam.* 11.4.1–2; there is nothing to indicate Decimus ever got his *supplicatio*.
28 Cic. *Fam.* 12.3.2; 12 23.3. On Cannutius, see *MRR* 2.323–4.
29 Cic. *Fam.* 12.23.2; Nic. Dam. 123–8; Vell. 2.60.3; Suet. *Aug.* 10.3; Plut. *Ant.* 16.7; App. *B. Civ.* 3.39; Dio 45.8.2; cf. Wardle 2014, 123; Toher 2017, 406–7.
30 Brunt 1971, 480–1.
31 Cic. *Att.* 15.12.1–2; cf. Nic. Dam. 111; Plut. *Cic.* 44.1.
32 Cic. *Fam.* 12.2.3.2.
33 Cic. *Att.* 16.8.1–2. Octavian purchases an army: Cic. *Att.* 16.11.6; Nic. Dam. 136–9; App. *B. Civ.* 3.40; Dio 45.12.1–2.
34 Cic. *Phil.* 3.4; 5.22; Dio 45.13.2.
35 News from the east: Cic. *Att.* 15.13.2; cf. Vell. 2.62.3–4; Plut. *Brut.* 24.1–2; App. *B. Civ.* 3.24; Dio 47.21.1; Tempest 2017, 142–51.
36 *MRR* 2.317.
37 Cic. *Att.* 15.13.2; 16.8.2; *Fam.* 12.23.2; *Phil.* 3.3–5; 5.22; App. *B. Civ.* 43–4; Dio 45.12.1–2; 45.13.1–2.
38 *Mon. Anc.* 1.
39 On Caesar's rhetoric employing the idea of rescuing liberty, which he deployed during the civil war, see ch. III, p. 74.
40 Crassus: Plut. *Crass.* 6.1–4. Metellus: App. *B. Civ.* 1.80; Pompey: Cic. *Leg. Man.* 61; App. *B. Civ.* 1.80; cf. Seager 2002, 26.
41 Tatum 2020c, 209; Hurlet 2020, 176–9. In Cicero's *Third Philippic*, Octavian's personal initiative (*privato consilio*) is a weapon to be deployed against Antony's tyranny (*dominatio*): *Phil.* 3.5; 3.29; 3.34.
42 Cic. *Att.* 16.8.1; 16.9; 16.11.6; 16.15.3.

43 App. *B. Civ.* 3.42.
44 Brunt 1988, 257–65; Osgood 2006, 43–7; Keaveney 2007, 37–55; Brice 2020.
45 Cic. *Fam.* 11.20.1: *laudandum adulescentem ornandum tollendum.*
46 Larks: see ch. VI, pp. 144.
47 Cic. *Att.* 16.15.3; App. *B. Civ.* 3.42.
48 Antony in Rome: Cic. *Phil.* 3.15–26; 5.23; 13.19; App. *B. Civ.* 3.45; Dio 45.13.3–4.
49 Cic. *Phil.* 3.20.
50 Cic. *Phil.* 3.15; cf. Borgies 2016, 56–63; 260–6.
51 Cic. *Phil.* 3.21.
52 App. *B. Civ.* 3.45.
53 Cic. *Phil.* 10.22; App. *B. Civ.* 3.46; 3.66.
54 Cic. *Fam.* 10.28.1; *Phil.* 3.11; 3.24; 5.24; 5.30; 13.19; App. *B. Civ.* 3.46; Dio 45.13.5.
55 Magnino 1984, 160; on Hercules' sanctuary, see Giuliani 2008/9 and Giuliani 2016.
56 Cic. *Phil.* 13.19.
57 Cic. *Fam.* 10.28.1; App. *B. Civ.* 3.46.
58 Brunt 1971, 481.
59 *Fam.* 11.5.1–2; 11.7.1–2; 11.6a.
60 On the events of this session, see Cic. *Phil.* 3 and *Phil.* 4; *Fam.* 10.28.2; 10.31.4; 11.6.2–3; 11.6a; 12.22a.1; 12.25.2; App. *B. Civ.* 3.47; Dio 45.15.2.
61 Cic. *Phil.* 3.3–14; *Phil.* 11.26–8 (Brutus and Cassius); cf. Arena 2012, 261–6; Tatum 2020c, 193–4.
62 Cic. *Phil.* 3.37–9; cf. Dio 45.15.1–2.
63 Cic. *Rep.* 3.33; Asc. 68–9C; cf. Tatum forthcoming.
64 Cic. *Phil.* 5.5; Cotyla latter became one of Antony's legates: *MRR* 2.355.
65 Cic. *Phil.* 4.1.
66 App. *B. Civ.* 3.47. Dio observes the same inconstancy but attributes it to the natural perversity of the human condition: Dio 45.11.2–4.
67 Cic. *Fam.* 10.28.1–2.
68 Cic. *Fam.* 12.4.1.
69 Senatorial aversion to men deemed too powerful: Epstein 1987, 56–8.
70 Mutina and related events: Drumann-Groebe 1899, 155–227; Holmes 1928, 37–57; Charlesworth 1934, 13–9; Syme 1939, 172–5; Frisch 1946, 159–292; Rossi 1959, 90–4; Bengtson 1977, 101–18; Huzar 1978, 105–14; Chamoux 1986, 137–54; Kienast 1999, 31–5; Matijević 2006, 238–321; Osgood 2006, 51–8; Lintott 2008, 385–407; Goldsworthy 2010, 221–8; Southern 2010, 106–7; Halfmann 2011, 81–8.
71 Cic. *Fam.* 12.5.2.
72 *MRR* 2.352.
73 Cic. *Phil.* 5–14; Vell. 2.61.4; Suet. *Aug.* 10.2–4; Flor. 2.15.3; Oros. 6.18.3; App. *B. Civ.* 3.49; Dio 45.36.3; 46.35.2.
74 *RRC* 489.2–3.
75 Cic. *Phil.* 13.22.
76 Schumacher 2018, 102.
77 Cic. *Fam.* 10.31 (Pollio); 10.8; 10.7 (Plancus); cf. 10.6. Decimus Brutus on Pollio: Cic. *Fam.* 11.9.1.
78 Cic. *ad Brut.* 2.3.4; *Phil.* 5.1; 5.35–53; 6.1–3; 6.16; App. *B. Civ.* 3.50; Dio 45.17.1–9; 45.19; 45.22.5; 46.26.7; 46.29.2.
79 App. *B. Civ.* 3.50.
80 Vell. 2.64.4; App. *B. Civ.* 4.17.
81 App. *B. Civ.* 3.51; cf. Fischer 1999, 34–5; Schultz 2021, 82–3. On the theatrics of dressing in mourning, see Hall 2014, 40–63.

82 Cic. *Phil.* 5.5.

83 Cic. *Phil.* 6.14; cf. 11.13.

84 Both App. *B. Civ.* 2.61 and Dio 46.29.4 report that Antony was offered Macedonia instead of Cisalpine Gaul, but this is an error perhaps sparked by Cic. *Phil.* 7.3.

85 Cic. *Fam.* 10.28.3; 12.5.3; *Phil.* 8.22; 13.29—see esp. *Phil.* 9.

86 Cic. *Phil.* 8.25–7; App. *B. Civ.* 3.62–3; Dio 46.30.3–4; 46.35.3.

87 Cic. *Phil.* 7.1–4.

88 Cic. *Fam.* 12.4.1; *Phil.* 13.36–7.

89 Cic. *Phil.* 8; 10.17–9; 12.11–7; 13.5; 13.23; 13.26; 14.1–3; 14.8; Dio 46.29.5; 46.31.2; 46.36.2.

90 App. *B. Civ.* 3.66; Dio 46.31.1–32.1. Cic. *Phil.* 7.23, by contrast, insists the municipalities were delighted to comply.

91 *MRR* 2.335; 2.345.

92 *MRR* 2.346; cf. Tempest 2017, 147–51.

93 *MRR* 2.342.

94 Cic. *ad Brut.* 2.5.3–5; 1.2a.2; 1.3.31.3a; cf. Tempest 2017, 156–62.

95 *MRR* 2.344.

96 Cic. *Fam.* 12.7; 12.14.4; *ad Brut.* 2.4.2; *Phil.* 11.16–9; 11.21–5; Dio 47.29.5.

97 Cic. *Fam.* 12.7.2; 12.11.1; 12.14.4; *ad Brut.* 2.33.3; *Phil.* 11.27; cf. *MRR* 2.343; Tempest 2017, 165–8.

98 Cic. *Phil.* 12 (*passim*); 13.36; 13.47–8; Dio 46.32.1–4; cf. Hall 2007.

99 Cic. *Phil.* 7.5.

100 Cic. *Phil.* 13. Cicero's letter to Lepidus: *Fam.* 10.27; his hopeful correspondence with Plancus: *Fam.* 10.6; 10.10.

101 Lintott 2008, 445–7. On Antony's letter, see Matijević 2006, 260–8; Tatum 2020c, 194–207 (assembling previous scholarship).

102 Cic. *Phil.* 13.22.

103 Cic. *Phil.* 13.23; 13.26; 13.35; 13.38–40; 13.48.

104 Cic. *Phil.* 13.24 (Hirtius, Octavian, and Decimus); 13.40 (Cicero).

105 Cic. *Phil.* 13.33.

106 Cic. *Phil.* 13.26; 13.30; 13.32; 13.38; 13.42.

107 Seager 1972; Meier 1980, xxxii–xliii; 163–90; Brunt 1988, 443–502; Mouritsen 2017, 144–5; Tatum 2020c, 200–2.

108 Cic. *Phil.* 5.32.

109 Cic. *Phil.* 13.39; 13.47.

110 Cic. *Fam.* 10.33.1; *ad Brut.* 2.4.5.

111 Cic. *Phil.* 13.26.

112 Cic. *Phil.* 13.34.

113 Cic. *Phil.* 13.30: *victum Ciceronem ducem habuistis.*

114 Cic. *Phil.* 7.2–4; cf. Caes. *B. Civ.* 1.9.3; 1.9.5.

115 Cic. *Phil.* 13.47.

116 Cic. *ad Brut.* 2.1; cf. Dio 46.35.6.

117 Battle of Forum Gallorum: Cic. *Fam.* 10.30; 10.33.3–4; *ad Brut.* 1.3a; *Phil.* 14.26–7; 14.36–7; Suet. *Aug.* 10.3; Plut. *Cic.* 45.3; *Ant.* 17.1; App. *B. Civ.* 3.66–70; Dio 46.37.4–5.

118 Cic. *Fam.* 10.30.

119 Cic. *Phil.* 14; App. *B. Civ.* 3.74; Dio 46.38.1–2.

120 Battle of Mutina and aftermath: Cic. *Fam.* 10.11.2; 10.17.2; 10.33.4; 11.9.1; 11.10.2; 11.13.1–2; 12.25a; *ad Brut.* 1.2.2; 1.3a; 1.4.1; Vell. 2.61.3–4; Suet. *Aug.* 10.3–4; 11; Plut. *Cic.* 45.3–4; *Ant.* 17.1–2; App. *B. Civ.* 3.71–6; Dio 46.33.5; 46.38.5–7; 46.39.1.

121 Plut. *Ant.* 17.3–6; Pelling 1988, 161.

122 Cic. *Fam.* 11.9.1–2; App. *B. Civ.* 3.76; Dio 46.40.

123   Cic. *Fam.* 10.33.4; 11.13b; *Phil.* 14.9.

CHAPTER VIII

1   On the formation of the triumvirate and the proscriptions, see Drumann-Groebe 1899, 232–8; Holmes 1928, 57–75; Charlesworth 1934, 19–22; Syme 1939, 176–201; Frisch 1946, 293–305; Rossi 1959, 94–8; Bengtson 1977, 119–34; Huzar 1978, 114–21; Chamoux 1986, 154–90; Pelling 1996, 1–5; Kienast 1999, 35–41; Matijević 2006, 332–70; Osgood 2006, 58–88; Lintott 2008, 408–24; Pasquali 2009, 122–33; Goldsworthy 2010, 228–33; 245–8; Southern 2010, 108–26; Halfmann 2011, 88–99; Welch 2012 164–82.
2   App. *B. Civ.* 3.75; Dio 46.40.1–46.41.3.
3   Cic. *ad Brut.* 1.4.4; 1.15.9; Plut. *Brut.* 22.3; cf. Ortmann 1988, 423–9.
4   Cic. *ad Brut.* 1.3a; 1.5.1; 1.15.8–9; Vell. 2.62.4–5; 2.64.4; Dio 46.39.3; 46.41.4.
5   Nep. *Att.* 9.1–10.6; cf. Fischer 1999, 35–7; Allély 2012, 94–100; Schultz 2021, 83.
6   Plut. *Ant.* 18.2–6.
7   Allély 2004, 105–20.
8   Cic. *Fam.* 10.17.1; 10.18.3; 10.21; 10.23; 10.33.4; 10.34.1; 11.9; 11.10.3; 11.13.3; Vell. 2.63.1–4; Plut. *Ant.* 18.1–8; App. *B. Civ.* 3.72; 3.81; 3.83–4; 3.97; Dio 46.51.4; 46.53.1–2.
9   Cic. *Fam.* 11.13a; Vell. 2.63–4; Plut. *Brut.* 28.1; App. *B. Civ.* 3.96–8; Dio 46.53.
10   Ortmann 1988, 395–417.
11   Cic. *Fam.* 11.14.2.
12   Cic. *ad Brut.* 1.10.1; App. *B. Civ.* 3.85; Dio 46.51.5.
13   *MRR* 2.348.
14   *MRR* 2.346.
15   Cic. *Fam.* 12.10.1; *ad Brut.* 1.12.1–2; 1.15.9; 1.18.6; Vell. 2.64.4; App. *B. Civ.* 3.96; Dio 46.51.4.
16   Cic. *Fam.* 10.24.6; *ad Brut.* 1.4a.2; Suet. *Aug.* 26.1; Plut. *Brut.* 27.2; App. *B. Civ.* 3.82; 3.88; Dio 46.42.2–43.4.
17   *MRR* 2.336.
18   App. *B. Civ.* 3.94; Dio 46.47.5.
19   App. *B. Civ.* 3.95.
20   App. *B. Civ.* 3.96; Dio 46.52.3–4.
21   Dio 46.49.1.
22   *MRR* 2.337; cf. Welch 2014.
23   Dio 46.48.4; 47.12.2; 48.17.1.
24   Ten Men: Cornell 1995, 272–92; Sulla: Seager 1994, 197–205.
25   Bleicken 1990; Lange 2009, 18–26; Vervaet 2020.
26   Dio 51.21.6.
27   Triumviral decree: *Lib. colon.* 212–3; Hinrichs 1969, 540–1; Bleicken 1990, 41–2.
28   *MRR* 2.337–8; cf. Hinard 1985, 227–318; Welch 2019. Appian's version of the triumvirs' decree: *B. Civ.* 4.8–11.
29   Suet. *Aug.* 27.1; Dio 47.8.1; cf. Borgies 2016, 147–56.
30   App. *B. Civ.* 4.27 (Pollio); 4.40 (Plancus).
31   Fischer 1999, 37–9; Schultz 2021, 87–9.
32   Lepidus Paullus: Suet. *Aug.* 16.8; Dio 54.2.1; L. Caesar: Plut. *Ant.* 20.5–6; App. *B. Civ.* 4.37; Atticus: Nep. *Att.* 10.1–6.
33   Sen. *Suas.* 6.17 (Livy); 6.24–5 (Pollio); Plut. *Cic.* 47–9; App. *B. Civ.* 4.19; cf. Roller 1997; Gowing 2013.
34   García Morcillo 2020; see ch. X, pp. 232–33.

35 App. *B. Civ.* 4.34; Dio 47.14.2.

36 Val. Max. 8.3.3; Quint. 1.1.6; App. *B. Civ.* 4.32.3; cf. Fischer 1999, 39–40; Schultz 2021, 89–90.

37 See ch. V, 108–9.

38 *MRR* 2.358.

39 Brunt 1971, 488–92.

40 *RRC* 492.1–2; 493.1.

41 *RRC* 494.1–46; cf. Buttrey 1954.

42 *MRR* 2.358–9; on the census and its significance, see Lintott 1999, 115–20; Clemente 2022.

43 Sulpicius Rufus: *MRR* 2.273; Val. Max. 6.7.3 (his Julian wife).

44 Ferriès 2020.

45 *RRC* 489.5; 489.6. This interpretation is commonplace: recent advocates include Woytek 2003, 478 and 360; Ferriès and Delrieux 2017, 360; Rowan 2019, 82; Carbone 2020, 44–6. For a survey of earlier scholarship, see Fischer 1999, 160–4.

46 *RPC* 1.3139 and 3140; on the background of this view, see the discussion by Schultz 2021, 14–6.

47 … OYIANΩN; evidence assembled in Head 1906, 213.

48 *RRC* 514.1.

49 See the essential discussions of Delia 1991, 201–2, and Schultz 2021, 14–6.

50 Drumann-Groebe 1899, 280–2; Holmes 1928, 80–9; Charlesworth 1934, 19–22; Syme 1939, 202–7; Bengtson 1977, 135–52; Huzar 1978, 125–8; Chamoux 1986, 191–223; Pelling 1996, 5–8; Kienast 1999, 42–4; Osgood 2006, 88–104; Pasquali 2009, 133–44; Goldsworthy 2010, 248–60; 245–8; Southern 2010, 126–63; Halfmann 2011, 99–103; Welch 2012 195–7; Tempest 2017, 173–210.

51 Cassius and Brutus in the east: *MRR* 2.360–1. Death of Gaius: *MRR* 2.342. The Liberators' rapacity: Kirbihler 2013; Tempest 2017, 173–91.

52 Plut. *Brut.* 38–40; App. *B. Civ.* 4.86–102; Dio 47.35–7.

53 *MRR* 2.362; cf. Welch 2012, 179.

54 Welch 2012, 182–95.

55 Plut. *Brut.* 38; App. *B. Civ.* 102–4; Dio 47.35–6.

56 First battle of Philippi: Vell. 2.70.1–3; Suet. *Aug.* 13.1; 91.1; Flor. 2.17.9–13; Oros. 6.18.5; Plut. *Brut.* 41–3; *Ant.* 22; *Caes.* 69.12; App. *B. Civ.* 4.109–13; Dio 47.42.1–46.5.

57 Plut. *Brut.* 47.2–3; App. *B. Civ.* 115–7; Dio 47.48.4.

58 Charlesworth 1934, 24.

59 Second battle of Philippi: Vell. 2.70.4–5; Suet. *Aug.* 13.1; Plut. *Brut.* 49; *Ant.* 22; *Caes.* 69.13–4; App. *B. Civ.* 4.125–9; Dio 47.48.3–5.

60 Vell. 2.71.1 (*non aliud bellum cruentius caede clarissimorum virorum fuit*); App. *B. Civ.* 4.137; Dio 47.39.1; cf. Verg. *G.* 1.489–97; Brunt 1971, 485–8.

61 App. *B. Civ.* 4.138; Dio 47.39.1–5.

62 On the aftermath of the battle, see Drumann-Groebe 282–2; Holmes 1928, 89–90; Charlesworth 1934, 25–7; Bengtson 1977, 149–52; Huzar 1978, 127–30; Chamoux 1986, 220–3; Pelling 1996, 9–10; Osgood 2006, 96–104; Pasquali 2009, 143–4; Goldsworthy 2010, 259–61; Southern 2010, 163–5; Halfmann 2011, 104–5; Welch 2012, 203–6.

63 Suet. *Aug.* 13.1; Plut. *Brut.* 53.4; *Comp. Dion Brut.* 5.1; *Ant.* 22.6–8; App. *B. Civ.* 4.135; variations in these accounts originate in subsequent, unhistorical elaborations. It is probably best to discount the story that, on Octavian's orders, Brutus' head was lopped off and sent to Rome (Suet. *Aug.* 13.1; Dio 47.49.2), though he may have urged it. In his autobiography, however, Octavian insisted that he never prevented a condemned man's remains from being restored to his family (Ulpian *Dig.* 48.24.1 = Aug. *De Vita Sua* fr. 3 in *FRHist*), possibly, as suggested by Scott, in reaction to invective originating at Philippi (Scott 1933, 23).

64 Plut. *Brut.* 50.3.

65 Plut. *Ant.* 3.10–1.

66 Plut. *Brut.* 53.4.

67 Lucullus: Val. Max. 4.7.4. Gibba: Vell. 2.17.2; cf. Woodman 1983, 172; *MRR* 2.340. The identities of these two figures, or whether they are in fact distinct figures, is not wholly certain. Velleius' Varro, it has been suggested, may be an otherwise unattested brother of M. Terentius Varro Lucullus (cos. 73) (so Hellegouarc'h 1982, 217, a view elaborated by Hinard 1985, 528–31); if so, we may have to do with the same man in both passages. Or he may be A. Varro Murena (aed. 44) (so Sumner 1978, 191).

68 See, for instance, the accounts of the death of M. Marius Gratidianus (pr. 85), variously attributed to Sulla or Catiline, at the tomb of Q. Lutatius Catulus (cos. 102): e.g., Cic. *Tog. Cand.* frr. 5. 14. 15; Asc. 84, 87, 90C; Sall. *Hist.* 1.36; 48.14McG; Liv. *Per.* 88; Val. Max. 9.2.1; Luc. 2.160–73; Sen. *Dial.* 5.18.1–2; Plut. *Sull.* 32.2; cf. Tatum 2018, 203–4.

69 Plut. *Brut.* 28.1–2; *Ant.* 22.6; cf. Pelling 1988, 173; Moles 2017, 269. Octavian's human sacrifices after the fall of Perusia: Suet. *Aug.* 15; Dio 48.14.3–5; cf. Scott 1920, 23–8; Wardle 2014, 137–8; Borgies 2016, 163–9.

70 Amnesty: Dio 47.49.2; App. *B. Civ.* 4.135. Allied forces: App. *B. Civ.* 3.79; 4.75; 4.88; 4.136; cf. Cic. *Phil.* 10.13.

71 In the view of some, however, Octavian and Antony remained implacable towards all the proscribed even in the aftermath of Philippi: e.g., Bengtson 1977, 151; Osgood 2006, 104; Welch 2012, 204.

72 On the triumvirs' legal capacity to pardon the proscribed, see Bleicken 1990, 46–7.

73 App. *B. Civ.* 4.38; 4.137 (explicit that the forces on Thasos surrendered to both triumvirs); *MRR* 2.364; 368. Not everyone on Thasos accepted the triumvirs' pardon: several officers escaped (App. *B. Civ.* 5.2).

74 App. *B. Civ.* 5.4.

75 App. *B. Civ.* 5.7.

76 App. *B. Civ.* 4.46; cf. *MRR* 2.364.

77 App. *B. Civ.* 5; Dio 48.2.3; cf. Brunt 1971, 488–9.

78 See ch. VII, 168.

79 Vell. 2.74.1; Suet. *Aug.* 13.3; App. *B. Civ.* 5.3; 5.12; Dio 48.1.2–2.2; cf. *MRR* 2.358. On Lepidus' activities, see Allély 2004, 143–5.

80 App. *B. Civ.* 5.56 indicates that Sextus did not take control of Sardinia until 40.

81 Dio 48.2.2. Definition of *provincia*: StR 1.51; Lintott 1999, 101–2; Giovannini 2015, 126–8.

82 Plut. *Ant.* 23.1; App. *B. Civ.* 4.120. On the donatives promised to the triumvirs' troops, see Botermann 1968, 50–1; Keppie 1983, 42; Keaveney 2007, 121.

83 Calculations of Philippi's survivors and of veterans entitled to plots of land can only be approximate; see Brunt 1971, 488–93.

84 App. *B. Civ.* 4.3; see ch. X, pp. 232–3.

85 Founding a colony: Brunt 1971, 294–300; Keppie 1983, 87–100.

86 It is obvious that not all donatives were paid, or at least not paid in full. In 41 Octavian made a show of making gifts to needy veterans (App. *B. Civ.* 5.13), and when Antony and Octavian met at Brundisium during the following year angry soldiers complained that they had not yet received their bounties (Dio 48.30.2).

87 On Lepidus' management of Rome in the absence of his colleagues, see Allély 2004, 134–42.

88 App. *B. Civ.* 5.12; Dio 48.3.1.

89 Dio 48.2.2.

90 Suet. *Aug.* 13.1 (*cum Antonius Orientem ordinandum . . . recepisset*); Dio 48.2.1–2; cf. Vell. 2.74.1. On the nature of Antony's eastern command, see Halfmann 2011, 104–5.

91 Dio 48.2.4.

92 During Antony's absence from Italy pressure from his brother, his wife, and the veterans obliged Octavian to include Antony's close associates in the founding of individual colonies in order to signal Antony's role in settling the veterans: App. *B. Civ.* 5.14; see Keppie 1983, 58–61.

93 On this important distinction, see Pelling 1996, 9–10; Lange 2009, 20, 29.

94 App. *B. Civ.* 5.3; Dio 48.2.3.

95 On the first day of his consulship Censorinus celebrated a triumph for his defence of Macedonia, the particulars of which are not preserved (*MRR* 2.386). His successor, Asinius Pollio, also earned a triumph for his campaign against the Parthini (*MRR* 2.387). On the disposition of Antony's troops after Philippi, see Brunt 1971, 497.

96 Celebrations after Philippi: App. *B. Civ.* 5.3; cf. Polyb. 6.39.1–11; Watson 1969, 114–7; Goldsworthy 1996, 276–9.

97 *RPC* 1646: *Antoni iussu colonia Victrix Philippensis.* On the foundation of Victrix Philippensis, see Strab. 7. fr. 41; Dio 51.4.6; Dig. 1.15.8.8; *RPC* 1646, 1647, 1648, 1649; Collart 1937, 224–7 and 235; Brunt 1971, 598–9; Papazoglou 1979, 357–8; Daubner 2014, 112–3; Rowan 2019, 100–2. This colony was later re-founded as Iulia Augusta Philippi (*RPC* 1650).

98 On Paquius' status, see Wiseman 1971, 249. He, like Antony, appears on the colony's coinage (see the previous note).

CHAPTER IX

1 Plut. *Brut.* 46.1; App. *B. Civ.* 4.118.

2 *RPC* 1551; 1552 (games); 1553; each coin honouring both Antony and Octavian. *RPC* prefers a date of 37 for these coins (followed by Papazoglou 1979, 328; Papazoglou 1988, 206–7; Voutiras 2011, 46): two issues exhibit an E which, it is argued, indicates the fifth year of the city's Antonian era (three undatable Thessalonian inscriptions confirm an Antonian era: *IG* X,2.1.83, 109, 124); but there is no reason to assume the city commenced an Antonian era before Antony returned to the east as its permanent viceroy in 39; the time to celebrate both triumvirs was immediately after Philippi. Perhaps the E indicates *freedom* (*eleutheria*; cf. Papazoglou 1988, 206; Voutiras 2011, 459 and 461).

3 *RPC* 1545 and 1546.

4 Moles 1983; Gosling 1986 (L. Brutus (cos. 509) was inspired to free the republic by the oracle at Delphi: Liv. 1.56.7–12; Dion. Hal. *Ant. Rom.* 4.69.2–4). Coins exhibiting the tripod and cauldron: *RRC* 498; 499; 500; 502; cf. Hollstein 1994; Rowan 2019: 66–71.

5 Antony's promise: Plut. *Ant.* 23.4. Apollo as watchword: employed by the Liberators before the first battle at Philippi (Dio 47.43.1); employed by Brutus before the second battle (Plut. *Brut.* 24.7); employed by Antony and Octavian (Val. Max. 1.5.7); Moles 1983, 250–1, makes a strong argument for preferring Valerius Maximus (followed by Hollstein 1994, 129).

6 Dio 47.20.4; Brutus and Cassius in Athens: *MRR* 2:321–2; Habicht 1997, 356–9; Tempest 2017, 144–59; Worthington 2021, 233–4.

7 τὸν θεῖον Καιπίωνος: *I. Délos* 1622, a dedication to Apollo by the *demos* of the Athenians and the inhabitants of Delos. After his adoption by Q. Servilius Caepio in 59, Brutus' legal name became Q. Servilius Caepio Brutus; cf. Tempest 2017, 25.

8 Day 1942, 120–76; Larsen 1938, 422–35; Habicht 1997, 315–65.

9 Green 1990, 564–5; Gruen 1992, 223–71; Spawforth 2012, 59–81; Kralli 2016.

10 Errington 1988; Habicht 1997, 328–3. Parigi 2013 argues for a small Roman presence.

11 Wallmann 1989, 220–4; Keinast 1995, 193; Fontani 1999, 194; Halfmann 2011, 106; a different view in Worthington 2021, 234–6.

12 Plut. *Ant.* 23.2. Only Plutarch furnishes an account of this winter. On various problems attending this passage, see Pelling 1988, 208–9; Pelling 2002, 354; Tatum 2020a.

13 Asinius Pollio is routinely cited as the source for Plutarch as well as for Appian's account of this period: Gabba 1956, 225–8; Pelling 2002, 12–24. Views along these lines must now be at least somewhat qualified: Drummond 2013, 439–44; Westall 2018. Matters are further complicated by the likelihood that Appian was also a reader of Plutarch: Pelling 2002, 36 n. 75.

14 Vell. 2.74.1; Suet. *Aug.* 13.3; App. *B. Civ.* 5.3; 5.12; Dio 48.1.2–2.2.

15 On Plutarch's literary motives here, see Pelling 1988, 208–9; Pelling 2002, 354; Tatum 2020a.

16 Cic. *Q. Frat.* 1.1.26; *Att.* 5.21.7; Suet. *Aug.* 52.1. Evidence is assembled by Cerfaux and Tondriau 1957, 279–85; Bowersock 1965, 150–1; Tuchelt 1979, 45–118; Price 1984, 42–3; Frija 2017.

17 Chaniotis 1995; Ma 2003; van Nijf 2013; Daubner 2018.

18 Hellenistic ruler cult and its Roman applications: e.g., Price 1984; Smith 1988; Chaniotis 2003.

19 Evidence assembled and discussed by Robert 1984, 472–89; Le Guen 2006; Perrin-Saminadayar 2004; Perrin-Saminadayar 2009. Formal receptions by (i.a.) ephebes granted to Roman officials, designated 'friends and benefactors' or 'friends and allies': *IG* II² 1006.21 (122/1 BC); 1008.13 (118/7 BC); 1011.18–9 (106/5 BC); 1028.14–5 (100/99 BC); 1029.10 (94/3 BC); 1030.12 (94/3 BC).

20 Kroll nos. 137 and 138; cf. Kroll 1993, 57–8; 84–7; on Apollo's tripod as a symbol of liberty in Rome, see above.

21 Heracles and the tripod: Woodford and Boardman 1990. Heracles and Athena: Boardman 1990. Antony and Heracles: Plut. *Ant.* 4.2; cf. 36.7; 60.5; cf. Michel 1967, 114–29; Smith 1988, 137; Huttner 1995.

22 Antony and Hercules on Roman coinage: *RRC* 494.2a and 2b (gold coins minted at the commencement of the triumvirate).

23 Moles 1983, 32–45; Pelling 2002, 143–70.

24 Plut. *Ant.* 23.2.

25 So (e.g.) Tarn 1934, 52; Raubitshek 1946; Pélékidis 1962, 255; Kienast 1995, 194–5; Habicht 1997, 362.

26 So (e.g.) Bengtson 1977, 155–6; Pelling 1988, 176; Kienast 1995, 193; Habicht 1997, 360.

27 Date: Mikalson 1975, 54–61. Too late for Antony: Clinton 1989, 1506. Athenian refusal to reschedule the mysteries even for Roman senators: Cic. *De orat.* 3.75. On the Eleusinian Mysteries, see Parker 2005, 342–63, assembling sources and secondary literature.

28 Date: Mikalson 1975, 120–2. On the Lesser Mysteries, see Parker 1996, 188–91; Parker 2005, 341–5.

29 Apollod. *Bibl.* 2.5.12; Diod. Sic. 14.14.2; Plut. *Thes.* 30.5; cf. Parker 1996, 98–100.

30 Plut. *Thes.* 33.2. Fourth-century diplomatic deployment of Heracles' Athenian citizenship: Parker 1996, 226–7, assembles the evidence.

31 Mikalson 1975, 34; cf. Parker 2005, 253–69.

32 Games for Roman officials: Syracusan games in honour of M. Claudius Marcellus (cos. I 222): Cic. *Verr.* 2.2.51, 154; Plut. *Marc.* 32; for Flamininus (cos. 198): Plut. *Flam.* 15–6; *Syll.*³ 592. 11; in 117 Lete in Macedonia celebrated games in honour of the quaestor M. Annius (otherwise unknown): *Syll.*³ 700; games in 97 for Q. Mucius Scaevola (cos. 95): *OGIS* 437–9; Cic. *Verr.* 2.2.51; *Div.* 757; Ps.-Asc. 202 and 262 St.; games in honour of Lucullus: Plut. *Luc.* 23.2; games for Sulla: *IG* II² 1039. 57; *SEG* 22.110. 57; *SEG* 13.279; Price 1984, 42–6.

33 Raubitshek 1946, 148–9; Kirchner 1948: plate 43; Pélékidis 1962, 255; Habicht 1997, 362. The dating of this inscription relies on the chronology established by Dinsmoor 1931.

34 [καὶ διηγωνίσθαι ἐν τοῖς] ἀγῶσιν ἐν τε τοῖς Θησιήο[ις καὶ Ἐπιταφίοις ὁμοὲ]ως δε κ[α]ὶ ἐν τοῖς Ἀντωνήοις τοῖς Πανα- / [θηναικοῖς Ἀντω]νίου θεοῦ νέου Διονύσο[υ - - - -]ου Ἀνθεστηριῶνος τῇ ἑπτακαιδεκάτῃ (*IG* II² 1043.22–3).

35 Viz. Παναθηναίοις Ἀντωνίου.

36 Raubitshek 1946, 149 insists that the inscription's reference to Anthesterion is unrelated to the Antoneia, but the lacuna separating them appears too narrow for the introduction of a new event.

37 Kienast 1995, 194–5, adducing *Ciris* 25 (but see Lyne 1978, 112, whose very different explanation of the passage is a better one) and Himerius *Orat.* 3 (on which see Panella 2007, 253–5; this is an event of the fourth century of our era and so hardly pertinent).

38 On Antony and Athens, see, further, Tatum 2020a.

39 Antony held an audience in Bithynia before journeying to Ephesus: Joseph. *AJ* 14.301; *BJ* 1.242. This sequence is rejected by Magie 1950, 1278.

40 Antony arranged for the construction of 200 ships during his occupation of Asia: App. *B. Civ.* 5.55.

41 *MRR* 2.386 (Censorinus); 2.387–8 (Pollio); cf. App. *B. Civ.* 5.75, describing Antony's military exertions in defence of Macedonia when he returned to the east in 39.

42 *SEG* 44.529; cf. Nigdélis 1994.

43 It is possible that Antony left two legions in Syria, inasmuch as that was the usual republican deployment there, but there is no evidence for it (the certainty expressed in many accounts, e.g., Sherwin-White 1983, 302, is misleading). Cassius, when he departed for Philippi, left one legion in Syria which Antony later collected (App. *B. Civ.* 4.63).

44 Dio 48.26.3 identifies Plancus as the Asian governor who fled to the islands, but Plancus arrived in his province too late for that. Turius, known as a legate only from numismatic evidence (*RPC* 1.2270; 1.2272), is almost certainly Antony's man in Asia: Grant 1946, 244–9; *MRR* 1.366, 382, 385. Doubts, however, have been expressed by Ferriès 2007, 524–5.

45 Brunt 1971, 497.

46 See further Brunt 1971, 497–8; 502–3.

47 Joseph. *AJ* 14.301; *BJ* 1.242.

48 App. *Mithr.* 61; cf. Kallet-Marx 1995, 261–90.

49 Caes. *B. Civ.* 3.105; Plut. *Caes.* 48.1; Dio 42.6.3; cf. Magie 1950, 405–7; Pelling 2011, 376–9.

50 Str. 14.1.42; Plut. *Caes.* 48.1; Dio 41.62.2–63.4; 42.6.3; cf. Magie 1950, 405–7. Previously the Pompeians had confiscated the properties of men closely linked to Caesar: Kirbihler 2013, 352–3.

51 Dio 42.49.1–5; cf. Magie 1950, 413.

52 Plut. *Ant.* 24.4; cf. Pelling 1988, 180, observing the conventional elements in Plutarch's elaboration of the procession attending Antony.

53 Weinstock 1971, 296–7. Caesar a god made manifest: *Syll.*³ 760 = *I. Eph.* 251.

54 App. *B. Civ.* 5.4; Dio 48.24.1–8.

55 Dio 48.39.1–2; *SEG* 12.149 (cf. Geagan 2011, 137); *IG* II² 1043; Kroll nos. 140, 141, 142; cf. Kroll 1993, 102–3; Rowan 2019, 102–4; see ch. XI, pp. 269–71. Appian never mentions Antony's pose as New Dionysus.

56 Pelling 1988, 179, followed by Lebreton 2009, 199.

57 The agency of the Ephesians is crucial to any correct understanding of this episode: see, early on, Drumann-Groebe 1899, 283; Craven 1920, 23; Tarn 1932, 149. At the same time, Antony's collaboration remains important: Rossi 1959, 110–3 (Rossi suggests that Antony's identification with Dionysus began in Athens); Chamoux 1986, 235. Too often the Ephesians' Dionysiac celebration is attributed solely to Antony's initiative: e.g., Cerfaux and Tondriau 1957, 297–8; Buchheim 1960, 14–5; Michel 1967, 126–8; Marasco 1987, 25–30; Pasquali 2009, 146–7; Halfmann 2011, 108–12; Roddaz 2012, 130–1. Jeanmaire 1924,

esp. 248–52, followed by Taylor 1931, 109–11, and Wallmann 1989, 224–8, argues that Cleopatra was the prime mover behind Antony's assumption of the identity of Dionysus at Ephesus (and thereafter).

58 Buchheim 1960, 14–5; Wallmann 1989, 222–4; Pasquali 2009, 146–7; Halfmann 2011, 108–12.

59 Cerfaux and Tondriau 1957, 148–61; 170–201; Nock 1972, 134–52; Burkert 1985, 161–7; 293–5; Smith 1988, esp. 37–8 and 123–4; Habicht 2017, 107–8; 18–20.

60 Diod. Sic. 4.4.4; Plin. *NH* 7.191.

61 Smith 1988, 123.

62 App. *B. Civ.* 5.4; Str. 14.1.23; cf. Rigsby 1996, 385–93.

63 App. *B. Civ.* 5.4.

64 *I. Eph.* 4324 = *RS* 35 (the most important discussion of this inscription). See also Weinstock 1971, 402–4; Price 1984, 76–7; Madsen 2016, 288–90.

65 *MRR* 2.358; see ch. VIII, pp. 187–8. Antony was not formally inaugurated as *flamen* until 39: Plut. *Ant.* 33.1.

66 *I. Eph.* 4324.1–3 (excerpted): Θέλετε κελεύτε ἵνα Μᾶρκος Ἀν | [τωνιος ---] . . . [--- τὴν ἱεριμ]νημονήαν θεοῦἸουλίου . . .

67 Kirbihler and Zabrana 2014; Kirbihler 2020, 198–201.

68 Joseph. *AJ* 14.306–13 (the Liberators' impiety: *AJ* 14.309–10). On Josephus' access to this correspondence, see ben Zeev 1998, 402.

69 Joseph. *AJ* 14.311.

70 Joseph. *AJ* 14.314–8 (the Liberators' impiety: *AJ* 14.315; their unconstitutional seizure of power: *AJ* 14.316; peace: *AJ* 14.318).

71 Joseph. *AJ* 14.323 indicates that letters similar to these were promulgated in Syria.

72 Buchheim 1960, 14–5, correctly observes that Antony did not expect to inspire the east by way of promulgating purely Roman values. But inspiration was not the sole purpose of his eastern programme, nor was his propaganda aimed only at the east.

73 Plut. *Ant.* 24.4–5; cf. Lebreton 2009.

74 App. *B. Civ.* 5.7 reports that, as Antony made his circuit through Rome's eastern dominions, 'he imposed heavy tribute on each of them'.

75 App. *B. Civ.* 5.6; Dio 48.24.1; cf. Plut. *Ant.* 24.7–8 (confused). Discussion: Broughton 1938, 585–6; Rostovtzeff 1941, 1005–9. The levy imposed by Cassius: App. *B. Civ.* 4.74.

76 Plut. *Ant.* 24.5–6.

77 Charisius ap. Keil, *Gramm. Lat.*, vol. 1, 146. This work's purpose comes solely by way of inference: it is cited by Charisius only by its title; cf. Wallmann 1989, 220–2; Borgies 2016, 179–80. Plutarch's familiarity with Messalla's works: Pelling 1988, 29; *FRHist.* 1.468.

78 *Mon. Anc.* 24.1.

79 The sensible suggestion of Rostovtzeff 1941, 1007 and 1580.

80 Broughton 1938, 562–4. In 47 Caesar reduced Asia's tribute by a third (Plut. *Caes.* 48.1; App. *B. Civ.* 5.4.19; cf. Dio 42.6.3), but it is unclear whether this remission took as its benchmark the province's normal rate or an increased rate imposed by Pompey during the civil war; cf. Pelling 2011, 379. On Roman money and the contemporary value of its sums, see ch. I, n. 9.

81 Although Antony cites the Roman practice of taxing Asia on the basis of a tithe (App. *B. Civ.* 5.4), we learn nothing about the calculations he employed in setting the costs of his levy.

82 Broughton 1938, 565; cf. Rostovtzeff 1941, 464–72. On Antony's levy in Syria, see App. *B. Civ.* 5.10.

83 Antony's alleged mistreatment of the Peloponnese is preserved: Vell. Pat. 2.77; App. *B. Civ.* 5.72; 5.77; 5.80; Dio 48.36.5; cf. Rostovtzeff 1941, 1012–3; Bengston 1977, 155; Hoffmann 2011, 106.

84 Rostovtzeff 1957, 308–11; 680–1.

85 App. *B. Civ.* 5.6–7; 5.75; Dio 48.24.1.

86 There is no reason to take seriously Plutarch's statement that Antony imposed more than one levy or the claim, attributed by Plutarch to the orator Hybreas, that Antony's agents raised 200,000 talents; cf. Pelling 1988, 181. The exchange between Hybreas and Antony, if indeed it ever took place, belongs not in 41 but in 33: Buchheim 1960, 12–3; cf. Plut. *Ant.* 56.1; Pelling 1988, 181.

87 Dio 47.36.4.

88 App. *B. Civ.* 5.7.

89 Amorgus is a possibility (*IG* xii 5.38; xii *Suppl.* no. 38); cf. Pelling 1996, 11 n. 30; so, too, Aphrodisias; cf. Reynolds 1982, 48–50.

90 App. *B. Civ.* 5.7.

91 On the provincial operations, including lending, of the *publicani*, see ch. II, pp. 39–41.

92 For all its exploitation by Rome, the east remained rich. Still, one had to get one's hands on its wealth. In the aftermath of Actium, when Octavian was able to appropriate, first, Antony's enormous treasury, and subsequently Egypt's wealth, he introduced so much cash into Italy that it drastically affected the economy: Suet. *Aug.* 41.1; Dio 51.21.4–5; Oros. 6.19.9; cf. Dillon 2007; Elliott 2020, 117–26.

93 App. *Mithr.* 62–3; Plut. *Sull.* 25.2; *Luc.* 7.5; 20.4. Initially local capitalists played a significant role in raising the loans needed to satisfy Sulla: Sherwin-White 1983, 247–8; Kallet-Marx 1995, 275; Brunt 2001, 3–4. On the impact of the region's subsequently ballooning debts, see Kallet-Marx 1995, 276–8.

94 Since the outbreak of civil war between Caesar and Pompey, Rome had been afflicted by a credit crunch, the severity of which cannot have been improved by the triumviral proscriptions. See further Frederiksen 1966; Crawford 1985, 193–4; Verboven 1997; Verboven 2003; Woytek 2003, esp. 392–412; Ioannatou 2006, 72–94; Rollinger 2009, 177–85; Woytek 2016; Harris 2019, esp. 168–9; 175–80.

95 Str. 14.1.41 records one instance of a friend of Antony profiting during the levy (unless this episode also derives from Messalla's hostile pamphlet). It would have been astonishing to contemporaries had Antony not aided his friends, local or Roman, in enriching themselves. For their part, the Liberators worked closely with cooperative Greek elites: e.g., C. Cassius Artemidorus, honoured by Ephesus (*SEG* 34.1085; cf. Kirbihler 2013, 360–2). As for Antony's Roman associates, profitable arrangements, including loans, were hardly unusual: when in 88 the Romans restored Nicomedes III to the throne of Bithynia, he relied on loans made by Roman commanders and officers for the bribes he had to pay in order to curry favour with Roman forces in Asia (App. *Mirthr.* 11; cf. Rollinger 2009, 124–7).

96 Dillon 2007, who assembles the evidence.

97 Dio Chrys. *Or.* 31.66; cf. Kienast 1999, 456–7. At the same time, the victorious Octavian imposed his own punitive levies in the east: Dio 51.2.1.

98 Dio 48.24.3.

99 After his victory, Sulla and his supporters regarded anyone who had entered into a business relationship with the Marian leadership as guilty of a serious offence: App. *B. Civ.* 1.96.

100 The depredations of the Liberators: Broughton 1938, 582–4; Rostovtzeff 1941, 1002–5; Magie 1950, 422–6; Kirbihler 2013; Tempest 2017, 175–93.

101 See ch. II, p. 40.

102 *Publicani* victimized during civil war: Caes. *B. Civ.* 3.31.1–2; 3.103.1; App. *B. Civ.* 2.92; Dio 42.6.3; see Ürögdi 1968, 1201; Badian 1972, 71–2; 116–7.

103 Even after his severe levy in Asia, Sulla obliged the cities to billet and supply his army: Plut. *Sull.* 25.2; Tac. *Ann.* 4.56.2; cf. Kallet-Marx 266 n. 27.

104 App. *B. Civ.* 5.55; cf. Morrison 2016, 148–9.

105 Caes. *B. Civ.* 3.31.1–2; 3.103.1.
106 Andreau 1999, 117.
107 The details (and even the extent) of these kinds of transactions remain controversial: Andreau 1999, 88–9; Harris 2011, 2223–54; Kay 2014, 107–28; 235–65.
108 Ample funds, including liquid assets, remained held in Rome. Keeping in reserve large quantities of hard currency was both a factor in and an effect of the debt and credit crisis afflicting Rome since the outbreak of the civil war between Pompey and Caesar (Dio 41.38.1; cf. Frederiksen 1966; Crawford 1985, 193–4; Woytek 2003, 9–82; Collins and Walsh 2015). Any loans structured around eastern polities at this time should be distinguished from the loans imposed by Octavian on temples in Italy: some of these loans contributed to donatives (App. *B. Civ.* 5.22) but most funded the operating costs of Octavian's military forces (App. *B. Civ.* 5.24; 5.26; cf. Dio 48.12.4).
109 Crawford 1985, 249; Woytek 2003, 466.
110 *MRR* 2.323; cf. Roddaz 1988; Ferriès 2007, 52–6.
111 E.g., Drumann-Groebe 1899, 284; Holmes 1928, 91; Tarn 1934, 33; Broughton 1938, 585–6; Magie 1950 437–8 (and often repeated thereafter).
112 Dio 48.30.2. There were no funds for compensating the dispossessed; nearly all funds reaching Italy from the east went out as donatives: App. *B. Civ.* 5.15.
113 Will 1982, 539–40; Börm 2016; cf. Börm 2019.
114 Joseph. *AJ* 14.312.
115 On the relationship between Rome and its client kings, see Braund 1984; van Wijlick 2021, 209–25.
116 Magie 1950, 351–78; Sherwin-White 1983, 226–34; Kallet-Marx 1995, 323–34; Seager 2002, 60–2; Sartre 2005, 37–44.
117 Braund 1984, 55–122.
118 *B. Alex.* 65–6; cf. *MRR* 2.286; Magie 1950, 405–15; Mitchell 1993, 36–7; Sartre 2005, 50–1.
119 Str. 13.4.3; Dio 42.46.4; 42.47.5; 42.48; cf. Magie 1950, 1259; Sullivan 1990, 158–9.
120 *B. Alex.* 66 (with Magie 1950, 1264); Str. 12.3.35; 12.3.38; Dio 51.2.3.
121 *B. Alex.* 67–8; cf. Magie 1950, 406; 1260; Sullivan 1990, 164–9.
122 Ariobarzanes: Magie 1950, 410–1; Sullivan 1990, 177–80; Antiochus: Sullivan 1990, 193–7; Tarcondimotus: Dio 41.63.1; Magie 1950, 410; Sullivan 1990, 187–91; Julia: *OGIS* 753 = *IGRP* III 901.
123 *B. Alex.* 66; Cic. *Att.* 13.2a.2; Magie 1950, 410–1; Sullivan 1990, 180–2.
124 Börm 2016.
125 Plut. *Ant.* 24.1–2; App. *B. Civ.* 5.7; Dio 48.24.1.
126 Deformation carried on by later polemicists: Borgies 2016, 267–76.
127 Preserved by Martial: see Mart. 11.20.3–4; ch. X, p. 250.
128 App. *B. Civ.* 5.7; cf. Str. 12.2.11; Tac. *Ann.* 2.42.2; Dio 49.32.2; see Sullivan 1990, 181–2.
129 Marasco 1987, 15–7; Borgies 2016, 268–76. Antony was intimately connected to the family of the father of Glaphyra's son by way of his friendship with Archelaus, who was briefly king of Egypt: see ch. II, pp. 46–7.
130 Tarn 1934, 34. In describing Antony during this time, Plutarch claims 'he was immersed in abundant leisure and peace' and was soon distracted from his responsibilities by pleasure (*Ant.* 24.2–3).
131 Rhodes: App. *B. Civ.* 5.7; Dio 47.36.4; Antony also released Rhodes from his eastern levy; Athens: App. *B. Civ.* 5.7; 5.30; Thasos' possession of Sciathos and Peparaethos went back to an award made by Sulla (*RDGE* 20 and 21).
132 A possible implication of Dio 54.7.2; cf. Habicht 1997, 361 n. 101.
133 These Athenian possessions were left intact by Sulla: the evidence is assembled by Ferguson 1911, 454; cf. Habicht 1997, 311–3.

134   Pałuchowski 2005 assembles the relevant epigraphical and numismatic evidence. As for Cydas the Cretarch, this name is too common in Crete to be confident of his identification with Antony's juror.

135   Lambrinoudakis 1989; Lambrinoudakis 1991; Ridgway 2000, 275–7; Mosch 2005, 146–7.

136   On the history of the Antiope myth, see Joyce 2001; Mosch 2005, esp. 151–5.

137   [----]τωι θεῶι Καίσαρι; cf. Lambrinoudakis 1989, 343.

138   Plut. *Ant*. 75.4–5; Pelling 1988, 303–4.

139   Augustus and Dionysus: e.g., Galinsky 1996, 316–7; 330–1.

140   The triumvirs' vow in Rome: Dio 47.36.4. The Rhodian Dirce of Apollonius and Tauriscus was acquired and shifted to Rome by Asinius Pollio: Plin. *NH* 36.34. Octavian's cameo appearance: Ridgway 1999, 519; Stewart 2001, 469–70. One need not accept the view, asserted both by Ridgway and Stewart, that the Rhodian Dirce is more or less contemporary with the Naxian General, a view that actually undercuts the point of the Naxian General's quotation, which, to be effective, must refer to a well-known piece. The more common (and more likely) view is that the sculpture by Apollonius and Tauriscus belongs to the second century and reflects Pergamene euergetism (Kunze 1998; Mosch 2005), a pedigree that, if true, can only have underscored the Naxian General's assertion of Antony's majesty.

141   Roddaz 2012, 130–1.

142   Plut. *Ant*. 24.2; cf. Bowersock 1965, 10; Wille 1967, 336–7; Pelling 1988, 177–8. Köhler 1996, 125, makes the point that anyone taking on the role of Dionysus must be attended by musicians and performers, a reality that doubtless encouraged Plutarch's disapproval of Antony's companions. Cicero's prior criticism of Antony's artistic companions: *Phil*. 5.15; 8.26.

143   The Romans' moral qualms about musicians: Wille 1967, 326–7; 332–6. Objections to artistic friends: e.g., Plut. *Sull*. 2.4; 33.3; 36.102 (Sulla); Q. Cic. *Comm. Pet*. 10 (Catiline); Tac. *Hist*. 2.72 (Nero); Suet. *Titus* 7.2 (Titus); cf. Tatum 2018, 206–7. Sulla's friendship with Q. Roscius Gallus (Macr. *Sat*. 3.14.3). Caesar's friendship with Hermogenes Tigellius: Cic. *Fam*. 7.24; *Att*. 13.49.1; Porphyrio *ad* Hor. *Serm*. 1.2.1; 1.3.4; cf. Gowers 2012, 92.

144   See, for instance, Plut. *Brut*. 21.6, recording how, even during the difficult politics of his praetorship, Brutus journeyed to Naples in order to enlist Greek performers for his games. On the importance of games for Roman office-seekers, see Tatum 2018, 6–7.

145   Csapo 2010, 168–204.

146   Antony and performers in Rome: Cic. *Phil*. 2.62–7; 2.101; 5.15; 8.26.

147   P. Brit. Libr. Inv. 137 = *RDGE* 57. A highly damaged inscription, originating in Tralles, preserves a part of the letter's opening; cf. Poljakov 1989, 105.

148   Other testimonia for this Synod are discussed by Fauconnier 2016, 79–80. Scholarship on this letter is assembled by *RDGE* 57; Ricciardetto 2012; Fauconnier 2016 (who argues convincingly for an association of athletes). The Wreathed Winners are identified by some with the Artists of Dionysus (on whom see: Pickard-Cambridge, 1968, 279–321; Le Guen 2001; Aneziri 2003; in 32 Antony lavished favours on the Artists: Plut. *Ant*. 56.7–57.1) or, it is suggested, this group included winners from a broad range of competitions. It is sometimes argued that the Synod's privileges should be dated to 32: see, e.g., Brandis 1897, 516; Ebert 1987; Fauconnier 2016, 78. The Synod was likely honoured on the occasion of games performed in Antony's honour: Potter 1999, 271–2 (cf. Suet. *Iul*. 42), repeated by Fauconnier 2016, 88.

149   *I. Eph*. vii. 24101 = *SEG* 31.952; cf. Knibbe 1981.

150   Boethius: Str. 14.5.14; cf. Bowersock 1965, 47–8.

151   Fontani 1999; Aneziri and Damaskos 2004; Daubner 2015.

152   Plut. *Flam*. 16.3.

153 Errington 1988, 153–6.
154 *Chios* 15 = *IGRP* 4.1703.
155 Marcellus: Plut. *Marc.* 30.4; Scipio: Cic. *Verr.* 2.5.185; Verres: Cic. *Verr.* 2.2.160.
156 Upon his death in 36 he was succeeded by his son, Mithridates II, who fought for Antony at Actium: Sullivan 1990, 197–8.
157 Antiochus was still in power in 38: Str. 16.2.3; Plut. *Ant.* 34.5–7; Joseph. *BJ* 1.321–2; Dio 48.41.5; 49.20–2; cf. Bowersock 1965, 57–8; Sullivan 1990, 193–7. Lycomedes: Str. 12.3.35; 12.3.38; Dio 51.2.3; cf. Bowersock 1965, 48. Iamblichus was executed by Antony on the eve of Actium: Dio 50.13.7; 51.2.2; cf. Buchheim 1960, 21–2; Bowersock 1965, 47; Sullivan 1990, 200–2. Tarcondimotus: Plut. *Ant.* 61.2; Dio 51.2.2; cf. Bowersock 1965, 46–7; Sullivan 1990, 187–91; Mustafa 2001. Malichus: Plut. *Ant.* 61.3; Dio 48.41.5; 49.32.5; cf. Bowersock 1965, 57; Sullivan 1990, 211–3.
158 Caesar and Antioch: Jones 1971, 457 n. 46. Caesar and Laodicea: *RPC* 1.4379 and 4380 (coins issued by Iulius Laodicea). Antony and Laodicea: App. *B. Civ.* 5.7.
159 Str. 12.3.4. When this happened is unclear: Magie 1950, 435, suggests a later date.
160 Str. 13.4.3; Dio 42.46.4; 42.47.5; 42.48.4; cf. Bowersock 1965, 50–1; Sullivan 1990, 159–60.
161 Buchheim 1960, 15–20; Sullivan 1990, 70–2; 206–7; Sharon 2017, 114–5. Ptolemy's death: Joseph. *AJ* 14.330. His domains: Str. 16.2.10; 16.2.18.
162 Adiatorix: Cic. *Fam.* 2.12.2; Str. 12.3.6; 12.3.35; cf. Magie 1950, 436; Bowersock 1965, 44–5; Sullivan 1990, 171.
163 *RPC* 1.4338; 1.4336; 1.4337; 1.4338; 1.4339.
164 Jones 1940, 129–31.
165 Cnidus: Plut. *Caes.* 48.1.
166 The link between civic freedom and the Romans' recognition of sound local government was a strong one: Dmitriev 2005, 308–12.
167 Joseph. *AJ* 14.297; App. *B. Civ.* 5.10; cf. Buchheim 1960, 27.
168 App. *B. Civ.* 5.10. Buchheim 1960, 27, believes Antony removed them more on account of their Parthian sympathies than their connection with Cassius.
169 Marion installed by Cassius: Joseph. *BJ* 1.238; *AJ* 14.297. Hostilities against Herod: Joseph. *BJ* 1.237–8; *AJ* 14.297–9. Antony's letter to Tyre: Joseph. *AJ* 14.315; cf. Buchheim 1960, 18; Pelling 1996, 11 n. 34; Sharon 2017, 145–7.
170 A Roman habit: Jones 1940, 170–1; Bernhardt 1985, 268; Dmitriev 2005, 309–17 (who introduces important qualifications to this view).
171 Dio 49.19.2–3; cf. Buchheim 1960, 21.
172 Amaseia: Str. 12.3.39. Megalopolis: Str. 12.3.37; cf. Jones 1971 n. 39. Zela: Str. 12.3.37. Caranitis: Str. 12.3.37. Amisus: Str. 12.3.14; the city quickly fell into the power of an autocrat named Strato, a figure unlikely to be denominated a king by Strabo (so Magie 1950, 1284, a view confirmed by a detailed study of Strabo's vocabulary of autocratic rule: C.P. Jones 2017; cf. Jones 1971, 427 n. 37, who takes Strabo's reference to be to Strato). Only in the case of Amisus is Antony mentioned in any source, but he is the likeliest Roman candidate for these actions: Jones 1971, 167–9.
173 *RPC* 1.2020, an issue which pictures the queen on the obverse, Heracles on the reverse; see Str. 12.3.37; 12.4.3; App. *Mithr.* 117; Jones 1971, 162–3 and 427 n. 39. It appears she was succeeded by another queen, Orodaltis: *RPC* 1.2021.
174 Str. 12.3.38; 12.3.40; cf. Jones 1971, 167 and 426 n. 39. Alternatively, the demotion of these cities could have taken place during Antony's resettlement of the east after his return in 39.
175 Antony's settlement of Pontus in 39: Str. 12.3.14; Dio 49.32–3; Jones 1971, 166–7; Magie 1950, 434–6; Mitchell 1993, 38–9; Marek 2006, 40–1; Madsen 2009, 30.
176 Str. 12.3.1; App. *Mithr.* 114.

177 Sullivan 1990, 164–9.
178 The year of the kings' deaths is made clear at Dio 48.33.4–5. Although Dio 48.33 mostly discusses events taking place in 40, at 48.33.4 he turns to occurrences 'in the prior year' (ἔν τε τῷ πρὸ τούτου ἔτει); he cites Castor's elevation at 48.33.5—still occupied with 41. At Dio 48.34.1, he continues with the retrospective 'these were the events during those two years'. The deaths of Attalus and Deiotarus, however, are routinely misdated to 40.
179 Dio 48.33.5; cf. Bowersock 1965, 51 (but see preceding note); Sullivan 1990, 169–70.
180 Cic. *Deit.* 29–33.
181 Brutus' friendship with Deiotarus: Cic. *Att.* 14.1.2; *Brut.* 5.21; Tac. *Dial.* 21.6; Plut. *Brut.* 6.6; Dio 47.24.3; cf. Moles 2017, 98–9.
182 Cic. *Att.* 14.12.1; *Phil.* 2.93–5. The amount alleged was 10,000,000 sesterces.
183 Mitchel 1993, 36.
184 App. *B. Civ.* 4.88; Dio 47.48.2.
185 Sullivan 1990, 169–70.
186 Dmitriev 2005, 195–6.
187 Joseph. *AJ* 15.76.
188 On Antony's service in Syria and his close relationship with Antipater and his sons, see ch. II, pp. 43–4.
189 Antipater and Hyrcanus during the Alexandrian War: Joseph. *BJ* 1.187–93; *AJ* 14.127–36.
190 Joseph. *BJ* 1.194; *AJ* 14.127–39; cf. Sharon 2017, 125–7.
191 Joseph. *AJ* 14.219–22; cf. Sharon 2017, 140–1.
192 Joseph. *BJ* 1.219–41; *AJ* 14.272–300; cf. Sharon 2017, 141–6.
193 Joseph. *BJ* 1.242; *AJ* 14.301–3.
194 Joseph. *AJ* 14.304–5.
195 Joseph. *AJ* 14.306–13.
196 Joseph. *AJ* 14.314–22.
197 Joseph. *AJ* 14.309. Sophocles' *Thyestes*: *AP* 9.98.2. This image was made familiar in Rome by way of Accius' *Thyestes*: fr. 13Klotz; see, further, Boyle 2017, 359.
198 See ch. VII, p. 162.
199 Joseph. AJ 14.309: τῶν εἰς θεοὺς ἀνομημάτων; cf. Lev. 17:16; 20:14; Deut. 15:9.
200 Joseph. *BJ* 1.243–5; *AJ* 14.324–6.
201 Joseph. *BJ* 1.245–7; *AJ* 14.327–9.
202 Plin. *Ep.* 10.96.3.
203 Plut. *Ant.* 26.1.
204 Plut. *Ant.* 25.2–3; App. *B. Civ.* 3.78; 4.59; 4.61; 4.63; 4.74; 5.8; Dio 47.31.4; cf. Cic. *Fam.* 12.11.1; cf. Will 1982, 537–9; Roller 2010, 75–9.
205 Joseph. *AJ* 15.89; *Ap.* 2.57; App. *B. Civ.* 5.9 (locates Arsinoe at Miletus); Dio 48.24.2 (not Arsinoe at Ephesus but Cleopatra's 'brothers').
206 Cic. *Att.* 14.13.6, reacting to *Att.* 14.13a; cf. Tatum 2017, 67–9. On Antony's propensity for epistolary aggression, see Plut. *Ant.* 78.3.
207 Hor. *Carm.* 2.3.1–2: *aequam memento rebus in arduis/servare mentum.*
208 App. *B. Civ.* 5.8; see ch. II, p. 52.
209 See ch. II, p. 52.
210 Plut. *Ant.* 58.6.
211 Cic. *Att.* 15.15.2 (*reginam odi*).
212 Socrates of Rhodes, *BNJ* 192 F1; Plut. *Ant.* 26–7. Some elements in Plutarch's version of Cleopatra's advent may have been lifted from Alexandrian ceremonies; cf. Pelling 1988, 188.
213 Fraser 1972, 238–40; Höbl 2001, 97–8; 107–8; Cheshire 2007; Caneva 2012, esp. 92–4; Kunst 2012, 96–9; Carney 2013, 98–100; Michel 2018. Other queens, in other kingdoms,

also identified themselves with Aphrodite: e.g., Laodice III, worshipped in Iasos as Aphrodite Laodice: see Ma 2000, 223–4; 333–5.

214   Cleopatra's statue: App. *B. Civ.* 2.102; Dio 51.22.3; cf. Ashton 2005, 57–8; 142–6; Kunst 2012, 98. Its invocation by way of Cleopatra's procession: Jeanmaire 1924, 249.

215   A frequent assertion: e.g., Staehlin 1921, 754–5; Volkmann 1953, 51; 77; Kleiner 2005, 99–100; cf. 151–4; Wyke 2007, 206–7; Roller 2010, 72.

216   Aly 1992, 52; Tatum 2008, 117–9. Westall 1996, 106–7, in a highly perceptive discussion, concludes that it was Octavian, not Caesar, who first deposited Cleopatra's statue in the temple; this same conclusion is reached by Gruen 2003, 259, but see also Williams 2001, 196–7.

217   Ashton 2005, 142–6; Walker 2008. After Actium, Octavian did not remove Cleopatra's statue: Dio 51.22.3.

218   Plut. *Ant.* 26.5; cf. Volkmann 1953, 93–6.

219   Jeanmaire 1924; Śniezewski, 134–5; Couvenhes 2013, 235; Strootman 2014, 243–4; Borgies 2016, 297–9.

220   App. *B. Civ.* 5.8.

221   Rossi 1959, 110–3; Buchheim 1960, 22–5; Marasco 1987, 20–5; Halfmann 2011, 122–4; Roddaz 2012, 131. Other discussions include: Drumann-Groebe 1899, 284–6; Holmes 1928, 91–2; Tarn 1932, 39–40; Bengtson 1977, 161–4; Huzar 1978, 153–4; Chamoux 1986, 241–7; Pelling 1996, 12; Chauveau 2002, 41–4; Pasquali 2009, 151–3; Goldsworthy 2010, 265–9.

222   Joseph. *AJ* 15.89; *Ap.* 2.57; App. *B. Civ.* 5.9; Dio 48.24.2; cf. Volkmann 1953, 91–6; Roller 2010, 76–9; Sartre 2018, 159–66.

223   Plut. *Ant.* 25.1; cf. Debevoise 1938, 108; Buchheim 1960, 14–5; 20–1; Bengtson 1977, 158–9; Chamoux 1986, 239–40; Marasco 1987, 13–4; Pelling 1996, 12–3; Pasquali 2009, 153; Goldsworthy 2010, 284; Southern 2010, 170–1; Halfmann 2011, 124–5.

224   Plut. *Ant.* 23.1; 25.1.

225   Dio 47.27.5; Cic. *Att.* 14.9.3; see, further, *MRR* 2.297; Sherwin-White 1983, 302. On Bassus, see Nicolet 1974, 810–1.

226   *MRR* 2.343.

227   App. *B. Civ.* 47.30.3; Dio 47.30.3.

228   Dio 48.24.2; Florus 2.9.4; cf. App. *B. Civ.* 4.6.3.

229   App. *B. Civ.* 4.88; 4.99; but cf. 4.63 and the doubts expressed by Sherwin-White 1983, 302 (although it is puzzling, if Sherwin-White is correct, that Cassius should simultaneously dismiss his Parthian cavalry *and* send Labienus to request Parthian aid). According to Dio 48.24.5, Orodes spent too long temporizing to be able to deliver any reinforcements. On Parthian involvement with the republican cause, see van Wijlick 2021, 68–74.

230   Hirrius: Caes. *B. Civ.* 3.82.4. Orodes' response: Dio 41.55.3–4; 42.2.5.

231   Vell. 2.53.1; Plut. *Pomp.* 76; App. *B. Civ.* 2.83; cf. Seager 2002, 167–8.

232   App. *B. Civ.* 4.59.

233   Rome and Parthia during the civil war: Debevoise 1938, 104–8; Sherwin-White 1983, 290–5; Nabel 2019; Schlude 2020, 76–84.

234   Dio 48.24.7; cf. Magie 1950, 431.

235   App. *B. Civ.* 5.9–10; cf. Hekster and Kaizer 2004.

236   A common suggestion: e.g., Buchheim 1960, 28; Bengtson 1977, 158; Chamoux 1986, 247–8; Pelling 1996, 12; Pasquali 2009, 153; Goldsworthy 2010, 284; Halfmann 2011, 124–5. Appian believed Antony's campaign stimulated the Parthian invasion of 40 (*B. Civ.* 5.9).

237   Dio 48.24.7.

238   Goldsworthy 1996, 248–82.

239 Dio 48.25.1–2.

240 *MRR* 2.384. His origins: Syme 1939, 80.

241 Dio 48.24.7; 48.25.1–2; Str. 14.2.24.

242 Antony's celebrated rapport with his men: Plut. *Ant.* 4.4–7.

243 Criticism: Dio 48.24.1–2; 48.24.6–8. Antony in Alexandria: Drumann-Groebe 1899, 287–8; Holmes 1928, 92; Tarn 1932, 40–1; Bengtson 1977, 164–5; Huzar 1978, 154–5; Chamoux 1986, 248–54; Pelling 1996, 12–3; Chauveau 2002, 44–7; Pasquali 2009, 157–8; Goldsworthy 2010, 269–71; Southern 2010, 180–2. Cleopatra: Volkmann 1953, 96–9; Roller 2010, 79–87; Sartre 2018, 166–70.

244 Fraser 1972.

245 Popularity: Plut. *Ant.* 3.10–1; cf. 29.4. Praetorian guard: App. *B. Civ.* 5.10 with Brunt 1971, 497. Alexandrian sensibilities regarding large, foreign armies: Caes. *B.Civ.* 104.1; Plut. *Pomp.* 77.6 (Pompey in Egypt); Caes. *B. Civ.* 106.4–5; Gabinius: see ch. II, p. 52; Plut. *Caes.* 48.7–8; cf. Dio 42.34.1 (Caesar in Egypt).

246 Fraser 1972, 89–90; 122.

247 App. *B. Civ.* 5.11; cf. *B. Civ.* 5.9–10; Appian's account is probably modelled on Plutarch's account of Antony's first winter in Athens: Tatum 2020a.

248 Dio 48.24.1–3; 48.27.1–2; cf. Joseph. *AJ* 13.1.324.

249 Plut. *Ant.* 28–30.1.

250 Ravished: Plut. *Ant.* 28.1; cf. Pelling 1988, 193. Antony depicted by Plutarch as a youth (*meirakion*): Pelling 1988, 193–7. By Appian, too, in his account of Cleopatra's audience at Tarsus: *B. Civ.* 5.8. Stereotypical depictions of aristocratic youthful hijinks: Laes and Strubbe 2014, 137–40. Youthful indiscretions, even violent ones, venial: e.g., Cic. *Inv.* 2.37; *Cael.* 28; 30; 42; Suet. *Ner.* 26; cf. Austin 1960, 84 and 102; Tatum 2011, 169–70; Dyck 2013, 129 (assembling further evidence); see ch. I, p. 17.

251 Plut. *Ant.* 29.2–4; on this species of aristocratic misbehaviour, tolerated when perpetrated by the young, see McDaniel 1914.

252 Plut. *Ant.* 29.7.

253 Monarchs and the politics of the court: Herman 1997, 212; Strootman 2014, 93–110; 145–64; 177–84. Cleopatra's court: Ashton 2005, 115–25.

254 Roller 2010, 80–3; cf. Ager 2017, 174. Close though Cleopatra and Antony may have become that winter, 'she did not . . . succeed in making herself indispensable', as Tarn puts it (Tarn 1932, 41). In autumn 37 Antony summoned Cleopatra for a meeting at Antioch (Plut. *Ant.* 36.1); see ch. XII, pp. 285–6.

255 Roller 2010, 100 (he suggests the Donations of Alexandria as the occasion for these gifts).

256 Plut. *Ant.* 28.3–7.

257 Plut. *Ant.* 28.2.

258 Philo, *Flacc.* 136; cf. Pelling 1988, 195.

259 Strootman 2014, 152–6; 175; esp. 188–91. Kings as big eaters and drinkers: Plut. *Mor.* 624a. Philosophers, by contrast, and generals on campaign were expected to avoid eating more than was necessary for nourishment: evidence assembled by Woodman 1983, 53–4.

260 Plut. *Caes.* 48.6; Suet. *Iul.* 52.1.

261 Plut. *Ant.* 28–30.1; App. *B. Civ.* 5.9–11; Dio 48.24.1–3; 48.27.1–2; cf. Borgies 2016, 254. Cleopatra is written into the Perusine war by way of Fulvian jealousy: Plut. *Ant.* 30.2; App. *B. Civ.* 5.19; 5.66.

262 App. *B. Civ.* 5.52.

263 Cic. *Fam.* 15.1.5.

264 By way of comparison, when Cicero was proconsul in Cilicia he relied for information on various dynasts, not all of whom were reliable: Cic. *Fam.* 15.1.1–3; 15.2.1; 15.4.7. On

the methods employed by provincial governors in order remain informed of movements within and outside their provinces, see Austin and Rankov 1995, 89–91; 94–7; 142–84.

CHAPTER X

1 Dio 48.6.2.

2 Syme 1939, 207–8; Gabba 1971; Roddaz 1988; see, i.a., Huzar 1978, 132; Kienast 1999, 44–5; Ferriès 2007, 186–7; Lange 2009, 27–8; Welch 2012, 218–30.

3 App. *B. Civ.* 5.19; 5.27; 5.29–30; 5.39; 5.43. Freedom: Dio 48.13.6.

4 Antony and the Perusine crisis: Drumann-Groebe 288–303; Holmes 1928, 92–100; Tarn 1934, 27–9; Syme 1939, 207–12; Rossi 1959, 128–30; Buchheim 1960, 29–34; Harris 1971, 299–303; Bengtson 1977, 167–71; Huzar 1978, 130–4; Chamoux 1986, 254–9; Kienast 1999, 42–5; Pelling 1996, 14–6; Ferriès 2007, 178–200; Pasquali 2009, 153–6; Southern 2010, 182–5; Goldsworthy 2010, 272–4; Halfmann 2011, 126–8; Mangiameli 2012, 174–201. The most important discussions are Groag 1915, 43–51; Gabba 1971; Roddaz 1988; Wallmann 1989, 89–135; Osgood 2006, 159–82; Welch 2012, 218–30.

5 Plut. *Ant.* 30.6; App. *B.Civ.* 5.55; cf. Roddaz 1988, 320; Gowing 1992, 77–84; Welch 2012, 221; Osgood 2014, 61–4.

6 Ennius represented Discord as 'a virago, born of hell, clad in a general's cloak' (*corpore tartarino prognato paluda virago*: Ann. *fr.* 220–1 SK). Was this striking and famous image employed against Fulvia in propaganda designating her the cause of the Perusine War?

7 Hallett 1977; Welch 1995, 193–4; Cluett 1998, 82–4; Fischer 1999, 40–7; Ferriès 2007, 405–8; Osgood 2014, 61–4; Schlutz 2021, 92–103.

8 Plut. *Ant.* 30.6; Dio 48.28.3; cf. App. *B. Civ.* 5.42; 5.54; Scott 1933, 24; cf. Livadiotti 2013, esp. 87–8.

9 Ferriès 2007, 431–2; Cresci Marrone 2014.

10 Octavian interrogates Lucius over Antony's role in the Perusine crisis: App. *B. Civ.* 5.54. Best to move on: App. *B. Civ.* 5.62.

11 Nep. *Att.* 20.4. Roman correspondence: Hall 2009; White 2010; Wilcox 2012; Rollinger 2014; Bernard 2017.

12 Schröder 2018.

13 Cic. *Att.* 5.19.1 (from Rome to Cybistra in 46 days); *Att.* 6.1.22 (Epirus to Laodicea in 48 days); *Att.* 6.2.6 (Rome to Laodicea in, at best, 60 days).

14 Cic. *Fam.* 5.6.1.

15 Cic. *Att.* 5.21.1; cf. Austin and Rankov 1995, 102–7; García Riaza 2020, 283–9.

16 App. *B. Civ.* 4.3; see ch. VIII, p. 185.

17 Triumviral decree: *Lib. colon.* 212–3; Hinrichs 1969, 540–1; Bleicken 1990, 41–2. Justifications: Laignoux 2013; Laignoux 2015; Ferriès 2016.

18 App. *B. Civ.* 4.2; cf. 5.12.

19 Salmon 1970; Keppie 1983, 49–52; Roselaar 2010, esp. 58–46.

20 *MRR* 2.75–6, esp. App. *B. Civ.* 1.96; 1.100; Salmon 1970, 128–32; Brunt 1971, 300–12; Harris 1971, 259–67; Seager 1994, 203–5.

21 App. *B. Civ.* 5. 5.

22 Gabba 1971, 141. Augustan regrets: e.g., Verg. *Ecl.* 1; *Ecl.* 9; Prop. 4.1.127–30; Hor. *Epist.* 2.2.49–52; cf. Osgood 2006, 108–51.

23 Planning for the new colonies began almost immediately by way of the appointment of land commissioners (*geonomoi*) (Dio 47.14.4). Plancus was apparently active in organizing one of the planned colonies: *ILS* 886 (... *agros divisit in Italia | Beneventi* ...), although this activity is sometimes located later than his consulship (e.g., Keppie 1983, 59). It is a secure

inference that Lepidus, triumvir and consul in this year, was also involved in carrying out, indeed in overseeing, the triumvirs' policy. On the significance of Lepidus' dual offices in 42, see Bleicken 1990, 41; his role in carrying out triumviral policies is reviewed by Allély 2004, 133–4. A different view is taken by Brunt 1971, 328, who argues that distributions did not begin until 41.

24 Calculations of Philippi's survivors and of veterans entitled to plots of land can only be approximate; see Brunt 1971, 488–93.

25 Founding a colony: Brunt 1971, 294–300; Keppie 1983, 87–100.

26 Dio. 48.6.3.

27 App. *B. Civ.* 5.12.

28 Dio 48.3.3.

29 Dio 48.6.2–3.

30 *Ecl.* 1; *Ecl.* 9; Osgood 2006, 109–44.

31 App. *B. Civ.* 5.12–3; 5.18; Dio 48.8–9. Violence in the countryside persisted: it remained a problem in 36 (App. *B. Civ.* 5.132).

32 After Actium, when Octavian once again turned to dispossessions in order to install his veterans in Italy, he compensated the evicted with payments or resettled them in colonies abroad: Dio 51.4.6; *Mon. Anc.* 16.1. The triumvirs lacked the resources for either form of compensation.

33 It is no accident that coins minted by Octavian's moneyers celebrate historic soldierly successes: *RRC* 513 and 514.

34 *MRR* 2.377–8; Brunt 1971, 326–31; Keppie 1983, 58–60. Lucius and colonization: see ch. VI, p. 157.

35 Six further legions: App. *B. Civ.* 5.22.

36 Illness: App. *B. Civ.* 5.12; 5.14; Dio 48.3.1. Compromise: App. *B. Civ.* 5.14.

37 Keppie 1983, 66–7.

38 App. *B. Civ.* 5.14; 5.22; cf. Keppie 1983, 62–4.

39 App. *B. Civ.* 5.15; 5.18; Dio 48.3–5; 48.8.1; cf. Welch 2012, 226–7; *MRR* 2.373.

40 On these military commands, see App. *B. Civ.* 5.50–1; Dio 48.10.1; *MRR* 2.372–6 (official titles are not always preserved by our sources); cf. Brunt 1971, 491–6.

41 Two legions owed to Octavian: App. *B. Civ.* 5.3; Dio 48.2.3.

42 App. *B. Civ.* 5.18; Dio 48.9.4–5. A possible illustration of Octavian's response is L. Memmius, who was *frumenti curator* and also responsible for allocating properties in the colonization of Luca: *ILS* 887; cf. *MRR* 2.485; Brunt 1971, 328.

43 App. *B. Civ.* 5.18. Appian's ὁ δὲ λεὼς ἀπέκλειε τὰ ἐργαστήρια refers to the Roman practice of shuttering *tabernae* in protest, including protests associated with political violence; cf. Tatum 1999, 29; 143–8; Russell 2016b.

44 Nicolet 1966, 389–422; Scuderi 1989; Deniaux 1993; Bleicken 1995, 26–32; Patterson 2006a; Patterson 2006b; Lomas 2012; Dench 2013; Tatum 2018, 87–8; 174–6; 226–7; Roselaar 2019; Santangelo 2019.

45 Tatum 2018, 16–9; 243–4; Santangelo 2019.

46 Q. Cic. *Comm. Pet* 31.

47 Frier 1985, esp. 52–98; Stewart 1995, 74–5; Paterson 2006b; Lomas 2012; Santangelo 2016; Tatum 2018, 244.

48 Tatum 2018, 16–9; 243–4.

49 Tatum 2018, 19–49; Hölkeskamp 2020, 43–62.

50 Cic. *Att.* 8.13.2.

51 Cic. *Att.* 16.3.1: … *deseremur ocius a re publica quam a re familiari.*

52 Canvassing and elections in 43: App. *B. Civ.* 4.18; Plut. *Cic.* 49.1. Elections during the triumviral period, see Bleicken 1990, 43–6; Pina Polo 2020, 52–7. The triumviral senate: Ferriès 2020.
53 Plut. *Ant.* 30.1; Dio 48.4.1–6; cf. *MRR* 2.370–1; Ferriès 2007, 181; Schultz 2021, 92–3.
54 *MRR* 2.323; cf. Roddaz 1988; Ferriès 2007, 52–6.
55 App. *B. Civ.* 5.19; 5.21; 5.27; Dio 48.4.1; 48.10.3; cf. 48.14.3–4; Gabba 1971, 148–9; Roddaz 1988, 336–7. On the vulnerability of Italian aristocrats during civil war, see Santangelo 2016.
56 This is the highly influential view of Gabba 1971 and Roddaz 1988; cf., i.a., Ferriès 2007, 186–7; Lange 2009, 27–8; Welch 2012, 218–30; Vervaet 2020, 41. On the diverse quality of Lucius' following, see Ferriès 2007, 191–5. We can safely reject the deprecations of Lucius' enemies, who attributed his actions to base motives, claiming that he and Fulvia were resentful of Octavian for excluding them from exploiting their clout and for somehow preventing them from enriching themselves amid the dispossessions (Dio 48.5.1–2).
57 App. *B. Civ.* 5.19.
58 App. *B. Civ.* 5.54.
59 App. *B. Civ.* 5.30–1.
60 Wallmann 1989, 96–7; Pelling 1996, 15; Osgood 2006, 160–1; 165; Schultz 2021, 94–5.
61 Suet. *Tib.* 4.2.
62 Cic. *Off.* 1.20; 2.73–8; 3.21–4; Vell. 2.89.4; cf. Brunt 1988, 305–6; 346–9; Wood 1988, 111–9; Annas 1989.
63 Brunt 1988, 330–4; Ferriès 2007, 182.
64 App. *B. Civ.* 5.12.
65 Caesar's confiscations: Cic. *Phil.* 2.103–5; 13.32; Dio 42.20.1. His rejection of Sulla's policy of seizing land: App. *B. Civ.* 2.94. His provincial colonies; *MRR* 2.294 (esp. Suet. *Iul.* 42.1); cf. Brunt 1971, 255–9; 589–601; Jehne 1987, 139–52; 343–7.
66 *AE* 1996.534, with Panciera 2006, 965–75 (one need not accept Panciera's argument that Octavian's punishment of Nursia came after Actium). *Libertas* (ἐλευθερία) in Nursia: Dio 48.13.6.
67 Dio 48.7.1–2; cf. App. *B. Civ.* 5.20. On the difficulties confronted by both Lucius and Octavian in communicating with soldiers and keeping them on one's side, see Mangiameli 2012, 174–201. Dio, relying on Octavian's propaganda, claims that, in reality, Lucius and Fulvia abandoned the veterans' interests (Dio 48.5.1–2); consequently, although he records the details of Lucius' programme, Dio makes it clear that he deems it a dishonest one. Influenced by Dio, modern scholars often conclude that Lucius' policy constituted a danger to the colonists' interests: e.g., Holmes 1928, 100; Syme 1939, 208; Groag 1915, 49; Gabba 1971, 146–7; Keinast 1999, 45; Roddaz 1988, 337–8; Wallmann 1989, 96–7; Osgood 2006, 161–5. Livadotti 2013 detects in Appian an ambiguity that owes itself to the historian's conflicting sources.
68 See ch. VI, pp. 105–6.
69 Contemporary fears of a permanent triumvirate: App. *B. Civ.* 5.12. In the end, Octavian resorted to propaganda very like Lucius' in order to rally Italy against Antony: Gabba 1970, XXIXC; Livadotti 2013, 75.
70 App. *B. Civ.* 5.19.
71 App. *B. Civ.* 5.19; 5.39; 5.43; cf. Dio 48.5.1–2.
72 App. *B. Civ.* 5.19; cf. Plut. *Ant.* 30.1.
73 App. *B. Civ.* 5.19; see, further, Schultz 2021, 97–100.
74 App. *B. Civ.* 5.43; Dio 48.7.3; cf. Wallmann 1989, 96–8; 111–3.
75 Dio 48.8.1.

76 *Epist.* 2.2; Osgood 2006, 212–9.

77 Dio 48.8–9.

78 Keppie 1983, 91–6.

79 Veteran displeasure: Dio 48.8–9. Concession to the veterans' relations: Dio 48.9.3.

80 Green 1996 goes so far as to argue that the divine benefactor of the *First Eclogue* is actually Lucius and not Octavian.

81 App. *B. Civ.* 5.19.

82 Suet. *Aug.* 62.1; Dio 48.5.2–4. Inasmuch as the soldiery, especially the men loyal to Antony, played an important role in his betrothal to Claudia (Suet. *Aug.* 62.1; Plut. *Ant.* 20.1; Dio 46.56.3), Octavian, in divorcing Claudia, ran something of a risk with the troops; he obviously made his purposes clear to them in such a way that they were not affronted.

83 Ferriès 2007, 187–90.

84 As observed by Suet. *Aug.* 62.1. Contemporary criticisms of Octavian's sexual predilections: Wardle 2014, 438–9; 405; Borgies 2016, 261–6. The propriety of preserving an ex-wife's reputation: Treggiari 1991, 464–5. For a different take on this divorce, see Schultz 2021, 94.

85 Dio 48.10.1.

86 Octavian's exactions: App. *B. Civ.* 5.22. Triumviral exactions from cities: *MRR* 2.372; 3.376. Pollio: Macrob. *Sat.* 1.11.22.

87 App. *B. Civ.* 5.20; 5.24; Dio 48.10.1.

88 Dio 48.10.2–4.

89 App. *B. Civ.* 5.26; cf. Dio 48.45.1.

90 App. *B. Civ.* 5.26; 5.53; Dio 48.20.4–5; 48.22.1–23.5. Welch 2012, 222, attributes these disturbances to Antony.

91 App. *B. Civ.* 5.20; Dio 48.10.2.

92 Keppie 1983, 139–40; cf. Gabba 1970, 44.

93 Gell. 10.3.1–3 (the event is undated); cf. Roth 2019.

94 Colloquium sites carefully staged: Cornwell 2020, 155–8; García Riaza 2020, 293–8.

95 App. *B. Civ.* 5.20; cf. Dio 48.5.2.

96 Dio 48.10.3.

97 On Antony's silence, and Appian's reaction to it, see Mangiameli 2008/9. Dio 48.27.1 maintains that Antony remained abreast of affairs in Italy, although this passage is far from clear: Dio, admittedly en passant, puts Antony's familiarity with Lucius' activities on a par with his familiarity with the invasion of Syria by Labienus, which took place in spring 40.

98 App. *B. Civ.* 5.21.

99 App. *B. Civ.* 5.60. On Cocceius, see Ferriès 2007, 373–4. Caecina's identity eludes: see *MRR* 3.43, suggesting he is Octavian's agent cited at Cic. *Att.* 18.18.1; on the distinguished equestrian Caecinae, see Nicolet 1974, 812–4.

100 Groag 1915, 49.

101 Lucius' tour: Dio 48.10.3. The Philippi agreement the focus of controversy: App. *B. Civ.* 5.22; Dio 48.12.1.

102 App. *B. Civ.* 5.21; cf. Schultz 2021, 96.

103 App. *B. Civ.* 1.94; cf. Plut. *Sull.* 32.

104 Cic. *Cat.* 1.8.

105 Cic. *Agr.* 2.78. The Praenestines ultimately petitioned Tiberius to make their town a municipium instead of a colony (Gell. 16.3.5): is this evidence, as Salmon suggested (Salmon 1970, 131), of enduring bitterness over Sulla's treatment?

106 Dio 48.11.1. The question arises: did Lepidus make an appearance in Praeneste? App. *B. Civ.* 5.21 suggests his sympathy with Fulvia's cause (cf. Schultz 2021, 96): the symbolism

of Lepidus' making his way to Praeneste, if it occurred, could only have been striking. Allély 2004, 146, however, argues that, throughout the Perusine crisis, Lepidus' support for Octavian was total.

107 App. *B. Civ.* 5.21; Dio 48.10.2–3.
108 App. *B. Civ.* 5.32; Dio 48.12.2–4.
109 Dio 48.5.14; 48.6.4–5.
110 App. *B. Civ.* 5.22; Dio 48.6.1; 48.11.3; 48.12.1.
111 App. *B. Civ.* 5.22.
112 App. *B. Civ.* 5.28–9.
113 App. *B. Civ.* 5.29.
114 App. *B. Civ.* 5.27
115 App. *B. Civ.* 5.24.
116 App. *B. Civ.* 5.31; 5.40; 5.46; cf. Brunt 1971, 495.
117 On Lucius' forces, see Brunt 1971, 494–8. Brunt suggests (unconvincingly in my view) that Lucius may have continued to command an army of some size after his triumph and that, instead of raising six legions in Italy, he conscripted soldiers who could fill the ranks of his existing legions.
118 App. *B. Civ.* 5.27.
119 Or, perhaps, *Titisienus* Gallus; cf. Ferriès 2007, 524.
120 App. *B. Civ.* 5.30; Dio 48.13.2; 48.13.5.
121 App. *B. Civ.* 5.52: this embassy, because it remained with Antony throughout his winter in Alexandria, never reported to Octavian.
122 App. *B. Civ.* 5.29–31; Dio 48.13.3–5; Florus 2.16. Combès 1966, 75, proposes that in this instance (as Appian states) the people and not the troops declared Lucius imperator, but he cannot be right. See the discussion by Allély 2012, 105–7.
123 App. *B. Civ.* 5.31.
124 Dio 48.13.5.
125 Florus 2.16; cf. Allély 2012, 107.
126 Dio 48.13.5.
127 App. *B.Civ.* 5.27; 5.29.
128 App. *B. Civ.* 5.31. On Barbatius, see *MRR* 3.34; Ferriès 2007, 342–3.
129 Barbatius' coins in 41: *RRC* 517.1–3 (designating Barbatius Q.P.). Gellius' coins in 41: *RRC* 517.7–8 (designating Gellius Q.P.). Nerva's coins in 41: *RRC* 517.4–5 (designating Nerva PROQ.P.). On the position *quaestor pro praetore*, see Lintott 1999, 114–5; Pina Polo and Díaz Fernández 2019, 188–91.
130 *MRR* 2.399.
131 Cic. *Phil.* 3.3.
132 *I.Kaunos* 110: ταμίαν καὶ ἀντιστράτηγον καὶ ἀγορανόμον ἀποδειγμένον; cf. Marek 2006, 294–6. Barbatius as aedile: *ILS* 9261.
133 Pina Polo and Díaz Fernández 2019, 193–5. See also the important discussion by Badian 1983.
134 Admittedly, as Ferriès 2007, 343, astutely observes, Barbatius need not have been dishonest even if he and Antony were not on good terms.
135 Aurei: *RRC* 517.1 (obverse: head of Antony; reverse: head of Octavian); denarii: 517.2 (Antony and Octavian); 517.3 (obverse: head of Antony; reverse: head of *L. Antonius Cos*). The coins of Gellius and Nerva (see above) bear the same features. On his own behalf, Antony minted coins celebrating his brother's consulship: *RCC* 516.
136 Barbatius' armada is unattested, but in Brundisium, after the fall of Perusia, five warships were available for Fulvia's and Plancus' retreat to Antony: App. *B. Civ.* 5.50.

137 *RRC* 516; 517.4–6 (solidarity with Lucius); *RRC* 517.7–8 (solidarity with Octavian). Haymann 2016 offers a useful discussion of these coins. Beilage 2019, 142–4, is unconvincing. After Actium, Barbatus supervised the founding of a colony (*RPC* nos. 2261 and 2262), but this hardly constitutes evidence that he became a partisan of Octavian when he returned to Italy in 41, pace Ferriès 2007, 142–3.

138 Plut. *Ant.* 28–30; App. *B. Civ.* 5.9; 5.34; 5.36; Dio 48.27.1.

139 Drumann-Groebe 303; Holmes 1928, 100; Buchheim 1960, 30–1.

140 Welch 2012, 218–30.

141 Gabba 1971, 146–7; Roddaz 1988, 342–3.

142 Groag 1915, 49–51.

143 Pasquali 2009, 153–6; Halfmann 2011, 126–8.

144 Syme 1939, 215; Pelling 1996, 15–6.

145 App. *B. Civ.* 5.31.

146 App. *B. Civ.* 5.19; 5.39; 5.43; Dio 48.5.1–2.

147 App. *B. Civ.* 5.30.

148 Dio 48.13.6.

149 App. *B. Civ.* 5.31; Dio 48.14.1–2; cf. Reinhold 1933. Perusine leadership hostile to Octavian: Harris 1971, 302. No preparations for Lucius' arrival: App. *B. Civ.* 5.34 (by contrast, Dio 48.14.2 insists Perusia was well provided for a siege).

150 App. *B. Civ.* 5.33; *MRR* 2.371.

151 According to Appian, late in the siege Octavian indicated that he intended to treat Lucius leniently: *B. Civ.* 5.40.

152 App. *B. Civ.* 5.33.

153 Dio 48.22.3. Fulvia during the Perusine War: Fischer 1999, 40–7; Schultz 2021, 96–101.

154 App. *B. Civ.* 5.38.

155 Scott 1933, 23–8; Wallmann 1989, 122–7.

156 *CIL* 11.6721; Hallett 1977; see the edition by Benedetti 2012 (who assembles previous scholarship).

157 Lucius: Benedetti 2012, no. 33 (*L. Antoni calve peristi*). Octavian: e.g., Benedetti 2012, no. 29 (*laxe Octavi sede*); no. 30 (*salve Octavi felas*); no. 31 (*peto Octaviani culum*). Fulvia: Benedetti 2012, no. 32 (*peto landicam Fulviae*).

158 Invective against women in Roman society: e.g., Cooper 1992, esp. 151–5; Edwards 1993, 49–62; Hemelrijk 1999, 84–92; Tatum 2011.

159 Mart. 11.20 quotes Octavian's poem in lines 3–8. This epigram, doubtless contemporary and attributed either at the time or later to Octavian, need not be authentic (in the late republic, political poems circulated with unreliable attributions: e.g., Cic. *Q. Fr.* 1.3.9). For commentary see Hollis 2007, 284–6 (who believes this poem antedates the siege). Later in life Octavian made a practice of composing epigrams: Suet. *Aug.* 85.2; Plin. *Ep.* 5.3.5. Octavian's Fescennine verses against Pollio (Marc. 2.4.21), which prompted the latter's witty response (*at ego taceo. non est enim facile in eum scribere qui potest proscribere*) were composed sometime during the triumviral period and are frequently dated during the Perusine crisis. But certainty is impossible; see Hawkins 2017.

160 Mart. 11.20.3–8: *quod futuit Glaphyran Antonius, hanc mihi poenam / Fulvia constituit, se quoque uti futuam. / Fulviam ego ut futuam? quid si me Manius oret / pedicem? faciam? non, puto, si sapiam. / 'aut futue aut pugnemus' ait. quid, quod mihi vita / carior est ipsa mentula? signa canant!*

161 Caes. *B. Civ.* 1.9.2: *sibi semper primam fuisse dignitatem vitaque potiorem.*

162 Suet. *Iul.* 51.

163 Charles and Anagnostou-Laoutides 2012, 1083–6.

164 Makhlaiuk 2020, 222–3.

165 Non. 6.21: *calvitur dictum est frustratur: tractum a calvis mimicis, quod sint omnibus frus-tratui*; cf. Reich 1903, 23; 470; 578; Wüst 1932, 1747–8; Nicoll 1963, 87–90. On mime in the late republic, see Panayotakis 2010, 1–16.

166 Suet. *Aug.* 68.

167 Treggiari 1991, 262–90.

168 Benedetti 2012, nos. 1 and 2.

169 Borgies 2016, 269–71, however, discerns in Octavian's epigram an attack on Antony's masculinity.

170 App. *B. Civ.* 5.234–9; Dio 48.14.3; cf. *MRR* 2.381.

171 Vell. 2.75–6; Tac. *Ann.* 5.1; Suet. *Tib.* 4.2; Dio 48.15.3–4. He soon abandoned Sextus, join-ing Antony in the east (Suet. *Tib.* 4.3; Dio 54.7.2).

172 App. *B. Civ.* 5.40–9; cf. Dio 48.14.3–5; *MRR* 2.379.

173 Scott 1933, 27–8; Borgies 2016, 159–63; Wardle 2014, 137–8.

174 Prop. 1.21; 1.22. Perusia Augusta: Harris 1971, 315–6; Eck 1995.

175 App. *B. Civ.* 5.54.

176 Later in the year, during Octavian's open conflict with Antony, he regarded Julia as a reli-able intermediary between himself and her son: App. *B. Civ.* 5.63.

177 Vell. 2.76.1–3; App. *B. Civ.* 5.50; cf. *B. Civ.* 5.63; Dio 48.15.1–16.2.

CHAPTER XI

1 Dio 48.24.4–25.4; Joseph. *AJ* 13.13.3–9; *BJ* 1.13.5–9; cf. Plut. *Ant.* 30.1–3; App. *B. Civ.* 5.65.

2 *MRR* 2.384.

3 Str. 14.2.24; Dio 48.25.1–2.

4 Plut. *Ant.* 30.1–2; Dio 48.27.3–5.

5 Dio 48.26.1–5; cf. Craven 1918, 78–83; Debevoise 1938, 108–21; Magie 1950, 430–2; Bengtson 1974, 13–6; Sherwin-White 1983, 302–5; Marasco 1987, 30–6; Sullivan 1990, 309–13; van Wijlick 2021, 106–16.

6 Plut. *Ant.* 32.1; App. *B.Civ.* 5.50; Dio 48.15.2; 48.27.3–4.

7 Plut. *Ant.* 30.1–5; App. *B. Civ.* 5.52; Dio 48.27.4. During the civil war, Libo had proved himself a valuable commander to Pompey; after Pompey's defeat, he accepted Caesar's pardon but was later proscribed by the triumvirs; consequently, he joined Sextus, by then his son-in-law: cf. Syme 1986, 255–6; *MRR* 3.187; Welch 2012, 112–5.

8 App. *B. Civ.* 5.52.

9 App. *B. Civ.* 5.50.

10 Marasco 1987, 31–6.

11 *MRR* 2.384.

12 Magie 1950, 430–2; Bengtson 1974, 13–4; Sherwin-White 1983, 302–3; Marasco 1987, 31–6; Sullivan 1990, 309–13; Bivar 2008, 57; Sharon 2017, 149–55; Schlude 2020, 84–5.

13 Dio 48.26.3, correcting Plancus to Turius: *MRR* 1.382 and 385.

14 Str. 12.8.16; 14.2.24.

15 Aphrodisias: Reynolds 1982, 96–106; Alabanda: Dio 48.26.3–4; Str. 14.2.24; Miletus: Reynolds 1982, 51; Mylasa: Dio 48.26.3–4; *RDGE* 60; Stratonicea: Tac. *Ann.* 3.62.2.

16 Drumann-Groebe 1899, 303–16; Holmes 1928, 101–8; Charlesworth 1934, 43–7; Syme 1939, 215–22; Rossi 1959; 130–3; Buchheim 1960, 35–46; Gabba 1971, 152–5; Bengtson 1974, 171–9; Huzar 1978, 135–41; Chamoux 1986, 258–69; Kienast 1995, 46–50; Pelling 1996, 17–21; Osgood 2006, 187–225; Pasquali 2009, 157–68; Goldsworthy 2010, 274–9; Southern 2010, 187–95; Halfmann 2011, 130–8; Welch 2012, 230–51; Lange 2020.

17 Welch 2012, 233–6.
18 App. *B. Civ.* 5.55; 5.59. On Domitius' legions, see Brunt 1971, 486–9 and 497.
19 Fufius' death and its consequence: *MRR* 2.382. On the legions now available to each triumvir, see Brunt 1971, 496–7.
20 No communication from Antony: App. *B. Civ.* 5.63.
21 Suet. *Nero* 3.1 (condemned but innocent); App. *B. Civ.* 5.62 (condemned but innocent); Cic. *Phil.* 2.27; 2.30; Dio 48.7.4–5; 48.54.1; cf. Carlsen 2006, 68–75.
22 A different explanation of Antony's pivot is furnished by Welch 2012, 235.
23 App. *B. Civ.* 5.52; cf. Dio 48.29.1–2.
24 App. *B. Civ.* 5.62; on this passage and its usefulness for uncovering the propaganda of the moment, see Wallmann 1989, 141–6.
25 Suet. *Nero* 3.1; App. *B. Civ.* 5.62.
26 App. *B. Civ.* 5.55.
27 App. *B. Civ.* 5.56; 5.59–61.
28 App. *B. Civ.* 5.58; there is no evidence these soldiers arrived in Italy before peaceful relations were restored between Antony and Octavian.
29 App. *B. Civ.* 5.56; Dio 48.27.5.
30 App. *B. Civ.* 5.59; 5.61; 5.62; cf. Welch 2012, 235–6.
31 App. *B. Civ.* 5.53; 5.59.
32 Syme 1986, 247–9.
33 A survey of Octavian's possible motives is furnished by Berdowski 2020.
34 App. *B. Civ.* 5.53.
35 Suet. *Aug.* 62.
36 App. *B. Civ.* 5.53; Dio 48.20.4.
37 Brunt 1971, 498.
38 Dio 48. 28.2.
39 App. *B. Civ.* 5.57–8; Dio 48.28.1.
40 App. *B. Civ.* 5.58; Dio 48.28.1.
41 App. *B. Civ.* 5.49.
42 App. *B. Civ.* 5.59; 5.61; Dio 48.28.3.
43 App. *B. Civ.* 5.59; 5.61.
44 Schultz 2021, 102–3.
45 App. *B. Civ.* 5.64–64.
46 Dio 48.18.1 (Octavian's contempt for Sextus); App. *B. Civ.* 5.72 (Sextus' expectations).
47 App. *B. Civ.* 5.66; 5.68.
48 App. *B. Civ.* 5.67–8.
49 Dio 48.29.1.
50 Dio 48.30.4.
51 Dio 49.18.1–5; cf. App. *B. Civ.* 5.127; see also Dio 48.46.4; 50.1.4–5; cf. Gowing 1992, 188–9; Borgies 2016, 180–1.
52 App. *B. Civ.* 5.65.
53 Reynolds 1982, 38–9.
54 Reynolds 1982, 38–106.
55 Octavian a property owner: Reynolds 1982, 38. *Vicinitas*: Tatum 2018, 226–7.
56 Antony was, for instance, patron of Bononia: Cic. *Fam.* 12.5.2; Suet. *Aug.* 17.2. We know very little of his involvements in the western provinces, although his service under Caesar furnished him opportunities. So, too, his legislation in Rome. In the case of Genetiva Iulia (Urso), although this colony in Spain was planned by Caesar, it was ultimately founded in 44 through an Antonian law (*Lex Ursonensis* CIII); this obviously established an important relationship between Antony and the city, perhaps making him a patron (*Lex Ursonensis*

XCVII); cf. *Roman Statutes* 445. Even after Brundisium Antony will have continued to cultivate connections like these.

57 Ziethen 1994; Eilers 2002, 161–81; Jehne 2015.

58 Dio 48.31.3; Inscr. Ital. 13.1.1b; Degrassi 1954, 109; cf. Cornwell 2017, 45–7; Schumacher 2018, 93–5; Lange 2020, 139–42.

59 *Pax* and victory: Harris 1979, 35–6; Clark 2007a, 159–61; Cornwall 2017, 11–42. *Ovatio* a response to capitulation: Dion. Hal. *Ant. Rom.* 9.36.3; Gell. 5.6.20–1 (*deditione repente*).

60 Fischer 1999, 68.

61 Dio 48.31.3; Treggiari 1991, 493–5. The circumstances of Octavian's marriage to Livia involved similar issues: Dio 48.44.1.

62 Fischer 1999, 79–81. There is no reason to take seriously the suggestion (Kienast 1995, 42) that Octavian sought this marriage tie in the expectation that his sister would act as an informant in Antony's household.

63 *RRC* 527.

64 *RRC* 528.

65 *RCC* 529.

66 *ILS* 3784; cf. *AE* 2008.294 (a statue and altar to Concordia dedicated by Casinum in October of 40).

67 Dio 48.30.2–3.

68 App. *B. Civ.* 5.67.

69 Dio 48.34.1–4.

70 App. *B. Civ.* 5.68.

71 Verg. *Ecl.* 4.1–3; 7–13. There is no need here to dilate on the problematic idea of literary patronage in ancient Rome: see White 1993. On Virgil's relationship with Pollio, see Cairns 2008.

72 See, e.g., Tarn 1932; DuQuesnay 1976; Coleman 1977, 150–4; Clausen 1994, 119–30; Osgood 2006, 193–201; Havener 2016, 61–71 (who reviews recent criticism). An independent view is offered by Pelling 1996, 19.

73 The *puer* is variously identified: for a survey, see Coleman 1977, 150–2. In 39 Octavia gave birth to a daughter.

74 Serv. Auc. *ad Ecl.* 4.11.

75 DuQuesnay 1976, 30–1, puts the dramatic and actual date of the poem after Brundisium on that grounds that Pollio was unable to take up his consulship until after hostilities between Octavian and Antony were ended. But this is misleading. During the republic, it was necessary for a consul-designate to be in Rome at the time of his investiture in order to meet his sacred obligations; failure to do so, however, did not per se prevent him from entering office but instead vitiated his actions as consul; scrupulousness in this matter, however, appears to have declined during the final years of the republic; cf. Mommsen, *StR* 1.615; Konrad 2004, 300–340; Vervaet 2014, 300–340. Caesar entered his second consulship outside Rome (Caes. *B. Civ.* 3.1.1; App. *B. Civ.* 2.48) and his fourth consulship while in Spain (Dio 43.33.1). Later, Augustus entered his consulship while abroad more than once (Suet. *Aug.* 26.3). We do not know what was deemed necessary amid the irregularities of the triumvirate: Antony became consul in 34, for a single day, without coming to Rome (Dio 49.39.1), and L. Flavius became suffect consul in 33 while serving under Antony in the east (Dio 49.44.3).

76 See, for instance, Putnam 1970, 136–65; Leach 1974, 216–32; Coleman 1977, 152.

77 Burrow 1997 furnishes a basic survey.

78 Hor. *Ep.* 7. 1–2: *quo, quo scelesti ruits? aut cur dexteris / aptantur enses conditi?*

79 For a rehearsal of criticism of this poem, see Watson 2003, 266–71.

80 On the difficulties of this poem, see Watson 2003, 479–88.

81 Dio 48.32.1.
82 App. *B. Civ.* 5.66; Dio 48.33.2–3; cf. *MRR* 2.383.
83 Dio 48.32.1.
84 Dio 48.26.3; cf. *MRR* 2.382.
85 App. *B. Civ.* 5.65; Dio 48.39.2; Plut. *Ant.* 33.1 is confused; cf. Bühler 2009, 109–16. Ventidius' initial forces: Brunt 1981, 503.
86 Dio 48.40.6.
87 *Lex Fonteia* (*RS* no. 36), a still puzzling inscription. It was promulgated by C. Fonteius Capito (cos. 33), probably, at the time, a tribune of the *plebs*; cf. *MRR* 3.93. On Nicias, see Bowersock 1965, 56–6.
88 Joseph. *BJ* 1.282–5; *AJ* 14.381–5.
89 Joseph. *BJ* 1.289; *AJ* 14.394; cf. *MRR* 2.389.
90 *MRR* 2.386.
91 Nic. Dam. 96.
92 Dio 48.34–5.
93 App. *B. Civ.* 5.66 (reconciliation); 5.67 (win the war).
94 Dio 48.31.1–6.
95 App. *B. Civ.* 5.69.
96 Our evidence for the date of the pact of Misenum is inconclusive; the best analysis is by Reynolds 1982, 70–1. Betrothal: Dio 48.38.3.
97 Vell. 2.77.3; App. *B. Civ.* 5.74; Dio 48.37.1–9; cf. Welch 2012, 250–1.
98 Welch 2012, 242.
99 Syme 1939, 221–2; Gabba 1971, 155–6; Ferriès 2007, 204–7.
100 Our sources, although less than satisfactory regarding details, are clear enough on the central point: App. *B. Civ.* 5.73; Dio 48.36.4–5; 50.10.1; cf. Lange 2009, 29–31; Vervaet 2010, 83–7; Welch 2012, 243–4.
101 *MRR* 2.258.
102 Potential conflicts over property: App. *B. Civ.* 5.74. Romans were unnerved by any potential instability provoked when dishonoured or deprived aristocrats returned home: see Cicero's discussion of the perils presented by returning exiles at *Off.* 2.81–3; Cicero, when consul, opposed rehabilitating the sons of the proscribed: *Quint.* 11.1.85.
103 See below, ch. XI, pp. 282–3.
104 App. *Ill.* 28. The most important discussion is Vervaet 2010, 87–9; cf. Gabba 1970, lxviii–lxxix. This matter remains highly controversial, and most historians prefer the view that the triumvirate was intended to expire at the end of 33, even if they disagree over whether Octavian surrendered the office at that time. Vervaet 2010 reviews the issues.
105 App. *B. Civ.* 5.95; Dio 48.54.6; cf. Lange 2009, 31–3.
106 Plut. *Ant.* 33.1.
107 *I. Eph.* 4324 = *RS* 35; see ch. IX, p. 206.
108 Koortbojian 2013, 41–5.
109 Plutarch's notice that Antony was inaugurated as a favour to Octavian, however, reflects his personal construction of the episode: Pelling 1988, 206.
110 Cic. *Fin.* 5.65.
111 Treggiari 1991, 38; 467–70; Bradley 1996.
112 Plut. *Ant.* 54.1–5.
113 Antony's family: Schultz 2021, 104–6. Antony's children by Fulvia were with him at Tarentum in 37: Plut. *Ant.* 35.8.
114 Plut. *Ant.* 31.1.
115 *MRR* 2.388; cf. Sherwin-White 1983, 298–306; Bühler 2009; Sheldon 2010, 57–61; van Wijlick 2021, 106–8.

116 Dio 48.49.1.

117 *MRR* 2.388–9.

118 Pollio's triumph: *MRR* 2.387–8. His brief campaign against the Parthini: Dio 48.41.7. Pollio's triumph could have taken place in 39 or 38; sound arguments for 39 are furnished by Bosworth 1972, 466. Syme 1986, 273, suggests C. Cocceius Balbus, suffect consul in 39, as Pollio's successor: an Athenian inscription records that he, too, was hailed *imperator* (*IG* II². 4110).

119 Reynolds 1982, 75.

120 App. *B. Civ.* 5.75.

121 Plut. *Ant.* 33.6–34.1; App. *B. Civ.* 5.76; Dio 48.39.1–2; cf. Tatum 2020a.

122 Plut. *Ant.* 60.6; cf. Hurwit 1999, 278.

123 Drumann-Groebe 1899, 322–6; Holmes 1928, 108–10; 120–3; Tarn 1934, 51–5; Syme 1939, 259–63; Rossi 1959; 147–9; Buchheim 1960, 49–83; Gabba 1971, 152–5; Bengtson 1974, 49–83; Huzar 1978, 156–68; 173–5; Chamoux 1986, 270–80; Marasco 1987, 37–63; Wallmann 1989, 177–83; 220–38; Pelling 1996, 21–2; Pasquali 2009, 169–75; Goldsworthy 2010, 279–88; Southern 2010, 196–202; Halfmann 2011, 139–46; Worthington 2021, 234–41.

124 App. *B. Civ.* 5.75.

125 Syme 1986, 273.

126 *MRR* 2.392.

127 *MRR* 2.393.

128 *MRR* 2.389.

129 Antony cheats Sextus: Dio 48.39.1; *De vir. Ill.* 84.4. Octavian interferes: Dio 48.46.1. Octavian claims Antony joins him in renouncing the Misenum agreement: App. *B. Civ.* 5.80. Propaganda conflict: Scott 1933, 3–5; Gabba 1970, 132–3; Marasco 1987, 40–1; Gowing 1992, 188–9; Borgies 2016, 201–6. Antony's alleged mistreatment of this region is often taken for granted: e.g., Drumann-Groebe 314; Rostovtzeff 1941, 1012–3; Bengtson 1977, 155; Halfmann 2011, 106.

130 App. *B. Civ.* 5.77.

131 Plut. *Ant.* 67.3; Paus. 4.3.1; 8.8.2; cf. Owens 1976, 726; Bowersock 1965.

132 Balzat and Millis 2013; cf. Spawforth 1996.

133 Larsen 1938, 726.

134 Balzat and Millis 2013.

135 Dio 48.39.1.

136 Socrates of Rhodes, *BNJ* 192 F 2.

137 *IG* II² 1043; see ch. IX, p. 202.

138 Plut. *Ant.* 33.9.

139 Kroll no. 143; cf. Kroll 1993, 102–3.

140 Hemelrijk 1999, 104–8 assembles the evidence.

141 *SEG* 12.149; cf. Raubitshek 1946 (whose suggestion that Octavia was worshipped as Athena Polias should be rejected); Geagan 2011, 137. On the role of benefactor in the regal ideology of Greek cities, see Ma 2000, 206–11.

142 *RPC* 1.2202; 1.2202. Even Octavian is implicated in Antony's Dionysiac imagery on an Ephesian coin—*Classical Numismatic Group*, 94 (18 September 2013), lot 999 (see Ferriès and Delrieux 2017, 367)—which depicts the triumvirs in jugate on its obverse and Dionysiac motifs on its reverse.

143 App. *B. Civ.* 5.76.

144 Athenian honours for Octavia: Plut. *Ant.* 57.2. Public appearances with Antony: App. *B. Civ.* 5.76.

145   *RPC* 1.1454; 1.1463. On Antony's Fleet Coinage (so-called owing to its imagery), see Crawford 1985, 270–1; Rowan 2019, 86–8; Carbone 2020 (assembling previous scholarship and discussing questions of chronology).

146   *RPC* 515.

147   Sextus: *RRC* 511/1. Octavian: *RRC* 534/2. Discussion: Powell 2002; Welch 2012, 182–90. The suitability of such images for signaling *pietas* may lie in their relationship with family *imagines*; see the speculative but suggestive remarks by Woytek 2014, 58–61.

148   *RPC* 1.1455; 1.1459; 1.1460; 1.1462; 1.1464; 1.1468; 1.1469.

149   *RPC* 1.1456; 1.1461; 1.1465; 1.1470.

150   Thonemann 2015, 145–68.

151   *RPC* 1.2202; presumably Octavia should be viewed as the divine consort of the New Dionysus (Wood 1999, 48–9). It is possible that a coin of Ephesus (*RPC* 1.2574) portrays a solitary Octavia—the identification is urged on stylistic grounds (the figure is unnamed)—but this must remain highly uncertain.

152   Octavia on Antony's coinage: Fischer 1999, 171–215; Wood 1999, 41–53. The influence of Antony's coinage on imperial portraits: Ferriès and Delrieux 2017.

153   Plut. *Ant.* 33.7; App. *B. Civ.* 5.76.

154   Plaut. *Pers.* 99; Ter. *Ad.* 535.

155   Scott 1933, 45–6; Borgies 2016, 297–303.

156   Sen. *Suas.* 1.7; Dio 48.39.2. Fabrication: Tarn 1934, 54; Nock 1972, 204. This story does not gain credence from Octavia's deification in Athens, *contra* Raubitshek 1946.

157   Theopomp. *BNJ* 115 F31; Rhianus fr. 1 (Powell).

158   Clem. Al. *Protr.* 4.54; cf. Plut. *Dem.* 26.5; Mastrocinque 1979, 265. A different view of this passage is taken by O'Sullivan 2008.

159   *RDGE* 27 (Stratonicea); Reynolds 1982, documents 6, 8, and 9 (Aphrodisias); *Milet.* 1.3 no. 126 (Miletus); Reynolds 1982, document 7 (Rhodes, Lycia, Laodicea, Tarsus); cf. Magie 1950, 1282.

160   Ateporix: Str. 12.3.37; cf. Magie 1950, 435; 1285. Nicias: Str. 14.2.19; Suet. *Gramm.* 14; Magie 1950, 1278. Strato: Str. 12.3.14; Magie 1950, 1284. Hybreas: Str. 14.2.24; cf. Bowersock 1965, 5–6. Cleon: Str. 12.8.8–9.

161   Str. 12.8.16; 14.2.24; cf. Magie 1950, 433; 1282–3; Sullivan 1990, 161–3.

162   Str. 12.6.3–4; App. *B. Civ.* 5.75; cf. Magie 1950, 433; 1282–3.

163   On the Romans' conception of its empire, see ch. II, pp. 35–6.

164   Badian 1958, 289.

165   Magie 1950, 418. Cic. *Phil.* 11.30 will not support the argument that Cilicia had been disestablished by 44.

166   Magie 1950, 434; Sullivan 1990, 190; Mustafa 2001; see ch. IX, p. 211.

167   Dio 48.40.6.

168   On Antony's reorganization of Cilicia, see Marasco 1987, 50–6 (assembling sources and scholarship).

169   Marasco 1987, 52–3; Roller 2010, 90–5.

170   *RPC* 1.908a–g; 909a–o; 910a–e; 911a–s; 912a–g; 913a–b; 914; 915; 916; 917; 918; cf. Buttrey 1983; Crawford 1985, 253. Roman administration of the Cyrenaica down to Actium is attested by *RRC* 546.

171   Rigsby 1996; España-Chamorro 2012.

172   Rostovtzeff 1957, 308–11; 680–1.

173   Perl 1970; Perl 1971; Sanders 1982, 6–11; Bowsky 2002; Pałuchowski 2005; Chevrollier 2016. There is no reason to believe that, when Octavian and Antony came to blows, Gortyn favoured the former and Cnossos the latter; cf. Bowsky 2001. This reform may well have originated with Caesar: see ch. VI, pp. 140–1.

174   Str. 12.3.14; App. *B. Civ.* 5.75; Dio 49.32–3; Magie 1950, 434–6; Buchheim 1960, 49–51; Jones 1971, 166–7; Marasco 1987, 47–9; Mitchell 1993, 38–9; Marek 2006, 40–1; Madsen 2016, 30.
175   App. *B. Civ.* 5.75.
176   App. *B. Civ.* 5.75; Magie 1950, 433; 1282–3; Sullivan 1990, 161–3.
177   Str. 12.3.41; Plut. *Ant.* 61.1; 63.3; Dio 50.13.5; Str 12.3.41; Magie 1950, 434; Marasco 1987, 48.
178   Str. 12.5.1; App. *B. Civ.* 5.75; Dio 49.32.3; Magie 1950, 433; 1282–3; Bowersock 1965, 51; Sullivan 1990, 169–74.
179   Str. 12.3.28: the modern district in Turkey is now called Vezirköprü.
180   Str. 12.3.38; cf. Magie 1950, 434–5. On Lycomedes, see ch. IX, p. 211.
181   Str. 12.3.39; cf. 12.3.14—each to be read with Magie 1950, 1284–5.
182   Str. 12.3.37, but see Magie 1950, 1283, for difficulties in unpacking this passage.
183   App. *B. Civ.* 5.75.
184   On Antony's manpower at this time, see Brunt 1971, 502–7.
185   See ch. II, pp. 39–40.
186   P. Bingen 45; cf. Minnen 2000. Not Cleopatra's autograph: Sarri 2018, 168.
187   Plut. *Ant.* 56.3–4.
188   Zimmermann 2002.
189   *MRR* 3.50; cf. Val. Max. 6.2.12.
190   Wiseman 1971, 222.
191   Bean 1954, 93.
192   Suet. *Aug.* 62.2; Dio 48.34.3; this divorce, perhaps controversial at the time, stimulated later polemic from Antony's supporters; cf. Wardle 2014, 407; Borgies 2016, 264–6.
193   Dio 48.44.1–2.
194   App. *B. Civ.* 5.77.
195   App. *B. Civ.* 5.77–80; Dio 49.46.1–4.
196   App. *B. Civ.* 5.80.
197   App. *B. Civ.* 5.80.
198   Plut. *Ant.* 34.5–7; Dio 49.20.5–49.21.1–2.
199   Oros. 6.18.32; Joseph. *AJ* 14.15.8–9; *BJ* 1.16.7.
200   Sherwin-White 1983, 306, is a distinguished example; further discussion at Marasco 1987, 43–6 (Marasco suggests Antony won Antiochus over through diplomacy) and van Wijlick 2021, 199–203.
201   Dio 48.41.5.
202   Ventidius a theme in anti-Antonian propaganda: Reinhold 1988, 49–50; Pelling 1988, 231; Wallmann 1989, 234–8; Borgies 2016, 362.
203   Plutarch's literary agenda: Pelling 1988, 231; Tatum 2020a, 452–6; at Plut. *Ant.* 34.8 Antony's decency is affirmed: 'he returned to Athens and then honoured Ventidius as he deserved'.
204   It appears Antony at least entertained the possibility of crossing into Parthia by way of Zeugma, in which case the loyalty of Samosata was indispensable: see ch. XII, pp. 290–1.
205   Dio 49.23.1–4; cf. Huzar 1978, 175; Marasco 1987, 45; Sullivan 1990, 197.
206   Tarn 1934, 53.
207   Bowersock 1965, 57–8; Sullivan 1990, 197–8.
208   Dio 48.41.6; cf. Str. 16.2.14.
209   Brunt 1971, 503.
210   Plut. *Ant.* 34.8; *MRR* 2.393; *RRC* 531 commemorates Ventidius' acclamation as *imperator*: he appears on the reverse, Antony on the obverse. Ventidius died soon afterwards and received a state funeral (Gell. 15.4.4), another Antonian advertisement.

211   Dio 48.41.5.
212   *MRR* 2.389; 2.393.
213   *MRR* 2.394.
214   *MRR* 3.391; cf. Welch 2012, 262–7.
215   App. *B. Civ.* 5.80; Dio 48.43.1; 48.53.5–6.
216   Dio 48.54.7.
217   App. *B. Civ.* 5.92.
218   App. *B. Civ.* 5.92; Dio 48.49.4.
219   *MRR* 2.393; 397–8; 412–3; cf. Sharon 2017, 155–65. Sosius' triumph took place in 34.
220   Dio 48.41.6; 49.22.3; cf. Str. 16.2.14.
221   Strab. 11.3.5; Plut. *Ant.* 34.10; Dio 49.24.1; cf. Sherwin-White 1983, 307; Marasco 1987, 70–3; van Wijlick 2021, 181–7.
222   Caesar: Suet. *Caes.* 44.3. Gabinius: see ch. II, p. 46.
223   Plut. *Ant.* 35.1–8; App. *B. Civ.* 5.93–5; Dio 48.54.1–7; *MRR* 2.396. Drumann-Groebe 1899, 327–8; Holmes 1928, 112–3; Tarn 1934, 54–5; 58–9; Syme 1939, 224–6; Rossi 1959; 148–9; Bengtson 1974, 182–3; Huzar 1978, 142–3; Chamoux 1986, 281–4; Wallmann 1989, 199–210; Kienast 1995, 50–4; Pelling 1996, 24–7; Osgood 2006, 242–3; Pasquali 2009, 175–9; Goldsworthy 2010, 289–90; Southern 2010, 202–4; Halfmann 2011, 145–7; Welch 2012, 268–9; Lange 2009, 31–3.
224   Gabba 1970, xv.
225   Plut. *Ant.* 35.1–8; App. *B. Civ.* 5.92–3; Dio 48.52.1–7; cf. Gabba 1970, xxxvi; Gowing 1992, 195.
226   Dio 48.54.1.
227   Syme 1939, 225–6, speculates sensibly that Antony 'may have hoped that his military genius as well as his ships would be enlisted to deal with Pompeius. But Octavian would have none of it'. It is perhaps relevant that, not long before his friendly invasion of Italy, Antony minted coins on the obverse of which he is depicted, in full length, as a general resting his foot on a ship's prow, an obvious claim of mastery of the sea; on the reverse is a lion holding a sword in its mouth, the seal, according to Plutarch (*Pomp.* 80.7), of Pompey the Great: cf. *RRC* 533.1 with Crawford's commentary on p. 743.
228   App. *B. Civ.* 5.97.
229   Octavian's failure to deliver: App. *B. Civ.* 5.134.
230   Suet. *Nero* 5.1; Dio 48.54.4.
231   Suet. *Aug.* 63.4; Dio 48.54.4; 51.15.5.
232   Allély 2004, 179–81.
233   These constitutional issues remain controversial: it is often maintained that the triumvirs backdated the extension of their office and therefore the triumvirate was set to expire in 33, but here I follow the persuasive, in my view decisive, arguments of Gabba 1970, lxvii–lxxix and Vervaet 2010, 80–97 (who accumulates earlier scholarship).
234   App. *Ill.* 28.
235   *CIL* 6.2028c.
236   The cynicism of Dio 48.54.3–6, in this instance, is worth taking seriously; cf. Drumann-Groebe 1899, 328; Rossi 1959, 149; Pasquali 2009, 179.

CHAPTER XII

1   Joseph. *AJ* 15.8–10; *BJ* 1.357; Plut. *Ant.* 36.4; Dio 49.22.6.
2   Joseph. *AJ* 15.92; *BJ* 1.440; Dio 49.32.5; Porphyry *BNJ* 260 F2; cf. Sullivan 1990, 207–8; Sharon 2017, 149–50; van Wijlick 2021, 167–72.

3   Cleopatra's gains: Joseph. *AJ* 15.79; 15.92–6; *BJ* 1.360–2; Plut. *Ant.* 36.1–2; Dio 49.32.2–5; cf. Buchheim 1960, 64–68; Marasco 1987, 52–8; Volkmann 1953, 116–20; Will 1982, 543–9; Höbl 2001, 241–2; Roller 2010, 90–6; Sartre 2018, 178–91; van Wijlick 2021, 130–6.

4   Marasco 1987, 52–3.

5   Plut. *Ant.* 36.1.

6   Plut. *Ant.* 36.5; Dio 49.32.4.

7   Roller 2010, 95; Sartre 2018, 191.

8   Liv. *Per.* 132; Dio 49.32.5.

9   Dio 49.32.5 is our sole source for Cleopatra's acquisitions in Crete and the Cyrenaica. Even if she made some gains, this Roman province subsisted; see ch. VI, pp. 140–1 and XI, pp. 271–5.

10 Joseph. *AJ* 15.79; 15.91–4; 15.95; 15.258.

11 Plut. *Ant.* 36.4; Dio 49.32.4; cf. Pelling 1988, 218–9; Wallman 1989, 256–62.

12 Examples include Letronne 1848, 90–3; Kromayer 1894, 582–4; Tarn 1934, 55 and 66; Volkmann 1953, 116–8; Bengtson 1977, 194; Chamoux 1986, 285–6; Sartre 2018, 192–3. Holmes 1928, 127–31, rehearses the controversy down to his day, and Ager 2013, who rejects the idea that Cleopatra and Antony ever married, assembles further references.

13 Roller 2010, 167–8, argues (unpersuasively) that Cleopatra was a Roman citizen.

14 Caes. *B. Civ.* 3.110.2.

15 Scott 1933, 41–4; Borgies 2016, 276–80; Aufrère 2018, 48–50.

16 Verg. *Aen.* 8.688: … *sequiturque—nefas—Aegypta coniunx.*

17 Liv. *Per.* 131: *Antonius … uxoris loco … habere coeperat.* Str. 17.1.11: Ἀντώνιος … ἐξετίμησεν ἐπὶ πλέον τὴν Κλεοπάτραν, ὥστε καὶ γυναῖκα ἔκρινε καὶ ἐτεκνοποιήσατο ἐξ αὐτῆς. Vell. 2.82.4.

18 Cleopatra Antony's lover: Plut. *Ant.* 31.3; 53.9–10. Cleopatra Antony's wife: *Comp. Dem. Ant.* 4.1; cf. Pelling 1988, 219–20.

19 Sen. *Suas.* 1.6: Ὀκταουία καὶ Ἀθηνᾶ Ἀντωνίῳ· *res tuas tibi habe* (a formula for divorce). Seneca explains the joke by reporting that Antony 'had both Octavia and Cleopatra as a wife'.

20 Athenaeus, in clarifying a notice in Socrates of Rhodes, describes Cleopatra as married to Antony: Ath.147f; cf. Eutropius 7.6; Servius *ad Aen.* 7.684; Oros. 6.19.11.

21 Suet. *Aug.* 69.2. Suetonius, for tactical reasons (he wants the reader to credit its criticisms of Augustus), describes this as a friendly letter (*scribit … familiariter*).

22 Cic. *Off.* 1.134; cf. Corbeil 2002.

23 On the correct sense of *uxor mea est* in this letter (it is a query not a statement), see Kraft 1967; Moles 1992.

24 Adams 1982, 190–1.

25 Ov. *Rem. Am.* 399–404 (lines 402–4: *ineas quamlibet ante velim;/quamlibet inuenias in qua tua prima voluptas/desinat*).

26 Dunkle 1967; Holt 1988; Baragwanath 2008, 153–4.

27 Lucretia: Liv. 1.57–9; cf. Ogilvie 1965, 218–20. Verginia: Liv. 3.44–9; cf. Ogilvie 1965, 476–9.

28 Wardle 2014, 443, proposes identifications.

29 Roller 2010, 100.

30 Ager 2013, 147–8 (extensive references assembled in n.38; add Sartre 2018, 192–3).

31 *RPC* 4094, 4095, 4096. Cleopatra's denomination as Newer Goddess remains a difficulty: see Bonner and Nock 1948; Nock 1972, 150; Howgego 1993, 203; Sartre 2018, 133–4.

32 Mints: Butcher 2004, 55–7; Oliver and Parisot-Sillon 2013; Aumaître 2018.

33 *RPC* only tentatively dates these coins to 36; Neumann 2021, 122–3 is highly cautious. In favour of 36: i.a. Butcher 2004, 55–7; Oliver and Parisot-Sillon 2013, 258–61; Oliver and Aumaître 2017; Aumaître 2018; Rowan 2019, 94–6; Carbone 2020, 36 (all with further

references). This dating inevitably hangs on the special circumstances of Cleopatra's reception. Emphasis is also placed on a hiatus at Antioch in the production of tetradrachms bearing the name and image of Philip Philadelphus, the last Seleucid ruler of Syria. After Syria's annexation, Rome permitted or encouraged the minting of these so-called Posthumous Philips (Butcher 2004, 53; McAlee 2007, 64–6; Neumann 2021, 117–22). A significant gap in their production occurs from 36–31. Our tetradrachms, it is urged, explain this cessation: they were produced to fill it (Oliver and Parisot-Sillon 2013, 258–61; Aumaître 2018). But prior to 36 more than one year-length gap in the production of Posthumous Philips is observable. Consequently, a gap of one or even two years or so could hardly be remarkable. Which leaves no decisive argument for dating our coins to 36.

34 Allotee de la Fuÿe 1904.
35 Buttrey 1954, 97. One need not accept all Buttrey's arguments regarding these coins to be persuaded on their dating: Antony's Fleet coinage (see ch. XI, pp. 270–1) extends to 35, after which (or, just possibly, during which) year it makes the best sense to locate Octavia's numismatic replacement by Cleopatra. Carbone 2020, 51, citing Amandry 1990, 80–3, dates the Fleet coinage to 38–37, but Amandry 1990, 83, concedes that any date down to 35 is possible for these coins.
36 *RRC* 539.
37 Dio 49.25.1.
38 Plut. *Ant.* 37.3.
39 Plut. *Ant.* 37.1–2; Dio 49.23–4.
40 Justin 42.4.10–5.2; Plut. *Ant.* 37.1–2; Dio 49.23.2–5.
41 Aug. *Mon. Anc.* 29.2; Suet. *Aug.* 21.3; cf. Cooley 2009, 242–3; Wardle 2014, 177–81.
42 See ch. II, pp. 47–51.
43 *MRR* 2.224; 2.230; cf. Sherwin-White 1983, 282–90; Bivar 1983, 49–57; Sampson 2008, 94–107; Sheldon 2010, 29–49; Weggen 2011.
44 *MRR* 2.229.
45 Bivar 1983, 56; Sheldon 2010, 50–6; Schlude 2012; van Wijlick 2021, 67–8.
46 Brunt 1971, 503–4; Malitz 1984; Syme 1999, 174–92; Pelling 2011, 436–8; van Wijlick 2021, 65–8; see ch. V, p. 107.
47 Sherwin-White 1983, 210.
48 Our sources are rarely interested in auxiliary forces and so we are not told when or how Antony acquired his Gallic and Iberian squadrons. Perhaps these men had long been serving in the east. Or perhaps, as their identifications suggest, they were acquired from Spain and Gaul. Antony's political connections in these regions, especially Gaul, may have played a role in recruiting these units—such contacts were often important in activating auxiliaries—but, if so, Octavian's cooperation will have been indispensable. On auxiliaries and their recruitment, see Prag 2015. Sherwin-White 1983, 315, suggests that Antonius' Iberian cavalry were raised by Canidius in Asian Iberia.
49 Brunt 1971, 503–4; Sherwin-White 1983, 311; Pelling 1988, 223; van Wijlick 2021, 120–1.
50 Plut. *Ant.* 37.3. These included Polemo, who joined the expedition: Plut. *Ant.* 38.6; Dio 49.25.4.
51 Plut. *Ant.* 37–51; Dio 49.24–32; cf. *MRR* 2.400.
52 Plut. *Ant.* 37.6.
53 Tatum 2011, 183–4; *FRHist.* 424–5.
54 Honoured by Augustus: Sen. *Clem.* 1.10.1. Honoured by Horace: *Carm.* 2.2.
55 Dio 49.39.2.
56 Sen. *Suas.* 1.7.

57 Dramatic elements: night combat: *Ant*. 47.4–5; 48.4–6; fraternization: *Ant*. 40.2–5; 46.1–3; Parthian awe: *Ant*. 39; Parthian appreciation: *Ant*. 49.3; mysterious guide: *Ant*. 41.1–4; mysterious diplomat: *Ant*. 46.4–7; 48.1–3; cf. Pelling 1988, 221.

58 Plut. *Ant*. 59.6–8 = Dellius *FRHist*. fr. 2.

59 Pelling 1988, 10–26; 220–1.

60 Antony evokes the comparison at Plut. *Ant*. 45.12; cf. Pelling 2002, 15 and 38–9.

61 Sources for Antony's invasions: Plut. *Ant*. 37–51; Dio 49.24–49.32; cf. *MRR* 2.400. Discussion: Kromayer 1896; Drumann-Groebe 1899, 329–37; Craven 1918, 111–42; Holmes 1928, 123–8; Tarn 1934, 71–5; Debevoise 1938, 121–33; Syme 1939, 264–5; Buchheim 1960, 76–9; Bengtson 1974; Bengtson 1977, 184–205; Huzar 1978, 176–80; Chamoux 1986, 289–99; Marasco 1987, 65–75; Wallmann 1989, 262–8; Pelling 1996, 30–4; Pasquali 2009, 183–90; Goldsworthy 2010, 293–320; Southern 2010, 211–8; Sheldon 2010, 65–80; Halfmann 2011, 153–62; K.R. Jones 2017; van Wijlick 2021, 116–25.

62 Plut. *Ant*. 38.1; Dio 49.25.1.

63 Str. 11.3.4; cf. Plut. *Ant*. 37.3; Dio 49.25.1. This move on Antony's part is sometimes regarded as a feint (e.g. Kromayer 1896, 100–1; Holmes 1928, 125; Bengtson 1974, 22) but this seems unlikely: Sherwin-White 1983, 309; van Wijlick 2021, 119–20.

64 Sherwin-White 1983, 311.

65 Plut. *Ant*. 37.5–38.1; Liv. *Per*. 130; cf. Pelling 1988, 224.

66 Plut. *Ant*. 38.2.

67 Plut. *Ant*. 47.1. Antony's route: Sherwin-White 1983, 312–3. Alternatives have been proposed: e.g., Holmes 1928, 123–8; Tarn 1934, 73–4. The site of Phraaspa, indicated by literary sources (Str. 11.13.3; Plut. *Ant*. 38.2; 50.1; Livy *Ep*. 130), remains undiscovered.

68 Plut. *Ant*. 38.1.

69 Sherwin-White 1983, 313. Profitable Roman plundering is obliquely suggested by an episode in Plutarch's narrative: *Ant*. 48.3–4; see, too, Plin. *NH* 33.83 (a golden statue seized as plunder during the Parthian campaign: *Antonii Parthicis rebus*), although this garbled anecdote may refer to actions that took place during Antony's attack on Armenia in 34.

70 Dio 49.24.2.

71 According to Dio, Artavasdes could have come to Statianus' aid but refused (Dio 49.25.5). In later propaganda, Antony claimed that Octavian had tampered with Artavasdes' loyalties: Dio 49.41.5; cf. Scott 1933, 37.

72 Dio 49.33.2; 49.44.2.

73 The baggage train must have come close to arriving when it was attacked: Pelling 1988, 226.

74 Dio 49.26.1–2.

75 According to Plutarch, Phraates feared desertions (*Ant*. 40.2)—or perhaps something worse, if Plutarch's claim reflects information about tensions between the king and his vassals that were exacerbated by the Romans' pertinacity; cf. Pelling 1988, 228.

76 Plutarch's choice of words at *Ant*. 41.3 (appropriating an expression from Xenophon) suggests these villages were prosperous places; cf. Pelling 1988, 231.

77 Plut. *Ant*. 46.4–7.

78 Pelling 1988, 232–3, assembles parallels.

79 Pelling 1988, 232.

80 *RRC* 541.

81 Plut. *Ant*. 44.3–5; cf. Pelling 1988, 233–4.

82 Flor. 2.20.9 indicates a march through Cappadocia. It is uncertain just where the troops wintered. Syria seems likeliest.

83 Dio 49.31.4.

84 Syme 1939, 64, a view shared by Roddaz 2012, 125–7.

85 Eminent examples include: Huzar 1978, 179–80; Pelling 1996, 34; Osgood 2006, 305; Pasquali 2009, 190; Roller 2010, 80.

86 Fundamental is Rosenstein 1990; quotation on page 172.

87 J.H. Clark 2014.

88 Dio 49.33.1.

89 In recognition of Polemo's loyalty and the part he played in bringing over Artavasdes, Antony added Lesser Armenia to his domain: Dio 49.33.2; 49.44.3.

90 Plut. *Ant.* 61.3. Betrothal: of Iotape and Alexander: Dio 49.44.2. Thereafter, doubtless at Antony's insistence, Iotape lived in Alexandria: Dio 51.16.2. Prior to Actium, according to Dio, Artavasdes was captured by Phraates (Dio 49.44.4), but this conflict probably took place after Antony's defeat (Sullivan 1990, 297–300); if Artavasdes was captured, he either escaped or was released, because he took refuge with Octavian (*Mon. Anc.* 32.1) and was established by him as king of Lesser Armenia (Dio 51.16.2; 54.9.2).

91 Vell. 2.82.3 (*victoriam vocabat*); Florus 2.20.10 (*quasi vicisset*).

92 Octavian attacks Antony's Parthian expedition at Dio 50.27.5.

93 Verg. *Aen.* 8.686 (Antony appears at the battle of Actium, depicted on the shield of Aeneas); Serv. *ad Aen.* 8.686: *quia primo vicerat Parthos*. Horace, by contrast, lumps Antony and Crassus together as Romans crushed by the Parthians (*Carm.* 3.6.9–10).

94 Rumours: App. *B. Civ.* 5.133; Dio 49.33.1–2.

95 van Wijlick 2021, 121–2, offers a useful summary of the difficulties in reckoning Antony's losses.

96 Dio 49.32.1.

97 *MRR* 2.399–400; Welch 2012, 261–79.

98 *MRR* 2.400.

99 App. *B. Civ.* 5.130.

100 App. *B. Civ.* 5.132.

101 Sextus' popularity: Vell. 2.79.6.

102 App. *B. Civ.* 5.132.

103 Vell. 2.81; App. *B. Civ.* 5.128–9; Dio 49.13–5.

104 App. *B. Civ.* 5.127; Dio 49.11.1.

105 Vell. 2.80; Liv. *Per.* 129; Suet. *Aug.* 16.4; App. *B. Civ.* 5.124–6; Dio 49.14.6–15.6.; cf. Allély 2004, 239–46.

106 Wardle 2014, 145.

107 Liv. *Per.* 129 perhaps suggests *abrogatio*, but this is unlikely (this was a decree that annulled a law *in toto*); *obrogatio* and *derogatio*, although poorly understood, were senatorial actions neutralizing a part of an existing law: Cic. *Rep.* 3.33; Asc. 68–9C; cf. Tatum forthcoming.

108 Vell. 2.88.

109 App. *B. Civ.* 5.132.

110 Scott 1933, 34; Borgies 2016, 207–8.

111 Betrothal: Dio 44.53.6. Preparations for marriage: App. *B. Civ.* 5.93.

112 Vell. 2.88.4.

113 *OGIS* 377. This explanation of Antonia Euergetes originated with Mommsen 1872; it is widely accepted, by (i.a.) Tarn 1934, 78; Syme 1939, 262; Huzar 1978, 230; Goldsworthy 2010, 329; Southern 2010, 36; Roller 2010, 91.

114 The phrase belongs to Sherwin-White 1973, 309–10.

115 Thonemann 2004, esp. 148–9; cf. Dessau 1913; Magie 1950, 1130 n. 60; Bowersock 1965, 8 n. 4.

116 *MRR* 2.408–9; cf. Bengtson 1977, 209–13; Halfmann 2011, 162–4; Welch 2012, 279–84.

117 App. *B. Civ.* 5.144.

118 Wallmann 1989, 268–74; Pasquali 2009, 196–8; Borgies 2016, 180–2.

119 Dio 49.18.6–7.

120 According to Dio, Antony later offered to abdicate (Dio 49.41.6; 50.7.1–2). It is, however, very likely that in 35 Antony associated himself with Octavian's declaration that, after the completion of the campaign against Parthia, both men would demit office.

121 App. *B. Civ.* 5.132.

122 Taylor 1954, 518.

123 Although Cleopatra is occasionally located alongside Antony (e.g., Chemoux 1986, 309; Goldsworthy 2010, 320), neither Plutarch's fantastic account of the ruses she put to work in playing on Antony's affections (Plut. *Ant.* 53.6–7) nor Josephus' account of their exchanges during this year regarding Herod (*AJ* 15.23–79) is a satisfactory basis for believing Cleopatra was in Antony's company when he left Alexandria.

124 Plut. *Ant.* 52.1–3; 53.1–2; App. *B. Civ.* 5.133–45; Dio 49.33.1–4.

125 Millar 1964, 89–90; Reinhold 1988, 9–11. Lintott 1997, 2505–11. On this problem in Dio's treatment of the Armenian campaign, see Buchheim 1960, 120–1 (n. 209).

126 Joseph. *AJ* 15.23–79; cf. Sullivan 1990, 126; Roller 2010, 119–21; Goldsworthy 2010, 300–1; Sartre 2018, 136–8.

127 Plut. *Ant.* 53.1–4; App. *B. Civ.* 5.138; Dio 49.33.4; cf. Drumann-Groebe 1899, 338–9; Holmes 1928, 130; Tarn 1934, 76–8; Syme 1939, 265; Volkmann 1953, 128–36; Buchheim 1960, 84–8; Bengtson 1977, 208–9; Huzar 1978, 181; Chamoux 1986, 306–9; Marasco 1987, 76–82; Wallman 1989, 274–80; Pelling 1996, 39; Fischer 1999, 98–101; Osgood 2006, 336–8; Pasquali 2009, 192–5; Roller 2010, 97–8; Goldsworthy 2010, 324–7; Southern 2010, 221–2; Halfmann 2011, 165–6; Sartre 2018, 202–3.

128 App. *B. Civ.* 5.138 describes Octavia as 'spending the winter in Athens', but if she spent the winter of 36/5 in Athens while Antony was in Alexandria with Cleopatra, it is nothing short of astonishing that we hear nothing else of this insult. Presumably this notice is somewhat garbled and Octavia came east intending to remain through the winter of 35/4. Gabba 1970, 231, however, places Octavia in Athens during the winter of 36/5.

129 Plut. *Ant.* 53.1; cf. Pelling 1988, 244.

130 This is the highly influential view of Syme 1939, 265. By contrast, Buchheim 1960, 86–8, proposed that it was something in Octavian's letter to Antony 'regarding the government', mentioned by App. *B. Civ.* 5.132, that stimulated estrangement.

131 Plut. *Ant.* 54.1–5; 57.4–5.

132 Antony instructs Octavia to await him (προσμένειν): Plut. *Ant.* 53.2 with Buchheim 1960, 85.

133 Dio 49.33.4; cf. Pelling 1988, 244–5.

134 App. *B. Civ.* 5.138 reports that Sextus very nearly gained possession of this cavalry as it made its way to Antony. This is our sole synchronization between Octavia's visit and the campaign against Sextus, but it suffices to make it clear how long the lag was between Octavia's arrival and her later dismissal.

135 Plut. *Ant.* 54.1–5; cf. Pelling 1988, 248–9; Borgies 2016, 276–80. Halfmann 2011, 165–6, however, rejects the idea that, at the time, Octavian was perturbed by Antony's treatment.

136 *RPC* 1.4741; 4742; 4771; cf. 4094; 4095; 4096; 924 and 925 do not carry portraits; *RRC* 543. *RPC* 1.4752 is a possible jugate portrait, but see Meshorer 1987/87, who argues that this coin depicts Cleopatra and Caesarion.

137 Smith 1988, 133–4.

138 See, recently, Oliver and Parisot-Sillon 2013, 264–6; Aumaître 2018.

139 Buttrey 1954, 108; see also the useful observations in Beilage 2019, 145–6.

140 Plut. *Ant.* 60.2–3; 86.5; Dio 50.5.2–3; 50.5.2–50.15.2.

141 Charisius ap. Keil, *Gramm. Lat.*, vol. 1, 104.

142 Dio 50.15.2, a notice accepted as genuine by (e.g.) Hurwit 1999, 278, but rejected by Pelling 1988, 265–6.

143 Plut. *Ant.* 86.5; cf. *OGIS* 195.

144 Hor. *Carm.* 1.37.21; cf. *Epod.* 9.11–6.

145 Dio 50.4.1; 50.5.3.

146 Syme 1939, 274.

147 Plut. *Ant.* 53.5–10; 59.3.

148 Plut. *Ant.* 53.5–10.

149 Plut. *Ant.* 60.1; Dio 50.5.3.

150 Plut. *Ant.* 58.11.

151 Plut. *Ant.* 58.10.

152 Plut. *Ant.* 58.11; Dio 50.5.1–2; 50.6.1; 51.9.5.

153 Syme 1939, 274.

154 Dio 49.39.1; cf. *MRR* 2.410.

155 Plut. *Ant.* 50.6–7; Dio 49.39–40; 49.44; *MRR* 2.411; cf. Drumann-Groebe 1899, 339; Tarn 1934, 78–9; Holmes 1928, 136–7; Buchheim 1960, 90–1; Bengtson 1977, 214–6; Huzar 1978, 181–2; Chamoux 1986, 310–2; Marasco 1987, 82–5; Wallmann 1989, 284–8; Pelling 1996, 39–40; Pasquali 2009, 199–201; Goldsworthy 2010, 329–30; Halfmann 2011, 169–72; Southern 2012, 223–6; Wijlick 2021, 187–90.

156 Tac. *Ann.* 2.3.1. Octavian defamation: Scott 1933, 37; Wallmann 1989, 284–91. Dellius the emissary: Dio 49.39.2–3.

157 Unattested specifically but by 31 Antony was *IMP IIII* (*RRC* 545). His victory in Armenia is the obvious moment for the acclamation. Antony remains *IMP III* on RCC 542, which Crawford dates to 33, but this issue is better dated to 34: *MRR* 3.115; cf. Schumacher 2018, 93–126.

158 Patterson 2015.

159 Arrangements: Dio 49.44.1–3. Alexander Helios king of Armenia: Plut. *Ant.* 54.7; Dio 49.41.3. Iotape: Dio 49.44.2; 51.16.2. Roman troops based in Media Atropatene may lie behind Josephus' mistaken report that in 34 Antony marched into Parthia (Joseph. *BJ* 1.362–3).

160 On the family of Artavasdes of Armenia, see the concise account in Cooley 2009, 230–2; cf. Sullivan 1990, 289–91.

161 Tac. *Ann.* 2.3–4.

162 Badian 1968, 82–4; Seager 2002, 62; Morrell 2017, 82–4; Fezzi 2019, 82–5.

163 Dio 51.16.2; cf. Tarn 1934, 78.

164 Dio 49.38.1; cf. Reinhold 1988, 72.

165 Plut. *Ant.* 54.1–5; cf. Pelling 1988, 248.

166 Vell. 2.82.4; Plut. *Ant.* 50.6; 54.4–9; Dio 49.40.3–4; 49.41.5; cf. Tarn 1934, 79–83; Holmes 1928, 136–7; Volkmann 1953, 140–7; Rossi 1959, 149–52; Bengtson 1977, 216–20; Huzar 1978, 182–4; 196–200; Will 1982, 549–51; Chamoux 1986, 312–25; Marasco 1987, 87–94; Wallmann 1989, 288–96; Pelling 1996, 40–1; Höbl 2001, 243–4; Osgood 2006, 336–9; Pasquali 2009, 201–4; Goldsworthy 2010, 330–4; Roller 2010, 99–100; Southern 2010, 227–9; Halfmann 2011, 172–6; Sartre 2018, 204–11.

167 Dio 51.5.5 (execution of Artavasdes); 51.16.2 (his family in Alexandria after Actium); cf. Reinhold 1988, 38–9.

168 On the processions of Hellenistic monarchs, see Rice 1983; Erskine 2013 (assembling bibliography); Strootman 2014, 233–46 (244–6 on Antony's entrance to Alexandria).

169 Liv. 45.32.8–11; Plut. *Aem.* 28.3–5.

170 Cic. *Prov. cons.* 15; *Pis.* 92; Suet. *Nero* 2.1; Florus 1.37; cf. Beard 2007, 266–72.

171 Theoc. *Id.* 17; cf. Hunter 2003. Roman society was replete with pageantry put to work in the manifestation of power: see, e.g., Hölkeskamp 2020 (and references there assembled).

172 'Queen of kings who are her sons': *RRC* 543: *Cleopatrae reginae regum filiorum regum.*

173 Strootman 2010; Strootman 2014, 230–2.

174 *RRC* 543: *Cleopatrae reginae regum filiorum regum.*

175 *RRC* 541.1 and 541.2.

176 See, for instance, Plin. *NH* 7.139–40, where it counts as one of the ten greatest and most hoped for accomplishments of a great man's life.

177 Ager 2013 is decisive. Much is sometimes made of *RPC* 5752, a bronze issue from Dora in Syria which dates to 34/33. This coin exhibits a jugate image of a diademed Cleopatra with a male figure routinely identified as Antony. On this coin, however, Cleopatra is in the foreground: the male figure is unmistakably the junior partner. Better, then, to identify the male as Caesarian (so Meshorer 1986/87) or as Ptolemy Philadelphus, monarch in Syria by that year according to the Donations.

178 Suet. *Iul.* 77.1.

179 Roller 2010, 100.

180 *OGIS* 195; cf. Fraser 1957. On the Guild, see ch. IX, pp. 226–7.

181 Athen. 6.235e–235e; Pollux 10.35.

182 Plut. *Ant.* 86.5.

183 *Suda*, s.v. ἡμίεργον. This notice may be confirmed by Dio 51.15.5, an unclear passage which appears to report that Antyllus was executed by Octavian even though he took refuge at a *heroon* of Antony; cf. Fraser 1972, vol. 2, 68–9.

184 Str. 13.1.30; 14.1.14; Plin. *NH* 34.58.

185 Str. 17.1.9; Plut. *Ant.* 69.6–7; cf. Fraser 1972, vol. 2, 66–7; Pelling 1988, 291.

186 Antony's popularity in Alexandria: Plut. *Ant.* 29.4; cf. Fraser, vol. 1, 90.

CHAPTER XIII

1 Dio 49.41.4–6. Embedded in these events is a reference by Dio to actions taking place in 32 (Dio 49.41.4). For this reason, Kromayer 1896, 40, concluded *all* the events reported in this passage belong to 32, an opinion that recurs frequently.

2 App. *Ill.* 27–8.

3 Dio 49.38.4.

4 App. *Ill.* 25; cf. *MRR* 2.281.

5 Octavian's campaign in Illyricum: *MRR* 2.407; 411; 415.

6 App. *Ill.* 28 puts the award of this triumph in 33; Dio 49.38.1 locates it in 35, after the first season of campaigning, but this is very likely to be another of Dio's dislocations; cf. Schmittenenner 1958, 218.

7 So, rightly, Kromayer 1896, 37 and 39. On 33 and 32, see Drumann-Groebe 1899, 342–6; Holmes 1928, 135–47; Tarn and Charlesworth 1934, 90–9; Syme 1939, 276–93; Volkmann 1953, 147–70; Rossi 1959, 152–63; Bengtson 1977, 219–29; Huzar 1978, 200–16; Chamoux 1986, 331–46; Wallmann 1989, 296–323; Pelling 1996, 48–54; Kienast 1999, 62–70; Osgood 2006, 323–72; Pasquali 2009, 204–18; Lange 2009, 49–71; Goldsworthy 2010, 340–55; Southern 2010, 229–39; Roller 2010, 134–7; Halfmann 2011, 177–97; Sartre 2018, 230–44.

8 Dio 49.41.4.

9 Dio 49.41.5: καὶ ἐκείνῳ [viz. Antony] τῶν νικητρίων ἐφθόνει.

10 *MRR* 2.412–3; 416. On the date for Claudius' and Cornificius' triumphs, see Degrassi 1947, 570 and *MRR* 2.419.

11 Strong 1968; Morgan 1971; Tatum 2008, 80–98; Hölkeskamp 2020, 97–113.

12 Shipley 1931, 24–32. Octavian's dedication: Dio 49.43.8; cf. *Mon. Anc.* 19.1. Agrippa's ae-dileship: *MRR* 2.415; cf. Roddaz 1984, 145–66.

13 See, for instance, Cic. *Att.* 4.16.8: *gratius . . . gloriosius . . . gloriosissimam* (all of public buildings).

14 Roller 2007.

15 Cic. *Att.* 4.16.8.

16 Dio 49.42.3.

17 Dio 49.41.6.

18 See ch. XI, pp. 282–3. Even if one prefers the view that the triumvirate expired at the end of 33, Antony's proposal came early.

19 App. *B. Civ.* 5.132.

20 Caes. *B. Civ.* 1.9.3; 1.9.5; Hirt. *B. Gall.* 8.52.4; Vell. 2.48.2–3; Plut. *Pomp.* 58.5; *Caes.* 30.1–2; *Cat. min.* 51.7; App. *B. Civ.* 2.27; Dio 40.62.3; cf. Caes. *B. Civ.* 1.32.8; App. *B. Civ.* 2.143; Dio 41.12.2; see ch. III, p. 70.

21 Cic. *Phil.* 7.2–4; 8.25; 13.47; cf. Tatum 2020c, 205–7.

22 Suet. *Aug.* 28.1.

23 Plut. *Ant.* 56.1; Dio 49.44.2–3.

24 Brunt 1971, 507.

25 Dio 50.9.1.

26 *MRR* 2.415.

27 Plut. *Ant.* 58.2; Dio 50.2.2; 50.10.4–6; 51.3.3.

28 Cic. *Inv. rhet.* 1.34–6; 2.28–31; 2.177–8; *Rhet. Her.* 3.10–5; cf. Corbeil 2002; Craig 2004; Arena 2007.

29 The superb formulation of Syme 1939, 149.

30 Cic. *Off.* 1.134; Quint. 6.3.8.

31 Tatum 2011, with further examples and earlier scholarship.

32 Charlesworth 1933; Scott 1933; Wallmann 1989, 249–333; Roddaz 2012; Borgies 2016, esp. 287–316.

33 Plut. *Ant.* 55; Dio 50.1.3–2.1.

34 Human sacrifice: Suet. *Aug.* 15; Dio 48.14.4; cf. Wardle 2014, 137–8. Testimonia for trium-viral abuse collected in Scott 1933; Wallmann 1989; and Borgies 2016.

35 Messala: Charisius ap. Keil, *Gramm. Lat.*, vol. 1, 104; 129; 146; Plin. *NH* 33.50; Pollio: Charisus ap. Keil, *Gramm. Lat.*, vol. 1, 80; Scott 1933, 48–9; Bosworth 1972.

36 Plin. *NH* 14.148; cf. Scott 1929; Huzar 1982; Geiger 1989. Pliny's expression *de ebrietate suo* (*On his drunkenness*) may not be the title of the work but Pliny's description of it, an obser-vation I owe to Chris Pelling.

37 Ov. *Pont.* 1.1.23; Tac. *Ann.* 4.34.5; Suet. *Aug.* 7.1; 16.2; 63.2; 69.2; Plut. *Ant.* 78.3; cf. Cugusi 1970, 236–69.

38 Suet. *Aug.* 63.2.

39 Polyb. 14.11.1; cf. Strootman 2017.

40 McCoy 2006, 178–81; Strong 2016, 62–96.

41 Multicultural origins: Cic. *Rep.* 3.25; *Off.* 1.35; Dench 2005; Gruen 2006; Gruen 2013. Open to outsiders: Cic. *Off.* 3.47; Balsdon 1979; Noy 2000; Coşkun 2005.

42 Dio 49.43.5.

43 Hor. *Carm.* 1.37.6–12.

44 Hor. *Epod.* 9.11–6 (excerpts).

45 Verg. *Aen.* 8.678–700 (excerpts).

46 Dio 50.25.2–4.

47 Plut. *Ant.* 56.4–5; 61.1–2; Dio 50.6.6.

48 It is sometimes suggested that in the Third Sibylline Oracle we possess evidence for a wider, regional hope that, under Cleopatra's leadership, Rome's domination might end and an age of universal peace and prosperity take its place: Tarn 1932; cf. Pelling 1996, 51 (duly qualified); Roller 2010, 169–71; Sartre 2018, 242–3. This is unlikely: Gruen 2016, 459–63, is decisive on the matter. After Actium, Octavian often strained himself to convince the east that he was in no way hostile to Hellenism: Bowersock 1965; Hose 2018.
49 Suet. *Aug.* 28.1; Dio 49.41.6; 50.7.1–2.
50 Dio 50.22.3–4.
51 Syme 1939, 275 and 460; versions of this assessment recur frequently.
52 Syme 1939, 280–2; Ferriès 2007, 274–87.
53 Plut. *Ant.* 58.1–2; Dio 50.2.2; 50.10.4–6; 51.3.3.
54 Macr. *Sat.* 2.4.29.
55 Dio 49.41.4.
56 Complaints about this alleged dispatch may have formed part of Octavian's later speeches before the senate: Dio 50.2.6; 50.3.2.
57 Dio 50.2.3.
58 Kromayer 1894, 41–2, whose chronology of 32 remains fundamental, prefers to locate this event in January, but it makes better sense to follow Kolbe 1914, 280–3, and date Sosius' attack to February.
59 Dio 50.2.3–4.
60 Dio 50.2.5–7; we do not know how many senators accompanied the consuls; Dio says 'not a few', in Greek a specimen of litotes that routinely indicates 'very many'; cf. K-G 182–3.
61 Dio 50.3.2.
62 Vervaet 2010; cf. App. *Ill.* 28; Gabba 1970, lxvii–lxxix.
63 *Mon. Anc.* 7.1.
64 Doxographies of this much-debated matter can be retrieved from Reinhold 1988, 224–5; Bleicken 1990, 14–6 and 68–82; Osgood 2006, 243; Lange 2009, 53–60; Vervaet 2010; Vervaet 2020.
65 E.g., Kromayer 1894, 2–21; Syme 1939, 270–1.
66 Vervaet 2020, 26–32 (with testimonia and detailed bibliography).
67 Suet. *Aug.* 28.1.
68 Plut. *Ant.* 56.1–3; Dio 50.3.2.
69 Vell. 2.84.2.
70 Cic. *Att.* 15.15.2.
71 Cic. *Att.* 14.1.2.
72 Pelling 1988, 256.
73 Plut. *Ant.* 56.3.
74 Plut. *Ant.* 56.4. Plutarch believes, probably wrongly, that Canidius supported Cleopatra owing to a bribe.
75 Plut. *Ant.* 58.4; Dio 50.3.2.
76 Plut. *Ant.* 56.1–3; 61.5; cf. Brunt 1971, 503–7.
77 Plut. *Ant.* 56.6–57.1. On the Artists of Dionysus and related guilds, see Pickard-Cambridge 1968, 279–321. On Antony's support for these artistic guilds, see Cayla 2017.
78 Plut. *Ant.* 57.1–3; cf. Dio 50.15.2.
79 Plut. Ant. 57.4–5; Dio 50.3.2. The date of the divorce is reported by Eus. *Chron.* 2.140.
80 Vell. 2.83.1–3; Plut. *Ant.* 58.4; Dio 50.3.2.
81 Disapproval of Plancus: Vell. 2.83.1–3.
82 Suet. *Aug.* 17.1; Plut. *Ant.* 58.6: Dio 50.3.3–5.
83 Champlin 1991 is fundamental; see also ch. VI, pp. 130–2.
84 Plin. *Ep.* 8.18.1.

85 Lucian *Nigr.* 30.
86 Plut. *Sull.* 38.2; *Pomp.* 15.3; cf. Champlin 1991, 14–5.
87 Cic. *Att.* 1.16.10.
88 Cic. *Phil.* 2.40.
89 Paul *Sent.* 4.7; 5.25.
90 Discussion and doxography in Crook 1957; Johnson 1978; Sirianni 1984; Borgies 2016, 313–6.
91 See, for instance, Cic. *Att.* 3.12.2; 3.15.3; 11.16.1; *Q. Fr.* 1.3.9; *Ad Brut.* 2.5.3–4.
92 See ch. XII, pp. 287–8.
93 Crook 1957.
94 Crook 1957, 37.
95 Schulz 1951, 321–3; Kaser 1971, 757–61.
96 Dio 51.15.5; cf. Fraser 1972, vol. 2, 68–9.
97 Price 1984, 32–40.
98 Habicht 2017, 145–9.
99 Pind. *Nem.* 3.21; Hdt. 2.44; Diod. Sic. 4.39.1; Paus. 2.10.1; cf. Stafford 2010.
100 Plut. *Ant.* 58.1.
101 Plut. *Ant.* 58.2; Dio 50.2.2; 50.10.4–6; 51.3.3.
102 Plut. *Ant.* 60.1; Dio 50.4.3–4; Dio 50.20.5. On possible constitutional remedies available to Octavian, see Cic. *Rep.* 3.33; Asc. 68–9C; cf. Tatum forthcoming.
103 Suet. *Aug.* 17.2; App. *B. Civ.* 4.38; 4.45; Dio 50.4.3–4.; cf. Allély 2012, 110–2.
104 Plut. *Ant.* 60.1; Dio 50.4.3–5; 50.6.1.
105 Beard, North, and Price 1998a, 132–4; Beard, North, and Price 1998b, 7–8. The fetial rite an Octavian adaptation or concoction: Wiedemann 1986; Rüpke 1990, 105–7.
106 He was certainly a *fetialis* later in his life: *Mon Anc.* 4.7.
107 Lange 2009, 79–90.
108 *Mon. Anc.* 25.2; cf. Cooley 2009, 215–7; Kearsley 2013.
109 Syme 1939, 284–7; Mouritsen 1998; Dench 2005, 184–7; Patterson 2006b; Bispham 2007, 405–46; see, also, the essays in Jehne and Pfeilschifter 2006.
110 Cic. *Phil.* 7.20 (*consensus Italiae*: Cicero often employs the expression when speaking for Italy); 10.19 (*tota Italia*).
111 Linderski 1995, 147–53, 642–4; Linderski 2007, 615–6; Wardle 2014, 149–50; Borgies 2016, 287–316.
112 Suet. *Aug.* 17.2; Dio 50.6.3.
113 Dio 50.9.2. Dio suggests Antony planned to invade Italy but was deterred. This is unlikely.
114 Str. 8.4.3; Dio 50.11–3.
115 Dio 50.9.3; cf. Plut. *Ant.* 60.4.
116 Plut. *Ant.* 60.2–4; Dio 50.9.5–6.
117 *RPC* 1.1245; Kroll 1997, 127; Haug 2008.
118 *MRR* 2.420.
119 Brunt 1971, 501; 504–8; Lange 2011, 612–5.
120 Drumann-Groebe 1899, 352–7; Holmes 1928, 147–8; Tarn 1934, 100–6; Volkmann 1953, 170–84; Bengtson 1977, 230–43; Huzar 1978, 216–21; Chamoux 1986, 342–64; Pelling 1996, 54–9; Kienast 1999, 70–1; Osgood 2006, 371–84; Pasquali 2009, 233–8; Lange 2009, 73–93; Goldsworthy 2010, 360–9; Southern 2010, 240–7; Roller 2010, 137–40; Halfmann 2011, 198–216; Sartre 2018, 244–8.
121 Vell. 2.84–5; Suet. *Aug.* 17.2–3; Plut. *Ant.* 60–68; Dio 50.10–35; sources for the Actium war assembled at *MRR* 2.422–3; cf. Kromayer 1899; Pelling 1996, 54–9; Lange 2011.
122 Lange 2011, 612.
123 Plut. *Ant.* 68.7.

124   Plut. *Ant.* 63.6–8; Dio 50.14.4–50.15.3.

125   Out of the multiple reconstructions of the strategy and tactics of the battle of Actium, the best remain Kromayer 1899 and Pelling 1996, 57–9.

126   Plut. *Ant.* 68.2 reports that no more than 5,000 perished in this battle, an unexpectedly small figure. In his account, Dio does not count the casualties; instead, he extends himself in describing the battle's horrors: Dio 50.34–35.

127   Vell. 2.85.2–86.2; Dio 51.4.6; Hyg. Grom. 177.11; cf. Keppie 71983, 9–80.

128   Syme 1939, 297.

129   On this crucial point, Goldsworthy 2010, 364; 368–9.

130   Plut. *Ant.* 68.6–8; 72.1; Dio 51.2.1–2; 51.4.1–2; cf. Josephus. *AJ* 15.187–96; *BJ* 1.387–93 (Octavian in Rhodes); Octavian in Ephesus: Sherk 1969, 297–8 (Sherk no. 58.III); 301–2.

131   Suet. *Aug.* 17.3; Dio 51.3.5–7; 51.4.3–8; conspiracy: Vell. 2.88.

132   Dio 51.5.1–2.

133   Drumann-Groebe 1899, 358–64; Holmes 1928, 158–65; Tarn 1934, 106–11; Volkmann 1953, 184–93; Bengtson 1977, 244–51; Huzar 1978, 221–7; Chamoux 1986, 364–75; Pelling 1996, 59–65; Osgood 2006, 385–90; Pasquali 2009, 238–43; Goldsworthy 2010, 370–80; Southern 2010, 247–52; Roller 2010, 140–6; Halfmann 2011, 217–23; Sartre 2018, 249–60.

134   Plut. *Ant.* 69.1–3; Dio 51.5.3–6.

135   Plut. *Ant.* 71.1–2.

136   Cleopatra's physician, Olympus, for instance, composed an account of the final days in Alexandria (*BNJ* 198); other literary figures could also claim autopsy and their works also circulated immediately and widely: Griffin 1986, 46–7; Pelling 1988, 28–9; 293–4; Borgies 2016, 324–47.

137   Plut. *Ant.* 69.6–7; cf. Str. 17.794; Pelling 1988, 291.

138   Plut. *Ant.* 69.3–5; Dio 51.6.3–4.

139   *MRR* 2.421.

140   Dio 51.7.2–7.

141   Dio 51.5.5; 51.6.2.

142   Plut. *Ant.* 71.3; Dio 51.6.1.

143   Plut. *Ant.* 71.4; Ter. *Ad.* 6–7; cf. Pelling 1988, 295–6.

144   See ch. II, pp. 50–2.

145   Plut. *Ant.* 72.1–2; 73.14; Dio 51.6.4–6; 51.8.1–7.

146   Plut. *Ant.* 74.1; Dio 51.9.1–4.

147   Plut. *Ant.* 74.2–75.1; Dio 51.9.5–51.10.2.

148   Suet. *Aug.* 17.3–4; Vell. 2.87.1; Plut. *Ant.* 75.2–77.7; Dio 51.10.3–11.1; Oros. 6.19.4.

149   Sh. *A&C* 4.15.53–60; Plut. *Ant.* 77.7; cf. Pelling 1988, 307–8.

150   EJ 49.

CHAPTER XIV

1   Octavian and the aftermath: Vell. 287.1–3; Suet. *Aug.* 17.1–18.2; Plut. *Ant.* 78.5–87.9; Dio 51.11.1–51.17.8; cf. Drumann-Groebe 1899, 364–75; Holmes 1928, 165–71; Tarn 1934, 108–13; Volkmann 1953, 187–203; Bowman 1996; Pelling 1996, 63–5; Kienast 1999, 73–7; Goldsworthy 2010, 381–9; Roller 2010, 146–56; Sartre 2018, 249–92.

2   Chauvinistic Octavian: Suet. *Aug.* 18.1; Dio 51.16.5.

3   Crassus: Ferriès 2007, 359–62; Ovinius: Oros. 6.19.20; cf. Ferriès 2007, 450–1.

4   Tac. *Ann.* 2.59 (*dominationis arcana*).

5   Sources assembled by Drumann-Groebe 1899, 383–4.

6 Bowersock 1965, 42–61.

7 Syme 1939, 425–7; Raaflaub and Samons 1990, 4287–30.

8 Tac. *Ann.* 4.44. It is not clear whether he was buried in the Mausoleum of Augustus or the ancestral tomb of the Octavii; cf. Woodman 2018, 237.

9 Pelling 1988, 325. Antony's Roman children: sources assembled at Drumann-Groebe 1899, 380–2.

10 See ch. I, pp. 12–3.

11 Plut. *Cic.* 49.6; Dio 51.19.3; Octavia's role is proposed by Flower 2006, 116–21; cf. Patrechko 2016.

12 *Mon. Anc.* 34.1–2. On the Augustan imaginary of his ending the civil wars, see Havener 2016, 51–150.

13 *Mon. Anc.* 34.3.

14 Augustus, the restoration of the republic, and its controversies: Crook 1996, 73–7; Galinsky 1996, 42–79; Kienast 1999, 78–98; Cooley 2009, 256–62; Ferrary 2009; Vervaet 2010; Richardson, 2012, 81–91; Havener 2016, 186–92; Moatti 2018, 251–69.

15 Tac. *Ann.* 1.2.

16 Antony and love poetry: Griffin 1986, 32–47. Plutarch and Antony: Pelling 1988, 10–18.

Abbreviations

AE	*L'année épigraphique*
BNJ	Worthington, I., et al. *Brill's New Jacoby.*
CIL	*Corpus inscriptionun Latinarum.* 1863–. Berlin.
Chios	McCabe, Donald F. 1986. *Chios Inscriptions: Texts and List.* Princeton.
Drumann-Groebe 1899	Drumann, W., and Groebe, P. 1899. *Geschichte Roms in seinem Übergang von der republikanischen zur monarchischen Verfassung, oder Pompeius, Caesar, Cicero und ihre Zeitgenossen,* vol. 1. Berlin.
EJ	Ehrenbert, V., and Jones, A.H.M. 1949. *Documents Illustrating the Reigns of Augustus and Tiberius.* Oxford.
Fayoum I	Bernand, É. 1975. *Recueil des inscriptions grecques du Fayoum,* vol. 1: *La "Méris" d' Hérakleidès.* Leiden.
FRHist	Cornell, T.J. (ed.). 2013. *The Fragments of the Roman Historians.* Oxford.
H-S	Hofmann, J.B., and Szantyr, A. 1972. *Lateinische Syntax und Stilistik,* 2nd ed. Munich.
I. Délos	*Inscriptions de Délos.* 1926–. Paris.
I. Eph.	Wankel, H., et al. 1979–1984. *Die Inschriften von Ephesos,* 8 vols. Bonn.
IG X	Edson, C. 1972. *Inscriptiones Graecae, X: Inscriptiones Epiri, Macedoniae, Thraciae, Scythiae, pars II, fasc. 1: Inscriptiones Thessalonicae et viciniae.* Berlin. Papazoglu, F., Milin, M., and Ricl, M. 1999. *Inscriptiones Graecae, X: Inscriptiones Epiri, Macedoniae, Thraciae, Scythiae, pars II, fasc. 2: Inscriptiones Macedoniae septentrionalis. Sectio prima: Inscriptiones Lyncestidis, Heracleae, Pelagoniae, Derriopi, Lychnidi.* Berlin.
IG XII	Hiller, F., et al. 1895–2003. *Inscriptiones Graecae, XII: Inscriptions insularum maris Aegaei praeter Delum.* Berlin.
IG II²	Kirchner, J. 1913–1940. *Inscriptiones Graecae II et III: Inscriptiones Atticae Euclidis anno posteriores,* 2nd ed. Berlin.
IGRP	Cagnat, R., et al. 1901–1927. *Inscriptiones graecae ad res romanas pertinentes,* 3 vols. Paris.
I.Kaunos	McCabe, D.F. 1991. *Kaunos Inscriptions. Texts and List.* Princeton.
ILLRP	Degrassi, A. 1963–1965. *Inscriptiones Latinae Liberae Rei Publicae.* Florence.
ILS	Dessau, H. 1954. *Inscriptiones Latinae Selectae,* 2nd ed. Berlin.
Inscr. Ital.	*Inscriptiones Italiae.* 1931–. Rome.
Keil, *Gramm. Lat.*	Keil, H. 1857. *Grammatici Latini,* 8 vols. Leipzig.
K-G	Kühner, R., and Gerth, B. 1898. *Ausführliche Grammatik der griechischen Sprache,* vol. 2. Leipzig.
LTUR	Steinby, E.M. (ed.). 1993–2000. *Lexicon Topographicum Urbis Romae.* Rome.
MAMA	*Monumenta Asiae Minoris Antiquae.* 1928–. Manchester.
McG	McGushin, P. 1994. *Sallust: The Histories,* vol. 2. Oxford.

MRR	Broughton, T.R.S. 1951–2. *Magistrates of the Roman Republic*, vols. 1–2. New York. 1986. *Magistrates of the Roman Republic*, vol. 3. Atlanta.
OGIS	Dittenberger, W. 1903–1905. *Orientis Graeci Inscriptiones Selectae.* 2 vols. Leipzig.
ORF⁴	Malcovati, H. 1967. *Oratorum Romanorum fragmenta liberae rei publicae*, 4th ed. Turin.
Philae	Bernand, A., and Bernand, É. 1969. *Les inscriptions grecques de Philae: I–II.* Paris.
RDGE	Sherk, R.A. 1969. *Roman Documents from the Greek East.* Baltimore.
RE	Pauly, A., Wissowa, G., and Kroll, W. (eds.). 1893–1980. *Paulys Real-Encyclopädie der classischen Altertumswissenschaft.* Stuttgart and Munich.
RS	Crawford, M.H. (ed.). 1996. *Roman Statutes.* London.
RPC	Burnett, A., Amandry, M., and Rilollès. P.P. 1992. *Roman Provincial Coinage, part 1: From the Death of Caesar to the Death of Vitellius (44 BC–AD 69).* London.
RRC	Crawford, M.H. 1974. *Roman Republican Coinage.* Cambridge.
Salamine XIII	Pouilloux, J., Roesch, P., and Marcillet-Jaubert, J. 1987. *Salamine de Chypre, XIII. Testimonia Salaminia, 2. Corpus épigraphique.* Paris.
SEG	*Supplementum Epigraphicum Graecum.*
StR.	Mommsen, T. 1887. *Römisches Staatsrecht*, 3 vols. Leipzig.
Straf.	Mommsen, T. 1899. *Römisches Strafrecht.* Leipzig.
Syll.³	Dittenberger, W., et al. 1915–1924. *Sylloge inscriptionum graecarum.* Leipzig.

Bibliography

Adams, J.N. 1982. *The Latin Sexual Vocabulary*. Baltimore.

Ager, S.L. 2013. 'Marriage or Mirage? The Phantom Wedding of Cleopatra and Antony', *CPh* 108: 139–55.

Ager, S.L. 2017. 'Symbol and Ceremony: Royal Weddings in the Hellenistic Age', in A. Erskine, L. Llewellyn-Jones, and S. Wallace (eds.), *The Hellenistic Court: Monarchic Power and Elite Society from Alexander to Cleopatra*. Swansea: 165–88.

Aigner, H. 1976. 'Zur Wichtigkeit der Waffenbeschaffung in der späten römischen Republik', *Grazer Beigräge* 5: 1–24.

Alexander, M.C. 1990. *Trials in the Late Roman Republic, 149 BC to 50 BC*. Toronto.

Alexander, M.C. 1993. 'How Many Roman Senators Were Ever Prosecuted? The Evidence from the Late Republic', *Phoenix* 47: 238–55.

Alexander, M.C. 2002. *The Case for the Prosecution in the Ciceronian Era*. Ann Arbor.

Allély, A. 2004. *Lépide, le triumvir*. Paris.

Allély, A. 2012. *La declaration d'hostis sous la République romaine*. Paris.

Allotee de la Fuÿe, F.-M. 1904. 'Monnaies Arsacides Surfrappées', *Revue Numismatique* 8: 174–96.

Aly, A.A. 1992. 'Cleopatra and Caesar at Alexandria and Rome', in G.P. Carratelli, G. Del Re, N. Bonacasa, and A. Etman (eds.), *Roma e l'Egitto nell'antichità classica: Atti del I Congresso Internazionale Italo-Egiziano*. Rome: 47–61.

Amandry, M. 1990. 'Le monnayage en bronze de Bibulus, Atratinus et Capito: Une tentative de romanisation in Orient. III', *Revue Suisse de Numismatique* 69: 65–96.

Ando, C. 2000. *Imperial Ideology and Provincial Loyalty in the Roman Empire*. Berkeley and Los Angeles.

Andreau, J. 1999. *Banking and Business in the Roman World*. Cambridge.

Aneziri, S. 2003. *Die Vereine der dionysischen Technite im Kontext der hellenistischen Gesellschaft: Untersuchungen zur Geshichte, Organisation und Wirkung der hellenistischen Technitenvereine*. Stuttgart.

Aneziri, S., and Damaskos, D. 2004. 'Städtische Kult im hellenistichen Gymnasion', in D. Kah and P. Scholz (eds.), *Das hellenistische Gymnasion*. Berlin: 247–71.

Annas, J. 1989. 'Cicero on Stoic Moral Philosophy and Private Property', in M. Griffin and J. Barnes (eds.), *Philosophia Togata I: Essays on Philosophy and Roman Society*. Oxford: 151–73.

Arena, V. 2007. 'Roman Oratorical Invective', in W. Dominik and J. Hall (eds.), *A Companion to Roman Rhetoric*. Malden: 149–60.

Arena, V. 2012. *Libertas and the Practice of Politics in the Late Roman Republic*. Cambridge.

Ashton, S.-A. 2005. *Cleopatra and Egypt*. Oxford.

Astin, A. 1958. *The Lex Annalis before Sulla*. Brussels.

Astin, A. 1978. *Cato the Censor*. Oxford.

Aufrère, S.H. 2018. 'Genèse de l'hubris barbare de la dernière reine lagide', in S.H. Aufrère and A. Michel (eds.), *Cléopâtre en Abyme: Aux frontiéres de la mythistoire et de la littérature*. Paris: 1–135.

Aumaître, H. 2018. 'Çléopâtre VII Théa et l'Orient antonien: Les émissions monétaires au portrait de la derniére souveraine lagide', in S.H. Aufrère and A. Michel (eds.), *Cléopâtre en Abyme: Aux frontières de la mythistorie et de la littérature*. Paris: 217–42.

Austin, N.J.E., and Rankov, N.B. 1995. *Exploratio: Military and Political Intelligence in the Roman World from the Second Punic War to the Battle of Adrianolple*. London.

Austin, R.G. 1960. *M. Tulli Ciceronis Pro M. Caelio Oratio*. Oxford.

Balsdon, J.P.V.D. 1939. 'Consular Provinces under the Late Republic', *JRS* 29: 57–73; 167–183.

Badian, E. 1958. *Foreign Clientela (264–70 B.C.)*. Oxford.

Badian, E. 1959. 'The Early Career of A. Gabinius (Cos. 58 B.C.)', *Philologus* 103: 78–99.

Badian, E. 1964. *Studies in Greek and Roman History*. Oxford.

Badian, E. 1968. *Roman Imperialism in the Late Republic*. Ithaca.

Badian, E. 1972. *Publicans and Sinners: Private Enterprise in the Service of the Roman Republic*. Ithaca.

Badian, E. 1983. 'The Silence of Norbanus: A Note on Provincial Quaestors under the Republic', *AJPh* 104: 156–71.

Badian, E. 1984. 'The Death of Saturninus', *Chiron* 14: 101–47.

Badian, E. 1988. 'The Clever and the Wise: Two Roman *Cognomina* in Context', in N. Horsfall (ed.), *Vir Bonus Discendi Peritus: Studies in Celebration of Otto Skutsch's Eightieth Birthday*. London: 6–12.

Badian, E. 1990. 'The Consuls, 179–49 BC', *Chiron* 20: 371–413.

Badian, E. 2004. 'The Pig and the Priest', in H. Heftner and K. Tomaschitz (eds.), *Ad fontes! Festschrift für Gerhard Dobesch zum 65. Geburtstag am 15. September 2004, dargebracht von Kollegen, Schülern und Freunden*. Vienna: 263–72.

Balmaceda, C. 2017. *Virtus Romana: Politics and Morality in the Roman Historians*. Chapel Hill.

Balsdon, J.P.V.D. 1979. *Romans and Aliens*. London.

Balzat, J.-S., and Millis, B.W. 2013. 'M. Antonius Aristocrates: Provincial Involvement with Roman Power in the Late 1st Century B.C.', *Hesperia* 82: 651–72.

Bane, R.W. 1971. *The Composition of the Roman Senate in 44 B.C.* Ann Arbor.

Baragwanath, E. 2008. *Motivation and Narrative in Herodotus*. Oxford.

Baronowski, D.W. 2011. *Polybius and Roman Imperialism*. London.

Baraz, Y. 2018. 'Discourse of Kingship in Late Republican Invective', in N. Panou and H. Shadee (eds.), *Evil Lords: Theories and Representations of Tyranny from Antiquity to the Renaissance*. Oxford: 43–60.

Bean, G.E. 1954. 'Notes and Inscription from Caunus (Continued)', *JRS* 54: 85–110.

Beard, M. 1990. 'Priesthood in the Roman Republic', in M. Beard and J. North (eds.), *Pagan Priests: Religion and Power in the Ancient World*. London: 17–48.

Beard, M. 1994. 'Religion', in J.A. Crook, A. Lintott, and E. Rawson (eds.), *The Cambridge Ancient History*, 2nd ed., vol. 10. Cambridge: 729–68.

Beard, M. 2007. *The Roman Triumph*. Cambridge, Mass.

Beard, M., North, J., and Price, S. 1998a. *Religions of Rome*, vol. 1. Cambridge.

Beard, M., North, J., and Price, S. 1998b. *Religions of Rome*, vol. 2. Cambridge.

Beck, H. 2005. *Karriere und Hierarchie: Die römische Aristokratie und die Anfange des cursus honorum in der mittleren Republik*. Berlin.

Beck, J. 2011. 'Consular Power and the Roman Constitution: The Case of *Imperium* Reconsidered', in H. Beck, A. Duplá, M. Jehne, and F. Pina Polo (eds.), *Consuls and the Res Publica: Holding High Office in the Roman Republic*. Cambridge: 77–96.

Beck, H. 2020. 'Republican Elites: Patricians, Nobiles, Senators and Equestrians', in V. Arena and J. Prag (eds.), *A Companion to the Political Culture of the Roman Republic*. Malden: 347–61.

Beilage, M. Große. 2019. 'Four Observations on Mark Antony and the Triumviral Narrative', *AHB* 33: 142–8.

Bell, A. 2004. *Spectacular Power in the Greek and Roman City*. Oxford.

Benedetti, L. 2012. *Glandes Perusinae: Revisione e aggiornamente*. Rome.

Beneker, J. 2012. *The Passionate Statesman: Eros and Politics in Plutarch's Lives*. Oxford.

Beness, J.L. 2000. 'The Punishment of the *Gracchani* and the Execution of C. Villius in 133/132', *Antichthon* 34: 1–17.

Beness, L., and Hillard, T. 2013. '*Rei Militaris Virtus ... Orbem Terrarium Parere Huic Imperio Coegit*: The Transformation of Roman *Imperium*', in B.D. Hoyos, *A Companion to Roman Imperialism*. Leiden: 127–40.

Bengtson, H. 1974. *Zum Partherfeldzug des Antonius*. Munich.

Bengtson, H. 1977. *Marcus Antonius: Triumvir und Herrscher des Orients*. Munich.

Béranger, J. 1972. 'Les jugements de Cicéron sur les Gracques', *ANRW* 1.1. Berlin: 733–63.

Berdowski, P. 2020. 'Why Octavian Married Scribonia', *Klio* 102: 601–16.

Bernard, J.-E. 2017. *La sociabilité épistolaire chez Cicéron*. Paris.

Bernhardt, R. 1985. *Polis und römische Herrschaft in her späten Republik: 149–31 v. Chr.* Berlin.

Berry, D. 1996. *Cicero: Pro P. Sulla Oratio*. Cambridge.

Bessone, L. 2012. 'I Lupercali del 44: Una revisitazione', *Acta Classical Universitatis Scientiarum Debreceniensis* 48: 35–57.

Ben Zeev, M.P. 1998. *Jewish Rights in the Roman World*. Tübingen.

Billows, R.A. 2009. *Julius Caesar: The Colossus of Rome*. London.

Bispham, E. 2007. *From Asculum to Actium: The Municipalization of Italy from the Social War to Augustus*. Oxford.

Bispham, E. 2016. 'The Civil Wars and the Triumvirate', in A.E. Cooley (ed.), *A Companion to Roman Italy*. Malden: 90–102.

Bivar, A.D.H. 2008. 'The Political History of Iran under the Arsacids', in E. Yarshater (ed.), *The Cambridge History of Iran*, vol. 3, part 1. Cambridge: 21–97.

Bleicken, J. 1990. *Zwischen Republik und Prinzipat: Zum Charakter des Zweiten Triumvirats*. Göttingen.

Bleicken, J. 1995. *Cicero und die Ritter*. Göttingen.

Blom, H. van der. 2010. *Cicero's Role Models: The Political Strategy of a Newcomer*. Oxford.

Blom, H. van der. 2016. *Oratory and Political Career in the Late Roman Republic*. Cambridge.

Blösel, W. 2011. 'Die Demilitarsierung der römishen Nobilität von Sulla bis Caesar', in W. Blösel and K.-J. Hölkeskamp (eds.), *Von der 'militia equestris' zur 'milita urbana': Prominenzrollen und Karrierefelder im antiken Rom*. Stuttgart: 55–80.

Blösel, W. 2016. 'Provincial Commands and Money in the Late Roman Republic', in H. Beck, M. Jehne, and J. Serrati (eds.), *Money and Power in the Late Republic*. Brussels: 68–81.

Boardman, J. 1990. 'Herakles with Athena', *LIMC* 5.1: 143–54.

Bonnefound-Coudry, M. 1989. *Le Sénat de la république romaine de la guerre d'Hannibal à Auguste: Pratiques déliberatives et prise de decision*. Rome.

Bonner, C., and Nock, A.D. 1948. 'Neotera', *HTR* 41: 213–15.

Bonner S.F. 1977. *Education in Ancient Rome: From the Elder Cato to the Younger Pliny*. Berkeley and Los Angeles.

Borgies, L. 2016. *Le conflict propagandiste entre Octavien et Marc Antoine: De l'usage politique de la vituperatio entre 44 et 30 a.C.n.* Brussels.

Börm, H. 2016. 'Hellenistische Poleis und römischer Bürgerkrieg: Stasis in griechischen Osten nac den Iden des März (44 bis 39 v. Chr.)', in H. Börm, M. Mattheis, J.F. Wienand, and F. Santangelo (eds.), *Civil War in Ancient Greece and Rome: Contexts of Disintegration and Reintegration*. Stuttgart: 99–125.

Börm, H. 2019. *Mordende Mitbürger: Statis in hellenistischen Polies*. Konstanz.

Bosworth, A.B. 1972. 'Asinius Pollio and Augustus', *Historia* 21: 441–73.

Botermann, H. 1968. *Die Soldaten und die römische Politik in der Zeit von Caesars Tod bis zur Begründung des Zweiten Triumvirats*. Munich.

Bowersock, G.W. 1965. *Augustus and the Greek World*. Oxford.

Bowman, A.K. 1996. 'Egypt', in A.K. Bowman, E. Champlin, and A. Lintott (eds.), *The Cambridge Ancient History*, 2nd ed., vol. 10. Cambridge: 676–702.

Bowsky, M.W.B. 2001. 'Gortynians and Others: The Case of the Antonii', *Eulimene* 2: 91–119.

Bowsky, M.W.B. 2002. 'Reasons to Reorganize: Antony, Augustus and Central Crete', in E. Dabrowa (ed.), *Tradition and Innovation in the Ancient World*. Krakow: 25–65.

Boyle, A.J. 2017. *Seneca: Thyestes*. Oxford.

Bradley, J. 2017. 'The Consular Provinciae of 44 BCE and the Collapse of the Restored Republic', *Hermes* 145: 174–94.

Bradley, K.R. 1996. 'Remarriage and the Structure of the Upper-Class Roman Family', in B. Rawson (ed.), *Marriage, Divorce, and Children in Ancient Rome*. Oxford: 79–98.

Bradley, M. 2012. 'Crime and Punishment on the Capitoline Hill', in M. Bradley and K. Stow (eds.), *Rome, Pollution and Propriety: Dirt, Disease and Hygiene in the Eternal City from Antiquity to Modernity*. Cambridge: 103–21.

Braund, D. 1984. *Rome and the Friendly King*. London.

Braund, D.C. 1998. '*Cohors*: The Governor and His Entourage in the Self-Image of the Roman Republic', in R. Laurence and J. Berry (eds.), *Cultural Identity in the Roman Empire*. London: 10–24.

Brendel, O.J. 1962. 'The Iconography of Marc Antony', in M. Renard (ed.), *Hommages à Albert Grenier*. Brussels: 359–67.

Brenk, F. 2017. *Frederick E. Brenk on Plutarch, Religious Thinker and Biographer*. Leiden.

Brennan, T.C. 2000. *The Praetorship in the Roman Republic*. Oxford.

Brennan, T.C. 2014. 'Power and Process under the Republican "Constitution"', in H. Flower (ed.), *The Cambridge Companion to the Roman Republic*, 2nd ed. Cambridge: 19–53.

Brice, L.L. 2020. 'Indiscipline in the Roman Army of the Late Republic and Principate', in L.L. Brice (ed.), *New Approaches to Greek and Roman Warfare*. Hoboken: 113–26.

Broughton, T.R.S. 1938. 'Roman Asia', in T. Frank (ed.), *An Economic Survey of Ancient Rome*. Baltimore: 499–916.

Broughton, T.R.S. 1991. *Candidates Defeated in Roman Elections: Some Ancient Roman 'Also-Rans'*. Philadelphia.

Brunt, P.A. 1971. *Italian Manpower, 225 B.C.–A.D. 14*. Oxford.

Brunt, P.A. 1982. 'Nobilitas and Novitas', *JRS* 72: 1–17.

Brunt, P.A. 1988. *The Fall of the Roman Republic and Related Esssays*. Oxford.

Brunt, P.A. 1990. *Roman Imperial Themes*. Oxford.

Brunt, P.A. 2001. *Roman Imperial Themes*. Oxford.

Bücher, F. 2009. 'Die Erinnerung an Krisenjahre: Das exemplum der Gracchen im politischen Diskurs der späten Republik', in K-J. Hölkeskamp (ed.), *Eine politische Kultur (in) der Krise? Die 'letzte Generation' der römischen Republik*. Munich: 99–114.

Buchheim, H. 1960. *Die Orientpolitik des Triumvirn M. Antonius: Ihre Voraussetzungen, Entwicklung und Zusammenhang mit den politischen Ereignissen in Italien*. Heidelberg.

Bühler, D. 2009. *Macht und Treue: Publius Ventidius: Eine römische Karriere zwischen Republik und Monarchie*. Munich.

Burckhardt, L.A. 1990. 'The Political Elite of the Roman Republic: Comments on Recent Discussions of the Concepts of Nobilitas and Novus Homo', *Historia* 39: 89–98.

Burkert, W. 1985. *Greek Religion*. Cambridge, Mass.

Burrow, C. 1997. 'Virgils, from Dante to Milton', in C. Martindale (ed.), *The Cambridge Companion to Virgil*. Cambridge: 79–90.

Butcher, K. 2004. *Coinage in Roman Syria: Northern Syria, 64 BC–AD 253*. London.

Buttrey, T.V. 1953. *Studies in the Coinage of Marc Antony*. Princeton.

Buttrey, T.V., Jr. 1954. 'Thea Notera on Coins of Antony and Cleopatra', *Museum Notes of the American Numismatic Society* 6: 95–109.

Calboli, G. 1997. 'The Asiatic Style of Antony: Some Considerations', in B. Czapla, T. Lehmann, and S. Liell (eds.), *Vir bonus dicendi peritus: Festschrift für A. Weishe zum 65. Geburtstag*. Wiesbaden: 13–26.

Cairns, F. 1979. *Tibullus: A Hellenistic Poet at Rome*. Cambridge.

Cairns, F. 2008. 'C. Asinius Pollio and the *Eclogues*', *CCJ* 54: 49–79.

Campanile, D. 2007. 'L'assemblea provincial d'Asia in età repubblicana', in G. Urso (ed.), *Tra oriente e occidente: Indigeni, Greci e Romani in Asia Minore*. Pisa: 129–40.

Caneva, S.G. 2012. 'Queens and Ruler Cults in Early Hellenism: Festivals, Administration, and Ideology', *Kernos* 25: 75–101.

Carbone, L.F. 2020. 'Mark Antony and the Bronze Revolution in the East', in A. Powell and A. Burnett (eds.), *Coins of the Roman Revolution, 49 BC–AD 14: Evidence without Hindsight*. Swansea: 43–78.

Carlsen, J. 2006. *The Rise and Fall of a Noble Family: The Domitii Ahenobarbi 196 BC–AD 68*. Odense.

Carney, T.F. 1961. *A Biography of C. Marius*. Rome.

Carney, E.D. 2013. *Arisinoë of Egypt and Macedon*. Oxford.

Carotta, F., and Eickenberg, A. 2011. 'Liberalia tu accusas! Restituting the Ancient Date of Caesar's *funus*', *REA* 113: 447–67.

Cavaggioni, F. 1998. *L. Apulieo Satunino: Tribunus plebis seditiosus.* Venice.

Cayla, J.-B. 2017. 'Antoine, Cléopιâtre, et le technites dionysiaques à Chypre', *Bulletin de Correspondance Hellénique* 141: 313–36.

Cébeillac Gervasoni, M., and Lamoine, L. 2003. *Les élites et leurs facettes: les élites locales dans le monde hellénistique et romain.* Rome.

Cerfaux, L., and Tondriau, J. 1957. *Le culte des souverans dans la civilisation Gréco-romaine.* Paris.

Chamoux, F. 1986. *Marc Antoine, dernier prince de l'Orient grec.* Paris.

Champlin, E. 199. *Final Judgments: Duty and Emotion in Roman Wills 200 B.C.–A.D. 250.* Berkeley and Los Angeles.

Chaniotis, A. 2011. 'The Ithyphallic Hymn for Demetrios Poliorketes and Hellenistic Religious Mentality', in P.P. Iossif, A.S. Chankowski, and C.C. Lorber (eds.), *More Than Men, Less Than Gods: Studies on Royal Cult and Imperial Worship.* Leuven: 157–95.

Charles, M.B., and Anagnostou-Laoutides, E. 2012. 'Galba in the Bedroom: Sexual Allusions in Suetonius' *Galba*', *Latomus* 71: 1077–87.

Charlesworth, M.P. 1933. 'The Fragments of Propaganda of Mark Antony', *CQ* 27: 172–7.

Charlesworth, M.P. 1934. 'The Avenging of Caesar', in S.A. Cook, F.E. Adcock, and M.P. Charlesworth (eds.), *The Cambridge Ancient History*, vol. 10. Cambridge: 1–30.

Chauveau, M. 2002. *Cleopatra: Beyond the Myth*, trans. D. Lorton. Ithaca.

Cheshire, W.A. 2007. 'Aphrodite Cleopatra', *Journal of the American Research Center in Egypt* 43: 151–91.

Chevrollier, F. 2016. 'From Cyrene to Gortyn. Notes on the Relationship between Crete and Cyrenaica under Roman Domination (1st Century BC–4th Century AD)', in J.E. Francis and A. Kouremenos (eds.), *Roman Crete: New Perspectives.* Oxford: 11–26.

Chrissanthos, S.G. 2001. 'Caesar and the Mutiny of 47 B.C.', *JRS* 91: 63–75.

Clark, A.J. 2007a. *Divine Qualities: Cult and Community in Republican Rome.* Oxford.

Clark, A.J. 2007b. 'Nasica and *Fides*', *CQ* 57: 125–31.

Clark, J.H. 2014. *Triumph in Defeat: Military Loss and the Roman Republic.* Oxford.

Clausen, W. 1994. *A Commentary on Virgil, Eclogues.* Oxford.

Clemente, G. 2022. 'The *Census*', in V. Arena and J. Prag (eds.), *A Companion to the Political Culture of the Roman Republic.* Malden: 193–205.

Clinton, K. 1989. 'The Eleusinian Mysteries: Roman Initiates and Benefactors', *ANRW* 2.18.12: 1499–1539.

Cluett, R.G. 1998. 'Roman Women and Triumviral Politics, 43–37 B.C.', *EMC* 42: 67–84.

Cole. S. 2013. *Cicero and the Rise of Deification in Rome.* Cambridge.

Coleman, R. 1977. *Vergil: Eclogues.* Cambridge.

Collart, P. 1937. *Philippes, Ville de Macédoine, depuis ses origines jusqu'à la fin de l'époque romaine.* Paris.

Collins, A., and Walsh, J. 2015. 'Debt Deflationary Crisis in the Late Roman Republic', *Ancient Society* 45: 125–70.

Combès, R. 1966. *Imperator: Recherches sur l'emploi et la signification du titre d'imperator dans le Rome républicaine.* Paris.

Connolly, J. 2007. 'Virile Tongues: Rhetoric and Masculinity', in W. Dominik and J. Hall (eds.), *A Companion to Roman Rhetoric.* Malden: 83–97.

Cooley, A.E. 2009. *Res Gestae Divi Augusti:* Text, *Translation, and Commentary.* Cambridge.

Cooper, K. 1992. 'Insinuations of Womanly Influence: An Aspect of the Christianization of the Roman Aristocracy', *JRS* 82: 150–64.

Corbeil, A. 2002. 'Ciceronian Invective', in J. May (ed.), *Brill's Companion to Cicero: Oratory and Rhetoric.* Leiden: 197–218.

Cornell, T.J. 1995. *The Beginnings of Rome: Italy and Rome from the Bronze Age to the Punic Wars (c. 1000–264 BC).* London.

Cornwall, H. 2017. *Pax and the Politics of Peace: From Republic to Principate.* Oxford.

Cornwall, H. 2020. 'A Framework of Negotiation and Reconcilation in the Triumviral Period', in F. Pina Polo (ed.), *The Triumviral Period: Civil War, Political Crisis and Socioeconomic Transformations.* Zaragoza: 149–70.

Coşkun, A. 2005. 'Inklusion und Exklusion von Fremden in den Gerichtsreden Ciceros', in S. Harwardt and J. Schwind (eds.), *Corona coronaria: Festschrift für Hans-Otto Kröner zum 75. Geburtstag.* Hildesheim: 77–98.

Cottier, M., Crawford, M.H., Crowther, C.V., Ferrary, J.-L., Levick, B.M., Salomies, O., and Wörrle, M. (eds.). 2008. *The Customs Law of Asia.* Oxford.

Courrier, C. 2014. *La plèbe de Rome et sa culture (fin du IIe siècle av. J.-C.–fin du Ier siècle ap. J.-C.).* Rome.

Couvenhes, J.-C. 2013. 'Le *basilikon sympion* de Cléopâtre à Tarse et Antonine *neos Dionysos* à Athènes', in C. Grandjean, A. Heller, and J. Peigney (eds.), *À la table des rois: Luxe et pouvoir dans l'oeuvre d'Athénée.* Rennes: 229–50.

Craig, C.P. 2004. 'Audience Expectations, Invective, and Proof', in J. Powell and J. Patterson (eds.), *Cicero the Advocate.* Oxford: 187–214.

Craven, L. 1918. *Antony's Oriental Policy until the Defeat of the Parthian Expedition.* Columbia.

Crawford, M. H. 1985. *Coinage and Money under the Roman Republic: Italy and the Mediterranean Economy.* Berkeley and Los Angeles.

Cresci Marrone, G. 2014. 'Spigolatura triumvirale: Il procuratore Manio nella lotta fra Marco Antonio e il giovane Cesare', *Paideia* 69: 47–63.

Cristofoli, R. 2008. *Antonio e Cesare: Anni 54–44 a.C.* Rome.

Cristofoli, R. 2019. 'I *chirographa Caesaris* e l'altalenante rapporto tra Marco Antonio e il senato nella primavera del 44 a. C.', *Giornale Italiano di Filologia* 71: 177–203.

Crook, J. 1957. 'A Legal Point about Mark Antony's Will', *JRS* 47: 36–8.

Crook, J.A. 1996. 'Political History, 30 B.C. to A.D. 14', in A.K. Bowman, E. Champlin, and A. Lintott (eds.), *The Cambridge Ancient History*, 2nd ed., vol. 10. Cambridge: 70–112.

Csapo, E. 2010. *Actors and Icons of the Ancient Theater.* Oxford.

Cugusi, P. 1970. *Epistolographi Latini Minores*, vol. 1. Turin.

Culham, P. 1989. 'Archives and Alternatives in Republican Rome', *CPh* 84: 100–115.

Damon, C. 1992. 'Sex. Cloelius, *Scriba*', *HSCPh* 94: 227–50.

Daubner, F. 2014. 'On the Coin Iconography of Roman Colonies in Macedonia', in N.T. Elkins and S. Krmnicek (eds.), *Art in the Round: New Approaches to Ancient Coin Iconography.* Rahden: 109–19.

Daubner, F. 2015. '*Gymnasia*: Aspects of a Greek Institution in the Hellenistic and Roman Near East' in M. Blömer, A. Lichtenberger, and R. Raja (eds.), *Religious Identities in the Levant from Alexander to Muhammed: Continuity and Change*. Turnhout: 33–46.

Daubner, F. 2018. 'Peer Polity Interaction in Hellenistic Northern Greece: *Theoria* Going to Epirus and Macedonia', in H. Börm and N. Luraghi (eds.), *The Polis in the Hellenistic World*. Stuttgart: 131–57.

Davenport, C. 2019. *A History of the Roman Equestrian Order*. Cambridge.

Day, J. 1942. *An Economic History of Athens under Roman Domination*. New York.

Day, S. 2017. 'The Date and Scope of M. Antonius Creticus' Command against the Pirates', *Historia* 66: 298–330.

Debevoise, N.C. 1938. *A Political History of Parthia*. Chicago.

Degrassi, A. 1947. *Fasti Consulares et Triumphales: Inscriptiones Italiae* 13.1. Rome.

Degrassi, A. 1954. *Fasti Capitolini*. Rome.

Delia, D. 1991. 'Fulvia Reconsidered', in S.B. Pomeroy (ed.), *Women's History and Ancient History*. Chapel Hill: 197–217.

Dench, E. 2005. *Romulus' Asylum: Roman Identities from the Age of Alexander to the Age of Hadrian*. Oxford.

Dench, E. 2013. 'Cicero and Roman Identity', in C. Steel (ed.), *The Cambridge Companion to Cicero*. Cambridge: 122–37.

Dench, E. 2018. *Empire and Political Cultures in the Roman World*. Cambridge.

Deniaux, E. 1988. 'Cicéron et la protection des cites de l'Illyrie du sud et de l'Épire, Dyrrachium et Buthrote', *Iliria* 18: 143–64.

Deniaux, E. 1993. *Clientèle et pouvoir à l'époque de Cicéron*. Paris.

Deniaux, E. 2005. 'Antoine en 44 av. J.-C.: Propositions de lois et recherches de clientèles', in P. Sineux (ed.), *Le législateur et la loi dan l'Antiquité: Homage à Françoise Ruzé*. Caen: 215–23.

Denniston, J.D. 1926. *M. Tulli Ciceronis in M. Antonius Orationes Philippicae, Prima et Secunda*. Oxford.

De Souza, P. 1999. *Piracy in the Graeco-Roman World*. Cambridge.

Dessau, H. 1913. 'De reginia Pythodoride et de Pythodoride iuniore', *Ephemeris Epigraphica* 9: 691–6.

Dettenhofer, M.H. 1992. *Perdita Iuventus: Zwischen den Generationen von Caesar und Augustus*. Munich.

Dillon, J.N. 2007. 'Octavian's Finances after Actium, before Egypt: The CAESAR DIVI F / IMP CAESAR Coinage and Antony's Legionary Issue', *Chiron* 37: 35–48.

Dinsmoor, W.B. 1931. *The Archons of Athens in the Hellenistic Age*. Cambridge, Mass.

Dmitriev, S. 2005. *City Government in Hellenistic and Roman Asia Minor*. Oxford.

Draycott, J. 2012. 'Dynastic Politics, Defeat, Decadence and Dining: Cleopatra Selene on the So-Called "Africa" Dish from the Villa della Pisanella at Boscoreale', *PBSR* 80: 45–64.

Drew-Bear, T. 1972. 'Deux décrets hellénistiques d'Asie Mineure', *BCH* 96: 435–71.

Driediger-Murphy, L.G. 2018a. *Roman Republican Augury: Freedom and Control*. Oxford.

Driediger-Murphy, L.G. 2018b. 'Falsifying the Auspices in Republican Politics', in H. van der Blom, C. Gray, and C. Steel (eds.), *Institutions and Ideology in Republican Rome: Speech, Audience and Decision*. Cambridge: 183–202.

Drogula, F.K. 2019. *Cato the Younger: Life and Death at the End of the Republic*. Oxford.

Drummond, A. 1989. 'Rome in the Fifth Century II: The Citizen Community', in F.W. Walbank, A.E. Astin, M.W. Frederiksen, R.M. Ogilvie, and A. Drummond (eds.), *The Cambridge Ancient History*, 2nd ed., vol. 7, part 2. Cambridge: 172–242.

Drummond, A. 1995. *Law, Politics and Power: Sallust and the Execution of the Catilinarian Conspirators*. Stuttgart.

Duff, T.E. 2004. 'Plato, Tragedy, the Ideal Reader and Plutarch's *Demetrius and Antony*', *Hermes* 132: 271–91.

Dugan, J. 2005. *Making a New Man: Ciceronian Self-Fashioning in the Rhetorical Works*. Oxford.

Dunkle, J.R. 1967. 'The Greek Tyrant and Roman Political Invective of the Late Republic', *TAPhA* 98: 151–71.

DuQuesnay, I.M. Le M. 1976. 'Virgil's Fourth *Eclogue*', *PLLS* 1:25–99.

Dyck, A.R. 2013. *Cicero: Pro Marco Caelio*. Cambridge.

Earl, D.C. 1963. *Tiberius Gracchus: A Study in Politics*. Brussels.

Earl, D.C. 1967. *The Moral and Political Tradition of Rome*. Ithaca.

Ebert, J. 1987. 'Zum Brief des Marcus Antonius an das κοινὸν Ἀσίας', *APF* 33: 37–42.

Eck, W. 1995. 'Augustus und Claudius in Perusia', *Athenaeum* 83: 83–90.

Edwards, C. 1993. *The Politics of Immorality in Ancient Rome*. Cambridge.

Edwards, C. 1996. *Writing Rome: Textual Approaches to the City*. Cambridge.

Eilers, C. 2002. *Roman Patrons of Greek Cities*. Oxford.

Elliott, C.P. 2020. *Economic Theory and the Roman Monetary Economy*. Cambridge.

Epstein, D.F. 1987. *Personal Enmity in Roman Politics, 218–43 B.C.* London.

Errington, R.M. 1988. 'Aspects of Roman Acculturation in the East under the Republic', in P. Kneissl and V. Losemann (eds.), *Alte Geschichte und Wissenschaft: Festschrift für Karl Christ zum 65. Geburtstag*. Darmstadt: 140–57.

Erskine, A. 1994. 'The Romans as Common Benefactors', *Historia* 43: 70–87.

Erskine, A. 2013. 'Hellenistic Parades and Roman Triumphs', in A. Spalinger and J. Armstrong (eds.), *Rituals of Triumph in the Mediterranean World*. Leiden: 37–55.

España-Chamorro, S. 2012. 'The *Procurator Campaniae* and the "Lands of Capua" on Crete', *Annual of the British School at Athens* 116: 1–21.

Evans, J.D. 1990. 'Statues of the Kings and Brutus on the Capitoline', *Opuscula Romana* 18: 99–105.

Evans, R.J. 1994. *Gaius Marius: A Political Biography*. Pretoria.

Evans Grubbs, J.A. 1995. *Law and Family in Late Antiquity: The Emperor Constantine's Marriage Legislation*. Oxford.

Fantham, E. 1975. 'The trials of Gabinius in 54 B.C.', *Historia* 24: 425–43.

Farney, G.D. 2004. 'Some More Roman Republican "Also Rans"', *Historia* 53: 246–50.

Fauconnier, B. 2016. 'Athletes and Artists in an Expanding World: The Development of Transregional Associations of Competitors in the First Century BC', in C. Mann, S. Remijsen, and S. Scharff (eds.), *Athletics in the Hellenistic World*. Stuttgart: 73–93.

Ferguson, W.S. 1911. *Hellenistic Athens: An Historical Essay*. London.

Ferrary, J.-L. 1999. 'À propos de deux passages des Pilippiques', *Archiv für Relgionsgeschichte* 1: 215–32.

Ferrary, J.-L. 2009. 'The Powers of Augustus', in J. Edmondson (ed.), *Augustus*. Edinburgh: 90–136.

Ferriès, M.-C. 2007. *Les partisans d'Antoine: Des orphelins de César aux complices de Cléopatre*. Bordeaux.

Ferriès, M.-C. 2009. '*Luperci* et *lupercalia* de César à Auguste', *Latomus* 68: 373–92.

Ferriès, M.-C. 2012. 'L'ombre de César dans le politique du consul Marc Antoine', in O. Devillers and K. Sion-Jenkis (eds.), *César sous Auguste*. Paris: 55–72.

Ferriès, M.-C. 2016. 'Les confiscations durant les guerres civiles, une arme supplémentaire ou un mal necessaire?', in C. Chillet, M.-C. Ferriès, and Y. Rivière (eds.), *Les confiscations, le pouvoir et Rome de la fin de la République à la mort de Néron*. Bordeaux: 139–63.

Ferriès, M.-C. 2020. '*Senatorum . . . Incondita Turba* (Suet. *Aug.* 35.1): Was the Senate Composed so as to Ensure Its Compliance?', in F. Pina Polo (ed.), *The Triumviral Period: Civil War, Political Crisis and Socioeconomic Transformations*. Zaragoza: 71–98.

Ferriès, M.-C., and Delrieux, F. 2017. 'Un tournant pour le monnayage provincial romain d'Asie Mineure: Les effigies de matrones romaines, Fulvia, Octavia, Livia et Julia (43 a.C.-37p.C.)', in L. Cavalier, M.-C. Ferriès, and F. Delrieux (eds.), *Auguste e l'Asie Mineure*. Bordeaux: 357–83.

Fezzi, L. 2003. *Falsificazione de documenti pubblici nella Roma tardorepubblicana (133–31 A.C.)*. Florence.

Fezzi, L. 2019. *Pompeo: Conquistatore del mondo, difensore della res publica, eroe tragico*. Rome.

Fischer, R.A. 1999. *Fulvia und Octavia: Die beiden Ehefrauen des Marcus Antonius in den politischen Kämpfen der Umbruchszeit zwischen Republik und Principat*. Berlin.

Flaig, E. 2003. *Ritualisierte Politik: Zeichen, Gesten und Herrschaft in alten Rom*. Göttingen.

Flamerie de Lachapelle, G. 2011. *Clementia: Recherches sur la notion de clémence à Rome, du début du 1er siècle a.C. à la mort d'Auguste*. Paris.

Flower, H.I. 1996. *Ancestor Masks and Aristocratic Power in Roman Culture*. Oxford.

Flower, H.I. 2006. *The Art of Forgetting: Disgrace and Oblivion in Roman Political Culture*. Chapel Hill.

Flower, H.I. 2014. 'Spectacle and Political Culture in the Roman Republic', in H. Flower (ed.), *The Cambridge Companion to the Roman Republic*, 2nd ed. Cambridge: 377–98.

Fontani, E. 1999. 'Il filellenismo di Antonio tra realtà storica e propaganda politica: Le ginnasiarchie ad Atene ad Alessandria', *Studi Ellenistici* 12: 193–210.

Fournier, J. 2010. *Entre tutelle romaine et autonomie civique: L'administration judicaire dans les provinces héllenophones de l'empire romain (129 av. J.-C.–325 apr. J.-C.)*. Paris.

Frederiksen, M.W. 1966. 'Caesar, Cicero and the Problem of Debt', *JRS* 56: 128–41.

Fraser, P.M. 1957. 'Mark Antony in Alexandria. A Note', *JRS* 47: 71–73.

Fraser, P.M. 1972. *Ptolemaic Alexandria*. Oxford.

Frier, B. 1985. *The Rise of the Roman Jurists: Studies in Cicero's Pro Caecina*. Princeton.

Frija, G. 2017. 'Les honneurs des cités d'Asie aux proches des gouverneurs', in A. Heller and O.M. van Nijf (eds.), *The Politics of Honour in the Greek Cities of the Roman Empire*. Leiden: 272–90.

Frisch, H. 1946. *Cicero's Fight for the Republic: The Historical Background of Cicero's Philippics*. Copenhagen.

Frye, R. N. 1984. *The History of Ancient Iran*. Munich.

Gabba, E. 1956. *Appiano e la storia delle guerre civili*. Florence.

Gabba, E. 1970. *Appiani Bellorum Civilium Liber Quintus*. Florence.

Gabba, E. 1971. 'The Perusine War and Triumviral Italy', *HSCPh* 75: 139–60.

Gabba, E. 1994. 'Rome and Italy: The Social War', in J.A. Crook, A. Lintott, and E. Rawson, E. (eds.), *The Cambridge Ancient History*, 2nd ed., vol. 9. Cambridge: 104–28.

Galinsky, C. 1996. *Augustan Culture: An Interpretive Introduction*. Princeton.

Garcea, A. 2012. *Caesar's* De Analogia: Edition, *Translation, and Commentary*. Oxford.

García Morcillo, M. 2020. '*Hasta infinita*? Financial Strategies in the Triumviral Period', in F. Pina Polo (ed.), *The Triumviral Period: Civil War, Political Crisis and Socioeconomic Transformations*. Zaragoza: 379–97.

García Riaza, E. 2020. 'Information Exchange and Political Communication in the Triumviral Period: Some Remarks on Means and Methods', in F. Pina Polo (ed.), *The Triumviral Period: Civil War, Political Crisis and Socioeconomic Transformations*. Zaragoza: 281–300.

Gauthier, P. 1985. *Les cites grecques et leur bienfaiteurs*. Paris.

Geagan, D.J. 2011. *The Athenian Agora: Inscriptions: The Dedicatory Monuments*. Princeton.

Geiger, J. 1989. 'An Overlooked Item in the War of Propaganda between Octavian and Antony', *Historia* 29: 112–4.

Gelzer, M. 1968. *Caesar: Politician and Statesman*, trans. P. Needham. Cambridge, Mass.

Gelzer, M. 1969. *Cicero: Ein biographischer Versuch*. Wiesbaden.

Giovannini, A. 2015. *Les institutions de la République romaine des origines à la mort d'Auguste*. Basel.

Giuliani, C.F. 2008/9. 'Santuario di Ercole Vincitore a Tivoli: Le fontane sulla fronte del tempio', *Atti della Pontificia Accademia Romana di Archeologia* 81: 109–27.

Giuliani, C.F. 2016. 'Santuario di Ercole Vincitore a Tivoli. 3, L'architettura', *Bollettino d'Arte* 101: 1–50.

Gleason, M. 1995. *Making Men: Sophists and Self-Presentation in Ancient Rome*. Princeton.

Goldbeck, H. 2010. *Salutationes: Die Morgenbegrüßungen in Rom in der Republik und der frühen Kaiserzeit*. Berlin.

Goldsworthy, A. 1996. *The Roman Army at War, 100 BC–AD 200*. Oxford.

Goldsworthy, A. 2010. *Antony and Cleopatra*. New Haven.

Goodenough, E.R. 1928. 'The Political Philosophy of Hellenistic Kingship', *YCS* 1: 55–104.

Gosling, A. 1986. 'Octavian, Brutus and Apollo: A Note on Opportunist Propaganda', *AJPh* 107: 586–9.

Gotter, U. 1996. *Der Diktator ist tot! Politk in Rom zwischen den Iden des März und der Begründung des Zweiten Triumvirats*. Stuttgart.

Gowers, E. 2012. *Horace: Satires Book 1*. Cambridge.

Gowing, A.M. 1992. *The Triumviral Narratives of Appian and Cassius Dio*. Ann Arbor.

Gowing, A.M. 2013. 'Tully's Boat: Responses to Cicero in the Imperial Period', in C. Steel (ed.), *The Cambridge Companion to Cicero*. Cambridge: 233–50.

Gradel, I. 2004. *Emperor Worship and Roman Religion*. Oxford.

Grant, M. 1946. *From Imperium to Auctoritas*. Cambridge.

Green, P. 1990. *Alexander to Actium: The Historical Evolution of the Hellenistic Age*. Berkeley and Los Angeles.

Green, R.P.H. 1996. 'Octavian and Vergil's *Eclogues*', *Euphrosyne* 24: 225–36.

Greenidge, A.H.J. 1901. *The Legal Procedure of Cicero's Time*. London.

Grillo, L. 2012. *The Art of Caesar's Bellum Civile:* Literature, *Ideology, and Community.* Cambridge.

Grillo, L. 2015. *Cicero's* De Provinciis Consularibus Oratio. Oxford.

Griffin, J. 1986. *Latin Poets and Roman Life.* Chapel Hill.

Griffin, M.T. 2013. *Seneca on Society: A Guide to* De Beneficiis. Oxford.

Groag, E. 1915. 'Beigräge zur Geschichte des zweiten Triumvirats', *Klio* 14: 48–68.

Gruen, E.S. 1965. 'The Lex Varia', *JRS* 55: 59–73.

Gruen, E.S. 1974. *The Last Generation of the Roman Republic.* Berkeley and Los Angeles.

Gruen, E.S. 1992. *Culture and National Identity in Republican Rome.* Ithaka.

Gruen, E.S. 2003. 'Cleopatra in Rome: Facts and Fantasies', in D. Braund and C. Gill (eds.), *Myth, History and Culture in Republican Rome: Studies in Honour of T.P. Wiseman.* Exeter: 257–74.

Gruen, E.S. 2006. 'Romans and Others', in N. Rosenstein and R. Morstein-Marx (eds.), *A Companion to the Roman Republic.* Malden: 459–77.

Gruen, E.S. 2008. 'Cleopatra in Rome: Facts and Fantasies', in M.M. Miles (ed.), *Cleopatra: A Sphinx Revisited.* Berkeley and Los Angeles: 37–53.

Gruen, E.S. 2013. 'Did Romans Have an Ethnic Identity?', *Antichthon* 47: 1–17.

Gruen, E.S. 2016. *The Construct of Identity in Hellenistic Judaism: Essays on Early Jewish Literature and History.* Berlin.

Habicht, C. 1997. *Athens from Alexander to Antony.* Cambridge, Mass.

Habicht, C. 2017. *Divine Honors for Mortal Men in Greek Cities: The Early Cases.* Ann Arbor.

Halfmann, H. 2011. *Marcus Antonius.* Darmstadt.

Hall, J. 2007. 'The Rhetorical Design and Success of Cicero's *Twelfth Philippic*', in T. Stevenson and M. Wilson (eds.), *Cicero's Philippics: History, Rhetoric, and Ideology.* Auckland: 282–304.

Hall, J. 2009. *Politeness and Politics in Cicero's Letters.* Oxford.

Hall, J. 2014. *Cicero's Use of Judicial Theater.* Ann Arbor.

Hallett, J.P. 1977. '*Perusinae Glandes* and the Changing Image of Augustus', *AJAH* 2: 151–71.

Harders, A.-C. 2015. 'Consort or Despot? How to Deal with a Queen at the End of the Roman Republic and the Beginning of the Principate', in H. Börm (ed.), *Antimonarchic Discourse in Antiquity.* Stuttgart: 181–214.

Harders, A.-C. 2017. 'Familienbande(n): Die politische Bedeutung von Verwandtschaft in der römischen Republik', in M. Haake and A.-C. Harders (eds.), *Politische Kultur und soziale Struktur der Römischen Republik: Bilanzen und Perspektiven.* Stuttgart: 197–214.

Harries, J. 2007. *Law and Crime in the Roman World.* Cambridge.

Harris, W.V. 1971. *Rome in Etruria and Umbria.* Oxford.

Harris, W.V. 1979. *War and Imperialism in Republican Rome, 327–70 B.C.* Oxford.

Harris, W.V. 2019. 'Credit-Money in the Roman Economy', *Klio* 101: 158–89.

Haug, E. 2008. 'Local Politics in the Late Republic: Antony and Cleopatra at Patras', *American Journal of Numismatics* 20: 404–20.

Havener, W. 2016. *Imperator Augustus: Die diskursive Konstituierung der militärischen persona des ersten römischen princeps.* Stuttgart.

Haymann, F. 2016. 'Der Perusinische Krieg und die Münzen für Marcus Antonius im Jahr 41', in F. Haymann, W. Hollstein, and M. Jehne (eds.), *Neuere Forschungen zur*

Münzprägung der römischen Republik. Beiträge zum internationalen Kolloquium um Residenzschloss Dresden 19–21. Juni 2014. Bonn: 215–44.

Hawkins, T. 2017. 'Pollio's Paradox: Popular Invective and the Transition to Empire', in L. Grig (ed.), *Popular Culture in the Ancient World.* Cambridge: 129–48.

Head, B.V. 1906. *A Catalogue of the Greek Coins of Phrygia.* London.

Heichelheim, F.M. 1938. 'Roman Syria', in T. Frank (ed.), *An Economic Survey of Ancient Rome,* vol. 4. Baltimore: 121–258.

Hekster, O., and Kaizer, T. 2004. 'Mark Antony and the Raid on Palmyra: Reflections on Appian, *Bella Civilia* V, 9', *Latomus* 63: 70–80.

Hellegouarc'h, J. 1963. *Le vocabulaire latin des relations et des partis politiques sous la république.* Paris.

Hellegouarc'h, J. 1982. *Velleius Paterculus, Histoire Romaine,* vol. 2. Paris.

Henderson, J. 1999. *Writing Down Rome: Satire, Comedy, and Other Offences in Latin Poetry.* Oxford.

Hemelrijk, E.A. 1999. *Matrona Docta: Educated Women in the Roman Elite from Cornelia to Julia Domna.* London.

Herman, G. 1997. 'The Court Society of the Hellenistic Age', in P. Cartledge, P. Garnsey, and E. Gruen (eds.), *Hellenistic Constructs: Essays in Culture, History, and Historiography.* Berkeley and Los Angeles: 199–224.

Herzog, E. 1876. 'Die lex sacrata und das sacrosanctum', *Jahrbücher für classische Philologie* 22: 139–50.

Hinard, F. 1985. *Les proscriptions de la Rome républicaine.* Rome.

Hinard, F. 2011. *Rome, la dernière République: Recueil d'articles.* Paris.

Hinrichs, F.T. 1969. 'Das legale Landversprechen im Bellum Civile', *Historia* 18: 521–44.

Hoff, M.C. 1989. 'Civil Disobedience and Unrest in Augustan Athens', *Hesperia* 58: 267–76.

Höbl, G. 2001. *A History of the Ptolemaic Empire.* London.

Hölkeskamp, K.-J. 2004. *Senatus Populusque Romanus: Die politische Kultur der Republik— Dimensionen und Deutungen.* Stuttgart.

Hölkeskamp, K.-J. 2010. *Reconstructing the Roman Republic: An Ancient Political Culture and Modern Research.* Princeton.

Hölkeskamp, K.-J. 2014. 'Under Roman Roofs: Family, House, and Household', in H.I. Flower (ed.), *The Cambridge Companion to the Roman Republic,* 2nd ed. Cambridge: 101–26.

Hölkeskamp, K.-J. 2017. *Libera Res Publica: Die politische Kultur des antiken Rom— Positionen und Perspektiven.* Stuttgart.

Hölkeskamp, K.-J. 2020. *Roman Republican Reflections: Studies in Politics, Power, and Pageantry.* Stuttgart.

Hollis, A.S. 1996. 'Octavian in the Fourth Georgic', *CQ* 46: 305–8.

Hollis, A.S. 2007. *Fragments of Roman Poetry, c. 60 BC–AD 20.* Oxford.

Hollstein, W. 1994. 'Apollo und Libertas in der Münzprägung des Brutus und Cassius', *Jahrbuch für Numismatik und Geldgeschichte* 44: 113–33.

Holmes, T.R. 1928. *The Architect of the Roman Empire.* Oxford.

Holt, P. 1988. 'Sex, Tyranny, and Hippias' Incest Dream', *GRBS* 39: 221–41.

Holtzman, B., and Salviat, F. 1981. 'Les portraits sculptés de Marc-Antoine', *Bulletin de Correspondence Hellénique* 105: 265–88.

Hopkins, K. 1983. *Death and Renewal*. Cambridge.

Hose, M. 2018. 'Augustus' Eintritt in die griechische Literatur', *Hermes* 146: 23–40.

Howgego, C. 1993. 'Rev. of A. Burnett, M. Amandry, and P.P. Ripollès, *Roman Provincial Coinage I: From the Death of Caesar to the Death of Vitellius (44 B.C.–A.D. 69)*', *JRS* 88: 199–203.

Hunter, R. 2003. *Theocritus: Encomium of Ptolemy Philadelphus*. Berkeley and Los Angeles.

Hurlet, F. 2020. 'The *Auctoritas* and *Libertas* of Augustus: Metamorphosis of the Roman Res Publica', in C. Balmaceda (ed.), *Libertas and Res Publica in the Roman Republic*. Leiden: 170–88.

Hurwit, J.M. 1999. *The Athenian Acropolis: History, Mythology, and Archaeology from the Neolithic Era to the Present*. Cambridge.

Hutchinson, G.O. 1998. *Cicero's Correspondence: A Literary Study*. Oxford.

Huttner, U. 1995. 'Marcus Antonius und Herakles', in C. Schubert, K. Broderson, and U. Huttner (eds.), *Rom und der griechische Osten: Festschrift für Hatto H. Schmitt zum 65. Geburtstag*. Stuttgart: 103–12.

Huzar, E.G. 1978. *Mark Antony: A Biography*. Minneapolis.

Huzar, E. 1982. 'The Literary Efforts of Mark Antony', *ANRW* 2.30.1: 639–57.

Ijalba Pérez, P. 2009. 'La familia Antonia descendiente de Antón, hijo de Heracles: La manipulación de un mito', *Studia Historica. Studia Antiqua* 27: 177–96.

Ioannatou, M. 2006. *Affaires d'argent dans la correspondance de Cicéron: L'aristocratie sénatoriale face à ses dettes*. Paris.

Jacóme, P.M. 2013. 'Bacchus and Felines in Roman Iconography: Issues of Gender and Species', in A. Bernabé, M.H. de Jáuregui, A.I.J. San Cristóbal, and R.M. Hernández (eds.), *Redefining Dionysus*. Berlin: 516–40.

Jacotot, M. 2013. *Question d'honneur: Les notions d'honos, honestum et honestas dan la République romaine antique*. Rome.

Jeanmaire, H. 1924. 'La politique religieuse d'Antoine et de Cléopatre', *Revue Archéologique* 19: 241–61.

Jehne, M. 1987. *Der Staat des Dictators Caesar*. Cologne.

Jehne, M. 2011. 'The Rise of the Consular as a Social Type in the Third and Second Centuries BC', in H. Beck, A. Duplá, M. Jehne, and F. Pina Polo (eds.), *Consuls and the Res Publica: Holding High Office in the Roman Republic*. Cambridge: 211–31.

Jehne, M. 2015. 'From *Patronus* to *Pater*: The Changing Role of Patronage in the Period of Transition from Pompey to Augustus', in M. Jehne and F. Pina Polo (eds.), *From Clientelae in the Roman Empire: A Reconsideration*. Stuttgart: 297–320.

Jehne, M. 2016. 'The Senatorial Economics of Status in the Late Republic', in H. Beck, M. Jehne, and J. Serrati (eds.), *Money and Power in the Late Republic*. Brussels: 188–207.

Jehne, M., and Pfeilschifter, R. (eds.). 2006. *Herrschaft ohne Integration? Rom und Italien in republikanischer Zeit*. Frankfurt.

Jewell, E. 2018. 'Like Father, Like Son? The Dynamics of Family Exemplarity and Ideology in (Fragmentary) Republican Oratory', in H. van der Blom, C. Gray, and C. Steel (eds.), *Institutions and Ideology in Republican Rome: Speech, Audience and Decision*. Cambridge: 267–82.

Johnson, J.R. 1978. 'The Authenticity and Validity of Antony's Will', *Antiquité Classique* 47: 494–503.

Jones, A.H.M. 1940. *The Greek City from Alexander to Justinian*. Oxford.

Jones, A.H.M 1971. *The Cities of the Eastern Roman Provinces*, 2nd ed. Oxford.

Jones, C.P. 2017. 'Strabo and the "Petty Dynasts"', in L. Cavalier, M.-C. Ferriès, and F. Delrieux (eds.), *Auguste et l'Asie Mineure*. Bordeaux: 349–56.

Jones, K.R. 2017. 'Marcus Antonius' Median War and the Dynastic Politics of the Near East', in J.M. Schlude and B.B. Rubin (eds.), *Cross-Cultural Interactions of the Parthian Empire*. Oxford: 51–63.

Jordan, B. 'The consular *provinciae* of 44 BCE and the collapse of the restored Republic', *Hermes* 145: 174–94.

Joyce, L.B. 2001. 'Dirce Disrobed', *CA* 20: 221–38.

Kajanto, I. 1965. *The Latin Cognomina*. Helsinki.

Kallet-Marx, R. 1995. *Hegemony to Empire: The Development of the Roman Imperium in the East from 148 to 62 B.C.* Berkeley and Los Angeles.

Kaser, M. 1971. *Das römische Privatrecht*, vol. 1, 2nd ed. Munich.

Kaster, R.A. 2005. *Emotion, Restraint, and Community in Ancient Rome*. Princeton.

Kaster, R. A. 2006. *Cicero: Speech on Behalf of Publius Sestius*. Oxford.

Kay, P. 2014. *Rome's Economic Revolution*. Oxford.

Kearsley, R. 2013. 'Triumviral Politics, the Oath of 32 BC and the Veterans', *CQ* 63: 828–34.

Keaveney, A. 2005. *Sulla: The Last Republican*, 2nd ed. London.

Keaveney, A. 2007. *The Army in the Roman Revolution*. London.

Keppie, L. 1983. *Colonisation and Veteran Settlement in Italy 47–14 B.C.* London.

Kienast, D. 1995. 'Antonius, Augustus, die Kaiser und Athen', in D. Dietz, D. Henning, and H. Kaletsch (eds.), *Klassisches Altertum, Späntike und frühes Christentum, Adolf Lippold zum 65. Geburtstag gewidmet*. Würzburg: 191–222.

Kienast, D. 1999. *Augustus: Prinzeps und Monarch*, 3rd ed. Darmstadt.

Kim, L. 2017. 'Atticism and Asianism', in D.S. Richter and W.A. Johnson (eds.), *The Oxford Handbook of the Second Sophistic*. Oxford: 41–66.

Kirbihler, F. 2013. 'Brutus et Cassius et les impositions, spoliations et confiscations en Asie mineure durant les guerres civiles (44–42 a.C)', in M.-C. Ferriès and F. Delrieux (eds.), *Spolier et confisquer dan le monds grec et romain*. Chambéry: 345–66.

Kirbihler, F. 2020. 'Ruler Cults and Imperial Cults at Ephesus: First Century BCE to Third Century CE', in D. Schowalter, S. Ladstätter, S.J. Friesen, and C. Thomas (eds.), *Religion in Ephesus Reconsidered*. Leiden: 195–210.

Kirbihler, F., and Zabrana, L. 2014. 'Archäologische, epigrapfische, und numismatische Zeugnisse für den Kaiserkult im Artemision von Ephesos', *JÖAI* 83: 101–31.

Kirchner, J. 1948. *Imagines Inscriptionum Atticarum: Ein Bilderatlas epigraphischer Denkmäler Attikas*, 2nd ed. Berlin.

Kleiner, D.E.E. 1992. *Roman Sculpture*. New Haven.

Kleiner, D.E.E. 2005. *Cleopatra and Rome*. Cambridge, Mass.

Klotz. A. 1919. 'C. Iulius Caesar', *RE* 10: 186–275.

Knibbe, D. 1981. 'Quandocumque quis trium virorum rei publicae constituendae: Ein neuer Text aus Ephesus', *ZPE* 44: 1–10.

Knopf, F. 2018. *Die Partizipationsmotive de plebs urban aim spätrepublikanischen Rom*. Berlin.

Koenen, L. 1993. 'The Ptolemaic King as a Religious Figure', in A. Bulloch, E.S. Gruen, A.A. Long, and A. Stewart (eds.), *Images and Ideologies: Self-Definition in the Hellenistic World*. Berkeley and Los Angeles: 25–115.

Köhler, J. 1996. *Pompai: Untersuchungen zur hellenistischen Festkultur*. Frankfurt am Main.

Kolbe, W. 1914. 'Der zweite Triumvirat', *Hermes* 49: 273–95.

Konrad, C.F. 1984. 'A note on the stemma of the Gabinii Capitones', *Klio* 66: 151–56.

Konrad, C.F. 1994. *Plutarch's Sertorius: A Historical Commentary*. Chapel Hill.

Konrad, C.F. 1996. 'Notes on Roman Also-Rans', in J. Linderski (ed.), *Imperium Sine Fine: T. Robert S. Broughton and the Roman Republic*. Stuttgart: 103–43.

Konrad, C.F. 2004. 'Vellere signa', in C.F. Konrad (ed.), *Augusto augurio: Rerum humanum et divnarum commentationes in honorem Jerzy Linderski*. Stuttgart: 169–203.

Konrad, K. 2022. *The Challenge to the Auspices: Studies on Magisterial Power in the Middle Roman Republic*. Oxford.

Koortbojian, M. 2013. *The Divinization of Caesar and Augustus: Precedents, Consequences, Implications*. Cambridge.

Kraft, K. 1967. 'Zu Sueton, Divus Augustus 69,2: M. Anton und Kleopatra', *Hermes* 95: 496–9.

Kralli, L. 2016. 'Attitude to Hellenistic Athens: "To Sneer or to Revere?"', in A. Powell and K. Median (eds.), *The Eyesore of Aigina: Anti-Athenian Attitudes across the Greek, Hellenistic, and Roman Worlds*. Swansea: 163–85.

Kroll, J. 1972. 'Two Hoards of First-Century BC Athenian Bronze Coins', Αρχαιολογικον Δελτιον 27: 86–120.

Kroll, J. 1993. *The Greek Coins: Athenian Bronze Coinage, 4th–1st Centuries B.C.*, The Athenian Agora, vol. 26. Princeton.

Kroll, J. 1997. 'Traditionalism versus Romanization in Bronze Coinages of Greece, 42–31 BC', *Topoi* 7: 123–36.

Kromayer, J. 1894. 'Kleine Forschungen zur Geschichte des zweiten Triumvirats', *Hermes* 29: 556–85.

Kromayer, J. 1896. 'Kleine Forschungen zur Geschichte des zweiten Triumvirats IV: Der Partherzug des Antonius', *Hermes* 31: 70–104.

Kroymayer, J. 1899. 'Kleine Forschungen zur Geschichte des zweiten Triumvirats VII: der Feldzug von Actium und der sogenannte Verrath der Cleopatra', *Hermes* 34: 1–54.

Kunst, C. 2012. 'Isis Aphrodite: Annäherungen an eine panhellenische Gottheit', *Mediterraneo Antico* 15: 83–102.

Kunze, C. 1998. *Der Farnesische Stier und die Dirkegruppe des Apollonios und Tauriskos*. Berlin.

Lacey, W.K. 1986. *Cicero: Second Philippic Oration*. Warminster.

Ładoń, T. 2016. 'Mark Antony's Forefathers: Comments on the Role of the gens Antonia in the Final Period of the Roman Republic', in D. Słapek and I. Luć (eds.), *Marcus Antonius: History and Tradition*. Lublin: 131–46.

Laes, C., and Strubbe, J. 2014. *Youth in the Roman Empire: The Young and Restless Years?* Cambridge.

Laignoux, R. 2013. 'Justifier ou contester les confiscations des guerres civiles: L'économie discursive des sanctions patrimoniales à Rome dans les années 44–31 a.C.' in

M.-C. Ferriès and F. Delrieux (eds.), *Spolier et confisquer dans les mondes grec et roman*. Chambéry: 367–85.

Laignoux, R. 2015. 'Politique de la terre et guerre de l'*ager* à la fin de la République: Ou comment César et les triumvirs ont "inventé" des terres pour leurs vétérans', *MEFR* 127: 397–415.

Lambrinoudakis, V. 1991. 'The Sanctuary of Iria on Naxos and the Birth of Monumental Greek Architecture', *Studies in the History of Art* 32: 172–88.

Lambrinoudakis, V. 1989. 'Neues zur Ikonographie der Dirke', in H.-U. Cain, H. Gabelmann, and D. Salzmann (eds.), *Festschrift für Nikolaus Himmelmann*. Mainz am Rhein: 341–50.

Lange, C.H. 2009. *Res Publica Constituta: Actium, Apollo, and the Accomplishments of the Triumviral Assignment*. Leiden.

Lange, C.H. 2020. 'Civil War and the (Almost) Forgotten Pact of Brundisium', in F. Pina Polo (ed.), *The Triumviral Period: Civil War, Political Crisis and Socioeconomic Transformations*. Zaragoza: 127–48.

Lange, H.L. 2011. 'The battle of Actium: A Reconsideration', *CQ* 61: 608–23.

Lapryionok, R. 2010. 'Tiberius Gracchus: Die Gestalt des demokratischen Reformers in der antiken Literatur', in V.V. Dement'eva and T. Schmitt (eds.), *Volk und Demokratie in Altertum*. Göttingen: 143–7.

Latte, K. 1960. *Römische Religionsgeschichte*. Munich.

Lausberg, H. 1990. *Handbuch der literarischen Rhetorik*, 3rd ed. Stuttgart.

Larsen, J.A.O. 1938. 'Roman Greece', in T. Frank (ed.), *An Economic Survey of Ancient Rome*. Baltimore: 259–498.

Leach, E.W. 1974. *Vergil's Eclogues: Landscapes of Experience*. Ithaca.

Lebreton, S. 2009. 'Dionysos Ômèstès (Plutarch, *Thémistocle*, 13; *Antoine*, 24)', in L. Bodiou, V. Mehl, J. Oulhen, F. Prost, and J. Wilgaux (eds.), *Chemin faisant: Mythes, cultes et société en Grèce ancienne; Mélanges en l'honneur de Pierre Brulé*. Rennes: 193–203.

Le Gall, J. 1953. *Recherches sur le culte du Tiber*. Paris.

Le Guen, B. 2001. *Les associations de technites dionysiaques à l'époque hellénistique*, 2 vols. Nancy.

Le Guen, B. 2006. 'L'accueil d'Athéniôn, messager de Mithridate VI, par les Artistes dionysiaques d'Athènes en 88 av. J.-C', *Studi Ellenistici* 19: 333–63.

Lennon, J. 2012. 'Pollution, Religion and Society in the Roman World', in M. Bradley and K. Stow (eds.), *Rome, Pollution and Propriety: Dirt, Disease and Hygiene in the Eternal City from Antiquity to Modernity*. Cambridge: 43–58.

Lentano, M. 2008. 'Bruto o il potere delle immagini', *Latomus* 67: 881–99.

Lentano, M. 2009. 'Il debito di Bruto: Per un'antropologia del nome proprio nella cultura romana', *MD* 63: 59–89.

Letronne, J.-A. 1848. *Recueil des inscriptions grecques et latines de l'Égypte*, vol. 2. Paris.

Leurini, L. 2000. 'Osservazioni, vecchie e nuove, su Rhian. Fr. 1 Powell', in M. Cannatà Fera and S. Grandolini (eds.), *Poesia e Religione in Grecia: Studi in Onore di G. Aurelio Privitera*. Naples: 385–97.

Levick, B.M. 2015. *Catiline*. London.

Linderski, J. 1986. 'The Augural Law', *ANRW* 2.16.3. Berlin: 2146–312.

Linderski, J. 1995. *Roman Questions I: Selected Papers*. Stuttgart.

Linderski, J. 2007. *Roman Questions II: Selected Papers*. Stuttgart.

Lindsay, H. 2009. *Adoption in the Roman World*. Cambridge.

Lintott, A. 1968. *Violence in Republican Rome*. Oxford.

Lintott, A. 1970. 'The Tradition of Violence in the Annals of the Early Roman Republic', *Historia* 19: 12–29.

Lintott, A. 1993. *Imperium Romanum: Politics and Administration*. London.

Lintott, A. 1994. 'Political History, 146–95 B.C.', in J.A. Crook, A. Lintott, and E. Rawson (eds.), *The Cambridge Ancient History*, 2nd ed., vol. 10. Cambridge: 40–103.

Lintott, A. 1997. 'Cassius Dio and the History of the Late Roman Republic', *ANRW* 2.34.3: 2497–523.

Lintott, A. 1999. *The Constitution of the Roman Republic*. Cambridge.

Lintott, A. 2008. *Cicero as Evidence: A Historian's Companion*. Oxford.

Liou-Gille, B. 1997. 'Les leges sacratae: Esquisse historique', *Euphrosyne* 25: 61–84.

Livadiotti, U. 2013. 'Lucio Antonio, Appiano e la propaganda augustea', *Seminari Romani de Cultura Greca* 2: 65–92.

Lomas, K. 2012. 'The Weakest Link: Elite Social Networks in Republican Italy', in S.T. Roselaar (ed.), *Processes of Integration and Identity Formation in the Roman Republic*. Leiden: 197–213.

Loraux, N. 1980/81. 'L'acropole comique', *Ancient Society* 11–12: 119–50.

Lundgreen, B. 2004. 'Use and Abuse of Athena in Roman Imperial Portraiture: The Case of Julia Domna', in J. Eiring and J. Mejer (eds.), *Proceedings of the Danish Institute at Athens IV*. Aarhus: 69–91.

Lyne, R.O.A.M. 1978. *Ciris: A Poem Attributed to Vergil*. Cambridge.

Ma, J. 2000. *Antiochus III and the Cities of Asia Minor*. Oxford.

Ma, J. 2003. 'Peer Polity Interaction in the Hellenistic Age', *Past and Present* 180: 9–40.

Madsen, J.M. 2009. *Eager tone Roman: Greek Response to Roman Rule in Pontus and Bithynia*. London.

Madsen, J.M. 2016. 'Cassius Dio and the Cult of Iulius and Roma at Ephesus and Nicaea', *CQ* 66: 286–97.

Magdelain, A. 1984. 'Paracidas', in *Du châtiment dans la cite: Supplices corporels et peine de mort dans le mond antique*. Rome: 549–70.

Magie, D. 1950. *Roman Rule in Asia Minor*. Princeton.

Magnino, D. 1984. *Appiani Bellorum Civilium Liber Tertius*. Florence.

Mahy, T. 2013. 'Antonius, Triumvir and Orator: Career, Style, and Effectiveness', in C. Steel and H. van der Blom (eds.), *Community and Communication: Oratory and Politics in Republican Rome*. Oxford: 329–44.

Makhlaiuk, A.V. 2020. 'Emperors' Nicknames and Roman Political Humour', *Klio* 102: 202–35.

Malitz, J. 1984. 'Caesars Partherkrieg', *Historia* 33: 21–59.

Mangiameli, R. 2008/9. 'Le lettere scomparse di Antonio dall'oriente (41–40 a.C.)', *Atti dell'Istituto Veneto de Scienze, Lettere ed Arti* 168: 239–67.

Mangiameli, R. 2012. *Tra duces e milites: Forme di comunicazione politica al tramonto della Repubblica*. Trieste.

Manuwald, G. 2007. Cicero, *Philippics 3–9*, 2 vols. Berlin.

Manuwald, G. 2018. *Cicero: Agrarian Speeches*. Oxford.

Marasco, G. 1987. *Aspetti della politica di Marco Antonio in Oriente*. Florence.

Marco Simon, F. 2011. 'The *Feriae Latinae* as Religious Legitimation of the Consuls' *Imperium*', in H. Beck, A. Duplá, M. Jehne, and F. Pina Polo (eds.), *Consuls and Res Publica: Holding High Office in the Roman Republic*. Cambridge: 116–32.

Marek, C. 2006. *Die Inschriften von Kaunos*. Munich.

Marshall, A.M. 1999. 'Atticus and the Eastern Sojourn', *Latomus* 58: 56–88.

Martin, P.M. 2015. 'Cicéron et le *regnum*', *REA* 117: 447–62.

Mason, S. 2016. 'Josephus as a Roman Historian', in H.H. Chapman and Z. Rogers (eds.), *A Companion to Josephus*. Hoboken: 87–107.

Mastrocinque, A. 1979. 'Demetrius tragodoumenos (Propaganda e letteratura al tempo di Demetrio Poliorcete)', *Athenaeum* 67: 260–76.

Matijević, K. 2006. *Marcus Antonius, Consul-Proconsul-Staatsfiend: Die Politik der Jahre 44 and 43 v. Chr*. Rahden.

Matijević, K. 2014. 'The Caesarian Opposition against Mark Antony after the Ides of March', in. R. Cristofoli, A. Galimberti, and F. Rohr Vio (eds.), *Lo spazio del non-allineamento a Roma fra tarda Repubblica e Prima Principato: Forme e figure dell'opposizione politica*. Rome: 41–58.

McAlee, R. 2007. *The Coins of Roman Antioch*. Lancaster.

McCabe, D.F. 1991. *Kaunos Inscriptions. Texts and List*. Princeton.

McCall, J.B. 2002. *The Cavalry of the Roman Republic: Cavalry Combat and Elite Reputations in the Middle and Late Republic*. London.

McCoy, M. 2006. 'The Politics of Prostitution: Clodia, Cicero, and the Social Order in the Late Roman Republic', in C.A. Farone and L.K. McClure (eds.), *Prostitutes and Courtesans in the Ancient World*. Madison: 177–85.

McDaniel, W.B. 1914. 'Some Greek, Roman and English Tityretus', *AJPh* 35: 52–66.

McDonnell, M. 2006. *Roman Manliness: Virtus and Republican Rome*. Cambridge.

McGinn, T.A.J. 1991. 'Concubinage and the *Lex Julia* on Adultery', *TAPhA* 121: 335–75.

McGushin, P. 1994. *Sallust: The Histories*, vol. 2. Oxford.

Meier, C. 1980. *Res Publica Amissa: Eine Studie zu Verfassung und Geschichte der späten römischen Republik*, 2nd ed. Wiesbaden.

Merrill, N.W. 1975. *Cicero and Early Roman Invective*, diss. University of Cincinnati.

Meshorer, Y. 1986/87. 'The Coins of Dora', *Israel Numismatic Journal* 9: 59–72.

Meyer, E.A. 2004. *Legitimacy and Law in the Roman World: Tabulae in Roman Belief and Practice*. Cambridge.

Michel, A. 2018. 'Cléopâtre et l' "île d'Aphrodite": Enjeux politiques et idéologiques de l'île de Chypre au crepuscule de la dynastie lagide', in S.H. Aufrère and A. Michel (eds.), *Cléopâtre en abyme: Aux frontières de la mythistoire et de la littérature*. Paris: 243–65.

Michel, D. 1967. *Alexander als Vorbild für Pompeius, Caesar und Marcus Antonius: Archäologische Untersuchungen*. Brussels.

Millar, F. 1964. *A Study in Cassius Dio*. Oxford.

Mitchell, S. 1993. *Anatolia: Land, Men, and Gods in Asia Minor*, vol. 1. Oxford.

Mikalson, J.D. 1975. *The Sacred and Civil Calendar of the Athenian Year*. Princeton.

Minnen, P. van. 2000. 'An Official Act of Cleopatra (With a Subscription in Her Own Hand)', *Ancient Society* 30: 29–34.

Moatti, C. 1997. *La raison de Rome: Naissance de l'esprit critique à la fin de la République (IIe-Ier siècle avant J.-C.)*. Paris.

Moatti, C. 2018. *Res Publica: Histoire romaine de la chose publique*. Paris.

Moles, J. 1983. 'Fate, Apollo, and M. Junius Brutus', *AJPh* 104: 249–56.

Moles, J. 1992. 'Plutarch, Vit. Ant. 31.3 and Suetonius, Aug. 69.2', *Hermes* 120: 245–7.

Moles, J. 2017. *A Commentary on Plutarch's Brutus*, with additional notes by C. Pelling. Newcastle.

Möller, M. 2004. *Talis oratio-qualis vita: Zu Theorie und Praxis mimetischer Verfahrenin der griechisch-römischen Literaturkritik*. Heidelberg.

Momigliano, A. 1942. 'Camillus and Concord', *CQ* 36: 111–20.

Mommsen, T. 1872. 'De titulo reginae Pythodoridis Smyrnaea', *Ephemeris Epigraphica* 1: 270–6.

Moretti, L. 1954. 'ΚΟΙΝΑ ΑΖΙΑΣ', *RFIC* 82: 276–89.

Morrell, K. 2017. *Pompey, Cato, and the Governance of the Roman Empire*. Oxford.

Morrell, K. 2018. 'Cato, Pompey's Third Consulship and the Politics of Milo's Trial', in H. van der Blom, C. Gray, and C. Steel (eds.), *Institutions and Ideology in Republican Rome: Speech, Audience, Decision*. Cambridge: 165–80.

Morrell, K. 2019. ' "Who Wants to Go to Alexandria?" Pompey, Ptolemy, and Public Opinion, 57–56 BC', in C. Rosillo-López (ed.), *Communicating Public Opinion in the Roman Republic*. Stuttgart: 151–74.

Morrison, J.S. 2016. *Greek and Roman Oared Warships, 399–30 BC*. Oxford.

Morstein-Marx, R. 2004. *Mass Oratory and Political Power in the Late Roman Republic*. Cambridge.

Morstein-Marx, R. 2012. 'Political Graffiti in the Late Roman Republic: Hidden Transcripts and Common Knowledge', in C. Kuhn (ed.), *Politische Kommunikation und öffentliche Meinung in der antiken Welt*. Heidelberg: 191–217.

Morgan, M.G. 1971. 'The Portico of Metellus: A Reconsideration', *Hermes* 99: 480–505.

Morgan, M.G. 1990. 'Politics, Religion and the Games in Rome, 200–150 B.C.', *Philologus* 143: 14–36.

Morstein-Marx, R. 2009. '*Dignitas* and *res publica*: Caesar and Republican Legitmacy', in K.-J. Hölkeskamp (ed.), *Eine politische Kultur (in) der Krise! Die 'letzte Generation' der römischen Republik*. Munich, 115–40.

Morstein-Marx, R. 2021. *Julius Caesar and the Roman People*. Cambridge.

Mosch, H.-C. von. 2005. 'Dirke, Thyiaden und der thebanische Dionyos zu den Dirkegruppen zwischen Rom und Kleinasien', *Numismatica e Antichità Classiche* 34: 141–80.

Mouritsen, H. 1998. *Italian Unification: A Study in Ancient and Modern Historiography*. London.

Mouritsen, H. 2017. *Politics in the Roman Republic*. Cambridge.

Münzer, F. 1909. 'Fabius', *RE* 6: 1739–43.

Murphey-O'Connor, J. 2012. *Keys to Jerusalem: Collected Essays*. Oxford.

Mustafa, H.S. 2001. 'Tarkondimotos, seine Dynastie, seine Politik und sein Reich', in *La Cilicie: espaces et pouvoirs locaux (IIe millénaire av. J.-C. – IVe siècle ap. J.-C.). Actes de la Table Ronde d'Istanbul, 2-5 novembre 1999*. Istanbul: 373–80.

Nabel, J. 2019. 'Remembering Intervention: Parthia in Rome's Civil Wars', *Historia* 68: 327–52.

Neumann, K.M. 2021. *Antioch in Syria: A History from Coins (300 BCE–450 CE)*. Cambridge.

Newman, R. 1990. 'A Dialogue of Power in the Coinage of Antony and Octavian (44–30 B.C.)', *AJN* 2: 37–63.

Nicoll, A. 1963. *Masks, Mimes and Miracles: Studies in Popular Theatre*. New York.

Nicolet, C. 1966. *L'ordre Équestre a l'époque républicaine (312–43 av. J.-C.)*, vol. 1. Paris.

Nicolet, C. 1974. *L'ordre Équestre a l'époque républicaine (312–43 av. J.-C.)*, vol. 2. Paris.

Nicolet, C. 1985. 'Plèbe et tribus: Les statues de Lucius Antonius et le testament d'Auguste', *MEFRA* 97: 799–832.

Niebuhr, B.G. 1830. *Römische Geschicte*, 2nd ed., vol. 2. Berlin.

Nock, A.D. 1972. *Essays on Religion and the Ancient World*. Oxford.

Nörr, D. 1989. *Aspekte des römischen Völkerrechts: Die Bronzetafel von Alcántara*. Munich.

North, J.A. 2006. 'The Constitution of the Roman Republic', in N. Rosenstein and R. Morstein-Marx (eds.), *A Companion to the Roman Republic*. Oxford: 256–77.

North, J.A. 2008. 'Caesar at the Lupercalia', *JRS* 98: 144–60.

Noy, D. 2000. *Foreigners at Rome: Citizens and Strangers*. Swansea.

Oakley, S.P. 1997. *A Commentary on Livy Books 6–10*, vol. 1. Oxford.

O'Donnell, J.J. 1992. *Augustine: Confessions*, 3 vols. Oxford.

Ogilvie, R.M. 1965. *A Commentary on Livy, Books 1–5*. Oxford.

Oliver, J., and Aumaître, H. 2017. 'Ántoine, Cléopâtre et le Levant: Le témoignage de monnaies', in L. Bricault, A. Burnett, V. Drost, and A Suspène (eds.), *Rome et les provinces: Monnayage et histoire; Mélanges offerts à Michel Amandry*. Bordeaux: 105–22.

Oliver J., and Parisot-Sillon, C. 2013. 'Les monnayages aux types de Cléopâtre et Antoine: Premiers résultats et perpsectives', *Bulletin de la Société française de numismatique* 68: 256–68.

Ortmann, U. 1988. *Cicero, Brutus und Octavian–Republikaner und Caesarianer: Ihr gegenseitiges Verhältnis im Krisenjahr 44/43 v. Chr*. Bonn.

Osgood, J. 2006. *Caesar's Legacy: Civil War and the Emergence of the Roman Empire*. Cambridge.

Osgood, J. 2014. *Turia: A Roman Woman's Civil War*. Oxford.

O'Sullivan, L. 2008. 'Marrying Athena: A Note on Clement *Protrepticus* 4.54', *CJ* 103: 295–300.

Owens, E.J. 1976. 'Increasing Roman Domination of Greece in the Years 48–27 B.C', *Latomus* 35: 718–29.

Pakter, W. 1994. 'The Mystery of *cessio bonorum*', *Index* 22: 323–42.

Pałuchowski, A. 2005. 'Le koinon crétois au temps du government de Marc Antoine à l'Est', *Eos* 92: 54–80.

Panayotakis, C. 2010. *Decimus Laberius: The Fragments*. Cambridge.

Panciera, S. 2006. *Epigrafi, epigrafia, epigrafisti: Scritti vari editi e inedita (1956–2005) con note complementari e indici*. Rome.

Panella, R.J. 2007. *Man and the Word: The Orations of Himerius*. Berkeley and Los Angeles.

Papazoglou, F. 1979. 'Quelques aspects de l'histoire de la province de Macédoine', *ANRW* 2.7.2: 302–69.

Papazoglou, F. 1988. *Les villes de Macédoine à l'epoque romaine*. Athens.

Parigi, C. 2013. 'The Romanization of Athens: Greek Identity and Connectivity between Athens and Rome in the 1st Century BC', in L. Bombardieri, A. D'Agostino, G. Guarduci, V. Orsi, and S. Valentini (eds.), *Identity and Connectivity: Proceedings of the 16th Symposium on Mediterranean* Archaeology, *Florence, Italy, 1–3 March* 2012. Florence: 447–55.

Parker, R. 1996. *Athenian Religion: A History*. Oxford.

Parker, R. 1998. *Cleomenes on the Acropolis*. Oxford.

Parker, R. 2005. *Polytheism and Society at Athens*. Oxford.

Pasquali, J. 2009. *Marcus Antonius: Todfeind Ciceros und Rivale des Octavianus*. Frieburg.

Paterson, J. 2006a. 'Rome and Italy', in N. Rosenstein and R. Morstein-Marx (eds.), *A Companion to the Roman Republic*. Malden: 606–24.

Patterson, J. 2006b. 'The Relationship of the Italian Ruling Classes with Rome: Friendship, Family Relations and Their Consequences', in M. Jehne and R. Pfeilschifter (eds.), *Herrschaft ohne Integration? Rom und Italien in republikanischer Zeit*. Frankfurt: 139–54.

Patterson, L. 2015. 'Antony and Armenia', *TAPhA* 145: 77–105.

Patrechko, O. 2016. 'Mark Antony's *damnatio memoriae* and the Foundation of the Principate', in D. Słapek and I. Luć (eds.), *Marcus Antonius: History and Tradition*. Lublin: 200–14.

Pelling, C. 1988. *Plutarch: Life of Antony*. Cambridge.

Pelling, C. 1996. 'The Triumviral Period', in A.K. Bowman, E. Champlin, and A. Lintott (eds.), *The Cambridge Ancient History*, 2nd ed., vol. 10. Cambridge: 1–69.

Pelling, C. 2002. *Plutarch and History: Eighteen Studies*. Swansea.

Pelling, C. 2010. *Plutarch: Rome in Crisis*, with I. Scott-Kilvert. London.

Pelling, C. 2011. *Plutarch: Caesar*. Oxford.

Perl, G. 1970. 'Die römische Provinzbeamten in Cyrenae und Creta zur Zeit der Republik', *Klio* 52: 319–54.

Perl, G. 1971. 'Die römische Provinzbeamten in Cyrenae und Creta zur Zeit der Republik', *Klio* 53: 369–79.

Perrin-Saminadayar, É. 2004. 'L'accueil officiel des rois et des princes à Athènes à l'époque hellénistique', *BCH* 128–9: 351–75.

Perrin-Saminadayar, É. 2009. 'La preparation des entrées royales et impériales dans les cites de l'Orient hellenophone, d'Alexandre le Grand aux Sévères', in A. Bérenger and É. Perrin-Saminadayar (eds.), *Les entrées royales et impériales: Histoire, representation et diffusion d'une cérémonie publique, de l'Orient ancient à Byzance*. Paris: 67–90.

Pickard-Cambridge, A.W. 1968. *The Dramatic Festivals of Athens*, 2nd ed. Oxford.

Pina Polo, F. 2006. 'The Tyrant Must Die: Preventative Tyrannicide in Roman Political Thought', in F. Marco Simón, F. Pina Polo, and J. Remesal Rodíguez (eds.), *República y Ciudadanos: Modelos de participación cívica en el mundo antiguo*. Barcelona: 71–101.

Pina Polo, F. 2011. *The Consul at Rome: The Civil Functions of the Consuls in the Roman Republic*. Cambridge.

Pina Polo, F. 2020. 'The Functioning of the Republican Institutions under the Triumvirs', in F. Pina Polo (ed.), *The Triumviral Period: Civil War, Political Crisis and Socioeconomic Transformations*. Zaragoza: 50–70.

Pina Polo, F., and Díaz Fernández, A. 2019. *The Quaestorship in the Roman Republic.* Berlin.

Poljakov, B. 1989. *Die Inschriften von Tralleis und Nysa, I: Die Inschriften von Tralleis.* Bonn.

Potter, D.S. 1999. 'Entertainers in the Roman Empire', in D.S. Potter and D.J. Mattingly (eds.), *Life, Death, and Entertainment in the Roman Empire.* Ann Arbor: 256–325.

Potter, D.S. 2011. 'Holding Court in Republican Rome (105–44)', *AJPh* 132: 59–80.

Powell, A. 2002. ' "An Island amid the Flame": The Strategy and Imagery of Sextus Pompeius, 43–36 BC', in A. Powell and K. Welch (eds.), *Sextus Pompeius.* Swansea: 103–34.

Prag, J.R.W. 2015. 'Auxilia and Clientelae: Military Service and Foreign Clientelae Reconsidered', in M. Jehne and F. Pina Polo (eds.), *Foreign Clientelae in the Roman Empire: A Reconsideration.* Stuttgart: 281–94.

Price, S.R.G. 1984. *Rituals and Power: The Roman Imperial Cult in Asia Minor.* Cambridge.

Putnam, M.C.J. 1970. *Virgil's Pastoral Art: Studies in the Eclogues.* Princeton.

Raaflaub, K. 1974. *Dignitatis contentio: Studien zur Motivation und politischen Taktik im Bürgerkrieg zwischen Caesar und Pompeius.* Munich.

Raaflaub, K. 2003. 'Caesar the Liberator? Factional Politics, Civil War, and Ideology', in F. Cairns and E. Fantham (eds.), *Caesar against Liberty? Perspectives on His Autocracy.* Cambridge: 35–67.

Raaflaub, K.A., and Ramsey, J.T. 2017. 'Reconstructing the Chronology of Caesar's Gallic Wars', *Histos* 11: 1–74.

Raaflaub, K.A., and Samons, L.J. 1990. 'Opposition to Augustus', in K.A. Raaflaub and M. Toher (eds.), *Between Republic and Empire: Interpretations of Augustus and His Principate.* Berkeley and Los Angeles: 417–54.

Ramsey, J.T. 1994. 'The Senate, Mark Antony, and Caesar's Legislative Legacy', *CQ* 44: 130–45.

Ramsey, J.T. 2001. 'Did Mark Antony Contemplate an Alliance with His Political Enemies in July 44 B.C.E. ?', *CPh* 96: 253–68.

Ramsey, J.T. 2003. *Cicero: Philippics I–II.* Cambridge.

Ramsey, J.T. 2004. 'Did Julius Caesar Temporarily Banish Mark Antony from His Inner Circle?', *CQ* 54: 161–73.

Ramsey, J.T. 2005. 'Mark Antony's Judiciary Reform and Its Revival under the Triumvirs', *JRS* 95: 20–37.

Ramsey, J.T. 2016. 'How and Why Was Pompey Made Sole Consul in 52 BC', *Historia* 65: 298–324.

Ramsey, J.T., and Licht, A.L. 1997. *The Comet of 44 B.C. and Caesar's Funeral Games.* Philadelphia.

Ranouil, P.C. 1975. *Recherches sur le patriciat: 509–366 av. J.-C.* Paris.

Raubitschek, A.E. 1946. 'Octavia's Deification at Athens', *TAPhA* 77: 146–50.

Rawson, B. 1974. 'Roman Concubinage and Other *De Facto* Marriages', *TAPhA* 104: 279–305.

Rawson, E. 1985. *Intellectual Life in the Late Roman Republic.* Baltimore.

Rawson, E. 1991. *Roman Culture and Society.* Oxford.

Rawson, E. 1994a. 'Caesar: Civil War and Dictatorship', in J.A. Crook, A. Lintott, and E. Rawson (eds.), *The Cambridge Ancient History*, 2nd ed., vol. 9. Cambridge: 424–67.

Rawson, E. 1994b. 'The Aftermath of the Ides', in J.A. Crook, A. Lintott, and E. Rawson (eds.), *The Cambridge Ancient History*, 2nd ed., vol. 10. Cambridge: 478–90.

Reich, H. 1903. *Der Mimus: Ein litterar-entwickelungsgeschichtlicher Versuch*. Berlin.

Reinhold, M. 1933. 'The Perusine War', *Classical Weekly* 26: 180–2.

Reinhold, M. 1988. *From Republic to Principate: An Historical Commentary on Cassius Dio's Roman History Books 49–52 (36–29 B.C.)*. Atlanta.

Reynolds, J. 1982. *Aphrodisias and Rome*. London.

Ricciardetto, A. 2012. 'La letter de Marc Antoine (SB I 4224) écrite au verso de l'Anonyme de Londres (P. Brit. Libr. Inv. 137 = MP³ 2339)', *APF* 58: 43–60.

Rice, E.E. 1983. *The Grand Procession of Ptolemy Philadelphus*. Oxford.

Richardson, J.S. 1994. 'The Administration of the Empire', in J. Crook, A. Lintott, and E. Rawson (eds.), *The Cambridge Ancient History*, 2nd ed., vol. 9. Cambridge: 564–98.

Richardson, J.S. 2000. *Appian: Wars of the Romans in Iberia*. Warminster.

Richardson, J.S. 2012. *Augustan Rome 44 BC to AD 14: The Restoration of the Republic and the Establishment of the Empire*. Edinburgh.

Richardson, L., Jr. 1992. *A New Topographical Dictionary of Ancient Rome*. Baltimore.

Ridgway, B.S. 1999. 'The Farnese Bull (Punishment of Dirke) from the Baths of Caracalla: How Many Prototypes?', *JRA* 12: 512–20.

Ridgway, B. S. 2000. *Hellenistic Sculpture II: The Styles of ca. 200–100 B.C.* Madison.

Rieger, H. 1991. *Das Nachleben des Tiberius Gracchus in der lateinischen Literatur*. Bonn.

Rigsby, K.J. 1976. 'Cnossus and Capua', *TAPhA* 106: 313–30.

Rigsby, K.J. 1996. *Asylia: Territorial Inviolability in the Hellenistic World*. Berkeley and Los Angeles.

Rizzelli, G. 2006. 'Antonio e Fadia', in G. Traina (ed.), *Studi sull'età di Marco Antonio*. Lecce: 201–20.

Robert, L. 1984. 'Documents d'Asie Mineure', *BCH* 108: 467–532.

Roddaz J.-M. 1984. *Marcus Agrippa*. Paris and Rome.

Roddaz, J.-M. 1988. 'Lucius Antonius', *Historia* 37: 317–46.

Roddaz, J.-M. 2012. 'Marc-Antoine: Myth, propagande et realites', in L.-M. Günther and V. Grieb (eds.), *Das imperial Rom und der hellenistische Osten: Festschrift für Jürgen Deininger zum 75. Geburtstag*. Stuttgart: 115–38.

Rohr Vio, F. 2019. *Le Custodi del Potere: donne e politica alla fine della repubblica romana*. Rome.

Roller, D.W. 2007. 'The Lost Building Program of Marcus Antonius', *L'Antiquité Classique* 76: 685–6.

Roller, D.W. 2010. *Cleopatra: A Biography*. Oxford.

Roller, M.B. 1997. 'Color-Blindness: Cicero's Death, Declamation, and the Production of History', *CPh* 92: 109–30.

Roller, M.B. 2018. *Models for the Past in Roman Culture: A World of Exempla*. Cambridge.

Rollinger, C. 2009. *Solvendi su⸱¹ nummi: Die Schuldenkultur der späten römischen Republik im Spiegel der Schriften Ciceros*. Berlin.

Rollinger, C. 2014. *Amicita sanctissime colenda: Freundschaft und soziale Netzwerke in der späten Republik*. Trier.

Roselaar, S.T. 2010. *Public Land in the Roman Republic: A Social and Economic History of Ager Publicus in Italy, 396–89 BC*. Oxford.

Roselaar, S.T. 2019. *Italy's Economic Revolution: Integration and Economy in Republican Italy*. Oxford.

Rose, H.J. 1927. 'Mox', *CQ* 21: 57–66.

Rosenstein, N.S. 1990. *Imperatores Victi: Military Defeat and Aristocratic Competition in the Middle and Late Republic*. Berkeley and Los Angeles.

Rosenstein, N.S. 2006. 'Aristocratic Values', in N. Rosenstein and R. Morstein-Marx (eds.), *A Companion to the Roman Republic*. Malden: 365–82.

Rosenstein, N.S. 2008. 'Revolution and Rebellion in the Later Second and Early First Centuries BC: Jack Goldstone and the "Roman Revolution"', in L. de Ligt and S. Northwood (eds.), *People, Land and Politics: Demographic Developments and the Transformation of Roman Italy, 300 BC–AD 14*. Leiden: 605–29.

Rosenstein, N.S. 2020. 'Armies and Political Culture', in V. Arena and J. Prag (eds.), *A Companion to the Political Culture of the Roman Republic*. Malden: 236–47.

Rosillo-López, C. 2017. *Public Opinion and Politics in the Late Roman Republic*. Cambridge.

Rosillo-López, C. 2022. *Political Conversations in Late Republican Rome*. Oxford.

Rossi, R.F. 1959. *Marco Antonio nella lotta politica della tarda repubblica romana*. Trieste.

Rostovtzeff, M. 1941. *The Social and Economic History of the Hellenistic World*. Oxford.

Rostovtzeff, M. 1957. *The Social and Economic History of the Roman Empire*. Oxford.

Roth, R. 2019. 'Sympathy with Allies? Abusive Magistrates and Political Discourse in Republican Rome', *AJPh* 140: 123–66.

Rowan, C. 2019. *From Caesar to Augustus (c. 49 BC–AD 14): Using Coins as Sources*. Cambridge.

Rüpke, J. 1990. *Domi militiae: Die religiose Konstruktion des Krieges in Rom*. Stuttgart.

Rüpke, J. 2012. *Religion in Republican Rome: Rationalzation and Ritual Change*. Philadelphia.

Rüpke, J. 2014. 'Roman Religion', in H. Flower (ed.), *The Cambridge Companion to the Roman Republic*, 2nd ed. Cambridge: 213–29.

Rüpke, J. 2018. *Pantheon: A New History of Roman Religion*. Princeton.

Russell, A. 2016a. *The Politics of Public Space in Republican Rome*. Cambridge.

Russell, A. 2016b. 'Why Did Clodius Shut the Shops? The Rhetoric of Mobilizing a Crowd in the Late Republic', *Historia* 65: 186–210.

Ryan, F.X. 2003. 'Der für die Priesterwahlen vorgeschriebene Zeitpunkt', *Studia Humaniora Tratuensia* 4: 1–2.

Saller, R.P. 1994. *Patriarchy, Property and Death in the Roman Family*. Cambridge.

Salmon, E.T. 1970. *Roman Colonization under the Republic*. Ithaca.

Salway, B. 1994. 'What's in a Name? A Survey of Roman Onomastic Practice from 700 BC to AD 700', *JRS* 84: 124–45.

Sampson, G.C. 2008. *The Defeat of Rome: Crassus, Carrhae, and the Invasion of the East*. Philadelphia.

Sanders, I.F. 1982. *Roman Crete. An Archaeological Survey and Gazetteer of Late Hellenistic, Roman and Early Byzantine Crete*. Warminster.

Santangelo, F. 2007. *Sulla, the Elites and the Empire: A Study of Roman Policies in Italy and the Greek East*. Leiden.

Santangelo, F. 2013. *Divination, Prediction, and the End of the Roman Republic*. Cambridge.

Santangelo, F. 2016. 'Performing Passions, Negotiating Survival: Italian Cities in the Late Republican Civil Wars', in H. Börm, M. Mattheis, J.F. Wienand, and F. Santangelo (eds.), *Civil War in Ancient Greece and Rome: Contexts of Disintegration and Reintegration.* Stuttgart: 127–58.

Santangelo, F. 2019. 'Municipal Men in the Age of the Civil Wars', in K.-J. Hölkeskamp, S. Karataş, and R. Roth (eds.), *Empire, Hegemony or Anarchy? Rome and Italy, 201–31 BCE.* Stuttgart: 237–58.

Sarri, A. 2018. *Material Aspects of Letter Writing in the Greco-Roman World, 500 BC–AD 300.* Berlin.

Sartre, M. 2005. *The Middle East under Rome.* Cambridge, Mass.

Sartre, M. 2018. *Cléopâtre: Un rêve de puissance.* Paris.

Schiff, S. 2010. *Cleopatra: A Life.* New York.

Schlude, J.M. 2012. 'The Parthian Response to the Campaign of Crassus', *Latomus* 71: 11–23.

Schlude, J.M. 2020. *Rome, Parthia, and the Politics of Peace: The Origins of War in the Ancient Middle East.* London.

Schmitthenner, W. 1973. *Oktavian und das Testament Cäsars: Eine Untersuchungen zu den politischen Anfängen des Augustus,* 2nd ed. Munich.

Scholz, P. 2011. *Den Vätern folgen: Sozialisation und Erziehung der republikanischen Senatsaristokratie.* Berlin.

Scholz, U.W. 1963. *Der Redner M. Antonius.* Erlangen.

Schröder, B.-J. 2018. 'Couriers and Conventions in Cicero's Epistolary Network', in P. Ceccarelli, L. Doering, T. Fögen, and I. Gildenhard (eds.), *Letters and Communities: Studies in the Socio-Political Dimensions of Ancient Epistolography.* Oxford: 81–102.

Schultz, C.E. 2021. *Fulvia, Center Stage: Power Politics at the End of the Roman Republic.* Oxford.

Schulz, F. 1951. *Classical Roman Law.* Oxford.

Schulz, R. 1997. *Herrschaft und Regierung: Roms Regiment in den Provinzen in der Zeit der Republik.* Paderborn.

Schumacher, L. 2018. *Historischer Realismus: Kleine Schriften zur alten Geschichte.* Göttingen.

Schwartz, D.R. 2016. 'Many Sources but a Single Author: Josephus' *Jewish Antiquities*', in H.H. Chapman and Z. Rogers (eds.), *A Companion to Josephus.* Hoboken: 36–58.

Scott, K. 1920. 'Octavian's Propaganda and Antony's *De Sua Ebrietate*', *CPh* 24: 133–41.

Scott, K. 1933. 'The Political Propaganda of 44–30 B.C.', *MAAR* 11: 7–49.

Scuderi, R. 1989. 'Significato politico delle magistrature nelle città italiche del I sec. A.C.', *Athenaeum* 67: 117–38.

Scuderi, R. 2015. 'I potere di un nome. *Puer . . . qui omnia nomini debes*', *Athenaeum* 103: 492–507.

Scullard, H.H. 1981. *Festivals and Ceremonies of the Roman Republic.* Ithaca.

Seager, R. 1972. 'Factio: Some Observations', *JRS* 87: 41–53.

Seager, R. 1994. 'Sulla', in J.A. Crook, A. Lintott, and E. Rawson (eds.), *The Cambridge Ancient History,* 2nd ed., vol. 9. Cambridge: 165–207.

Seager, R. 2002. *Pompey the Great,* 2nd ed. Oxford.

Sedley, D. 1997. 'The Ethics of Brutus and Cassius', *JRS* 87: 41–53.

Shackleton Bailey, D.R. 1968. *Cicero's Letters to Atticus*, vol. 4. Cambridge.

Shackleton Bailey, D.R. 1977. *Cicero Epistulae ad Familiares*, vol. 1. Cambridge.

Sharon, N. 2017. *Judea under Roman Domination: The First Generation of Statelessness and its Legacy*. Atlanta.

Shatzman, I. 1971. 'The Egyptian Question in Roman Politics (59-54 B.C.)', *Latomus* 30: 363–69.

Shatzman, I. 1975. *Senatorial Wealth and Roman Politics*. Brussels.

Sheldon, R.M. 2010. *Rome's Wars in Parthia: Blood in the Sand*. London.

Sherk, R.K. 1969. *Roman Documents from the Greek East: Senatus Consulta and Epistulae to the Age of Augustus*. Baltimore.

Sherk, R.K. 1984. *Rome and the Greek East to the Death of Augustus*. Cambridge.

Sherwin-White, A.N. 1973. *The Roman Citizenship*, 2nd ed. Oxford.

Sherwin-White, A.N. 1983. *Roman Foreign Policy in the East, 168 B.C. to A.C. 1*. Norman.

Sherwin-White, A.N. 1994. 'Lucullus, Pompey, and the East', in J.A. Crook, A. Lintott, E. Rawson (eds.), *The Cambridge Ancient History*, 2nd ed., vol. 9. Cambridge: 229–73.

Shipley, F.W. 1931. 'Chronology of the Building Operations in Rome from the Death of Caesar to the Death of Augustus', *MAAR* 9: 7–60.

Siani-Davies, M. 2001. *Cicero's Speech Pro Rabirio Postumo*. Oxford.

Sigmund, C. 2014. *Königtum in der politischen Kultur des spätrepublikanischen Rom*. Berlin.

Simelon, P. 1985. 'À propos des émeutes de M. Caelius Rufus et de P. Cornelius Dolabella (48–47 av. J.-C.)', *Les Études Classiques* 53: 387–405.

Simonton, M. 2017. *Classical Greek Oligarchy: A Political History*. Princeton.

Siranni, F.A. 1984. 'Was Antony's Will Partially Forged?', *Antiquité Classique* 53: 236–41.

Smith, C.J. 2006a. *The Roman Clan: The Gens from Ancient Ideology to Modern Anthropology*. Cambridge.

Smith, C.J. 2006b. '*Adfectio Regni* in the Roman Republic', in S. Lewis (ed.), *Ancient Tyranny*. Edinburgh: 49–64.

Smith, R.R.R. 1988. *Hellenistic Royal Portraits*. Oxford.

Śniezewski, S. 1998. 'Divine Connections of Marcus Antonius in the years 43–30 BC', *GB* 22: 129–44.

Soraci, C. 2018. 'Diritto latino, cittadinanza romana e municipalizzazione: Transformazioni graduali e progressive in Sicilia tra Cesare e Augusto', *Dialogues d'histoire ancienne* 44: 37–58.

Southern, P. 2010. *Mark Antony: A Life*. Stround.

Southern, P. 2012. *Mark Antony: A Life*. London.

Spaeth, B.S. 1996. *The Roman Goddess Ceres*. Austin.

Spawforth, A.J.S. 1996. 'Roman Corinth: The Formation of a Colonial Elite', in A.D. Rizakis (ed.), *Roman Onomastics in the Greek East: Social and Political Aspects*. Athens: 167–82.

Spawforth, A.J.S. 2012. *Greece and the Augustan Cultural Revolution*. Cambridge.

Stadter, P.A. 2015. *Plutarch and His Roman Readers*. Oxford.

Staehlin, F. 1921. 'Kleopatra', *RE* 21: 750–81.

Stafford, E. 2010. 'Herakles between Gods and Heroes', in J.N Bremmer and A. Erskine (eds.), *The Gods of Ancient Greece: Identities and Transformations*. Edinburgh: 228–44.

Steel, C. 2012. 'The *lex Pompeia de provinciis* of 52 B.C.: A Reconsideration', *Historia* 61: 83–93.

Steel, C. 2013. *The End of the Roman Republic, 146 to 44 BC: Conquest and Crisis.* Edinburgh.

Stevenson, T. 2015. *Julius Caesar and the Transformation of the Roman Republic.* London.

Stewart, A. 2001. Rev. of C. Kunze, *Der Farnesische Stier und die Dirkegruppe des Apollonios und Tauriskos*, 1998. *Gnomon* 73: 468–70.

Stewart, R. 1995. 'Catiline and the Crisis of 63–60 BC', *Latomus* 54: 62–78.

Strauss, B. 2015. *The Death of Caesar: The Story of History's Most Famous Assassination.* New York.

Strong, A.K. 2016. *Prostitutes and Matrons in the Roman World.* Cambridge.

Strong, D.E. 1968. 'The Administration of Public Building in Rome during the Late Republic and Early Empire', *BICS* 15: 97–109.

Strootman, R. 2010. 'Queen of Kings: Cleopatra VII and the Donations of Alexandria', in M. Facella and T. Kaizer (eds.), *Kingdoms and Principalities in the Roman Near East.* Stuttgart: 140–57.

Strootman, R. 2014. *Courts and Elites in the Hellenistic Empires.* Edinburgh.

Strootman, R. 2017. 'Eunuchs, Renegades and Concubines: The "Paradox of Power" and the Promotion of Favorites in the Hellenistic Empires', in A. Erskine, L. Llewellyn-Jones, and S. Wallace (eds.), *The Hellenistic Court: Monarchic Power and Elite Society from Alexander to Cleopatra.* Swansea: 121–42.

Sullivan, R.D. 1990. *Near Eastern Royalty and Rome.* Toronto.

Sumi, G.S. 2005. *Ceremony and Power: Performing Politics in Rome between Republic and Empire.* Ann Arbor.

Sumner, G.V. 1971. 'The Lex Annalis under Caesar (continued)', *Phoenix* 25: 357–71.

Sumner, G.V. 1978. 'Varrones Murenae', *HSCPh* 82: 187–95.

Suolahti, J. 1955. *The Junior Officers in the Republican Period: A Study on Social Structure.* Helsinki.

Süss, W. 1920. *Ethos: Studien und älteren griechischen Rhetorik.* Leipzig.

Sussman, L.A. 1998. 'Antony the *Meretrix Audax*: Cicero's Novel Invective in *Philippic* 2.44–46', *Eranos* 96: 114–28.

Swain, S. 1996. *Hellenism and Empire: Language, Classicism, and Power in the Greek World, AD 50–250.* Oxford.

Swain, S. (ed.). 2007. *Seeing the Face, Seeing the Soul: Polemon's Physiognomy from Classical Antiquity to Medieval Islam.* Oxford.

Syme, R. 1939. *The Roman Revolution.* Oxford.

Syme, R. 1980. 'No Son for Caesar?', *Historia* 29: 422–37.

Syme, R. 1982. 'Clues to Testamentary Adoption', *Tutili* 4: 397–410.

Syme, R. 1984. *Roman Papers*, vol. 3. Oxford: 1236–50.

Syme. R. 1986. *The Augustan Aristocracy.* Oxford.

Syme, R. 1988. *Roman Papers*, vol. 4. Oxford: 159–70.

Syme, R. 1999. *The Provincial at Rome and Rome and the Balkans 80 BC–AD 14.* Exeter.

Tan, J. 2017. *Power and Public Finance at Rome, 264–49 BCE.* Oxford.

Tarn, W.W. 1932. 'Alexander Helios and the Golden Age', *JRS* 22: 135–60.

Tarn, W.W. 1934. 'The Triumvirs', in S.A. Cook, F.E. Adcock, and M.P. Charlesworth (eds.), *The Cambridge Ancient History*, vol. 10. Cambridge: 31–65.

Tarn, W.W., and Charlesworth, M.P. 1934. 'The War of the East against the West: The Break', in S.A. Cook, F.E. Adcock, and M.P. Charlesworth (eds.), *The Cambridge Ancient History*, vol. 10. Cambridge: 90–9.

Tatum, W.J. 1990. 'Publius Clodius Pulcher and Tarracina', *ZPE* 83: 299–304.

Tatum, W.J. 1996. 'The Regal Image in Plutarch's *Lives*', *JHS* 96: 135–51.

Tatum, W.J. 1999. *The Patrician Tribune: Publius Clodius Pulcher*. Chapel Hill.

Tatum, W.J. 2008. *Always I Am Caesar*. Malden and Oxford.

Tatum, W.J. 2009. 'Roman Democracy?', in R.K. Balot (ed.), *A Companion to Greek and Roman Political Thought*. Malden: 214–27.

Tatum, W.J. 2013. 'Campaign Rhetoric', in C. Steel and H. van den Blom (eds.), *Community and Communication: Oratory and Politics in Republican Rome*. Oxford.

Tatum, W.J. 2015. 'The Practice of Politics and the Unpredictable Dynamics of Clout in the Roman Republic', in D. Hammer (ed.), *A Companion to Greek Democracy and the Roman Republic*. Malden: 257–73.

Tatum, W.J. 2017. 'Intermediaries in Political Communication: *Adlegatio* and Its Uses', in C. Rosillo-López (ed.), *Political Communication in the Roman World*. Leiden: 55–80.

Tatum, W.J. 2011. 'Invective Identities in Pro Caelio', in C. Smith and R. Corvino (eds.), *Praise and Blame in Roman Republican Rhetoric*. Swansea: 165–79.

Tatum, W.J. 2015. 'The Practice of Politics and the Unpredictable Dynamics of Clout in Republican Rome', in D. Hammer (ed.), *A Companion to Greek Democracy and the Roman Republic*. Malden: 257–73.

Tatum, W.J. 2018. *Quintus Cicero: A Brief Handbook on Canvassing for Office*. Oxford.

Tatum, W.J. 2020a. 'Antonius and Athens', in F. Pina Polo (ed.), *The Triumviral Period: Civil War, Political Crisis and Socioeconomic Transformations*. Zaragoza: 451–73.

Tatum, W.J. 2020b. 'Gang Violence in the Late Roman Republic', in G.G. Fagan, L. Fibiger, M. Hudson, and M. Trundle (eds.), *The Cambridge History of World Violence, Vol. 1: The Prehistoric and Ancient Worlds*. Cambridge: 400–417.

Tatum, W.J. 2020c. 'A Great and Arduous Struggle: Marcus Antonius and the Rhetoric of Libertas in 44–43 BC', in C. Balmaceda (ed.), *Libertas and Res Publica in the Roman Republic*. Leiden: 189–215.

Tatum, W.J. 2020d. '*Cherchez la femme*? Fadia in Plutarch's *Life of Antony*', *Antichthon* 54: 127–40.

Tatum, W.J. 2022. '88 BCE', in V. Arena and J.R.W. Prag (eds.), *A Companion to the Political Culture of the Roman Republic*. Chichester: 555–67.

Tatum, W.J. forthcoming. '*Non iure rogata*: The People, the Senate, and the Rule of Law in Republican Rome', in E. Cowan, K. Morrell, A. Pettinger, and M. Sevel (eds.), *The Rule of Law in Ancient Rome*. Oxford.

Taylor, A.J.P. 1954. *The Struggle for Mastery in Europe, 1848–1918*. Oxford.

Taylor, L.R. 1931. *The Divinity of the Roman Emperor*. Middletown.

Taylor, L.R. 1960. *The Voting Districts of the Roman Empire*. Rome.

Tempest, K. 2011. *Cicero: Politics and Persuasion in Ancient Rome*. London.

Tempest, K. 2017. *Brutus: The Noble Conspirator*. New Haven.

Thonemann, P.J. 2004. 'Polemo, Son of Polemo (Dio, 59.12.2)', *Epigraphica Anatolica* 37: 144–50.

Thonemann, P. 2005. 'The Tragic King: Demeterios Poliorketes and the City of Athens', in O. Hekster and R. Fowler (eds.), *Imaginary Kings: Royal Images in the Ancient Near East, Greece and Rome*. Stuttgart: 63–86.

Thonemann, P. 2015. *The Hellenistic World: Using Coins as Sources*. Cambridge.

Toher, M. 2004. 'Octavian's Arrival in Rome, 44 B.C.', *CQ* 54: 174–84.

Toher, M. 2017. *Nicolaus of Damascus: The Life of Augustus and The Autobiography*. Cambridge.

Tramunot, M. 2009. *Concubini e concubine nell'Italia romana*. Rome.

Treggiari, S. 1981. 'Concubinae', *PBSR* 49: 59–81.

Treggiari, S. 1991. *Roman Marriage: Iusti Coniuges from the Time of Cicero to the Time of Ulpian*. Oxford.

Treggiari, S. 2007. *Terentia, Tullia and Publilia: The Women of Cicero's Family*. London.

Tuchelt, K. 1979. *Frühe Denkmäler Roms in Kleinasien: Beiträge zur archäologischen Überlieferung aus de Zeit der Republik und des Augustus*. Tübingen.

Tyrrell, R.Y., and Purser, L.C. 1894. *The Correspondence of M. Tullius Cicero*, vol. 4. Dublin.

Ürögdi, G. 1968. 'Publicani', *RE Suppl.* 11: 1184–208.

van Nijf, O.M. 2013. 'Ceremonies, Athletics and the City: Some Remarks on the Social Imaginary of the Greek City of the Hellenistic Period', in E. Stavrianopoulou (ed.), *Shifting Social Imaginaries in the Hellenistic Period: Narrations, Practices, and Images*. Leiden: 311–38.

van Wijlick, H. 2021. *Rome and the Near Eastern Kingdoms and Principalities, 44-31 BC*. Leiden.

Várhelyi, Z. 2011. 'Political Murder and Sacrifice: From the Roman Republic to Empire', in J.W. Knust and Z. Várhelyi (eds.), *Ancient Mediterranean Sacrifice*. Oxford: 125–41.

Vé, K.K. 2016. 'Les liens entre les Lupercales et Romulus dans la tradition romaine', *Bulletin de l'Association Guillaume* Budé 2: 96–113.

Verboven, K. 1997. 'Caritas Nummorum: Deflation in the Late Republic', *MBAH* 16: 40–78.

Verboven, K. 2002. *The Economy of Friends: Economic Aspects of Amicitia and Patronage in the Late Republic*. Brussels.

Verboven, K. 2003. '55–44 BC: Financial or Monetary Crisis?', in E. Lo Cascio (ed.), *Credito e moneta nel mondo romano*. Bari: 49–68.

Vervaet, F.J. 2014. *The High Command in the Roman Republic: The Principle of summum imperium fro 509 to 19 BCE*. Stuttgart.

Vervaet, F.J. 2010. 'The Official Position of Imperator Caesar Divi fillius from 31 to 27 BCE', *Ancient Journal* 40: 79–152.

Vervaet, F.J. 2020. 'The Triumvirate *Rei Publicae Constituendae*: Political and Constitutional Aspects', in F. Pina Polo (ed.), *The Triumviral Period: Civil War, Political Crisis and Socioeconomic Transformations*. Zaragoza: 23–48.

Veyne, P. 1983. 'La folklore à Rome et les droits de la conscience publique sure la conduite individuelle', *Latomus* 42: 3–30.

Volk, K. 2021. *The Roman Republic of Letters: Scholarship, Philosophy, and Politics in the Age of Cicero and Caesar*. Princeton.

Volkmann, H. 1953. *Kleopatra: Politik und Propganda*. Munich.

Voutiras, E. 2011. 'Des honneurs divins pour Marc Antoine à Thessalonique?', in P.P. Iossif, A.S. Chankowski, and C.C. Lorber (eds.), *More Than Men, Less Than Gods: Studies on Royal Cult and Imperial Worship*. Leuven: 457–73.

Vuković, K. 2018. 'The Topography of the Lupercalia', *PBSR* 86: 37–60.

Walbank, F.W. 1984. 'Monarchies and Monarchic Ideas', in F.W. Walbank and A.E. Astin (eds.), *Cambridge Ancient History*, 2nd ed., vol. 7.1. Cambridge: 62–100.

Walker, S. 2008. 'Cleopatra in Pompeii?', *PBSR* 76: 35–46.

Wallace-Hadrill. A. 1994. *Houses and Society in Pompeii and Herculaneum*. Princeton.

Wallmann, P. 1989. *Triumviri Rei Publicae Constituendae: Untersuchungen zur politische Propaganda im Zweiten Triumvirat (43–30 v.Chr.)*. Frankfurt.

Wardle, D. 2009. 'Caesar and Religion', in M. Griffin (ed.), *A Companion to Julius Caesar*. Malden: 100–111.

Wardle, D. 2014. *Suetonius: Life of Augustus*. Oxford.

Wardle, D. 2018. 'Baby Steps for Octavian: 44 B.C.', *CQ* 68: 178–91.

Watson, G.R. 1969. *The Roman Soldier*. Ithaca.

Watson, L. 2003. *A Commentary on Horace's Epodes*. Oxford.

Weggen, K. 2011. *Der lange Schatten von Carrhae: Studien zu M. Licinius Crassus*. Hamburg.

Weinrich, O. 1932. 'Zu Virgils Vierter Ecloge, Rhianos und Nonnos', *Hermes* 67: 359–63.

Weinstock, S. 1971. *Divus Julius*. Oxford.

Welch, K. 1995. 'Antony, Fulvia, and the Ghost of Clodius in 47 B.C.', *Greece & Rome* 42: 182–201.

Welch, K. 2012. *Magnus Pius: Sextus Pompeius and the Transformation of the Roman Republic*. Swansea.

Welch, K. 2014. 'The *Lex Pedia* of 43 BCE and Its Aftermath', *Hermathena* 196/97: 137–61.

Welch, K. 2015. 'Programme and Narrative in *Civil Wars* 2.118–4.138', in K. Welch (ed.), *Appian's Roman History: Empire and Civil War*. Swansea: 277–304.

Welch, K. 2019. 'Selling Proscriptions to the Roman Public', in C. Rosillo-López (ed.), *Communicating Public Opinion in the Roman Republic*. Stuttgart: 241–54.

Welwei, K.-W. 2001. 'Lucius Iunius Brutus: Zur Ausgestaltung und politischen Wirkung einer Legende', *Gymnasium* 108: 123–35.

Westall, R. 1996. 'The Forum Iulium as representation of Imperator Caesar', *Mitteilungen des Deutschen Archäologischen Instituts* 103: 83–118.

Westall, R. 2018. 'The Sources for the Civil Wars of Appian of Alexandria', in K. Welch (ed.), *Appian's Roman History: Empire and Civil War*. Swansea: 125–67.

Westall, R.W. 'Date of the Testament of Ptolemy XII', *Richerche di Egittologia e di Antichità* 11: 79–94.

White, P. 1993. *Promised Verse: Poets in the Society of Augustan Rome*. Cambridge, Mass.

White, P. 2010. *Cicero in Letters: Epistolary Relations of the Late Republic*.

Wiedemann, T. 1986. 'The *Fetiales*: A Reconsideration', *CQ* 36: 478–90.

Wilcox, A. 2012. *The Gift of Correspondence in Classical Rome: Friendship in Cicero's Ad Familiares and Seneca's Moral Epistles*. Madison.

Will, E. 1982. *Histoire politique du monde hellénistiqu (323–30 av. J.-C.)*, 2nd ed., vol. 1. Nancy.

Wille, G. 1967. *Musica Romana: die Bedeutung der Musik im Leben der Römer*. Amsterdam.

Williams, J.H.C. 2001. '"Spoiling the Egyptians": Octavian and Cleopatra', in S. Walker and P. Higgs (eds.), *Cleopatra of Egypt from History to Myth.* Princeton: 190–9.

Wirszubski, C. 1950. *Libertas as a Political Idea at Rome during the Late Republic and Early Principate.* Cambridge.

Wiseman, T.P. 1971. *New Men in the Roman Senate 139 B.C.–14 A.D. 14.* Oxford.

Wiseman, T.P. 1987. *Roman Studies.* Liverpool.

Wiseman, T.P. 1994a. 'The Senate and the Populares, 69–60 B.C', in J.A. Crook, A. Lintott, and E. Rawson (eds.), *The Cambridge Ancient History*, 2nd ed., vol. 10. Cambridge: 327–67.

Wiseman, T.P. 1994b. 'Caesar, Pompey, and Rome', in J.A. Crook, A. Lintott, E. Rawson (eds.), *The Cambridge Ancient History*, 2nd ed., vol. 9. Cambridge: 368–423.

Wiseman, T.P. 1995. 'The God of the Lupercal', *JRS* 85: 1–22.

Wiseman, T.P. 2009. *Remembering the Roman People: Essays on Late-Republican Politics and Literature.* Oxford.

Wiseman, T.P. 2014. 'The Legend of Lucius Brutus', in J.H. Richardson and F. Santangelo (eds.), *The Roman Historical Tradition: Regal and Republican Rome.* Oxford: 120–45.

Wisse, J. 1995. 'Greeks, Romans and the Rise of Atticism', in J.G.J. Abbenes, S.R. Slings, and I. Sluiter (eds.), *Greek Literary Theory after Aristotle: A Collection of Papers in Honour of D.M. Schenkeveld.* Amsterdam: 65–82.

Wissowa, G. 1902. *Religion und Kultus der Römer.* Munich.

Wood, N. 1988. *Cicero's Social and Political Thought.* Berkeley and Los Angeles.

Wood, S.E. 1999. *Imperial Women: A Study in Public Images, 49 B.C.–A.D. 68*, rev. ed. Leiden.

Woodford, S., and Boardman, J. 1990. 'Herakles and Apollon/Apollo', LIMC 5.1: 133–142.

Woodman, A.J. 1983. *Velleius Paterculus: The Caesarian and Augustan Narrative (2.41–93).* Cambridge.

Woodman, A.J. 2018. *The Annals of Tacitus: Book 4.* Cambridge.

Woods, D. 2019. 'Fulvia and the Lion', *Revue Belge de Numismatique et de Sigillographie* 165: 252–8.

Worthington, I. 2021. *Athens after Empire: A History from Alexander the Great to the Emperor Hadrian.* Oxford.

Woytek, B. 2003. *Arma et nummi: Forschungen zur römischen Finanzgeschichte und Münzprägung der Jahre 49 bis 42 v. Chr.* Vienna.

Woytek, B. 2014. 'Heads and Busts on Roman Coins: Some Remarks on the Morphology of Numismatic Portraiture', *Revue Numismatique* 171: 45–71.

Woytek, B. 2016. 'Exactions and the Monetary Economy of the Late Roman Republic: A Numismatic Perspective', in C. Chillet, M.-C. Ferriès, and Y. Rivière (eds.), *Les confiscations, le pouvoir et Rome de la fin de la République à la mort de Néron.* Bordeaux: 183–97.

Wüst, E. 1932. 'Mimus', *RE* 15.2: 1727–48.

Wyke, M. 2007. *The Roman Mistress: Ancient and Modern Representations.* Oxford.

Yakobson, A. 1999. *Elections and Electioneering in Rome: A Study in the Political System of the Late Republic.* Stuttgart.

Yakobson, A. 2017. 'Consuls, Consulars, Aristocratic Competition in the People's Judgment', in M. Haake and A.-C. Harders (eds.), *Politische Kultur und soziale Struktur der römischen Republik: Bilanzen und Perspektiven.* Stuttgart: 497–516.

Yavetz, Z. 1983. *Julius Caesar and His Public Image*. London.

Zevi, F. 2017. 'I Fasti di *Privernum* all luce della collaborazione Filippo Càssola', in M. Chiabà and L. Cristante (eds.), *Il sussurro di una brezza leggera: Ricordo di Filippo Càssola*. Trieste: 5–18.

Zevi, F. 2016. 'I Fasti di Privernum', *ZPE* 197: 287–309.

Ziethen, G. 1994. *Gesandte vor Kaiser und Senat: Studien zum römischen Gesandtschaftswesen zwischen 30 v. Chr. und 117 n. Chr.* Sankt Katharinen.

Zimmermann, K. 2002. 'P.Bingen 45: Eine Steuerbefreiung für Q. Cascellius, adressiert an Kaisarion', *ZPE* 138: 133–9.

Index

For the benefit of digital users, indexed terms that span two pages (e.g., 52–53) may, on occasion, appear on only one of those pages.

Pompeius Magnus Pius, Sex. (cos. des. 35), 94–95, 97, 101, 105, 125, 134, 138–39, 167, 181–82, 185–86, 189, 191, 193, 228, 233, 236–37, 248–49, 250, 252, 253–58, 260, 262–65, 266–67, 269, 275–76, 277–78, 279–83, 299–301, 302–3, 304, 305, 306, 310, 320–21, 323
Pompey the Great. See Pompeius Magnus, Cn.
Pomponius Atticus, T., 5, 34–35, 36, 39–40, 62–63, 93, 98, 126, 137–38, 161–62, 180, 185–86, 230, 235
pontiffs/pontifex maximus, 59–60, 70, 123–24, 134, 275, 299–300
Pontus, 8–9, 11, 12, 46, 89, 94–95, 210, 213, 215–16, 220–21, 239–40, 271–72, 273. See also Mithridatic Wars
poor Romans. See lower orders
Poppaedius Silo, Q., 262–63, 268
Porcius Cato, M. (cos. 195–Cato the Elder), 31
Porcius Cato, M. (pr. 54–Cato the Younger), 26–28, 62, 65–69, 73–74, 94–95, 254
Praeneste, 242
praenomen, 5–6
praetorship, 4–5, 7–8, 10, 58, 99, 123, 135–36, 140, 146, 149, 150, 152–54, 166, 173, 234, 262, 264
praevaricatio, 53–54
prefect, urban. See urban prefect
prefectures, 34–35, 39–40, 43–44
prestige . See dignitas
Priene, 330
professio, 26, 67
profiteering. See corruption
Propertius (Sex. Propertius: poet), 250
proscriptions, 9, 10, 22, 172–73, 185–87, 191–93, 194, 206, 208–9, 233, 237, 238–39, 264, 302, 334–35
prosperous Romans. See First Class; aristocracy
provinces, 35–38, 49–50, 168–71, 191, 194, 209–10, 237, 240, 262, 263–64, 271–74, 346. See also provincial administration
provincia/provinciae. See provinces
provincial administration, 23–26, 33, 34–46, 47–50, 81, 84–85, 101, 136–43, 154, 188–90, 194–95, 197–98, 202–5, 206–11, 214–19, 222–27, 240, 262–63,

266–67, 268, 271–74, 305, 340. See also provincial elites
provincial commands, 33, 49–50, 62, 65–68, 130, 132–33, 134–35, 154, 158–59, 168–72, 188–90, 258–59, 348–49
provincial elites, 37–41, 44–46, 73, 101, 136–43, 194–95, 198, 207–8, 211, 214, 215, 217, 258–59, 262, 268, 272–73, 301, 313, 321–22, 340
provincial governors. See provincial administration
Prusias (Cius), 215–16
Ptolemy, Ituraean ruler, 215
Ptolemy, king of Mauretania, 346–47
Ptolemy XII (Auletes), 41, 42, 45, 46–52, 84, 139, 220–21
Ptolemy XIII, 84–85, 217
Ptolemy XIII, pretender, 219
Ptolemy XIV, 101
Ptolemy Caesarion. See Caesarion
Ptolemy Philadelphus, 284–85, 314, 318, 346–47
public building, 99–100, 319–20
publicani, 24–25, 26, 37–41, 44–46, 203, 207–9, 273–74, 311–12. See also equestrian order; financiers
Publicius Malleolus, C. (q. 80), 25
Pupius Piso, M. (pr. 44), 92
Puteoli, 146
Pythodoris Philomater, 301
Pythodorus of Tralles, 203, 301

quaestorship, 4–5, 7–8, 9–10, 33, 34, 55–56, 57–59, 62–65, 71, 244–46
Quinctilis, 105–6, 150, 151
Quinctius Flamininus, T. (cos. 198), 36–37, 214
quindemviri (Roman priesthood), 59–60
Quirinus, 107–8

Rabirius Postumus, C., 47–48, 49, 50–52, 53, 101
Raetia, 158–59
Ravenna, 62, 64
regnum. See kingship in Rome
religion, Greek, 198, 199, 200–1, 203–5, 268–70. See also pageantry, Hellenistic
religion, Roman, 4, 7–8, 48, 50–51, 59–61, 75, 86, 94–95, 99–100, 104–10, 116–19,